# THE ACCOMMODATED JEW

# THE
# ACCOMMODATED
# JEW

### ENGLISH
### ANTISEMITISM
### FROM BEDE TO MILTON

## KATHY LAVEZZO

CORNELL UNIVERSITY PRESS
*Ithaca and London*

First published 2016 by Cornell University Press

Printed in the United States of America

Library of Congress Cataloging-in-Publication Data

Names: Lavezzo, Kathy, author.
Title: The accommodated Jew : English antisemitism from
    Bede to Milton / Kathy Lavezzo.
Description: Ithaca : Cornell University Press, 2016. |
    Includes bibliographical references and index.
Identifiers: LCCN 2016013027 | ISBN 9781501703157
    (cloth : alk. paper)
Subjects: LCSH: Jews in literature. | Antisemitism in
    literature. | English literature—Old English, ca.
    450–1100—History and criticism. | English literature—
    Middle English, 1100–1500—History and criticism. |
    English literature—Early modern, 1500–1700—History
    and criticism. | Antisemitism—England—History. |
    Jews—England—History.
Classification: LCC PR151.J5 L39 2016 |
    DDC 820.9/3529924—dc23
LC record available at https://lccn.loc.gov/2016013027

Cornell University Press strives to use environmentally responsible suppliers and materials to the fullest extent possible in the publishing of its books. Such materials include vegetable-based, low-VOC inks and acid-free papers that are recycled, totally chlorine-free, or partly composed of nonwood fibers. For further information, visit our website at www.cornellpress.cornell.edu.

Cloth printing      10 9 8 7 6 5 4 3 2 1

# ❧ CONTENTS

# ❧ ILLUSTRATIONS

# ❦ ACKNOWLEDGMENTS

I am delighted to acknowledge the many forms of support I received for this book.

I am very grateful for the financial support, including a book subvention, that the University of Iowa provided for my project. I am also thankful that the Jean and Samuel Frankel Center for Judaic Studies funded a six-month fellowship at the Institute for Advanced Judaic Studies at the University of Michigan.

Several people helped me reconstruct and reimagine the layout, built environments, and social aspects of English cities. Robert Halliday, Margaret Statham, Betty Millburn, Abby Antrobus, Keith Cunliffe, Caroline Barron, and Sylvia Cox assisted my research on medieval Bury; Giles Darkes at the British Towns Historic Atlas assisted my work on Chaucer's London. Cath D'Alton prepared many maps for the book. Margaret Gamm, Paula Balkenende, Bethany Davis, and Lindsay Moen, librarians at both the University of Iowa Map Library and Special Collections and Archives department, helped locate several maps used in the book.

I owe a huge debt to several scholarly collectives. Both current and former graduate students and colleagues at my home institution, the University of Iowa, supported me through their friendship and by serving as generous readers and interlocutors: Bluford Adams, Tom Blake, Eric Gidal, Lena Hill, Stephanie Horton, Rebekah Kowal, Priya Kumar, Irene Lottini, Erin Mann, Chris Merrill, Judith Pascoe, Laura Rigal, Phil Round, Miri Rubin, Michael Sarabia, Arne Seim, Lara Trubowitz, Chris Vinsonhaler, and Doris Witt. I owe special thanks to Naomi Greyser, Miriam Gilbert, David Cunning, Garrett Stewart, Jon Wilcox, Claire Sponsler, and, most of all, Alvin Snider. Two residencies at the Obermann Center for Advanced Studies helped get the project going and complete it. Thanks especially belong to Teresa Mangum and Jay Semel for their support. The astonishing cohort at both the Frankel Institute for Advanced Judaic Studies and the University of Michigan provided support and feedback at a crucial time. Special thanks go to my research assistant, Shayna Goodman, and to Lois Dubin, Todd Endelman, Deborah Dash

Moore, Anita Norich, Cathy Sanok, Michael Schoenfeldt, Doug Trevor, and Jonathan Freedman. Since the start of the project, members of the Medieval Writers' Workshop have offered expert feedback and key support. I especially thank Elizabeth Allen, Jessica Brantley, Andrea Denny-Brown, Lisa Cooper, Seeta Chaganti, Bobby Meyer-Lee, Dan Birkholz, and Kellie Robertson.

Over the years, many other friends and colleagues offered advice, conversed, read drafts, and helped in other crucial ways: Suzanne Akbari, Pompa Banerjee, Anke Bernau, Lawrence Besserman, Benjamin Braude, Jody Enders, Aranye Fradenberg, Richard Helgerson, Geraldine Heng, Christopher Kendrick, Marcia Kupfer, Jennifer Hellwarth, Seth Lerer, Emma Lipton, David Matthews, Julie Mell, Andy Merrills, Mark Miller, Paul Remley, Pinchas Roth, Andy Scheil, John Sebastian, Jim Shapiro, Bob Stacey, Sarah Stanbury, Sylvia Tomasch, Elaine Treharne, Nick Vincent, Marina Warner and Mimi Yiu. I am also grateful to Meagan Loftin at the University of Washington and Carol Pasternack at UCSB for inviting me to present my work at their institutions; I received invaluable feedback on both occasions. Former Cornell editor Peter Potter chose superb readers; Lisa Lampert-Weissig and Andrew Galloway's comments substantially shaped the development of this book. Many thanks belong to staff at Cornell University Press—Mahinder Kingra, Karen Hwa, Susan Barnett, Bethany Wasik, and Deborah Oosterhouse—for their assistance in editing and producing the book.

I am particularly indebted to Anthony Bale, Heather Blurton, Jeffrey Jerome Cohen, Theresa Coletti, John Ganim, Hannah Johnson, Stacy Klein, Steven Kruger, and Keith Lilley for their exceptional support.

My greatest debt is to my family. Nina Lavezzo-Stecopoulos cheerfully endured my highs and lows while working on the project. More importantly, she was and is a constant source of joy. It's impossible to calculate what I owe my partner in love and scholarship, Harry Stecopoulos. Harry helped shape this book from the start; he challenged me to think more critically and more ambitiously about the scope, nuances, and implications of my topic. Mary Lavezzo supported the project from the start. I dedicate this book to my dad, John Lavezzo, whom I dearly miss. Through his work ethic, optimism, and strength, he embodied virtues that are fundamental to thriving in any walk of life.

Sections of chapter 1 appeared as "Building Antisemitism in Bede," in *Imagining the Jew in Anglo-Saxon Literature and Culture*, ed. Samantha Zacher (Toronto: University of Toronto Press, 2016); portions of chapter 2 appeared as "Shifting Geographies of Antisemitism: Mapping Jew and Christian in Thomas of Monmouth's *Life and Miracles of St William of Norwich*," in

*Mapping Medieval Geographies: Geographical Encounters in the Latin West and Beyond, 300–1600,* ed. Keith D. Lilley (New York: Cambridge University Press, 2014); sections of chapter 4 appeared as "The Minster and the Privy: Rereading the Prioress's Tale," in *PMLA* 126, no. 2 (2011): 363–82. The publishers of these works have kindly granted permission to reprint.

# ❧ ABBREVIATIONS

| | |
|---|---|
| EETS | Early English Text Society |
| JEGP | *Journal of English and Germanic Philology* |
| JHS | *Jewish Historical Studies* |
| JMEMS | *Journal of Medieval and Early Modern Studies* |
| MED | *Middle English Dictionary* |
| NM | *Neuphilologische Mitteilungen* |
| OED | *Oxford English Dictionary* |
| PQ | *Philological Quarterly* |
| RS | Rolls Series |
| SAC | *Studies in the Age of Chaucer* |
| SEL | *Studies in English Literature, 1500–1900* |
| TJHSE | *Transactions (& Miscellanies) of the Jewish Historical Society of England* |

# ❧ THE ACCOMMODATED JEW

# Introduction

Lock up my doors, and when you hear the drum
And the vile squealing of the wry-necked fife,
Clamber not you up to the casements then
Nor thrust your head into the public street
To gaze on Christian fools with varnished faces;
But stop my house's ears—I mean my casements—
Let not the sound of shallow foppery enter
My sober house.

—Shakespeare, *Merchant of Venice*, 2.5.28–35

Upon leaving his home to dine with gentiles, Shylock gives his daughter instructions that reveal much about this notorious literary Jew.[1] With his perception of music as a hateful cry emanating from a deformed ("wry-necked") object or person, Shylock aggressively—and tragically—denigrates festivity and "merriment."[2] Instead of inhabiting "the world of comedy and love," Shylock is all business.[3] Figurative language proves too imprecise for the moneylender. When he clarifies that "ears" refer to his home's "casements," Shylock exhibits the same legalistic certainty and exacting literalness that prompt both his strict adherence to the terms of Antonio's bond and his foiling by Portia.[4] Shylock's preference for pared-down and frugal speech over metaphoric excess speaks to his status as not only a capitalist but also a kind of Puritan.[5] Disdaining the sensual extravagances of the Venetian Catholic majority, whom he denigrates as inebriated "fools with varnished faces," Shylock is a "sober," temperate, and bourgeois ascetic.[6]

But above all, this passage manifests Shylock's deep and abiding identification with the built environment through which he enacts his anticomic and Puritanical sobriety: his home. Emphatically, the house is his: "*my* doors," "*my* house's ears," "*my* casements," "*my* sober house." A possible rationale for Shylock's possessive domesticity appears just before this passage, where he seems to analogize his home and Jessica. "Loath to go"

1

from his house and dine with the "prodigal Christian" Antonio, he tells her: "my girl, / Look to my house" (2.5.15–16). The repetition of "my" in Shylock's directive yokes the "girl" to the "house," suggesting his concern over leaving her there. Yet the subsequent passage, with its use of the possessive only in relation to the house, suggests otherwise. Shylock seems less concerned with his daughter than with maintaining the integrity of the edifice in and of itself. It is not so much human but architectural violations he fears. Shylock worries not that his daughter will hear "the sound of shallow foppery," but rather that such merriment will cross the threshold of his "sober house." Indeed, Jessica figures in the passage as not so much a chaste vessel needful of protection but a mobile and aggressive entity, a woman who might "clamber . . . up to the casements." Shylock's worry that Jessica will "thrust" her head out of the window "into the public street" implies her affinity with the problematic excesses enacted in Venetian thoroughfares. She prompts his fear over the violation of the house from within.

Why is Shylock so attached to his domicile? Shylock's identification with his home partly speaks to "the plight of many transnational migrants" who endeavored during the Early Modern period to create a zone of domestic stability in foreign locales.[7] Yet at the same time that the financier's domesticity might induce us to empathize with him as part of an alien minority, it also enhances Shylock's negative characterization. As Roy Booth observes, Shylock's "sober" house resonates with long-standing English libels about Jewish homes.[8] According to those libels, inside the confines of their houses, Jews commit such anti-Christian acts as attack the Eucharistic host, desecrate crucifixes, defile statues of Mary, and ritually murder boys in mockery of the Crucifixion. Shakespeare most clearly engages such libels in act 4, when Nerissa implicitly risks her own ritual murder as she, playing the part of a boy, visits "old Shylock's house" to have the banker sign the deed granting half his wealth to Jessica and Bassanio (4.2.11).[9]

However, Shylock's earlier directive to Jessica construes his house not so much as a potential site of ritual murder, but as an embodiment of Jewishness itself. For centuries, Christians had characterized the Jews' rejection of Christianity as an intentional locking up of the senses—in particular, a willful blindness—to a revealed "truth."[10] The currency of this idea in early modern England emerges in John Foxe's claim, in a sermon Shakespeare knew and possibly cites in *Merchant*, that Jews "wil not only not acquaint themselues with the trueth, being layd open before their eyes, but *will wittingly shut vp their senses* from the beholding thereof."[11] Foxe offers an architectural riff on Jewish enclosure when, elsewhere in the sermon, he complains to the Jews that, were Jerusalem restored, they would "streight and restrain all worship due vnto God, within the walles of your Temple only, as it were, lockt fast in some closet."[12] The "lockt fast" Jewish temple can never come to pass, Foxe writes, because it would violate the claim in Malachi 1:11 that "the time should come, when the Lord of hosts should be worshipped in all places," a prophecy that Christianity fulfills.[13]

Shakespeare departs from Foxe in associating Shylock not with a sealed-up temple but with a closed house; moreover, Shylock doesn't so much deny Christianity as oppose Venetian festivity and hedonism. At the same time, though, Shakespeare draws on Foxe's implicit linkage of self-barricading Jews and closed-up buildings by having the house personify Shylock. No line fosters this connection between Jews' "*shut vp . . . senses*" and their "lockt fast" built environments more than Shylock's injunction that Jessica "stop my house's ears—I mean my casements." As we have seen, the passage suggests a linguistic precision, the merchant's legalistic investment in the clarity of literal "casements" over figurative "ears." Yet Shylock's phrasing also suggests the slippage, twinning, and conflation of person and building: "my casements" implies how Shylock's body is a house, and "my house's ears" suggests how Shylock's house is a body. The passage indicates both the Jew's precision and its opposite: *confusion* on Shylock's part over just what is being shut up, his home or himself.

Shakespeare of course urges that conflation by embedding the word "lock" in Shylock's name, which proclaims the rigidly closed stance of the lender toward the prodigal Venetian majority.[14] Later, during the trial scene, Shakespeare further stresses Shylock's hard closure when the Duke pities Antonio for having "come to answer / A stony adversary, an inhuman wretch, Uncapable of pity, / void and empty / From any dram of mercy" (4.1.3–6). When the Duke calls Shylock a "stony adversary," he cites a prime way that Christian writers, appropriating the reference to the Jew's "heart of stone" in Ezekiel 36:26, tied Jewish unbelief to what amounted to an inhuman shutting down of the senses.[15] Peter the Venerable (d. 1156) exemplifies this trend when he ponders of the Jew, "whether that person is human from whose flesh the heart of stone is not yet removed."[16] By describing how Shylock's stoniness makes him "void and empty" of mercy, the Duke portrays him in the same way that Shylock perceives his home and himself: closed off from and unsympathetic to the lives of the greater Venetian world, the very stance that leads Jessica to deride her home as "hell" (2.3.2). Shylock is so hardened and closed to Venetian prodigality and liveliness, so stonily bound to his "law," that he *is* at some level his insensate, closed-up, and "sober" house.

The English association of the Jew with a closed built environment is longstanding. The practice predates ritual-murder and related libels, to about a millennium before the 1600 printing of *Merchant*, during the time of the Venerable Bede (673–735).[17] Both Bede and another Anglo-Saxon writer, Cynewulf, tie the Jew to the space of a sepulcher or grave, closed and/or empty locations that adumbrate the lifelessness of Shylock's home. Later English works resonate more closely with Shakespeare's image. Dating from the twelfth to the seventeenth centuries, texts ranging from Thomas of Monmouth's Latin pseudo-hagiography *The Life and Miracles of St. William of Norwich* (ca. 1154–74), to boy-martyr myths like the legend of Adam of Bristol (ca. 1225) and the Vernon manuscript *Child Slain by Jews* (ca. 1400), to plays like the Croxton *Play of the Sacrament* (ca. 1461), Christopher Marlowe's *The Jew of Malta* (1592), and *Merchant* all offer a geography of identity—that is, a mutual constitution of self and space—that locates the Jew in a domicile.[18] These and related texts comprise the focus of *The Accommodated Jew*.

Accommodate, a Latin-based word with many meanings in current and earlier parlances, signifies in my book most obviously through its association, starting around the time of *Merchant*, with housing.[19] From Thomas of Monmouth's *Life* onward, my primary texts focus on Jews who are *accommodated*, that is, who have found lodging in a host country. Insofar as they are accommodated or housed, the Jews depicted in early English texts offer a geography of Jewish identity that departs from what may be a more familiar linkage of Jews and space in antisemitic literature: the legend of the Wandering Jew. That legend, whose mobile protagonist embodies the territorial upheavals of the Jewish diaspora, only became popular in Europe during the seventeenth century. Before that time, English literary texts featured not the wandering but the accommodated Jew.[20] At least on the face of it, Jewish stasis, privacy, and domesticity concern these texts more than Jewish mobility, dispersal, and instability.

This isn't to say that medieval and Renaissance texts depict safe havens for a displaced people: far from it. Countering representations of the always mobile and unsettled Jew, yet supporting the Christian fantasies of Jewish iniquity that often inform that image of Jewish wandering, English texts view Jewish houses and related spaces as covers for crime and sacrilege. From the ritual murder of a Norwich boy in Thomas of Monmouth's "hagiography" to the host desecration staged by the Croxton play and the multiple traps set by Marlowe's Barabas, Jewish households in English texts frequently serve as the setting for anti-Christian violence. Following Anthony Bale's work on Christian devotion, we might say that the house serves in these texts as a key tool in imagining the Jew as Christian persecutor.[21] Insofar as English texts stress the mythic dangers posed by Jews, their poetics of accommodation authorizes and urges its geographic opposite: isolation, confinement, and exile. Jews, these texts imply, should not enjoy stable habitation or indeed any place among Christians, due to the anti-Christian uses to which they put their houses.

The political stakes of early English images of the "Jew" serve as a disturbing reminder of the precocity and persistence of anti-Jewish activity in England.[22] Such behavior may hail as far back as the Anglo-Saxon period, when Jews lived not in England, but in many other areas in Europe, including Italy, Iberia, and Gaul.[23] Factors including the proximity of European Jews to the island—in the case of Gaul, just across the channel—have prompted scholars to postulate that Jews were "deliberately excluded from the country" during that period.[24] Only after 1066, when William I brought Jews from Rouen to his newly conquered realm, did Jews begin to inhabit England.[25] While some Jews and Christians seemed to have enjoyed a neighborly, positive interaction, a little more than a century after the conquest, in 1189–90, the island was the setting for *the* major pogrom of the twelfth century.[26] The attacks erupted during Richard I's coronation in London, spread throughout the land, and culminated in the death of an estimated 150 Jews in York.[27] Less than three decades later, in 1218, England was the first country to force Jews by law to wear a badge, following Canon 68 of the Fourth Lateran Council.[28] Then, in 1290, England became the first country to expel forcibly its Jewish residents.

A rare glimpse at Anglo-Jewish experience during this period emerges in the Hebrew poetry of Norwich writer Meir ben Elijah.[29] Writing in the late 1270s, Meir poignantly records the horrors of Anglo-Jewish oppression on the eve of the expulsion. Yoking the persecution of Anglo-Jews to their remote location in England, far from Israel, he despairingly asks in one poem "Have you forgotten, my God, to be merciful? When will you gather your people / scattered to the corners of the earth like children that lack the light."[30] Balancing such evocations of despondency are hopeful and triumphant moments such as a passage in another poem where Meir proclaims: "My song, be strong with the words of my mouth. / Even in Egypt's bondage [i.e., English oppression], I shall soar."[31] Those lines appear in one of a series of sixteen poems through which Meir connoted Jewish power, strength, and grandeur during a time of English depredation and abuse.

The one-hundred-year period between the 1189–90 pogroms and the 1290 expulsion, marked by a series of shameful "firsts" for England, constitutes the indisputable nadir of Christian-Jewish interaction in English history. However, later centuries also suggest a uniquely English antagonism toward Jews. From the sixteenth to the mid-seventeenth century, while other European nations opened their borders to Jewish immigrants, English authorities notably resisted any official admission policy. Jews living in England during that time were forced to do so under cover, as conversos or Christian converts. Only in the second half of the seventeenth century did state officials begin to debate "readmission," though the position of Jews throughout that century and beyond remained in many respects tenuous and provisional.[32]

What kind of role could English literary texts have played in motivating such anti-Jewish activity? If the impact of such texts on readers was restricted to an imaginative and/or emotional sphere, that antisemitic literature would have had no role in historical efforts by the English to reject Jews.[33] At the same time, it may be no accident that the precocity of English anti-Jewishness matches that of antisemitic English literary production. Thomas of Monmouth's pseudo-hagiography is the earliest extant boy-martyr legend and, as Robert Stacey points out, "nowhere else would ritual crucifixion stories enjoy the widespread credence they claimed in England."[34] That writers ranging from Thomas to Shakespeare generated texts that, to varying degrees, could be seen as urging an English rejection of contemporary Jews is clear. For example, while the former refers to the prospect of Jewish extermination, the latter implicitly supports Jewish exile via Shylock's absenting from the final act of the play.[35] Along with orally circulated myths and other cultural products, such texts at times contributed to the sociopolitical climate evinced by the expulsion and other shameful acts. A pointed example of the impact of antisemitic fictions on Jews occurred in 1255, when the death of a Lincoln boy named Hugh prompted a libel about his ritual murder. "[O]n the basis," as Geraldine Heng puts it, "of a community belief in Jewish guilt and malignity," the state authorized the execution of nineteen Jews for Hugh's "martyrdom."[36] Antisemitic fictions at times enjoyed real-world agency, affecting the lives of historical Jews.

By calling certain English texts "antisemitic" and asserting their connection to anti-Jewish actions during the Middle Ages and Renaissance, I do not intend to evoke, anachronistically, a monolithic phenomenon. Antisemitism emerged as a term only in the nineteenth century, long after the texts I analyze were produced. I nevertheless use the term (which I do not hyphenate due to the fictional nature of the "Semite") to stress the offensive and constructed nature of Christian images of Jews.[37] Even the earliest Christian conceptions of Jews speak not so much to the realities of "Judaism as a historical or lived religion," but to what David Nirenberg calls "Judaism as a figure of Christian thought, a figure produced by the efforts of generations of thinkers to make sense of the world, a figure projected into that world and constitutive of it."[38] While later narratives about Jewish ritual murder and host desecration may be more outrageously elaborate than the ideas of Judaism promulgated by patristic writers like Augustine, they resemble them in their fantastic and derogatory nature.

To stress the mythic quality of antisemitism is not to erase its heterogeneity and contingency. Rather, like historical acts of aggression against Jews, offensive cultural constructions emerge from particular moments and locations.[39] Attending to the specific contexts that gave rise to antisemitic texts reveals various and even conflicting motivations that affirm how antisemitism is no singular and unchanging entity but rather a complicated, unpredictable, and contradictory phenomenon. Far from a straightforward and obvious aspect of Christian culture, far from an attitude whose outlines are so familiar as to merit no more than a pat acknowledgment (i.e., the idea that "of course" Christians hated Jews), antisemitism merits close, critical, and historicized study. While undeniably repugnant, careful analysis of antisemitism teaches us about the heterogeneity of Christian notions of identity and interaction, and the presence of contingencies and entanglements that give us some hope for the future.

This book addresses such complexity and overlap by taking seriously the spatial and geographic dimensions of early English texts. As the depiction of Shylock's house in *Merchant* indicates, closed and private "Jewish" locations serve in these works as an implicit metaphor or allegory for the nature of the "Jew." Shylock's closed casements imply his alterity and antipathy to Christians. Insofar as the texts I analyze use space to portray Jews as dangerous or degraded others, they offer an early example of a phenomenon analyzed by cultural geographers Neil Smith and Cindy Katz. In an important 1993 essay, the two theorists focus upon the critical vogue for spatial metaphors like "'positionality,' 'locality,' 'grounding,' 'displacement' 'territory,' [and] 'nomadism.'" As Smith and Katz point out, "metaphor works by invoking one" seemingly familiar and straightforward "meaning system to explain or clarify another," more complex, meaning system.[40] Writers have long used space to explain difficult concepts. An ancient habit of thinking that might recall certain aspects of the antisemitic house metaphor is the use of buildings as figures for human identity. In the *Timaeus*, Plato uses a citadel to describe how the heart, reason, and mortal soul defend against the body "being injured by something from outside, or possibly even by an internal appetite."[41] Later, Jewish writers such as Philo of Alexandria (25 BC–AD 50) and Christian writers like Paul (e.g., 1 Cor. 3:16) would continue to liken persons to castles, temples, and other buildings.[42] When we turn to the Middle Ages, as Jill Mann puts it, "the field of examples is vast" and encompasses lengthy and detailed architectural allegories that enumerate various components of a church, monastery, castle, etc. to help readers comprehend and ponder identities such as that of Christ, the Virgin Mary, a monk, or a nun.[43]

However, as Katz and Smith stress, while writers have at times used spatial metaphors to pin down, fix, and clarify concepts, the fact is that space is a much more complicated entity.[44] Space is not clear, stable, and given, but rather multiple, contradictory, contingent, and shifting. Classical and medieval texts suggest this complexity when, for example, the fortified castles used to describe chastity "cannot help," as Mann observes, but carry "the implications of action, of attack and defense," or when writers from Ovid to Chaucer evoke fame through "fantastic buildings which defy the notion of stability in every possible way."[45] Due to its inherent complexity, space ultimately doesn't so much assist as problematize any effort to determine identities, whether that of the virgin, the monk, or the "Jew."[46] Shakespeare certainly connotes such complexity via Shylock's house. As we have seen, the very architectural closure that connotes a carnal Jewish blindness also makes Shylock a figure for the very bourgeois trends—sobriety, domesticity, thrift, Puritan asceticism—that defined Shakespeare's England. Further complications arise when Shylock's faith in architectural solidity proves mistaken. Soon after he reiterates that Jessica lock up the house— "shut the doors after you. / Fast bind, fast find" (2.5.48–49)—she departs from it with two Christians youths and her father's money onto the streets of Venice and ultimately the island of Belmont.

The way that Shylock's house doesn't so much confirm his "stony" Jewishness but open him up to multiple and contradictory significations exemplifies how careful attention to the depiction of physical space in antisemitic texts allows us to apprehend their complexity and contradictions. What Henri Lefebvre calls "the multiplicity of space" enables a more nuanced understanding of identity formation than easy oppositions of good Christian and bad Jew. The mutual constitution of selves and spaces is a fraught endeavor marked by heterogeneity, change, overlap, and slippage.[47] Careful attention to spatial complexity, moreover, allows for interpretations that not only elucidate the causes and outcomes of antisemitism but also suggest alternate narratives. In the case of *Merchant*, the contradictory nature of Shylock's house shores up a counterplot in Shakespeare's play, in which the Jew isn't only demonized enemy but also sympathetic victim, in which the object of critique isn't so much Jews but Protestant asceticism.

In order to unpack how space both fosters and troubles the antisemitism at work in English texts, I engage in both historical contextualization and close formal analysis of their representation of physical locations. The intersection between imagined and historical spaces is crucial to my methodology. Often, the subtle and indirect nature of the counternarratives I identify may raise the question of how much writers consciously intended, and readers or auditors readily comprehended, them. Any answer to the question of the availability of a counterintuitive reading to a medieval or early modern context is necessarily speculative. Arguments about the political unconscious of cultural works, of the antinomies of representation, and of the "crossover" capacity of texts urge the legitimacy of reading against the grain of literary texts, including antisemitic writings.[48] My project, with its attention to what we might call the "spatial unconscious" of medieval and early modern texts, is in the spirit of such critical methodologies. My aim isn't always to ascertain precisely how aware a medieval or early modern writer, reader, or theatergoer was of a certain interpretation and its historical context. Rather I seek primarily to demonstrate how attention to spatial complexity enhances our understanding of the medieval and early modern past in its variety, contingency, and open-endedness, that is, of how unacknowledged and emergent understandings existed alongside more official and traditional accounts of identity and lived experience. The likelihood that a medieval or Renaissance reader did not identify ambiguity in a text doesn't mean that we should ignore such tensions, particularly when ethics and politics prompt our inquiry.

## Shifting Geographies of Antisemitism and the Hereford Map

In order to develop further my methodology, I use as a conceptual springboard not a medieval literary text but a more explicitly geographic artifact: the Hereford *mappa mundi* or world map (figure 1).[49] Produced ca. 1285, around the time of the expulsion, the map offers a useful starting point for pondering the spatial politics of the Jewish–Christian dynamic in medieval England. As David Leshock has observed, the Hereford map offers two versions of the "Jew": the biblical Jews whom Christians claimed as predecessors (called alternately *populus israel* or *filiorum israel*), and contemporary Jews, labeled *Iudei*, who are rejected as carnal idolaters and associated with another demonized group, Muslims.[50] Not only does the map construct contemporary Jews as religious others by associating them with idolatry, but it also maps out that alterity by locating the *Iudei* in Asia, just west of the Red Sea, and at a considerable remove from the Christian West (figure 2).

In reality, of course, contemporary Jews openly lived throughout Europe when the map was created. By imaginatively exiling Jews from the West, the Hereford mapmaker suggests, in part, just how upset gentiles were by the sheer existence of Jews in Christian territory. Theologically, contemporary Jews confronted Christians with a disturbing paradox: the sheer ongoing presence in the world of God's former chosen people—Jesus, after all, was a Jew—who nevertheless denied the validity of Christianity. If Christianity,

**FIGURE 1.** Hereford world map, ca. 1285. Hereford Cathedral, Hereford. By permission of the Mappa Mundi Trust and Dean and Chapter of Hereford Cathedral.

as theologians stressed, grew out of yet supplanted Judaism, what were Jewish remnants of that older religiosity doing in the world? Why had they not converted? Augustine provided an early and influential answer to such questions when he claimed that, through exile and scattering, God both punished the Jews (by depriving them of a stable dwelling and of liberty) and provided Christians with living embodiments of the Old Testament and its prophecies regarding Christ. Blind to how their religious books typologically affirm the ancient roots of the Christian message, dissenting Jews became in Augustine's thought less sentient beings than insensible forms of

FIGURE 2. *Iudei* on the Hereford map. By permission of the Mappa Mundi Trust and Dean and Chapter of Hereford Cathedral.

providential technology. Diaspora constitutes, in effect, God's universal ad campaign. "For if that testimony of the Scriptures existed only in the Jews' own land," writes Augustine, "and not everywhere, then, clearly, the Church, which is everywhere, would not have it to bear witness in all nations to the prophecies which were given long ago concerning Christ."[51] Augustine's Jews are omnipresent, global, and highly public billboards proclaiming the Christian message, "milestones" who "point the way to travelers walking along the route" to salvation, who themselves remain "inert and unmoving" until their final conversion during the Last Judgment.[52]

But no images of blind Jewish signposts dot the spaces of Britain or any other western location on the Hereford map. In its absenting of Jews from England, the map reflects how arguments for coexistence had lost their cachet in England. By erasing Jews from European lands that in fact were occupied by Jews, the map presents an offensive cultural fantasy. Such a geography of intolerance accords with the message Kathleen Biddick and Suzanne Conklin Akbari identify in other examples of medieval Christian visual and textual culture. Through acute readings of maps and texts such as the *Siege of Jerusalem* (ca. 1370–90) and Mandeville's *Travels* (ca. 1350–70), Biddick and Akbari demonstrate how Christian *temporal* claims about an outmoded Jewish people, blindly clinging to an old, outdated law, prompted *geographic* images of containment, exile, and erasure.[53] As Biddick observes, the temporal "cut" entailed by the claim that Christianity had superseded Judaism entails a correlating spatial cut or division of Christians from Jews. The Hereford *mappa mundi* offers an extreme example of such fantasies of exile for its English mapmaker. That is, while all of Europe is devoid of Jews, the situation of England on the northwestern world border—the furthest of all western locales from Asia—suggests how the island epitomizes the "ideal" separation of Jews from Christians.

However, if we shift our attention from mapping of bodies on the Hereford map to its portrayal of buildings, we can complicate the idea that the map empties England of Jews. On the entirety of what the map calls *Britannia Insula*, no persons appear whatsoever. Instead the map crams England full of *spaces*: place names, mountains, hills, waterways, and above all, city icons (figure 3). One of the earliest surviving efforts to chart the British Isles in detail, the Hereford map depicts some twenty-five place-icons that denote English cities via images of crenellated castles, towers, and dome-topped cathedrals. The three largest icons refer to London, Chester, and Lincoln, and of those cities, Lincoln stands out for its size and "intricate" design.[54] An image of Lincoln Cathedral—a square topped by a large rectangular tower and shorter towers—appears perched on a hilltop over the river Witham (figure 4). Left of the cathedral is a crenellated wall before three stone structures. Their crenellations suggest that those built environments are the towers of Lincoln castle. But what is especially noteworthy about the image is how the stone structures move up to the cathedral at an angle that doesn't so much suggest the castle, which occupies a plain, but rather the "house-lined street" that leads up to the cathedral, that is, the thoroughfare that begins as the Strait and then becomes Steep Hill.[55]

I stress the street leading up to the cathedral on the place-icon because of the strong Jewish associations of Lincoln at the time of the expulsion, when it "was by far the most affluent and most numerous of the English communities" of Jews (figure 5).[56] To this day two late twelfth-century structures on Steep Hill are linked with Jews, a stone synagogue and the "luxurious" upper-hall stone house of Belaset, daughter of Solomon of

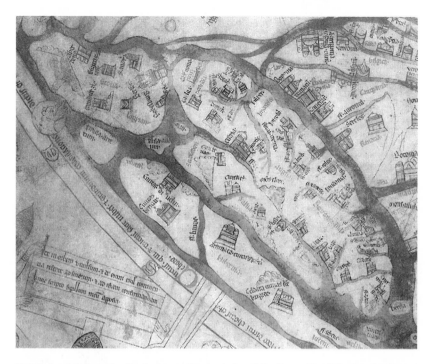

**FIGURE 3.** Britain on the Hereford map. By permission of the Mappa Mundi Trust and Dean and Chapter of Hereford Cathedral.

Wallingford (figure 6).[57] Belaset's ca. 1170–80 home occupies the junction of the Strait and Steep Hill and is one of the earliest extant town houses in England; shops occupied the first floor, whose richly decorated door and windows are still evident.

Further down the hill, on the eastern side of the Strait, stood an even more impressive home, that of Josce of Colchester's daughter Floria, described in expulsion lists as "optima domus cum duabus shopis et pulcro exitu" (the best house with two shops and a beautiful entrance).[58] North and perpendicular to the crossing of the Strait and Steep Hill lay Brancegate, now Grantham Street, where many Jews settled.[59] The expulsion property lists record how both Jacob of Brancegate and Manser of Bradeworth each had "a good house, well built" there, and Josce of Colchester had a well-built home with "two chambers."[60] According to the hundred rolls, during the twelfth century, all of the property on the west side of Steep Hill within the South Gate of the Upper Town was owned by England's greatest financier, Aaron of Lincoln.[61] Aaron's home occupied the top of Steep Hill, in the protection of the Bail, and faced what is now the square between the castle and the cathedral.

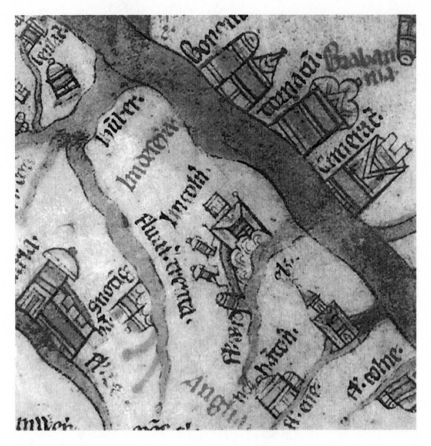

**FIGURE 4.**    Lincoln on the Hereford map. By permission of the Mappa Mundi Trust and Dean and Chapter of Hereford Cathedral.

Could the Lincoln place-icon refer to those Jewish houses? It is of course true that place-icons are just that, icons. Houses on maps usually perform the generic and iconographic work of simply indicating that a place is a city. But, as we have seen, the Lincoln place-icon is notably elaborate and includes elements that accurately reflect such particulars as Lincoln Cathedral, Steep Hill, the river Withum, and the castle. Such details have prompted scholars, especially Malcolm Parkes, to speculate that the Richard identified on the map as its creator was either from Lincoln or was well acquainted with the city.[62] Evidence suggests that perhaps the mapmaker even shared ink with Jewish scribes in artistic workshops in Lincoln.[63] The likelihood that the mapmaker lived in Lincoln and worked alongside Jews supports the prospect that the stone houses lining Steep Hill on the place-icon might refer to Jewish residences on that street.

UPPER TOWN
LOWER TOWN
Cathedral
Castle
N
1 Aaron's house
2 Jew's/Belaset's house
3 Synagogue/ Garmston House
4 Castle
5 Cathedral
6 Steep Hill
7 The Strait
8 High Street
9 Stonebow Arch
10 Brayford Pool
11 Fossdyke Canal
12 River Witham
13 St Paul-in-the-Bail
14 St Benedict's
15 Grantham Street
16 St George's
17 St Martin's

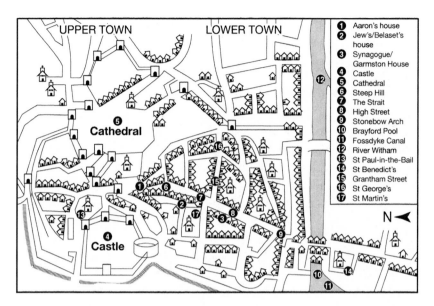

**FIGURE 5.** Plan of medieval Lincoln. Map by Cath D'Alton. Adapted from Hillaby and Hillaby, *Palgrave Dictionary of Medieval Anglo-Jewish History*, 209.

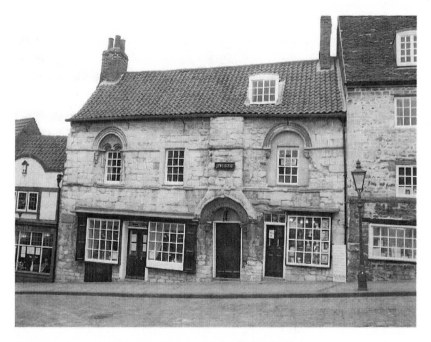

**FIGURE 6.** Ca. 1170–1180 home of Belaset of Wallingford in Lincoln.

And yet, regardless of such evidence, should we even endeavor to link the stone structures on the place-icon to houses owned by Jews in Lincoln, when such a connection risks supporting what has become a problematic chestnut? An ongoing myth about Jews in medieval English cities is that they had a special association with stone houses. Cecil Roth writes that "Jews were pioneers in the art of domestic architecture" and "were apparently among the first to introduce the use of stone houses for ordinary occupation into England."[64] Popular English mythology, moreover, maintains that *all* medieval stone houses on the island belonged to Jews.[65] While Roth celebrates Anglo-Jews' contribution to English architecture, popular generalizations seem to support long-standing stereotypes about the Jew's stony nature. Of course, in theory the stone house could serve as a metaphor for the virtuous fortification of the Jew from dangerous and corrupting influences in the manner of the *Timaeus*, medieval allegories and *The Merchant of Venice*. But more likely is the prospect that the folk association of Jews with stone houses emerges from and lends credence to negative stereotypes. For example, the lofty physicality of certain stone buildings supports the supposed association of the "Jew" with materialism and greed. And the sturdy and castle-like walls surrounding those structures make them lasting public memorials to the supposedly stony interiority of the "Jew," who firmly closes himself off from the Christian majority and its religion.

Mindful of such issues, I nevertheless put the Lincoln place-icon into conversation with medieval Anglo-Jewish habitation. Somewhat ironically, though, I find the icon useful not only because its details resonate with where Jews actually lived in medieval Lincoln, but also because those same details affirm the ambiguity of the medieval stone house as a marker of human identity. The buildings dotting Steep Hill on the icon tell us nothing about the religious affiliation of their residents. There is, for example, no image of a synagogue on the icon, just a series of houses, none of which bear markers of a Christian and/or Jewish owner. While such factors might seem to militate against linking the buildings to Jews, it is that very ambiguity that counters myths about the Jewishness of stone dwellings and instead connotes the more complex historical reality of Anglo-Jewish life. As historian Sarah Rees Jones and archeologists John Schofield and Alan Vince have shown in their analyses of high medieval habitation patterns, Jews hardly had a monopoly on domestic stone architecture in England.[66] In Lincoln and other cities like York and London, Christians built and occupied numerous stone homes. And even if, as Roth and others suggest, Jews played an important role in establishing stone architecture on the island, there was nothing "Jewish" about those structures. The form and design of Jewish homes borrowed from the majority community.[67] Thus when Jews occupied stone houses, those homes didn't set them apart in any way from Christians.

Indeed, regardless of what kind of house they occupied, Jews in medieval England lived a life defined not by architectural and other kinds of geographic separation, but rather spatial contiguity and intimacy. While we can refer to Anglo-Jewish neighborhoods during this period, we cannot speak of ghettoes, which first emerged in Europe well after the 1290 expulsion.[68] Neither a walled enclosure nor any kind of geographic form of segregation marked off Jewish buildings from their Christian counterparts in medieval England. Rather, as such scholars as Vivian Lipman and Jeffrey Jerome Cohen stress, Jews and Christians shared space on streets and street blocks, living often alongside one another as neighbors.[69]

The ambiguity of the Lincoln place-icon resonates with such aspects of medieval Anglo-Jewish habitation. The similitude of the three houses on the icon reflects the generic nature of all stone houses in England and allows us, in accord with Jewish–Christian neighboring, to imagine them as occupied just by Christians, just by Jews, or by a combination of the two. The prospect that all three icons leading up to the cathedral are Christian homes is clearly the safest interpretation. Viewed as depicting only "Christian" built environments in an English city that once openly housed Jews, the Hereford map would participate in the architectural appropriations of the expulsion, which entailed the massive acquisition of Jewish property by the Crown. Such a reading would of course also reinforce how the entire map exiles Jews from western space.

A far more oppositional and risky reading would interpret the place-icon in light of the reality of preexpulsion neighboring in Lincoln, identifying one or two of the buildings leading up to the cathedral as "Jewish" dwellings. By associating some of the houses on the icon with Jewish residents, we discover in it a means of undoing interpretively the overt "othering" program of the map, whose *Iudei* or Jews appear only in the east and are cast as idolaters. While images of persons suggest how the map posits English isolation from Jews, images of buildings allow us to view the map as acknowledging a "Jewish" presence on the island.

By describing two different options for reading the Lincoln place-icon, I mean to stress the multiplicity of space, both as it existed in preexpulsion England and as the Hereford map imagines it. In the same way that, as scholars such as Schofield and Jones suggest, places like York or London functioned in not a monolithic but a complex manner, I emphasize here and throughout this book the multivalence and multiplicity of historical and imagined spaces. The goal here often isn't to determine how literary texts "resolve" societal dilemmas through spatial metaphor but to explore how the spaces in those texts confirm and even intensify social problems and possibilities.

## Jews, Christians, and Urban Conduits

As my reading of the Lincoln icon indicates, this book approaches Jewish houses and other built environments not as static and clearly delineated spaces, but as shifting and permeable sites that exist in dynamic and destabilizing relation to a larger, heterogeneous field that assumes urban, regional, national, and even global dimensions. Crucial to my analysis of that spatial complexity are depictions of flow and movement in early English antisemitic culture. The Lincoln place-icon refers to such spatial mobility via the road where the three houses and the cathedral appear. Like other infrastructural features such as waterways, the thoroughfares connecting built environments and public squares evince their permeability and imply the journeying of persons and other entities in and out of doorways and other thresholds. As mediums of movement and interaction, roads can variously consolidate and query identities.[70] Viewed one way, the connective capacity of a road could foster Christian community; for example, a road might enable the joint movements of Christians to and from a church or other site of communal gathering. But roads can also foster unexpected and disruptive links. A Christian might take a road to enter a Jewish household, or vice versa. Roads thus speak to the potential for contact between various residents, interactions that would render domiciles and other sites heterogeneous, mixed, and changing spaces.

Roads and other medieval avenues of transport suggest how the spatial flows stressed in recent work on contemporary spaces aren't altogether new. Insights like sociologist John Urry's stress on how "the heterogeneous, uneven and unpredictable mobilities of people, information, objects, money, images and risks" manifested by "global fluids" resonate with earlier historical flows.[71] Movement not only characterizes late capitalism but also applies to the medieval and Renaissance world, albeit with less intensity and on a smaller scale. This book considers how literary depictions of space on a host of scales—ranging from microspaces within buildings to highly public and global locations—intersect with such instances of medieval and Renaissance mobility.

While the chapters that follow consider how antisemitic texts engage with several kinds of destabilizing flows, such as the movement of individual persons, groups of people, and even sewage, they particularly stress the flow of goods and capital and their attendant effect on spatial dynamics. When, as early as the ninth century, surplus goods emerged in the medieval West and laid the groundwork for a money economy, that new commercial system manifested itself spatially, in urban form. Scholars of the "new urban sociology" such as David Harvey and Manuel Castells emphasize the importance of the contemporary, postindustrial city over other geographic units, such as the region or nation, due to its privileged role in the circulation of capital.[72] Ironically, though, even as postindustrial technologies have made the metropolis more important than ever before, because the city is a prime nodal point for the relay of global economic flows, it functions as a kind of negative space that is always in the process of emptying itself. The medieval city hardly evinces quite that level of self-negating intensity and scale of flow. We need only think of the encircling of medieval cities by walls to affirm their difference from the permeable postindustrial metropolis. But then again, neither was the medieval city altogether different from contemporary urban space. Work by scholars including economic historians Rodney Hilton and R. H. Britnell and archeologists Schofield and Vince demonstrates how the medieval English city was not so much a coherent and bounded entity but an "urban field" defined by commercial interaction between a city and its greater environs.[73] As the example of London attests, it is partly due to its commercial basis that the medieval form of England's metropole offers us "a fractured landscape, a locality irreconcilably plural," at whose "perimeter . . . flux, activity and border crossing was rife."[74]

One individual whose commercial practices evinced such urban destabilizations is Aaron of Lincoln, the financier who owned a block of properties on Steep Hill, the topographical feature so important to the representation of Lincoln in the Hereford map. Aaron helped finance the building of cathedrals, abbeys, and episcopal palaces in Lincolnshire (possibly Lincoln Cathedral), Yorkshire, and other locales in England. The banking practices of Aaron, who maintained residences in both Lincoln and London, reveal the circulation of capital from the Jewish house into English cities, where it participated in the construction of the seeming architectural opposite of the Jewish house, a Christian church. Aaron's financing projects thus add another interpretive dimension to the Lincoln icon on the Hereford map, showing how its road connects the church at the top of Steep Hill to not just Christian but also Jewish residences. Aaron shores up how the physical components of a Christian church—for example, walls, sculpture, windows—speak to unstable flows of capital.

Of course, in citing Aaron's role in medieval English urban economies, I risk reinforcing antisemitic ideas about the "economic" Jew, that is, the idea that there was some sort of essential relationship of Jews to capitalism as a materialist practice.[75] Essentialist notions of the economic Jew refer to a materialism that is part and parcel of Jewishness, something that inheres to all Jews. Such a view has roots in Pauline hermeneutics and its stigmatization of Jews as inherently carnal, fleshly, material, and literal.[76] Christian godliness, Paul stressed to converts from Judaism in his epistles, involves a faith-based spiritual sensibility. Because Christians, Paul claimed in Romans 8:9, "are not in the realm of the flesh but are in the realm of the Spirit," they supplant Jewish carnality—for example, the physical inscription of the body via circumcision—with new and superior spiritual counterparts. Paul's interpretive method proved so influential that Christianity emerged as a religion whose very coherence hinged on its supposed supersession of a materialism that it stigmatized as Jewish. Shylock evinces the long life of that stereotype in his grasping desire for either monetary payment or a pound of flesh in return for his loan to Antonio, as does the depiction in the Hereford map of contemporary Jews worshipping an idol that excretes money.

But while Christians claimed to supplant such "Jewish" materialisms with a higher, spiritual-order mode of being, Christian history tells a very different story. As Marx insinuated in his complex screed "On the Jewish Question," the official version of Christianity—like the nineteenth-century political state—is "unreal, imaginary" insofar as its mystical elements have no existence in an ineluctably material world.[77] Any claim about Christian spirituality—like notions of political community—is, Marx asserts, mere sophistry, the *"political lion's skin"* that covers over profane, material practices that in reality dominate life and are the practical basis of both Christianity and the political state.[78] Notoriously—perhaps facetiously—Marx equates the actual nature of Christianity with Judaism, confronting Christian readers with the idea that the Jewishness they have long demonized as grasping, selfish, and carnal is in actuality their own nature. Nirenberg reframes this insight in a non-Marxist and more religious register when he writes that Pauline supersession "would have the effect of stigmatizing and 'Judaizing' vast areas of human life—letter, law, flesh—that are difficult to transcend in this world."[79]

Let me be clear: my position in this study is that there is nothing especially "Jewish" about capitalism or any materialist practice. The historical participation of Jews in commerce has nothing to do with any innate association of Jews with the carnal. Whatever role Jews have played in capitalism over time has arisen from a host of changing and various contingencies. Included in those contingencies in England are factors—such as royal policy and hardening ecclesiastical attitudes toward usury—that forced or encouraged many Jews into certain occupations during the High Middle Ages.[80] Also included in those contingencies is how, in later centuries, diaspora happened to situate some Jews in a mercantile position.[81] By stressing the contingent and partial nature of any Jewish involvement in capital, I don't mean to suggest that that phenomenon was solely reactive; even as some Jews were forced into certain occupations, others actively participated in and even shaped trade and commerce.[82] Rather, I mean to stress how careful attention to historical and geographic particulars erodes fantasies of the economic Jew by demonstrating how capitalism is a phenomenon in which *some* people, hailing from *all* religious and ethnic identities, have participated, at various levels of intensity and success.[83]

Indeed, if we turn to historical work on the period between the conquest and the expulsion, England stands out for its complex economic *entanglement* of Jews and the Christian Crown.[84] William the Conqueror appears to have brought Jews into the realm for financial reasons.[85] Starting at least as early as the twelfth century, Anglo-Jews were called "the King's Jews" because they were protected and controlled by English kings who both taxed them and assumed their loans and property after their death.[86] The Jews' status as a "Royal Milch-Cow" helped the king oppose the nobility, a fact that led to the promulgation of anti-Jewish legislation by nobles.[87] Over the course of the thirteenth century, when taxation and other abuses made Jews no longer profitable for English kings, they ceased to enjoy royal projection. Edward I's decision to sponsor the expulsion resulted partly from the Jews' economic uselessness, and partly from the new material benefits resulting from the Crown's evolving relationship with Parliament. Edward I received an unprecedentedly large tax in exchange for granting expulsion.[88]

Thus what seem to be uniquely English and Christian carnalities help account for Jews' movement in and out of English space during the Middle Ages. While the greed of England's new Christian conqueror brought Jews onto the island after 1066, the avarice of Edward I helped prompt the forced migration of Jews from the island in 1290. The example of Aaron of Lincoln affirms, moreover, how such material connections and overlaps were not restricted to the English Crown. Members of the English clergy, persons invested in architectural materialisms like the massive cathedrals for which the Middle Ages is famous, enacted such projects with the aid of Jewish lenders.

I argue that close attention to the shifting and complex urban geographies of antisemitic texts reveals such a radical entangling of Christian and non-Christian, Jew and gentile. My analysis thus reads the accommodated Jew as not only the imagined perpetrator of boy-martyr and other libels, but also a figure of new and destabilizing urban economies. I begin by tracking how English antisemitic texts construct "Jewish" buildings as a locus of urban problems ranging from violent crime to greedy acquisition. The architectural counterpart to the Jewish house in those texts typically is the communal space of a church, where Christians worship such "victims" of Jewish hostility as a ritually murdered boy or Christ in the host. Through such mappings of Jew and Christian onto different urban structures, English writers oppose a Jewish private sphere to a Christian public sphere, and contrast Jewish violence with Christian veneration. But the very spatial terms through which English writers perform their antisemitism bind Christian and Jew as much as they divide them. To oppose, for example, a Jewish home and a Christian church is to assume an urban geography whose complex web of infrastructural conduits and economic flows challenges the opposition on which antisemitism depends.

Such connective currents erode notions of particularly "Jewish" or "Christian" locations and assert instead how a space like a Jewish home uncannily mirrors its seeming Christian opposite. For all English writers' overt stress on the Jew's house as a site that counters Christian welfare, they use that built environment to ponder, at an antisemitic and architectural remove, Christian problems. At the same time that the events imagined to transpire inside the Jewish households of English texts clearly affirm long-standing ideas about Jewish danger, they point less directly to fraught urban and commercial Christian behaviors such as mob violence and greedy acquisition.

"Accommodated" in my title thus extends beyond practices of lodging and lending to the word's primary association from the classical period onward with adaptation, repurposing, and flexibility. Cicero and later writers invoked such a meaning of "accommodate" when they described the adaptation of the self to others' needs—for example, gearing a speech to the interests and tastes of a particular audience.[89] Contemporary rhetorics of accommodation resonate with those early valences, with their stress on accommodating buildings and rooms for disabled or transgender persons. With the exception of a discussion in chapter six of arguments favoring "readmission," and its coda, on Eliza Davis's correspondence with Charles Dickens, this book traces no such ethical adaptations and adjustments. The English texts I analyze are hardly interested in the needs of a Jewish minority in a majority Christian west. Instead, English writers adapt their antisemitic constructions to their own gentile concerns and interests. Starting with Thomas of Monmouth, English writers accommodate the "Jew" to respond to new socioeconomic conditions in medieval and early modern England.

Such antisemitic "accommodations," I contend, urge a revision of the usual scholarly stress on supersession when analyzing antisemitism. Scholarly work on early images of the "Jew" often takes as its starting point Pauline supersession and goes on to uncover how Christianity—to cite Steven Kruger's important formulation—is "haunted" by a Jewishness it claims to have moved beyond.[90] But antisemitic writers such as Chaucer and Marlowe invert and reverse this temporal dynamic, construing the Jew as not only a sign of a renounced carnal past, but also a charged harbinger of a material future. With the advent of trade and related spheres of economic influence, English texts increasingly connote Jewish carnality in order to manage emerging bourgeois concerns over the city, commerce, and other issues. While supersessionist discourse renders the Jew outmoded, atavistic, and other in his carnality, this more protosecular discourse aligns Jewish materialism with modern trends—for example, a profit economy—that undo fantasies of Christian spiritual supremacy and cohesion.

## Mapping Antisemitism across Time

Spanning some nine centuries, the texts covered in this book disclose a long history of continuity and contradiction in literary mappings of Jew and Christian. While the sweeping, historicist reach of this project affirms the persistence of certain tropes, especially the association of the "Jew" with closed and lethal built environments, it also demonstrates the complexity and contingency of the fate of Jews in English society. By generating readings attuned to the particulars of the time and place where these texts emerged, this book attends to how various social issues prompted English writers to employ spatial tropes for different reasons. For example, while monastic well-being troubles Thomas of Monmouth, urban sanitation concerns Chaucer, and domesticity interests the Croxton-writer. A long historical look also enables an awareness of how changing times can loosen or tighten the boundaries demarcating identities. In the case of plays like Croxton or *The Jew of Malta*, the increasing prominence of capitalism allows for greater acknowledgment of how the dangerous Jewish house isn't Jewish at all, but a figure for Christian materialism. In other examples, rising capitalism and other developments such as the Protestant Reformation don't prompt a more open stance toward religious others. Thus for Milton, the Protestant turn that proves compatible with Hebraism also entails an antisemitic rejection of readmission.

Chapter 1 analyzes the unstable geography of Christian and Jew during the Anglo-Saxon period, before the burgeoning of commerce, when other materialisms proved unavoidable and even desirable for a newly converted English people. I take as my starting point how the Venerable Bede and poet

Cynewulf construct Christianity by asserting its alterity and opposition to an idea of Jewish carnality that draws on and modifies Pauline supersession. Bede and Cynewulf demonstrate how, before the Jews' arrival in England, English writers proved especially fascinated by the intimacy of biblical Jews to privileged spaces like Solomon's Temple or the setting of the Crucifixion. The spatial paradox that emerges in their texts in a sense turns supersession on its head. Bede's love of the temple and Queen Helena's intense interest in finding out from a Jew the location of the cross constitute less the Christian supplanting of a degraded Jewish carnality than a Christian reliance on exalted Jewish materialisms. Instead of exiling outmoded Jewish materialisms from Christian space, these Anglo-Saxon texts seek to bring privileged and venerable Jewish materialisms into a new Christian world that seems somehow wanting without them.

While that dynamic would persist beyond the time of Cynewulf and Bede, the material concerns informing their works also would transmute into the more commercial issues analyzed in subsequent chapters. Turning to English antisemitic texts produced during the advent of the city and a money economy, I examine how such developments prompted a heightened focus not so much on venerable Jewish sites like Solomon's Temple but on houses and related spaces associated with contemporary Jews. My study begins with an analysis of Thomas of Monmouth's ritual murder libel as a fraught monastic response to the massive urban changes that occurred in Norwich over the course of the twelfth century. A member of a cloister (Norwich Cathedral close) ministering to an unwieldy urban population, Thomas manages his vexed status as a city monk through the figure of a Jew who "monkishly" closes his home to Christians. Thomas's displacement of his monastic fear of the crowd onto the "Jew" is no easy linear process, however, but takes mediated form as he moves in his antisemitic narrative through a variety of interconnected urban spaces that reveal the complexities and contradictions of an animosity that includes, but is hardly limited to, Jews. Careful attention to such slippages reveals how medieval antisemitism was a layered and multidimensional process in which national or global spaces intertwined with local and private spaces. In England, ideologies of expulsion emerge through mundane, small, and overlooked locations like a doorway, a wooden post, or a sewage drain, microspaces that exist in intimate infrastructural relation to larger sites within towns, the nation, and the greater world.[91]

The following three chapters maintain this focus on urban geography but analyze vernacular texts concerned more with commerce than with human aggregation. Largely if not entirely lay productions, Chaucer's *Prioress's Tale*, the Croxton *Play of the Sacrament*, and Marlowe's *The Jew of Malta* feature

Jews whose danger is as economic as it is religious. Writing after 1290 and before readmission, these writers demonstrate how antisemitic lore flourished *after* Jews officially had left the island. Spanning the Middle Ages and Renaissance, their texts offer a shared notion of Jewish carnality that challenges received notions of periodization.

Chapter 3 centers on Chaucer's *Prioress's Tale*, a text that epitomizes the architectural dualism introduced in chapter 2. While Thomas's *Life* and other English antisemitic texts oppose the public and holy space of a Christian church to the private and dangerous location of a Jewish house, Chaucer contrasts the Christian minster where a boy martyr rests to arguably the most debased built environment imaginable, the abject space of a privy used by Jews. The latrine partly speaks to the tale's unique focus on moneylending as a specifically Jewish and allegedly filthy practice. However, the privy serves as no straightforward emblem of imagined Jewish perfidy. By contextualizing the *Prioress's Tale* in terms of the cultures of sanitation, building, and lending with which Chaucer was closely associated, I read the latrine as a symptom of infrastructural flows that undermined any effort to conceive of a coherent Christian subject. Foremost among such destabilizing flows is the inspiration for my analysis, an anecdote in which Aaron of Lincoln jokes about the reliance of church builders on Jewish financiers. While no friend to Jews, Chaucer nevertheless reproduces the "money trail" described by Aaron when, in the *Prioress's Tale*, the body of a dead boy covered with Jewish excrement is carried in a procession to the nearest conventual minster.

In my next chapter, I turn from English ritual-murder tales to the host-desecration libel staged by the Croxton *Play of the Sacrament*. Unlike other host-desecration dramas, Croxton intertwines host desecration with commerce. Only in this play does Jonathas, the chief merchant of the Jews, barter with a Christian trader over the price of the host. Only in Croxton is host desecration preceded by the staging of mercantilism in a Christian house. I consider how the play's economic dimensions would have been all the more resonant when performed in the Great Market of Bury St. Edmunds, due not only to the feel, smell, sound, and sight of market life, but also to the looming presence of Moyse's Hall. The grandest secular building in Bury, Moyse's Hall was associated with Jews but not via ritual-murder, host-desecration, or other antisemitic libels. Instead, folklore claimed the building contained "hidden treasure" controlled by Jews from afar. Ultimately, by teasing out the interplay of commerce in both the play and the town of Bury, I suggest how Croxton doesn't so much affirm the miraculous Christic properties of the host as use the Eucharist to ponder the slippages, oppressions, and possibilities of life under capital.

Marlowe's early modern remapping of the Jew and urban space comprises the focus of chapter 5. *The Jew of Malta*, I argue, enacts a spatial contradiction. While, since the fall of the Second Temple, Jews had been associated with spatial instability and vulnerability, Marlowe places a Jew in Malta, the most fortified location in Europe. A Hospitaller bastion, Malta served as a charged military barrier between the Christian and Muslim-governed portions of the Mediterranean. Complicating claims that Barabas is a figure of containment, I view him as a canny destabilizer of even Maltese hyperfortified space: he locates a city sewer through which Turks may invade Malta, he puts a defunct monastery to secular uses, and he even, hammer in hand, engages in a home-improvement project on his third and final residence. Crucial to my reading is how the counting house—a bourgeois "little room" that seems to epitomize Barabas's identity as greedy encloser—is instead a porous site that informs virtually every built environment in the play. In his staging of how Christian locations in Malta are doubles of Barabas's counting house, Marlowe responds to, revises, and critiques notions we see centuries earlier, in Thomas, Chaucer, and the Croxton playwright. A full understanding of Marlowe's achievement necessitates attending to the long literary history of antisemitism in England.

My final chapter turns to the "readmission" debates of the seventeenth century, when the English shifted from telling stories about Jewish houses to contemplating the accommodated Jew in earnest. During this period the link between Jews and materiality acquired new urgency in England, as the participants in Oliver Cromwell's Whitehall Conference pondered making a place, literally, for Jews on the island. I track in the chapter how, for writers both Jewish and Christian, the prospect of reaccommodating Jews in England proved fraught. Amsterdam rabbi Menasseh ben Israel urged readmission through both polemical writings and his own prominent residence on the Strand, even as his Messianism precluded any deep attachment to any place other than Israel. Protestant polemicist William Prynne amassed evidence favoring keeping Jews out of England that ironically created a valuable archive of a former Jewish presence on the island. I close by considering how John Milton, famous for never weighing in on readmission, offers his view on accommodating Jews in *Samson Agonistes* (1671). While its focus on Judges places biblical Jews at center stage, the generic form of the play denies that Jewish presence: *Samson Agonistes* is a closet drama never intended for performance on a physical stage.

Milton's displacement of even stage Jews speaks to how the great Hebraist was also a Puritan whose asceticism gave new life to the Pauline rejection of "Jewish" carnality under supersession. Nine centuries after Bede, Milton echoes his supersessionism in the form of Samson, an iconoclastic figure who, despite his own rejection of idolatries, exhibits a materialism that merits his interment in his father Manoa's home. Like Bede, Milton associates domestic life with Christians not Jews; for both writers, the only "housing" Jews merit is a tomb akin to Manoa's sepulchral home. The uncanny similitude of the tomb-like Jews of Bede and Milton's Samson radically undermine traditional takes on periodization and evince disturbing continuities traversing nearly a millennium.

But if Bede and Milton speak to the regrettable persistence of the idea that "Jewish" carnality is so antithetical to Christianity as to merit Jews' absenting from England altogether, other writers covered in this study reveal a substantially different relation between Christian and Jew. Sensitive to how the profit motive clashed with Christian theology, writers like Chaucer and the Croxton-playwright use the "Jew" to distance themselves from and worry over the domesticated yet globalizing mercantilism that we now identify as preeminently English.[92] Thus at the same time that the houses featured in antisemitic libels are settings for Jewish violence against Christian boys and the Eucharistic host, they also allow for a mediated inquiry into such protobourgeois issues as privacy, inwardness, and urban trade. Ultimately, my project tracks the central place of the "Jew" in the slow process by which the English accommodated themselves and negotiated their relationship to the bourgeois, profit-minded, and domesticated sensibility they came to embrace and embody. In the reviled figure of the filthy and grasping Jew, whose home was a lethal trap for innocent Christian victims, this "nation of shopkeepers" removed themselves from and grappled with the very domesticated and mercantile identity we now view as eminently English.[93]

# Sepulchral Jews and
# Stony Christians

*Supersession in Bede and Cynewulf*

## Stone and Supersession

Arguably, the primary form of religious difference that occupied the minds of Anglo-Saxon Christians was paganism. One of the two writers on which this chapter focuses, Bede, was born in 672/73, less than a hundred years after the Gregorian mission to convert the Anglo-Saxons and only decades after Celtic missionaries joined that effort.[1] We know very little about Cynewulf, the poet whom I pair with Bede. He likely was an ecclesiastic and seems to have flourished a generation or more after Bede.[2] But we can be sure that during Cynewulf's life, paganism continued to lurk not far from Christianity, especially with the onset of Viking invasions. Both Bede's and Cynewulf's works confirm this interest in pagans. Texts like Bede's *Ecclesiastical History* (ca. 731) and Cynewulf's *Fates of the Apostles* evince a deep investment in the apostolic mission of extending the Roman Christian *imperium* to its English border, where a newly converted Germanic and, later, Norse people were asked to renounce long-held polytheistic attachments.[3]

However, Jews were just as much if not more of a concern for Anglo-Saxon Christians. This was not due to the presence on the island of Jews, who did not inhabit England until after the Norman Conquest, but rather to the proximity of Judaism and Christianity. While Anglo-Saxon writers like Bede and Cynewulf didn't live alongside Jews, they were keenly cognizant of both their status as

God's original chosen people, whose holy books formed the basis of Christianity, and the vexing fact that contemporary Jews did not follow the new Christian religion. Thanks to the close and difficult relationship between Christianity and Judaism, Jewishness haunted Christian life and thought. As Andrew Scheil and other scholars affirm, fundamental to Anglo-Saxon writers' efforts to negotiate their relationship to the Jew was an ideology of supersession or, in a more strictly textual register, a typological hermeneutic.[4] According to supersession, which first emerged in the complex intertwining of "ontology, hermeneutics, anthropology, and christology" in Paul's epistles, Jews adhere to an outmoded carnality and literal-mindedness that Christianity supplants with its embrace of the spirit and figurative thinking.[5] For example, in 2 Corinthians 3:3, Paul contrasts the literal inscription of the old law on the tablets containing the Ten Commandments to the figurative writing of the new law by "the Spirit of the living God" on "the fleshly tables of the heart."[6] Later writers, most influentially Augustine, invoked a version of supersession to manage the problematic priority—that is, the exalted venerability—of the Hebrew Bible. Persons, places, and events in the Old Testament, Augustine and other theologians asserted, both look toward and are superseded by their counterparts in Christian history, although Jews fail to grasp such a relationship due to the literal mindset that their carnality entails.[7] Supersession, to be sure, was not unique to Anglo-Saxon writers but appears in Christian discussions of Jews produced throughout the medieval West. However, Bede and Cynewulf engaged supersession in spatial ways that both set them apart from previous writers and adumbrate English notions of Jews and geography evinced in later texts.

For anyone familiar with contemporary Anglo-Saxon studies, my emphasis on space and Jews will bring to mind the topic of migration. Important work by scholars such as Scheil, Patrick Wormald, Nicholas Howe, and Samantha Zacher has made clear how the Anglo-Saxons exhibited a distinctive interest in the Israelites of Exodus, whose migratory experience and chosen status offered a template for understanding Anglo-Saxon identity.[8] My discussion diverges from such work by taking as its starting point the Anglo-Saxon interest in not migration but Jerusalem and, more particularly, the privileged materialisms associated with that holiest of sites. Instead of attending to expansive tribal movements, this chapter tracks smaller-scale investments in the former Jewish homeland and the exalted objects and buildings located there.[9]

My analysis centers on Bede's Latin exegetical work *On the Temple* (ca. 729–31), which interprets the description in 3 Kings 5:1–7:51 of Solomon's erection of the Temple of Jerusalem, and Cynewulf's Old English poem

*Elene*, which retells the legend of the discovery of the "true" cross.[10] Bede, one of the most sophisticated, nuanced, and brilliant thinkers in medieval Christianity, offers an excellent starting point for examining supersession, a rhetoric that informs nearly all the works covered in this book. Cynewulf's *Elene* complements and supplements Bede by showing how an Anglo-Saxon writer understood supersession not in a Latinate and theological register, but rather in a vernacular and explicitly literary context. In what follows, I slowly tease out the stakes, slippages, and tensions informing both Bede's and Cynewulf's accounts of Jews and "Jewish" materialism. I take as my premise the belief that while we already know that supersession is both omnipresent in early Christian writings and doomed to failure, its articulation in certain places and periods generates lines of development and breakdown that diverge and overlap in important and telling ways. In the case of Bede and Cynewulf, their charged engagements with supersession and "Jewish" places contribute both to our understanding of Anglo-Saxon material culture and to the important role that ideas of the Jew played in such materialisms.[11]

As we shall see, in many respects, both Bede and Cynewulf affirm the usual Christian elevation of the spirit over matter and letter. At the start of *On the Temple*, Bede claims he will locate "the spiritual mansion of God" in the "material structure" of the temple, foregrounding his interest in reading the building typologically, or what Christian theologians later would describe as "in the *accommodated* sense."[12] And *Elene* features a Jew, Judas, whose carnal investment in the well-being of his fellow Jews prevents him from assisting Queen Helena in her quest to uncover the cross as a vehicle of faith. However, other aspects of those works exhibit Christian materialisms that both shed light on important aspects of the Anglo-Saxon world and radically undermine the usual denigration of the Jew as carnal. These elements hint at a fuller picture of early Christian identity in England than supersession would, on the face of it, suggest. Effectively turning the import of supersession on its head, these texts reveal how Christians not only are carnal but also are fascinated by and even envious of what emerges as not a debased but rather a privileged Jewish materialism.

Crucial to my analysis of Bede's and Cynewulf's spatial rhetorics of supersession is their engagement with a material long associated with the "carnal" Jew, stone. Stone plays a central role in Paul's elevation of Christian over Jew; in 2 Corinthians 3:7–8, he describes how the Christian life-giving "ministry of the spirit" supersedes a Jewish "ministry of death" that was "engraved with letters upon stone."[13] Paul elaborates on the Jew's stony materialism, writing that Jewish minds are hardened—their senses ossified, dull, and unchanging—so much so that "to this day" they are incapable of "beholding the glory of the Lord" witnessed under Christianity.[14] Stonily clinging to a carnal mentality, Paul's Jews are cognitively handicapped, incapable of comprehending new Christian truths.[15] While ideas of the stone-hearted or stony Jew appear in writings in medieval England and elsewhere, Bede offers a distinctively architectural and notably offensive version of this rhetoric in a sermon that I pair with his temple exegesis.[16] In this homily, Bede connotes the Jew's lithic materialism via the degraded space of a tomb closed by a stone. Cynewulf makes a similar move in *Elene* by linking Judas's stony carnality to the notorious moment when Queen Helena tortures him in a grave-like pit for refusing to help her find the cross.

Both Bede's and Cynewulf's texts depict what I call the "sepulchral Jew," the idea that the Jew's recalcitrant investment in the dead letter of the old law merits his association with a grave or tomb-like space. I argue that, by using Bede's and Cynewulf's respective depictions of the stony, sepulchral Jew as a heuristic for both *Elene* and *On the Temple*, we gain an important means of tracking the geopolitical stakes of those writings, that is, their conception of the place of both Christians and Jews in the contemporary world. Bede's and Cynewulf's sepulchral Jews adumbrate the tomb-like houses of Shylock in *Merchant* and Manoa in *Samson Agonistes*. They also look toward the political acts of displacement that would occur in England in 1290. In the same way that the expulsion removed Jews from English soil, Bede's tomb and Cynewulf's pit exile the carnal Jew from Christian life, consigning him to a stony space of death located underground or inside a rocky escarpment. Indeed, the offensive image of the sepulchral Jew the writers connote lends chilling support to theories that during the Anglo-Saxon period, Jews were "deliberately excluded from the country."[17]

Importantly, however, even as the depiction of stone in Bede and Cynewulf points to a disturbing burial or entombment of the Jew, it also undermines the very rhetoric of supersession on which that spatial rejection is based. A close look at Bede's interpretations of the stones of Solomon's Temple reveals moments where he proves invested in that building material in ways that point to the role of stone monuments and architecture in establishing the faith in England. Such links suggest how not just Roman but also Jewish materialisms shaped Christianity on the island, where religious sought both to incorporate England within an imperial Roman *ecclesia* and to bring the holy, Jewish spaces of Jerusalem to their isolated island. Cynewulf's *Elene* exhibits similar contradictions, though those tensions emerge more overtly in relation to the materialism of Anglo-Saxon secular culture and Germanic paganism. Namely, references to the stones used in a building program led by Queen Helena, a Roman queen who also resembles Anglo-Saxon aristocrats, expose her deep investment in "Jewish" materialisms. Taken together, Bede's and Cynewulf's works give us a new vantage point for appreciating how the Anglo-Saxons' conversion to Christianity entailed no easy supplanting of pagan carnality with a pure and ascetic-minded Christian spirituality, but rather involved the messy and necessary entanglement of pagan, Christian, and Jewish materialisms.

## Supersession and the Sepulchral Jew

Bede's engagement with supersession appears in one of his fifty homilies on the Gospels. Likely late career products, the sermons are organized into two volumes and are found in their entirety in two ninth-century parchment continental manuscripts (Boulogne, Bibliothèque municipale, MS 75, 339 fols.; Zurich, Zentralbibliothek, MS C. 42, 81 fols.).[18] The sermon, the tenth of volume 2, focuses on an Easter pericope or gospel passage from Luke where the evangelist recounts how, after the Crucifixion, Mary Magdalene and other women wishing to anoint Christ's corpse with spices "found the stone rolled back from the sepulcher. And going in, they found not the body of the Lord Jesus" (Luke 24:2–3). As Bede does throughout his homilies, he teases out several meanings of the episode for his fellow monks.[19] Bede begins with the historical sense, by reminding his readers that Matthew's gospel "tells us that an angel came down from heaven and rolled the stone away from the mouth of the tomb"; the angel, Bede stresses, did not move the stone to "make a way for the Lord to go out, but so that the open and empty space of the tomb might divulge to human beings that he had risen again."[20] The usual function of a sepulcher—to protect a corpse—does not pertain to Christ, whose Resurrection rendered the built environment unnecessary. Indeed, Christ's triumph over the physical world and mortality is such that he didn't need his tomb opened by an angel in order to depart from it. The angel turns away the stone not to assist Jesus but to disclose his Resurrection to those left on earth. Instead of sheltering Christ, the empty sepulcher manifests Christ's transcendence of material objects like tombs. Physical absence signifies as spiritual presence in Bede's reading of the homily. Through its obsolescence, the tomb morphs into a vehicle of faith.

Bede elaborates on Christ's triumph as he considers the spiritual meanings of the passage. Employing the pericope to assert supersession, Bede writes that "mystically, the rolling away of the stone implies the disclosure of the divine sacraments, which were formerly hidden and closed up by the letter of the law. For the law was written on stone" (II.10, 90).[21] Echoing Paul, Bede reads rolling away the stone as a figure for the revelation of a higher, spiritual

Christian order, one that displaces and supplants a Jewish law that is bound to a literal and earthly sensibility. Bede's use of stone to connote Jewish carnality is twofold. The letter of the law is both "written on stone" in the manner of the Ten Commandments and covers over or encloses the new law in the manner of a tomb. The sealed tomb signifies the Jews' inability to see or witness the new law, while its architectural function—the sheltering of a corpse—signifies the lethal nature of the old law, as articulated by Paul's claim that "the letter kills." Bede engages in a kind of historical sleight of hand here. For Jews, that is, Mary Magdalene and the other Marys, are portrayed in the Gospels as the first to learn of the Resurrection from the angels at the tomb. But Bede, exhibiting a pattern of thought analyzed by Kruger, depicts the women as somehow always already Christian.[22]

Members of the Christian faithful, Bede continues, mystically reenact the work performed by the angel: "when we acknowledge our faith in the Lord's passion and resurrection, his tomb, which had been closed, is opened up" (II.10, 90).[23] In contrast, Jews and pagans "continue to be like a tomb still closed by a stone. They are not capable of entering to see that the body of the Lord has disappeared by his rising, because by the hardness of their infidelity they are prevented from becoming aware that a dead person, who has destroyed death's right of entry and has already passed into the heights of the heavens, cannot be found on earth" (II.10, 90–91).[24] In his account of the unbeliever's hermeneutic blindness, Bede technically refers to both Jews and pagans. Yet his primary focus on the former group emerges in their stony *duritia* or hardness of infidelity, as well as his focus on Jewish law just prior to this moment.[25] Here, as in his likening of the stone covering the tomb to the old law, Bede draws his trope from 2 Corinthians. In the same way that Paul writes that Jews' minds "were hardened" or ossified, "for to this day the same veil remains when the old covenant is read," Bede renders the Jew hermeneutically blind and lithic. In Bede's homily, as in Paul's epistle, the Jew embodies the dead literalism of the old law in the manner of the stone of the Ten Commandments. Bede intensifies the trope not only by describing the Jew's heart as hard and ossified but also by comparing the Jew to a tomb still closed by stone. In Bede's sermon, while Christians mystically open Christ's tomb anew, Jews become like sealed tombs in their stubborn adherence to a carnal perspective that prevents them from comprehending the Resurrection. Rendering Bede's sepulchral Jew especially degrading is its presentation in the context of supersession. When occupied, a tomb has its uses, ranging from the ordinary function of sheltering a corpse to grander purposes such as memorialization. For a Christian ascetic—such as Cuthbert, whose biography Bede wrote—the sepulchral, reclusive, and closed space of the hermit's cell or monk's cloister presented an appealing otherworldliness.[26] But here, in the context of the tomb abandoned by Christ, a closed sepulcher is superfluous and useless, connoting the Jew's outmoded carnality.

If we turn from Bede's Latin sermon to Cynewulf's Old English poem *Elene*, we find the poet similarly using a tomb to indicate the Jew's stony materialism and resulting hermeneutical incapacity. Richly combining travel, landscape, archaeology, and architecture, *Elene* is a verse account of the apocryphal story of the finding of the cross during the reign of Constantine the Great, who some English writers claimed was born in Britain.[27] In the legendary tale, Constantine's mother Helena travels to Jerusalem and eventually finds both the beams on which Christ died and the nails of the cross. Of the three Old English versions of the invention legend that exist, only Cynewulf's text features a Jew and yokes finding the cross to the problem of Jewish unbelief.[28] In *Elene*, the queen turns to the Jew, Judas, for help in her quest, but due to his stony carnality, he at first resists helping her. However, after Helena tortures him in a pit redolent of Bede's tomb, Judas relents, assists Helena, and eventually becomes the bishop of the emperor's newly conquered territory of Jerusalem.

*Elene* is located in a single late tenth-century manuscript known as the Vercelli Book (fols. 121r–133v), where it comprises one of several poems that mingle with twenty-three Old English prose sermons.[29] In many respects those poems, as Scheil points out, develop literary themes laid out in the homilies.[30] One such theme is that of the stony Jew. The sixteenth sermon in the codex relates how Christ's divinity was evident not only to humans but to all of creation; even the stones recognize Christ, including many stones of the temple, which fell out of the sanctuary and burst apart at the time of the Crucifixion.[31] But the "hard-hearted" Jews' stubbornness is such that it trumps even the hardness of stones; they "wished not to recognize him, and they were harder than any stones due to their counsel" ("And hineþonne hwæðreð forheardydan heortan Iudeas hine ne woldon ongitan, ac hie wæron heardran þonne ænige stanas, ac hie for ðan næfre to hira ræde gecyrran ne meahton").[32] Cynewulf's *Elene* develops this offensive notion and also builds on and complicates references to the lithic in his likely source, the so-called *Acta Cyriaci*.[33] Complicating a relationship only hinted at in his sources and touched on in Vercelli 16, Cynewulf's citations of stone, both literal and metaphoric, create in *Elene* richly various, overlapping, and even contradictory depictions of a stony and "Jewish" carnality.

A stony hard-heartedness is vital to Judas's identity in the poem, and at least initially it sets him apart from other Jews. Before Judas appears in *Elene*, Cynewulf recounts a meeting between five hundred Jews and Helena.

During this gathering, the queen berates the Jews as "wræcmæcggas" ("miserable men," 387a) who know the prophets yet deny that God's son was born in Bethlehem (386–95).[34] Helena evokes the familiar stereotype of a willful hermeneutical blindness to Christian truth. But the Jews' response posits a scenario that in certain ways is more far disturbing: they claim that they have no idea what sin they have committed. In other words, we find in *Elene* not willfully blind Jews—Jews whose ancestors knew Christ as one of their own and rejected him as their savior—but instead Jews who are utterly ignorant of Christianity and Christ's existence. This is not the first time Helena has met with Jews in the poem; rather she assembled them before her on three earlier occasions. During those encounters, the queen exhibited a keen Christian cognizance of and vested interest in Jewish law and the Hebrew Bible (288a–292b; 333a–368a). In contrast to Helena's intense awareness of Judaism, the Jews are oblivious of the new Christian order and its fraught relation to them and their ancestors. The problem facing Helena at this point in the poem isn't so much the Jews' denial that Jesus was God, but that Jews are so disinterested in Christian history and the Gospels that Jesus has no place in their historical record or collective memory.

Judas, however, knows of what the queen speaks, and he is remarkably firm in resisting her aid. He tells his fellow Jews after their royal summons that Helena seeks information about the cross on which Christ died and stresses that "the need is great that we set our hearts firmly" ("Nu is þearf mycel / þæt we fæstlice ferhðstaðelien," 426b–427b) to hide both the murder and the location of the cross (419–30a). Judas's desire to conceal evidence of Jewish anti-Christian violence adumbrates the conventions of later ritual-murder legends, where "martyred" boys are hidden in forests, wells, and privies. These lines also mark the first time that Cynewulf associates Judas with hard-heartedness. His likely Latin source, the so-called *Acta Cyriaci*, doesn't mention solidly fixed hearts and has Judas simply urge that no one reveal the information.[35] Making Judas's resistance especially noteworthy is his awareness of not only the historical Jesus but also his divinity, thanks to firsthand knowledge passed down from his grandfather Zachaeus and father Simon (436–531a). Recounting a dialogue between his ancestors, Judas relates how Zachaeus, who lived in Jerusalem during Christ's lifetime, tried to convince his fellow Jews not to hang the man they all knew was "the true son of the creator" ("soð Sunu meotudes," 461). Judas's knowledge of the "truth" of Christianity seems to render him all the more obstinate in refusing to assist Helena. Indeed, in urging his fellow Jews to set their hearts on secrecy, he opposes both what he knows to be a fact and the wishes of his forbearers. Zachaeus tells Simon to "speak quickly" ("snude gecyð," 446b) about the cross if asked about it, and Simon likewise counsels Judas never to speak ill of Christ (522–28). Ignoring the import of his personal paternal hotline to Christianity, Judas asks the Jews to lie and ensure that, in an ironic choice of phrase, the "teachings of our fathers" ("fæderlican lare," 431b–432a) are not abandoned. Importantly, Judas is notably carnal in his adherence to Judaism. While Zachaeus "turned from the world" ("wende hine of worulde," 440a) to support Christ, and Simon urges his son to speak well of Jesus so that he will merit "eternal life" ("ece lif," 526b) in heaven, Judas trains his attention on *middangeard* or earth (435a), worrying that the "nobles of Israel" ("Israhela æðelu," 433) may rule ("ma ricsian," 434b) there no longer. The needs of the tribe trump the patrilineal plot.[36]

Once Judas enlightens his fellow Jews about Christ, they finally possess the knowledge Helena seeks. Thus when the queen soon reassembles them before her, they can exhibit a stony resistance toward her, which they do. The queen asks them "where the prince suffered, the true son of the creator for the love of souls" ("hwær se þeoden geþrowade, soðsunu meotudes for sawla lufan," 563–64), only to receive a response that highlights the Jews' newfound stubbornness:

> Heo wæron stearce, stane heardran,
> noldon þæt geryne rihte cyðan
> ne hire andsware ænige secgan,
> torngeniðlan þæs hio him to sohte
> ac hio worda gehwæs wiðer-sæc fremedon,
> fæste on fyrhðe.
>
> *(565–70a)*

[They, her bitter foes, were stiff, harder than stone; [they] did not want rightly to reveal that secret nor give any answer to her about what she sought from them, but they offered opposition to her words, firm in heart.]

Following Judas's advice and echoing his own hard-heartedness, the Jews are "firm in heart" in their unwillingness to assist Helena. Indeed, they are, as Cynewulf stresses in a line that resonates with Vercelli 16, "harder than stone."[37] Cynewulf implicitly contrasts Jewish obduracy with Christ's generosity. While, as the queen tells the Jews, Jesus lovingly gave up his life, they refuse to give over their knowledge about that sacrifice. As E. Gordon Whatley points out, Cynewulf's "careful wording" of Helena's query intersects with the language the poet uses to describe the Jews' response, tying their stony obduracy toward the queen to the deicide charge.[38] That is, insofar as their hard resistance makes them "bitter foes" of Helena's Christian cause, the Jews repeat the opposition of their ancestors toward Christ.

This moment in *Elene* supports the dominant image of Jews in the poem. Jews first appear in the narrative when a newly converted Constantine learns how Jesus was hung ("waes ahangen," 180a) on the cross "in envy through malice" ("æfstum þurh inwit," 206a–207a), thanks to the powers of the Devil "over the Jewish race" ("Iudea cyn," 209a). This image of the Jews as evil agents of Christ's suffering and death receives more stress when Judas tells his fellow Jews how their ancestors out of hate ("purh hete," 424a) and with "furious minds sent the holy one to his death by their own hand" ("on þone halgan handa sendan / to feorhlege fæderas usse / þurh wraðgewitt," 457–59a) and sought to inflict Christ with suffering ("sarum settan," 479). Helena's exchange with the Jews, with its characterization of them as "active antagonists," merges this notable stress on the Jews as enemies of Christ with claims about their stony obduracy, rendering it an ongoing feature of Jewish identity.[39]

Further confirmation of this association of the Jews' lithic resistance with their violent aggression toward Christianity emerges in Judas's speech and its account of the Protomartyr Stephen's martyrdom. Describing how "stones were thrown" ("stanum worpod," 492b) at Stephen after Saul/Paul ordered that Stephen be destroyed with stones ("stanum . . . abreotan," 509b–510a), Judas connotes stone as an anti-Christian weapon. When, a bit later, Cynewulf characterizes as ossified the Jews who resist Helena, he echoes the stones of Stephen's martyrdom, suggesting their association. The Jew's lithic mind, Cynewulf implies, is an anti-Christian weapon akin to the literal stones thrown at Stephen. Such a reading of the weapons of Stephen's martyrdom as figures of Jewish obstinacy was well established in Anglo-Saxon discourse and evoked by writers including Bede and Arator.[40]

If the Jews' obduracy resonates with the stony violence of both Christ's death and Stephen's martyrdom, Helena responds with equal aggression by threatening to burn them in a fierce, hellish fire if they remain silent. Fearing death, the Jews give Judas over to the queen as an informant. The charged confrontation that ensues begins with Helena warning Judas that resistance will prompt the death of both his body and soul. Judas responds:

"Hu mæg þæm geweorðan þe on westenne
meðe ond meteleas morland trydeð,
hungre gehæfted 7 him hlaf 7 stan
on gesihðe bu geweorðað,

strea[r]c 7 hnesce, þæt he þone stan nime
wið hungres hleo, hlafes ne gime,
gewende to wædle 7 þa wiste wiðsæce,
beteran wiðhyccge, þonne he bega beneah?"

*(611–18)*

["How can that happen for the one in the wilderness, (who) treads the
moorland weary and without food, tortured by hunger, and for whom
both bread and stone, the hard and the soft, both appear together to his
vision, that he should take the stone for refuge from hunger and heed
not the bread, turn to poverty and refuse the food, scorn the better
when he has both at his disposal?"]

Read in tandem with his earlier speech, Judas's evocation of stone before
Helena presents the reader with a contradictory cluster of associations ranging from carnality, obstinacy, and sacrifice to salvation. Ironically, this "stony"
(i.e., stubbornly carnal) man tells Helena that he disregards stone; he explains
how a starving man alone in the wild will prefer sustenance—the *hlaf*, that is,
the loaf or bread—over deprivation, here embodied by inedible stone. Judas's
description of bread as soft or *hnesce* and stone as hard or *strearc* furthers their
respective associations with an easy existence where life is supported and a
difficult life devoid of nourishment.[41] As Whatley points out, Judas tells Helena that he is drawn toward a comfortable life on earth, suggesting how he
is open to assisting her.[42] But Judas's words seem to be a ploy, since he goes
on to resist Helena for sixty-five lines, until she resorts to torturing him in a
dry well. Judas, in other words, will actually choose the "stone" in supporting
his Jewish cause; he endures deprivation for the sake of his tribe, even as he
claims to prefer sustenance.

At the same time, as Whatley also observes, Judas's words are, from a figural
perspective, "apt."[43] For in overtly embracing "bread" or food, Judas reveals
his carnal "Jewish" nature. In claiming to prefer bread—in asserting his desire
to live on earth—Judas admits his stubborn "Jewish" investment in this world
over the next. Viewed in this light, Judas reiterates the worldly stance he
assumed when he advocated to his fellow Jews that they maintain Jewish
rule on earth by keeping quiet. When he implies to Helena that he chooses
life over death, Judas thus signifies his investment in a "Jewish" carnality, his
figurative stoniness.[44] A look at the two closest biblical analogues to the passage affirms how Judas reveals his materialism. In the Sermon on the Mount,
as described in Matthew 7:9 and Luke 11:11, Jesus asks his disciples, "what
man is there among you, of whom if his son shall ask for bread, shall reach for

a stone?" Jesus follows that literal question with a figurative query as he tells the disciples: "If you then being evil, know how to give good gifts to your children: how much more will your Father who is in heaven, give good things to them that ask him?" (Matt. 7:11; Luke 11:13). Bede, following Augustine, interprets this passage as figuring supersession, with stone signifying the Jew's *duritia cordis* or hard heart and bread indicating eternal life.[45] Judas supports this construction of the Jew in his "stony" preference for literal bread over the "bread" of spiritual life offered by his own father and grandfather.

After Helena exchanges with Judas more words that confirm his resistance to her cause, she tries a new strategy to enlist his help: torturing him in an empty pit.[46] Finding Judas "stiðhycgende" ("stiff- or hard-minded," 683a) in his refusal to assist her,

Heht þa swa cwicne corðre lædan,
scufan scyldigne—scælcas ne gældon—
in drygne seaðþær he duguða leas
siomode in sorgum seofon nihta first
under hearmlocan hungre geþreatod,
clommum beclungen.

*(691–96a)*

[She then ordered him led away alive by a company and the guilty one pushed—the servants did not hesitate—into a dry well where, lacking retinue, he abided in sorrow for the space of seven nights, tormented in prison with hunger, bound with fetters.]

Helena's action reveals her canny awareness of how Judas's carnality puts him in a double bind. Judas vehemently desires to preserve Judaism and Jewish authority on earth. Yet the carnality associated with Jewishness implies a limit to what Judas will do to defend his people and their law. In other words, *Elene* posits the question: insofar as Jewishness is aligned with a love of this world, will a Jew go so far as to sacrifice himself or herself—to leave this world, renounce her physical being—to ensure the continuation of Judaism? The alacrity with which the Jews offer up Judas in order to avoid death by burning indicates that this is not the case. Helena's decision to throw Judas in the pit suggests how she is sensitive to this conundrum, and Judas's actions confirm how he is caught in a web of carnal attachments. For seven days Judas starves, suggesting how he used his bread and stone speech as a mere ruse. But ultimately, unlike figures such as Stephen who actually die for their faith, Judas eventually submits to his will to live.

When he calls out from the pit for release "from the torment of hunger" ("fram hungres geniðlan," 701a), it turns out that Judas's bread and stone speech accurately reflected his carnal attachment to literal bread over and above the needs of his tribe.

The pit, Helena's strategic response to Judas's stony carnality, presents the reader with a complex image that lends itself to multiple interpretations. Here I touch on one meaning in particular: its resonance with Bede's tomb-like Jew. As we have seen, in Bede a sealed tomb indicates the Jew's stony, stubborn closure to Christian spiritual truths. Cynewulf's pit isn't a closed tomb, but it is a grave-like space. The seven days Judas spends in the empty hole constitute a kind of living death that gives Judas a taste of the eternal death he faces if he remains obdurate.[47] Moreover, like Bede's tomb-like Jew, the sepulchral pit indicates how Judas is "dead" to Christian spirituality. Devoid of sustenance, the pit figures the absence of Christian "bread"—spiritual food—in Judas's life. Thus while *Elene* doesn't explicitly liken Judas to the pit in the manner of Bede's idea of the Jew *as* tomb, Cynewulf's stress on Judas's stony, stubborn carnality does imply how he is sepulchral and occupies a stance that mirrors the grave containing him. In this light, Helena seems to be torturing Judas by submerging and surrounding him with a literal manifestation of his spiritual emptiness.

Both Bede and Cynewulf suggest a disturbing Anglo-Saxon geopolitical stance toward the Jew. As I noted in the Introduction, Augustine famously conceived of the Jews' exile from Jerusalem and subsquent geographic dispersal as both divine punishment and grounds for toleration. God scattered the Jews throughout the world, Augustine argued, because they embodied the biblical books that prophesy and confirm the validity of Christianity. But Bede and Cynewulf offer a geography of supersession where the Jew's stony, stubborn attachment to the dead letter of the law prompts not his scattering but his entombment or burial. Both Bede's and Cynewulf's sepulchral Jews suggest how their Anglo-Saxon creators wish that the contemporary Jewish unbeliever is not just exiled from Jerusalem but evacuated from the spaces of earthly habitation altogether. Imagined as not only stone-hearted but also occupying a stony space of death, the sepulchral Jew cedes the outside world to Christianity.[48]

## Christ's Absence, Spiritual Presence, and Biblical Buildings in Bede

Both Cynewulf and Bede stress the empty and dead space of the Jew. But what of the empty space of the Christian? To return to Bede's Easter homily, the sermon juxtaposes the closed tomb of the Jew to a Christian space, Christ's tomb, which is itself empty. The story of Easter is one of

divine transcendence—of Jesus' triumph over the material, mortal world—
*and* the absence that results from the Resurrection. Bede registers that
troubling void by recounting how the women at the tomb were "sad-
dened at the disappearance of Jesus's body" (II.10, 91).[49] He also indicates
how Christian sorrow over the continued absence of the physical "presence of our Maker" persists and "afflicts" both himself and his brothers,
who "endure the hardship of exile" from "the eternal joys of the citizens
on high" who share space with God (ibid.).[50] While contemporary Jews
endure exile from the historical Jerusalem, Christians on earth suffer exile
from the heavenly Jerusalem. Cynewulf, in *Christ II*, similarly states of the
Christians left behind after Christ's ascension into heaven, "their spirit
was sad, / hot around the heart, their mind mourning, / because they no
longer could see the one so dear / under heaven" ("Him wæs geomor sefa /
hat æt heortan, hyge murnende, / þæs þe hi swa leofne leng ne mostun /
geseon under swegle").[51] The dilemma Bede and Cynewulf raise here problematizes their respective images of the sepulchral Jew. In the case of *Elene*,
Judas's deprivations during his time spent underground in the pit in certain
respects pale in comparison to the separation in the world above of Christians from God. While those who die in imitation of Christ—for example,
martyrs like Stephen—enjoy immediate access to the New Jerusalem, the
rest of the Christian community, such as Helena and her son Constantine,
must wait, in exile on earth, until mortality brings them to that privileged
space. The earth, viewed in terms of the Resurrection, is in a sense one giant
empty tomb: a site devoid of the lively spirituality and divine presence of the
New Jerusalem which pious Christians aspire to enter. In the remainder of
this chapter, I track how Bede and Cynewulf respond to the problematic
emptiness of Christian space, and the ironic place of the "Jew" in efforts to
imagine a strong and rich Christian existence on earth.

In his Easter sermon, Bede comforts auditors who feel despondent at
Jesus' absence, stating that they must "have not the slightest doubt" that
during such moments of sadness, angels are "invisibly" present to them in
the manner of those whom the women encountered at the tomb, bringing
"them the remedy of consolation by disclosing the fact of [Christ's] resurrection" (II.10, 91).[52] Bede thus counters the problem of physical absence by
invoking an unseen yet real spiritual presence that affirms Christ's occupation of heaven. Bede goes on to cite Paul on the frequent arrival on earth
of "ministering spirits" who assist the saved (Hebrews 1:14), singling out a
particular place where and occasion when such spirits frequent Christians:

Nevertheless, we should believe that the angelic spirits are especially
present to us when we give ourselves in a special way to divine services,

that is, when we enter a church and open our ears to sacred reading, or give our attention to psalm singing or apply ourselves to prayer or celebrate the solemnity of the mass. . . . We are not permitted to doubt that where the mysteries of the Lord's body and blood are being enacted, a gathering of the citizens from on high is present—those who were keeping such careful watch at the tomb where [Christ's] venerable body had been placed, and from which he had departed by rising.

(II.10, 91–92)[53]

Bede's account of how the same angels who were at the tomb make a special point of visiting Christian believers in a church during the consecration of the host engages both the spiritual (invisible angels) and the physical (a church). The faith is practiced not in a void but in a built environment. Living on earth after the Resurrection entails both believing in spirits and relying on concrete edifices.

That Bede viewed architecture as crucial to Christian practice emerges in his *Ecclesiastical History* (hereafter *EH*), where, in his account of the dissemination of the faith in Britain, preaching goes hand-in-hand with building churches (cf. 1.26, 76–77, and 2.3, 142–43).[54] That stress hardly surprises, insofar as, since Constantine's era, the construction of Christian buildings—and demolition of non-Christian edifices—was fundamental to conversion, even aggressively so. Thus, in a letter included in the *EH*, Gregory the Great, citing Constantine as his exemplar, instructs the newly converted king to "overthrow" his pagan subjects' "buildings and shrines" (1.32, 112–15).[55] Bede's own appreciation of churches as "concrete manifestations of missionary advance" emerges not only in this letter but also his account in the *EH* of Æthelbert and other kings like Ecgfrith and Oswald who assisted in church building or restoration.[56] Especially notable is Bede's description of King Edwin's spiritual development—his journey from student of the faith to baptized member of the Christian community—as a process intertwined with the progressive building of a church from a hastily built and impermanent timber structure to a fine edifice made of stone (2.14, 186–87).[57]

However, in the Christian-cum-pagan Anglo-Saxon world described in the *EH*, the idea of a Christian built environment was fraught. Another, even more famous, Gregorian epistle included by Bede in his *EH* suggests how the Anglo-Saxons' lingering pagan attachments prompted a certain missionary resistance to tearing down heathen buildings and erecting Christian structures in their stead. Apparently writing to Abbot Mellitus not long after he wrote Æthelbert, Gregory urged that "the idol temples of" the pagan Anglo-Saxons "should by no means be destroyed, but only the idols in them," which clerics will replace with altars and relics (1.30, 106–9). Gregory's original instruction that Æthelbert demolish pagan temples invests the materiality of built environments with particular value. Pagan temples are part and parcel of paganism and therefore must be demolished, just as erecting new religious edifices proves key to establishing Christianity (1.30, 108–9). That violent architectural policy reflects the coercive nature of conversion during this period in England and elsewhere. But when faced with the "stubborn minds" of the Anglo-Saxons, Gregory shifts tack, stating that they may retain their temples, since physical buildings are not really intrinsic to Christianity but rather serve as mere settings for what really matters, the faith and its rituals (ibid.).

Bede reflects Gregory's stance toward buildings in his Easter homily, where his primary interest is not churches per se, but rather the presence inside them of members of the faithful—the "living stones" of the "spiritual church" described in 1 Peter 2:5—and their invisible angelic companions. That perspective also informs one of his sermons on the dedication of a church. Glossing the reference in John 10:23 to Jesus "walking in the temple, in Solomon's portico" during the feast of the dedication, Bede writes that if Christ

> did not disdain to walk round the portico where a mortal and earthly king, albeit the most powerful and wisest one, was once accustomed to stand and pray, how much more greatly does he desire to inspect and enlighten the innermost recesses of our hearts—if he regards them as equivalent to the portico of Solomon, that is, if he regards them as having the fear of him which is the beginning of wisdom. We must not suppose that only the building in which we come together to pray and celebrate the mysteries is the Lord's temple, and that we ourselves, who come together in the Lord's name, are not more fully his temple and are not so named, since the Apostle clearly says, *You are the temple of the living God; as God says, "I will live in them and walk among them."*
>
> *(II.24, 241–42).*[58]

Invoking the logic of supersession, Bede stresses how it is not the "building" where Christians pray but people who epitomize the new Christian practice that has supplanted Judaism. Christ desires far more to enter "the innermost recesses" of the heart—that is, a figurative architectural space located inside the believer—than any literal building, whether Solomon's

Temple or a physical church. Bede's elevation of the heart as edifice over any physical church exists in tension with his stress in the *EH* on Christian building programs. Or to put it more precisely, his investment in living and not literal stones helps explain why Bede in the *EH* values physical buildings yet doesn't bestow on them notable praise and attention.[59]

There is, however, one kind of building upon which Bede does lavish attention: the biblical Jewish buildings discussed in *On the Temple* and other works such as *On the Tabernacle* (ca. 721–25), an interpretation of the account in Exodus 24:12–30:21 of the erection of the Mosaic tabernacle, and *On Ezra and Nehemiah* (ca. 725–31), an exegesis of Ezra-Nehemiah's portrayal of the postexilic construction of the Second Temple.[60] Those texts mark, in Jennifer O'Reilly's words, "the culmination of a lifetime's thought and writing on biblical built environments: the closest parallels to *De Templo* occur in three of Bede's own gospel homilies."[61] Rendering Bede's interest in Jewish edifices all the more striking is its unprecedented nature. While Jews had long subjected the temple to allegorical interpretation, until Bede no Christian writer had devoted sustained attention to either that edifice or the tabernacle.[62] The "first Christian exegete to produce complete verse-by-verse commentaries on these subjects," Bede broke "new ground" in the history of Christian exegeses.[63] Highly popular works that went on to exert an influence over Christian allegories and even Christian architecture for centuries after Bede's death, *On the Temple*, *On the Tabernacle*, and *On Ezra and Nehemiah* were without precedent and parallel during the period of their production.[64]

What accounts for this unusual interest in Jewish buildings?[65] Two books at Bede's home abbey of Wearmouth-Jarrow were likely influences: the *Codex Grandior*, the ca. 547 Old Latin bible that Cassiodorus commissioned at his monastery at Vivarium and Abbot Ceolfrith (ca. 642–716) apparently transported from Italy to England; and another pandect partially modeled on the *Codex Grandior*, the *Codex Amiatinus*, which was created at Wearmouth-Jarrow and Ceolfrith presented to the pope in 716.[66] The opening leaves of the *Codex Grandior* contained images of the temple and tabernacle.[67] At least a decade before he wrote his architectural exegeses, Bede probably helped make the *Codex Amiatinus*, which opens with an image of the tabernacle based on that fronting the *Codex Grandior* (figure 7).

Mary Carruthers demonstrates how images like the sanctuaries in the *Codex Amiatinus* and its exemplar demonstrate the role of built environments in monastic spirituality, especially "various kinds of memory work for medi-tation and prayer."[68] Monks used building plans as "meditation machine[s]" to inspire and shape their prayers and theological works.[69] The situation of

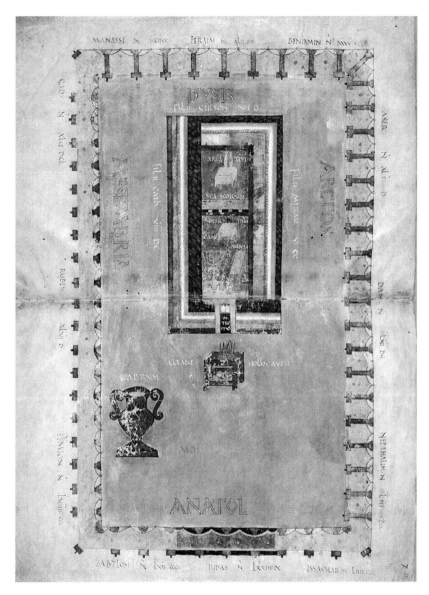

**Figure 7.** The tabernacle. Florence, Biblioteca Medicea Laurenziana, MS Amiatino 1, cc. 2v–3r. By permission of MiBACT.

the tabernacle and temple at the start of the bibles at Bede's abbey encouraged such a relationship between buildings and interpretive Christian pondering.[70]

Alongside the two codices at Wearmouth-Yarrow, another rationale for Bede's exegeses emerges in the fact that he wrote about biblical buildings while writing the *EH*. Insofar as the temple and tabernacle serve in Bede's work as prompts for spiritual thinking, they spoke to the ultimate purpose of the missionary work described in the *EH*: the creation of solid "living stones"—a firmly faithful church—in an erstwhile pagan Anglo-Saxon England. As Scott DeGregorio puts it, "the idea of building a house for God parallels Bede's historical account of the foundation of the *ecclesia gentis Anglorum* in the *Ecclesiastical History* . . . suggesting that Bede may have envisioned a massive exegetical-historical project on a set of interrelated themes which he deemed particularly pressing."[71] Thus the Jewish edifices of the Hebrew Bible not only assist monastic meditation but also contribute to the national program of strengthening the faith in a newly converted Anglo-Saxon England.

Interestingly, the *EH* refers to the utility of still another Jewish structure in fostering the faith in England. In Gregory's letter to Mellitus, the pope, after advocating retaining heathen temples, instructs the abbot to allow new converts also to continue, with modifications, the pagan practice of animal sacrifice: "on the day of the dedication or festival of the holy martyrs, whose relics are deposited there, let them make themselves *tabernacula* from the branches of trees around the churches which have been converted out of shrines, and let them celebrate the solemnity with religious feasts" (1.30, 108–9).[72] As Flora Spiegel points out, Gregory's "description of the huts as *tabernacula*, and his couching these instructions [elsewhere in the letter] in the context of the Israelites' reception of the Law after their forty-year sojourn in the desert, all suggest an explicit reference to the Jewish festival of Sukkot."[73] Sukkot, or the Feast of Tabernacles, commemorates Israel's wandering in the desert by creating outdoor temporary booths akin to those inhabited by Jews during the Exodus. Because Sukkot was a prominent public festival in Roman society and due to Gregory's involvement in Jewish communities, he very likely "was aware of early medieval Jewish traditions for celebrating the holiday."[74] Spiegel links Gregory's instruction that missionaries organize proto-Sukkot feasts to the pope's theory that the new converts should come to Christianity incrementally, first by identifying with Jews and then later with Christianity.[75] Thus Gregory didn't deride contemporary Jews as wholly irrational and blind beings but situated them on "the middle position on the spectrum of rationality between Christians and practising pagans" like the Anglo-Saxons.[76] Archaeological evidence suggests that missionaries carried out Gregory's injunction. Brian Hope-Taylor's excavation of a settlement at Yeavering, Northumbria, revealed at least four "rectangular wattle huts, each measuring approximately six feet by twelve feet," which were erected one after the other on the same location as "intentionally temporary structures."[77]

Both the pseudo-Sukkot huts described by Gregory and Bede's exegeses of biblical buildings suggest a uniquely architectural role played by the
"Jew" in Anglo-Saxon Christianity. While for Gregory that architectural
utility worked in overtly material ways that replicated contemporary Jewish ritual building practices, for Bede, the materials of long-gone biblical
structures functioned in a more figurative vein, as prompts for conceiving
of Christianity. Viewed in tandem with his Easter homily, Bede's exegeses
of the temple and tabernacle present a complex and contradictory engagement with the space of the Jew. While Bede connotes the uselessness of
the sepulchral Jew in his sermon, he demonstrates in his exegeses the
utility of Jewish built environments in "building up" symbolic Christian
locations. Alongside the idea of the lethal and barren Jew-as-tomb, Bede
suggests the fecundity of biblical Jewish spaces, from which a slew of
Christian meanings proliferate.

It is this figurative or allegorical approach to literal buildings that
overtly informs Bede's architectural exegeses. Early in *On the Temple*,
Bede announces his intention of finding "the spiritual mansion of God
in the material structure [of the temple]" (6).[78] Similarly, in *On the Tabernacle* Bede writes that "we must reflect for a little while upon the text
of the material letter itself, *so that* we shall be able to discuss the spiritual
sense with greater certainty" (my emphasis).[79] Everywhere, Bede's architectural exegeses testify to his spiritualizing thrust.[80] Through ingenious
allegories, Bede links Old Testament buildings to mystical sites associated
with "the past, present and future states of the Ecclesia," that is, Christ
as cornerstone, the living church of the faithful on earth, the sanctuaries
created in the heart of individual pious persons, and their eternal home
in heaven.[81]

Of the manifold spiritual meanings Bede finds in biblical sanctuaries, his account of both the living stones of the church and the heart
as temple counter the problem of Christ's absence with which I began
this section. But here, instead of stressing a compensatory angelic presence, Bede emphasizes the sheer fullness of the faith in the world. For
example, when describing the conversion work of the evangelists and,
later, missionary practice under Rome, Bede associates Christianity
with a wondrous fullness and expansiveness. Thus in *On the Tabernacle*,
"the width of the boards" of the tabernacle mystically signify "the
expansion of the faith and the sacraments, which formerly lay hidden
among the one Israelite people but through" the ministry of the apostles
and their successors "came [to fill] the wideness of the whole world"
(66).[82] And, in *On the Temple*, the four wheels on each of the ten bases

of the temple figure how, "with the Lord's help through the instrumentality of the apostles, the word of the Gospel filled all the regions of the world in a short space" (97).[83] Elsewhere, Bede's account of the erection of individual temples in Christian hearts suggests how, while Christ may be gone, believers nevertheless enjoy a mystical intimacy with the divine. In *On the Tabernacle*, the grate in the middle of the tabernacle altar figures the "place for the Lord" prepared by the elect "in the inmost affections of their hearts, where they gather thoughts devoted to him" (92).[84] Here, as in his homily on the dedication of a church, Bede's rhetoric originates in Paul's idea—in, for example, 1 Corinthians 3:16 and 6:19—on the relationship between the temple and individual believers.[85] Bede is unique, however, in stressing the extreme intimacy enjoyed by Christians; while Paul generally associates individual persons with the temple, Bede specifies God's presence not only in the core of a person's being—the heart—but moreover in its "inmost affections" and "innermost recesses."[86]

Such moments in Bede's exegeses reveal a spatial paradox: the discrete and limited physical buildings of the Hebrew Bible figure their geographic inverse. The very materials that made the biblical sanctuaries bounded edifices accessed only by Jews mystically signify the spread of the faith to persons throughout all the earth. Christ may be in heaven, but the faith spreads everywhere, to even the most intimate locations of the self. But as the Easter homily evinces, the miraculous reach of the faith is neither as universal nor as intimate as it appears. While God travels widely under Christianity, he never resides in a "Jewish" space. Biblical Jews had special access to a building enlivened by nothing less than God's presence. But Jews who deny Christianity, instead of enjoying their ancestors' privileged architectural intimacy with God, suffer the opposite and are exiled from God like "a tomb still closed by a stone."[87] Due to their hardened and resolutely carnal hearts, Jews are trapped inside an empty and spiritually barren space of death. The lively fecundity of spiritual truths figured by the temple and tabernacle are apparent only to Christians and are hidden from the literal-minded and tomb-like Jew. Bede's figural method thus wrenches the privileged architecture of the bible away from contemporary Jews and transfers it to Christians, while rendering the "architecture" of contemporary Jewish identity as debased as possible. Thanks to the Christian's sensitivity to the spirit and the Jew's enslavement to the letter, the former enjoys a vital plenitude and the latter suffers emptiness, lack, and death.

## Loving Stone: Christian Materialism
## and Bede's Architectural Exegeses

Bede's architectural exegeses hinge on supersession: higher, spiritual meanings supplant the literal spaces of the tabernacle and temple. And yet, as critics such as Jill Robbins and Steven Kruger have made clear, the promulgators of Christian hermeneutics always register the value of the "old" Jewish perspectives they claim to supplant.[88] Christian spirituality never truly trumps its Jewish material counterpart; rather, the material dimensions of Jewish historical life persist in the "new," figural interpretation. In "Figura," Erich Auerbach suggests such an interrelation, writing that "Figural prophecy implies the interpretation of one worldly event through another; the first signifies the second, the second fulfills the first. Both remain historical events; yet both, looked at in this way, have something provisional and incomplete about them; they point to one another."[89] Auerbach suggests the dialectical and interdependent quality of the Christian–Jewish analogies generated in works like *On the Temple, On the Tabernacle,* and *On Ezra and Nehemiah.* Insofar as the temple and its Christian meanings "point to one another," the figural turn is always incomplete.

While this instability always informs Christian hermeneutics, it seems to especially emerge in Bede, whose fascination with the materiality of Jewish built environments is palpable and undeniable. As Charles Jones points out, throughout his architectural exegeses "Bede has a master's interest in the literal meaning despite his preacher's aim to surmount it."[90] At the start of *On the Tabernacle,* Bede makes that interest explicit when he stresses how it is important to discuss the *circumstantiae* referred to by Paul in 1 Corinthians 10:11, that is, particulars regarding time, place and the physical nature of things.[91] In keeping with this methodology, Bede goes on to preface his figural interpretations with close attention to the materials of the tabernacle and its contents. *On the Temple* engages in a similar interpretive method, as Bede attends to each tiny literal aspect of Solomon's Temple. In Arthur Holder's words, "Every part of the structure . . . every detail of ornament, every number, measurement or point of the compass described in the biblical accounts" of Solomon's Temple "presented Bede with a mystery of Christ or the Church."[92] Bede's interest in getting an accurate grasp of the physical details of the tabernacle and temple is such that, when possible, he supplements his discussion by citing extrabiblical sources, such as Cassiodorus and Josephus.[93]

Bede suggests otherwise, of course. Statements such as his aforementioned claim about how he seeks "the spiritual mansion of God in the material structure" (6) of the temple would seem to affirm how his hermeneutic really looks "through an object rather than at it."[94] Yet Bede's marked investment in the physical components of biblical built environments suggests the inverse: that he was drawn to the inherent physicality of those buildings; that he repeatedly, even obsessively, looked *at* them as objects.[95] Indeed, Bede's figural interpretations demonstrate an attention to physical details so minute and so scrutinizing that it effectively renders the temple and tabernacle imaginative presences in his reader's mind's eye. Thus even as Bede stresses building the living Christian church, he brings long-gone Jewish built environments to vivid imaginative life. Bede's exegetical works make virtually visible for his Anglo-Saxon readers the spaces of the temple and tabernacle.[96]

Why would Bede exhibit such a marked visual investment in those buildings? One answer lies in the problem voiced in his Easter homily: the empty nature of Christian space after the Resurrection. The issue of Christ's absence may have been particularly pressing for Bede, given the sheer novelty and instability of the faith in England during this period. We may speculate that the notably tenuous nature of Anglo-Saxon Christianity might have rendered him especially attracted to the idea of "grounding" Christian practice by imaginatively importing to England certain privileged Jewish materialisms. In other words, the proximity of the pagan in Anglo-Saxon England may have inspired a compensatory effort to gain an intimacy with the one true God via the exalted spaces of the Jew.

And exalted those spaces were. No Christian church matched the privileged materialism of the temple and tabernacle, the most exalted buildings in human history. In the case of the former building, the material privilege of the temple extended to its supremely hallowed lithic foundation. As Cristiana Whitehead points out, "reputed to lie at the centre of the world, the great temple rock" on which Solomon's Temple stood "was considered the oldest part of creation: the first point of dry land, beneath which all the waters of the earth were gathered and controlled."[97] Beyond its association with the "germinal point of creation," the temple's privileged materialism emerges in how its physical components and form were dictated by none other than God, as recorded by scripture (1 Chron. 28:11–19).[98] Most importantly, both the temple and the tabernacle enjoyed unsurpassed distinction as houses of God. Each holy sanctuary embodies how, during the time of the old law, faith was bound up with a certain material, geographic, and communal exclusivity: only in Jewish spaces did God reside, only Jews could enjoy a physical proximity to the divine. The tabernacle and temple epitomize how biblical Jews were as close to God as possible, that is, they enjoyed a relationship so intimate that he deigned to inhabit man-made shelters located in Jewish communities.[99]

Bede's clear attraction to the privileged materiality of the temple and tabernacle qualifies his celebration of the angelic and other spiritual presences that define Christian life in the wake of the Resurrection. Merely stressing living stones and the temple of the heart—for all Bede's statements to the contrary—proves insufficient and requires a supplementary attention to privileged biblical architecture. That investment in the literal, in turn, undermines the rhetoric of supersession, with its claim that Christian spirituality supplants Jewish materialism. Indeed, there are ways in which Bede's attention to the letter doesn't merely trouble but inverts the logic of supersession. While supersession refers to a shift from a lesser Jewish to a higher Christian plane, Bede's materialism suggests the deficiencies of the new Christian order when compared to its Jewish predecessor.

Beyond his overall scrutiny of the materials of the temple and tabernacle, one aspect of Bede's exegeses seems to especially undermine his rhetoric of supersession: his investment in the stones of the temple. As we have seen, stones were a favored means by which Christians connoted a debased Jewish carnality. In his Easter sermon, Bede viscerally indicates the stubbornness, imperceptiveness, and even inhumanity of Jews by likening them to hard and insentient stone. Solomon's Temple, however, offers an entirely different and exalted brand of stoniness. While the stony Jew is closed off and blind to Christian truths, the stones of the temple merit careful attention. Bede's attraction to stones appears in a section of *On the Temple* on 1 Kings 5:18, where he describes how the church lays "large precious stones . . . in the foundation" of the "temple" of the faithful when it sets before the people exemplary Christians, who "cling in a special way by the virtue of humility to the Lord . . . persevering unflinchingly with invincible constancy of spirit like squared stones" (16).[100] While Bede denigrates the stony obstinacy of the Jew, here he celebrates the stony immutability of exemplary Christians, whom he compares to the hard stones of the temple.[101] Bede's figurative reading circles back to its material prompt. The foundation stones figure faithful Christians who in turn are "like squared stones." Living during an Anglo-Saxon era when the faith was indeed shaky, Bede proves attracted to stony permanence.[102]

Bede's appreciation of the durability of the temple's stones emerges especially in his discussion in *On the Temple* of 1 Kings 6:18. His exegesis begins by describing how the supreme durability of the stones of the temple walls signifies the "living stones" of the saints "cemented to each other by the strength of their faith in the one and the same rule" (41).[103] Then Bede ponders the place of stone in the old law and another building material—wood—in the new law:

because the law was written in stone whereas the teaching of the Gospel was confirmed by the wood of the Lord's passion, so too the people

were circumcised by a flintstone in the foreskin whereas we are conse-
crated by the sign of the cross on the forehead. The stone walls of the
temple or the floor paved with most precious marble can quite appro-
priately be taken as a type of those who lived faithfully and perfectly
in the law, whereas the planks of cedar or fir can signify the righteous
of the New Testament who in their desire to go after the Lord deny
themselves and take up their cross daily and follow him.

*(41)*[104]

While under their law inscribed on stone (i.e., the Ten Commandments)
Jews literally alter their bodies through circumcision by flint, Christians
symbolically mark themselves with the sign of the cross. But the Christian
event memorialized by that symbolic gesture has its physical elements: the
wooden beams on which Christ died. Bede develops this relationship by
linking the "planks of cedar or fir" of the temple to righteous Christians
who "take up their cross" and identifying the stone walls of the temple as
figures for righteous Jews "who lived faithfully and perfectly" in the old
law. Thus while Bede earlier imbued Christians with stony permanence,
now he likens them to ordinary, impermanent wood and links devout biblical Jews with the very stony permanence he had just a few lines earlier
associated with the saints. Of course, the more fragile and mutable nature
of wood is part of Bede's theological point. A key Christian paradox is that
God deigned to become man and take on impermanent, mortal flesh.[105]
But I would suggest that because Bede's reference to the wood of the cross
comes on the heels of a passage so clearly invested in stone's permanence,
the association of Christianity with timber is problematic. I'm not suggesting here, of course, that stone is inherently superior to wood; no material object has any essential value. Many aspects of Anglo-Saxon material
culture—buildings, furnishings, and artifacts—attest to the value of wood.
Yet, within the particular context of *On the Temple*, Bede's realignment of
Christians with wood proves disturbing.[106]
    Bede's association of righteous Jews with the stone walls of the temple
contradicts another earlier moment in his exegesis, a section on 1 Kings 6:3
where he linked the portico with righteous Jews and the temple itself to
Christians. That earlier designation of the entrance as a figure of holy Jews
both grants them their historical priority (since one reaches the portico first
when entering the temple) and exiles them from the space of the temple
itself.[107] But in his reading of 1 Kings 6:18, as we have seen, Bede associates
Jews with the stone used for the whole temple. Cognizant of this issue, Bede

states "Nor should there seem to be any conflict between this and what we said above to the effect" (41–42).[108] Such seeming inconsistencies are fine, and indeed are central to his exegetic program: "in the different materials there is a manifold repetition of the same figures" (42).[109] But despite such assurances, Bede seems uncomfortable with the turn his analysis has taken and goes on to engage in some rapid and rather confusing maneuvering. First, he writes that the stone walls signifying righteous Jews pertain to the portico, not the temple, and that the cedar of the portico represents the Jews who "with greater perfection" (42) led a Christian life before Christianity.[110] Then, turning to the interior of the temple, Bede links Christians who sacrifice all for God with the stone wall of the temple and states that people who are content merely to do the minimum necessary to enter heaven signify its wooden board work.[111] Bede shifts rapidly between interpretations, moving between associating first Jews then Christians with stone, with wood, with inner and outer temple, finally resting upon the association of the holiest Christian with the most durable material entity, the stone of the temple proper.

The finest writer-scholar of his generation (if not the entire Anglo-Saxon era), Bede evinces such exceptional hermeneutic skill, creativity, control, and nuance in his corpus that the interpretive instability present in this passage from *On the Temple* seems especially unusual and telling. To be sure, the slippery nature of Bede's exegesis partly confirms his own stress on the "manifold" or multiple nature of exegetical interpretation. But his rapid maneuvering also suggests a kind of hermeneutic volatility stemming from his materialist discomfort with the direction his analysis has taken. In other words, the fact that those frequent hermeneutical shifts immediately follow Bede's association of Jews with stone and Christians with wood suggests how that material binarism—lithic Jew and ligneous Christian—troubles him. The fact that Bede's exegesis culminates and settles on the association of stone with the holiest of Christians seems to confirm how his hermeneutic shifts are prompted by an investment in stone. When viewed alongside Bede's portrayal of the sepulchral Jew, this passage clarifies the contradictory nature of Christian denigrations of a "Jewish" carnality. Stone, far from embodying the outmoded and lethal old law, proves appealing to arguably the greatest scholar of the new law during the eighth century. We glimpse here how Bede loved not only the living stones of the Christian church but also the literal stones of the Jew.

An important historical counterpart to this passage in *On the Temple* emerges in the religious functions of stone during the Anglo-Saxon period.[112]

Stone was so crucial to Anglo-Saxon Christianity that "at least on the richest monastic sites, the really revolutionary change" effected by the introduction of the religion in England "was the revival, for the first time since the Romans left, of technologies for building and carving in stone."[113] The colossal crosses at Ruthwell and Bewcastle were without parallel in Europe when they were erected during the seventh and eighth centuries. Emblems of the Crucifixion, the sculptures served as important and complex loci of Christian ritual, performance, and contemplation. Carved with text—including the words iterated by the speaking cross of *The Dream of the Rood*—those lithic monuments offer a different take on the Christian celebration of "living stones," by pointing us not to souls but to animated objects. Just as, if not more, significant than those sculptures was the stone architecture introduced by missionaries, who restricted the practice to buildings associated with the church.[114] Bede's home at Jarrow and its sister monastery at Monkwearmouth (founded ca. 673) lie at the center of this ecclesiastical building program.[115]

Critics including Nicholas Howe stress the Roman investments evinced by those stone structures. Such factors as the reuse of stones originally used for Hadrian's wall to build St. Peter's and Benedict Biscop's fondness for churches built in the Roman style make clear that Bede appreciated the Roman connections of Jarrow's buildings and even viewed the monastery as "a type of Rome set at the end of the road that led from the papal city to Northumbria."[116] But it is also important to consider the possible Jewish meanings that Jarrow and its stone edifices held for Bede. The language of Christian architecture suggested such a relationship, insofar as the word *templum* was used to refer to a church since the fourth century.[117] Jarrow and Wearmouth may have taken the link between Christian and Jewish buildings one step further by basing certain architectural components on Solomon's Temple. One such feature is what Cramp describes as "an elaborately decorated covered walk or passage" in Wearmouth, "which led south from" St. Peter's church (founded AD 674) to other monastic buildings.[118] Paul Meyvaert suggests that that walkway was influenced by the *porticus* in the image of the temple Cassiodorus had painted in his *Codex Grandior*.[119] Meyvaert also suggests that the *caenaculae* or upper stories of St. Peter's were modeled on those at Solomon's Temple.[120] Holder notes how "one of the most striking features" of Solomon's Temple, that is, "its great height in proportion to its length and breadth, would have been duplicated in a general way" by the height of the walls of St. Peter's.[121] In addition, Ian Wood suggests that St. Paul's church at Jarrow was built to echo the physical form and makeup of Solomon's Temple.[122]

In part, we can view the possible modeling of Christian architecture on Jewish precedents as a function of monastic spirituality. In the same way that, as Carruthers stresses, the image of the tabernacle in the *Codex Amiatinus* may not so much represent an actual building than offer a rhetorical *ductus* or traveling in and out of the "'places' of a mental schema," the buildings of Wearmouth and Jarrow may have served as cues for spiritual meditation.[123] But we would be wrong to stress only the spiritual side of the equation and view the built environments at Wearmouth-Jarrow as nothing more than mental prompts. As we have seen, Bede's exegeses suggest that he didn't only look "through" but also "at" the materials of the temple; surely he felt the same way about the monastic stone structures where he spent the majority of his life.[124] But that materialism isn't explicit and extensive. Any overt embrace of Christian buildings would shore up a version of the degraded materialism Bede attributes to Jews, as well as the idolatry from which he sought to wean erstwhile pagans.[125] Instead he inadvertently offers us a glimpse at his Christian materialism as it emerges in the hermeneutic instability of *On the Temple*.

## Stony Christians and the Suffering Jew in *Elene*

In Bede's exegeses of Jewish buildings, Christian materialism exists in tense relation to an abiding and overt investment in monastic spirituality and the "living stones" of a newly converted Anglo-Saxon church. Cynewulf similarly exhibits a fraught stance toward the place of materialism in Christianity, most significantly in *Christ II*. While, as I mention above, the poem depicts the sadness of those left behind when Christ ascended into heaven, Cynewulf doesn't endeavor to resolve materially this absence. Indeed Cynewulf evinces little overall interest in physical space. As Johanna Kramer observes, "Cynewulf's approach to teaching Ascension theology" in *Christ II* "differs from the concrete, materially grounded, and spatially conceived imagery used to teach it in most Anglo-Saxon literature and art."[126] The emphasis on the "cerebral and theoretical" in *Christ II*—above all the poem's stress on "realiz[ing] a spiritual ascension"—contrasts starkly with *Elene*, a poem that explicitly portrays Christianity accommodating the carnal and worldly.[127] *Elene* opens with warfare between the Roman emperor Constantine and the invading Huns, Hrethgoths, and Franks. As the great monastic prose writer, the monk Ælfric of Eynesham, puts it in his account of the three estates, Constantine is a worldly warrior or *woruldcempa* who fights carnal foes and performs worldly battles or *woruldlicum*, as opposed to a "servant of God" such as Bede or Ælfric, who "battles spiritually against invisible foes."[128] The "true cross" on which *Elene* centers partakes in Constantine's carnal battles. Only when he receives a vision of the cross and then uses a crucifix as his battle standard does the emperor overcome the invaders (99b). Later on, the nails of the cross serve a similarly worldly function when they are used for the bridle of Constantine's horse, allowing him to overcome all enemies (1177a–1188a).

Cynewulf develops the carnal associations of the cross on several registers. For one thing, the cross Constantine sees in his vision possesses a magnificent materiality like the cross in another Vercelli manuscript poem, *The Dream of the Rood*.[129] In the same way that the dreamer in the latter poem beholds a cross covered in gold and gems, the emperor in *Elene* witnesses a *crux gemmata*, a radiant, glorious object "bright with gems" ("frætwum beorht"; 88b) and "adorned with gold" ("golde geglenged"; 90a).[130] Secondly, Constantine's interest in the cross after his conversion is abidingly literal-minded. Thankful that God through the cross "gave me glory and success in war against the hostile ones" ("me tir forgeaf, / wigsped wið wraðum"; 164b–165a), Constantine seeks to return the favor and glorify God by uncovering the original artifact. Here *Elene* resonates with the English cult of the true cross, which emerged from multiple impulses, spiritual and material.[131] Devotees viewed the cross as a kind of portal to heaven, a means of healing bodily ailments, and/or a way of reenacting the scene of the Crucifixion. Central to such beliefs was an investment in the wood of the cross, as the movement of both pilgrims to Jerusalm and relics to England attests.[132] The investment in the materiality of the cross was such that relics even were thought to turn the wood of the reliquaries containing them into the actual wood of the cross.

Both the cult of the true cross and the particular investment in the literal cross portrayed in *Elene* should be understood, at least partly, in terms of the issues raised in Bede's Easter homily and, to a lesser extent, Cynewulf's *Christ II*, with their acknowledgment of the material absences that inform post-Resurrection life on earth. *Elene* refers to Christ's departure from earth when Constantine learns of the ascension (185b–188b). As we have seen, Bede responds to this problem by stressing the compensatory presence of invisible spirits on earth and the sheer fullness of the faith. The cult of the cross evinces a desire to access on earth a material artifact with Christic associations, an object that in a sense was the closest thing to Christ on earth. *Elene* centers on the Roman imperial archaeological project that made the cult possible.[133]

Rendering the quest for the cross in *Elene* all the more worldly is its resonance with the secular warfare that initiates the poem. Introduced as Christ killers whose burial of the cross is of a piece with deicide, Jews function in the poem as new, specifically religious enemies for Constantine to defeat through the proxy of his mother, Helena. As with the battle against the Huns, Hrethgoths, and Franks, the "battle" against the Jews is worldly and geopolitical. The Jews' rule "ofer middangeard" will end upon the Christians' discovery of the cross (434a). In the same way that Constantine fights the invaders with swords, arrows, and spears, Helena travels to Jerusalem with a band of "mighty men, war-brave heroes" ("leodmægen, guðrofe hæleþ"; 272b–273a) who are loaded with weaponry.[134] The queen doesn't actually fight the Jews in a full-blown war, but her encounter with them has martial and materialist elements.[135] Royally enthroned, bedecked with golden ornamentation that mirrors the decorations on the cross revealed to her son (329b–331b), and supported by her armed band of warriors, Helena threatens the Jews with bodily harm and ultimately employs physical torture to obtain the material object she seeks.

Crucially, however—and as Helena's torture of Judas affirms—the Jews aren't simply enemies of Christianity, but also radically important mediums by which the queen gains access to the cross. At the same time that Helena hates the Jews she also desperately needs their—or more precisely Judas's—help.[136] Judas's role as the lynchpin to Helena's materialist project presents us with another version of the privileged Jewish materiality witnessed in Bede's exegetical works. That is, Helena's intense interest in Judas—like Bede's acute investment in the temple and tabernacle—speaks to a Christian fascination with, desire for, and even envy of the Jew's physical intimacy with the divine. In the same way that the Jews of the bible shared space with a God who deigned to inhabit their man-made sanctuaries, direct Jewish access to God continued into Christian history, as related by the New Testament. The Gospels describe how Jesus was Jewish and lived among Jews. Christian teaching demonized Jews as killers of Christ. But the presence of Jews at the Crucifixion, as eyewitnesses to that pivotal historical event, imbued them with an enviable proximity to the divine that all believers living after Christ's death and Resurrection lacked.[137] It's Judas's genealogical—that is, material—link to that time and place, via his father and grandfather, that makes him so valuable to Helena.[138] In the same way that Bede's exegesis brings virtual versions of the temple and tabernacle to earth, Helena works to bring "Christ"—or an object closely tied to Christ—back to earth via Judas. In Helena's intense and carnal interest in Judas, we discover the contradictory nature of supersession as an ideology that embraces the materiality it claims to trump and, conversely, proves anxious over the spirituality it purports to embrace. Symbolically taking up the cross or simply marking oneself with the sign of the cross is not sufficient in *Elene*; only the material cross will do, and only a Jew can deliver the goods.

Because Helena's recovery project hinges on a contemporary Jewish informant, the image of the sepulchral Jew in *Elene* departs from its counterpart in Bede. Bede's Jew is tomb-like because his carnality has no place in the new spiritual order on earth. In contrast, the pit in *Elene* is pivotal to the queen's materialist project. Only by starving Judas does Helena finally learn the location of the true cross. Tellingly, once Judas unearths the cross, it, like its counterpart in *The Dream of the Rood*, enjoys an exalted materiality. Like the speaking and suffering cross of *Dream*, the cross Judas finds in *Elene* has physical abilities that render it more than just the object on which Christ died but rather a "metonymic recovery of the Lord's presence."[139] For example, when the cross reveals itself as such by miraculously reanimating a dead boy, it repeats the miracle with which Christ manifested his divinity, the raising of Lazarus in John 11:1–44. By bringing back the deceased youth the cross discloses its Christ-like powers; by uncovering the cross Judas thus seems to enable another resurrection of Christ, though here "Christ" in the cross doesn't ascend to heaven but remains on earth.

Once Constantine learns of the discovery, he commands Helena to build a "temple of the Lord" ("tempel dryhtnes"; 1009b) on Calvary. Helena goes into action:

> Þa seo cwen bebead cræftum getyde
> sundor asecean, þa selestan,
> þa þe wrætlicost wyrcan cuðon
> stangefogum, on þam stedewange
> girwan Godes tempel, swa hire gasta weard
> reord of roderum; heo þa rode heht
> golde beweorcean 7 gimcynnum,
> mid þam æðelestum eorcnanstanum,
> beset[a]n searocræftum 7 þa in seolfren fæt
> locum belucan.
>
> *(1018a–1027a)*

[Then the queen ordered the men skilled in their craft to be sought out individually, those [who were] the best, those who could work most wondrously in the joining of stones, to make on that field the temple of God, as the protector of souls had told her from the heavens. She then commanded that the rood be adorned with gold and precious stones, with cunning studded with the noblest stones, and then locked up in a silver vessel with locks.]

Helena's construction program starkly contrasts with the depiction of Christian architecture in Bede's architectural exegeses. As we have seen, Bede stresses not literal churches but the living stones of the faithful. However, and in keeping with its depiction of a materialist Christian investment in the cross, *Elene* imagines Elena literally reenacting the original building of the Jerusalem temple. In the same way that Solomon, imbued with divine wisdom, oversaw the construction of the First Temple, Helena supervises the erection of the *tempel* as God instructs her from above ("swa hire gasta weard / reord of roderum," 1023a). Just as Solomon's Temple featured the use of dressed stone (1 Kings 5:15–17), Helena has men skilled in joining stone or *stangefogum* build her temple. And just as God entered the temple in an inner room containing the ark of the covenant (1 Kings 8:10–11), the Christ-like cross inhabits an elaborately decorated chest located inside Helena's temple. Instead of depicting the Christian typological fulfillment and supplanting of Jewish materialisms, *Elene* portrays the re-creation on earth of the physicality of both Christ and the Jewish temple.[140]

However, in *Elene*, this yoking of worldliness to Christianity is far from smooth or easy, given Cynewulf's stress on both figural interpretation and Jewish–Christian relations. As scholars have noted, Helena berates the Jews who assemble before her for their interpretive failings. Klein points out how "the unconverted Jews in the poem are depicted . . . as strictly literal readers, obdurately impervious and willfully blind to symbolic meaning" within their own biblical books. Since Helena castigates the Jews for their carnal approach to the bible, interpreting the queen "on a strictly literal level would be misguided, for it would, in fact, be to read her precisely as do the Jews in the poem."[141] The same insight, of course, applies to Helena's antagonist, Judas. Yet when read figuratively, the meanings of those key personages prove unstable and ambiguous. The poem overtly encourages its readers to celebrate Helena's materialisms and denigrate Judas's materialisms: the queen's quest for the literal cross and building of literal churches render her holy, while Judas's carnal love of his tribe makes him an enemy of Christendom. But if we view those figures allegorically, their identities become slippery and shifting, so much so that at times Helena verges on becoming a "Jewish" villain and Judas comes to resemble a "Christian" hero. Such moments remind us that Cynewulf is also the author of the ascetic-minded *Christ II* and suggest that he may have had qualms about his subject matter in *Elene*, concerns that prompted him to render his characters ambiguous via allegory.

The built environments of the poem lie at the center of this hermeneutic instability, starting with the pit. As we have seen, the pit performs symbolic work akin to Bede's tomb, insofar as its empty and sepulchral nature suggests how Judas both lacks Christian sustenance, that is, the "bread" described in the Sermon on the Mount, and is "dead" to Christianity. But the symbolism of the pit hardly stops here. At the same time that the pit symbolizes Judas's stony, lethal, and "Jewish" carnality, it also suggests his status as a type of Christ.[142] As we have seen, Jews are introduced in *Elene* as Christ killers and violent persecutors, a view that encompasses the Jews who bury the cross and resist helping Helena. But once Judas enters the pit, he shifts from "Jewish" persecutor to a figure whose suffering links him not so much to Jesus' enemies but to Jesus himself, as well as other suffering Christians.

Of course, his eventual release from the pit puts an end to Judas's "Christian" suffering. However, that very movement in and out of the dry well connotes still other Christian valences. In the bible, heroic figures are thrown into cisterns not for any crime they have committed, but due to the abuse of others.[143] Thomas Hill, the first critic to call serious attention to the figural aspects of *Elene*, points out how Judas's liminal time in the pit resonates specifically with the account in Genesis 37:24 of Joseph being thrust into a cistern by his brothers and subsequent rescue, a sequence that exegetes typically read as "a figure of Christ's entombment, descent into hell, and resurrection."[144] The cross in *Elene*, buried then unearthed, also figures the movement of Christ in and out of hell. And Judas, by dint of his journeying in and out of the pit, is a kind of double of the cross. Other moments in the Vercelli manuscript, namely *The Dream of the Rood*, reinforce this alignment of Judas-in-the-pit with the buried cross. In *Dream*, the speaking cross describes the "terrible fate" ("egeslic wyrd") suffered by it and the other two crosses as "men buried us in a deep *pit*" ("Bedealf us man on deopan seaþe," my emphasis).[145] Judas's resonance with not only Joseph but also the cross suggests how the pit in *Elene* serves a typological function akin to that of the pit in a much later medieval English text, the *Prioress's Tale*. But while in the *Prioress's Tale* it is a Christian schoolboy who is thrown into and rescued from a pit—mirroring the harrowing of hell—here it is a Jew.

In the same way that Judas paradoxically gains Christian valences during this episode, Helena acquires contradictory meanings as she tortures him in the pit. While in hagiography saints are sufferers not persecutors, *Elene* "violates the normal conventions of hagiography" in having a saint "compel credence by physical force."[146] In the master plot to which all hagiographic narratives refer, the Crucifixion narrative, the role of persecutor is attributed to the Jew, with Christ in the position of sufferer. Ironically, Helena stresses that dichotomy in her dialogue with the Jewish assembly, when she alludes to how Christ suffered for love of souls ("ge þrowade . . . for sawla lufan"; 563b–564b) even as she threatens to oppress them. Helena indicates that paradox yet again when she issues to Judas a threat—"I swear by the Son of the creator, the crucified god, that you will be killed by starvation in front of your kinsmen" ("Ic þæt geswerige þurh sunu meotodes, / þone ahangnan god, þæt ðu hunger scealt / for cneo-magum cwylmed weorðan"; 686–88)— that recalls Christ's alignment with the very public victimhood and suffering that Judas will soon undergo.

Critics have suggested how Helena's harsh words make her a militant *mater ecclesia*.[147] Her gender and maternal function, which authorities such as Isidore of Seville tied closely to matter, certainly help explain why she came to supplant Constantine as the finder of the cross in versions of the *Inventio* legend; who better to uncover a material object—and work with the supremely carnal Jew—than a woman?[148] Insofar as Helena is a matriarchal warrior, the pit may resemble a kind of disciplinary "womb" through which Judas is reborn into Christianity. Yet a look at the links between the pit in *Elene* and the pits depicted in the bible complicates this view, since it is never the case that a beneficent figure in the bible places someone in a pit. Indeed, *Elene* itself imbues burial with negative associations. In the same way that their refusal to assist Helena loops back toward the Crucifixion, by keeping the cross hidden underground "the Jews are, in a sense, reenacting the crucifixion, extending their original crime."[149] Resonating with those nefarious acts of burial—and adumbrating the Jewish villains in ritual-murder libels who hide their Christian victims in wells and pits—Helena's "burial" of Judas in the pit suggests yet another way she exhibits the "Jewish" aggression normally associated with the deicide charge.

With his ambivalent portrayal of Helena and Judas as figures who are both Jewish and Christian, Cynewulf may be acknowledging his own, probably monastic, investment in the otherworldly and spiritual. Both the cerebral elements of *Christ II* and the epilogue to *Elene*, with its forceful contemptus mundi and encoding of that message in runes spelling out Cynewulf's identity, suggest how the poet doesn't utterly endorse the Christian materialism at the forefront of *Elene*.[150] In keeping with this antimaterialist bent, Cynewulf encodes in *Elene* a subtle denigration of the secular aspects of his world somewhat in the manner of Ælfric who, by yoking his aforementioned account of the three estates to a sermon on the Jewish warriors of Maccabees, denigrates as Jewish and "insufficient" the carnal values of the Anglo-Saxon members of the second estate.[151]

A telling sign that Cynewulf criticizes Helena for her "Jewish" materialisms is the rhetoric of stone in the poem. As we have seen, the poet expands on his sources to stress the stony nature of Jewish carnality via the Jews' lithic refusal to assist Helena, Judas's preference for figurative stones and literal bread over Christian spiritual sustenance, and the stones that martyred Stephen. Such moments go beyond Paul's idea of the stony Jew's inability to see Christian truth to the still more offensive association of the stony Jew with deicide and anti-Christian violence. After such a noteworthy stress on the pejorative associations of stone, what are we to do with the stones that proliferate later in the poem, when Helena erects the temple? Cynewulf expands considerably on his likely source to stress the place of not living but literal stones in this construction program. While the *Acta Cyriaci* refers to stones only once, Cynewulf does so three times. The Latin legend mentions how Helena adorned the cross with precious stones or *lapidibus praetiosis*.[152] Cynewulf not only refers to the *stangefogum* or stone joining performed by the masons who build the temple, but also stresses twice the adorning of the cross with stones (*gimcynnum* or gemstones, and *eorcnanstanum* or noblest stones).

Taken one way, such references may support Christian materialism, that is, the idea that stones and other physical objects and literal spaces aren't so much antithetical to Christianity but rather may be appropriated for distinctly Christian ends. Instead of being deployed to destroy Stephen, these stones create a Christian edifice.[153] But Cynewulf's unusual stress on the "Jewishness" of stone problematizes such a reading and suggests instead how Helena's construction program, with its focus on literally reproducing Solomon's Temple, doesn't so much supersede but extend and continue the materialism of the Jew.[154] Cognizant of the necessarily material nature and worldly associations of Christianity both during the time of Constantine and in his own Christian moment, Cynewulf doesn't reject such practices outright but instead subtly critiques them by suggesting Helena's paradoxical Jewishness.

I end by considering how Cynewulf may acknowledge his fraught relation to Helena and Christian materialism by identifying himself—as a Christian poet—with Judas. Robert DiNapoli has pointed to original aspects of Cynewulf's account of Judas's ancestral knowledge, especially its use of the word *leoðorun* ("wise counsel given in song," 522b), that align Judas with poetic wisdom.[155] DiNapoli contends that Judas's ancestral affiliation with poetry mirrors that of Cynwulf and showcases his status as the representative of a pagan Anglo-Saxon literary tradition in conflict with a new Christian literary mode.[156] While I agree with DiNapoli that Judas is portrayed as a kind of poet-figure, I would argue that the link between poet and Jew shores up not so much Cynewulf's identification with a native pagan tradition, but something altogether different: his difficult position as an ecclesiastic— a member of the first estate learned in spiritual wisdom—writing a poem about Christian materialisms. After all, the paternal poetic tradition with which Judas is aligned is one that stresses the otherworldly. Paradoxically, Judas does become otherworldy and sacrificial (and Christ-like) as he resists Helena, yet he gives in to her carnal Christian quest to find both the cross and, later, the nails. Could Cynewulf be encoding in Judas's resistance and ultimate submission his own qualms about celebrating Helena and writing this carnal poem?

Cynewulf's possible identification with Judas and his subtle criticism of Helena don't necessarily render *Elene* any less antisemitic than critics such as Scheil or Estes claim it is. Cynewulf criticizes Helena by shoring up her problematic "Jewishness." Cynewulf's identification with Judas is more complex. While Cynewulf may identify with Judas as a figure compelled or forced into the service of worldly Christian rulers, that connection doesn't mean that he feels a particular sympathy with Jews.[157] In other words, and in a move that in some respects looks toward the gentile cross identification with Jews in modernist writings as analyzed by Brian Cheyette and Jonathan Freedman, Cynewulf may be drawn to Judas not so much as a Jew per se, but as a member of a people who were in a sense the ultimate outsiders.[158] In the difficulties posed by the Jew's strangeness to and isolation from a larger Christian community, Cynewulf may have seen parallels with his own status in Anglo-Saxon England as an ascetic in an unavoidably material and worldly milieu. Is the pit, after all, so different from a monastic cell?

# CHAPTER 2

# Medieval Urban Noir

*The Jewish House, the Christian Mob, and*
*the City in Postconquest England*

If Bede and Cynewulf's sepulchral imagery signals a disturbing English refusal to give contemporary Jews a space in which to live, the reality of Jews' ongoing presence in Christian lands became evident to the English as never before after 1066, when William the Conqueror brought Ashkenazic Jews from Rouen to the island.[1] Jews first lived in London, eventually moving to other locations, and especially to urban sites they perceived as safe, as a reference to rural violence by Rabbi Elijah Menahem of London attests.[2] Over the course of the twelfth century, Jews inhabited over thirty towns and cities such as Lincoln, York, Newcastle, Exeter, Hereford, and Bungay (figure 8).[3] No longer a remote and regrettable reality for Christians like Bede, the Jewish presence in Christendom finally was palpable in England, prompting Dominic of Evesham (fl. 1125) to observe, some sixty years after 1066, how "every city in every place supports this race within itself."[4]

Anglo-Jews were small in number. Between only two thousand and three thousand Jews lived in England at the time of the expulsion.[5] But despite their small numbers, Jews were nevertheless prominent, due to their tendency to live in city centers, near marketplaces and royal castles.[6] Moreover, as Vivian Lipman has shown, Jewish residences weren't set apart from but lay side by side with and at times were surrounded by gentile homes.[7] That centrality and contiguity likely disturbed certain members of the Christian

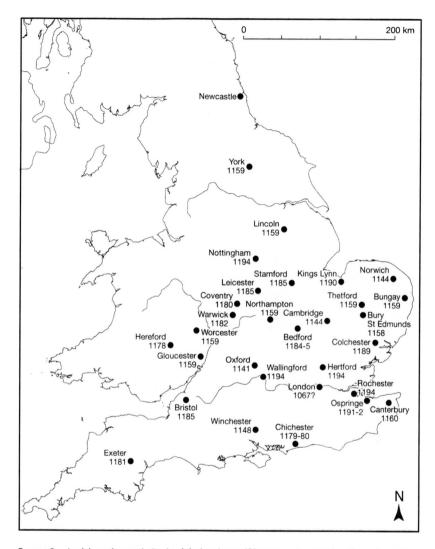

**FIGURE 8.** Jewish settlement in England during the twelfth century. Most dates refer to the earliest recorded reference to Jews in that location. While no hard evidence confirms a Newcastle community prior to 1200, it is possible that one existed. Map by Cath D'Alton. Adapted from Mundill, *King's Jews*, xiv.

majority. As Keith Lilley demonstrates, Normans and other leaders strategically organized medieval cities to support Christian concepts of the nature of the universe. Crucial to medieval Christian ideas of *cosmopolis* was the idea that "being on the 'inside,' at the core, marked out those at the center from those on the 'outside,' on the edges of society" in moral, political, and social terms.[8] Such notions emerge in twelfth- and thirteenth-century *mappae mundi* that imagine a providentially arranged macrocosm in which Jerusalem is "the spiritual center of the earth and 'deviant' Others [are] situated around its edges."[9] Exemplifying that politicized geography on an urban scale, the Anglo-Norman microcosm of Norwich situated its most powerful Christian population (i.e., the Normans) at its center and pushed disenfranchised Anglo-Scandinavian populations to town borders.[10] England's new Jewish population, however, by inhabiting the center or "Jerusalem" of towns and cities, challenged received majority ideas about the divine ordering of the macrocosm and microcosm.

During this period of Jewish–Christian cohabitation, English writers continued to write about biblical buildings.[11] Bede's allegorical exegeses became canonical and were widely incorporated into patristic glosses on the bible. New allegories of the temple-tabernacle appeared, particularly during the twelfth century, from writers who at times turned to Jews for "assistance" in confirming their typological readings.[12] But alongside such writings about long-gone Jewish buildings, images of contemporary Jewish built environments begin to appear during this period in English texts, many of which gave new life to old eastern legends about the Virgin Mary.[13] Instead of portraying, as Bede and Cynewulf do, entombed Jews, monastic writers such as William of Malmesbury, Nigel of Canterbury, and William Adgar portray Jews who are accommodated in both houses and, less frequently, synagogues. Taking English readers into imagined Jewish spaces, miracles of the Virgin produce the Jew as not merely an unbeliever but also an active enemy of Christianity. For example, in "Toledo," after Mary warns church-goers that the Jews are crucifying her son anew, they break into a Jewish building— usually a synagogue but also "the homes of the felonious Jews"—where they find a waxen image of Christ, which the Jews have abused in mockery of the Crucifixion.[14] And in "The Jewish Boy," a Jewish youth accompanies his Christian playmates on Easter Sunday to Mass, where he receives the host.[15] When the boy's father learns what happened, he furiously tosses his son into an oven, where Mary miraculously preserves the child.[16] In these texts, built environments are fundamental tools in the performance of Jewish animosity toward Christianity.[17] Under the cover of a house or synagogue, the imagined Jews of these texts wage war against Christianity by reenacting Christ's death and violently defying Christian ritual.

The popularity of such myths in England results from not only the new Jewish presence on the island but also larger shifts that were happening there and in Europe. As scholars including Robert Chazan and R. I. Moore have shown, factors such as the racialist elements of Urban II's crusade rhetoric, socioeconomic tensions between Christians and their Jewish neighbors, and concerns over the hermeneutic agency evinced by the Talmud prompted a heightened Christian animosity toward Jews.[18] The most significant initial manifestation of that animosity was the tragic massacre in 1096 of whole communities of Rhineland Jews by European knights and local commoners during the First Crusade. According to Chazan, an important impetus for the pogroms was an extremist version of crusader doctrine that saw addressing Jewish unbelief as a core component of the crusader ideal.[19] Jews, their attackers claimed, were, like Muslims, enemies of Christianity. Indeed, as Anna Sapir Abulafia observes, it is during the eleventh and twelfth centuries that "over and above the accusation of killing Christ, Jews were increasingly accused of murdering Christ deliberately and not out of ignorance."[20] But unlike Muslims, who lived far away in Jerusalem, the Jews were geographically proximate to European Christians. Answering the call to, as the monk Ralph put it in a sermon for the Second Crusade, "avenge the Crucified upon his enemies who dwell among you," crusaders attacked their Jewish neighbors.[21] Crusading, the attackers believed, begins at home, with the Jewish enemies in their midst.

Marian miracle tales helped flesh out antisemitic crusader fantasy by providing mythic "knowledge" of how Jews weren't only the ancestors of Christ killers, but a people who actively opposed Christianity behind the closed doors of houses and synagogues. The Jews, these tales suggest, are a far cry from the affirmative public embodiments of Old Testament prophesies described by Augustine. No Christian billboards, Jews emerge in Marian miracles as secret enemies of Christendom who, while lacking a stable home, nevertheless take advantage of the privacy accorded by what habitations they do have. Mary may seem to alleviate such fears when she effects the conversion of Jews in tales such as "The Jewish Boy."[22] But the Jewish threat exposed by Mary often seems to exceed her miraculous powers. Through their fantasies of Jews both colluding to attack images of Christ and killing their own children for participating in Christian ritual, "The Jewish Boy" and "Toledo" imply how the threatening Jewish other requires rooting out and removal. To return to the mapping of medieval English cities, such texts indicate that Jews are not just unbelievers but violent aggressors who should be removed from urban centers and indeed Christian space altogether. The offensive fantasy of the sepulchral Jew doubtless would have appealed to the promulgators of such myths, insofar as it confirmed how the only proper location for a Jew in Christian lands is a grave.

A medieval accusation that, far more than "The Jewish Boy" or "Toledo," fostered fears in England over a Jewish threat was the claim that, in Norwich, close to Easter in 1144, Jews abducted and killed a twelve-year-old

Christian boy named William. William's uncle, Godwin Sturt, initially leveled the charge, the first of its kind in history; but the most important figure
associated with the libel is Thomas of Monmouth.[23] A Benedictine monk
who became affiliated with the Norwich Cathedral Priory in 1146, Thomas
promotes William as an English martyr in his Latin pseudo-hagiography, *The
Life and Miracles of St. William of Norwich* (ca. 1154–74, hereafter *Life*).[24] The
*Life* appears in a single Cistercian manuscript, Cambridge, University Library,
Additional MS 3037, which was copied as late as 1200, probably at Sibton
Abbey in Suffolk.[25] The contents of CUL Add. MS 3037 reflect Thomas's
overt goal of establishing the Norwich boy's sanctity. Both the other English
saints' lives in the manuscript and the presence in the book of a Canon of the
Mass connote William's status as a type of Christ.[26] In the process of making
his case for William's sainthood, Thomas also puts in written form, for the
first time in the medieval West, a full-blown account of what scholars now
refer to as the ritual-murder or boy-martyr libel: the charge that Jews collude
to seduce Christian boys into Jewish homes where they are ritually tortured
and killed in mockery of the Crucifixion.[27] In boy-martyr myths, which
would proliferate in England during the Middle Ages and beyond, the Jewish
threat imagined by Marian miracle tales resonates in a newly jarring manner.[28]
Instead of imagining Jews reenacting the Crucifixion through a statue or by
attacking a Jewish child, those tales imagine Jews using the cover of a domicile
to harm a Christian boy. Here Thomas introduces what would become, in
Roy Booth's words, "the Jew's house of popular legend: a sanguinary trap, into
which innocents are lured, and bled to death in ritualized murder."[29]

Versions of the libel would provide a spurious rationale for anti-Jewish
attacks in medieval England, most notoriously, the state-sponsored execution of nineteen people for their supposed involvement in the "martyrdom" of Hugh of Lincoln in 1255.[30] But Thomas not only initiated a trend
that entailed further accusations and tragic punishments, but also offered an
image of Jewish society that opposed the very idea of an Anglo-Jewry. By
constructing the Jewish home as a radically inhospitable site, where Christian
boys expecting kindness instead meet their deaths, Thomas countered any
notion—Augustinian or otherwise—of the benefits of toleration. Why, the
*Life* implies, should England—or any Christian society, for that matter—host
Jews when Jews are so lethally inhospitable to Christians? That intolerance
comes to a head in a highly disturbing moment in Thomas's text, when a
Jew purportedly involved in William's death surmises that if their crime is
discovered, "our people will then be totally eliminated (*funditus exterminabi-
tur*) from the realm of England. Indeed, and what is extremely terrifying
to us, we and our wives and little ones will be handed over to the Gentiles

as victims, be carried off to death, be given to utter destruction (*dabimur in exterminium*)."[31] The passage uncannily adumbrates later English anti-Jewish actions, namely the 1290 expulsion and, closer to Thomas's time, the only major pogroms of twelfth-century Europe, which began at Richard I's 1189 coronation in London, spread throughout the realm, and culminated in the massacre of hundreds of Jews at York in 1190.[32] While certainly there are no easy and straightforward connections between those events and the *Life*, we can't ignore the likelihood that Thomas's myth and later libels helped encourage horrific acts of English aggression against Jews.[33]

As scholars have shown, the *Life* addresses a host of issues particular to its time and place. Those issues include the need for a patron saint at Norwich Cathedral Priory, the monk's wish for fame as promoter of William's sanctity, his interest in the problem of how to unite and celebrate a radically divided postconquest England, Thomas's critical stance toward certain twelfth-century intellectual currents, his shared concern with other monks over adolescent identity, and the monk's wish to generate via William's *passio* a local version of the passion to which Christians were everywhere devoted.[34] We can better understand many of those issues and uncover still other problems informing the *Life* by taking seriously its geographic elements. Thomas urges such a geographical approach insofar as the *Life* not only stresses the home where William purportedly was killed, but also reads that house against other sites, above all other locations in Norwich. Norwich as a city is very much at issue in Thomas's text, and especially its first two books, which describe William's murder and its aftermath. In his account of William's death, discovery, and eventual veneration as a martyr, Thomas takes his readers on a tour of Norwich and its environs, through narrow passageways leading to the domestic site of William's murder, outside the town to the local forest, Thorpe Wood, where his corpse is deposited, to the urban thoroughfares through which his body is taken in a great procession to Norwich Cathedral, where a Requiem Mass occurs followed by a burial in the monks' cemetery. Later the body is transported to the chapter house and then to its final resting place, the cathedral itself. The *Life*, in other words, is not simply a hagiography or boy-martyr libel, but also a city text, a document as invested in reimagining medieval Norwich as it is in demonizing Jews.[35]

Unlike his contemporaries such as William fitz Stephen and Lucian, figures who wrote laudatory accounts of London and Chester, Thomas locates both good and evil in the city he describes: Norwich in the *Life* is a site that gave rise to both a boy saint and a Jewish menace.[36] However, close attention to the imagined spaces of the *Life* reveals an urban dynamic that is more nuanced and contradictory than the simple opposition of holy boy and wicked Jew. Ultimately, the Jewish home figures in the *Life* as less a particularized site of Jewish menace than a monastic response to larger problems in the emerging city of Norwich. Through the Jewish house, in other words, Thomas routs his own issues as a monk living in an urban location. That mapping of monastic issues onto the Jew becomes visible when we consider how, when viewed geographically, monks aren't altogether different from the Jews Thomas demonizes: the *Life* portrays the Jewish home as closed to Christians in somewhat the same way that monks cloistered themselves from the greater world. To put it another way, in his stress on the Norwich Jews' efforts to seclude themselves from the prying eyes of their gentile neighbors, Thomas aligns Jewishness with a spatial separation that recalls the coenobitic ideal of monasticism.

I argue that Thomas renders his Jews monkish in order to manage his own bifurcated identity as a monk *and* a member of an episcopal see located at the center of a medieval city. Thomas's Norwich had undergone radical changes since the conquest. Shortly after 1066, the new Norman elite razed native Anglo-Scandinavian homes and churches to make way for a French borough (ca. 1071–75), a stone castle (ca. 1120), and a stone cathedral priory, whose main building was completed by 1148.[37] Within that reconfigured Norman cityscape, a market-driven and episcopally administered lay population burgeoned.[38] At the start of the 1100s, around five thousand people lived in Norwich. By the end of the century, the number of people may well have tripled.[39] That dense and heterogeneous secular population spilled into Thomas's cathedral priory. Far from enjoying isolation, monks like Thomas found "the urban market" at their "doorstep." In Roberta Gilchrist's words, "every day pilgrims, merchants, and secular servants mingled at [the] thresholds" of the cathedral.[40] All of which is to say, the entirety of Norwich in a sense threatened monastic identity. And yet monks like Thomas served that city, assisting residents' needs, promoting their faith, and giving them a cathedral in which to worship.[41]

Unable to express openly his hostility toward the urban population to which he ministered, Thomas indirectly registers his resistance to "hosting" city residents by ascribing that inhospitableness to Jews. In the Jewish exiles of Norwich, Thomas found an urban community who, far more than monks, was both other to the lay majority and displaced from its preferred habitation. The long-standing absence of Jews in England may have meant that when they finally arrived shortly after 1066, "they were," in Robert Stacey's words, "aliens in medieval England to a more profound degree than perhaps anywhere else in western Europe."[42] As a community exiled from its homeland of Jerusalem, making do in a less-than-ideal location, the Jews imagined by Thomas allow him to register his fraught relationship with Norwich's Christian majority at an antisemitic remove by suggesting that the only thing truly awry with the city is its Jewish minority. That displacement is no easy linear process, however, but takes mediated form as Thomas weaves his narrative through a variety of interconnected spaces that point to problems that are hardly limited to Jews. Thus, at the same time that Thomas's text uses antisemitism to imaginatively overcome concerns over the emerging city, the *Life* also registers the reality of disorder as an issue endemic to urban life. Ultimately, Thomas's text registers his anxious realization that, even if the Jews left Norwich (which they eventually were forced to do, in 1290), problems pertaining to that city and its dense multitude of Christians would remain. In this manner, the *Life* urges its placement alongside not only other boy-martyr myths and related antisemitic legends but also satirical accounts of English medieval cities penned by such writers as the Benedictine monk Richard of Devizes. When read as a critical city text, the *Life* adumbrates the deplorable actions of urban groups—against Jews, monks, and other lay Christians—later in the twelfth century and beyond.

Epitomizing such monstrous urban behaviors are the 1190 pogroms that began in London and culminated in York. I close the chapter by considering the important account of the attacks by the Augustinian canon William of Newburgh (ca. 1136–ca. 1198), who in many respects makes explicit the urban criticisms that Thomas only hints at in his account of Norwich. A monk like Thomas, but one who lived at a distance from urban centers, William has no problem denigrating cities as places that counter everything a monk embraces. If the cloister is an otherworldly space strictly ordered around contemplation and pious self-denial, the city is an all too worldly place where greedy carnality fosters rampant disorder and violence. In his *History of English Affairs*, William doesn't so much pinpoint a particular urban problem that needs rooting out in the manner of the demonized Jews and houses of Thomas's *Life*, but rather offers a wholesale condemnation of the city qua city.

## Medieval Urban Noir

A brief look at Richard of Devizes's account of the urban context for the ritual-murder myth he relates in his *Cronicon* will help prepare the way for my discussion of the *Life* as a city text. The *Cronicon* was composed two decades after Thomas finished his *Life*, when tales of ritual murder had gained a popular currency in England.[43] Accusations had been leveled at Jews about boys killed in Bury St. Edmunds, Gloucester, Bristol, and possibly Winchester.[44] Demonstrating how ritual-murder charges had become so prevalent in England as to merit parody, the *Cronicon* is a brilliantly allusive and satirical text. The *Cronicon* is famous for its early account of London, which Richard portrays as no esteemed capital but rather the very worst place on earth. A microcosm of global evil—where "whatever evil or malicious thing that can be found in any part of the world" exists in a single urban location—London is a city worth avoiding at all costs. What especially characterizes London in the *Cronicon* is its dense gathering of diverse criminal personages, from "crowds of pimps" to an "infinite" quantity of "parasites." "All sorts of men," the text asserts, "crowd together there from every country under the heavens. Each race brings its own vices and its own customs to the city. No one lives in it without falling into some sort of crime. Every quarter of it abounds in grave obscenities."[45] Richard's London presents no unproblematic cosmopolitanism but rather evinces in "every quarter" a medieval English version of the Roman underworld Horace describes in his *Satires*: "Actors, jesters, smooth-skinned lads, Moors, flatterers, pretty boys, effeminates, pederasts, singing and dancing girls, quacks, belly-dancers, sorceresses, extortionists, night-wanderers, magicians, mimes, beggars, buffoons: all this tribe fill all the houses."[46]

However, in a move in keeping with Richard's allusive, slippery, and satirical methodology throughout the *Cronicon*, he does not voice his critique of London directly but puts it in the mouth of a French Jew. Conversing with a poor Christian orphan in France, the Jew convinces the boy to travel to England, claiming that as long as he avoids dens of iniquity such as London, the boy will find "terram lacte et melle manantem" or "a land flowing with milk and honey." The Jew convinces the boy to emigrate to Winchester, which he portrays as idyllic, only to provide the Jewish inhabitants of the city with a young Christian victim.[47] The boy and a friend move to the town, where the orphan works in a Jewish household until Good Friday, when he disappears. The friend goes to the house and accuses the Jewish inhabitant of crucifying the boy. Standing before a crowd that has gathered outside the residence to witness the friend's strident accusations, the boy proclaims: "this Jew is a devil; this man has torn the heart out of my breast; this man has cut the throat of my only friend, and I presume he has eaten him, too."[48]

The *Cronicon*, it would seem, only imagines widespread urban degeneration in England to mitigate that threat through the ritual-murder libel. The account of London's riffraff is spoken by a duplicitous Jew, an unreliable narrator whose ulterior motives reveal that wrongdoing, far from abounding in every corner of English cities, lurks under the cover of a Jewish home. In England, the only "crime" experienced by the boy and his friend is in the Jew's home, where the boy was last seen according to the friend and a corroborating witness. The friend's accusations before the crowd infuse the Jewish domicile with a conspiratorial, criminal, and even cannibalizing Jewish domesticity.

The meaning of Richard's chronicle, however, is hardly this straightforward. As scholars note, the *Cronicon* is a parodic, "allusive," "scurrilous," and even proto-deconstructive text whose tendency to offer "open-ended contrasting of different points of view" destabilizes meaning in the vein of Menippean satire.[49] For example, Richard undercuts the seeming truth behind the French Jew's efforts to lure the orphan to England—a truth that the orphan's friend stridently proclaims—by never confirming the fate of the missing boy. After the friend unleashes his nasty diatribe, "the story," as Heather Blurton puts it, "rushes to its denouement: the only witness is unreliable, there is no body, the judge is bribed, and the matter is dropped."[50] Moreover, the French Jew qualifies his praise of Winchester by telling the orphan that the one flaw in its citizenry is their propensity toward lying, a charge that implicates none other than Richard himself as a monk of St. Swithin's.[51] What is a reader to believe, if everyone—not only the figures Richard portrays but also the monastic writer himself—proves unreliable?

Ironically, the prime dissimulator in this episode—the French Jew—turns out to be most trustworthy figure. As Nancy Partner points out, the Jew, for all his associations with duplicity, "figures as the authentic voice of worldly urban experience . . . who expresses views about English towns consistent with Richard's own remarks elsewhere in the *Cronicon*," a decision that may reflect Richard's own cynicism, sophistication, admiration of pagan Romans (whom the French Jew approximates), and knowledge that Jews were "the most consistently urban of medieval populations."[52] Insofar as the French Jew ultimately enjoys the most authentic voice in this section of the *Cronicon*, he alludes to the repressed reality behind the ritual-murder libel, a narrative of widespread gentile misbehavior akin to those performed by the undesirables of London.[53]

As one of the objects—if not the prime object—of Richard's satire, Thomas's *Life* presents itself as no parody but an "accurate" account of the urban terrors posed by Jews. That narrative begins three days before Passover in 1144, when a messenger from the Jews approaches William, who had moved to Norwich from the country to develop his craft of skinning.[54] Claiming to be the cook for the archdeacon of the cathedral precinct, the messenger offers William a job in the kitchen with great potential for advancement.[55] William takes the messenger to his mother Elviva, who eventually permits William to go with the man.[56] The next day the messenger travels by the home of William's aunt Liviva and tells her that the mother had entrusted the boy to him. Suspicious about precisely what the Jews are doing with her nephew, Liviva sends her daughter on an information-gathering mission. The girl, Thomas tells us, "went out in order to discover their route, and she followed them from a distance, as they turned, taking secret alleyways. Following in this way she watched them at last enter secretly into the house of a certain Jew, and noticed them immediately shut the door behind them. Having seen this, she returned to her mother and informed her of what she had seen."[57] Thomas then recounts the sordid treatment of William in the Jewish home. William's Jewish hosts at first treat him *blande* or courteously.[58] But the next day, when the Jews return to the house after singing Passover hymns in their synagogue, they commence their attack. In salacious detail, Thomas describes the "manifold and wretched ways" ("varii ac miserabiles . . . modi") the Jews maltreat William.[59] Those torments culminate in the boy's crucifixion and death "in mockery of the Passion of the Cross."[60]

In Richard's London, a heterogeneous group of undesirables "fill every house."[61] But Thomas limits Norwich misbehavior to a single Jewish house, the home of a man identified later as a wealthy lender called either Eleazar or Deulesalt.[62] By crucifying a young man, the Jews perform a second crucifixion, but not the public spectacle described in the Gospels. Rather, William's martyrdom occurs in a secret and domesticated Calvary, re-created in the dark Jewish underbelly of Norwich, a site accessible only by private passageways. In imagining Norwich's Jews as lurking behind private alleys, Thomas departs radically from their actual pattern of habitation. The Jewish presence in Norwich is recorded in documents starting in the 1130s.[63] Like their coreligionists elsewhere on the island, the Jews of Norwich were small in number—at their peak, in the early thirteenth century, around two hundred—but centrally located and thus prominent.[64] Most lived south and southeast of the new Norman marketplace, the source of their livelihood, and also within close reach of the new Norman castle, where they could seek protection and rights from the Crown and its representatives (figure 9).[65] Jews also lived side by side with Christians; consider, for example, the string of medieval properties located near the market, east of Haymarket and south of Saddlegate, which is now White Lion Street (figure 10). From the corner of Haymarket and Saddlegate moving eastward lay five properties owned by Christians, followed by two properties owned by Jews during the 1250s and 1260s. Immediately south of a Christian corner property were several Jewish homes.[66] Elsewhere in town, outside the Jewry, on Conesford (now called King Street) near the river Wensum, was the still extant home of the most prominent Norwich Jew, Isaac (ca. 1125–1235).[67]

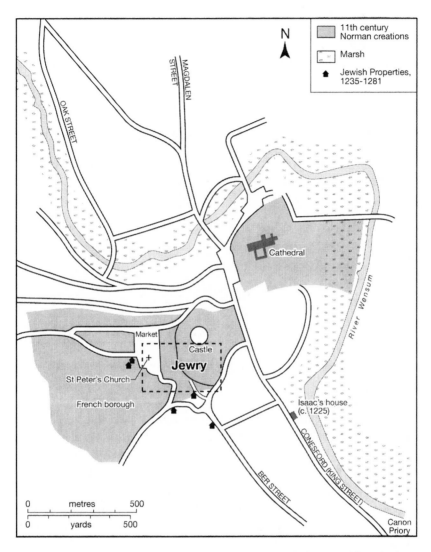

**FIGURE 9.** Twelfth-century Norwich. Map by Cath D'Alton. Adapted from Rawcliffe and Wilson, *Medieval Norwich*, map 2.

Unlike their historical counterparts, Thomas's Jews live in dwellings that are notable for their obscurity. Thomas's ascription to Jews of a secrecy they historically lacked may speak to the status of his text as proto–detective story. As Gavin Langmuir points out, the first two books of the *Life* involve tracking down and uncovering the nefarious activities imagined to transpire in Jewish homes.[68] As a covert affair, the ritual-murder legend affords the prototabloid pleasure of peering beyond closed doors to witness a horrifying series of

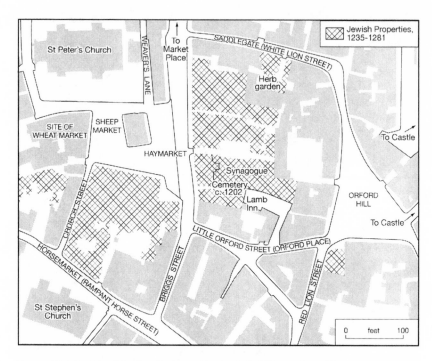

**FIGURE 10.** Section of the Norwich Jewry. Map by Cath D'Alton. Adapted from Lipman, *Jews of Medieval Norwich*, figure 13.

tortures. The house, however, with its "keen sense of domestic detail," serves in Thomas's narrative as more than a means to voyeuristic fascination.[69] Its material components are also constitutive of Jewish animosity. For example, evidence culled after William's death from "most definite and clear signs of the affair" indicate that the youth was nailed and bound by cords directly onto its "posts."[70] The building is not merely the setting for William's martyrdom; its very timber supports buttress the crucified William. Of a piece with Jewish violence is the very stuff of the Jewish house.[71]

Even more than its posts, the doors of the house participate in Thomas's construction of Jewish menace. Repeatedly depicted by Thomas in the process of being closed, those architectural elements enact a certain Jewish animosity toward Christians. As we have seen, an identification of Jewish hostility with enclosed spaces informs earlier images of Jews, from Bede and Cynewulf's sepulchral Jews to the homes and synagogues covering over anti-Christian violence in "Toledo" and "The Jewish Boy." But the *Life* is unprecedented in its scrutiny of the Jewish sealing of apertures.[72] Thomas stresses the entrance to the house through his initial reference to the cousin seeing and hearing it closed, and a reminder a bit later in the text of how she saw "that the door immediately was firmly closed behind him."[73] Thomas also emphasizes the door located inside the domicile, leading to the room where William is tortured. In a section of the *Life* providing a series of arguments "proving" that Jews killed William, Thomas describes how the Jews' Christian maidservant, while passing a pot of boiling water over to the Jews in the room, "through the chink of the door managed to see the boy fastened to a post. She could not see it with both eyes," Thomas informs us, "but she did manage to see it with one."[74] The maid's prying curiosity results in revulsion at the torture she witnesses: "Having seen this, she shuddered at the sight. She shut that eye and they shut the door."[75]

Thomas's unique stress on Jewish doors, like his depiction of private alleys, attributes secrecy to what was historically a rather open and public Jewish population. At the same time, the closed doors in the *Life* might speak to the reality of a city center where Jews and Christians lived alongside each other, often with very little space separating their dwellings.[76] Such close quarters might produce an anxious curiosity about a neighbor's private goings-on. All of which is to say, in the absence of substantial geographic boundaries separating Jews and Christians in medieval Norwich, domestic thresholds could gain a special resonance, both in lived experience and in urban texts like the *Life*. As Mary Douglas points out in her work on social rituals of pollution, thresholds, such as building entrances or—shifting scales downward—bodily entrances like mouths or eyes, are charged and vulnerable sites symbolizing "points of entry or exit to social units" in a culture.[77] A door, when open, could serve as a conduit of hospitable connection between Jews and Christians or of even more intense Jewish–Christian mixings, such as the union of lovers.[78] The Norwich Jews imagined by Thomas, however, open their doors to a Christian youth only to close them, trapping and killing their guest. Teasing out the architectural phenomenology of Jewish aggression signified by the closed or closing door, Thomas describes how William's cousin, through the dual sensory registers of sight and sound, experiences the door closing, and encourages his readers to imagine the maid struggling to peer into the room while the door is momentarily ajar. Antisemitism emerges in the *Life* not only through images of Jews killing Christians, but also through the closing of a door, the aggressive sealing of the Jewish domicile from Christian eyes and ears in the manner of a barricade dividing one enemy camp from another.[79]

Thomas's perception of a door as a sign of hostility was shared by his medieval culture. For example, Isidore of Seville's influential *Etymologies* (ca. 636) align doors with aggression by punning the Latin for door (*ostium*) with the words for both impeding (*obstare*) and enemy or foreigner (*hostium*).[80]

Exemplifying Isidore's claim that some "say doorway is so called because it detains an enemy (*ostis*, i.e. *hostis*), for there we set ourselves against our adversaries," Thomas describes Jews repeatedly closing to Christians the door of the domicile where they torture William. Thomas possibly signposts the linguistic slippage between architecture and attack—between domestic seclusion and a warlike animosity—through his medieval Latin. By spelling door with an "h" (*hostium*) and calling Jews the "christiani nominis hostes" or "enemies of the Christian name," Thomas renders the words for door and enemy nearly identical.[81] Regardless of whether Thomas's pun on *hostium* and *hostes* is intentional, the two terms nevertheless prove mutually constitutive in the *Life*. In repeatedly shutting the doors of their home to Christians, the Jews provide architectural proof of Thomas's racialist sentiment that they possess an "inborn hatred of the Christian race" that makes them constitutionally incapable of friendly exchange and cohabitation with Christians.[82]

Doors aren't the only apertures crucial to Thomas's myth of Jewish animosity. When the maidservant witnesses William's torture, the architectural threshold of the door works in conjunction with the bodily aperture of the eye, as if the horrific nature of the scene merits the use of two protective barriers. The woman's eye—pruriently open and peering into the room then closing in fright as the Jews shut the door—demonstrates how Thomas uses buildings and bodies to connote an adversarial relationship between Jews and Christians.[83] He makes a similar move by describing how the Jews commence their torture of William by gagging his mouth. William's gagging, Thomas claims, happens while the unsuspecting boy is eating dinner. In a move that reiterates the pattern set up by the doors, the Jews initiate a hospitable movement of nourishment into William's mouth, only to aggressively stop up that aperture by seizing William and "insert[ing] into his open mouth an instrument of torture."[84] Isidore portrays the mouth as a door mapped onto the body, writing that "the mouth (*os*) is so called because through the mouth as if through a door (*ostium*) we bring food in and throw spit out, or else from that place food goes in and words come out."[85] In keeping with this idea of mouths and doors as charged thresholds, Thomas's text turns to the boundaries of both the Jewish home and William's body to make Jews demonized others. In contrast to the maid, who protectively walls herself off from the room where William is tortured, the Jews aggressively seal William off from both the Christians that might rescue him (though the maid is clearly not ready for such an act of heroism) and the food that will nourish him.

Rendering William's gagging all the more resonant as a sign of Jewish aggression is the particular object that the Jews use, a device "vulgo teseillun dicitur" or "called by the commoners a teasel."[86] The use of a teasel to produce Jews as sealers of vital, life-giving flows is telling. As Anthony Bale points out, Thomas's reference to the teasel is one of two moments in which his vocabulary takes a notably English and local turn.[87] For Bale, the vernacularity of the teasel offers "key coordinates around which the reader can apprehend and remember" William's story as a local version of "Passional martyrdom."[88] We can press further the local valences of a teasel and consider how its presence in the *Life* contributes to its negative construction of Jews. Teasels—a kind of prickly thistle—were cultivated in England for use by fullers to raise the nap on cloth.[89] In Norwich's vital manufacturing sector, cloth making was a key industry, along with William's own trade of leatherworking.[90] The teasel thus was an important object in the Norwich economy. So too were Jews vital to commerce in the city. Norwich Jews held various occupations and worked as educators, physicians, household servants, vintners, cheesemongers, fishmongers, traders, pawnbrokers, and, above all, financiers.[91] As Jeffrey Cohen affirms with respect to that final role, as bankers Jews were "the lifeblood of Norwich's commercial prosperity."[92] Through William's gagging, however, Thomas imaginatively inverts the Jews' historical relationship to the Norwich economy. The urban population that infused capital into that city, thereby creating and stimulating economic flows in Norwich, is imagined to oppose commercial vitality on multiple fronts. Beyond the sheer act of murdering one of the city's young workers—and luring the boy into the Jewish house under the false pretense of economic advancement—the Jews stop up William's mouth with the teasel, perversely employing it not for its intended manufacturing use but as an instrument of torture.

## Christian Multitudes and Public Space in the *Life*

Thomas's stress on closed doors and dark alleys shores up the status of the medieval city as a site with a dark underbelly, a place that attracts a criminal element engaged in spurious actions in secluded locations. Such an anxiety over secrecy and private life may well have been endemic to medieval cities, where diverse populations gathered and cohabitated in tight spaces. But a dark, hidden, and dangerous Jewish quarter is by no means the only aspect of Norwich imagined by Thomas in the first two books of the *Life*. Events like judicial proceedings, ecclesiastical synods, and Christian rituals showcase the public side of Norwich and imbue it with a beneficent Christian aura that contrasts with the seedy private regions of the city. A prime example is the crowds that fill the city on Holy Thursday, the day after William's purported martyrdom. Thomas writes that after killing William, his abductors are forced to delay transporting the boy's corpse out of town, because "That day was the day of absolution, Maundy Thursday, on which a crowd of penitents of the whole diocese customarily gathered in the mother church of Norwich, and the streets of the whole city were then visited by an unusual multitude of people wandering about."[93] Having dwelt extensively upon the sordid details of William's torture, Thomas opens his text outward, to the open squares or *platee* of Norwich, where Christian ritual is the order of the day. The gathering of Christians in both the cathedral and streets of Norwich suggest communal flows that starkly contrast with the closed environment of the Jewish domicile. As an exceptionally large group crowding all of the city's streets, the Holy Thursday multitude also affirms the dominance of the Norwich Christian majority over its Jewish minority. Through its sheer size, the Christian public of Norwich opposes Jewish mobility and intentionality, unwittingly transforming what was a trap for William into a temporary prison for his attackers.

Thomas's effort to distinguish Christian from Jewish spaces culminates in his account of William's funeral and burial. Thomas tells us how, after the body is discovered in Thorpe Wood, the bishop of Norwich, Everard of Calne, instructed some monks to retrieve the corpse for burial. When the monks returned from the forest,

> so vast a multitude of the common people met them that you would have thought very few had stayed behind in the city. And so, that precious and desired treasure was carried with immense delight of clergy and people, and was received by the venerable chapter of the monks in a procession, was led into the Cathedral Church, and was placed with its bier before the altar of the Holy Cross. . . . A Requiem Mass for the faithful was sung solemnly by the monks and the whole Church was filled from front to back with a crowd of townspeople.[94]

Even more than the Holy Thursday crowds, the Norwich multitudes attending the funeral infuse that ritual with a public nature that contrasts with the secrecy surrounding William's murder. The boy's abduction involved clandestine movements in dark alleys, but his translation entails a procession in broad daylight. While a few Jewish men torture the boy in the seclusion of a home, a host of monks sings William's Requiem Mass before an audience so great that it fills the entire church from end to end. Later, during William's burial, we are told "the cemetery was filled with thousands of people" so that "the area was hardly large enough for those who kept coming in."[95] The opposition of public and private, of cathedral and home, of ritual veneration and ritual murder, all set the Christians of Norwich apart from their Jewish counterparts. The supersession of Christianity over Judaism emerges in the public spectacle of a multitude of Christians revering a dead boy. That is, the scale of Christian practice, heightened all the more by its public performance in and around the massive Romanesque cathedral, overshadows and diminishes the isolated act of ritual murder in an ordinary Jewish home. The passage exemplifies the idea that Christianity inaugurated a radical shift in the scale of the saved, from a tiny group of chosen people to, as Peter the Venerable puts it, "a plenitude of peoples."[96]

Thomas's crowds recall Bede's stress in his architectural exegeses on how Christians spread throughout and fill up the world. But he departs from Bede in stressing the literal space where those "living stones" of the church gather. Crucial to Thomas's construction of a beneficent Christian majority is the episcopal-priory complex, which emerges in his cartography as the most prestigious and holy site in Norwich. While the closed door of the Jewish home registers Jewish–Christian animosity, the open and capacious space of the cathedral reveals a hospitable affinity between the monks and the pious multitude venerating William, presenting what Robert Stacey describes as "a triumphant closure to" a tale that began with Jewish perfidy.[97] Here, at the cathedral and its immediate environs, Thomas depicts, in Jeffrey Cohen's words, a "culminating moment of civic unity"; of the throng of clergy, monks, and laity present at the funeral, Thomas proclaims, "however different they may have been in lifestyle and in sex, [they] were nevertheless all as one as they watched."[98] Jewish aggression doesn't so much harm the city as reinforce the unity and piety of its Christian majority.

Through his representation of the cathedral close and its architectural other, the Jewish home, Thomas imagines Norwich as a place where the worst and best of deeds can be mapped with clarity and precision. While a second crucifixion occurs in single "Jewish" location, public displays of pious fellowship abound in the city, and especially the magnificent and ample spaces of the cathedral close. Yet this is hardly the whole story, for Thomas's image of Christian communal union under the aegis of a welcoming and capacious cathedral close idealizes the relationship of the town to what was in fact an intimidating and even brutal force. Founded in 1098, when the East Anglian see was transferred from Thetford to Norwich, the cathedral-priory complex comprised one of several changes in the city that testified to its new Norman governance. As James Campbell puts it, "Norwich was more changed by the Norman Conquest than it had ever changed before (in so short a time); or than it was ever to change again."[99] While the new castle and marketplace spoke to the new secular leadership of the city, the cathedral complex asserted the dominance of Norwich by its new mother church.

The first Norwich bishop, the Norman Herbert de Losinga, appropriated "a vast site" encompassing a substantial portion of the original Anglo-Saxon town, areas "on the precinct's western fringe . . . and rural properties."[100] Monastic lands thus stretched over the city, as the monumental cathedral soared above it. The Romanesque cathedral, the primary signpost in a city devoid of street signage, has been compared by Eric Fernie to "the Gothic cathedrals of northern France of the later twelfth and thirteenth centuries," which in turn "have often been compared to skyscrapers or to American and soviet spacecraft in their scale, their cost and their impact on the contemporary imagination."[101] In all likelihood a "staggering sight" for anyone who witnessed it, Norwich Cathedral evinced in architectural terms the bishop's and monks' sway over the city.[102]

The authoritative role of the cathedral complex in shaping the lives of Norwich's Christian masses reveals how at stake in the *Life*'s image of Christians dominating Jews is also the issue of Christians dominating Christians. Thomas's images of crowds gathering at the mother church is not simply a depiction of communal unity but bears traces of a charged intra-Christian power dynamic. Not just any group of Christians overshadows and supplants the Jewish minority of Norwich, but "living stones" who cluster around and are governed by religious authorities. The Holy Thursday crowds gather to seek absolution from their spiritual leaders, affirming the authority of the monks. The multitude that fills "the whole Church . . . from front to back" is led by the monks who sing William's Requiem Mass.

## Shifting Scales of Antisemitism: From the Local to the Global

The medieval domination of the Christian masses by the ecclesiastical elite was not only a matter of urban or parish control. The twelfth century witnessed an unprecedented wave of consolidation on the part of the entire Western church, spearheaded by popes bent on codifying Roman authority.[103] From the conquest through the end of the century, the papacy gradually extended its influence into England.[104] In Norwich, the "increasing contact between England and Rome" at times codified the power of the episcopal see.[105] During the first half of the twelfth century, for example, popes Innocent II and Honorius II repeatedly granted certain administrative powers and lucrative offerings to the cathedral priory.[106] Norwich Cathedral also embodied these ties between England and Rome. Herbert began work on the cathedral two years after a 1094 trip to the Vatican. He went to Rome "to seek absolution from Pope Urban for the simoniacal purchase of his see," reflecting the reforming efforts that characterized this period.[107] Once he returned to England, the bishop followed architectural precedent to fashion the see as an arm of the Roman mother church.[108] The bishop obtained a site for the complex "with terrain reminiscent of the papal complex" and ensured that the dimensions of the cathedral approximated those of old St. Peter's basilica.[109]

Wholeness and universality were key ideals during this period of consolidation.[110] Gregory VII and other reformers sought to create a homogeneously Christian society united in a shared relationship to Rome. The reformers' efforts to generate an organic Christian "us" prompted a new emphasis on Jews as "them," as religious outsiders.[111] Thomas's depiction of Christian unity over and against Jewish danger seems to affirm this ideal. Both the universal nature of William's veneration (he stresses how all of the city's Christian population seems to attend his Requiem Mass and funeral) and containment of William's worshipers by a space patterned after St. Peter's would seem to endorse Roman authority.

Yet Rome was no friend to William's emerging cult. While Alexander III (1159–81) enthusiastically endorsed the canonization of Thomas Becket, he gave no such support to William, who was never canonized by Rome.[112] Thomas responds to Rome's disregard for William at the opening of book 2 of the *Life*. Responding to critics who claim that it is rash to worship William as a saint because "the church universal" hasn't recognized him, Thomas stridently challenges the notion of a united and universalizing church:

> If indeed those who worship the memory of those saints whom the whole world does not recognize are to be accused of presumption, then you would find few or none who would not incur that blame. And I would assert as true that, apart from the glorious Virgin Mother of God and John the Baptist and the Apostles, it can be said of few saints that knowledge of them is widespread in all the lands where the religion of the Christian name flourishes. Truly, is it possible that all those whom Rome herself venerates, Gaul and Britain accept for worship too? Is it true that the name of the most blessed king and martyr Edmund and the glorious confessor Cuthbert, famed in all parts of England, is known to the people of Greece and Palestine? Briefly to conclude, is it true that the whole of Europe also is used to celebrate all those which Asia or Africa hold as famous? If it were so, or rather because it is firmly so, what sort of blame is incurred by those who celebrate with fitting veneration someone whom the Church does not know or worship universally?[113]

Unlike the many moments in the *Life* when Thomas imagines Norwich on its own spatial terms, here he jumps scales from that single English city to "all the lands where the religion of the Christian name flourishes." His account of the cult of saints, referencing the world and its three continents of Asia, Africa, and Europe, creates a verbal *mappa mundi* or world map. Unlike Thomas's imagined Norwich, this global perspective hardly presents a picture of Christian unity. In response to Rome's failure to canonize William, Thomas conjures a striking image of Christian heterogeneity. No universal collective headed by Rome, Christendom is a place where the vast majority of holy men and women receive only local and national forms of veneration. Thomas goes so far as to ascribe limited renown to not only English saints but also even those holy persons "whom Rome herself honors."

Thomas's turn from an urban to a global perspective is accompanied by a shift in his antisemitism. Jews are crucial to the monk's negotiation of the relationship between Norwich and Rome. Namely, Thomas resists Rome not only by depriving the mother church of her universal sway, but also by demonizing universalism itself as Jewish. This "Jewishing" of Roman corporatism emerges when Thomas states of the skeptic seeking Rome's approval that "a stony hardness obstructs the passages of his brain," and that "this is the way that a blind man strikes out."[114] Christian writers had denigrated Jews as blind and stone-like as far back as the New Testament. Justin Martyr (AD 100–ca. 165) exemplifies that trend when he proclaims to a Jewish interlocutor in his *Dialogue* "you are a people hard of heart, and without understanding, and blind, and lame, and sons in whom there is no faith."[115] By ascribing those stereotypically Jewish qualities to William's skeptics, Thomas produces as "Jewish" anyone who insists on a Rome-authorized network of saints.

Thomas offers an even more explicit account of the Jewishness of universalism in the most notorious passage of the *Life*, which offers the fifth piece of "evidence" affirming that Jews killed William. Through the fictional testimony of "Theobald, who was once a Jew, and afterwards a monk" ("Theobaldo, quondam iudeo et monacho postmodum"), Thomas offers a tale of Jewish global conspiracy as fraudulent and offensive as the modern era's Protocols of Zion.[116] According to Theobald,

> in the ancient writings of their ancestors it was written that Jews could not achieve their freedom or ever return to the lands of their fathers without the shedding of human blood. Hence it was decided by them a long time ago that every year, to the shame and affront of

Christ, a Christian somewhere on earth be sacrificed to the highest God, and so they take revenge for the injuries of Him, whose death is the reason for their exclusion from their fatherland and their exile as slaves in foreign lands.

Therefore, the leaders and rabbis of the Jews who dwell in Spain, at Narbonne, where the seed of kings and their glory flourishes greatly, meet together, and cast lots of all the regions where Jews lived. Whichever region was chosen by lot, its capital city had to apply that lot to the other cities and towns, and the one whose name comes up will carry out that business, as decreed. In that year, however, when William, the glorious martyr of God, was killed, it so happened that the lot fell on the men of Norwich, and all the communities of the Jews of England offered their consent by letters or by messengers for the crime to be performed at Norwich.[117]

Theobald's testimony creates a verbal world map by describing the spread of Jews from Jerusalem to the western territory of *Occitania* and its Jewish nodal capital of Narbonne, to the far western terrain of England, and finally the northern city of Norwich.[118] Like Thomas's account of the cult of saints, Theobald connotes the universal presence of Jews in the world. However, if Jews and Christians are both omnipresent, only one group possesses a successful organizational system. While blind to the Christian message and closed off from their gentile neighbors, the Jews imagined by Thomas are cannily cognizant of each other. In stark contrast to the Christian cult of saints, which lacks an effective means of spreading information (so that Romans are ignorant of English saints and the English are ignorant of Roman saints), the members of the Jewish cabal comprise a well-functioning corporate entity operating hierarchically on multiple spatial scales, from the seat of the "Royal seed," to the metropolis of a selected country, and the chosen city within that country. Thanks to their well-functioning network, the members of the Jewish cabal are at once cognizant of and amenable to the selection of William as its victim. Thus Christian discord and heterogeneity about saints contrasts with Jewish union and homogeneity over ritual murder. Not all Christians venerate William, but all Jews agree to kill him. Approximating Roman universalism, the Jewish cabal serves as dark double for papal ecclesiastical networking, and another means by which Thomas registers his resistance to consolidated global authority. Far from exemplifying a Christian social order, universalism is demonized in the *Life* as a "Jewish" phenomenon that is antithetical to true Christian practice.

## A Rose among (English) Thorns: Crowds and Cloistering in the *Life*

Instead of celebrating the universal church, Thomas embraces more local and national Christian communities. Thus in his account of the cult of saints, Thomas celebrates Edmund and Cuthbert, who are "renowned in every part of England." William is another national saint; Herbert de Losinga tells Thomas in a dream that through the boy's relics "the church of Norwich would be much exalted and become famous in the whole of England and venerated in the parts beyond the sea."[119] The world map evoked by Theobald's testimony contributes to this national program, insofar as it stresses not only the usual cartographic suspects (e.g., Jerusalem, Spain, and even Narbonne) but also Norwich, a city that never appears on medieval world maps. The utter absence of Norwich on medieval *mappae mundi* affirms its global insignificance; in the ranking of English cities, after all, Norwich was a long second to the capital of London.[120] But Theobald's report suggests otherwise. Of all the cities and towns that comprise the far-flung network of medieval Jewish habitation, it is Norwich that is chosen as the site of sacrifice.

To be sure, the fact that Jews put Norwich on the world "map" is problematic, given their demonized status. But William is not simply a victim of the cabal but also a blessed martyr. Early on in the narrative, Thomas states that it is his belief that "by the wish of divine providence," William was "predestined to martyrdom centuries ago."[121] In other words, while Rome hasn't yet recognized England's latest martyr, God singled him out long before his birth. Thomas foregrounds William's providential sacrifice by opening the *Life* with these lines: "When the mercy of divine piety desired to visit the province of Norwich—indeed the whole of England—and to give it in these new times a new patron, it gave a boy who was to be listed among the principal martyrs and to be honored by the entire company of saints."[122] From the start of the narrative, we learn that William's martyrdom signifies God's special favor to Norwich, or rather to "the whole of England."

Yet, in the lines that follow, Thomas seems to distinguish William from the English by stating that God caused William "to grow, little by little, as a fragrant rose among the thorns."[123] Is William somewhat of an exception to the rule regarding English behavior, a rose arising from English *spina* or thorns? Thomas's simile here, with its evocation of a single flower surrounded by a multitude of thorns, connotes the English masses, but hardly the submissive multitude seeking absolution on Holy Thursday, or the pious collective at the boy's Mass. On a plant, thorns are preponderant, prickly, and displeasing to handle. Thorns imply something dangerous about the many men and women of Norwich.[124]

A closer look at the crowds depicted in the *Life* confirms this prospect. In addition to the Holy Thursday and funeral collectives, Thomas describes the multitude that assembles once the rumor reaches the city that William's body has been discovered in Thorpe Wood:

> The city was shaken with a new disturbance and the streets were filled with restless crowds; and it was already claimed by many that only the Jews could do such things, especially at that time. And so many stood still, as if shocked by so novel and unusual a matter; many ran hither and thither, above all boys and youths, and, guided by divine will, they rushed to the wood in large groups in order to get a good view. Indeed, they sought and found and identified the marks of punishments on him and, having then considered the matter with care, certain of them believed that the Jews were not guiltless of the crime. Some even claimed to have been inspired by a certain presentiment. When they returned, those who had stayed at home came together in groups, and when they heard how things were, they rushed to see, and when they, too, returned, they testified about it to others. And so the whole of Saturday and the whole of Easter Day were occupied with people going and returning in successive throngs, and the whole city was engaged and amazed. Hence zeal of pious fervor incited everyone towards the destruction of the Jews; they would have already laid hands on them, but were held back by fear of Sheriff John, and remained calm for a while.[125]

The boys and young men exhibit a certain level of rationality through their careful inspection of the markings on William's corpse. Moreover, God draws them on, and it is a "pious fervor" that impels them "towards the destruction of the Jews." At the same time, however, the crowd, roused by an unusual agitation, is disturbing the peace (*tumultuantibus*). Many of its restless members are "running to and fro" (*discurrebant*) along the streets of Norwich, and back and forth between the city and wood. The carefully plotted spaces of Norwich threaten to become undone by the unruly Christian masses. Thomas betrays here a certain worried fascination with the mob.

Crowds have long occupied a fraught place in the history of Christianity, which originated as a religion with the open-air throngs gathering around Christ yet shifted during the Middle Ages to an institution bent on controlling and containing crowds.[126] Elias Canetti locates the roots of the church's antagonism toward crowds in the earliest heretical movements.[127] But in the *Life*, not heresy but imagined Jewish persecutors mobilize large groups of male youths. While the crowd at William's funeral is united in their love of the boy martyr, the boys in this episode are united in their hatred, that is, their desire to destroy the Jews of Norwich.[128] Canetti identifies a love of density as a prime trait of the crowd, whose tight mass enables a liberating union or equality, a release of "burdens of distance" and "distinctions."[129] Unlike the submissive Holy Thursday and funeral collectives, which Canetti would term a "closed crowd," the youths are an "open crowd" whose movements are difficult to control, "open everywhere and in any direction," and spread over territory with "ease and speed."[130] "Discharged" or released from "distances of ecclesiastical hierarchy," the boys relay information in an unmediated manner; "testimony" circulates between groups forming in the city and groups returning from the woods.[131]

Arguably more disturbing than those unsupervised boys is the crowd mobilized by William's mother. Upon learning that "her son was dead and buried in the wood," Elviva "immediately tore at her hair, clasped her hands repeatedly and ran like a lunatic, crying and wailing through the streets."[132] After traveling in this manner to her sister's home and learning from Liviva and Godwin that her son was killed in an unusual manner ("insolito more occisus fuerit"), Elviva determines

> that it was not Christians, but in truth Jews, who had dared to commit the crime in that way. She accepted these speculations with a woman's credulity; and she at once broke out in public with abuse of the Jews in word, noisy clamor and formal accusation. In this way, no doubt, the mother was influenced by the effect of a maternal instinct; here was a woman carried away by feminine and reckless daring. Again, whatever she suspected in her heart she took to be certain, and whatever she imagined she asserted, as if she had seen it with her own eyes; she conducted her roaming through small streets and large, and compelled by maternal suffering, she accosted everyone with horrible cries and asserted that her son had been seduced by fraud, kidnapped from her by cunning, and killed by the Jews. She turned the minds of all in this matter towards the suspicion of the truth; hence it was cried out also by the voices of all that all the Jews should be destroyed, root and branch, as the constant enemies of the Christian name and cult.[133]

The crowd's shared wish to exterminate all Jews—while unspeakably offensive and disturbingly prophetic of modern antisemitic genocide—is, horrifyingly, in keeping with Thomas's efforts to celebrate Christian unity and demonize Jews. Yet this episode also speaks to a Christian danger that exceeds any "approved" antisemitic aggression, thanks to William's mother. While the boys moving to and from Thorpe Wood at least exhibit a hint

of masculine rationality, Elviva is a stereotypically emotional and irrational woman, who determines Jewish guilt through her female willingness
("facilitate muliebri") to act on a hunch. The disorderly movements of the
mother's mind are mapped by Thomas onto "the streets and open places"
("uicos et plateas") of Norwich. Echoing the actions of the mother in "The
Jewish Boy," who, upon learning that her husband has placed her son in an
oven, with "disheveled" hair "wailed that she was in misery and filled the city
with her cries," William's mother runs like an *amens* or insane person through
the streets of Norwich, where she emits "dreadful screams" ("horrendos
clamores"), tears out her hair, and clasps her hands.[134] That, of all people, a
hysterical woman catalyzes the Christian masses renders that urban collective all the more disturbing for an inhabitant of the cathedral close. Here,
perhaps more than at any other moment in the *Life*, Thomas comes closest
to acknowledging the flimsiness of his tale of ritual murder by implying, in a
misogynistic vein, that the ritual-murder libel is as tenable as the beliefs held
by a discredited female authority.[135] At this point it appears that the prime
threat in Norwich isn't so much the Jews but the irrational, emotional, and
disorderly actions of the Christian majority.

While any ecclesiastic would find crowds worrisome, a monk like Thomas
would arguably be the most disturbed by them. Starting with its origins in
the desert fathers' efforts to escape urban corruption by seeking out desolate
spaces, monasticism has avoided the Christian masses and sought out solitude
and contemplation. We can glean the centrality of isolation to monasticism
by looking at Isidore's entry on monks in his *Etymologies*, which claims that
the Latin *monachus* derives from the Greek word for oneness. As Isidore puts
it, "if the word for monk means a solitary, what is someone who is alone
doing in a crowd?"[136] To paraphrase Isidore, if solitude epitomizes monasticism, what is a monk like Thomas doing celebrating crowds?

Clearly, Thomas celebrates crowds in the *Life* because his was no ordinary
sequestered monastery, but a hybrid space whose episcopal component exerted
itself forcefully into Norwich and the greater diocese, even as its monastic
component shunned contact with the world.[137] In architectural terms that
contradiction emerged through the presence in the complex of both the communal space of the cathedral and the closed space of the cloister. The term
"cloister" is derived from the Latin *claustrum*, whose meanings as "enclosure,
barrier, bolt or gate" indicate the stress laid upon geographic separation and
sequestration in monastic life.[138] We have seen barriers, of course, in Thomas's
narrative, in the Jewish door whose closure the monk so obsessively stresses.
By foregrounding the Jewish door as spatial barrier, Thomas downplays the
tensions that inform the relation between his religious home and its urban

milieu. Coenobitic aversion to the Christian masses—and to the urban public mission of the see—disappears as a problem in the *Life* as Thomas highlights Jewish barriers and strives to imagine the cathedral priory as a space that is open to the Norwich multitudes.

But as we have seen, Thomas proves far from comfortable with the crowds that gather in response to the discovery of William's body.[139] And a closer look at William's funeral reveals how even a pious crowd can prove problematic. The behavior of the monks during the Mass and the funeral procession affirm Canetti's insight that "the whole substance of the faith, as well as the practical forms of its organization," is geared toward subduing the crowd.[140] Solemnly chanting and moving in the measured steps of a procession, the monks endeavor to contain and control the incipient threat embodied by the massive group assembled at the ritual. Even more significant, however, is Thomas's description of how, after William's Requiem Mass, his body "was placed—after deliberation—between the choir screen and the monks' choir, lest the crowd of people (*turba populi*) pressing to kiss the bier—indeed, pushing with desire to see the body if possible—would be more of an impediment than a help to the brothers at work conducting the required funerary ritual of washing."[141] Threatening to impede the monk's ministrations, the Christian multitude no longer figures as a reassuring sign of local Christian union but instead signals discord. The moving press of Christians evinces an agitation that contrasts with the deliberate calm of the monks, by whom the Mass was "solenniter cantabatur" or "solemnly sung" and who soberly enact the ritual cleansing of William's body. Instead the mob recalls the disruptive actions of both the boys and Elviva in the city streets. Regardless of the good intentions indicated by their desire to kiss the bier, the members of the crowd threaten to be "an impediment" to the monks, and even perhaps pose a danger to William's corpse. The crowd risks being not unlike the Jews who hurt William in the first place.[142]

The crowd threatens the monks so much so that they use the *pulpitum* or choir screen to protect themselves and the corpse. The *pulpitum*, a charged interface between the monks and the laity, architecturally expresses the tension between the cloistering and communal impulses at play in the cathedral-priory. Following a plan typical of Benedictine conventual churches, the *pulpitum* of Norwich Cathedral, located at the third pier west of the crossing, divided the lay and monastic sections of the nave.[143] Ostensibly Norwich Cathedral fosters closed crowds, the limited and hence manageable multitudes tolerated by the church. But the monks' use of the rood screen suggests how the crowd venerating William is an "open crowd"—the growing press so feared by the church—that necessitates the use of supplementary boundaries beyond the walls of Norwich Cathedral.

Both the crowd's status as potential *impedimentum* or obstacle to the monk's ministrations, as well as Thomas's stress on the *pulpitum* as a means of hindering the multitudes from pressing upon William's corpse, return us to the Jewish door.[144] Of course the monks use the *pulpitum* to protect William's body while the imagined Jews of the *Life* use the door to hide William's ritual murder. But despite their differing uses, the Jewish door and Christian *pulpitum* yoke the monks to the Jews. Not unlike the Jewish door, which hides William and his attackers from the Christian public, the *pulpitum* barricades William from his lay admirers. The manner in which a few monks perform ritual actions on the corpse behind a barrier renders them uncannily similar to the Jews who ritually murder William behind closed doors. While the collective piety staged in the cathedral contrasts with the danger and secrecy of the Jewish domicile, here cathedral close and home converge. In that slippage between Christian cathedral and Jewish home, in the similarities that obtain between the Jewish door and Christian choir screen, we can glean how the *Life*'s antisemitism serves not only to imagine Christian unity but also to acknowledge problems in Thomas's own Christian community in Norwich. The *pulpitum* as barrier serves as a metaphor for the cloister and the status of not just Jews but also monks as a cloistered community, set apart from the Christian majority. The *pulpitum*, deployed to protect the monks and William from a potentially harmful Christian mob, shores up the fraught status of the complex as a site both open to and set against the Christian masses.

## Christian Mob Violence

A century after the *Life* was completed, the threat posed to Norwich monks by the Christian mob finally came to pass. Over the course of three days in August 1272, citizens attacked, burned, and plundered the cathedral precinct. Rioters destroyed the main entrance of the Ethelbert gate, burned most of the Norman buildings in the complex, and did considerable damage to the cathedral. The mob also killed "some thirteen people on the priory side," dragging several monks through the city's streets.[145] Norman Tanner, in his account of medieval cathedral–city relations, writes that it is unclear whether a period of "mounting tension or relatively harmonious relations" characterized the time between the founding of the cathedral and the riot.[146] Thomas's depiction of English crowds implies a history of such Christian-versus-Christian tensions.

As we have seen, the *Life* not only hints at intra-Christian tensions but also registers Christian–Jewish antagonism in an overt manner.[147] That manifest anti-Jewish sentiment may explain why, less than two decades after Thomas completed his work, his depiction of Christian multitudes bent on "the destruction of the Jews" would be tragically realized. The Norwich pogrom of 1190 comprised one of many attacks that began during the fall of the previous year, during Richard I's 3 September coronation. Although the king banned further attacks, they resumed when Richard departed England for the Third Crusade, spreading northward from January to March 1190 in cities including Norwich, Dunstable, Stamford, King's Lynn, and Lincoln.[148] They culminated on 16 March 1190 in York, on the Christian holy day of Palm Sunday and the Jewish holy day of *Shabbat ha-Gadol*.[149] We have little information about the Norwich pogrom beyond chronicler Ralph Diceto's cryptic statement that, in Norwich on 5 February 1190, "as many Jews as were found in their houses were butchered; some took refuge in the castle."[150] But another work, the *History of English Affairs* (1198–1201) of William of Newburgh, contains detailed information about the attacks in London and other sites. William, an Augustinian canon at Newburgh, Yorkshire, wrote in the fourth book of his chronicle what is the most important account of the attacks.[151]

William's account of the attacks merits our sustained attention as a narrative that develops and elaborates upon, even as it challenges and complicates, the image of the medieval city offered in Thomas's *Life*. As we have seen, Thomas attempts to limit city problems to the threat of ritual murder posed by Jews even as aspects of the *Life* admit worrisome aspects of the urban Christian majority. In contrast, William offers a more wholesale condemnation of the city and its masses, whether Christian, Jewish, or a mixture of the two. Adumbrating the economic concerns of later antisemitic texts like the Croxton *Play of the Sacrament* and *The Jew of Malta*, William depicts the city as a place that draws hordes of persons who are mobilized by a shared desire for profit. Thus while Thomas stresses the particular sinfulness of the Jew as boy killer, William showcases how the vast majority of city residents commit the commercial sin of greed. However, regardless of his unique stress on commerce, when William turns to the pogroms, his account of crowds—multitudes, as we shall see, that are catalyzed by both greed and still other complicating factors—brings to a head the urban problems hinted at by Thomas. In William's *History*, the destructive and disorderly crowd behaviors registered by the *Life* gain a near apocalyptic intensity that suggests how, due to their unruliness, multitudes paradoxically make and unmake the medieval English city. Radically challenging contemporary understandings of the city as a microcosmic instance of the providential ordering of all creation, William constructs the city as a sinful, disorderly, and self-annihilating space.

For all its clear hatred of urban masses, William's account of the city is not without contradiction. Certainly, William doesn't share Thomas's conflict over Christian collectives. While Thomas exhibits the fraught positioning of a monk ministering to a city, William seems to have lived what was to all intents and purposes a life of seclusion in Newburgh Priory, despite the public service to which canons ostensibly dedicated themselves.[152] The Augustinian canon's apparent investment in Cistercian piety, which emphasized ascetic isolation, together with his status-based elitism, rendered William an unabashed critic of the vulgar mob.[153] But while William clearly despised the masses, his stance toward the Jew was more ambivalent.

While Jews, William stresses, are sinners, their guilt hardly legitimates the pogroms of 1189–90. In attacking the Jews of York, William claims, the rioters fail to realize that "the perfidious Jew that crucified the Lord Jesus Christ is suffered to live amongst Christians, from the same regard to Christian utility, that causes the form of the cross of the Lord to be painted in the church of Christ; that is to say, to perpetuate the highly beneficial remembrance of the passion of the Lord amongst all the faithful; and while in the Jew we execrate that impious action, in that sacred form we venerate the Divine majesty with due devotion."[154] The Augustinian canon's advocacy of tolerance and particularly his citation of Psalm 59:12—"God shall let me see my desire upon my enemies. Slay them not, lest my people forget"—recall his founder Augustine's viewpoint.[155] Specifically, William draws on Bernard of Clairvaux's idea, articulated at the onset of the Second Crusade, that Jews should be tolerated because of their relation to the Crucifixion, as recorded in the Gospels.[156] That invocation of deicide is, to say the least, counterintuitive. Since the pogroms of the First Crusade, deicide was invoked to construct Jews as ongoing aggressors who merit Christian attack. Deicide, as we saw in the *Life*, also provides a framework for comprehending boy-martyr fantasies. William, following Bernard, rejects deicide as an act that Jews continue to perform on young male victims; he takes pains to dismiss English boy-martyr cults as unfounded. Instead, William imbues Jews with a utility that in some ways recalls Cynewulf's *Elene* and its investment in Judas as a link to the Crucifixion. Linking Jews to Crucifixion imagery and Christian built environments, William states that while they are "perfidious," Jews are nevertheless "highly beneficial" in the manner of the crosses "painted in the church of Christ." Due to their capacity to make English public spaces—like the interiors of English churches—memorials of Christ's sacrifice, Jews "live among Christians" because of their "Christian utility."[157]

Voicing traditional rhetoric, William claims that while Jews should be tolerated as reminders of the Crucifixion, "for their own iniquity they ought to live in servitude."[158] Like Augustine, William sees the proper place for Jews in Christendom as one of disciplinary submission and theological publicity; God scattered the Jews to both punish them and assist Christians in their piety. But the Jews described in the *History* hardly occupy their assigned subservient role in the world. Instead they inhabit cities where they—in a proto-Marxist move—epitomize the disorderly and disruptive effects of commerce. The prime indicator in William's *History* of the urban upheavals caused by the Jews' economic activity is their homes. Thus William, like Thomas in the *Life*, ties Jewish misconduct closely to the space of the Jewish domicile. For example, William describes how York's two leading bankers, Joceus and Benedict, "with profuse expense . . . built houses of the largest extent in the midst of the city, which might be compared to royal palaces; and there they lived in abundance and luxury almost regal, like two princes of their own people, and tyrants to the Christians, exercising cruel tyranny towards those whom they had oppressed by usury."[159] Here, Jewish urban menace isn't a matter of ritual murder but rather economic behaviors that draw on stereotypes of Jewish carnality and materialism. Insofar as the city in the *History* is a space defined by the market and profit, Jews embody those disruptive and oppressive commercial elements. "Lifting themselves up imprudently against Christ," Jews in England "inflict many sufferings upon the Christians" through harsh banking practices.[160] As usurers—that is, men who lend money at interest—Jews lead the way in making York not an urban microcosm mirroring a providentially ordered macrocosm but rather a small-scale version of a world turned upside-down.[161] Instead of serving the religious majority, as God "intended," Jews are "tyrants to the Christians."[162]

William portrays the Jewish homes of York as visualizing that usurious oppression in a manner not unlike the monumental edifices through which princes (or, as we have seen in Norwich, religious figures) articulated their power in a medieval city. Indeed Joceus's house, "from the magnitude and strength of its construction, might be said to be equal to a castle of no small size."[163] While the martial qualities of Joceus's fortresslike home recall the door-as-barrier of the Jewish house in the *Life*, its monumental scale resonates even more with the stone fortifications erected by the Christian leaders of English cities.[164] Amplifying how England's new Jewish population overturned received ideas of divine order and unity, Joceus and Benedict's houses are imposing and grand structures occupying York's most privileged locale, its city center, the urban counterpart to "Jerusalem" on world maps.

The Jews' rejection of the subservient social position allotted them by God prompts in William's *History* a providential and cosmic interpretation of the pogroms. Indeed, throughout this chronicle, William presents a providential take on history in which, time and time again, God chastens the sinful—regardless of religious identity—and restores proper order and equilibrium to the world.[165] Thus in the book immediately preceding William's account of the attacks, he offers a history of Jerusalem in which God repeatedly cleanses the Holy Land of sinners, Jewish, Muslim, and Christian.[166] And when he turns to the pogroms, William writes about the sinfulness of the Jews as a "perfidious people" at whose "insolence" in England God bridles.[167] William especially encourages readers to yoke the English attacks to larger cosmic, supernatural, and divine patterns by shaping his narrative in a manner that recalls Josephus's *Jewish War* ( *JW* ) (late 70s AD).[168] In the final books of the *JW*, Josephus describes the Roman siege and destruction of Jerusalem and the temple in AD 70, an event that medieval Christians viewed as a prime example of the Jews' providential subjugation.[169] Drawing on those books, William's *History* portrays the pogroms as exemplifying inevitable patterns of Jewish sinfulness and divine retribution.[170]

Yet seriously complicating this providential component of the pogroms is the cupidity of the Christian instruments who dole out divine discipline. The Christian attackers are themselves consumed by the urban greed associated with Jews. As Michael Kennedy puts it, while William locates multiple causes for the pogroms, the "basic motive for the violence was avarice. . . . In each of William's accounts of anti-Jewish violence, financial considerations are specified and in the York narrative one of the most vivid scenes is that of the leaders of the massacre ceremonially burning in the Minster the bonds which recorded their indebtedness."[171] While Jews may epitomize the materialism of the medieval city, avarice is so twined with urban formations that nearly all city dwellers exhibit the sin. William in effect presents here an early version of Marx's facetious claim about Christians' "Jewish" relation to capital. Thus, as Nicholas Vincent points out, when William describes how the mob in York lacks "any scruple of Christian conscience, thirsting out of greed for booty, for the blood of these perfidious (Jews)," the chronicler creates a "chiastic juxtaposition of opposites here, with greed preyed upon by the greedy, and with Christians shown behaving less like Christians than like stereotypical Jews."[172]

Thanks partly to his somewhat tolerant position toward Jews and his derision of the greedy Christian mob, William's account of the pogroms resists falling into neatly defined categories of sinful Jews and virtuous Christians performing God's will. Often fully equivocating on claims he has just made (or is about to make) about the providential nature of the event, William describes "with unhidden disgust the base motives and vile conduct of the Christian townspeople."[173] Thus immediately after claiming that the Jews "underwent by the just judgment of Christ this peril of their lives," William states that the attackers can "by no means be excused, who, by an unexpected commotion, inflicted slaughter on them."[174] Elsewhere William ironically states that while the attackers claimed "they were doing homage to God" in reality they lack "even the tiniest scruple of conscience."[175] William not only derides the attackers, but also empathizes with their Jewish victims; as Elisa Narin van Court observes, for all of their antisemitism, William's "records are relentless . . . in their detailed descriptions of Jewish suffering."[176]

Arguably the most charged of such contradictions is how the attackers oppose the very ordering mechanism associated with God's providential hand. Like the tyrannical York lenders Joceus and Benedict, the Christian crowd violates ideas of right relation. As much emerges, of course, in their greedy materialism itself, which turns "Christians" into "Jews," recalling the ambiguities of Cynewulf's depiction of materialist Christians in *Elene*. Moreover, a host of still other stereotypically Jewish traits—blindness, irrationality, hermeneutic insufficiency, and even ritual murder—are evinced repeatedly by the Christian attackers, bloodthirsty murderers who are affected by neither "the vigor of the laws, nor reason, nor humanity," and who, with their "blinded spirit," "perverted" the meaning of Psalm 58.[177] At the same time that the Christian attackers invert proper relations by exhibiting traits that make them "Jewish," the Jews whom they assail become "Christian." Like Judas in *Elene*, the victims of the pogroms at times resemble none other than the suffering Christ.

William links such religious slippages to urban issues primarily by focusing on how the Christians form a mob. In his thoroughgoing critique of the crowd, which he alternately calls a *turba*, *populis*, and *multitude*, William draws on Josephus, who in turn drew on Greek political thought and especially Plato for his image of the Judean mob.[178] In the same way that Josephus sees the Judean crowd as a fickle entity easily swayed by untrustworthy leaders, William at times depicts the Christian mob as "dupes of wealthy debtors of the Jews."[179] But William also goes beyond Josephus to speak to issues pertinent to his own historical moment and location, in a medieval England witnessing the rise of the city. Insofar as the city is defined by its dense assembling of persons—London's population, for example, had swelled by this time to some forty thousand persons—William exposes it as a volatile, unruly, and self-destructive entity.[180] Far more blatantly than the crowds in Thomas's *Life*, William's crowds exhibit the problems of unrest and destruction identified by Canetti. The extreme and variously iterated disorder of the mob radically undermines William's claims that the Jews' defeat expresses divine justice. How, that is, do the pogroms foreground the cosmic order when the very group that quells Jewish insubordination is itself deeply unruly?

As we have seen, in Thomas's *Life*, the crowds of boys and the urban collective marshaled by Elviva only imply their disregard for authority. William, however, explicitly states that the mob is presumptuous *(licentias)*, audacious *(audaces)*, and a "great and unparalleled . . . affront to his [i.e., Richard I's] royal dignity," linking them to Josephus's Judean mob and its rebellion against Roman authority.[181] But while the Christian mob shares the audacity of Josephus's Judean mob, it never suffers a version of their Roman subjugation. Richard proves to be no Titus toward his own rebelliously "Jewish" populace.[182] The crowd's defiance of Richard's authority first emerges in William's account of the origins of the pogroms during the coronation ceremony. William describes how the king prohibited the Jews "(by a proclamation, it is said) to enter the church while he was being crowned, or to enter the palace while the banquet was being held after the solemnity of the coronation."[183] Recalling the *pulpitum* set up by the monks, Richard endeavors to erect an impassable barrier around the spaces of his coronation ritual. But "the people, who were watching about the palace, began to crowd in. The Jews, who had mingled with the crowd, were thus driven within the doors of the palace."[184] The Jews' entry into the palace is what triggers the pogroms in London and beyond. While William's source, Roger of Howden, states that Jewish leaders intentionally disregarded the royal ordinance and approached the king with presents, William renders that violation not deliberate but a product of the crowds' very status *as* a crowd, a multitude so dense as to demolish all boundaries, orderings, and hierarchies—both external and internal. The crowd disregards the wishes of not only the king but also the Jews contained within the throng. It exemplifies the dangers posed by the radical "state of absolute equality" that Canetti associates with crowds, where "a head is a head, an arm is an arm, and differences between individual heads and arms are irrelevant."[185] Collapsed into and absorbed by the crowd, the Jews can do nothing to prevent their movement into the palace.

William's unique account of the Jews' accidental entry into the palace offers just one indicator of his keen interest in how crowds erode the spatial boundaries that organize urban society. Even as the *History* foregrounds the tragic destruction of human life—for example, William stresses how the rioters shed "human blood like water" and "destroyed with monstrous ferocity" their victims—that text also devotes special attention to the destruction of city mappings.[186] What emerges from that stress is the fragile condition of the organizational practices of any city in the face of the crowds that live there.

The crowd's urge to upset and undo outweighs William's providential message. When the rioters turn away from the coronation ceremony to wreak their fury on Jewish homes, their actions evoke not so much divine intention as hellish disorder. Initially the "raging people" who were "vigorously" attacking the houses fail to break into them due to their "stronger construction" ("fabrica firmior"). But the houses eventually succumb to the "horrible conflagration" ignited by the mob on their roofs.[187] In setting fire to the Jewish homes, the mob deploys a weapon with which it shares key properties: in Canetti's words, "the incalculable movements within [the crowd], the thrusting forth of an arm, a fist or a leg, are like the flames of a fire which may suddenly spring up on any side."[188] In the same way that the coronation crowd ignored the borders within and without itself, fire subverts and overrides divisions. William, adumbrating Canetti's insight that "fire joins what was separate, and in the shortest time possible," states of the fire set by the rioters: "Nor was the fire destructive to the Jews alone, though kindled especially against them; for knowing no distinction, it caught some of the nearest houses of the Christians also."[189] The historical absence of significant divisions (like a ghetto wall) between Jews and Christians in London would have encouraged the fire's spread from the former to the latter. But William doesn't stress that propinquity. Instead he emphasizes how, like the crowd at Richard's coronation, the fire blindly incorporates into itself contiguous objects, regardless of their Jewish or Christian association, "knowing no distinction."

William's account of the final, culminating tragedy at York may reiterate this message about the dangers of the crowd.[190] While the Christian rioters, as in previous pogroms in London and Lynn, break into and set fire to Jewish homes, most Jews avoid death by occupying the royal *arcem* or citadel, which may or may not have stood on the site of Clifford's Tower in contemporary York.[191] However, after several days "the capture of the castle was certain," because it was "surrounded" not only "by immense bands of ar[med] men," but also "siege engines."[192] Ultimately, some 150 Jews perished either through suicide or murder. William explicitly compares this horrible tragedy to Josephus's account of thousands of Jews' self-immolation at the fort in Masada. But while the vast majority of Jews at Masada ardently seek to kill themselves before the Romans reach them, such is not the case at York.[193] Because "many" present "went away, preferring to make trial of the clemency of their enemies, rather than die in this manner with their friends, the roof was set on fire, so that the flames, while a horrid deed was being done—for they were preparing their necks for the knife—might slowly gain strength among the solid timber, and deprive of life even those who had departed from the rest through love of life."[194] Fire also figures in Josephus's account of Masada. But while in Josephus, the leader Eleazar sets the fortress ablaze only after he is sure that all the Jews there have already died, in William, Jews set fire to the roof of the citadel to compel even Jews seeking mercy to partake in the leaders' self-destructive program.[195] Thus, like the conflagration created by the mob in London, and like the crowd outside the royal palace during Richard I's coronation, the swelling fire set by the multitude of Jews in York has no regard for the objects it consumes and into which it spreads. Undermining the urban dividers imagined by Thomas of Monmouth are the breached boundaries of William of Newburgh's city as conflagration.

Recent work on cities in an age of global information networks stresses the self-emptying nature of urban geography. Manuel Castells, for example, characterizes world cities like New York or London as "spaces of flow," which he contrasts with "spaces of places," that is, the modern city, up to the 1970s.[196] Epitomizing the city as a space of flow are locations, such as airports and malls, defined not by communal gathering but by movement and far-flung networks. This chapter suggests how English antisemitic texts speak significantly to the question of the nature of a city as a space. Thomas, at least overtly, confirms Castells's claims by imagining in his *Life* the medieval city as an organization of discrete places connoted by physical boundaries like the choir screen or the door of a Jewish home. The pogroms described in William's *History*, however, may provide a corrective to Castells's account, suggesting how, even at the time of its emergence in the West, the city was already defined as a space of flow. To be sure, there are important differences between the medieval chronicler and the contemporary theorist. While Castells concerns himself with global movements, William tracks movements within and between English cities. And the urban flow described by William is not so much productive of networks but rather destructive of not only urban space but also many human lives. Yet William's very stress on the city as a kind of nonspace, a site emptied of fixed meaning, resonates with and adumbrates accounts of the self-emptying global city. Due to his monastic investment in solitude and geographic separation, William views the emerging medieval city as a horrifying nonspace, where the fiery flow of bodies demolishes differences between persons and places. William characterizes the city as self-annihilating, an entity whose very burgeoning ironically leads to its disappearance.

$\mathscr{S}$ CHAPTER 3

# The Minster and the Privy

*Jews, Lending, and the Making of Christian*
*Space in Chaucer's England*

## English Commerce and Aaron of Lincoln

When Jews migrated to England, they inhabited a society whose commercial aspects, while at times hard to pin down, were nevertheless significant and even on the rise.[1] Georges Duby describes how, by the late 1100s, England and Europe witnessed the "take-off" of a profit economy that slowly but surely eclipsed a gift culture.[2] Factors including a growing population, the stabilization and centralization of state forms, and rapid urbanization provided favorable conditions for the rise of commerce in England from the late eleventh to the thirteenth centuries.[3] Merchants, peasants, magnates, and prelates worked together (if not always harmoniously) to generate agrarian surplus goods and exchange those products in various trading systems.[4] The changes wrought by this commercial turn included a shift from a monetized to a monetary system characterized by regular coin use and widely available credit, heightened specialization of production, and an increased chartering of markets and fairs.[5]

The rise of "money and commodities" in the medieval West, as Henri Lefebvre points out, generated "not only a 'culture,' but also a space." Namely, "the medieval revolution brought commerce inside the town and lodged it at the centre of a transformed urban space."[6] Epitomizing the new commercial thrust of medieval towns and cities were marketplaces, urban sites dedicated

explicitly and exclusively to trade. Masschaele describes the increasing prominence, from the twelfth century on, of marketplaces in English towns and
cities, as witnessed by both their centrality and their size (in some cases as
large as twelve thousand to thirty thousand square yards).[7] All medieval towns
contained one or more markets, which often assumed either a lozenge shape
on wide streets lined with deep and ample plots leading to narrow back lanes,
or a square form in towns formally organized as regular grids.[8] But whatever
their configuration, medieval markets were not discrete spaces. Rather, they
were linked through roads, alleys, doorways, conduits, and other infrastructural
components to the rest of the city, which itself constituted a kind of market.
"Trade and production," as Howard Saalman puts it, "went on in all parts of
the city: in open spaces and closed spaces; public spaces and private spaces."[9]
Unrestricted sites that in Lefebvre's words "opened up on every side onto the
surrounding territory," marketplaces in England comprised core components
of a commercialized urban field yoked to its agricultural surroundings, as well
as other towns and other countries, via an infrastructural network of roads
and waterways.[10]

The mapping of Anglo-Jewish residences placed Jews in intimate relation to the new urban geography that arose in tandem with commerce.
Jews tended to live in cities, and within those urban sites—which included
Bury St. Edmunds, Canterbury, Colchester, Exeter, Hereford, Lincoln, London, Norwich, Nottingham, Oxford, Winchester, and York—they typically
occupied homes located in or alongside markets.[11] In other places, such as
the coastal cities of Southampton and Bristol, Jews lived near quays, which
similarly served as important commercial centers.[12] Of course, Jewish settlement patterns belie easy generalization. English Jews lived alongside Christians in not only urban but also rural areas, and some Jews in cities lived at a
considerable remove from the main Jewish neighborhood.[13] Still, an abiding
consideration in Jewish habitation seems to have been economic opportunity
in the form of commerce.[14] In other words, Jews preferred to live near the
source of their livelihood, the urban market.

While the mapping of Jews in English cities speaks to their participation
in England's emerging economy, precisely what was that role? Robert Stacey
speculates that, after 1066, William I brought Jews from Rouen into England
to benefit from their commercial know-how. As "traders in luxury goods
and as dealers in plate and coin," Jews may have appealed to the conqueror
as persons who could assist in trade, convert martial spoils into currency, and
"keep a finger on the commercial pulse of London."[15] During the twelfth
century, under Henry I (ca. 1068–1 December 1135), Jews thrived through
their participation in an established and "specifically English" combination

of moneychanging, moneylending, and bullion dealing.[16] Yet when Stephen of Blois (ca. 1092/96–25 October 1154) assumed the throne, the chaos of his reign diminished opportunities and created hazards for gentile moneychangers and merchants even as it "increased demands for loans."[17] As a result, Jews may have been primarily identified with lending as early as 1154, and "by 1180, the balance of Jewish economic activity in England had already shifted decisively . . . toward a much more exclusive reliance upon moneylending."[18] Jews were hardly the only people lending during this time; in fact Christian financiers likely "were the pioneers in developing" the "essential elements of the thirteenth-century system of moneylending by bonds against gages (pledges)."[19] By 1200, however, factors including royal claims over usurers' estates, ecclesiastical critique, and the creation of the Jewish exchequer prompted Christians to leave lending in England exclusively to Jews.[20]

Both England's emerging commercial economy and its Jewish participants present a crucial context for the Latin city texts analyzed in the last chapter. Penned by twelfth-century monks and a coenobitic canon whose piety clashed with England's rising commercialism, those writings responded in a decidedly critical manner to Anglo-Jews' business practices. Thus in Thomas of Monmouth's *Life* of William, the man "in whose house" the Norwich boy purportedly dies is "the richest Jew of them all," the lender Eleazar or Deulesalt.[21] By allotting Norwich's most prominent financier a key role in William's death, Thomas implicitly connects lending and ritual murder, suggesting that the former practice somehow harms Christians in the manner of the latter.[22] Deulesalt, Thomas suggests, saps not only funds but also life itself from Christian boys. In keeping with this tacit identification of lending and ritual murder, William's avenger is Deulesalt's greatest debtor, the Norwich knight Simon de Novers. When Simon's financial troubles prompt Deulesalt's murder, Thomas interprets that crime as a providential retaliation for William's sacrifice. "Let the diligent reader here observe," Thomas points out, "how worthily God dealt out retribution," by having Simon's men lure Deulesalt into the woods and kill him, thus paralleling Deulesalt, "who with sacrilegious hands had enticed a Christian into his house and, having killed him, had him flung him into a wood."[23] William of Newburgh's *History of English Affairs* similarly denigrates Jews as financiers. But while Thomas links Jewish bankers to ritual murder, William portrays them as disruptive economic tyrants. In contrast to Deulesalt's home, which provides the setting for a Christian boy's "martyrdom," the imposing and grand mansions of Benedict and Joceus of York cited in William's *History* exemplify how those men resist the subservient role allotted to them by God and instead oppress and dominate Christians via harsh lending practices.

Jews in these texts, however, are hardly the only English residents criticized for their commercial practices. At the same time that Thomas and William denigrate Jewish lenders, they acknowledge how they were part of an economic system comprised mainly of Christians. Reflecting how the rising mercantile economy was met by a heightened clerical stress on "the bourgeois" sin of cupidity (even cupidity as *the* worst sin), both Thomas and William register greed's prominence in English cities.[24] Thus the Christian mob portrayed by William possesses a "greedy frenzy" or "rabies avara" that is so aggressive and destructive as to render not only Jewish mansions but also Christian homes and even the royal *arc* or castle vulnerable. By portraying avaricious Christians demolishing both Jewish and gentile buildings, William implies how the urban impulse to accumulate wealth is self-defeating. Jewish mansions inspire resentment that leads to their razing, and Christian greed leads to the eradication of Christian homes and castles.

While Thomas doesn't explicitly condemn Christians for their greed in the manner of William, he does acknowledge their commercial impulses. After all, it is the lure of a better job in the archdeacon's kitchen that impels young William of Norwich to follow a messenger to Deulesalt's home.[25] And while the boy's mother, Elviva, initially rejects the messenger's offer, greed ultimately trumps maternal concern. Endeavoring "to undermine maternal sentiment, and divert towards avarice the unreliable firmness of feminine fickleness, corrupted by the glitter of silver," the messenger removes three coins from his purse and convinces Elviva with those shining silver pieces to give over her son to him.[26] As those examples suggest, implicit in Thomas's *Life* is the idea that a profit motive informs existence everywhere in the burgeoning commercial center of Norwich. But like William of Newburgh, the monk doesn't so much render all Norwich residents alike in their greed, as stress how urban acquisitiveness tends to coalesce and gather in the Jewish home. In both cases, due to their avarice, Christians are drawn toward encounters with the Jewish other, whose domicile epitomizes in microcosm the dangers of the city.

Of course, in Thomas's work, the notable exception to his commerce-infused city is Norwich Cathedral close. Like Deulesalt's home, the religious precinct does contain "thesauros" or treasure, but while the Jew's wealth is literal, that of Norwich Cathedral is the "holy object" of William's corpse.[27] But when Thomas uses such urban spaces to perform his antisemitism, he links Christians and Jews as much as he divides them. Given how economic currents bound together all parts of a city, given how marketing was "the *raison d'être* of mediaeval towns," just how disassociated *were* churches from their urban milieu and its commercial thrust?[28] Far from occupying separate spheres, religion and economy at times intersected and informed one another.[29] Gervase Rosser describes how "trends in piety" in cities "gave rise to—and in turn were fed by—industrial specialisations, such as Nottingham's production of alabaster heads of St John the Baptist."[30] Geographic evidence of the intimacy of market and church emerges in cities such as York, where chandlers crowded "the approaches to the Minster with stalls selling candles, images, and *ex voto* wax limbs to pilgrims."[31] The Norwich Cathedral precinct was surrounded by commerce. The old market area of Tombland lay, in Gilchrist's words, at the "doorstep" of the cathedral; craftworkers and merchants labored alongside the upper inner court; stonemasons and bell-founders worked in the Prior's Fee, north of the precinct; and a fair, "from which the sacrist collected the rents from the stalls," took place on Pentecost in the lay cemetery and area known as Green Yard.[32] As these examples affirm, English churches and cathedrals were not sanctuaries from the urban but rather were connected to cities in terms that were as infrastructural as they were economic. Thomas acknowledges such an interpenetration of religion and commerce when he criticizes William's uncle, the priest Godwin Sturt, for selling for its miraculous healing powers the teasel used to torture his dead nephew.[33]

Perhaps the most telling evidence of the commercial and spatial ties binding church and city are the material components of English churches. The stone and mortar of cathedrals and abbeys offer physical evidence of the church's reliance on its emerging economy, and the Jews who came to monopolize English banking.[34] The commercial practices of two Jews reveal this relationship, the Aarons of Lincoln and York. Medieval England's greatest financier, Aaron of Lincoln (ca. 1125–86) had a "vast financial network of agents and clients" that extended to nearly every shire in the realm and included kings, earls, archbishops, priors, and abbots.[35] Nine Cistercian abbeys—Rievaulx, New Minster, Kirkstead, Louth Park, Revesby, Rufford, Kirkstall, Roche, and Biddlesden—owed Aaron massive amounts, "totaling well over £4,374 13s 4d."[36] Noting the foundation dates of the abbeys (between 1140 and 1152) and the amount of money lent them, Joseph Jacobs asks, "What does this mean but that these nine Cistercian abbeys would not have been built but for the financial assistance given by Aaron of Lincoln?"[37] Beyond those monasteries, Aaron helped finance at least two cathedrals, Lincoln and Peterborough.[38] A century later, Aaron of York (d. 1268) presents a similar narrative of ecclesiastical lending. Among the first immigrants to reestablish a Jewish community in York after the 1191 massacre, Aaron enjoyed commercial links tying him to "almost every shire in England."[39] Like Aaron of Lincoln, Aaron of York lent to abbeys, particularly "Yorkshire monastic houses," giving loans to seven or more abbots.[40] Local York tradition has referred to the Five Sisters Window in York Minster as the Jewish Window in remembrance of money lent by Aaron.[41]

The support provided by the two Aarons for ecclesiastical building programs clearly undermines Thomas's and other writers' efforts to set Christian churches apart from an urban danger linked with Jews. Inverting the architectural logic of ritual-murder myths, where churches are counterpoints to an imagined Jewish threat, the Jews who lent to abbots shore up the reality of the medieval city as a place saturated by and benefiting from commercial practices of which Jews are a part. By challenging the Christian notion of a dangerously insular Jewish domesticity and the Jew's house as lethal trap, ecclesiastical dependence on Jewish bankers opens up the Jewish dwelling, alerting us to its status as a site where capital not only accumulates but also flows into the material components of Christian edifices. The history of Anglo-Jewish lending thus gives new resonance to the status of the Jew as "the other within," a figure who is necessary and proximate to Christianity.[42] Not only was Judaism the religion out of which Christianity grew, not only were Hebrew holy books the basis of the New Testament, but also Jewish capital was built into the physical components of Christian churches and related buildings.[43]

Awareness of this Jewish–Christian dynamic emerges not only in names like York minster's Jewish Window but also in an oft-told anecdote attributed to Aaron of Lincoln. According to the story, recorded in *The Deeds of the Abbots of the Monastery of Saint Alban*, when Abbot Simon (1167–83) died, "Aaron the Jew who held us in his debt coming to the house of St. Alban in great pride and boasting, with threats boasted that it was he who made the window for our Saint Alban, and that from his own money he had prepared a lodging for the homeless saint."[44] The anecdote clearly denigrates Aaron. The banker's "great pride" or "superbia magna" makes him guilty of a deadly sin. Moreover, his "threats"—indicators of yet another mortal sin, the avarice of the grasping usurer—harken back to the oppressions that William of Newburgh and Thomas of Monmouth associate with Jewish lenders.[45]

At the same time, however, Aaron links Jewish lending practices to two sacred structures: a window, located possibly in the north transept of St. Alban's abbey church, and the large shrine that Simon commissioned for Alban's relics, a piece C. C. Oman calls "one of the most important examples of English art in the twelfth century" (figure 11).[46] However prideful, Aaron's boast about his funding of those two Christian artifacts radically complicates English associations of Jews with urban oppression. While William of Newburgh links Jews with an acquisitiveness that ultimately leads, in

**FIGURE 11.**    Drawing of the shrine of St. Alban. Matthew Paris, *Vie de Seint Auban* (ca. 1230–40). Dublin, Trinity College Library, MS 177, fol. 61r. By permission of The Board of Trinity College, Dublin.

the pogroms, to the destruction of not just Jewish houses but also Christian edifices, Aaron stresses how Jews created urban spaces and, indeed, enabled the fashioning of the most exalted of such sites. And while Thomas and others who promote ritual murder and similar libels imagine Jews as aggressive enemies of Christianity, Aaron shows how Jewish lenders, far from creating martyrs, subsidized the very churches that sheltered them.[47] In fact, by contributing to the erection of Alban's shrine, Aaron "prepared a lodging" or "hospitium praeparavit"—certainly a charged act when performed by a member of the diaspora—for one of England's most important martyrs and its first native saint.[48]

In what follows, I rethink the most well-known medieval English libel about Jews—Chaucer's *Prioress's Tale*—by reading it in terms of the ironies Aaron of Lincoln registers at St. Alban's. That is, I will interpret Chaucer's text as it relates to the currents of urban capital that yoked medieval Christian culture to its Jewish other. In the *Prioress's Tale*, a schoolboy's Marian hymn so offends the inhabitants of the Asian Jewry through which he passes that they conspire to murder him and hide his body in a "wardrobe" or privy.[49] But the Virgin Mary exposes their crime: hidden in the Jewish latrine, the dead "litel clergeon" miraculously resumes singing, drawing the attention

of Christians (7.503). By the end of the tale, the schoolboy's corpse, like
the "martyr" William's remains, is entombed in a local minster or monastic
church, while his Jewish attackers are brutally drawn and hanged.

Although early readers of the tale like Sherman Hawkins stressed its theological import, recent work by L. O. Aranye Fradenburg, Steven Kruger, Lisa
Lampert-Weissig, and others has analyzed the offensive image of Jews on
which the nun's devotional message depends.[50] As that scholarship has shown,
at the heart of the *Prioress's Tale* are images of flow, contact, and containment
that oppose imagined Christian purity to perceived Jewish danger. Thus
we find in Chaucer's text, in Kruger's words, "an opposition between the
Christian body, attacked but preserved, and the Jewish body, foul [and] justly
destroyed."[51] At the same time, contemporary scholarship identifies in the
tale what Anthony Bale describes as "elements which force ambiguous connections" between Christians and their supposed enemies.[52] In details such as
the beating the schoolboy fears he will receive for his unauthorized memoriz-
ation of the *Alma redemptoris mater*, and the monks' tearful convulsions upon
witnessing the boy's death, we find Christian counterparts to the cruelty
and physical paroxysms of the murderous and defecating Jews of the tale
(7.541–42; 7.677–78).[53] This is not to say that Chaucer's Prioress is a friend
to Jews. The *Prioress's Tale* is indisputably offensive and claims notoriety
as the most well-known antisemitic literary text from the entire medieval
period. But at the same time that Chaucer's Prioress demonizes Jews, her
tale also inadvertently proves critical of Christianity. In a move that reflects
the fact that Chaucer isn't a monk like Thomas or other religious, but a
secular man linked to emerging commercial professions, the *Prioress's Tale*
subtly undermines fantasies of a pure, distinct, and exalted Christian identity.

In keeping with the poet's own economic ties, links between Christians
and Jews in the *Prioress's Tale* emerge through not only bodily violence but
also the conduits of medieval commerce. I argue that by closely attending
to how the Prioress maps out the imagined city where she sets her tale, and
by analyzing how those urban spaces reflect the saturation of medieval life
by market forces, we find a crucial way of unpacking the fraught image of
Jew and Christian in that Canterbury tale. Like many English antisemitic
tales, the *Prioress's Tale* culminates in a church where a boy martyr resides; that
Christian site stands in opposition to a debased built environment associated
with Jewish menace, the latrine where the violated boy is hidden. Chaucer,
however, is hardly a writer invested in space as a stable entity. Work, for
example, by V. A. Kolve on the *Knight's Tale* and Kruger on the *Legend of Good
Women* makes clear Chaucer's interest in deconstructing geographic locations.[54] In the case of the *Prioress's Tale*, the minster and the privy, analyzed not

as fixed entities but as contingent, fluid spaces joined through the usurious infrastructure of the tale, suggest a materialist critique of notions of purely religious space. Ultimately, Chaucer's text imagines the Christian minster as not a sacred but a quotidian space possessed of material links to urban currents, among them the flow of capital associated with the Jewish lender.

## Jewish Presences in Chaucer's London

Set not in England but in an anonymous Asian city, the *Prioress's Tale* may seem to have little to do with the issues outlined above.[55] Moreover, when Chaucer wrote the tale, during the 1380s and 1390s, it had been some one hundred years since Edward I authorized the forced expulsion of all Jews from the realm.[56] Yet one of the striking aspects of English antisemitic culture is how, in Geraldine Heng's words, "*After* the Expulsion of Jews from England, in the absence of real Jews of the flesh is in fact when anti-Semitic literature exponentially increases."[57] Thanks to phenomena including homiletic writings, liturgical ritual, maps, manuscript illustration, drama, and libels such as ritual murder, "Jews" proliferated in England after 1290 as imposing virtual or imagined presences.[58] By writing an antisemitic text, Chaucer contributed to a regrettably popular national phenomenon.

In a passage near the end of the *Prioress's Tale*, Chaucer suggests how boy-martyr myths enjoyed a particular currency within that offensive culture. In an apostrophe that concludes her tale of the schoolboy's death, the nun asks for prayers from "yonge Hugh of Lyncoln," who "it is notable" (i.e., well known), was killed by "cursed Jewes" (7.684–85). The nun then explains that Hugh's story is familiar because he died "but a litel while ago" (7.686). Of all English boy-martyr libels, that of Little Saint Hugh had the most lethal consequences for Jews.[59] In 1255 Henry III ordered the execution in London of nineteen Jews supposedly associated with the crime.[60] The timing of both Hugh's death and the Jews' execution was hardly, as the Prioress asserts, "a litel while ago" but rather about 150 years before Chaucer wrote the tale. Yet the nun's claim about the newness of Hugh's death does imply how, thanks to the proliferation of boy-martyr libels, fantasies about a dangerous Jewish presence in England were fresh in the minds of the nation's fourteenth-century Christian population.[61]

The *Prioress's Tale* itself doesn't concern an English martyr like Hugh but a boy living in the distant East.[62] But by turning to Hugh at the end of her tale, the nun urges her auditors to connect the two figures.[63] Through a dual approach that engages both medieval Lincoln and the anonymous Asian city, Chaucer's text demonstrates how English antisemitism relies on both "the recollection of a pre-expulsion history, the presence of those Jews who needed to be removed," and the identification of an ongoing Jewish threat.[64] If the nun's reference to Hugh exemplifies how, as Kruger points out, the "continuing force" of 1290 hinges on a conjuring up of Jews from England's past, her story of the Asian Jewry shows how a pro-expulsion stance can rely on travel both through time and over space, to contemporary Eastern sites that evince the ongoing problem of Jewish criminality.

Beyond the nun's reference to Hugh, other features of her narrative suggest its interest in Jews and England. One such aspect is the layout of its imagined Asian city. The Prioress stresses how the Jewry is "free and open at eyther ende," so that along its main street "men myghte ride or wende" (7.493–94). The notable porosity of the Jewry comprises but one of many examples of how the *Prioress's Tale* emphasizes the idea of "the easy passage," in Fradenburg's apt formulation.[65] Insofar as its accessibility resonates with such details as the movement of song from the boy's throat, the ready flow of breast milk into the mouths of the babes (in the tale's prologue), and Mary's role as heaven's gate in the *Alma redemptoris mater*, the Asian Jewry speaks to varied issues of fluidity and infrastructure. At the same time, though, that the Jewry engages such themes, its openness returns us to the particulars of Jewish life in English cities. As we have seen, in Thomas of Monmouth's Norwich and all other English cities, Jews lived not in closed ghettos but side by side with Christians.

Chaucer surely was aware of Anglo-Jewish habitation patterns, in part due to his upbringing. The poet's childhood tenement in the Vintry Ward was just south of the main Jewish neighborhood of preexpulsion London (figure 12).[66] Jews in London largely settled in a large area north of Cheapside that extended east beyond Colechurch Lane (where Aaron of York had a home and where a synagogue existed during the twelfth century) to the western end of Lothbury (where Aaron of Lincoln had a house) and the southern end of Colman Street, north to Catteaton (or Catte) street, and west to Milk and Wood Streets.[67] Chaucer lived only about a thousand feet away from the Jewry, on Thames Street, just south of St. Martin's Church, between La Reole (now College Hill) and Little Elbow Lane (now little College Street).[68] Less than a five-minute walk from Chaucer's home was Colechurch Lane, renamed after 1290 *la Olde Iuwerie* or *la Elde Jurie*.[69] The renaming of Colechurch Lane as Old Jewry Lane exemplifies Paul Strohm's insight about how medieval urban space "is already symbolically organized by the meaning-making activities of the many generations that have traversed it."[70] When a young Chaucer strolled along it, Old Jewry Lane may well have reminded him of the Jews' vexed relation to England. The descriptor "old" proclaims the work of the expulsion and the discontinuous, former nature of Jewish life in the city, an absence acknowledged by the Prioress's placement of

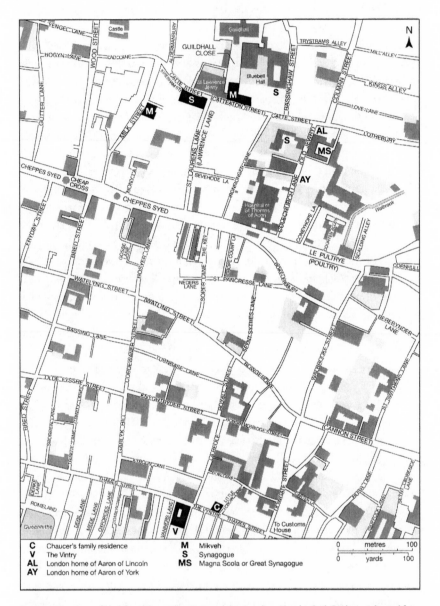

**FIGURE 12.** Area of Jewish settlement in preexpulsion London. Map by Cath D'Alton. Adapted from maps in Lobel, ed., *British Historic Towns Atlas,* vol. 3, *The City of London from Prehistoric times to c. 1520.*

Jews in Asia not England. Yet the noun "Jewry" memorializes how Jews once lived in London, rubbing shoulders with the gentile majority, a fact echoed by the English nature of the open passages depicted in the *Prioress's Tale*.[71]

Later, around the time of the *Canterbury Tales*, Chaucer lived in even closer proximity to a former Jewish neighborhood. From 1374 to 1386, he inhabited the eastern edge of London, in a residence above Aldgate (Eastgate). Several fourteenth-century records refer to the presence in the thirteenth century of a neighborhood called *la Porejewerie*, located directly south of Aldgate below the city wall.[72] Memorializing that second Jewish area was a street alternately called *Jurie Strete* or *Pore Jewerie Lane*, which stretched some 1,200 feet south of Aldgate along the city wall. Chaucer possibly used Pore Jewerie Lane every day as he traveled between his Aldgate home and his job at the Customs Office, located on Thamestrete east of Billingsgate and west of the Tower (figure 13). We might speculate that Chaucer's daily back-and-forth journey on Pore Jewerie Lane uncannily resembled the travels of the Prioress's little schoolboy, whose home and school lie on opposite sides of the Asian Jewry. It's possible, in other words, that the movements of the child, who "to scoleward and homeward . . . wente . . . thurghout the Juerie" (7.549), emerge from and refer to the understanding of Jewish–Christian relations Chaucer gleaned and perhaps imaginatively experienced on a quotidian basis in London, while walking down Pore Jewerie Lane and pondering, perhaps, how Jews once lived along the street.[73]

## Mapping Jews in English Antisemitic Texts

The possible parallels between the daily travels of Chaucer and the Prioress's clergeon help us glean how the *Prioress's Tale* journeys all the way to the East only to return to English territory. But to appreciate fully its English valences, we must consider how the tale engages with not only the physical spaces Chaucer traversed but also the imagined spaces of English writings, and especially the locales associated with Jews in Chaucer's sources and analogues. In this tale, Chaucer responds primarily to two genres. As the Prioress's reference to the Lincoln libel demonstrates, her tale offers a version of a ritual-murder myth and responds especially to that of Hugh. Legendary accounts of Hugh's death appear in four chronicles and an Anglo-Norman ballad that, as critics including Gavin Langmuir and Roger Dahood have demonstrated, point at the very least to a "general tradition" whose details Chaucer knew.[74] In addition, the *Prioress's Tale*, with its focus on the Virgin Mary's rescue of a Christian boy, broadly exemplifies Marian miracle tales like "Toledo" and "The Jewish Boy" and, more particularly, participates in "the largest single subgroup of miracles of the Virgin," tales involving the "Miracle of the Boy Singer."[75] The earliest extant boy-singer myth appears in an early thirteenth-century English manuscript (Oxford, Corpus Christi College,

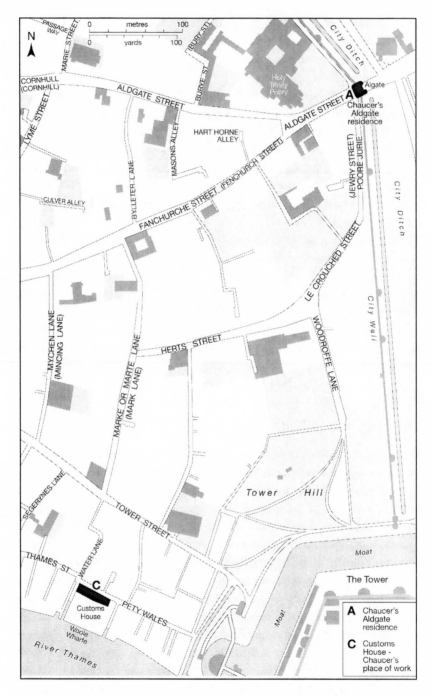

**Figure 13.** Chaucer's Aldgate residence. Map by Cath D'Alton. Adapted from maps in Lobel, ed.
*British Historic Towns Atlas*, vol. 3, *The City of London from Prehistoric times to c. 1520.*

MS 32, fol. 92r), though the legend is "pan-European in iteration" and exists in exempla, hagiographies, and miracle collections in Latin, Dutch, English, and Norse.[76] Chaucer's closest analogue is a Middle English story about a Parisian boy that appears in the Vernon manuscript (Oxford, Bodleian Library, MS Eng. Poet. a 1, fol. 124v).

Both Hugh of Lincoln and boy-singer narratives exemplify the persistence in English culture of the image of the Jew we traced first in Thomas's *Life* of William, that is, a figure whose dangerous nature is mutually constitutive with the closed domestic spaces he inhabits.[77] A gloss in five manuscripts containing the *Prioress's Tale* suggests such a linkage by citing lines from John of Garland's *Stella Maris* that describe how a Jew, "through bitter hatred" ("Diram per Inuidiam"), killed the singing boy and "buried him in his house" ("domo sua quem humauit").[78] Visually epitomizing this stress on the nefarious Jewish home is the Vernon manuscript version of the singing-boy myth (figure 14). Reflecting the voyeuristic desire to violate Jewish private space and witness prurient crimes, the manuscript features an illustration that dissolves two walls of the Jewish house in order to portray all key aspects of the murder narrative within that space.

On the far right side of the home the Jew beckons the boy with his right hand as he stands in his doorway, the folds of his fabric running parallel to the doorposts, an image that reflects the stress on the door of the Jewish home in boy-martyr libels.[79] Just left of this image, in the center of the home, is an image of the Jew slitting the boy's throat. On the far left of the domicile, we see the Jew placing the child's corpse headfirst into a privy. By crowding three images of both Jew and boy into a single image of the home—layering multiple narrative elements onto a single image—the illustration amplifies the status of the house as the setting for all elements of ritual murder, thus rendering that built environment an essential component in the enactment of imagined Jewish perfidy.

Beyond the multiple images of Jew and victim that crowd there, the house in the Vernon illustration contains only one piece of household "furniture," what Denise Despres aptly describes as "a gaping black privy."[80] Latrines are an important spatial feature of both boy-singer tales and Hugh of Lincoln legends. Ten of the thirteen boy-singer analogues cited by Laurel Broughton in her discussion of Chaucer's sources and analogues describe how the dead boy is deposited in a privy. For example, in keeping with the Vernon illustration is the accompanying Middle English text of the tale, which describes how the Jew "In to a gonge-put fer wiþ-Inne / þe child adoun þer-Inne he þrong" (he shoved the child down deep inside a toilet).[81] And the Anglo-Norman ballad

**FIGURE 14.**    Illustration accompanying *The Child Slain by Jews*. Oxford, Bodleian Library, MS. Eng. poet. a. 1, fol. 124v. By permission of the Bodleian Library, University of Oxford.

of Hugh also recounts how Jews decide to hide their Christian victim in a latrine or "chambre privé."[82] Privies also serve as important features of other boy-martyr myths, such as the thirteenth-century legend of Adam of Bristol, who is crucified "in cloaca" or in a latrine.[83]

The question of what those Jewish latrines signify is worth pondering at some length, since the *Prioress's Tale* also features one. In part, the privies of English antisemitic tales intensify the stress on Jewish secrecy that, as we have seen, emerged in the earliest ritual-murder libel through Thomas's obsessive attention to the closed door of Deulesalt of Norwich's home. Where better to hide evidence of ritual murder than in that most private of places, a privy?[84] Of course, to link medieval privies to issues of privacy counters the stereotype of the open, public character of waste during the medieval period. The notion that medieval people threw buckets of ordure in city streets or relieved themselves publically is still a widely held assumption. In Norbert Elias's well-known formulation, only in the Renaissance did western Europeans begin to privatize natural bodily functions.[85] But we can see how medieval people indeed associated latrines with privacy by looking at Isidore's *Etymologies,* which state that a "privy *(seccessus)* is so named because it is a private area, that is 'without access' *(sine accessu)*."[86] Middle English semantics similarly stress how the latrine isolates its occupant. The primary meaning of the noun *privy* (or *prive*) is privacy, secrecy, and secrets, and the second definition of the word is a latrine.[87] In keeping with the association of latrines with secrecy, a Latin singing-boy analogue of Chaucer's text describes how a Jew hides a dead boy in a privy "where nature purges itself in solitude" ("ubi natura se purgat per secessum"); the legend of Adam of Bristol describes how he is tortured and buried in a latrine hidden at the *back* of the Jewish home ("in domum anteriorem"); and the Vernon legend states that the Jew places the boy in a privy "Lest his Malice migte ben aspyet" (to hide his malice).[88]

However, the privileged privacy afforded by the privy only goes so far. To turn to another *Canterbury Tale,* the *Merchant's Tale,* while May uses a privy to peruse secretly and dispose of Damyan's letter, she certainly doesn't want to enter the latrine itself in the manner of the singing boy (4.1950–54). The privy thus speaks not only to medieval ideas of privacy but also to a medieval desire to isolate that which it rejects as polluting and contaminating. A debased space of exile—of double containment (room and toilet)—the privy enables the voiding of human waste from both body and household. Isidore in fact portrays excrement as so polluting that it must be physically isolated from the defecator herself. In a biological section of the *Etymologies,* he notes how the bodily mapping of the anus and the eyes protects people from their own polluting activities. The anus, Isidore claims, is located on "the backside and on the opposite side from the face, so that while we purge the bowels we may not defile the sense of sight."[89]

The material engineering of the privy in Chaucer's England supports Isidore's stress on defecation and excrement as polluting. The medieval latrine was a built environment consisting of three parts, "the seat, usually built over joists; the garderobe chute, often lined with boards, which was called a *pipe;* and the means of collection or disposal of the sewage below, usually a pit."[90] By the start of the thirteenth century the construction of privies in homes was regulated to hide the defecator and the excrement she produced. The ordinances required that cesspools walled with stone must be at least two and a half feet wide, and that cesspools walled with timber (sometimes called earth in the records of the Assize of Nuisance) had to be at least three and a half feet from neighboring properties.[91] Public latrines also sequestered medieval defecators via their placement on dead-end streets bearing names like "Easement Alley" and "Ordure Street."[92]

Reflecting this medieval rejection of waste, the imagined Jews of anti-semitic writings often employ the privy not only to hide but also perform their anti-Christian aggression. In those libels, Jews exhibit their maliciousness toward Christianity by placing a dead boy "in a place of vileness" ("in locum . . . vilitatis") or "in a place of utmost filth" ("in loco . . . immundissimo").[93] Several Marian legends specify how the Jews dump the child's corpse in a cesspit as "a reproach to" the Virgin whom the boy praised in song when he lived.[94] The Vernon legend showcases this aspect of the privy through its title, "Hou þe Jewes, in Despit of Ure Lady, þrewe a Chyld in a Gonge."[95] Dumping the child in the latrine thus colludes with other acts of hostility against Christians. Insofar as filth is, as Mary Douglas points out, "matter out of place," the latrines of antisemitic libels attribute to the Jew a desire to reject Christians as waste, as dross needful of dumping, hiding, and sequestra-tion in the manner of feces.[96] The preponderance of privies in Marian tales may prove especially telling in this regard. As scholars including Alexandra Cuffel have shown, some Jewish polemicists criticized Christianity by scoff-ing at the idea of God inhabiting a woman's womb, that is, a bodily location contiguous to the bowels and their filthy contents.[97] Legends about Jews denigrating the Virgin by placing Christian boys—themselves figures of Christ—in latrines resonate with those misogynistic polemics. Even more pointed are antisemitic tales, like Matthew Paris's account of Abraham of Berkhamsted, of Jews throwing images of Mary in privies.[98]

There is a crucial difference, however, between the filth featured in anti-Christian polemics and antisemitic libels: while Jewish polemicists stress the filth of Mary, the libels represent Jews immersing Christian objects in *their own* filth. Even as the Jews in the libels construe as filth the objects or persons they thrust in their latrines, the latrines themselves also refer to the filth of their users. Antisemitic narratives in effect equate Jews with filth. The Vernon manuscript illustration exemplifies this equation of Jews and ordure. Pointing out how "the cramped, dark and slightly receding space of the Jew's house underscores the link between this polluted place and the gaping black privy," Despres argues that the image establishes a synecdochic relationship between the privy and the house.[99] If, following Despres, the house is like the privy, then the inhabitant of the house—that is, the Jew—is like the excrement filling the latrine. In this manner boy-martyr myths construe excrement and defecation as key aspects of Jewish danger. Implicit in these tales is the idea of an urban Jewish menace that consists of not only violence (murdering boys) but also contamination: the threat of contact with Jewish excrement and with Jews *as* excrement. By producing the Jew as a reviled and polluting entity—as matter that is "out of place" yet nevertheless asserts itself onto the bodies of dead boys—the legends imply that Christians should rid themselves of Jews in the manner of waste. Like Bede's idea of the Jew as tomb, tales that link Jews with ordure construe them as "so fundamentally alien" that they "must be rejected." "Labeling something as filthy," William Cohen stresses, "is a viscerally powerful way of excluding it."[100] Written both before and after 1290, the legends support eradicating England—thus keeping England "clean"—of Jews.[101]

In the *Prioress's Tale*, the *only* Jewish built environment depicted is a privy. As the libel contained in the Vernon manuscript demonstrates, boy-singer tales typically depict a Jew leading his victim into his house. But Chaucer's text portrays the Jews hiring a "homycide" or assassin, who from the confines of not a home but a "privee place" in an alley, seizes the child "and heeld hym faste, / And kitte his throte, and in a pit hym caste" (7.567; 7.568–71). The Prioress goes on, with obscene clarity, to explain that this "pit" is "a wardrobe . . . Where as thise Jewes purgen hire entraille" (7.572–73). The nun's reference to a "Jewerye" at the beginning of her tale implies houses in the aggregate (7.488). However, the Prioress alludes to just one home in her tale—that of the Christian boy and his mother—when she refers to the schoolboy's travels "homward" from school (7.549). In Chaucer's narrative, we never see the accommodated Jew of other antisemitic tales. Instead, we peer into the Jewish latrine. By identifying Jews not with homes but with only a privy, the tale stresses that most defiling of built environments over any other. And through its obscene explication of the Jewish privy as a place "Where as thise Jewes purgen hire entraille," the tale associates Jews with defecation in an unprecedentedly explicit and straightforward manner.[102]

With its unprecedented showcasing of the Jewish latrine, the *Prioress's Tale* also intensifies the architectural opposition depicted in many English antisemitic texts. As we have seen, writers since Thomas of Monmouth contrasted dangerous Jewish homes with beneficent Christian churches. The sources and analogues of the *Prioress's Tale* are no different. All versions of the libel about Hugh of Lincoln recount how the boy's body was taken via a grand procession to Lincoln Cathedral. There, a multitude of Christians venerate the dead boy, whose body was, in Matthew Paris's words, "honorably buried in the church of Lincoln as if it had been the corpse of a precious martyr."[103] And in all of the singing-boy legends, the dead child is taken, very often with "gret solempnete" and ceremony by a large group composed of clergy and laity, through the streets of the city to a minster or cathedral church.[104] Reflecting the deep structure of English antisemitic literature, these texts exalt the Christian minster as the architectural opposite of the debased and dangerous Jewish home. The *Prioress's Tale*, by opposing the Christian church to not a home but a latrine, pushes this spatial dualism to its extreme.

A latrine—even a Christian latrine—is very much the architectural opposite of a church. While the most ordinary yet contaminating bodily functions occur in the privy, the most sacred and extraordinary Christian actions—the praise of God and the consecration of the host—occur in the church. Following Lefebvre, we might say that the privy epitomizes the quotidian building, a space that in literary terms offers "the prose of the world as opposed, or apposed, to the poetry" and collective joy of the monumental building that is the cathedral.[105] The socio-spatial politics of the privy only set it further apart from its architectural other. Minsters are inherently communal structures. Isidore of Seville writes that *ecclesia* "is a Greek word that is translated into Latin as 'convocation' (*convocatio*), because it calls (*vocare*) everyone to itself."[106] Exemplifying the public, Christian function of *ecclesia*, the conventual church of the *Prioress's Tale* gathers the "Cristene folk," lay and religious, of the Eastern city to honor the little schoolboy (7.614). In contrast, the privy isolates defecators as they engage in the basest of physical activities. The relationship of the minster and the pit to their urban settings further registers their respective public and private natures. The downward-looking privy, tellingly called a "pit" by the Prioress (7.571), and located in out-of-the-way places, goes underground to conceal the waste of the defecator. In contrast, medieval cathedrals are immense, eye-catching monuments possessed of a spectacular, heaven-scraping verticality that asserts their status as the most prominent of societal sites. What better way, then, to use buildings to connote Christian purity and Jewish danger than link the Jew to a latrine and the Christian to a church?

## The Flow of Usury in Medieval London and Chaucer's Writings

Through its latrine the *Prioress's Tale* also offers a far more strident version of the economic antisemitism present in prior libels. As we saw in the examples of Thomas's *Life* and William's *History*, earlier texts bind the demonized Jewish home to a critique of Jewish lenders, but curiously, none of Chaucer's closest sources and analogues feature financiers. In fact, most boy-singer myths do not specify the Jews' occupations at all, with the exception of three analogues, which refer to winemakers, cloth merchants, and pharmacists.[107] Some versions of the Hugh of Lincoln libel—most notably that by Matthew Paris—do posit Jewish financing as a given, but none of them offer anything along the lines of a pointed critique.[108] In contrast, the *Prioress's Tale* foregrounds and demonizes lending and profit in its very first stanza, which refers to the "foule usure" and "lucre of vileynye" practiced by Jews in the city where the tale is set (7.491). That stress on usury sets the *Prioress's Tale* apart from all other previous English libels.

Not only does Chaucer place an unprecedented stress on finance but he also has the nun label usury "foule," a word whose primary meaning is "dirty, filthy, soiled."[109] That association is emphasized further in both the Ellesmere and Hengwrt manuscripts via a Latin gloss, *turpe lucrum* or filthy lucre, for "lucre of vileyenye." Such descriptors both connote the sinfulness of usury and link it to the filthiest place portrayed in the tale, the latrine.[110] We have seen such a linkage of commercial wrongdoing and a Jewish built environment before. In William of Newburgh's *History*, Jewish mansions in York exhibit an oppressively excessive carnality that reflects critically on their avaricious owners: huge Jewish houses loom over medieval York in the same way that their owners' tyrannize Christians via harsh lending practices. William thus evokes Jewish greed through the corrupt yet admittedly grand material space of a manse. But the Prioress's architectural critique gains added traction by using not a house but the abject space of the latrine. The Jewish usurer, her tale implies, isn't just carnal but carnal in the vilest manner imaginable, as carnal as excrement.[111] While at some level William's readers might envy and admire the grand homes of York lenders, we can be sure that the Prioress's auditors had no such urge regarding the privy of the Jewry.

While the Prioress's antisemitic triad or cluster—in which Jews, filth, and lending all share in a demonized carnality—distinguishes the tale from its sources and analogues, it follows key aspects of Chaucer's culture. During a medieval period when commerce was on the rise, Christian writers often elevated the "bourgeois sin" of avarice to the deadliest of sins, a stance registered by Chaucer's Pardoner in his tale with its theme *radix malorum est cupiditas*.[112] Within that body of writing, profits acquired through usury—that is, the lending of money at interest—frequently were singled "out for special censure," as the Prioress's pairing of usury with "lucre of vileynye" or illicit gain affirms (7.491).[113] A host of different and at times conflicting attitudes toward usury existed; for the most condemnatory of writers, usury often epitomized a wrongheaded quest for monetary gain that the pious should revile as so much dung. Thus thirteenth-century English cardinal Stephen Langton called usury "dung and filth" in a sermon, and thirteenth-century French canon Jacques de Vitry recounts in an exemplum how God impels a donkey bearing the corpse of a Christian usurer to send "the cadaver flying into the dung beneath the gallows."[114] Closer to Chaucer's period, an even more arresting linkage of usury and defecation appears in a fresco of hell by Taddeo di Bartolo (ca. 1396). For the punishment of *usuraio*, Taddeo depicts an obese, white, nude, and prostrate usurer whose gaping mouth receives gold coins excreted by a naked, hairy, black, and grimacing devil (figure 15).

**FIGURE 15.** Taddeo di Bartolo, detail of fresco depicting scenes of hell, ca. 1396. Duomo, San Gimignano. Alinari/ Art Resource, NY.

In neither Taddeo's fresco nor the sermons of Jacques and Stephen is the usurer a Jew, a fact that reflects the presence of Christian lenders during the Middle Ages.[115] However, with notable frequency, medieval Christians from the twelfth century onward labeled Jews usurers, so often that a moneybag came to be second only to funnel hats and exaggerated physiognomic features in visual stereotypes of Jews.[116] There are, as we have seen, historical grounds for the linkage of Jews and finance in English artifacts. Jews in England came to dominate lending until Edward I outlawed the practice in 1275. But beyond their real history as lenders, Jews were imagined to be essentially, even racially, connected to lending. By the twelfth century, the term *judaizare*, which Christian writers had used earlier to signify heresy, meant charging interest.[117] Similarly, the Middle English word for Jews, "Jeuerie," also signified moneylenders as early as 1230.[118] The medieval terminology of usury demonstrates how "the Jew had become the 'stereotypical' moneylender in the eyes of most Christians, or at least in Christian writings," so much so that the "term 'usurer' . . . was considered practically synonymous with the term 'Jew.'"[119] It seems that lending was so tied to Jewishness that to lend was in some sense to become Jewish or at least to act "like a Jew."[120] Thus, it is possible that the auditors and viewers of the aforementioned sermons and fresco would have understood the filthy Christian usurers they depict—figures alternately immersed in, force-fed with, or equated with excrement—as somehow "Jewish."

A more explicit conceptualization of Jews as polluting usurers emerges in the French King Louis IX (1214–70) of France's statement "Let [the Jews] abandon usury or let them leave my land completely, lest it be further defiled by their filth."[121] That concept of the inherently avaricious, polluting, and usurious Jew would have been well known to Chaucer through artifacts such as the Hereford world map, discussed in the introduction (figure 1). That *mappa mundi*—like the *Prioress's Tale*—locates contemporary Jews in the Asian upper half of the terrestrial world. West of the Red Sea and notably far from European Christians, and contiguous to the Exodus of the Israelites, appears a group of men, one of whom has a stereotypical hooked nose (figure 2). Termed *Iudei*, the men worship a bestial idol defecating a string of coins.[122] In an England devoid of Jews but filled with images like that of the idolatrous Jews on the Hereford map, the equation of Jews with a foul materialism continued well after 1290 and into the Renaissance.

By incorporating into the *Prioress's Tale* such widespread ideas about the polluting Jewish usurer, Chaucer adds an element to his boy-singer legend that renders it uniquely and unprecedentedly antithetical to Aaron's joke. In confronting the monks of St. Alban's with the fact that their construction programs relied on Jewish capital, Aaron exposed how England's new urban economies were pervasive, so much so as to inform even its holiest sites. Indeed, Aaron's exposure of the economic transactions responsible for making St. Alban's shored up the mock aristocratic materialism of Christianity itself, manifested by its ornate windows, elaborate shrines, and soaring cathedrals. But instead of acknowledging the spread of England's emerging profit economy throughout Christian society, even its spectacular religious monuments, instead of acknowledging the *utility* of Jewish lenders in making Christian space, the *Prioress's Tale* rejects both usury and Jews as dangerously and aggressively polluting entities. In this legend more than any other English antisemtic libel, usury is at once projected onto the Jew and then rejected as ordure.

And yet the representation of polluting Jews, usury, and carnality in the *Prioress's Tale* is more complex and contradictory than this account of the tale suggests. How could it not be, given Chaucer's own immersion in the "world and ethos of commerce"?[123] A merchant's son who grew up in a London neighborhood populated by Italian bankers, Chaucer lived in a city whose thoroughgoing commercialization made abundantly clear the fantastic and wrongheaded nature of any notion of lending as a filthy and essentially Jewish practice.[124] More than any other English city, London reflected the saturation of Christian life by market forces. By the early fourteenth century, London had become a national center of consumption and the site for "most of the internal market in England in cloth, furs, wine and spices."[125] The preponderance of both shops and streets named after various businesses bespeaks London's dominance by trade during Chaucer's age. Principal streets such as Chepeside or Cornhill were occupied by hundreds of shops and booths; running back from those thoroughfares "were selds, bazaar-like enclosures often with stone walls which had stalls within them," and smaller streets and alleys, bearing names like Ironmonger Lane, Bred Street, and Hosyer Lane, which also contained shops.[126] As a Londoner, Chaucer was literally surrounded by markets.

To describe Chaucer as immersed in commerce, though, belies his own famous characterization of his spatial relationship to the city in his dream vision *The House of Fame* (1379–80). In a rare moment when Chaucer alludes to his place of habitation, during the second book of the poem, the poet offers an image of himself—articulated by a golden eagle scolding the character of "Geffrey"—as heavily isolated from London's commercial hustle and bustle. Presumably alluding to the apartment above Aldgate in which Chaucer lived from 1374 to 1386, the eagle bemoans to Geffrey "Thou goost hom to thy hous anoon, . . . sittest at another book, / Tyl fully daswed ys thy look; / And lyvest thus as an hermyte" (655–59). In this passage, Chaucer attributes to himself a bookishness that is bound up with a separation from his urban milieu that is nothing less than cloistral. The eagle's characterization of Chaucer's isolated home life suggests how the poet embraced a small-scale version of the isolation of London's monastic houses. The near thirty monasteries of London were stone structures "surrounded by a wall with its own gates. They were formidable topographical blockages, which had to be walked round, rarely through."[127] Like the monks and nuns of London, Chaucer distances himself from his urban milieu through his "sky-high," ivory tower–like home above Aldgate.[128]

Yet like those monastic built environments, Chaucer's home during the time he wrote *The House of Fame* actually undermined any desire for isolation, bookish or otherwise. As we saw in the case of Thomas of Monmouth's priory in Norwich, urban monasteries proved to be open to their city environs. In the case of London's monasteries, crucial to our understanding of their isolation or lack thereof is the fact that many of them existed on the border of the city, along its wall.[129] Exemplifying this location is the first post-conquest monastery, Holy Trinity Priory, located on Aldegatestrete and Leadenhall Street just northeast of Chaucer's home.[130] Taken one way, the location of Chaucer's home, like that of so many London monks and nuns, along the walls of London affirms notions of closure and seclusion. As Ardis Butterfield points out, "in some ways, the existence of a city wall gives apparent clarity to a notion of London: three miles long, and punctuated by six ancient . . . gates. . . . with a ditch eighty-foot wide beyond, the wall was strengthened in the thirteenth century and carefully maintained through the fourteenth."[131] But the wall, punctuated as it was by gates like Aldgate as well as waterways, ultimately testifies not so much to a defining seclusion but to an inescapable porosity. Living above Aldgate, on "the edges of the city," Chaucer was positioned—even more so than the many monks living along London's walls—to appreciate how his city was "not a self-enclosed space but rather the dynamic and open centre of an increasingly dispersed set of trade routes."[132] The immediate environs of Aldgate reinforced how London served as a locus of trade; among the residents "in the parishes within and without Aldgate"—people who "duellen almost at" Geffrey's "dores" in *The House of Fame*—were "fishmongers, butchers, potters, bakers, chandlers, goldbeaters, goldsmiths, fellmongers, vintners, saddlers, cordwainers, tawyers, brewers, hatters, spurries . . . merchants" and "moneyers."[133]

Chaucer wasn't merely surrounded by commerce; he participated in it. Indeed, Chaucer's jobs made him very familiar with the very business practice on which the *Prioress's Tale* focuses, lending. For twelve years, from 1374 to 1386, Chaucer worked in the London Customs Office regulating the import and export of goods, "back in the mercantile world in which he had been born."[134] As a controller of wool and other customs, Chaucer oversaw the shady practice of using custom revenues to repay the Crown's creditors.[135] Another job gave him still more contact with lending. Appointed the clerk of the king's works from 1389 to 1391, Chaucer collected from royal debtors to finance the building and repair of royal properties, including Saint George's Chapel in Windsor Castle.[136] Finally, Chaucer himself seems to have borrowed funds with some frequency; we know of five suits brought against him to recover debts between 1388 and 1399. His creditors included a London merchant and moneylender, Gilbert Mawfield, from whom Chaucer is recorded as borrowing, on 28 July 1392, twenty-six shillings eight pence, a loan he repaid one week later.[137]

Chaucer's involvement in commerce and lending places the *Prioress's Tale* in a new light. For one thing, it reminds us that, unlike the ecclesiastics Thomas of Monmouth and William of Newburg, Chaucer was a "New Man" whose secular identity gave him a unique vantage point on English antisemitic culture and its relationship to burgeoning commercial cities like London.[138] Chaucer's lay and commercial identity helps explain his unique stress on usury and suggests how he may not share with the Prioress her stereotyping of lending as inherently filthy and Jewish. We can never know for certain if Chaucer knew about Aaron's jest and the Anglo-Jewish financing of English cathedrals. But we can be sure that the poet's deep knowledge of and experience with commerce imbued him with a critical relationship to Christian culture.

We need only look elsewhere in Chaucer's literary corpus to learn that the Prioress has erred in defining lending as Jewish. As critics such as Lee Patterson and Patricia Eberle have observed, not only Chaucer's routine mercantile transactions but also his literary productions exhibit a commercial sensibility. For example, the same passage in *The House of Fame* where Chaucer imagines himself shut away reading in Aldgate also alludes to his "labour" making "rekenynges" at the Customs Office (652–53). And, returning to the *Canterbury Tales*, both the form and content of that work indicate the omnipresence of commerce and lending in the Christian West. All of the tales are, in Eberle's words, "conditioned, directly or indirectly, by the essentially commercial arrangement involved in Harry Bailey's conditions for the tale-telling game, by the continuing presence of [the businessman] Harry as fictional audience and judge of the tales, and by the point of departure and final destination of the group, Harry Bailey's tavern."[139] Indeed, a usurious logic of debt and repayment informs Bailey's game. Starting with Harry's request for a tale from the Monk that will "quite with the Knyghtes tale" (1.3119), the tale-telling competition becomes a "quitting" competition in which pilgrims strive to "quite" or match each other's stories and win the prize of a free meal. A primary meaning of *quiten* is to repay a debt, as signaled by Chaucer's friend John Gower, who writes of debtors, "Bot who that takth or gret or smal, / He takth a charge forth withal, / And stant noght fre til it be quit."[140] In the give-and-take of stories between pilgrims such as the Miller and the Reeve, and particularly in the pilgrims' attempts to outdo (or return with interest) others' tales, we find a literary version of the dealing out and repayment of goods in the medieval economy.

The "quitting" competition implicates all of Chaucer's pilgrims in a usurious literary game. Moreover, a Christian lender actually features in one tale, that of the Shipman who, not coincidentally, tells his tale immediately before the Prioress. With its story of the avaricious dealings of a Christian merchant just across the channel from England, in France and Flanders, the *Shipman's Tale* undermines the Prioress's effort to project usury onto a faraway Eastern location and attach it solely to Jews. Moreover, at smaller scales—those of the home and rooms within the home—the Shipman troubles the nun's fantasy of economic confinement. In the earliest recorded use of "counting house" in Middle English, the Shipman describes how the merchant goes "up into his countour-hous . . . to rekene with himself" (7.77–78), and

> His bookes and his bagges many oon
> He leith biforn hym on his counting-bord.
> Ful riche was his tresor and his hord,
> For which ful fast his countour-dore he shette.
>
> *(7.82–85)*

With its image of the "half miser and half hermit" merchant shutting his "countour-dore" "ful fast," to ensure that "no man sholde hym lette / Of his acountes," the tale connotes mercantile secrecy (7.85–87); later in the tale, the merchant reiterates his investment in privacy when he explains to his wife that "us chapmen" must "kepen oure estaat in pryvetee" (7.226, 7.232).[141] The merchant's investment in private domestic space resonates with the closed houses and hidden latrines of Jews hailing back to Thomas of Monmouth's ritual-murder libel. Though the merchant, of course, is no ritual murderer. By stressing how the merchant "leith biforn hym" many bags of treasure in the counting house, the tale doesn't so much engage longstanding tales of ritual murder as look ahead in English literary history, to the loot piled beside the Jew Jonathas at the start of the Croxton *Play of the Sacrament* and, even more precisely, *The Jew of Malta*, in whose first scene we see Barabas in his "little room" or counting house with "heaps of gold before" him.[142]

The image in the *Shipman's Tale* of a merchant secretly hoarding his wealth implies a certain spatial separation of mercantile greed from other spaces of Christian life. But Chaucer's text ultimately demonstrates how wealth accumulates not only in the little rooms of merchants (Jewish or gentile) but throughout the profit-driven worlds of medieval and Renaissance society. Chaucer tracks the presence of greed and carnality well beyond the seemingly confined space of the counting house. The French merchant's business ventures take him out of his home in St. Denis, first to Flanders, then to Paris. During those two journeys, the merchant—a professional lender—repays a debt to Lombard bankers to his economic advantage through the medieval system of the bill of exchange. When the merchant borrows twenty thousand shields in Bruges but repays the loan in Paris, he makes a one-thousand-franc profit from the exchange of currency from shields to francs.[143] Less professional but equally commercial and usurious practices occur in and around the merchant's home, showing, as Andrew Galloway puts it, "the extension of mercantilism on several fronts into realms not yet overtly commercialized."[144] In the merchant's residence, his "friend," a lecherous monk, receives sexual favors from the merchant's wife in exchange for helping her resolve her own financial debts. With its depiction of lending occurring not only in the marketplace but also in the home—between a housewife and a monk no less—the *Shipman's Tale* makes clear more than any other Canterbury tale just how cognizant Chaucer was of the thoroughgoing commercialism of his Christian society and its immersion in various kinds of illicit lending.

## Sanitation, Contamination, and the *Prioress's Tale*

In stressing how the Prioress's image of commerce intersects with other Chaucerian texts, I follow an important critical trend. Lampert-Weissig reads the *Prioress's Tale* alongside fragments 7 and 8 to identify "the figure of the hermeneutical Jew beyond the ghetto of the *Prioress's Tale*." In the case of the *Second Nun's Tale*, for example, Lampert-Weissig locates in that text a model of learned Christian piety that competes with and queries the idea of holy ignorance embraced by the Prioress.[145] In a similar vein, Miriamne Krummel reads the *Prioress's Tale* alongside tales such as the *Tale of Sir Thopas* to suggest how "Chaucer's corpus—when taken as a whole—complicates the sobriety generated by" the Prioress through its depiction of not just the stereotypical Jewish murderer but a "multidimensional Jewish figure."[146] Additionally, Lawrence Besserman analyzes *The House of Fame* and the preface to the *Treatise on the Astrolabe* to suggest Chaucer's "distance from the traditional theologically and socially motivated antisemitism" demonstrated in the *Prioress's Tale*.[147] A focus on lending in the *Canterbury Tales* similarly destabilizes the antisemitic fantasy promulgated by Chaucer's nun, by exposing a wide gap between the Prioress's antisemitic understanding of usury and that presented by the *Canterbury Tales* overall.

We can, however, destabilize the Prioress's image of commerce by looking not only beyond her tale, but also within it, and namely at its "foule" center, the privy. As we have seen, the Prioress constructs the Jewish usurer as filth by drawing upon the medieval culture of the privy, and its stress on containing and sequestering human ordure. Yet a closer look at defecation troubles such a project. Excrement is an abject yet irrepressible flow from the human body. As an excreted substance that indeed embodies movement, ordure belies any effort at sequestration, including the containment function of latrines. In the Prioress's privy, Chaucer found an apt symbol of the medieval Christian impulse to stem abhorrent flows and the futility of that wish.

Chaucer certainly was attuned to the fraught association of the privy with containment and contamination. The need for waste management assumed national proportions around the time that the poet was working on the *Prioress's Tale*, during the latter half of the 1380s. After the Merciless Parliament dissolved in June 1388, the Cambridge Parliament of that year demonstrated Richard II's effort to regain his authority by "cleaning up" the realm. The Crown both legislated against the dirty politics practiced by biased public officials and restricted the mobility of laborers, beggars, servants, and pilgrims. The king's cleanup plan also included the first sanitation act in English history, which endeavored to end the spread of sewage by removing "Annoyances, Dung, Garbages, Intrails, and other Ordure" from the "Ditches, Rivers, and other Waters, and also within many other Places" in the cities and suburbs of the realm.[148] Closer to home, Chaucer had personal experience in sanitation work, thanks to two royal appointments. As clerk of the king's works, he served as a property manager and contractor for the king and worked with laborers including the master mason, carpenter, joiner, and plumber.[149] And in 1390 Chaucer sat on a royal sanitation commission charged with the maintenance of "walls, ditches, gutters, sewers, bridges, streets, dams, and trenches on the Thames between Woolwich and Greenwich."[150]

Both Chaucer's administrative work in public health and the government's investment in controlling waste of various kinds help explain why the poet decided to have the Prioress deploy the latrine to confine her usurious Jews. The Prioress, we might say, seeks to manage the threat of the Jewish usurer much the way the fourteenth-century Crown responded to the "dangers" posed by human detritus, such as wandering beggars, laborers, servants, and pilgrims. Yet medieval English sewage systems—like government efforts to rid England of human waste—were far from foolproof. The London Assize of Nuisance records Londoners' complaints over faulty walls, gutters, and privies between 1301 and 1431.[151] Among the grievances heard by the assize justices is Ralph de Cauntebrigg's accusation that the sewage from his neighbor William's latrine "penetrates and defiles his [Ralph's] whole premises," and Andrew de Aubrey's complaint that his neighbors had removed a party-wall and roof enclosing their cesspit, "so that the extremities of those sitting upon the seats can be seen, a thing which is abominable and altogether intolerable."[152] If the *Shipman's Tale*, set largely in a French merchant's home, exposes the flow of usury into that domestic space, the assize demonstrates how another repellant flow had come home to medieval Londoners. Instead of enjoying the architectural sovereignty aimed at by the assize, which regulated matters such as the minimum thickness of walls and the distances between private cesspits and neighboring properties, the citizens of medieval London were susceptible to excremental currents within and without their houses.

Even London churches were susceptible to such filth. A 1358 entry in the Assize of Nuisance records a common sergeant's claim "on behalf of the commonality" that "men living in the churchyard" of Saint Lawrence Jewry, located on Catte Street (now Gresham), "throw dung and other refuse, and make their privies [near its entrance], which is an abomination to the mayor and aldermen and common people passing along the street."[153] Twentieth-century excavations at the churchyard unearthed evidence that it "was used in the 12th century, and no doubt earlier and later," as a dump: "rubbish including dress fastenings, metalworking waste, . . . stable refuse and human excrement."[154] Of the excavation, Schofield writes that it may indicate that the Saint Lawrence churchyard "had the character of a dung-heap, since worms had begun to be active."[155] This London church, in other words, presents us with historical evidence that undermines the notion of Christian purity promulgated by the *Prioress's Tale*, boy-singer narratives, and ritual-murder myths. While those gentile tales imagine Christian minsters as havens from material contamination (i.e., ordure, money, and Jews), Saint Lawrence Jewry was linked to polluting flows. While the Prioress opposes the minster to the privy, Saint Lawrence Jewry conflates the two built environments.

Reflecting that English failure to control and contain urban sewage, the latrine of the *Prioress's Tale* isn't a bounded and sequestered space but rather is open and spills into other locations. The permeability of the latrine emerges in the Prioress's prurient elucidation of what she means by "pit." When the nun explains "that in a wardrobe they hym threwe / Where as thise Jewes purgen hire entraille" (7.571–73), she opens up the privy to the gaze of the members of her audience. Peering into Jewish built environments and especially Jewish homes is a key component of English tales of Jewish perfidy.[156] But unlike other texts, the *Prioress's Tale* seems to cross a line of propriety in its visualization of the privy, where readers and listeners witness the excretions that—as Isidore reminds us—even the defecator is protected from seeing. In other words, at the same time that the Prioress violates the privacy of the privy, she enables the breeching and contamination of the mind's eye of both her pilgrim auditors and Chaucer's readers. Wordsworth deemed the Prioress's description of the pit so offensive that he censored it in his translation, which reads, "I say that him into a pit they threw, / A loathsome pit whence noisome scents exhale."[157] In Wordsworth's sanitized version, the pit doesn't quite become a latrine. Never exposed as a place of Jewish defecation, the pit is merely a site from which vile smells emanate. Wordsworth's act of censorship suggests how the filth associated with Jews leaks into and taints the language of Chaucer's text, so that the Prioress's words themselves must be erased from the narrative. In the vulnerability of the Prioress's narrative to contamination, we perceive how the violated privy enables the return of multiple repressed flows. The exposure of the privy reflects Chaucer's sensitivity to the impossibility of stemming all sorts of circulations, from the "entry of Jew and Christian into each other's bodies, worlds, rituals and texts" to equally problematic fluxes between Christians.[158]

## The Miracle of the Boy Singer, or Abject Christian Lending in the *Prioress's Tale*

If the Prioress's prurient impulse to clarify the nature of the pit opens it up to readers and auditors, thus contaminating them, it is her young protagonist, the little schoolboy, who allows for that pollution to occur in the tale itself. In keeping with the conventions of ritual-murder and boy-singer legends, prior to his burial, the schoolboy is "with honour of greet processioun . . . carien . . . unto the nexte abbay" (7.622–24). The transportation of a boy martyr to a church typically is an event that signals the triumph of Christian society over its Jewish minority. But in the case of Chaucer's narrative, aspects of the boy's journey suggest how it is not so much victorious and holy, as destabilizing and profane. The child, after all, was immersed in the excrement-filled latrine before his rescue.[159] While an analogue depicts the schoolboy's cleansing after his discovery, the *Prioress's Tale* includes no scene of washing, and thus suggests his abiding filthiness, a prospect reinforced by the alacrity of the schoolboy's interment: the local abbot and monks "sped hem for to burien him ful faste" (7.638).[160] His body covered in excrement, the child taken to the minster brings the ordure of the privy to that ostensibly holy place.

As we have seen, the *Prioress's Tale* links the filth of the privy to a Jewish and usurious carnality: Jews, moneylending, and excrement all cluster together in their abject physicality. The journey of the dirty child from privy to minster would suggest, then, both the "Jewish" and the "usurious" nature of the minster. Does the procession from latrine to church return us to Aaron of Lincoln's boast about St. Alban's shrine? The manner in which the boy carries the excrement of the latrine to the minster seems to map out a version of the money trail linking Jewish lenders to medieval churches. And yet there are important differences between the Jew's jest and Chaucer's tale. If the boy's journey links churches to Jewish lenders, it does so in a manner that doesn't so much celebrate a Jewish contribution to Christian architectural magnificence, as suggest that lending reduces Christian buildings to the base level of Jewish excrement. The tale seems to recall not Aaron's jest but the critique written by the most famous denigrator of church building programs, Cistercian abbot Bernard of Clairvaux (1090–1153).[161] In a section of his *Apology*

(ca. 1125) hailed by scholars as the single most important medieval commentary on religious art, Bernard, like Chaucer, yokes church buildings to
the cluster of lending, the "Jew," and filth. According to Bernard, greedy
"bishops, debtors to both the wise and unwise," build churches to generate
not "spiritual profit" but financial donations from awed and ignorant parishioners.[162] He sees in the physical grandeur of churches a turn away from
the "spiritual mansion of God" hailed by writers like Bede to a materialism
defined as Jewish.[163] Church magnificence is both atavistically Jewish—a
"bringing back of ancient Jewish rites"—and rejected as mere "dung."[164]
The culture of asceticism in medieval Christianity, epitomized by Bernard's
work, suggests how the generation of spectacular architectural monuments to
Christianity prove self-defeating; indeed, the more magnificent the minster,
the greater it approximates its seeming other, the Jewish pit.[165] Such a context
clarifies how, when the schoolboy is taken to the local minster, he brings to
that space a mirror of its "true" nature in the form of the "Jewish" and usurious fecal matter covering his body.

This is not to deny, however, that aspects of the procession in the *Prioress's
Tale* don't link so much as oppose the minster and the privy and, through
that architectural distinction, elevate holy Christian over sinful Jew. Foremost
among such demarcating aspects of the procession is the boy's song. As in all
boy-singer myths, the Jews' efforts to silence the child through murder and
then conceal that crime are countered by the Virgin Mary, who restores his
voice to the dead boy. The boy's mother, after waiting all night for him to
come home, seeks him out in the streets of the city; finally, through divine
inspiration, she approaches the privy and calls out after her son who, "with
throte ykorven lay upright" (on his back with his throat slit, 7.611) begins to
sing the *Alma redemptoris mater*. After his discovery and removal from the pit,
the violated schoolboy continues "syngynge his song alway" during the
procession to the local minster (7.622). As the singer of a Marian hymn, the
boy serves as an emblem of Christian purity over and against Jewish danger.
While the mapping of the lower regions of the Jewish body, particularly its
anal portal, produces the Jew as a carnal and filthy figure who belongs in a
latrine, the corporeal geography of the schoolboy shifts up, heavenward, to
the head and throat, out of which issues the *Alma redemptoris mater*. In other
words, the song maps onto the boy's body an exalted holy geography that
points toward the proper architectural setting for his corpse.[166] Thus in the
procession to the minster we witness a Christian teleology, in which the child
finally rests in the built environment that truly suits his holy song and its
miraculous continuation after the boy's throat is slit. Indeed, we can go further
and consider how the song not only affirms the tale's ecclesiastical teleology,

but also defies Jewish space through its territorializing and reterritorializing capacities. Chanted by the living boy as he enters into and departs from the Jewry, the *Alma redemptoris mater* is a refrain that violates the Jewish neighborhood by marking it out lyrically as a Christian space.[167] When, despite his severed throat, the boy miraculously resumes singing the hymn in the Asian city where the tale is set, he realizes the wondrous global advance of the Christian word celebrated in the nun's prologue: "O Lord, oure Lord, thy name how merveilous / Is in this large world ysprad" (7.453–54).

Yet finally the boy's song does not so much repress as respond to the economics of spiritual space with which we began. Mary miraculously restores the boy's voice when she places on his tongue a "greyn" (7.662). The grain is a detail original to Chaucer's version of the singing-boy legend. When an object appears in the mouth of the boy in the analogues, it is either a lily (as in the Vernon analogue), or a gem, or a pebble.[168] The question of what the grain signifies has inspired a wealth of scholarly speculation. The many meanings put forth by critics include a rosary bead and a pill used to cure speech loss, as well as two particularly resonant interpretations: the idea, articulated by Hawkins, that the grain represents the deeper "kernel" or nucleus of meaning located by medieval exegetes beneath the "chaff" or literal significance of a text, and many readers' association of the grain with the Eucharistic wafer.[169] No one will ever explain definitively the polyvalent grain. But we can add to the rich store of interpretations by considering how Mary's gift of the grain to the boy and its later removal by the abbot constitute the sole representation of a loan in the tale. While we are told the Jews are usurers, we only see them arrange for a murder. It is Mary who performs the only specific act of lending in the tale.

As a loaned object, the grain turns us away from medieval exegetes' stress on the "fruit and chaff" gleaned from textual interpretation to the particulars of the medieval economy. A cereal surplus enabled the commercial takeoff and attending push toward urban development described by Duby in his account of the medieval economy. In placing on the boy's tongue a grain, Mary thus puts in his mouth both an archetypal product of the greater agrarian world and a key element of the rise of the medieval city. Loans frequently entailed grain, which also, along with other staples such as oil and wine, was a stock example of a fungible good (whose use could not be separated from its substance) in medieval definitions and theories of usury in both scholarly and more popular texts.[170] For example, the fourteenth-century English preacher's manual *Fasciculus Morum*, following Pope Gregory IX's influential decretal *Naviganti* (1227–34), distinguishes between usurious and nonusurious loans through hypothetical examples of the loan of grain (*granum*), wine (*vinum*), and oil (*oleum*).[171]

But even as Mary's agrarian loan speaks to a fundamental aspect of the medieval economy, does her lending of the grain really suggest a Christian version of the usurious processes reviled by the Prioress? After all, Mary is no ordinary lender. A beneficent and wondrous figure, Mary departs dramatically from the stereotype of the sinful usurer. While moneylenders exhibit a foul materialism that, as Ambrose puts it, kills the life of the borrower, Mary's loan enables the boy's rescue from the latrine and restores his life.[172] Not a profit seeker but a "blisful mayden free" (7.660), Mary simply gives without asking for anything in return. Her figuration as a kind of holy creditor appears elsewhere in medieval culture. The thirteenth-century devotional work *The Mirror of the Blessed Virgin Mary* identifies "generosity countering avarice" among the meanings of "the fruit of Mary" and cites Bernard of Clairvaux's claim that while "any earthly thing [Mary] could have had from her father's house, all such possibilities were like dung to her, for she made profit from Christ."[173] An especially telling comparison of Mary to usurers appears in an early fourteenth-century tract on moneylending by Remigio of Florence (d. 1319). After a lengthy Aristotelian discussion of the how the usurer's profits represent an unnatural "breeding" of sterile money, Remigio opines how "many things that are shown to come into existence against nature are nevertheless in truth good. For the Virgin Mary, remaining a virgin, against nature brought forth her son Jesus."[174] Remigio's account of Mary's unnatural birthing of Christ resonates with the grain's unnatural restoration of life and song in the schoolboy. As the child puts it to the abbot of the convent to which he is taken, "by wey of kynde, / I sholde have dyed, ye, longe tyme agon" (7.649–50). In the same way that Remigio sets usurious breeding against Marian generation by describing the former act as sinful and the latter as "in truth good," the *Prioress's Tale* places the illicit actions of the tale's usurious and murderous Jews at variance with the wondrous and fertile outpourings fostered by Mary.

And yet this dichotomy of benevolent Virgin and dangerous Jew does not hold in either Remigio's text or the *Prioress's Tale*. The fact that Remigio is compelled to refer twice to the unnaturalness of Mary's maternal function suggests how he, like many medieval writers, was uncomfortable with her extraordinary maternal identity. As much could be said about the citation from Bernard in *The Mirror of the Blessed Virgin Mary*, with its odd formulation of Mary's profiting from Christ. The medieval notion of Mary as a kind of antiusurer evinced medieval writers' discomfort with her unnaturalness as much as it exemplified their praise for her generosity. We might speculate that in the *Prioress's Tale* the Marian loan that seems to oppose usury is no less problematic. After all, Mary's generosity leads to the spectacle of a near-decapitated singing boy. Is it possible that the monks are anxious to inter the boy not only because he reeks of the privy but also because his miraculous song disturbs them? While the miracle is not viscerally unclean like the privy, it nevertheless exemplifies the workings of abjection as described by contemporary theorists. "It is not lack of cleanliness or health that causes abjection," Julia Kristeva writes, "but what disturbs identity, system, order. What does not respect borders, positions, rules."[175] Producing noise from a throat that has been gruesomely "ykorven" to the "nekke boon" (7.649), the schoolboy is abjectly situated on the border between life and death. The child's song renders him a sort of zombie possessed of a disquietingly inexorable anthem. Thanks to Mary's generosity, the undead boy sings without stopping, "syngynge his song alway" (7.622) as he is removed from the latrine and taken "unto the nexte abbay" (7.624), making the Christian folk around him "wondre" (7.615), a Middle English verb that connotes not only awe and astonishment but also horror and loathing.[176] Relentless and stridently omnipresent, rendered unpleasantly "loude" so "that al the place gan to rynge" (7.613), the boy's song suggests how even a Christian liturgical refrain can oppress and contaminate.[177]

The abbot who uncovers the workings of the miracle also indicates its disturbing effects. After asking the boy to explain his strange actions, the monk learns that the child's compulsion to sing results from the Virgin's agrarian gift; as the boy puts it, "I synge, and synge moot certeyn, . . . 'Til fro my tonge of taken is the greyn" (7.663–65). Immediately the monk "His tonge out caughte, and took awey the greyn," enabling the child to "yaf up the goost" (7.671–72). The sudden violence of the abbot's removal of the grain may reflect negatively on the miracle. Instead of a wonder that merits praise and inspires joy, the song seems to be a disturbing and troubling event that requires instant termination. In putting an end to the boy's song, the abbot suggests the impropriety of that supernatural event to the minster. Reclaiming the minster from the undead singer, the abbot implies his preference that it shelter no wondrously singing boy but something more ordinary and profane: an excrement-covered corpse.[178]

In keeping with its association of the minster with everyday material realities, the *Prioress's Tale* offers no account of the ornamentation or exalted form of that structure. Beyond the altar before which the child's bier is set, the only space in the minster that the Prioress encourages us to imagine is its floor. After the abbot removes the grain and the child perishes, the monk "fil al plat upon the grounde" (fell flatly on the ground, 7.632–35); the members of the convent follow suit, lying on the "pavement," where they emit tears that may signify relief as much as grief and devotion, as the abject presence finally leaves their church (7.677). The tale's persistent gaze on the minster's floor, the humble surface on which people travel and under which sewers circulate, seems to emphasize the status of the church as a structure sharing earthly and ordinary characteristics with other built environments of the medieval city, even its privies. Though the tale does not advocate the demolition of sacred space in favor of the simple structures espoused by ascetics like Bernard—Chaucer, after all, was no monk—the absence of a gaze heavenward at the conclusion of the *Prioress's Tale* may urge a more grounded approach to sacred space, a perspective that reflects the writer's fourteenth-century mercantile society and the economic aspects of the *Canterbury Tales*. The *Prioress's Tale* suggests how a minster may be most attractive—and is certainly most livable—not in its divine and miraculous guises but in its ties to the mundane realities of lived existence. When the boy is silenced and the Marian miracle ends, the minster is restored to its quotidian identity as a Christian edifice like the English minster cited by the Prioress at the end of her tale, Lincoln Cathedral, an all-too-human space sponsored by loans from the financier Aaron of Lincoln.

The entombment of the boy is instructive in this regard.[179] The tomb, like the sealed container of the boy's chaste corpse "sowded" (7.579) to virginity, demonstrates how a space imagined as wholly bounded and impermeable results in morbidity.[180] Livable space, on the other hand, requires apertures and access to flows. To be sure, the quotidian habitability and permeability of the minster in the *Prioress's Tale* are far from universal and hardly extend to Jews. To rethink the minster as a livable location is not to make a case for the humane treatment of Jews, as their final depiction in the tale makes clear. Horrifyingly disenfranchised of space, the Jews "That of this mordre wiste" (7.630) are "with wilde hors" (7.632) drawn through the streets of the city and then hanged.[181] In collapsing the pit/minster divide and exposing the "Jewish" materialism of Christian built environments, Chaucer does not celebrate Jews and their contributions to either the medieval economy overall or church-building programs in particular. Rather, the *Prioress's Tale* reveals how antisemitic fantasy played a pivotal role in the slow and contradictory process by which the English negotiated their relationship with an emerging mercantile culture. Through offensive ideas about the filthy and usurious Jew, the *Prioress's Tale* worries over the reality of urban commerce and its spatial manifestation. The tale vacillates between multiple and conflicting locations, sites imagined alternately as bounded and open, opposite and identical. Alongside and in fraught relation with the contaminating and contained latrine is an open city defined by commercial flows reaching even into the built environment of a minster.

# ❧ CHAPTER 4

# In the Shadow of Moyse's Hall

*Jews, the City, and Commerce in the*
*Croxton* Play of the Sacrament

Scholars have often understood the fifteenth
century as a time of commercial decline in England.[1] The truly decisive
developments in trade and exchange, so the received historical account goes,
occurred centuries earlier, in the 1200s.[2] Then, in the wake of famine, plague,
and other fourteenth-century crises, the English population decreased and
"the whole economy shrank."[3] The next century witnessed further contraction, as money declined in supply and usage.[4] However, such statistics hardly
mean late medieval England was a commercial backwater. As Christopher
Dyer stresses, the initial thirteenth-century commercial "sea-change" in England
was profound and lasting.[5] It created a market mentality and economic
practices that "seeped into every corner of society, involving smallholders
as well as the better off, and extended into every region."[6] A transformation that thorough could hardly be undone in subsequent centuries. And,
despite setbacks, "the market maintained a high level of activity" during the
late medieval period; for example, credit proved crucial for persons of all
ranks, from the peasant to the Crown.[7] Demographic changes prompted the
growth of a "mature urban system" that "was developing in sophistication
and adjusting to new economic influences."[8] One such development was the
commons' increased consumption of clothing, housing, goods, and services, a
change that resulted partly from increases in real wages and spending power.[9]
Concurrent with rising consumerism was a burgeoning mercantile estate.

English merchants, in fact, formed such an important—if shifting—group, that they served as the greatest nonagrarian employer on the island.[10]

Contemporary literary texts reveal a variety of responses to the rise of commerce. For example, the notably jingoistic and colonialist poem *The Libelle of Englyshe Polycye* (1437) celebrates trade. Stressing the key role of English goods and English waters in a trade network encompassing Flanders, Spain, Portugal, Brittany, Prussia, Venice, Florence, and other locales, the *Libelle* advocates an expansionist policy based on national control over the channel, adjacent waters, and nearby territories like Ireland.[11] While the *Libelle* trains its gaze on international trade, two coming-of-age poems, "The Merchant and His Son" and the closely related "The Childe of Bristowe," endorse mercantilism by focusing on an individual boy's actions.[12] In each text, commerce proves so appealing as to prompt a gentle-born youth to renounce his own corrupt estate and assume a life of "marchandise" in the commercial hub and port town of Bristol.[13] Of course, not all texts embraced commerce. "The Merchant and His Son" and "The Childe of Bristowe" respond to the long-standing idea, fostered by estates satire and other texts, that merchants are greedy, dishonest, proud, and ungodly.[14] That such a critical view persisted emerges in the ballad "London Lickpenny," which recounts a penniless rural man's "nightmare visit" to London.[15] While walking through Westminster into the City, past stalls and shops along Cheapside, Candlewick, Eastcheape, and Cornhill, the speaker finds London awash in buying and selling. Cooks, grocers, mercers, drapers, butchers, fishmongers, innkeepers, and other sellers call on the man to purchase goods and services, but, as the ballad's refrain iterates, "for lacke of money" he may observe but never participate in urban trade.[16] "Sore a-hungred," the starved man returns to Kent through a journey that seems at once an exile from material plenitude and an escape from grasping consumerism.[17]

Like "London Lickpenny," the text analyzed in this chapter, the East Anglian drama the Croxton *Play of the Sacrament* (hereafter Croxton), makes clear the ongoing status of commerce as a problem during the fifteenth century.[18] Croxton survives in single copy, Dublin, Trinity College, MS F.4.20, fols. 338–56. Though the copy was made during the sixteenth century and bound up in TCD MS F.4.20 in the seventeenth century, internal evidence indicates that the play was written as early as 1461.[19] Croxton explicitly concerns an antisemitic religious topic: the libel that Jews desecrate the Eucharist. But its interest in commerce is clear.[20] While in the analogues of the play, a poor Christian woman, often a maid, sells the host to a Jew, in Croxton, a wealthy Christian merchant named Aristorius procures and sells the wafer to a Jew called Jonathas.[21] Trade also frames Croxton. The play opens with

paired monologues, in which Aristorius boasts about his commercial practice and Jonathas brags about his many goods. And the drama ends with
Aristorius, newly penitent about his greedy desire to profit from an unholy
bargain, agreeing to never buy and sell again. Such aspects of the play rightly
have prompted one critic to characterize Croxton as a drama that "rereads"
its sources "through the lens of 15th-century commerce."[22]

Scholarly work on mercantilism and Croxton falls roughly into two
camps. One group of scholars stresses how the play critiques trade in a
manner supportive of Christian ideals. Situating Croxton in the burgeoning
commercialism of its regional milieu of East Anglia, Victor Scherb points to
the play's interest in how the profit motive opposes Christian charity and
how, in more general terms, "mercantilism and its attendant materialism
can erode religious life."[23] Such readings highlight how Croxton separates
religion from economics, a claim that emerges in Derrick Higginbotham's
recent essay on nationalism and the play, where he writes that the Christian
merchant "can operate as an exemplar of Christianity only when he *divorces
himself* from the deracinating effects of his trade and returns to his native
land, his 'nacione'" (my emphasis).[24]

The second, poststructural, critical camp queries whether Christianity
and a cash system are in fact separable. Often focusing on the doctrine of
transubstantiation and the workings of a paper economy, critics such as Alexandra Reid Schwartz, David Lawton, and, most recently, John Parker argue
that Croxton stages a disturbingly irresolvable slippage between economic
and religious systems.[25] In much of this work, the key to Croxton's yoking
of Christianity to commerce is its status as theater. An art form that trades
in trickery and deceit, drama depends—like money and the host—on believing in certain substitutions (e.g., an actor and his role, the wafer and Christ,
money and real value). Following Sarah Beckwith's groundbreaking work
on Croxton's extravagant theatricality, many of those critics stress how, far
from authorizing Christian thinking, Croxton is "haunted by" and even
"rejoices in" the illusory or counterfeit nature of its genre, Christianity, and
commerce.[26]

As this scholarship makes clear, the intersection of Christianity and commerce is a crucial aspect of Croxton. Why, though, does the play interrogate
that relationship through the accommodated Jew? The main character of
Croxton is Jonathas, and its central action occurs in his home. There, Jonathas and other Jews attack the Eucharistic host and, after a series of spectacular miracles, convert to Christianity. For some critics, Jonathas's Jewishness is
inconsequential to Croxton's interrogation of commerce. Stressing the similarities between Jonathas and Aristorius, they contend that the play doesn't

so much convey antisemitism as demonstrate how "a mercantile system" can "shape every aspect of medieval life in its own image."[27] Such readings imply that Jonathas represents not so much a particularly *Jewish* brand of otherness but rather a more broadly understood difference. From this perspective, Jonathas could easily be possessed of other alterities whether religious (e.g., Muslim, pagan, heretic) or ethnic (e.g., French, Flemish, Spanish, etc.). What matters is the fact that, whatever its particular nature, Jonathas's difference dissolves under the influence of commerce.

However, far from signifying as yet another alterity eroded by the medieval economy, Jonathas demonstrates the unique utility of the "Jew" as a construct through which the English responded to commerce as a problem.[28] As we saw in the last chapter, attending the advent of commerce were fantasies about its "Jewishness" that persisted in England well after 1290. Through images like the coin-worshipping Jews on the Hereford map, tales like Chaucer's story of Jewish usurers, and even the vernacular lexicon itself (where the word for Jews also meant moneylending), the English imagined the Jewish other as closely bound up with money, profit, and trade. As these examples attest, the English intertwined Jews and commerce, opposing both to ideas of Christian unity, purity, and spirituality.

But importantly, understood in terms of its spatial aspects, medieval English antisemitism emerges as a complex phenomenon that involves no easy projection of the profit motive onto Jews but rather a mapping of economic currents that alternately separate, yoke together, and even conflate Christian and Jew. The spatial messiness of these texts reveals the very trend stressed by critics like Lawton and Parker: the impossibility of creating a "pure" space of Christian practice devoid of trade. English antisemitic texts thus evince an irresolvable tension between disavowing and acknowledging Christian commercial practice, between endorsing the fantasy of the "Jewishness" of commerce and exposing how the "Jew" is a construct that enables the suppression and management of Christian carnality. Lurking behind the antisemitism in these trade-focused texts is this question: Is the greedy merchant always somehow "Jewish," or just a corrupt Christian?

Croxton occupies a pivotal place among such antisemitic English texts, thanks to its unprecedentedly explicit mapping of links between the "Jew" and Christian commerce.[29] A quick comparison of the plotting of Jew and Christian in Croxton and the *Prioress's Tale* indicates the relative openness with which the play addresses Christian commerce in and through imagined Jews. The Prioress overtly isolates Jewish usurers through both her tale's Eastern setting and the confining space of the privy; in tension with this narrative of projection and confinement is an implicit acknowledgment of

Christian ties to a "Jewish" usuriousness through the flow of the excrement-covered schoolboy from the privy to the minster. What Chaucer only hints at, Croxton foregrounds. Namely, the play opens by not only pairing Christian and Jewish merchants but also having the former actually welcome the latter into his home. When Aristorius opens his doors to Jonathas and sits down with him in his hall, Croxton manifests the fluid and overlapping relation between Christian and Jew as no previous English antisemitic text ever had done before. The oft-noted similitude and cordial relation between the two merchants doesn't concern commerce's erosion of all brands of alterity, but rather thematizes a relationship that had for centuries quietly informed antisemitic English literature: the doubling of carnal Jew and grasping Christian. Whether that doubling endorses the "Jewishness" of greed or exposes that notion as construct is a tension that informs the play throughout.

Amplifying the destabilizing aspects of Croxton's depiction of Jews and Christians is their manifestation through the spatial conventions of medieval theater. Croxton seems to fit the pattern of the open-air "place and scaffold" play.[30] That staging technique involved one or more loci—typically a scaffold or an elevated stage—referring to particular locations where action occurs. Croxton seems to involve three loci: Aristorius's home, where the two merchants bargain over the host; Jonathas's home, where he and other Jews attack the host; and a church to which a bishop returns the host. Those loci may have stood on a *platea* or flat open space where characters move between stages and at times engage in dramatic action. That staging technique would inevitably intensify whatever spatial fluidity and indeterminacy the play already contains. For example, Croxton not only foregrounds startling flows like the entry of a Jew into a Christian home, but constitutes those domestic sites through destabilizing spatial currents. The scaffolds denoting each home weren't bounded and discrete spaces but porous sites in and out of which players moved directly onto the larger terrain of a town, city, or rural area. That larger geographic milieu would have signified in relation to the play, lending weight to, complicating, and even questioning the notion of stable identities.

Theories on just where Croxton was staged are conjectural. As Gail McMurray Gibson acknowledges, "to seek to uncover the lost historical context of a medieval play" such as Croxton "is necessarily a search for plausibilities rather than certitudes."[31] But however speculative, considering where Croxton may have been performed is a valuable exercise, in no small part because of the dynamic relation between the play and its locale. By interpreting the play in tandem with a possible staging location we can generate telling speculations about the nature, function, and significance of *both* entities. Read in this light, the drama and the site of its performance relate to each other not only as "play" and "historical context" but also, dialogically, as dense and complex analogues. Thanks to the way that Croxton engaged and overlapped with the site of its performance, it produced that site as itself performative, as an entity that merits attention and interpretation. Viewed as analogues, play and place need not be historically aligned to speak productively to each other.

This chapter interprets Croxton alongside the "urban analogue" of late medieval Bury St. Edmunds, a Suffolk monastic town of some five-thousand persons.[32] Scholars including Gibson and Lisa Lampert-Weissig have considered aspects of Bury that would have supported Croxton's overt celebration of Christianity, and the antisemitism and antimercantilism it subtends.[33] But like the city spaces staged in Croxton, fifteenth-century Bury was fraught and contradictory.[34] At the same time that the monastic town enshrined Christian belief (and housed the relics of a national saint), it also manifested the striking commercial developments outlined at the start of this chapter. Like London, Norwich, and other English cities, Bury was a place where religious impulses collided and coincided with more secular, economic interests. Moreover, Bury contained architectural and infrastructural notions of the "Jew" that in many respects intensified the heterogeneous, shifting, and contradictory nature of the city. Bury, like other medieval cities of course, was awash in images of a dangerous Jewish other; the town not only proliferated in images of deicidal Jews at the Crucifixion but also it had its own boy martyr, Robert. But Bury also contained urban markers of Jewishness that spoke to its thriving commercialism. No urban building performed such a destabilizing function more than Moyse's Hall. Moyse's Hall was the greatest secular structure in Bury; it occupied the central marketplace of the town and had long-standing associations with Jewish wealth. What meanings would accrue both to Croxton and Bury were the play performed in the town's Great Market, in the shadow of Moyse's Hall? I argue that, yoked spatially to each other, both play and city would have offered viewers a disturbing contradiction: an overt and triumphant "enshrining" of "the values of Christian community," *and* an acknowledgement of the impossibility of maintaining firm boundaries between commerce and religion, Christian and Jew.[35]

## Croxton and the Christian Mapping of Bury

Like the *Prioress's Tale*, Croxton sets its action at a remove from England, in Spain. The Banns, or proclamations read before the play, claim that it stages events that took place in 1461, in the mythical location of Heraclea, "the famous city of Aragon" (11–12). Yet Croxton clearly responds to English issues and, even more precisely, is "pointedly East Anglian in its topography of mind and purpose."[36] Jonathas uses English currency, "an hundder pownd" (one hundred pounds, 315), to purchase the host. The Jewish merchant also hails from "Surrey" (19), which may mean Syria but also sounds like the southeastern English county. Finally, supposedly while in "Heraclea," Jonathas somehow manages to encounter a Flemish doctor, Master Brandyche, who lives "a lytyll besyde Babwell Myll" (near Babwell Mill, 621), located just north of Bury. Such details affirm how Croxton's Spanish setting is by no means straightforward but instead, in Elisabeth Dutton's words, "appears to be Eraclea in the Aragonese kingdom of Suffolk."[37]

An East Anglian staging would of course have rendered the English aspects of Croxton all the more resonant for audience members. The Banns' reference to a performance "at Croxston" confirms that it was performed at one of the many Croxtons in the area, most likely a village two miles from Thetford in Suffolk.[38] The Banns also indicate that the play toured, so "this was not an exclusively 'Croxton' play of the sacrament."[39] The likelihood that Croxton was performed also in Bury is suggested by references to both Babwell Mill and a tollhouse near the north gate of the city. Since David Bevington first postulated a performance in Bury, many scholars, among them Gibson, John Wasson, Beckwith, and Lampert-Weissig, have followed suit.[40]

Mindful of how a particular space in Bury might intersect with Croxton, Gibson has narrowed the possible location and timing of the play to the feast of Corpus Christi (celebrating the real presence of Christ in the Eucharistic wafer) and the market and fair area called Mustowe.[41] Mustowe, which consists today of Angel Hill and Mustow Street, was situated west of the walls of Bury St. Edmunds Abbey, and just northwest of St. James, a church in the abbey precincts (figure 16). Gibson stresses how staging Croxton in Mustowe would have enhanced its orthodox valences. She posits two scaffolds for Jonathas and Aristorius's houses and the use of St. James for the final action of the play. Shifting from fake sets to a bona fide holy structure, the play's overt message regarding transubstantiation and the "efficacy of the priesthood" would have culminated as "the host," whose embodiment of Christ was just miraculously displayed in Jonathas's home, "is borne in triumph, in a version of a Corpus Christi procession, from the playing area to a church and then to an altar" where the Jews "kneel in contrition."[42]

Gibson stresses how that orthodox message produced by both play and locale had little to do with Jews. Rather, following Cecelia Cutts's influential reading, Gibson sees Jonathas and his fellow Jews as thinly veiled Lollards, Christian heretics who queried such aspects of Christianity as the priesthood,

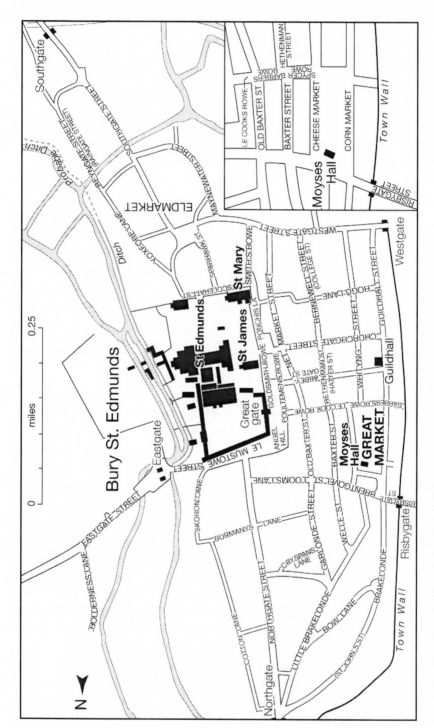

**FIGURE 16.** Map of Bury St. Edmunds. Map by Cath D'Alton. Adapted from Statham, *Book of Bury St. Edmunds*, 15.

pilgrimage, the sacraments, and especially the communion ritual and its attending doctrine of the real presence of Christ in the host.[43] By having Jonathas
first proclaim "familiar Lollard error" and then learn the "truth" of transubstantiation, Croxton "make[s] the opponents of Catholic Christianity witness
for the mysteries of the faith in spite of themselves."[44] Thus for Gibson—and
for many other readers who stress the anti-Lollard aspects of Croxton—in the
same way that the Aragon of the play isn't really Aragon but East Anglia, the
Jews of the play are not really Jews but Bury Lollards.[45]

While it's not clear that there were many Lollards living in late fifteenth-
century East Anglia, there is no question that in this pre-Reformation era
Christians had doubts about transubstantiation and other aspects of the
church.[46] But to read the Jew in Croxton only as a Lollard—or more broadly,
a generic Christian doubter—risks effacing antisemitism from the play.[47]
Similarly, by viewing the Jews of Croxton only as placeholders for Bury
Lollards and other Christian doubters, we elide the abiding presence of antisemitism in the town, where Jews were not merely present but "ubiquitous"
as imaginary or virtual constructs that the English had been invoking for
centuries.[48] In Bury and elsewhere, such antisemitic constructs ultimately
pertained to the Crucifixion and its image of Jews as Christ killers. Any
place where the passion was invoked and reimagined, whether through prayer,
ritual, or meditation, fostered the fantasy of a Jewish threat. In the many
churches of Bury, the events of the Mass prompted churchgoers to dwell
upon the Jews' purported role in Christ's death.[49] Beyond the Mass, depictions of the Crucifixion in texts, visual art, and/or sculpture contributed to
such a stereotype. For example, the famed Bury St. Edmunds cross, likely
located behind the main altar in the abbey church, promoted antisemitism
through features such as a side inscription stating that "the Jews laughed at
the pain of God dying."[50] And, as Anthony Bale has shown, because piety was
"part of the everyday devotion of the religious *milieu* of a fifteenth-century
household," not just churches, shrines, and chapels but homes were the site of
prayers and devotions fostering Christian antisemitism in Bury.[51]

The Crucifixion was made omnipresent to enrich devotion and enable
devotees to imagine Christ's suffering anew, in all places and with great
frequency. Such an effort, as Lampert-Weissig and Bale stress, made Christ's
suffering—and, by extension, Jewish aggression—eternal. Boy-martyr
and host-desecration libels only intensified this fantasy of the Jew as eternal
enemy of Christendom. The myth that contemporary Jews attack Christ-
like youths and Christ in the host suggested that all Jews wish to reenact their
ancestors' "crime." The latter fantasy flourished in East Anglia, due to not only the
cult of William of Norwich but also that of Little Robert of Bury, whom Jews

purportedly martyred in 1189. Family-centered, domestic practices fostered Robert's cult in Bury, as well as public locations such as the abbey and its chapel dedicated to the local boy martyr.[52] Both the cult of Little Robert and the overall devotion to the passion in Bury reveal a prominent antisemitic context for the host desecration staged by Croxton, suggesting how audience members would have understood Jonathas's attack on the host as demonstrating the ongoing aggression toward Christianity felt by all Jews.[53] Were Croxton performed in Bury, its staging of Jews desecrating the host would have participated in an antisemitic rezoning—a morphing of contemporary space into a virtual Calvary—that was happening everywhere in the city, from its churches during the Mass, to houses where residents prayed to Little Robert, or wherever a person might stop to contemplate a crucifix.

Indeed, Crucifixion devotion extended to the renowned and unique form of Bury's streets.[54] Two abbots, Baldwin (1065–97) and Anselm (1121–48), spearheaded what was *the* major Benedictine urban development of post-conquest England: the reorganization of Bury's layout according to a regular grid pattern based on root two (1: 2), and involving symmetrically placing pairs of streets at right angles to one main axis.[55] By aligning the prime axis of the city—Churchgate Street—with the axis of the abbey precinct (i.e., St. James Church and, east of that building, the abbey church), the abbots shaped Bury's topography in accordance to "cosmologically derived" notions of divine aesthetics and the primacy of Christianity in lived experience.[56] Insofar as the town's layout followed the monks' lead, the abbey quite literally determined the shape of everyday life in Bury. The right angles created by the east–west and north–south dimensions of the axes mapped out Christianity in their cruciform shape, which duplicated that of the abbey church and St. James.[57] The very organization of Bury's streets made present for town residents the pivotal event of the Crucifixion and, by implication, the concept of the deicidal Jew.[58]

## Mapping Commerce in Bury

But Bury was hardly a homogeneous location.[59] Commercial elements mingled alongside and even merged with the religious aspects of the city. Indeed, during a time of national economic contraction, Bury seems to have thrived, largely due to its role as a "major component in the south Suffolk cloth industry, which flourished in the Stour River Valley in the fifteenth and sixteenth centuries."[60] A key market center for the sale of finished cloth and other goods, Bury drew to itself, in Robert Gottfried's words, "not only local folk, but merchants from London, Norwich, King's Lynn, Great Yarmouth, and aliens from the Low Countries, Germany, and northern Italy."[61] In Bury, "devotion" to commerce was as omnipresent as devotion to the Crucifixion.

A closer look at Bury's grid layout affirms its shaping by both religious and economic forces. For example, while one of the city's prime axes (now Abbeygate Street), affirmed the primacy of Christianity by forming a focal point at its west end, where it joined the Great Gate of the abbey, the thoroughfare also served as "the main shopping street of the town."[62] The multiple names given to various sections of Abbeygate during the Middle Ages demonstrate its commercial use: moving west from the Great Gate, shoppers would pass through first Le Cook Rowe, then Barbour Rowe, and Spycer Rowe.[63] In conjunction with this axis stretching from the monastic precinct, Bury's economic bent emerged on streets along the northern, western, and southern borders of the abbey (i.e., every side of the precinct bordering the city itself). North of the abbey lay Eastgate Ward, where blacksmiths occupied Mustowe and the annual fair was held "just outside the abbey's walls and main gates" on the square.[64] Outside the western walls of the abbey, on either side of St. James, were (moving north to south) le Goverisrowe, Goldsmith's Street, and Smith's Row.[65] Directly south of the precinct was Southgate Ward, where commerce had thrived since preconquest times.[66] Goldsmiths, blacksmiths, fullers, and launderers were among the laborers who sold their goods and services there.[67]

The most important indicator of medieval Bury's market orientation was its designated marketplace, located east of what is now Cornhill, where the westernmost portion of Abbeygate (the medieval Spycer Rowe) led (figure 17).[68] Once established, this site became "the most striking feature about the 'new' Bury" and was noteworthy nationally as one of the two "great rectangular market places" in England.[69] A site whose very name proclaimed its importance, the Great Market rightly has been called "enormous" and "monumental in scale" by scholars: it took up a far larger space than the previous market and stretched some 350 feet from east to west and approximately 1/8 mile (or almost 700 feet) from north to south.[70] Occupying the edges of this ample square were, at various times during the late Middle Ages, a host of laborers, goods, services, and sellers: linendrapers, mercers, and spicers on the east, tanners and skinners on the north, ironmongers and a cornmarket on the west, and fishmongers on the south.[71] Inside the market was the tollhouse, where "the borough's bailiffs supervised the volume and quality of goods traded and collected their tolls," and multiple smaller markets consisting of rows of stalls.[72] The Great Market, in fact, was literally surrounded by businesses: "Of all the major merchants in Bury," Gottfried writes, "only the goldsmiths had their shops more than a few yards away."[73]

**FIGURE 17.** Moyse's Hall and Buttermarket, ca. 1879–88. Spanton Jarman Collection K505/0099. Reproduced by permission of the Bury St Edmunds Past and Present Society (Spanton Jarman Collection K505/0099).

The commerce around the abbey's borders, extending out westward on Abbeygate into the Great Market, affirms how Bury was organized not only to praise the Christian God but also to generate financial profit for its residents. The question of how those secular and religious elements intersected leads to no easy answers. The precise nature of the relationship between commerce and piety in the city was complex and fraught. From a theological perspective, the market—with its stress on material acquisition and profit—opposed the Christian virtues of spirituality, otherworldliness, and sacrifice. The spiritual dangers posed by Bury's commercial elements emerge in a ca. 1130–50 sculpture that originally formed part of a frieze on the West Front of the abbey church. The stone carving, called the *Doom*, portrays two demons pushing a writhing usurer into the mouth of hell; the man dons only a moneybag, and snakes bite at his genitals.[74] Through its portrayal of the doom that greedy sinners faced, the sculpture provided residents with a horrifying account of how a money economy opposed Christianity.

And yet, in practice, money hardly was divorced from Christian life. For example, Anselm, the same abbot who helped establish Bury's grid layout, also "had the right to hold a market confirmed and acquired the right to hold a fair."[75] The abbey, a massive property owner in Bury and the greater West

Suffolk region, profited from the rents it charged to burgesses.[76] Within the
marketplace, "not only did the abbey collect ground rents . . . on properties,
but . . . also took a second share on any wealth gained through commerce or
industry" via tolls and taxes.[77] The monks also were in the business of making money, through their supervision of a royal mint from the late tenth to
the fourteenth centuries.[78] Over the medieval period, when Bury merchants
and burgesses sought independence from the abbey and even endeavored to
create a secular corporation, monks actively defended and maintained their
powers over the city and the financial benefits associated with those rights.[79]
Such phenomena suggest the hypocritical nature of the *Doom* sculpture, situated as it was on the front of the church of an abbey whose residents were
immersed in materialism and commerce.

For lay residents, the message of the *Doom* was even more pressing. During
the fifteenth century, "virtually every major merchant in the borough" was a
moneylender; "indeed," Gottfried writes, "one of the distinguishing features
of Bury's mercantile elite was their role as financiers."[80] Probably due to
both troubled consciences and status consciousness, the spoils of commerce
spilled into Bury churches through other means than the monks' taxes. Merchants donated ample funds for church-building programs throughout East
Anglia. Still extant in St. Mary's Church, a block south of St. James, is one
of "two porches built in . . . honor" of Bury merchant John Nottingham,
who donated funds to rebuild the church after a fire during the fifteenth
century.[81] That example was hardly unique but instead reflects a general
trend in East Anglia, where the lucrative cloth trade played such a key role in
ecclesiastical building programs that residents came to refer to them as "wool
churches."[82] The term "wool churches" demonstrates the deep complexity and confused nature of the church–market relationship, which ranged
in Bury from the Christian demonization of trade, to merchants' attempts
to put their money to pious ends, and religious officials' efforts to swell the
coffers of the church.[83]

The key role of the "Jew" in managing the messy and even incoherent
relation between commerce and piety in Bury emerges when we return to
the *Doom*. While the carving is too severely eroded to allow for precise identification, the condemned man very likely was a Jew, given the fact that "a
moneybag is second only to the pointed hats and stereotyped physiognomi-
cal features as the most common attribute of a Jew in medieval art."[84] If the
*Doom* depicted a Jew, it provided residents with a means of disentangling
Christianity from the commercial aspects of Bury, by suggesting the inherent "Jewishness" of a money economy and its profit motive. Commerce, the
*Doom* may have implied, isn't really a Christian problem but instead is other

to Christian society in the manner of the Jew. Christian financiers in effect renounce their religion and embrace "Jewish" greed.

Antisemitic images like the *Doom* also would have provided late medieval Bury residents with an offensive hermeneutic for aspects of the city that recalled its former Jewish inhabitants. For a little over thirty years, during the second half of the twelfth century, Jews lived in Bury.[85] Then, in 1190, not long after the string of pogroms that began during Richard I's coronation and spread throughout England, a "pioneering and bloody expulsion" of the Jews of Bury occurred, one hundred years ahead of the national exile in 1290.[86] Members of the Bury Anglo-Jewry most likely inhabited a thoroughfare known during the late Middle Ages as Hethenmannestrete. Now part of Hatter Street, Hethenmannestrete ran parallel to the western wall of the precinct and traversed the two major axes of the city, Abbeygate and Churchgate. Hethenmannestrete thus was a key element of the town's grid design (figure 16).[87] The carving of the doomed Jewish moneylender on the front of the abbey church would have fostered an understanding of Hethenmannestrete as an example of how, when Jews entered Bury, they brought into the town—indeed, into Bury's very urban core—a damnable, and damnably "Jewish," commercialism and profit-mindedness. Hethenmannestrete supported that reading; the idea that Jews were materialists who "worshipped" money (cf. the Jews on the Hereford world map) complemented their status as *hethenes* or pagans. Further support for the link between Jews and sinful materialism was the nearness—just a block away—of the Jewry to the Great Market. The physical proximity of Hethenmannestrete to the market, of course, reflects the historical fact that many Bury Jews gained their livelihood from commerce. What I want to stress, however, is how Christian thinking like that presented in the *Doom* carving overlaid—or, better, replaced—historical reality with antisemitic fantasy: the idea that Jews were inherently connected to a sinful materialism that flourished in the marketplace.

However, the physical urban infrastructure of Bury not only supported but also troubled fantasies about the "Jewishness" of greed. For one thing, consider the irony of the location of Hethenmannestrete. Because the thoroughfare occupied a key north–south axis in Bury, the very street memorializing the "hethene" or pagan practices of "idolatrous" Jews paradoxically helped articulate the cruciform geometry of the city. Equally destabilizing is how the nearness of the Great Market to the Jewry suggests a more dialectical relation between the two sites than the *Doom* sculpture allows. That is, the spatial contiguity of the Jewry and market—as well as the sheer preponderance of Christians in the market—created a tension between the fantasy of the inherent "Jewishness" of commerce and the fact that Bury Christians were themselves deeply immersed in mercantile practices.

The image of the Jew connoted by Bury's complex urban topography complicates the account of the city's antisemitic practice as described by Lampert-Weissig and Bale. While the "Jew" generated via passion devotion is the great eternal and omnipresent "other," the "Jew" generated by economic antisemitism is a more slippery entity. To be sure, at times the stereotype of the greedy Jew returns us to the passion story. For example, medieval representations of Judas—the man who "sold" Christ for thirty pieces of silver—"conflate contemporary social tensions with the historical circumstances of Christ's passion."[88] But clearly this is not the whole story regarding antisemitic notions of "Jewish" commerce, which engage not only the Crucifixion but also a profit-minded medieval society. When viewed in light of their relation to new market forces, Jews aren't simply other to Christians, but are also like Christians. Understood in relation to the tangled mapping of profit and piety in a city like Bury, the offensive image of the greedy Jew shifts between serving as Christianity's other and its double.

## The "Jew" and the Treasure in Moyse's Hall

By far the most provocative intersection of Christians, Jews and, commerce in Bury emerges in *the* major secular building of the city, Moyse's Hall (figure 17).[89] Now a museum located at the northeastern corner of the Great Market (figure 16), Moyse's Hall is the oldest standing building in Bury and the oldest home in Suffolk.[90] Built ca. 1180, and composed of flint rubble dressed with stone, Moyse's Hall consists of two stories of nearly square fifty-by-fifty-feet floors. While a tradition dating at least back to 1768 claimed that the structure originally served as a synagogue, recent scholarship identifies the building as an important example of a "first-floor 'hall-and-solar' type" of Norman house.[91] The ground floor, the most impressive space in the building, divides into two rectangular rooms featuring separate sets of vaulting. The larger room, consuming over half the eastern side of the floor, opens onto the square and likely served as a shop. It features two aisles of three square bays of stone vaulting, consisting of mid- to late twelfth-century Gothic arches supported by two simply made Norman responds or columns. The smaller, western, section features three oblong bays of groined stone vaulting supported by mid-twelfth-century Romanesque arches. Apparently devoid of windows for security purposes, the room probably was used for storage. The first floor of Moyse's Hall, not directly accessible by the street, has a spacious main hall that probably was heated by a large fireplace.[92] The hall retains its original twelfth-century Romanesque windows. Before each window are two stone window-seats, featuring rolled edges and foot rests. On the exterior of the building, two stone arches surround those rectangular windows.[93] West of the hall is a smaller room that probably was used as a solar or bedding chamber. On the ground and first floors, behind the hall and undercroft, were possibly two additional chambers, though nothing remains of these rooms.[94]

During the fifteenth century, the King family owned Moyse's Hall. An eminent Bury household, the Kings lived on the upper floor of Moyse's Hall and leased the lower floor for multiple business ends, including a tavern and inn.[95] But—as the traditional identification of the building as a synagogue attests—Moyse's Hall originally may have been owned by Jews. The possible Jewish associations of Moyse's Hall were hotly debated during the late nineteenth century, when Rabbi Hermann Gollancz published an article opposing a plan to use the building as a fire station.[96] While Gollancz argued that Moyse's Hall was a synagogue, the argument that ultimately prevailed during that original debate was that of photographer Frank Haes. Haes claimed that, on the one hand, given the antisemitism present in Bury, no Jew would have dared lived in such a prominent building outside the Jewry, and, on the other hand, that "Moyse" was a common Suffolk Christian name.[97] Versions of Haes's argument persisted in subsequent discussions, most notably by Gottfried, who in his 1982 book stressed how the location and name of the building imply a Christian occupant and owner.[98] The fact that a recent reference book on medieval Anglo-Jews claims that the building was Christian demonstrates the persistence of this argument and may even suggest that the case is closed on the question of Moyse's Hall's Jewish connections.[99]

The fact remains, however, that arguments against and for the Jewishness of Moyse's Hall are not definitive. The debate is not over. For example, consider the tenuous nature of Gottfried's claim that "it is unlikely that a Jew ever lived" in Moyse's Hall, because it is "a few blocks . . . outside the ghetto" on Hethenmannesstrete.[100] But Jews in medieval England lived in neither walled ghettoes nor homogeneously Jewish locations. The location of Moyse's Hall, in fact, actually conforms to East Anglian patterns of Jewish habitation. As noted in chapter 2, Jews in Norwich not only had Christian neighbors but also lived well beyond the Jewry. The still extant home of Isaac fil Jurnet, another two-story twelfth-century stone dwelling, was located on King Street some five hundred meters southeast of the Norwich Jewry, and thus at a much farther remove than Moyse's Hall was from Hethenmannesstrete.[101] Moreover, the placement of Moyse's Hall directly on the Great Market, a locale that offered, even more than Hethenmannesstrete, "a first-class trading position," parallels the tendency of East Anglian Jews to live near markets.[102] Jews in Norwich lived in homes "near to the wheatmarket, the sheepmarket, and the horsemarket. Thus they were in the midst of the most populous part of the city."[103]

Like claims about location, those centered on names are not definitive. The earliest reference to the building as Moyse's Hall is a 1328 entry in the *Chronicles* of St. Edmund's Abbey, which describes how rioters "hastened to Moyse's Hall (*ad aulam Moysii*)."[104] As Edgar Samuel points out, the debate over naming centers on whether "ad aulam Moysii" refers to the common Suffolk surname of Moyse, the relatively uncommon Christian first name Moses, or the widely used Jewish first name of Moses.[105] Through his comparison of the sounding of Latin versions of both the surname "Moyse" and Hebrew Mosheh (Mosse in English), Samuel makes the provocative claim that the Latin reference in the chronicle "strongly hints at" the first name of a Jew.[106]

We have no hard evidence identifying Moyse's Hall with either a Christian or Jewish owner during the time of its construction in the twelfth century. Yet a more pertinent question for our purposes is not so much whether Jews actually lived in Moyse's Hall but if the fifteenth-century residents of Bury associated Jews with the building. Evidence of such a connection appears in a 1499 entry in the register of Cardinal and Archbishop of Canterbury John Morton (ca. 1420–1500). After Norwich bishop James Goldwell died in 1499, Morton administered the diocese *sede vacante*. Morton commissioned John Vaughan, D.C.L., to visit the Suffolk archdeaconry during this brief period; after a whirlwind visitation, Vaughan presided at court sessions, "where he heard the confessions or pleas of those whose sins had been reported to him during the visitation."[107] One such session, on 17 June 1499 in Ixworth Parish church, involved reports that "Marion Clerk, daughter of John and Agnes Clerk," engaged in various superstitious acts including healing, prophesying, and "revealing the whereabouts of hidden treasures."[108] A girl from Great Ashfield, about five miles east of Bury St. Edmunds, Clerk confessed to the charges regarding her abilities, which she claimed she acquired "from God and the Blessed Virgin and from the gracious fairies."[109] Clerk went on to elaborate on her occult skills, including her knowledge of "a hidden treasure in a place in Bury called 'Moises Halle' and that the Jews had custody of this treasure."[110] By means of a holly stick blessed by a local curate, Clerk said that she "would without doubt find hidden treasures, to wit a very valuable silver cross, a chalice and gold in great quantities."[111]

Clerk's testimony suggests that not only was Moyse's Hall associated with Jews during the time of Croxton's production, but also such links were so widespread as to circulate in the realm of folklore, and in a geographic area beyond the immediate confines of Bury, in the suburban village of Great Ashfield. Moreover, and in keeping with the building's location on the Great Market, Clerk's testimony links Moyse's Hall not to the deicidal Jews of Bury's Christian imaginary but to wealth, magic, and secrecy. The cross and chalice listed by Clerk do point to the Crucifixion, of course. But what Clerk stresses is how those items are material treasure; the cross is "very valuable" and part of a general hoard of precious goods including "gold in great quantities."[112] By identifying the hoard as "hidden," and presumably buried by Jews, Clerk's testimony resonates with the secrecy stereotypically applied to Jewish menace, witnessed in England as early as Thomas of Monmouth's myth of William's martyrdom. But here, lurking in a Jewish building is not anti-Christian violence, but material fortune. Moyse's Hall, as portrayed by Clerk, thus looks toward the home of Marlowe's Barabas, where, beneath a floor plank on its second story, the merchant has hidden "gold and jewels," and even, much later, Fagin's secreted watches and gems.[113] The notion of the hoarding Jew combines in Clerk's testimony with another concept, articulated by English writers such as Chaucer and Gower, of Jews' affinity for magic.[114] By claiming that Jews, despite their physical exile from Bury, nevertheless serve as guardians for the buried treasure in Moyse's Hall, Clerk attributes to Jews a certain mystical power over wealth.

If Clerk's testimony reflects widespread ideas, it radically alters our understanding of the already fraught topography of Bury. In Bury St. Edmunds, it seems, antisemitic fantasy not only made Jews virtually present as deicidal others, but also promulgated the idea of a magical Jewish presence tied to a particular building and its hidden treasure. A kind of fissure along Bury's Christian grid layout, Moyse's Hall challenges the idea that all Jews want to kill Christ—the building had no associations with ritual murder or host desecration—and replaces it with a notion of Jewish financial know-how. Images like the *Doom*, of course, also associate the Jew with money. But while the *Doom* viciously damns "Jewish" greed, Moyse's Hall speaks to a Christian fascination and wonder over hidden treasure and its mystical Jewish management. Moyse's Hall doesn't so much demonize the powerful and magical relation to wealth it ascribes to Jews as admit a Christian desire for that privileged material plenitude.

The greatest secular building in Bury, Moyse's Hall was no understated sign of Jewishness and wealth. The challenge it posed to stereotypes about demonized Jews and pious Christians was nothing less than monumental. In the Great Market where Moyse's Hall was situated, there also stood a basic stone cross. The market cross not only recalled the Crucifixion and its accompanying idea of Jewish persecutors, but also suggested how trade could somehow accommodate Christian virtues, and that Christ protected merchants.[115] Yet Moyse's Hall, to all intents and purposes, dominated the area, dwarfing the modest cross. Looming over and thus in a sense defining the square, Moyse's Hall served as an icon of Christian devotion to not God but money. And of course the market, with its proliferation of traders and goods, only confirmed that message. The Great Market served, as Gottfried stresses, as the secular counterpoint to Mustowe. The establishment of the two squares in Bury "took inspiration from an old merchant adage of two squares, one for God and one for commerce."[116]

The preponderance of money and goods circulating just outside the doors of Moyse's Hall went far in undermining the divide between those Jewish and Christian spaces. What separated Moyse's Hall from its immediate milieu wasn't so much its materialism as the fantasy of a mystical Jewish control over secret wealth. We might say, then, that Moyse's Hall functioned in Bury somewhat like a Christian church. Both sites contained hidden precious goods: buried treasure in Moyse's Hall and Christ's occult presence in the host. In somewhat the same way that a priest supposedly had the mystical power—as God's medium—over the divinity inside the host, Jews were thought to enjoy magical control over the wealth secreted in Moyse's Hall. I'm aware here of the slippage between objects hidden in an edifice and God hidden in an object. But I would posit nevertheless that at some level the mystery of Moyse's Hall and that of the host are analogous and productively comparable.

Croxton points to an even tighter relation between Christ in the host and treasure in a Jewish hall. As a host-desecration drama, the play stages a version of the widespread Christian idea that Jews aggressively and violently teased out the material secrets lurking inside the Eucharistic wafer. What then, if Croxton were staged not, as Gibson and other critics have suggested, in Mustowe, the square dedicated to God, but in Bury's "other" square, the Great Market? How would the commercial thrust of the Great Market and the mystical materialism of Moyse's Hall intersect with the instabilities immanent in the play? What might be the impact of staging Jonathas's interrogation of the host in the shadow of a great building where Jews supposedly controlled precious goods? Performed in this context, what secret relations—that is, relations pertaining to Bury's commercial bent—might emerge in the play, beyond its orthodox discovery of priestly authority?

## Staging Commerce in Croxton

Croxton opens by highlighting the prominence of commerce in the late medieval world. To be sure, Aristorius in his opening monologue first stresses not goods, but God. "Cryst that ys our Creatour," Aristorius proclaims,

"He maynteyn us with myrth that meve upon the mold" (Christ our Creator . . . sustains us with joy who move upon the earth, 81–82).[117] Yet, like "the boasting speeches of tyrants elsewhere in medieval drama," Aristorius ultimately seems more interested in the shaping presence on earth of not God but himself, "a merchante most might[y]" (85).[118] Aristorius nominally attributes his commercial power to the God who "maynteyn[s]" or sustains him (82); but the fact that he calls himself mighty no less than three times in the space of six lines suggests otherwise (85, 87, 90).[119] The merchant clarifies the geographic nature of his might as he devotes twenty lines to cataloging the sites "thorowght" (throughout) "all this world" where he both sets his "sale" (sail) and makes sales (116).[120] Aristorius's global ambitions are such that he even views entire countries as potential commodities; "wer a countré to by" (were a country up for sale), the merchant boasts, he wouldn't hesitate to purchase it (88).

Aristorius cites locales in Europe and Asia that reflect the presence of a world economic system during this period.[121] Bury merchants, like traders throughout England, hardly dominated that global network in the manner of Aristorius.[122] Yet, from the late fourteenth-century onward, they did at least participate in the world trade system, primarily by selling finished cloth overseas in "a Channel commercial sphere that included eastern England, the Low Countries and northwestern France."[123] Merchants from France, Brabant, Flanders, and other sites also came to Bury to purchase cloth and other goods.[124] Because Aristorius's speech includes many of those sites as well as "Brytayn" (Britain), it may have reminded spectators watching Croxton in the Great Market of both the world economic system he describes and their own association with it.[125] A performance in the Great Market might have made such connection explicit if an actor picked up a foodstuff or other good sold by a nearby vendor while speaking the line—"in Brytayn I am full bold" (I am very powerful in Britain, 98)—that directly implicates Bury in the commercial world Aristorius describes.

If "London Lickpenny" is any indication, the Great Market was filled with the sight of stalls, booths, and shops; the sounds of butter merchants, poultry traders, grain sellers, and other providers of goods and services hawking their wares; and the aromas of cheese, fowl, meats, tanned leather, and other goods. Such a display of carnal appetites and needs could have worked in tandem with the account of global trade described by Aristorius to query orthodox Christian mappings of space. As we have seen, elements like Bury's grid layout, by evincing an urban version of the divine ordering portrayed by *mappae mundi*, endorsed the unity of the Christian macrocosm and microcosm. But even on a non-market day, the Great Market was bursting not so much with God-centered but commerce-centered activity.[126] Working in tandem with Aristorius's opening lines, the sights, sounds, and smells of the market would have replaced the ideal unity of a divinely ordered world with its economic other: the repetition at global and urban scales of commercial flows.

In Aristorius's monologue, one word in particular might have registered for audience members the destabilizing influence of commerce in the world: the verb *rennen*. Before cataloging the sites where he trades, the merchant boasts that "In all maner of londys, without ony naye, / My merchaundyse renneth, the sothe for to telle" (In all kinds of lands, no one can deny / My merchandise runs, to tell the truth, 93–94). By foregrounding how his goods "renneth," the merchant employs a verb with disruptive spatial resonances. In addition to referring to the circulation of money and merchandise, *rennen* signifies various kinds of spatial flows, extensions, and revolutions, from the rolling of dice to the growth of a plant. In the context of Croxton and a Bury performance, the most resonant and jarring definition of *rennen* is the flow of a liquid, like water, oil, or mercury.[127] The idea that Aristorius's merchandise runs like water creates a spatial relation that is utterly dissimilar to the divine order depicted in medieval world maps and city plans. Unlike the straight lines and right angles of Bury's grid layout—or the global schema of T-O maps—liquid commerce spreads in all directions, disregarding and moreover eroding borders and divisions.

The flow of Aristorius's trade is such that it spills into Christendom's most sanctified spaces. When, for example, the merchant states "in Rome to Seynt Petyrs temple, / I am knowen certenly for bying and sellyng" (107–8), he situates commerce at the center of the medieval church, undermining the ostensible division between piety and profit. The merchant's reference to Old Saint Peter's basilica as a "temple" suggests how commerce erodes the Christian nature of the building. As a "temple," Saint Peters is less a site for the worship of the Christian God than, in keeping with the primary meaning of the Middle English word, idolatrous materialism in the form of trade.[128] As the play continues, it becomes clear how Christian mercantilism flourishes not only in Rome, but also in Aristorius's immediate milieu, where, seeking profit, he both controls his priest Isidore's movements and puts the host into circulation in the local economy.[129] While the merchant's sale of the host undoubtedly would have shocked many audience members, his sway over Isidore may not have, since Bury's most prominent merchants had chantry priests who served them.[130]

Importantly, of non-Christians, only Jews are included in Aristorius's trade. In a passage that adumbrates the key action of the drama, he boasts of his fame as a trader in "Jerusalem and in Jherico among the Jewes jentle" (105). The merchant's interaction with the Middle Eastern merchants breaches the line between Christian and Jew, a transgression intensified by Aristorius calling the Jews "jentle."[131] Beyond a desire to alliterate, the Croxton author may use "jentle" to generate a slew of contradictory ideas, all of which break down some kind of identificatory division: that the mercantile Jew is a non-Jew or gentile; that this usually debased other is of noble or gentle rank; and that the Jew exhibits gracious or gentle manners despite his stereotypical demonization. Regardless of the various valences of "jentle" at play in the passage, the line overall indicates how Aristorius's global trade, far from confirming ideas of Jewish alterity and separation, entails a certain openness to and familiarity with the "Jew."[132]

Further evidence of that openness emerges once Aristorius's monologue ends, when he instructs his clerk Peter Paul to search along the shore of Heraclea for news that "ony merchaunte be come to this reyn / Of Surrey or of Sabé or of Shelysdown" (any merchant has come to this realm / from Syria, or Saba or Chalcedon, 139–40). The eastern sites listed by Aristorius suggest how he intentionally "dispatches his servant to seek out the newly arrived Jewish merchants so that he might go so far as to welcome them into his home."[133] The status of the Jew in Croxton as an attractive, highly desired figure receives more confirmation when, a bit later in the play, we learn that Aristorius and Jonathas have known each other and traded prior to meeting about the host.[134] This is not to suggest that Croxton necessarily portrays Christian merchants as philosemitic, but that Aristorius's use of "jentle" in his opening monologue indicates his canny and calculated interest in Jews for purposes of profit.

The precise nature of the Jew's commercial allure becomes clearer when Jonathas, the "chefe merchaunte of Jewes" (chief merchant of the Jews, 196), performs his opening monologue. While Aristorious cataloged the global sites linked to his commercial practices, his Jewish counterpart offers an inventory of the precious goods in which he trades. In addition to gold and silver, Jonathas has an array of both "presyous stonys" (precious stones, 158), including diamonds, emeralds, pearls, sapphires, rubies, and amethysts, and an "abu[n]ddaunce of spycys" (an abundance of spices, 159), and exotic foods, such as ginger, cloves, oranges, and figs. Were this monologue listing Jonathas's goods performed in the scaffold denoting the Jew's house, the play would have departed from the usual mapping of "Jew" and "Christian" in English antisemitic texts. In ritual murder libels, Jews evince their hatred of Christianity by murdering boys in their houses and other private locations, while Christians demonstrate their piety by publically worshipping those "martyrs," who are often portrayed as metaphorical wealth: for example, Thomas of Monmouth repeatedly refers to William of Norwich as an *egregium thesaurum* or excellent treasure and the Prioress hails the schoolboy as a "gemme" and "emeraude" (emerald) of chastity, as well as a "ruby bright" of martyrdom. But the opening of Croxton complicates such associations by staging not the Jews' abuse of symbolic treasures like a boy martyr or Christ in the Host, but rather his love of literal goods.

Were Croxton performed in Mustowe, near St. James church, Jonathas's embrace of wealth would likely have supported stereotypes about the Jews' sinful carnality. A performance in the Great Market, in the shadow of Moyse's Hall, however, might have exposed a rather different English relationship to goods. For in the same way that Marion Clerk associates Jews with "gold in great quantities" and other "treasure" in Moyse's Hall, Croxton links Jonathas to "gold, sylver," and a host of other precious goods (158). If the actor playing Jonathas performed his lines on the scaffold denoting his home, the links between this moment in the play and Moyse's Hall would have been all the more resonant. Croxton is famous for the outrageous special effects that occur later in the drama, when, for example, an oven explodes to reveal a profusely bleeding Christ child. But maybe this early staging of Jonathas's speech is the play's first special effect. By staging the play near Moyse's Hall and depicting—perhaps spectacularly, if fake diamonds, gold, and other props were used—Jonathas's treasure-filled home, the play may have fulfilled Bury residents' desire to seek out, discover, and gaze on a "Jewish treasure" akin to that imagined to lurk inside the massive built environment looming over the Great Market. This scene thus might have yoked together two kinds of medieval "magic": folk notions of an occult Jewish control over buried treasure, and the theatrical tricks used by the medieval Christian stage. Like the holly stick that Marion Clerk intended to use as a divining rod, Croxton conjures the profane allure of the "Jew" in a commercialized Christian milieu present both in the Great Market and in the character of Aristorius.[135] Staged in the Great Market, this scene would have adumbrated Marlowe's proto-Marxist image of Barabas, "whose pursuit of wealth," in Stephen Greenblatt's formulation, "does not mark him out but rather establishes him—if anything, rather respectably—in the midst of all the other forces in the play."[136]

Only after it stages Jonathas's profane allure does Croxton turn to its thematic focus on host desecration. Interestingly, though, Jonathas doesn't conform to classic religious stereotypes. Jonathas's servants, to be sure, voice their desire to "be wreke" (be avenged [upon], 212) and "to bete byggly" (beat vigorously, 219) Christ in the form of the wafer. However, when

Jonathas introduces the topic of transubstantiation, his words hardly suggest deicide:

> The beleve of thes Cristen men ys false, as I wene,
> For they beleve on a cake—me thynk yt ys onkynd,
> And all they seye how the prest dothe yt bynd,
> And be the myght of hys word make yt flessh and blode,
> And thus be a conceyte they wolde make us blynd,
> And how that yt should be He that deyed upon the Rode.
>
> *(199–204)*

> [The belief of the Christian men is false, as I suppose,
> For they believe in a cake, which I think is unnatural,
> And all of them say how the priest conjures it,
> And by the might of his word transforms it into flesh and blood
> And thus by a trick they would make us blind
> And [make us believe] that it should be he that died on the cross.]

Jonathas doesn't attack Christ but instead queries the doctrine of transubstantiation and its claims about priestly authority. While his doubts echo Lollard critiques, they also engage and revise stereotypes about Jews. Christians had long claimed that Jewish unbelievers had a mental incapacity—an irrational "blindness"—that prevented them from seeing the truth of Christianity. Jonathas, however, attaches blindness to anyone who believes in transubstantiation. While the Eucharist is just a "cake" or inanimate wafer, the church "wold make us blynd" (would make us blind) to that reality "be a conceyte" (through a trick), that is, the ritual of the sacrament.[137] Turning the tables on stereotypes of Jewish incapacity and Christian revelation, Jonathas exhibits a skepticism that resonates with the lengthy—almost forty-line—disquisition on wealth that precedes this moment. In other words, with his querying of the actual value of the Eucharistic wafer, Jonathas seems less the deicidal or blindly unbelieving Jew than a clear-headed and successful merchant pondering whether he should include the host among his collection of precious goods.[138]

## Bourgeois Domesticity and Croxton

Jonathas goes on to confirm his mercantile stance toward transubstantiation when he tells his Jewish colleagues that he plans to acquire "the cake" by going "to see Arystories hall," where he will make a "bargayn wyth hym"

(223–28). This is precisely what happens next, in a scene that enacts an important staging shift from the scaffold depicting the Jewish home to that of the Christian domicile. By turning audience attention to Aristorius's home, a Croxton performance in the Great Market would have fostered a new dynamic between the spaces of the play and its greater urban environs. That is, while Jonathas's scaffold may have signified in relation to Moyse's Hall, Aristorius's scaffold likely would have accrued meaning through its interaction with other buildings, namely the many Christian homes on the square and its immediate environs in Risbygate Ward.[139]

Recent work on what Felicity Riddy calls medieval "burgeis" domesticity provides an important context for unpacking the possible meanings that would have accrued from such an interaction between Croxton and Bury houses.[140] After "the great transformation in urban building" during the twelfth and thirteenth centuries, the ideal of the pious household loomed large in England, narrowing "the distance between the domestic and the holy within bourgeois culture."[141] Reflecting the consumerism that shaped and fueled the fifteenth-century economy, household goods played a key role in that domestic piety, and often circulated between domestic and religious built environments.[142] Goldberg describes how bourgeois "homes contained religious images and painted hangings and their parish churches were filled with material objects that had formerly functioned for domestic use."[143] Even the production of wine and bread in urban houses and "the daily act of dining borrowed from church services some of the solemnity of ritual."[144] Late medieval Bury wills affirm how domestic goods could signify Christian faith. Among the items listed by residents are linen and worsted cloths "stained" or painted with holy images such as the coronation of the Virgin Mary.[145]

Aristorius's home, however, speaks not to sacred but to secular ideologies. Consider an exchange that occurs between him and Peter Paul before Jonathas arrives at his home. Having encountered Jonathas on his way to Aristorius's house, the servant informs his master that "The grettest marchante in all Surré / Ys come with yow to bey and sell" (The greatest merchant in all of Syria / is coming to buy and sell with you, 251–52). Aristorius responds by asking his servant to engage in a version of home decorating hardly befitting a pious Christian: "I prey thee rychely araye myn hall / As owyth for a marchant of pe banke. / Let non defawte be fownd at all" (Please decorate my hall richly / as befits a merchant of the bank. / Let no fault be found [there] at all, 259–61). The merchant's insistence that there be no "defawte" or fault whatsoever in his hall reflects, as Riddy points out, how "the pursuit of excellence" was a key bourgeois value associated with the medieval home, though clearly here that excellence is a matter of not religious but mercantile perfection.[146]

The play elaborates on that mercantile domesticity when Peter Paul tells Aristorius that he will depart "Hasterli to hange your parlor wyth pall / As longeth for a lordis pere" (Quickly to hang your parlor with a hanging / appropriate for a lord's peer, 264–65). The woven hanging hung by Peter Paul would have had a local resonance for a Bury audience in the Great Market. Echoing national trends, most of Risbygate's "prosperity rested in the sale and production of textiles."[147] By 1400, cloth "was the most valuable commodity traded in the" Great Market and by the late fifteenth century, "cloth production was of sufficient importance to attract London's Merchant Adventurers" and alien merchants to the Great Market.[148] As noted above, the religious hangings listed in Bury wills suggest how that commercial production could be directed toward pious ends. But here, in Croxton, the woven hanging adorning Aristorius's hall supports his own secular aims.[149] Not unlike the aristocratic feasts discussed in the *Mirrors for Princes* genre, the cloth adorning Aristorius's home is an object whose material splendor testifies to the magnificence of its owner as a man who counts lords among his peers.[150] Reiterating the global dynamic stressed in his monologue at the scale of the individual house, Aristorius's hall is given fully over to commerce.

Instead of confirming ideals about domestic piety, Aristorius's home reflects the fact that homes were closely tied to the commercial aspects of medieval cities.[151] An audience viewing Croxton in the Great Market would have been keenly aware of the mercantile function of Bury homes, since probably all of the shops on the edges of the market comprised part of a house.[152] Typically, urban shops occupied the front portion of a house and were formed primarily by projecting shutters over multiple arches that faced a street or market.[153] Croxton, though, points to a mercantile presence not just in the commercial frontage but also inside the home. Namely, the play features the hall, a large interior room that was in many respects the heart of the medieval household, "usually open to the rafters, often of two stories in height."[154] Sylvia Thrupp notes how inner rooms weren't entirely dedicated to pious ends, observing how "angels competed with heraldic beasts in the decoration of the household."[155] But such jostling of sacred and profane objects wasn't always necessary in medieval halls, as Mark Gardiner demonstrates. Home owners could store furniture and goods and remove certain objects as the occasion demanded.[156] As Gardiner's research indicates, the hall was not a static or fixed space but rather a flexible, multiuse space, not unlike a stage.[157] Croxton thus depicts in this scene a kind of play within a play: the "staging" by Peter Paul of Aristorius's mercantile might.

Crucially, Aristorius has Peter Paul "set the stage" for a Jew. It is precisely to impress Jonathas with his commercial magnificence that Aristorius has his servant decorate the home. Demonstrating the utility of antisemitism in responding to the complexities and contradictions informing bourgeois commercial life in late medieval England, Croxton's telling depiction of a mercantile household emerges in and through the "Jew." The scene demonstrates, on the one hand, a Jewish merchant's desire "to bey and sel" with a Christian merchant and, on the other hand, the latter's desire to barter with a Jew who is "the grettest marchante in all Surré." Like Jonathas's monologue, this scene evinces an antisemitism that departs from the stereotype of the deicidal Jew, stressing instead Jewish commercial know-how and material wealth. While, as Bale shows, "antisemitism literally begins at home" in medieval Bury through devotion to both the Crucifixion and the boy martyr Little Robert, Croxton stages a household where a Christian doesn't despise the Jew as Christian enemy, but rather cannily entertains him as an economic player.[158]

Aristorius's domestic performance of mercantile power has its desired effect. Upon arriving at the scaffold representing the merchant's house, Jonathas praises it as "semelé to se" (worthy or beautiful to behold, 266) and moreover hails Aristorius as the "myghtyest merchaunte of Arigon!" (267). After telling Jonathas "ye be wellcum unto myn hall," Aristorius fosters—for his own financial benefit—a cozy intimacy between himself and Jonathas, telling him "I pray yow come up and sit bi me, / And tell me wat good ye have to sell, / And yf ony bargeny mad may be made" (please come and sit next to me, / and tell me what goods you have to sell / and if any bargain may be made, 270–74). Sitting comfortably next to Aristorius possibly on chairs or, more likely, cushions, Jonathas begins to bargain with his fellow merchant, an act that culminates in the notorious haggling between the two over the price of the host.[159]

Both this scene and what follows mark a significant reversal of the image of the Jew that we have seen in boy-martyr libels such as Thomas's *Life* of William or the *Prioress's Tale*. In those narratives, the imagined threat of the Jew intertwines with his supposed capacity to lure Christian innocents into the domicile where they meet their death. Jonathas will conform partly to that geography of Jewish menace later in the play, when he and his peers attack the host in his home. But importantly, before Jonathas brings the host into his domicile he enters—or more accurately, he is welcomed into—a Christian home. In Croxton, therefore, prefacing and complicating the fantasy of the Jew performing in his home yet another version of the deicide charge is another antisemitic narrative located in not a Jewish but a Christian home. Only after Aristorius bargains with Jonathas over the price of the host and finally settles on one-hundred pounds does the usual story of anti-Christian violence in the Jewish home occur.

As the staging of the merchant's bargain as an intimate tête-à-tête between businessmen affirms, fundamental to this unholy trade between Jew and Christian is its private nature. Jonathas signposts that secrecy when he tells Aristorius, "I wold bartre wyth yow *in pryvyté* / On lytell thyng, that ye wyll me yt take / *Prevely* in this stownd" (I would trade with you secretly / a little thing that you will bring to me, / secretly, in this place, 276–78, my emphasis). Jonathas refers to Aristorius's home as a *stownd* or place where merchants may barter *prevely* or secretly. Jonathas's stress on privacy is telling on several registers. In part, it reflects how urban homes were not always the open and public sites famously described by Phillippe Ariès and Wytold Rybczynski but instead, as Riddy contends, served as the setting for the cultivation of an emerging bourgeois notion of interiority and private life.[160] Analyzing material including the Assize of Nuisance, vernacular romances, and travel literature, Riddy speculates that during the late Middle Ages in England, "there may have been a sense that the home is, and ought to be, an unwatched place to which access is by invitation only," and that the home is "a place of *secreta* that were not to be seen or heard by outsiders."[161] In other words, Moyse's Hall was not the only mysterious building in Bury; ordinary Christian houses had their secrets as well.

While a home's commercial frontage, as Richard Britnell observes, served as "an intermediate space between the public world of the market and the private world of the family home," the room Croxton features—the hall—afforded home-dwellers with greater privacy.[162] Halls, as Sarah Rees Jones points out, "were nearly always located away from the street frontage either on the ground floor accessed by a narrow lane off the street, or on the first floor of a house above storage and retail spaces."[163] Thus, from its start, the meeting between the two merchants in Croxton has been a private affair; theirs is not a transaction performed in the open and public space of the market, near charged sites of market surveillance and management like the tollhouse and guildhouse, but one that occurs in the hidden recesses of the home. We might speculate, then, that insofar as Croxton was a play performed in dialectical relation to its urban setting, the scaffold depicting the interior of Aristorius's home directed audience attention away from the visible public spaces of the Great Market and the liminal spaces of the shops fronting homes, to the "unseen" landscape of the city in the form of the withdrawn spaces of the merchant residence.[164] In the same way that Jonathas's scaffold may have revealed the hidden treasures of the Jew, Aristorius's scaffold reveals the hidden life of the Christian merchant.

And what viewers discover in that mercantile household—the "unholy" bargain struck by the two men—is hardly reassuring. The privilege of bourgeois privacy clearly has its dangers. Scholars, including James Davis and Mary Bateson, stress how hidden forms of trade, including commercial transactions in the home, were a source of concern in late medieval England.[165] Both the secular and religious authorities who regulated and taxed commerce associated "secret and hidden trade" with "fraud, price-raising and other crimes," and relied on "publicity in trade" as a means of inspecting goods, "securing foreigner's debt," and confirming contracts.[166] Powerful merchant burgesses like Aristorius were exempted from such regulations, which typically were aimed at outsiders.[167] Croxton, however, locates commercial corruption and deceit at the very top of the mercantile order, in the form of a great Christian merchant who secretly performs the worst kind of trade imaginable: selling Christ in the form of the host.

In keeping with the play's use of antisemitism to ponder mercantile domesticity, it is Jonathas who signposts the need to keep secret his transaction with Aristorius. The play's emphatic association of secrecy with Jonathas echoes long-standing stereotypes about the furtively dangerous Jew. As we have seen, English myths repeatedly depict the Jewish home as a site that hides anti-Christian aggression. Jonathas's investment in secrecy resonates with prior English ritual-murder myths even as it adumbrates the particular host desecration that will be staged in his domicile later in the play. Of course, the fantasy that danger lurks within the confines of the Jewish home has always had little to do with Jews; rather, such myths allow Christians to address their own urban behaviors at a remove. The fact that the "Jewish house" is never really a Jewish house but a projection of concerns over covert Christian practices suggests how we might push the history of bourgeois privacy back beyond the late medieval period proposed by Riddy, to the antisemitic city texts of the twelfth century.

Croxton strikingly emphasizes this doubling of Christian and Jewish built environments by having Jonathas voice the need for secrecy when he is in not his own home, but that of Aristorius. In this manner Croxton brings a Christian built environment and its occupant into the usual antisemitic narrative of nefarious secrecy. Jonathas's concern over secrecy reminds audience members that what they are about to witness—the haggling over the price of the host—is an act whose deeply illicit and sacrilegious nature requires covering up in the manner of the anti-Christian acts associated with Jewish homes.

Critics have long recognized how the opening monologues of Aristorius and Jonathas in Croxton parallel the two merchants, looking toward Portia's telling query in the *Merchant of Venice*: "Which is the merchant here, and which the Jew?" (4.1.163).[168] But I would add that just as important as the linking of Jewish and Christian merchants is the paralleling of Jewish and Christian homes in the play. The intersection of the two edifices leads to a portrayal of mercantile misbehavior or illicit trade as an act bound up with anti-Christian aggression. As Aristorius tries to make the biggest financial profit that he can from the host—turning both Christ into a commodity and himself into a figure of Judas—he and his home participate in and even parallel the "deicidal" actions staged later in Jonathas's domicile.[169] By portraying Jewish and Christian dwellings as analogously dangerous spaces, Croxton—more than any English text before it—showcases the utility of the "Jew" in literary responses to Christian urban life. In this play, fantasies about what happens behind the closed doors of the Jewish home in the medieval city openly intersect with concern over events taking place in Christian houses.

## The Agential Object, or the Host as Divine Redecorator

After he and Jonathas agree on a price for the host, Aristorius goes to the scaffold for the church and uses his priest's key to steal a Eucharistic wafer, which he then delivers to Jonathas. The Jew then tells his Christian colleague, "I shall kepe thys trusty treasure, / As I wold doo my gold and fee" (381–82). The Jewish merchant, in keeping with his earlier speech about transubstantiation, constructs the host as just another material good, a commodity that he will "kepe" (possess) and control in the manner of his gold and other "fee" (riches). Yet Jonathas's understanding of the host soon proves inaccurate, as it turns out to be no ordinary consumer item, but an extraordinary object possessed of miraculous transformative powers. Those miraculous transformations, famously, involve its bleeding and eventual morphing into an image of the Christ child. Evincing the collaboration of antisemitism with what Carolyn Walker Bynum describes as "a sort of religious materialism—a frenzied conviction that the divine tended to erupt into matter," Croxton "proves" (ironically, through theatrical tricks) the doctrine of transubstantiation.[170]

Yet importantly, in Croxton the host's miraculous powers involve not only its own transformation but also the remaking of other entities, namely Jonathas and his home. The wafer's transformative effect on the Jew is immediate: upon receiving the host Jonathas at once shifts from referring to it as a material good to addressing it as "thee" (383). Ironically, then, once Jonathas actually gets the host into his hands, an act that suggests his physical control over the wafer, the relationship between the Jew and object seems to reverse. Of course the host literally is inert and silent at this point in the play; only later does it bleed and turn into a speaking child. Nevertheless, the tiny wafer seems to figure as a supernatural presence that affects both the Jew's speech and, as the scene continues, his actions. Mirroring Aristorius's order to Peter Paul about decorating his hall, Jonathas asks his colleague Jason to "Sprede a clothe on the tabyll" in his hall (391), an act that resembles the placement, during the Mass, of the corporal on the altar during the Offertory.[171] Jonathas then lays the host on the table and, along with his fellow Jews, recites an overview of the Christian faith that approximates parts of the Canon of the Mass and the Apostles Creed (395–440).[172]

Ironically, then, it is not the Christian but the Jewish house that evinces the conflation of the domestic and ecclesiastical in medieval homes through the use of "religious images and painted hangings" and other material links to church culture.[173] While the pall hung by Aristorius's servant signifies the merchant's secular might before a Jewish guest, the cloth laid out in Jonathas's home is used in a seemingly pious manner: it "hosts" the host upon an altar-like table. Alongside the Christian conversion of the Jewish home is a kind of conversion of the Jews within it: presiding over the Eucharist along with his colleagues and reciting the Christian faith, Jonathas and his men come to resemble priests.[174] Built environments and selves prove mutually constitutive in this scene, exemplifying Patricia Yaeger's insights regarding the geography of identity.[175]

Instead of serving as a profit-making site like Aristorius's hall, the merchant houses of Bury, or Moyse's Hall, Jonathas's home thus undergoes a kind of divine remodeling project. A site magically controlled not by Jews from afar in the manner of Moyse's Hall, but by the divine Eucharistic object it houses, Jonathas's home gives rise to an inversion of the power dynamic staged in the previous scene. Aristorius's home demonstrates the capacity of market forces to infiltrate the interior recesses of a Christian home, where even the host is traded between merchants. Jonathas's home evinces Christ's power, working through the host, to remake, of all things, a Jewish household into a space supportive of Christian ideology. The fantasy acted out by the play is the idea that, even if commerce proliferates so much in a city that it entails reducing the host to a mere commodity, that mercantilism falters in the face of the real presence of Christ. Defying its construction as mercantile treasure, the host impels the deployment of objects in the household (e.g., a woven cloth and table) as signifiers of its sanctity and divinity. No passive object, the tiny wafer is a formidable home redecorator.

This is not to say that the remodeling of the Jewish home into a domestic "church" is straightforward and final. After Jonathas presides over a quasi Mass, he and his cohort then stab the wafer with daggers, enacting the libel that the Jew is an eternal Christian enemy. The space of the Jewish home in Croxton, therefore, gives rise to an odd complexity and hybridity. At the same time that it becomes a virtual Calvary, a site for the performance of an ancient Jewish aggression toward Christianity, that domicile also, ironically, becomes a holy and pious location where Jonathas behaves like a Christian figure.

That strange mixing of piety and aggression culminates in Jonathas's and the host's "crucifixion." After Jonathas stabs the host, its divinity emerges in spectacular, theatricalized form, perhaps through the special effect of a "tightly filled bladder inside the sacramental loaf."[176] Disturbed by the spectacle of a bleeding host and following the instructions of his colleagues, Jonathas picks up the wafer to toss it in a cauldron of boiling oil (497–98). But he cannot drop the wafer into the cauldron, because, to his horror, the host clings to his hand, an act that makes explicit how it is no passive and inert object but a reactive entity that defies appropriation. A distraught Jonathas proclaims: "Out! Out! Yt werketh me wrake! / I may not awoyd yt owt of my hond!" (Alas! Alas! It performs its vengeance on me! / I may not remove it from my hand!, 499–500). As Jonathas moves from the platform signifying his home onto the *platea* where he runs around with the host clinging to his hand, his friend Jason advises his fellows to "faste bynd hyme to a poste" (securely attach him to a post, 507). With hammer and nails the other men follow the order, and then pull away his arm only to have Jonathas's hand "hang styll with the Sacrament" (hang motionlessly alongside the Sacrament, 515b).

An outrageous and fascinating moment that sets Croxton apart from other host-desecration libels, this scene brims with interpretive possibilities. Taken one way, it seems to counter the divine remodeling of Jonathas's house with almost an apotheosis of the stereotype of Jewish domestic danger. Here, as in ritual-murder myths, the Jewish home is the setting for the reenactment of the Crucifixion, though the victim in Croxton isn't a boy but a wafer possessed of divine material vitality. The nailing of the Christic wafer to the post recalls the first English ritual-murder tale, where Thomas of Monmouth describes how William of Norwich was nailed on a *postis* or "post" in Eleazar's home.[177] The scene construes the Jewish home as a building whose very timber is bound up in aggression toward Christianity in the manner of the crucifixions that occur in ritual-murder tales. The additional nailing of Jonathas's hand to the post in some ways enhances this demonization of the Jewish house.

By rendering the Jew's appendage part of the physical substance of that built environment, the scene literalizes the equation of Jew and built environment in the long literary history of English antisemitism; it looks back to Bede's idea of the Jew as "a tomb still closed by a stone," and ahead to Shylock's famous line, "But stop my house's ears, I mean my casements."[178]

But does this scene really put an end to the divine redecorating of Jonathas's home? After all, as Nisse points out, the severing of Jonathas's hand from his body indicates "the bloody fragmentation of Jewish . . . agency."[179] Removing from the Jew the appendage most closely aligned with human agency indicates how the host is still the master of Jonathas's domain. And indeed, close attention to the spatial components of the episode—that is, the scale and the precise location of the attack—suggests how it returns us to the ideal of domestic piety associated with medieval homes. By staging an attack on not a living boy but Christ inside a tiny wafer, Croxton miniaturizes the Crucifixion.[180] That process of scaling down applies to Jonathas, too, since it is only his disembodied, inanimate hand that remains on the wall. Such aspects of the attack suggest how it resembles the domestic act of piety that many Bury Christians—as town wills attest—performed: hanging a crucifix in their homes.[181]

The host as crucifix—as a domestic reminder of Christ's suffering and Jewish persecution—returns us to the artifacts that promulgated religious antisemitism throughout Bury, as Bale and Lampert-Weissig have stressed. It connects the outrageous actions staged by Croxton to the household piety of Bury residents. But the crucifix in Jonathas's home is no ordinary Christian object, thanks to its incorporation of both the "holy matter" of the host and, importantly, the hand attached to that wafer.[182] As scholars such as Robert Homan point out, the yoking of Jonathas's hand to the host makes him not only the perpetrator but also the victim of anti-Christian violence.[183] Croxton, oddly and awkwardly, places the Jew on either side of the deicidal scenario. He is both the Jew who torments Christ and a figure of Christ tormented.[184]

I would argue, though, that another kind of suffering, one beyond that of the Crucifixion, might inform this scene, given the unique stress Croxton places on commerce. Croxton showcases merchants exhibiting a masterful, self-aggrandizing relation to commodities, from the precious gems and spices hoarded in Jonathas's house, to the Jew's perception of the host as a "cake," and Aristorius's deployment of the sumptuous hanging in his hall. Here Jonathas experiences his own commodification and objectification, the reduction of his hand to a dead thing hanging on a post. The contiguity and close intimacy of the disembodied hand to the host might seem to qualify my stress on its inert thingness; in other words, that intimacy might enable the hand to partake in the wafer's divine vitality. However, an equally plausible prospect is that the union of the dead appendage with the wafer *turned crucifix* shores up the oppressive effects even of "holy" commodities. In other words, the brutal severing of a hand that is attached to a "crucifix" may recall, at one level, how hands were used and abused in making goods like crucifixes, palls, and other domestic objects, and how such labor wreaked a toll on the medieval laborer.[185] Such a scenario suggests that we can expand the range of secrets exposed by Jonathas in Croxton. The Jew not only displays treasures like those imagined to lurk in Moyse's Hall and coaxes out the divinity buried inside the Eucharistic wafer, but also—and in tension with those other revelations—hints at the painful and dehumanizing effects of life under capital. Jonathas's subjection to a divine materiality in this scene perhaps speaks not so much to the Christian frenzy for holy matter described by Bynum but to a worry over the potential objectification of person in both Christian and economic discourse. Christianity had long demonized Jews and rationalized Jewish unbelief by imagining Jews as objects, especially insensate stone. While the cruelty of that process was by and large irrelevant to promulgators of the "stony" Jew stereotype and thus was disregarded by them, Croxton makes a spectacle of the pain entailed by Jonathas becoming a crucifix.

While the highly evocative nailing of the Jewish hand to the Christian wafer makes Jonathas a fascinatingly unstable figure, subsequent events impel both him and his household toward a more complete Christian conversion.[186] After a brief comedic interlude, Jonathas's colleagues place the hand and host in a cauldron of seething oil, which then explodes and reveals a bleeding Christ child, who then restores Jonathas's hand to his body. Instead of attacking Christ or inadvertently becoming Christ-like, Jonathas now worships the Christian deity.[187] While previously, Jonathas celebrated his own goods and praised the merchant Aristorius, now he exalts Christ through a string of exclamations beginning with "Oh Thow my Lord God and Savyowr, osanna!" (Oh Thou my Lord God and Savior, Hosanna!, 778–79).[188] The worship of the Christian God soon expands after Jonathas contacts the local bishop, who calls on "all my peple, with me ye dresse / for to goo see that swymfull syght" (all my people, with me prepare / to go to see that sorrowful sight, 888–89) of the bleeding child. When the bishop and his people arrive there, Jonathas's home seems to have become, to all intents and purposes, a house of God governed by a priest and filled with members of the Christian faithful. The Jewish house serves no longer as a site for the private circulation of profane commercial flows or anti-Christian violence, but instead witnesses the reproduction of the public piety of the church in the private sphere of the home. The fantasy offered by Croxton's final dramatic turn is thus not only the "truth" of transubstantiation, but also the myth that a commercialized urban space—and market-minded urban subjects—may be converted along orthodox Christian lines. Thus when the play, following the conventions of antisemitic city texts, stages a procession to the scaffold representing the "real" church, it presents an unusual movement from one identical space to another in a now homogeneously Christian city. The architectural opposition at the heart of many English antisemitic libels, holy minster versus debased Jewish domicile, recedes from view as the latter site becomes effectively a church.[189] In keeping with this urban fantasy, Aristorius transforms as well. After learning about the miraculous events that occurred in Jonathas's house, the Christian merchant confesses his deeds to the bishop, who responds by asking Aristorius "nevermore for to bye nor sell" (never again to buy and sell, 915). Croxton thus suggests how not just a heretical trading in hosts but *all* mercantilism partakes of sin. Linking Christian practice to the utter renunciation of commerce, Aristorius claims that he will "amende myn wyckyd lyfe" (amend my wicked life, 973) and dedicate himself to piety instead of profit.

## Universal Commercialism in Croxton

But Croxton, as many critics stress, is a play that resists offering a lasting resolution to the social problems it stages. For one thing, it exhibits a certain lack of confidence in the changes wrought in both merchants. Despite the fact that Jonathas converts, he exiles himself from the Christian community of the play, announcing that he and his fellows will "walke by contré and cost, / Owr wyckyd lyvyng for to restore" (walk by country and coast, / to compensate for our wicked lives, 964–65).[190] And Aristorius similarly declares: "take I my leave in thys place; / I wyll go walke my penaunce to fullfyll" (I take my leave from this place; / I will go walking to fulfill my penance, 976–77). Those two exiles repeat the events of 1290, but with a difference. Ejected from what is (despite its mythical Aragonese setting) to all intents and purposes an English city are not only Jews but also a Christian merchant. Jonathas's and Aristorius's respective exiles imply the insufficiency of conversion and penitence; for a city to remain Christian, it must be "cleansed" of both Jews and mercantilism.[191]

And yet Croxton doesn't so much advocate exile as render it problematic. The precise spatial nature of both mens' penitential journeys is difficult to pin down.[192] Although the play is set in Aristorius's homeland in Aragon, the merchant states that he will go "into my contré" (into my country, 972), a line that oddly registers the play's probable staging in East Anglia and the distance between that site and the Spanish locale where the play is officially set. Jonathas, on the other hand, is far from his Syrian homeland. Could his statement that he will undertake a voyage "by contré and cost" mean that he will return to the East to spread the Christian word? Additionally, it's unclear whether both men commit themselves to permanent exiles or temporary pilgrimages. By leaving open-ended where the merchants will go, how long they will be gone, and even the precise location of the site they are leaving, Croxton summons up a concept—exile—usually tied to fantasies of spatial purification and firm borders only to evoke geographic incoherence and dislocation.

And, of course, at the same time that the play leaves its Jews and Christians in a kind of floating, geographic limbo, it in no way assures spectators of the holy nature of the society that expels those two figures. When near the end of the play, in words echoing the language of Lateran IV, the bishop commands that the host be locked up in its pyx, Croxton acknowledges how, even without the corrupt presence of Aristorius and Jonathas, the medieval city still abounds in problematic and degrading flows from which the Eucharist needs protection. That ecclesiastical officers (from the Pope down, if Aristorius is to be trusted) are themselves corrupt raises the problem of whether even the host can ever be safeguarded from such currents.

Croxton ends with the bishop urging members of the faithful to avoid hellfire and attain heavenly bliss by following the Ten Commandments, then leading a rendition of the *Te Deum*, sung presumably not only by the performers but also by audience members. With its praise of God as the eternal father whom "all the earth worships" ("Te aeternum patrem omnis terra veneratur") the *Te Deum* suggests how Croxton performs the work of its continental counterparts, accusations and plays where, in Miri Rubin's words, "after a host desecration, the world was in better order."[193] But would the anthem and the bishop's words ring true, given the events they follow? As we have seen, Croxton enacts a hermeneutic slippage in which "the Jew" is not merely a figure for heterodox Christian doubters (like Lollards) but also mirrors orthodox Christians whose ventures in capitalism raise uncomfortable questions about Christianity's entanglement in a profit economy. I would argue that despite its final turns, Croxton doesn't so much overcome as reproduce the contradictions of its society. Croxton leaves viewers with a world in a state of disarray so massive and far-reaching that no mere hymn can resolve it. Trade and materialism are so ubiquitous in the secular and spiritual worlds staged by the play as to be annihilated only in a final global apocalypse; the exile of two merchants and the locking of a tabernacle can hardly eliminate the problem.[194]

And where better to stage such tensions than in the Great Market, where the abundance of buyers and sellers before Moyse's Hall would make clear the irony of the merchants' exiles? The omnipresence of trade in the square would have registered for theatergoers how buying and spending were hardly going to disappear in a medieval city; and the iconic, massive presence of Moyse's Hall would have signaled the flimsy nature of Croxton's divine remodelings. Insofar as Croxton may have been a discomfiting theatrical experience, Bury's commercial hub would have driven home the drama's destabilizing economic thrust. Moreover, the myth associated with that edifice—that Jews magically control the treasure in Moyse's Hall from afar— would have opposed Croxton's staging of Jewish exile with the idea of an ongoing Jewish presence in England, one related not to the exigencies of Christian passion devotion, but to the need to invoke "the Jew" when contemplating a disturbing reality: that Christianity isn't the spiritual community it purports to be but often manifests itself through a thoroughly carnal and commercializing religion.

## ❧ CHAPTER 5

# Failures of Fortification and the Counting Houses of *The Jew of Malta*

## Protected Christians and Vulnerable Jews

If, as Emily Bartels points out, the title of *The Jew of Malta* (1592) "demands that we consider what it means to be 'of Malta' while deciding what it means to be 'the Jew,'" the drama soon provides an answer.[1] Just one hundred lines into the play, Barabas soliloquizes about Jewish wealth, highlighting the singularly rich Jews inhabiting various lands: "There's *Kirriah Jairim*, the great Jew of *Greece*, / *Obed* in *Bairseth*, *Nones* in *Portugall*, / My selfe in *Malta*" (1.1.121–23).[2] We thus readily can understand Christopher Marlowe's title in economic terms. Because he is "wealthier farre then any Christian" as well as any other Jew on the island, Barabas is *the* Jew of Malta (1.1.124). However, if we consider Marlowe's play from a geographical perspective, the notion of a "Jew of Malta" proves more problematic and even contradictory. For, while Jews were notorious for their spatial disenfranchisement, Malta was famous for its spatial power and privilege. As we shall see after comparing the space of the Jew to the space of the island, their geographic disparity threatens to render the phrase "The Jew of Malta" something of a non sequitur.

At least since Augustine, Christians contended that God punished a sinful Jewish people by depriving them of spatial security. The biblical Barabas figured pivotally in such claims about the geography of Jewish guilt.[3] When the Jews chose to free the imprisoned radical Barabas instead of Jesus, taking the latter's "blood . . . on us and our children" (Matthew 25:25–26), they supposedly set themselves up for an eternal punishment with important spatial dimensions. Namely, as Marlowe's likely source, French explorer Nicolas de Nicolay (1517–83), puts it in his *The nauigations, peregrinations and voyages, made into Turkie* (1568), ever since the Jews told Pilate "hys blood bee vppon vs and our children . . . their sinne hath followed them and their successours throughout al generations" so that, from the siege of Jerusalem "vnto this present day," Jews "hadde at no time any certayne dwelling place vpon the face of the earth," and "alwayes gone straying dispearsed and driuen awaye from Countrie to countrie."[4] In this passage, from Nicolay's description of Constantinople, an Ottoman metropolis where many early modern Jews lived, the Jews' rejection of Jesus and embrace of Barabas prompted God to deprive them of not only Israel but also any "certayne dwelling place" or stable habitation on earth.

Ten years before Marlowe began writing *The Jew of Malta*, the protestant martyrologist John Foxe would elaborate publicly and with offensive ingenuity on the spatial aspects of Jewish disenfranchisement.[5] Delivered at the 1 April 1577 christening of Yehuda Menda, a Jew from North Africa, Foxe's sermon conceives of Jews as "always stuck at the present moment of the Crucifixion, in effect amalgamated with their ancestors" and thus forever suffering from the geographic consequences of their forbearers' crime.[6] Foxe brings to vivid life the utter destruction entailed by the siege of Jerusalem, when the temple was "consumed by fire, the altar throwen downe, and the citie put to the sacke and destroyed," so much so that not "one stone" was left "standing vpon an other of your whole citie."[7] He emphasizes the ongoing nature of such historical assaults on contemporary Jews, whose "habitations are become waste and desolate" and who "haue now neither citie nor temple, kingdome nor priesthode."[8] Jews, Foxe stresses, can't hope for any future resolution to their troubles. Although the Hebrew prophets foretold a time of "securite" and inhabiting "the land confidently" (Ezekiel 28:26), their texts require typological interpretation. Thus Ezekiel points not to the restoration of the Jews to Jerusalem but rather "to the spirituall king|dome of Israel" or heavenly Jerusalem.[9] Foxe's geographic understanding of Jewish disenfranchisement is such that it extends from actual buildings to architecturally conceived mentalities. The Christian spiritual fulfillment of biblical prophesies "doeth vn|ioynte and shyuer in pieces all the strong bulwarkes of your [Jewish] vnbeliefe, euen to the very bottome of the foundation."[10] Supersession, as portrayed by Foxe, lays siege to the Jewish mindset in in the manner of Jerusalem's attack; it causes the "bulwarks" of Jewish unbelief, however well fortified, to tremble and break apart.

The national and local contexts of Foxe's sermon would seem to support his claims. England supposedly evinced the spatial instability of the Jews, as a site from which they had been expelled for centuries. As James Shapiro has shown, the 1290 expulsion and its aftereffects loomed large in English minds during the sixteenth century, partly due to the exigencies of national fantasy.[11] As we shall discuss a bit later, Jews actually did live in Foxe's England and especially London. Nevertheless, during this period of nation building, definitions of Englishness often hinged on the fantasy that the island was devoid of Jews. The occasion for Foxe's sermon reinforced such a fantasy on a local level. After his baptism, Menda would find spatial security in the form of his new Christian home, the *Domus conversorum* on New Street (now Chancery Lane).[12] The example of Menda showed how the only way for a Jew to find a secure dwelling place in England was to cease being Jewish altogether.

Malta shared with England the dubious status of a site devoid of Jews. In 1492, the Crown of Aragon expelled Jews from Malta, "after a residence of fully fifteen hundred years."[13] Thus when Marlowe places Barabas and other Jews in "Malta" on an English stage, he ironically makes "Jews" (i.e., actors playing Jews) present on overlapping sites of Jewish exile.[14] Clearly, the sheer absence of Jews from sixteenth-century Malta renders Marlowe's title impossible. But what makes the idea of a "Jew of Malta" particularly fraught is the status of Malta as no ordinary place in Christendom but one associated with the extreme geographic opposite of the Jew's radical instability of habitation. Malta, that is, was famously associated with fortification. Nearly synonymous with spatial security, Malta epitomized "the art of fortification" during the sixteenth century.[15] The impetus for that security buildup was precisely the threat Marlowe stages in his play: Islamic imperialism. Turkish Muslims, unlike Jews, were religious others whose control of and dominance over space was a source of considerable fear for Christians. From its capital in what is now Turkey, the sixteenth-century Ottoman Empire circled the Mediterranean, from Algiers to Croatia, and extended deep into territories in Eastern Europe, the Middle East, and North Africa. Situated north of Tripoli and just south of Italy, Malta served as the great impediment between the Islam-governed eastern and Christian-controlled portions of the Mediterranean.[16] Upon setting up base in Malta in 1530, the Knights of the Order of St. John—entrusted with protecting Christendom from the spread of Islam—devoted themselves to fortifying the island and continued to do so "almost to the very time of their departure in 1798."[17] The knights first rebuilt and enlarged St. Angelo, which commanded the tip of the promontory of the Grand Harbor and protected their headquarters, the town of Il

Borgo or Birgu. Nicolay singles this fort out in his *Navigations* as "by art and nature almost inexpugnable," a military term meaning "impregnable" or "invincible."[18] Then, through their innovative work on both St. Elmo, on the edge of the Sciberras peninsula, and other forts, including Vittoriosa, St. Michael, and Senglea, the knights emerged as "consummate fortress builders" who took practices of fortification to an unprecedented extreme.[19] Even Ottoman rulers stressed Malta's supreme inviolability, with Suleiman the Magnificent (1494–1566) lamenting how "this cursed rock is like a barrier interposed between us and our possessions."[20]

Marlowe's title, when viewed in terms of Malta and Jews' respective relationships to space and territory, just doesn't seem to follow. In stark contrast to the "almost inexpugnable" castle of Malta, Jews lack spatial power, as witnessed by the expulsions in Malta, England, and elsewhere. If Malta stands for the construction of a firm and solid defense against the "infidel," the "Jew" epitomizes spatial weakness and vulnerability. And ironically, Marlowe's protagonist Barabas signposts that Jewish spatial disenfranchisement. As we have seen, Barabas's biblical namesake Barabbas figured crucially in the Jewish "crime" that led to the siege of Jerusalem and subsequent upheavals and dispersals. Barabas even refers to the siege in 2.3.10. Such aspects of the play suggest Marlowe's awareness of the spatial irony encoded in his title, *The Jew of Malta*: while early modern Malta was the most fortified site on earth, early modern Jews were stereotyped as the least protected people on earth.

However, a closer look at early modern understandings of both Malta and Jews reveals how the opposition of an impregnable island to a vulnerable religious other ultimately doesn't hold. When examined carefully, the relationship of both Malta and the Jew to space reveals a far more complex situation, in which the Hospitaller bastion proves vulnerable, and Barabas is empowered by a certain spatial sagacity and facility. Marlowe's cognizance of such complexities emerges most clearly in the final act of the play, when the Spanish governor of Malta, Ferneze, believing Barabas dead, orders that his corpse be flung over the city walls. Ferneze's physical "expulsion" of Barabas's body resonates with the long history of Christians forcibly exiling Jews from their lands.[21] But Barabas, rising from what was only a feigned death, inverts the received relationship between Jews and territory. Revealing a canny understanding of Maltese space and, particularly, the weaknesses of its supposedly impermeable fortifications, Barabas shows the Turks how to infiltrate the city walls by means of the city's sewage system. As his statement in the first scene of the play, "They say we are a scatter'd Nation; I cannot tell" (1.1.118), affirms, Barabas is a recursive figure who actively refuses exile. Undoing fantasies of Christian security, defense, and purity—and, as his assistance of the Turks suggests, revealing the limits of Ottoman geographic power—Barabas defiantly insists on being "The Jew of Malta."[22]

That Marlowe's imagined Jew enacts a "sequence of ironic contrasts" with received Christian thinking has been clear to scholars at least since the publication of G. K. Hunter's classic essay on Marlowe's theology.[23] Hunter acknowledges the temporal dimensions of those reversals in his reading of passages like Barabas's reference to "the Blessings promis'd to the Jewes" by Abraham (1.1.102). While Christianity tries to "remove the Old Testament from the Jews and shackle its prophecies and promises to the New Testament," so that Abraham's promise is directed toward Christians, Barabas reclaims Abraham for Jews, reinstating a link between the Jewish past and Jewish present.[24] In this chapter, I examine the spatial aspects of Barabas's subversive response to Christianity, which emerges not just in the Turkish invasion but also throughout the play, starting with its opening scene. Everywhere in *The Jew of Malta*, Barabas displays a spatial know-how and undermines notions of stable and coherent Christian locations. In the face of fantasies about Christians' privileged relationship to territory, Barabas aggressively situates himself in gentile locations and moreover exhibits a masterful control over those sites.

Questions of space and identity have, to be sure, figured prominently in critical work on Marlowe. Marjorie Garber, for example, has analyzed the showcasing of containers in all his plays: "Cave, wall, nunnery, monastery, cage, chariot, countinghouse, study, circle, cauldron—the list of literal enclosures is striking and consistent."[25] Like other Marlovian protagonists, Barabas uses space to trap other persons; but ultimately, enclosers like Barabas or Tamberlaine find themselves enclosed.[26] While Garber stresses the capacity of space to circumscribe and contain, other critics emphasize the instability of Marlowe's spaces and their borders. Stephen Greenblatt, for example, considers how Marlowe uses abstraction to secularize space in plays like *Tamberlaine* and *The Jew of Malta*, existentially reducing "the universe to the coordinates of a map."[27] As Greenblatt observes, secular and scientific approaches to space emerge ironically in Marlowe's plays as "desperate attempts at boundary and closure" that "produce the opposite effect," emptying selves and spaces of both meaning and agency.[28] Refining Greenblatt's formulation, Bartels claims that "Marlovian space is, in some ways, shapeless, but the lack of differentiation between its worlds functions on a less abstract level to suggest the meaninglessness not of space but of the bounds imposed upon it. The point is not that space is meaningless, but that the differences assigned to it are empty, overdetermined, or arbitrary at best."[29] The "bounds" to which Bartels refers are efforts to delimit identity, whether that of a place like Malta or stereotyped other such as Barabas, and they fail partly due to both their uncircumscribable cosmopolitanism and the multiplicity and incoherence of colonial constructions of identity.[30]

With Bartels, Greenblatt, and other critics, I stress the instability of space in Marlowe's work, which I read less in terms of cosmopolitanism, colonialism, and secularization, than in light of the destabilizing effects of greed, commerce, and related material flows.[31] I argue that Barabas, through his manipulation of Maltese space and his aggressive insertion of himself within that environment, offers a materialist critique of received Christian geopolitical thinking. Taking seriously the geographic ramifications of the Turkish Bashaw's oft-cited remark that "The wind that bloweth all the world" is "Desire of gold" (3.5.3–4), I view Barabas as a figure whose canny management of material currents—ranging from the flow of sewage to the circulation of precious goods, as well as the movements of profit-minded persons—connotes a world whose spaces are thoroughly destabilized by commerce. While historical Malta was famed as a great global boundary that protected Christian interests, the greedy and sordid flows of Marlowe's Malta suggest otherwise.

The location in *The Jew of Malta* that epitomizes this dynamic is Barabas's counting house. At the start of the play, the counting house seems to fix Barabas as a greedy Jewish other, the "encloser" analyzed by Garber. Yet ultimately that site doesn't so much contain and enclose but instead proves to be a porous location where the goods that define the Jewish merchant's profession pool and disperse. Moreover, thanks to Barabas's stratagems, by the end of the play virtually every locale it stages emerges as yet another version of the Jew's counting house. Thus in the same way, as Greenblatt points out in his Marxist reading, Barabas's pursuit of wealth makes him "not the exception to but rather the true representative of his society": the Jew's built environment proves prototypical of the layout and mapping of the world he inhabits.[32] It's no accident that Marlowe's play lacks any representation of the churches that feature in earlier English myths about Jews; the only kind of bona fide "house of worship" in *The Jew of Malta* is that of counting house.[33]

## Christians, Jews, and Failures of Fortification

Even before the play proper begins, *The Jew of Malta* foregrounds the ostensible powers of fortification. Just twenty-two lines into the prologue, the character of Machevil proclaims that "a strong built Citadell / Commands much more than letters can import" (1.1.22–23). Like the Hospitaller knights of Malta, Machevil, a figure who embodies popular thinking about Machiavellian iniquity, celebrates the mighty fortress. Yet the historical Machiavelli thought otherwise. Chapter 20 of *The Prince* stresses how "fortresses have not been seen to bring profit to any prince," a topic Machiavelli expounds on in his *Discourses* on Livy.[34] Citing examples of fortifications "lost either through the fraud of whoever guards them, or through the violence of whoever assaults them," Machiavelli emphasizes the fragility of citadels and city walls.[35] The plot of Marlowe's work, with its staging of the conquest of Malta by Turkish forces led by Barabas, clearly supports Machiavelli's insight and queries the claims of the Prologue's "Mac-Evil."[36]

Although historical Malta was never actually taken by the Turks, the history of the island does support Machiavelli's thesis. Marlowe's decision to stage Malta's conquest violates historical fact, but it broadly represents the deeper import of the island's architectural history, which reveals a highly fraught relationship to fortified buildings.[37] The Turks' most significant assault on the island, the nearly four-month Great Siege of 1565, left only remnants of the defenses erected by the Order. As Quentin Hughes puts it, "gaping holes were torn in all the defensive walls and rubble filled the ditches."[38] The ramparts of Fort St. Elmo, which the Turks breached and occupied, were broken "even down to the sheer rock on which the fort had been erected."[39] In the wake of that destruction emerged Valletta, a city that inaugurated "an ever-expanding chain of defense, that ultimately extended outwards to embrace the whole island."[40] Due to changing trends as well as developments in artillery, Valletta and other defenses were "subjected to repeated criticism."[41] In response to those intellectual "attacks," the design of Maltese fortresses "was subject to constant modifications and additions."[42] Both the Turkish decimation of Maltese defenses as well as the anxiety and criticism that informed subsequent efforts to make Malta impermeable suggest how the island didn't so much epitomize a faith in fortification as evince an anxious and critical querying of the capacity of any built environment to protect its inhabitants.

Just as a closer look at Malta complicates its association with spatial strength, deeper scrutiny of Jewish history and culture troubles the association of Jews with spatial weakness. To begin with, Christian accounts of Jewish geographic instability take as their starting point—the Siege of Jerusalem—a period in Jewish history noteworthy for its interest in fortification. During their war with the Jews, the Romans attacked fortresses like Masada and Antonia, as well as the defensive walls surrounding Jerusalem. Those built environments were products of the construction programs of Herod the Great and, before him, Jewish leaders—including Nehemiah and members of the Hasmonean dynasty—who sought to realize the prophets' call to rebuild Jerusalem after the destruction of the First Temple. In other words, well before Malta gained fame as a stronghold, before Christianity even emerged as a religion, Jerusalem enjoyed renown as a fortified city. Christian cognizance of Jerusalem's association with fortification is of long stead, and emerges in the many images of the walled city in medieval texts and maps such as the Hereford *mappa mundi*.[43] English Protestants were well aware of the venerable association of Jerusalem with walls and other physical defenses.[44] The Hebrew Bible or Old Testament describes the city as a "mighty fortress" and records Nehemiah and other leaders' building programs.[45] The popularity of Josephus and the 1558 English translation of "Yosippon" served to further associate Jerusalem with fortification during Marlowe's lifetime, as did plays like John Smith's *Destruction of Jerusalem* and Thomas Legge's *Solymitana Clades* (ca. 1579–88), and travel writings.[46] All of which is to say, the idea of Jewish dispersal wasn't so much a self-contained spatial concept as the outcome of a providentially ordained reversal, from a position of exceptional fortification and stability to its inverse.

Sixteenth-century Jews were deeply attuned to Israel's history of construction and demolition. Jewish travelers to the East faced Jerusalem's destruction head on. An account of Karaite visitors to Eretz Israel describes how they walked along the western wall of the temple and "all the gates of Jerusalem," where they "desired its stones and embraced its dust."[47] While only a small portion of Jews travelled to the Holy Land, many more pondered at a remove the fraught history of Jerusalem and its built environments. Through the ritual fast Tisha B'av, early modern Jews annually commemorated the destruction of both temples. Moreover, cognizance of the razing of Jerusalem was so omnipresent as to encompass everyday domestic lived experience. A Jewish custom, codified in a 1565 legal code penned by the Sephardic rabbi Joseph Karo (1488–1575), instructed Jews, when building houses, to leave a 1.5 foot square on one wall unpainted to memorialize Jerusalem's fall.[48] The custom of rendering part of the Jewish home incomplete opposes Christian stereotypes by showing how Jews themselves, actively and intentionally, destabilized the places they inhabited. Through those architectural unmakings, Jews brought a virtual fallen Jerusalem into their homes, located across the wide sweep of the diaspora.

Could early modern Jews' nuanced response to Jerusalem and fortification inform Marlowe's play? It's unlikely that Marlowe was aware of the domestic custom of leaving the Jewish home unfinished, though there is a chance that he knew about Tisha B'av, thanks to the Hebraism of post-Reformation England.[49] At the same time, however, Barabas's canny understanding of space—especially fortified space—resonates with the know-how of a

Jewish people possessed of a long and fraught relationship to defensive built environments. Over the course of the play, Barabas emerges as a Jew who has learned the hard lessons of Jewish architectural history. The merchant knows better than to believe that built defenses—even the technologically advanced fortifications of Malta—are impermeable. We thus have another way of understanding the logic behind Marlowe's decision to title his play *The Jew of Malta*. While the idea of the unfortified Jew in a supremely fortified space doesn't follow, who better to expose the vulnerability of Malta than a member of a people who knew all too well the weaknesses of defensive built environments?

## Material Flows and Porous Spaces

While Marlowe's play concerns failures of fortification, that phenomenon isn't realized primarily through the physical demolition of strongholds. The Turks do "give assault unto the wals" of Malta, and after their victory, survey "the ruin'd Towne and see the wracke" they caused (5.1.92; 5.2.19). But the key to the Turks' success isn't so much physical destruction as infrastructural knowledge, in the form of Barabas's intelligence about Malta's sewage system. "Feare not," the resurrected Barabas assures Calymath outside the walls of Malta, "for here against the Sluice, / The rocke is hollow, and of purpose digg'd, / To make a passage for the running streames / And common channels of the City" (5.1.88–91).[50] Barabas ensures a Turkish victory by leading "five hundred souldiers through the Vault" into the "middle of the Towne," where they will "Open the gates" for Calymath (5.1.93–95).

Barabas's expertise on sanitation systems, as well as his passage through the Maltese sluice and its excremental contents, undoubtedly resonates with English antisemitic associations of Jews with filth, such as the Jewish privy of the *Prioress's Tale*. The scene also seems to lump the Turks together with Barabas as filthy entities, since Calymath's men follow the Jew through the sewage channels of Malta. As Lloyd Kermode puts it, Barabas and the Turks "return through the channels that should only allow effluence to leave the jurisdiction—they are therefore dangerous excess to the city's safety, the city's political filth infecting the city structure."[51] However, here, as elsewhere in the play, Barabas undermines the very stereotypes he represents. The merchant doesn't so much link himself or Turks to excrement as highlight and take advantage of the *omnipresence* of filth—its passage through "common" or shared "channels"—in Maltese Christian society. While the Prioress, for example, through her obscene reference to "Jewes purgen hire entraille" (7.573) urges the Canterbury pilgrims to imagine defecating Jews, Barabas reminds us that not just Jews but everyone empties their bowels. Chaucer's text hints at such a relationship when the filth-covered schoolboy is taken via a procession into the local minster. Marlowe's point is far more explicit and radical: the filth in question is that of an entire city. The Jewish antihero identifies it as such and takes advantage of its urban management for the benefit of both himself and the Turks.[52]

Marlowe's stress on urban waste management would undoubtedly have resonated with theatergoers in London. As Holly Dugan stresses, sixteenth-century London experienced a sewage crisis that resulted from its sudden and massive population growth.[53] That crisis was met by a 1531 city commission entrusted with the task of ensuring "the drainage of London's surface waters into existing tributaries or common shores."[54] Such "running streams and common channels" were omnipresent and unavoidable for anyone in the city, a "proximity," Dugan stresses, that "was not a mark of failure or excess but rather urbanity: the sewers connected and defined the metropolis, demarcating its borders."[55] But importantly, waste channels didn't simply demarcate but also opened up London's borders; the river Walbrook "ran underneath London's ancient Roman wall into the heart of the early modern city, connecting Townditch, an open sewer that ran parallel to the wall, to the Thames."[56] In the flow of sewage beyond the boundaries of London we witness how the bodily discharges of city residents are repeated on a larger scale by the entire city. Thus, Marlowe's London managed the waste that exuded from the apertures of its individual citizens through urban openings in the same way that, in Marlowe's play, the sanitation requirements of Malta prompt authorities to "of purpose" dig out "the rocke" of what is otherwise an impregnable fortified wall, rendering it "hollow."

Barabas's manipulation of Malta's sewage system shows how material flows render even a hyperfortified city vulnerable. In the case of the Turkish invasion, the flow in question is that of sewage. But elsewhere in the play the dominant material coursing through Malta is the seeming opposite of excrement: gold and other desirable commodities. While Malta expels its sewage, it seeks wealth. Of course, from the traditional Christian perspective, the wealth sought by the greedy residents of Marlowe's Malta really should be rejected as so much ordure. We saw in the *Prioress's Tale* a medieval instance of such condemnation; numerous aspects of Marlowe's post-Reformation world reveal the persistence of that view. Such factors as the emptying of church coffers during the dissolution of the monasteries, the emergence of Puritan asceticism, the place of greed in works by reformist writers like Thomas More, Robert Crowley, and Thomas Lever, and the expansion of English mercantilism during the final decades of the sixteenth century rendered the problem of greed newly relevant to Marlowe's audience.[57] Anxieties over materialism gave new life to medieval morality plays, spurring works like parson and playwright William Wager's *Enough is as Good as Feast* (ca. 1569), whose allegorical figure Worldly Man is "a very dunghill and a sink of sin."[58] Marlowe echoes such denigrations when Barabas exposes the universal nature of Malta's sewage; because the only other universal aspect of the island (and the greater world) is "desire for gold," this scene implies the congruity of the two. The precious goods of Malta are not other to but of a piece with the detritus of the city.

Fundamental to the status of wealth as filth in the play is its disruptive effect on space. In Marlowe's Malta, commerce, like excrement, is predicated on flows, currents that necessitate the creation of urban openings, border crossings, and related forms of spatial destabilization. The idea that commerce unsettled space was hardly new to sixteenth-century drama. For example, in Wager's play the vice figure Couetouse "all strong walles . . . doost convince" (300), and "ouerthoweth flat, / The strongest walles and towers in a whole land" (923–24), and Greed's disciple, Worldly Man, accepts money from the "Straungers" who are "placed now in England . . . in euery Porte" and spurn the needs of needy natives, so that they "no houses can get" (986–87). Similarly, the usury play *The Three Ladies of London* (1584) describes how "vilde Usery" took "the fee-simple" of a man's "house and mill quite away."[59] Marlowe departs from such representations of avarice by portraying not only the spatial destabilizations suffered by victims of greed but also the unstable nature of the locations inhabited by the greedy.

## The Stage, Urban Space, and Global English Commerce

As we saw both in Thomas of Monmouth's *Life* and William of Newburgh's *History*, the English had been worrying over the destabilizing effects of a profit economy at least since the twelfth century. By Marlowe's time, commerce had expanded in scale considerably, so much so that it has been described as "the single most dramatic shift in English history in the early modern period."[60] Starting with Columbus's so-called voyages of discovery and "even before," there began a period of economic growth that led, over the next two centuries, to the creation of what scholars such as Immanuel Wallerstein call a capitalist world economy.[61] During the sixteenth century, the configuration of that developing global system of supply and demand entailed, as Daniel Vitkus puts it, "a chain of empires that stretched from the Habsburgs in Europe and the Americas, to the Ottomans in the Mediterranean, to the Safavid Persians, to the Indo-Timuri (or Mughal) empire in India, and on to China, Japan and the Spice Islands in the Far East."[62] Due to the Protestant Reformation and other factors, England did not enter into this world economic system in a significant way until the final decades of the century.[63] A German traveller to London in 1592 indicates England's new role in a global market when he writes of the city: "most of the inhabitants are employed in buying and selling merchandize, and trading in almost every corner of the world, since the river is most useful and convenient for this purpose."[64] The visitor, Duke Frederick of Wirtemberg, overstates England's place in the world economy; but as Jean Howard notes, he does accurately reflect the "perceptible commercial energy" of both England and its London metropolis, where commerce had expanded significantly beyond the northern European lands with which the English had traded during the late medieval period.[65] By Marlowe's time, English trade had expanded as far as Turkey, evincing how, ironically, goods and currency were actively crisscrossing the very east–west border that the Knights of St. John strove to erect and maintain from their headquarters in Malta.[66]

As Jean-Christophe Agnew and other scholars point out, the rise of capitalism and international commerce in England led to a heightened awareness of the relationship between trade and fluidity.[67] More than ever before, the "market" referred not so much to a discrete space—such as Cheapside—as to, in Crystal Bartolovich's words, "an abstracted and generalized *process* of exchange," a cognizance of the destabilizing mobility entailed by trade.[68] London manifested this mobility not so much through changes in its layout; even in 1600, the city remained still, to all intents and purposes, medieval in its urban form.[69] Rather, the sheer movement of persons and goods on thoroughfares, travelling in and out of the city, its neighborhoods, and its buildings, manifested London's heightened commercialism. While the increasing "redundancy" of the city walls shows how London was not so much a bounded city but an urban location defined by flow, nothing better evinced the flows entailed by English global economic expansion than the Thames, the river that, in Vitkus's words, "connected" London "to the open sea and thus to the world."[70] National shipping surveys demonstrate the key role of the Thames during this time of economic expansion. Between 1582 and 1629, when the total tonnage of the realm increased 70 percent, the cargo that shipped out of London on the Thames tripled in weight.[71]

The global commerce facilitated by the Thames entailed both outward and inward flows that not only pushed goods and persons—largely in the form of merchants—ever further beyond the confines of England, but also brought the world (or at least a sampling of it) to the island.[72] As Howard points out, "the expansion of overseas trade mandated a kind of forced cosmopolitanism, a recognition that one had to undertake certain kinds of negotiations with strangers in order to further one's own interests."[73] Elsewhere in the city, on Threadneedle Street, lay a key building pertaining to "London's arrival as a cosmopolitan center of international trade," the Royal Exchange that from its opening in 1571 brought together merchants "from France, the Netherlands, Italy, and Spain."[74] Known as "strangers," those foreign merchants were drawn to London due to what Howard aptly describes as "the pull of economic opportunity."[75] A 1568 London census describes those "strangers" as Dutch, French, Spanish, Italian, Danish, Scottish, Portuguese, "Jenoways" (possibly Genovese), Polish, and "Barbarian."[76] A 1593 census identified 7,113 strangers—an increase of over four thousand from 1500—from as far as Turkey, Morocco, and Hungary.[77] Those figures make all the more evident how, in London, commerce overrode religious and political efforts to create a bulwark between a Christian West and an Islamic East.

The destabilizing commercial currents of England may have loomed large in the minds of theatergoers attending the initial 1592 run of Marlowe's play at the Rose Theater. To be sure, in watching Marlowe's play at the Rose, playgoers didn't witness the manifest overlap of staged and actual urban commerce in the manner of Croxton. As we saw in the last chapter, because the medieval play was performed outdoors on scaffolds in open areas in a city, it could, when performed near shops and markets, speak quite explicitly to urban commerce and related issues. The Rose, in contrast, was a fourteen-sided structure whose walls separated viewers from its greater environs. However, as scholars of Elizabethan drama have stressed, not only the Rose but also the larger theatrical culture of which it was a part exemplified Elizabethan England's commercial aspects. The Rose was itself a highly commercial enterprise, one of several new public theaters, purpose-built permanent buildings where audience members—most of whom were themselves tradesmen—paid to watch dramatic performances; the profits were used to pay player-shareholders, playhouse owners like Henslowe, and hired workers.[78]

Moreover, despite its closed walls, the Rose prompted viewers to ponder commerce, both global and local, thanks to its location. (figures 18 and 19). Situated only four hundred feet from the south bank of the Thames, on the north side of Maiden Lane Rose Alley and about one hundred feet west of Horseshoe Alley, the Rose stood alongside bear-beating arenas, gardens, brothels and craft workers in the liberty known as the Clink.[79] Together with Paris Gardin, the Clink comprised the Southwark suburb of Bankside. Since the publication of Steven Mullaney's groundbreaking work on the place of the stage in early modern London, scholars have been attuned to how the situation of the Rose and other public theaters—like the Globe,

**FIGURE 18.** View of South Bank from the Agas map. *Source:* Agas, *Plan of London*. By permission of the University of Iowa Libraries, Iowa City. B: Billingsgate, G: Globe Theater, LB: London Bridge, R: Rose Theater.

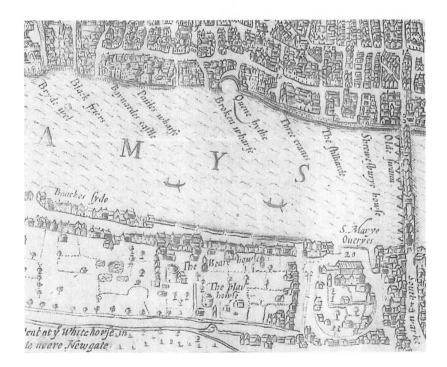

**FIGURE 19.** Detail from the map of London in John Norden's *Speculum Britanniae* (1593). The Rose Theater is referred to as "The Play howse."

the Curtain, and the Theater—in the liberties rendered them liminal sites. Located beyond the walls of London, those theaters transgressed notions of cultural propriety promulgated by city officials.[80] But in addition to stressing the liminality of the Clink, it is crucial to consider how the Rose's placement in that liberty necessitated travel on the part of London theatergoers. As John Schofield stresses, the location of theaters in the liberties during the early modern period in part "stemmed from an idea that to go to the theatre was to make a journey."[81] And the sights and sounds theatergoers encountered while traveling to and from the Rose generated important messages about economy and urban space.

A Londoner's journey to the Rose entailed direct contact with the Thames. Playgoers had two options: they could walk to the theater over London Bridge or travel there via a small boat, called a wherry, from the north bank of the river. The latter option obviously made theatergoers abundantly aware of the Thames as a global commercial artery, especially if they travelled from the east side of London Bridge, where the majority of commercial vessels loaded and unloaded their goods.[82] Medium and small ships docked directly at one of the Legal Quays, while most of the large, seagoing ships heading to and from global destinations anchored in the middle of the river and were unloaded by smaller vessels.[83] Audience members traveling over the bridge weren't quite as immersed in London's river commerce. However, not only did they pass through buildings that testified to London's commercial bent—what John Stow describes in his *Survey of London* as "large, fair, and beautiful buildings inhabitants [*sic*] for the most part rich merchants"—but also they could see the river itself through lookouts.[84] Travelers casting their eyes left of the bridge would have a good view of England's most important dock, Billingsgate, located about five hundred feet from the northern end of the bridge.

## The Place of the Jew in Marlowe's London

Londoners attending *The Jew of Malta* would have become attuned not only to the commercial bent of their city, but also the cosmopolitanism that accompanied global trade. Whether they crossed over London Bridge or took a river wherry, whether looming above or surrounded by boats, theatergoers would have seen and may have heard the voices of foreign-born merchants on vessels hailing from the Netherlands, Morocco, Europe, Iberia, Russia, and other locales. Such aspects of the phenomenology of theater travel suggest how, despite the walls surrounding the Rose, patrons would have a keen sense of the local historical counterparts to not only the commercial practices staged by *The Jew of Malta* but also the depiction in the play of Spanish Christians and Ottoman Turks. But what of Barabas, the Jew who stars in Marlowe's play? Would theatergoers have been cognizant of English parallels to Barabas and other Jews depicted in the play, beyond the convert Menda and other residents of the *Domus*? As we shall see, while Foxe's sermon and the 1290 expulsion suggest a total effacement of contemporary Jews from English space, during the sixteenth century, some Jews did in fact inhabit London and other English locations, where they played an important role in the expanding world economy.

While they are not officially identified as such in censuses, Portuguese Jews—known as New Christians, conversos, and Marranos—also comprised a portion of the "strangers" of sixteenth-century London.[85] A community whose family members in Portugal were forcibly baptized in 1496 and later fled their homes during the inquisition of 1537–40, these secret or crypto-Jews first migrated to Eastern Europe, Africa, and Turkey; later many travelled to Holland and, in much smaller numbers, to England, where they exchanged their "nominal Catholicism for nominal Protestantism" in London as well as other port cities like Bristol.[86] England's Marrano community was small, numbering "between eighty and ninety" and possibly more, if Jonathan Gil Harris is true in his speculation that, due to the strong ties of London's Jews to Antwerp, some of the Dutch immigrants listed in censuses are also crypto-Jews.[87]

Both the diminutive size of the Jewish community in England as well as its hidden nature reflect the relatively unique role of England in the history of Jewish–gentile interaction during this period. Many scholars see the final decades of the sixteenth century as initiating an important and exciting period of transformation in Jewish culture.[88] In France, Italy, the Netherlands, in areas of central and eastern Europe, and in the wide swath of the Ottoman Empire, Jewish communities flourished and grew, particularly in the arenas of learning, print, and trade. England, however, didn't participate significantly in that trend; as David Ruderman puts it, the "cultural profile" of Anglo-Jews "emerges distinctly only in the eighteenth century, and only at that century's end."[89] England couldn't figure in such a history since, unlike other regions in the world, it failed to accommodate any official and public Jewish presence. While elsewhere in the world Muslim and Christian authorities created policies that invited Jews into their regions and countries, no such invitation was forthcoming from Elizabeth (1533–1603) and her advisor William Cecil (1520–98). Only during the reign of James I (1566–1625) would the English initiate official efforts to bring Jews to the island. In other words, just as England stood at the vanguard of medieval antisemitism through factors such as the expulsion, the pogroms of 1189–90, and Thomas of Monmouth's boy-martyr libel, so too was Renaissance England slow to adopt the more "philosemitic" (if at times calculatedly so) gestures of other nations.[90] That early modern English resistance to Jews resulted from a slew of factors that include but are not limited to the idea that Jews threatened Christianity (as converters of Christians, ritual murderers), English economic prosperity (as greedy usurers, mercantile rivals), state welfare (as in the case of the queen's physician Roderigo Lopez), and national identity (i.e., the fantasy that "England" is defined by the absence of Jews there).

There is, however, much more to England's Portuguese Marrano community than its low "cultural profile" and official rejection by the Elizabethan state would suggest. Covertly, the queen, Lord Burghley, and other officials worked closely with and supported several conversos in London, one of whom I will discuss in some detail. And even though England's Jews were small in number, they nevertheless exemplified some of the dynamism and vitality of the early modern Jewish experience. Namely, English conversos demonstrated what Ruderman identifies as a key component of Jewish community during this period: mobility.[91] Reframing received associations of diaspora with hardship and oppression, Ruderman and other scholars such as Jonathan Israel stress how, even as gentile majority leaders oppressed Jews through forced exiles, Jews also actively engaged in a peripatetic lifestyle for intellectual, commercial, and religious purposes. Importantly, that canny approach to mobility encompassed the movements of the Sephardic community of Jews and crypto-Jews, including members of England's Portuguese Jewish community. In Ruderman's words, "the circulation and exchange of individuals, ideas, goods, and institutions defined the very core of the Sephardic diaspora," whose members understood cities not as stable spaces but as "node[s] of movement" and sites for the crisscrossing of multiple flows.[92] Sephardic Jews did not travel solely because of religious and political persecution. As "agents in an international system of trade," they "had reason to travel from place to place, covering long distances, repeatedly crossing regional zones of commerce and culture."[93] Thanks to the networks generated by their mobility, conversos facilitated the trafficking of goods via "maritime rather than overland routes" between a host of locales, and in so doing played a unique and important role in the commercial expansion of Europe.[94]

England's crypto-Jews were part of this dynamic and active trade. Jewish merchants such as George Añes (died ca. 1538) and his son Dunstan (ca. 1520–94), the physician Hector Nunez (1520–91), Gabriel Fernandes, Alvaro de Lima, Jeronimo Lopez, and Fernando del Mercado, through their ties to traders in Lisbon and Antwerp, served as mediators in the movement to northern Europe of goods from Iberian entrepôts.[95] The settlement patterns of many of those Jews reflect their role in global trade. Most of the

London streets where Jews lived—such as Duke's Place, Hart Street, Mark or Marte Lane, Crutched Friars Lane, and the Minories—were located in the wealthy and prominent ward of Tower Street, in an area that was bordered on the south by Tower Street, the north by Fenchurch Street, the west by Mincing Lane, and the east by the Minories (figure 20). The Tower Street Ward was very near (about two hundred yards from) the north bank of the Thames, where, at the twenty Legal Quays crammed between the Custom House and London Bridge, the vast majority of ships bringing goods in and out of the city moored.

How cognizant might Marlowe and other Londoners have been of the small converso community in the city? When the playwright moved in 1587 from Cambridge to Norton Folgate, he lived at a considerable remove (about a seven minute walk northwest) of the area on the east side of the city where most Marranos settled.[96] Yet the location of London's conversos nevertheless may have fostered an awareness of them on the part of Marlowe, as well as Londoners generally. Mark Lane, a street inhabited by conversos, was part of the route used for both royal processions and city pageants.[97] Due to the

**FIGURE 20.** Jewish settlement patterns in sixteenth-century London. Adapted from the Agas map. F: Fenchurch Street, H: Hart Street, LB: London Bridge, M: Mark Lane, T: Tower Street. *Source: Agas, Plan of London.* By permission of the University of Iowa Libraries, Iowa City.

popularity of those festive civic rituals, as well as executions on Tower Hill, Londoners frequently gathered in areas contiguous to the Marrano community, and hence may have been aware of their presence. Such factors may help account for the claim, articulated in the 1588 testimony of an inquisition informant, that the presence of crypto-Jews "is public and notorious in London."[98]

Evidence that Marlowe knew of London's Marrano population appears in *The Jew of Malta* itself, in the lines with which I began this chapter. Included among the rich Jews named by Barabas is *"Nones* in *Portugall,"* an apparent reference to the Portuguese converso Hector Nunez, who lived in London from ca. 1549 until his death in 1591.[99] The owner of what must have been large houses on Hart Street and later Mark Lane, Nunez was a distinguished physician, a leader in the Marrano community, and a man tied to high-ranking English officials, including the queen, her advisor Cecil, and Secretary of State Francis Walsingham.[100] In addition to working as a doctor, Nunez "engaged in foreign trade on a large scale."[101] Over the course of some thirty years, Nunez traded jewels, cloth, dyes, wine, spices, sugar, and other foodstuffs in Europe, North Africa, South America, and India.[102] Nunez's massive commercial ventures relied upon his connections to trading partners—who consisted of both relatives and other associates—in London, Antwerp, and Lisbon.[103] Thanks to those business ties, Nunez facilitated the movement of not only goods but also intelligence to England. It is said that he was the first person to notify Walsingham of the gathering of the Spanish Armada in Lisbon.[104]

It is precisely the global nature of the Jewish network with which Nunez worked that Marlowe stresses through Barabas's speech. To be sure, the monologue contains many fictive and stereotypical elements. Of all the men listed by Barabas, only "Nones" has a real-life sixteenth-century counterpart; both "Kirriah Jairim" and "Obed" seem to be taken from the book of Chronicles in the bible.[105] And, as Eric Griffin points out, the speech, "like the play more generally, reinscribes a culturally hyperbolic commonplace about 'Jewish' ability to accumulate wealth."[106] But alongside its mythic aspects, the passage does affirm a certain reality. By referring to Nunez in conjunction with himself and other prominent Jews around the world (*"Kirriah Jairim, the great Jew of Greece, / Obed* in *Bairseth* [possibly Beirut], . . . some in *Italy,* / Many in *France"* [1.1.121–24]) Barabas conjures a visual map of the global commercial system of which the converso merchants historically were a part.[107] Undermining stereotypes of the global dispersal of oppressed Jews, Barabas refers to an array of canny Jews, actively working together via a world trading system.

## Opening up the Counting House

If Barabas's speech touches on the new and exciting early modern reality of Jewish trade in a global network that encompassed England, Marlowe opens his play with a scene that supports a centuries-old stereotype. Notoriously, *The Jew of Malta* begins by revealing "*BARABAS in his Counting-house, with heapes of gold before him*" (1.1). As many critics observe, insofar as this initial image recalls the vice figures of morality plays, it immediately labels Barabas as a conniving and corrupt antichrist figure.[108] Yet while the glittering "heapes of gold" before Barabas would have appalled ascetic-minded Christians watching the play, that treasure surely would have appealed to the profit-minded members of Marlowe's London audience.[109] After all, as we have seen, English cities had long devoted themselves to trade, even as they had for centuries denied Jews any official role in that commercial activity. Marlowe's cognizance of how his nation could tolerate only a covert Jewish presence—the open secret described by the inquisition informant—helps explain his decision to place "Nones" not in England but in the Portuguese homeland to which Nunez fled in the 1540s. At the same time, Barabas and his treasure register how, while the English officially banned Jews from their island, they were more than willing to maintain a virtual Jewish presence in the form of mythic rich men like Barabas, performed by actors on English stages. The opening scene looks back to the start of the Croxton *Play of the Sacrament*, whose Jewish merchant Jonathas, like Barabas, appears first in his home and voices a monologue that catalogs his many precious and exotic goods. Both plays speak to an English fascination with and even attraction to fantasies about the "Jewish" accumulation of goods.

Furthermore, both *The Jew of Malta* and Croxton depict how greed prompts Christians to associate with Jews. In somewhat the same way that Jonathas's treasure impels the Christian merchant Aristorius to invite the Jew into his home, Barabas's wealth accounts for his presence in Christian Malta. As a Hospitaller knight puts it to the Jew in the second scene of act 1, "Thou art a Merchant, and a monied man, / And 'tis thy mony, Barabas, we [i.e., the Christian authorities of Malta] seeke" (1.2.52–53). Malta's investment in Barabas's wealth is such that, after Ferneze seizes the merchant's goods and his house, the Spanish governor tells Barabas "we will not banish thee," with the expectation that the Jew will "get more" riches and again benefit a greedy Spanish state (1.2.101–3). Clearly, neither the knight nor the governor exhibit the kind of hospitality that Aristorius extends to Jonathas. Aristorius warmly—if calculatedly—hosts his Jewish guest. In contrast, both Ferneze and the knight view Barabas and his wealth with a hypocritical mixture of greedy desire and religious scorn. While they allow Barabas to remain in Malta for financial reasons, they deride him for his "inherent sinne" and in particular the "monstrous sin" of "covetousnesse" (1.2.110; 1.2.124).

The irony of Maltese Christians denigrating Barabas for a sin they also embody is clear. What may be less obvious is how Marlowe maps out Christian greed by revising the imagined spaces of medieval English antisemitic writing. As we have seen, English writers construe Jewish and Christian identities in relation to urban sites and especially two built environments, the house and the church. Even Croxton, which features not only the Jew's house of antisemitic lore but also a Christian abode, juxtaposes those domestic sites with the church where the Eucharist is venerated. In contrast, no churches feature in Marlowe's play, because the piety associated with those buildings has no place in Malta, where everyone—whether Spaniard or Turk or Jew—worships money.

To be sure, there are ways in which the imagined geography of *The Jew of Malta* might seem to counter the idea that greed is universal. Namely, Marlowe suggests how greed is particular to Jews in Barabas's opening monologue, when the merchant refers to hiding "Infinite riches in a little roome," a phrase that connotes goods tightly crammed in a closed built environment (1.1.37). Counting houses were associated with the private accumulation of goods; for example, a 1577 translation of a sermon by Swiss reformer Heinrich Bullinger (1504–75) denigrates greedy merchants who "keepe themselues cloase in secreate counting houses," where "their baggs are their pillowes whereon they sleepe."[110] As critics such as Julia Lupton and Leslie Thomson point out, when the play was first performed at the Rose Theater, Barabas likely appeared in "the discovery space," a small opening within the tiring house wall that could "suggest secrecy or containment" and reinforce the idea that Barabas hides his wealth.[111] The closed geography of the counting house may seem at this point, at the start of the play, to refer not only to Barabas's secret wealth but also to his own identity; the boundaries of the counting house perhaps define the Jew and set him apart from others for his intense devotion to wealth.

But if Marlowe invokes the economic Jew in this scene, he soon problematizes that stereotype by having Barabas, immediately after he refers to the "little room," radically shift spatial scales. Most likely stepping beyond the discovery space onto the stage, Barabas asks

> But now how stands the wind?
> Into what corner peeres my Halcions bill?
> Ha, to the East? yes: See how stands the Vanes?
> East and by-South: why then I hope my ships
> I sent for *Egypt* and the bordering Iles
> Are gotten up by *Nilus* winding bankes:
> Mine Argosie from *Alexandria*,
> Loaden with Spice and Silkes, now under saile,
> Are smoothly gliding downe by *Candie* shoare
> To *Malta*, through our *Mediterranean* sea.
>
> *(1.1.38–47)*

Like Aristorius, the Christian merchant of Croxton who brags about how his merchandise "renneth" throughout the world, Barabas considers the movements of his own laden vessels in the Mediterranean.[112] Because they are the source of his wealth, the open movements of the Jew's ships don't so much contrast as intersect with the "secret" accumulation of riches in the counting house. The counting house is finally no closed space but is mutually constitutive with the flow of wealth in the greater commercial world, where a host of different persons trade and seek out profit. As Lisa Jardine points out, Barabas's description of his merchant ships traveling from Alexandria and Crete conjures a highly accurate image of the Eastern Mediterranean as it was visualized via early modern cartography.[113] Here, in the same way that the vast quantities of wealth in the counting house may have proven attractive to some audience members, Barabas's Mediterranean trade connections may have awed trade-minded persons in Marlowe's audience, living in a nation striving to expand its commercial purview farther and farther beyond the island. The play would have encouraged such a comparison when a merchant tells Barabas "Thy ships are safe, riding in *Malta* Rhode" (1.1.49), a line that imagines a harboring in Malta akin to the many dockings happening not far from the Rose along the Thames.

When Barabas instructs the merchant who notifies him of his ship's arrival to bring "threescore Camels, thirty Mules, / and twenty Waggons to bring up the ware" from his newly arrived ships (1.1.58–59), Marlowe adds to this first scene one more element that signals the playwright's interest in revising the imagined geography of earlier English antisemitic tales. Barabas arranges for a colossal procession of goods—a parade entailing over a hundred mechanical and animal conveyances—in the open thoroughfares of Malta.[114] Processions, as we have seen, are crucial to English antisemitic myths. But while the *Prioress's Tale*, Croxton, and other libels end in the triumphant procession of spiritual treasure (a boy or a host), *The Jew of Malta* begins with the grandiose procession of literal treasures. The fact that Barabas can stage his procession in such a spectacularly public manner evinces how he shares with Christians an admiration of material goods. This is not to deny that Barabas hides his wealth, but to distinguish his brand of secrecy from that displayed by the Jewish antagonists of earlier English antisemitic myths. Here the secrecy that in previous tales connotes the alterity of the Jew to Christians now indicates his similitude to the greater world of Malta. Barabas accumulates goods secretly—"warily garding that which I ha got" (1.1.185)—precisely because he knows that Christians love those goods too.

## The Jew's House of Malta

Christian interest in Barabas's goods soon becomes manifest when authorities, claiming they need to pay ten years' worth of tribute to the "Emperour of *Turkey*," seize Barabas's belongings (1.2.39). Ferneze appropriates both Barabas's goods and his home. As Park Honan observes, "Lightly, this echoes a major crisis in English history. When the kingdom's Jews were expelled in the thirteenth century, their houses, their farms, their lands—down to the last half-acre—were forfeited to the state."[115] Barabas's individual loss resonates with the disastrous, large-scale seizure of Jewish property in 1290 and the intertwining of that event with the greed of the medieval English Crown.[116] However, while Jews were expelled from England partly because they no longer proved profitable to the Crown, Spanish authorities in Marlowe's play retain Barabas on the island in the hope that he can generate still more wealth and further benefit them. As the play continues, the Spanish retention of Barabas as a mere generator of wealth, to put it mildly, proves mistaken. Barabas is no victim but a resourceful and cunning figure.

The merchant's skillful response to his maltreatment by the state involves murderous actions that support the association, implicit in the 1290 expulsion and in early modern England's failure to admit Jews in any official capacity, of the "Jew" with danger. Medieval libels of course gave imaginative "proof" of such notions with their depiction of Jews who are forever locked into the deicidal, anti-Christian stance associated with their ancestors. Unlike the Jews of medieval libels, however, Barabas doesn't reenact the Crucifixion by martyring boys or attacking Eucharistic wafers. Instead of attacking Christian doctrine in the manner of host-desecration or ritual-murder

myths, Barabas exhibits a highly destructive combination of greed, vengeful-
ness, and megalomania directed at not only Christians but also other gentiles.
The Maltese governor's son, the young man's friend, two friars, a slave, a
prostitute, a courtesan, hundreds of Spanish and Turkish troops, and an entire
convent of nuns all perish due to the merchant's stratagems. This image of
the Jew as a greedy and lethal figure builds on medieval stereotypes of dangerous "Jewish" materialisms and commercial practices, ideas that were still
very much in play in Marlowe's England. Thus in *Three Ladies of London* the
figure of Usury is a "hard-harted knaue" (2.175) of Jewish ancestry who
"kild" a man's "father with sorrow" (2.108), and the merchant Mercadorus
exemplifies how Christians "seeke to excel . . . in Iewisnes" (2.1436) through
execrable actions performed for "greedines of the mony" (2.1431).[117] Barabas in many respects engages and expands on the widespread stereotype that
greed is a treacherous and essentially "Jewish" phenomenon.[118]

Barabas performs his outrageous realization of myths of "Jewish" danger
through the domestic locations that typify medieval English antisemitism.
As we have seen, the great fear registered in so many medieval texts is that,
under the cover of their homes, Jews perform horrible anti-Christian deeds.
The accommodated Jew would continue to obsess Renaissance writers even
as notions of the precise danger lurking in the Jewish domicile shifted. With
the Reformation rejection of transubstantiation, anxiety over host desecration dissipated. Claims of ritual murder, in contrast, persisted. The libel was
told and retold in printed editions of Thomas of Monmouth's inaugural legend, Holinshed's *Chronicles*, and other histories such as Foxe's *Book of Martyrs*
and Hartmann Schedel's *Nuremberg Chronicle*, which illustrated its recounting
of Simon of Trent's alleged murder in "the Jew Samuel's house" via a horrific
woodcut.[119] In *The Jew of Malta*, Marlowe alludes to ritual murder at the end
of act 3, when friar Bernadine asks his fellow religious Jacomo "to exclaime
against the Iew" and latter asks, "What, has he crucified a child?" (3.6.49).[120]
After Marlowe, the proto-picaresque English novelist Thomas Nashe would
riff on ritual murder when the roguish protagonist of *The Unfortunate Traveler*
(1594), Jack Wilton, is nearly dissected alive in the house of a Jewish physician named Zacharie.[121] And of course Shylock's "sober" house also signified
in relation to the libel. As Roy Booth observes, when Nerissa, playing the
part of a boy clerk, travels to Shylock's home to retrieve Portia's ring "and
emerges safely," audience members would have breathed a sigh of relief.[122]

While Barabas never performs ritual murder, he certainly engages the
long-standing English interest in the accommodated Jew. Over thirty references to Barabas's home appear in the play, and the merchant's house figures
significantly in the plot of all five acts. Indeed, Barabas's home is so crucial

to the drama that Marlowe could easily have titled it not *The Jew of Malta* but *The Jew's House of Malta*. Playing with the trope of the Jewish house, Marlowe associates Barabas with not one but three domiciles that, over the course of the play, increase in grandeur and heft as the merchant's lethal effects magnify. Barabas's first house, an impressive built environment that one of the knights calls a "mansion," is appropriated by the state before Barabas can do anything there beyond the hoarding staged in the first scene (1.2.129). Barabas's second house is "as great and faire as is the Governors" and figures in the deaths of both his daughter's two suitors and two friars (2.3.14). By the end of the play, Barabas not only assumes ownership of the governor's home (i.e., the citadel of Malta) but also controls an erstwhile monastery, where all of the Turkish troops are "massacred" (5.5.106).

Like his infiltration of the city sewers, and the lengthy procession of his goods through the streets of Malta, Barabas's ever-expanding real estate holdings undermine the association of Jews with diaspora, dispersal, and exile and assert instead a masterful Jewish control over Christian territory. Of course, taken one way, Barabas's actions ultimately seem to support negative stereotypes about Jews and diaspora. By deploying his spatial savvy for nefarious ends, Barabas exemplifies why Jews should not live in Christian lands, whether in England, Malta, or elsewhere. Jews don't merit a stable habitation, the example of Barabas suggests, because they will use their accommodations to harm other people. Yet at the same time that Barabas affirms Christian myths about "Jewish" danger and its relation to built environments, he also serves an important social function. Namely, Barabas is a biting satirist and social critic whose relationship to space points not only to Jewish but also to Christian failings. Yes, Barabas attacks Malta, but he does so in a manner that satirizes the material dimensions of its Christian society.

## Conventual Commercialism and Barabas's First Home

Barabas performs that satirical work throughout the play, starting with his response to the state extortion of his wealth and home. When a Hospitaller knight advises Ferneze to appropriate Barabas's house, the knight frames that seizure of property in a manner that foregrounds traditional thinking about the geography of Christian piety, that is, the role built environments play in fostering Christian identity. "Grave Governor," the knight tells Ferneze, "Convert his mansion to a Nunnery, / His house will harbour many holy Nuns" (1.2.128–30). The knight's use of the verb "convert" suggests that Barabas's home will undergo a transformation as substantial as that wrought in the new Christian believer. The knight not only suggests that buildings are like persons but also implies, through the consonance linking "harbour" to "holy," that buildings foster certain modes of being, namely the ascetic piety of the Christian religious. No longer a mercantile home open to global trade, the convent will "harbour" in the manner of the earliest English definitions of that verb; it will "keep in safety or . . . protect" the nuns from worldly corruption and thus nurture their "holy" state.[123]

Importantly, the knight specifies that *female* religious will inhabit Barabas's house, a move that separates Marlowe's work from earlier English anti-semitic myths, which typically focus on men (boys, Christ in the host, and at times even monks). By redirecting our attention from men to women, Marlowe can offer a fuller and more nuanced response to Christian fantasies about space. Namely, the knight's linkage of the space of the convent with the vulnerable bodies of nuns recalls the prominent role of women in the many architectural allegories that were produced during the middle ages and renaissance.[124] Such allegories tended to feature women, in part due to their worry over the status of woman's sexual organ as an aperture or gateway.[125] Through its staging of the "harbored" nuns, Marlowe's play responds to a long tradition in which images of protected, sealed, and fortified spaces figure chastity and the holy woman. Converted into a convent, Barabas's home thus will not only protect the nuns but also serve as an architectural double for nuns themselves and their virginal bodies. The bulwarks of Malta, there-fore, aren't the only instance in Marlowe's drama when Christian identity emerges in relation to fortified space. In the same way that Malta suppos-edly separates the Christian West from the Ottoman East, convents separate women from men.

Barabas suggests otherwise, however, by shoring up the status of woman not as a sealed edifice but as a figure caught up in destabilizing material flows. The merchant instructs his daughter Abigail to pretend to convert to Chris-tianity, enter the convent, extract from it treasure that he has hidden under the second floor, and then return to him. When Abigail follows her father's orders, her movements in and out of the convent evoke not so much sealed cloisters but breached buildings and the secular notion of female identity those structures evoke, that is, the wandering, promiscuous woman. Abigail's wanderings, however, aren't so much erotic as commercial. She evinces a close relationship with capital both in the way her movements mirror that of Barabas's treasure and in her direct contact with that wealth. Moreover, Abigail herself is a kind of treasure. After she delivers the hidden wealth to her father from inside the convent, Barabas exclaims: "Oh my girle, / My gold, my fortune, my felicity. . . . Oh girle, oh gold, oh beauty, oh my blisse!"

(2.1.46–53). Barabas's list of beloved objects suggests their equivalence and interchangeability, a relationship further confirmed when he hugs his bags of gold instead of Abigail (2.2.53).[126] In contrast to the convent's evocation of woman as chaste virgin, Abigail connotes woman's status as a valuable object on the market.

This episode, however, doesn't so much juxtapose profane with pious notions of female space as invoke the secular to undermine the sacred. By hiding his treasure in his home, and deploying his daughter to recover it, Barabas generates a heuristic about the convent's "true" nature. Literally, the "Ten thousand Portagues, besides great Perles, / Rich costly Jewels, and Stones infinite" secreted in the structure are Barabas's possessions and thus refer to him (1.2.244–45). Viewed this way, the lingering presence of Jewish wealth in the convent may suggest the impossibility of conversion, architectural or otherwise.[127] As the merchant's reference to "Stones infinite" crammed beneath the plank suggests, the convent still resembles its Jewish predecessor, counting house and all (1.2.245). The cloister thus seems to remain stubbornly "Jewish" in the same way that Jewishness persists in the human converts like the conversos of London. Yet because the treasure was hidden in the house and lingers for a time there after it becomes a convent, the loot becomes, however briefly, associated with that space. Read as an integral if disavowed component of the nun's home, the treasure thus has the capacity to speak not so much to the process of conversion but to the actual nature of all convents. Hidden in the building, the treasure serves as a kind of carnal unconscious to the ostensibly spiritual space of the convent. Critics such as Greenblatt have noted how Marlowe renders the nuns carnal not only through multiple joking allusions to their promiscuity but also through their "new made Nunnery," whose existence resulted from the greedy appropriation of property.[128] Moreover, moving into that new convent requires the nuns to leave their former cloister and "stray . . . farre amongst the multitude" in the corrupt society of Malta (1.2.302; 1.2.305). Barabas's treasure indicates that Christian carnality. Situated tellingly in the foundational location of the convent's flooring, the treasure reveals how this built environment is corrupt from within, from the "ground" up.

The ironic manner in which Barabas marks the spot where his treasure lurks also refers to Christian carnality. Instructing Abigail how to retrieve the hoard, Barabas tells her "The boord is marked thus † that covers it," and makes the sign of the cross (1.2.350). The very idea of a cross in a Jewish home recalls the ritual-crucifixion myth. But in this secular and sardonic revision of that fantasy, the cross does not refer to the Crucifixion or the deicidal Jew. In the same way that Abigail feigns Christian conversion for monetary purposes, the cross indicates not the sacrifice on which Christianity ostensibly centers but rather material gain. "Religion," as Barabas puts it to his daughter, "Hides many mischiefs from suspition" (1.2.279–80). Importantly, those acts of religious feigning associated with Barabas's daughter and home also figure the false nature of Christianity itself. Both the convent and its residents offer a show of Christian asceticism that masks greedy impulses.[129] The convent only pretends to be a cloister, when it is in reality yet another counting house.

The affinity between convents and counting houses surely was a familiar concept to the Anglican members of Marlowe's audience. By Marlowe's time, convents and monasteries had been emptied of any sacred authority ascribed to them in medieval times and exposed as structures housing greedy and carnal persons. During the dissolution of the monasteries between 1536 and 1540, Henry VIII assumed control over eight hundred religious houses, while his chief minister Thomas Cromwell oversaw the painstaking and thorough removal of all material goods contained in monasteries, convents, friaries, abbeys, and conventual churches. A letter to Cromwell describes how the "commissioners" of the dissolution "were asked to assess the value, first, of the lead, bells, and other parts of the buildings that could be broken up before the sale of the 'mansion'; secondly, of all jewels, ornaments, moneys, stocks and stores."[130] With its account of state agents gathering up jewels, moneys, and other goods from a monastery—tellingly called a "mansion" in the letter—the missive imagines the convent less as an otherworldly cloister than as a place nearly identical to the home of a wealthy merchant like Barabas. Indeed, in much the same way that Barabas hides goods in a "little room" beneath a floor plank, English monks and nuns hid treasure in their cloisters and churches: three commissioners at Glastonbury abbey wrote Cromwell that "we have daily found and tried out both money and plate hid and mured up in walls, vaults, and other secret places, as well by the abbot and others of the convent."[131]

In the urban milieu where *The Jew of Malta* was first performed, the spatial changes wrought by the dissolution were palpable, and indeed constituted, in Schofield's words, "the fundamental change to the topography of London in the decades before 1600."[132] In a move that inverts the architectural conversion staged by the repurposing of Barabas's house for the nuns, monastic complexes throughout England were given over to secular uses.[133] Because most of the monasteries were built near the city walls, such changes were most visible to residents like Marlowe, who lived near London's borders. Before passing through Bishopsgate on his way into the city from Norton Folgate, Marlowe would have viewed on his right the transformed spaces of what was St. Mary Bethlehem priory; once in the city, the playwright passed on his left the newly transformed spaces of St. Helen's Priory; while visiting the Rose, Marlowe was near the former grounds of the priory of St. Mary Ovarie in Southwark. Of the three former convents, St. Helen's evinced the greatest transformation; in 1544 Thomas Kendall bought several buildings, which were used for the leathersellers company.[134] As the use of St. Helen's for a livery company demonstrates, to an extent, the massive topographic changes of the dissolution manifested hidden material elements of purportedly "holy" sites; while nuns and monks hid goods inside walls and other "secret places," tradesmen openly sought monetary gain. The repurposing of monasteries as urban palaces, industrial complexes, and even public theaters all looked back to the inauthentic nature of the piety of nuns and monks and their status as performers—as men and women feigning asceticism—who are in reality invested in material gain.[135] The dissolution, in other words, allowed for the morphing of covert Catholic avarice into explicit Protestant acquisition.[136] Marlowe of course couldn't aim "his corrosive representation of Christian hypocrisy" directly at his sixteenth-century London audience.[137] Instead of evincing how English Protestants had failed to move beyond Catholic materialism, he represents Spanish Catholics sharing in a "Jewish" carnality. Barabas, ostensibly the embodiment of an old "Jewish" carnality that Christianity supersedes in the manner of the convent supplanting the Jewish house, ultimately figures a Catholic corruption that, in turn, obliquely registers the new materialisms of Malta's insular double to the west, Reformation England.

## "As great and faire as is the Governors": Barabas's Second Home

After he recovers his treasure, Barabas defiantly announces his refusal to suffer the geographic instability ascribed to Jews: "I have bought a house / As great and faire as is the Governors; / And there in spite of *Malta* will I dwell" (2.3.13–15). Like his first home, Barabas's second dwelling allows him to expose the greedy materialisms linking Christians to their supposed Jewish others. In the first of two episodes associated with the house, it serves as the setting for the pursuit of Abigail by her two suitors, the Governor's son Lodowick and his friend Mathias. Here, Christian greed assumes a distinctly erotic cast.[138] Lodowick, eager to discover if Abigail is as beautiful as her suitor Mathias claims she is, asks "*Barabas*, canst helpe me to a Diamond?" (2.3.49). The youth evinces a greedy interest in Abigail as treasure that makes him the Jew's Christian double. After some lapidary-inflected wordplay on Abigail between the two men, Barabas indicates his willingness to give his daughter-diamond over to Lodowick, when he urges the suitor to "come to my house," where Abigail now lives, having left the convent (2.3.67). The merchant implores the governor's son to visit the Jew's home on increasingly warm terms, from the familial "come home" to the suggestive "be no stranger at my house" (2.3.92; 2.3.138). Barabas's request that Lodowick not be a stranger obviously is ironic; in many nasty asides to the audience, he derides Lodowick as his enemy (e.g., 2.3.42–43). But on another level, the merchant's words register the material affinities of Jew and Christian. Lodowick isn't "strange" or foreign to Barabas's house, insofar as he relates to that space in the grasping fashion that the merchant does: as the container of Abigail the "gem," that is, as yet another counting house and locus of greed. Barabas's new dwelling exposes how Jews and Christians are not alien but connected to each other by their materialisms.

Marlowe reinforces such links by having Lodowick arrive at the domicile at the same time that Abigail gives her father "letters come / From *Ormus*," that is, Hormuz, a Middle Eastern port city associated with both the gem trade and sexual licentiousness (2.3.225–26). The coincidental appearance of both the letters and the suitor implies how Lodowick's business at Barabas's house isn't altogether different from that conducted between the merchant and his colleagues in the Middle East. Like the counting house at the start of the play with its ties to global networks, Barabas's second home is open to gem trading—that is, literal jewels and Abigail as object—on both the Persian Gulf and in Malta. In keeping with its stress on the openness of Barabas's home to commercial flows, this scene emphasizes its front door. When he and Lodowick arrive at the house, Barabas calls from outside "What, ho, Abigall; open the doore I say" (2.3.224). After Lodowick enters Barabas peruses the letters while lingering outside the door, highlighting its status as the primary domestic portal, a site that, more than any other architectural feature of the house, manifests its intersection with outside commercial forces.

Barabas soon turns our attention to his front door again. Still lingering before the entrance, he encounters Mathias and tells him that Lodowick has been actively pursuing Abigail. Abigail's commodification intensifies as Barabas characterizes Lodowick's efforts to woo Abigail in commercial terms: the governor's son "sends her letters, bracelets, jewels, rings" (2.3.260). Abigail, however, refuses to "sell" herself. She "sends them backe," and

when he comes, she lockes her selfe up fast;
Yet through the key-hole will he talke to her,

While she runs to the window looking out
When you should come and hale him from the doore.

*(2.3.262–66)*

Barabas again emphasizes his front door, which now figures less as a gateway to trade than a built environment like the convent (i.e., a site whose fortification is bound up with the safeguarding of a woman's body). Merging home and girl, the merchant describes how, though Abigail "lockes her *selfe* up fast" (my emphasis), Lodowick manages nevertheless to "talke to her" through the "key-hole" of the front door. Here, more than at any other moment in the play, Barabas keenly attends to the various apertures of his dwelling, from its main entrance, to the tiny opening of the keyhole on the door, to the window above it. Multiple ironies emerge from the resulting image of the Jewish house. Jumping scales downward from the defense of a community to that of a person, Barabas describes how, even as Malta fortifies itself in fear of a Turkish siege, other attacks are occurring within the island, in the form of an erotic battle between the sexes.[139] Here not a Christian island but the home of a Jewish woman on that island is the object of Christian attack. And, in the same way that Malta doesn't enjoy a supreme inviolability, Abigail can't seem to shut out Lodowick, who delivers love-talk through the keyhole of the locked door while she, from her balcony, anxiously awaits Mathias's aid. Of course, this scene isn't really about the vulnerability of Barabas's home or his daughter. Lodowick hasn't actually laid siege to Abigail and the house; that notion is a fiction cunningly crafted by Barabas, who in fact has ordered his daughter to trick Lodowick into believing she loves him. The Jew's ultimate goal here is to lure the male suitors into a fatal duel. Yet in achieving that nefarious goal, Barabas sends up Christian fantasies about spatial security and cohesion, suggesting how the forces of lust—like the equally carnal forces of capital—can penetrate built environments regardless of their fortifications.

In act 2, Barabas's second home attracts Christian men drawn to the singular, matchless gem it contains: the "diamond" Abigail. In act 4, Barabas continues to use his home as the setting for the exposure of Christian materialisms, though the materialisms in question are not those of a layman like Lodowick, but rather belong to members of Christian fraternal orders. That exposure occurs when two friars accuse Barabas of engineering Lodowick's and Mathias's deaths. The merchant first attempts to gain the friars' favor by offering to turn Christian. Then Barabas sweetens the deal by offering to give over his riches upon his conversion:

> Cellers of Wine, and Sollers full of Wheat,
> Ware-houses stuft with spices and with drugs,
> Whole Chests of Gold, in Bulloine, and in Coyne,
> Besides I know not how much weight in Pearle
> Orient and round, have I within my house;
> At Alexandria, Merchandize unsold:
> But yesterday two ships went from this Towne,
> Their voyage will be worth ten thousand Crownes.
> In Florence, Venice, Antwerpe, London, Civill,
> Frankeford, Lubecke, Mosco, and where not,
> Haue I debts owing; and in most of these,
> Great summes of mony lying in the bancho;
> All this I'le giue to some religious house
> So I may be baptiz'd and liue therein.
>
> *(4.1.66–79)*

While the singular "gem" Abigail drew the young suitors to the merchant's home, here an array of goods—wine, spices, wheat, gold, and pearls—within the chambers and warehouses of Barabas's house entices the monks. Enhancing the sheer plenitude of Barabas's wealth is its global scattering. Wealth amasses not only in the Barabas's Maltese home but also in North Africa, Eurasia, and—in a line in the play that acknowledges England's participation in global profitmaking—as far west as London. The Jew lures the friars by promising them that "All this I'le giue to some religious house." Here, as with Barabas's first home-turned-nunnery, the differences between Catholic religious house and Jewish mansion fall away.[140] As the receptacle of Barabas's wealth, the religious house becomes yet another counting house. Tantalized, the brothers contend over whose fraternal order will reap the profits of the Jew's "conversion." First Jacomo exclaims, "Oh, good Barabas, come to our house"; then Bernardine immediately counters with "Oh, no, good Barabas, come to our house!" and Jacomo reiterates "Good Barabas come to me" (4.1.80–81; 4.1.90). Barabas then convinces Jacomo of his success, telling him "goe you home with me," and "come to my house" (4.1.92; 4.1.94). The rapid repetition of "come to my house" in the scene creates a kind of domestic jumble that confuses all three houses, emptying each of any distinctive character and imbuing them all with the self-interest and greedy flows that everywhere inform Marlowe's Malta.

The only act of hosting to which the exchange ultimately leads is Bernardine's arrival in Barabas's home. There, in the scene in the play that most resonates with antisemitic libels, Barabas's slave Ithamore strangles Bernardine. Bernardine's demise recalls how, in certain boy-singer legends, Jews kill monks inside their homes.[141] The geographic location of the friar's murder contributes to the resonance of that death with boy-singer libels. When, before the murder, Ithamore assures his master that "none can heare" Bernadine "cry he ne'er so loud," and Barabas responds "Why true, therefore did I place him there: / The other Chambers open towards the street" (4.1.139–41), Marlowe encourages his audience to imagine the most private, interior room of the Jew's domicile, probably the discovery space that served as Barabas's counting house in act 1. That stress on the domestic concealment of Jewish misconduct recalls how English libels train the reader's eye on architectural features that hide the crimes imagined to occur in Jewish houses: closed doors, sealed-up ovens, and, that most private of domestic locales, the latrine. But here, as elsewhere in the play, antisemitic tropes both appear in secular guise and receive satirical treatment. Stripping the myth of Jewish menace of its religious import, Barabas kills the friar not to mock the Crucifixion, test the host's divinity, or silence a Marian hymn, but to keep his role in the suitors' deaths a secret. And the friar is no boy martyr but a man defined by carnality.

## The "Homely Citadel": Barabas's Third Home

Insofar as *The Jew of Malta* exploits Christian anxieties over the Jewish home and the nefarious deeds purported to occur there, its final act brings such concerns to a head. Having led the Turks into Malta, Barabas becomes governor and moves into his third and final home, the citadel of the island and thus the most fortified of his dwellings. With this plot element, Marlowe imagines the religious other supposedly condemned to dispersal and spatial disenfranchisement enjoying the most privileged spatiality imaginable. Barabas finally seems to have become the "Jew" of "Malta" in its most straightforward (and paradoxical) meaning, that is, a Jew who controls the island and partakes in its renowned fortifications. The final scene of the play initially seems to confirm how Barabas has shifted from spatial destabilizer to a man who embraces spatial security and stability. The scene opens with Barabas "*with a Hammar above, very busie*," supervising a construction project in his new home (5.5). As Barabas asks the carpenters "How stand the cords? How hang these hinges, fast? / Are all the Cranes and Pulleyes sure?" he evinces a newfound interest in architectural reliability and solidity (5.5.1–2). "Leave nothing loose, all leveld to my mind," the merchant urges the workmen (5.5.3).

However, motivating Barabas's interest in architectural integrity is a notably disruptive enterprise. As Barabas explains to Ferneze, his "home-improvement" project is the construction in his citadel of "a dainty Gallery, / The floore whereof, this Cable being cut, / Doth fall asunder; so that it doth sinke / Into a deepe pit past recovery" (5.5.33–36). The addition to the citadel is part of a scheme in which Barabas plans to double-cross the Turks, regain the good graces of both Ferneze and Christian Malta, and receive "Great summes of mony" for his services (5.3.86). The merchant has invited Calymath to dine at the citadel, where he plans to trap the Turkish ruler as he walks along the trick passage.[142] Barabas thus has rendered his new home securely unreliable, with "sure" and "fast" mechanisms that will remove the ground from beneath the Turk's feet. The Jew's stratagem, like the murder of Jacomo in his second house, reiterates stereotypes about nefarious behavior inside the Jewish home. Yet here the victim is a Turk, and the Jewish house is deployed to benefit a Christian. Complicating matters further is the fact that, unbeknownst to Barabas, his house will assist Ferneze far more than the Jew realizes; the governor tricks the merchant into falling into the very domestic trap the Jew set for Calymath.[143] The Jewish home thus ultimately morphs into a vehicle for antisemitic violence, a hell-like place where Barabas suffers "intolerable pangs" inside a cauldron below the gallery (5.5.87).[144]

As many critics have noted, through Barabas's demise, Marlowe affirms traditional Christian thinking. In the same way that the Jew's first appearance in the play with piles of gold signaled his identity as a classic Vice figure, Barabas's descent mirrors the punishment accorded that villain in morality plays. The nature of Barabas's death also reinforces stereotypes about the "Jewish" nature of greed in the manner of the *Doom* sculpture discussed in the last chapter, with its image of a Jewish moneylender being thrust into the maw of hell. The location of the cauldron in the discovery space—where Barabas first appeared in his counting house—reinforces such associations, by reminding viewers how the Jew's grasping nature led to his destruction.

And yet, consideration of Marlowe's play as it relates to the long literary history of English antisemitism reminds us of the moral ambiguity of the play's ending. At the same time that Ferneze's trick shows how the ex-governor proves unwilling to view the Jew as an ally, it reveals how he is more than willing to imitate Barabas's spatial stratagem, and in so doing recall both the nefarious actions of the Jewish assassin in the *Prioress's Tale*, who throws the dead school-boy into a pit, and the ambiguous actions of the Christian queen who tortures the Jew Judas in a pit in *Elene*. When read against the conventions of English antisemitic writing, Ferneze hardly emerges as the pious wielder of justice.

Moreover, at the end of the play, when the Christians regain control of the island, the defeat of both Jew and Turk hardly reassures audiences through any triumphant establishment of an ideal social order. Thanks to his spatially inflected stratagems, Barabas has thoroughly dismantled the pieties of nuns, friars and members of Christian laity. Not unlike the Christian community portrayed in the Croxton *Play of the Sacrament*, Malta's Christian majority is itself caught up in materialistic flows. Such a message, as we have seen, applied to England as much as its insular counterpart in the Mediterranean world of the play. Marlowe hints at such a correlation in moments such as Barabas's payment in pounds by Ferneze. Both the commercial nature of the Rose, where viewers paid to watch the play, as well as the immediate environs of the play, where good-laden boats crowded the nearby Thames, would have encouraged viewers to understand Malta's Christian commercialism as a mirror of their own mercantile tendencies. I end this chapter by touching on one more aspect of English life that intersected with Marlowe's imagined Malta, namely the governing architectural image of the play, the counting house.

In 1571, the assistance court of the London Company of Carpenters ruled, in response to mayoral efforts to regulate and manage the "at large" construction of "compting houses," as well as "studies Jutties purprestures and penthowses," that carpenters who erect counting houses and similar additions must obtain "speciall licence firste" from the wardens and masters of the company.[145] With its criticism of the "at large" or unrestrained erection of counting houses in London, the court document suggests, as Schofield surmises, how "evidently many [counting houses] were being built" in the English capital.[146] Not only was the building of counting houses a "boom" area in the home-improvement industry (homes could contain as many as five of them), it also was conspicuous in its popularity; those built environments were additions erected "presumably on the outsides of buildings."[147] The trendiness of the counting house reflects how the expansion of English trade during the period heightened English merchants' accounting needs. It also complicates our understanding of the depiction of counting houses in *The Jew of Malta*. I've suggested that Marlowe satirizes the Christian society of Malta by staging its affinity with and connections to Barabas's counting house. Although Marlowe initially singles out Barabas as a greedy and nefarious figure by tying him to the space of the counting house and the riches it contains, he ultimately exposes the omnipresence of materialism—and counting houses—in both Malta and the greater world. The popularity of the English counting house, though, suggests how, even before Marlowe staged multiple links connecting Barabas's counting house to Maltese Christians, the opening scene of the play presented London viewers with a reflection of their own commercial predilections.

Intensifying the connection between Barabas's counting house and those of Elizabethan Christians is their small size. For example, the plan of a house on 31 Catteaton Street (now part of the site of Gresham College on Gresham Street) that appears in a 1612 survey by Ralph Treswell includes a roughly six-by-eight-foot counting house (figures 21 and 22).[148] The "Little Countinghouse" Treswell identifies over a parlor of the Clothworker's Hall on Mincing Lane likely was even smaller.[149] The use in the Rose of a small (8.5 by 6 feet) discovery space as Barabas's counting house thus reflects the modest physical dimensions of most early modern English counting houses, and the merchant's celebration of the gathering of "infinite riches in a little room" echoes the repeated characterization of counting houses as "little" in English surveys, wills, and inventories.[150] Audience members would have further cause to see Christian resonances in Barabas's counting house, thanks to the prominence of counting houses in literary texts. While the counting house, as an office space dedicated to records and bookkeeping, could represent the ideal ordering of a domicile, it typically serves as an iconic space of greed in sixteenth-century texts such as English cleric Edward Topsell's *Time's lamentation* (1599), which associates the rich man with his counting house.[151] The most canonical English depiction of the Christian counting house appears, as we have seen, in Chaucer's *Shipman's Tale*, which contains the earliest recorded use of the term "counting house" in English and exemplifies how the inclusion of counting houses in homes extends back to the fourteenth century.[152]

The English penchant for building counting houses and the English association of counting houses with greed not only revises our understanding of how theatergoers might have viewed the opening of *The Jew of Malta*, but also expands the possible resonances of the final act of the play. Namely, when Barabas finds himself burning inside the cauldron, the ironies of place informing that scene may have resonated personally with members of Marlowe's English audience. Because the cauldron was located in the same place as the counting house, the scene circles back to not only the space of the merchant's downfall but also a built environment English viewers knew all too well. Considered in terms of the overt religious message of the play, the English resonances of Barabas's counting house imply how the English members of Marlowe's audience were, like the Jew, damned. On the other hand, could Barabas's affinity with England's thriving commercial tendencies, a trend given architectural form in the frequent erection of counting houses, have led some audience members to view Barabas's demise with regret?

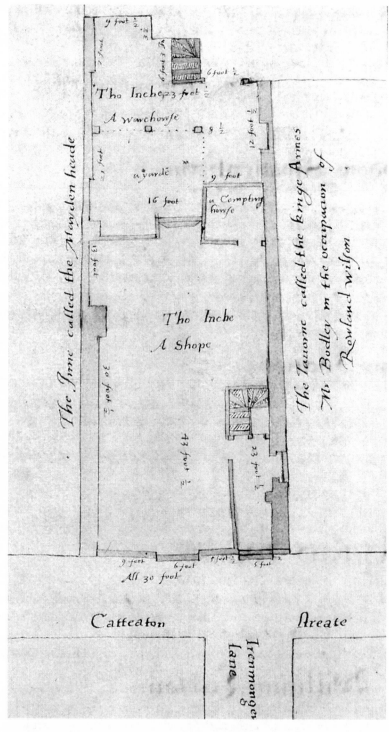

The following text appears within the plan:

9 foot ½

7 foot

6 foot ½

6 foot ½

Tho Inche 23 feet

A warehouse

23 feet

a yarde

16 foot

13 foot

9 foot

a Comptinge howse

12 foot ½

8 ½

The lone called the Mayden heade

30 foot ½

Tho Inche
A Shope

4 ¾ foot

23 feet ½

The Tauorne called the kinge Armes
Mr Bodley in the occupacion of
Rowland wilson

9 foot    6 foot    5 foot ½    5 foot
All 30 foot

Catteaton                Areate

Iremonger
lane

**FIGURE 21.** Plan of 31 Catteaton Street, now part of site of Gresham College, Gresham Street. Ralph Treswell, *A Survaye of all Lands and Tenementes belonging to the Worshipfull Company of Clothworkers of London . . .* (1612), fol. 32r. By permission of The Clothworkers' Company, London.

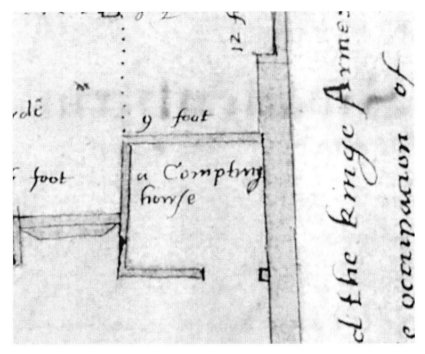

**FIGURE 22.** Detail of the counting house in Treswell's drawing of Catteaton Street. By permission of The Clothworkers' Company, London.

Could the substitution of the hellish cauldron for the gem-filled counting house have felt at some level wrong to Marlowe's commerce-minded audience members?

Among all of the London houses surveyed by Ralph Treswell, one stands out as especially impressive: a residence, known as The Leadenporch, located on the north side of Catteaton street (now Gresham Street), facing Ironmonger Lane. As Schofield notes, "Treswell's description of the interior in 1612 includes the most frequent use in these surveys of the word 'fair.'"[153] As noted above, this home exemplifies the London penchant for counting houses; along the east wall of the house, behind its shop, is what Treswell identifies as "a Compting howse." The home also seems originally to have been a smaller stone house (of roughly 3.5 by 30.5 feet) that was formerly inhabited by Jews. Catteaton Street was part of the main Jewish neighborhood of preexpulsion London. The home would have been immediately southwest of a private synagogue on Basinghall Street and just east of the mikveh on the north side of Catteaton. The history of that house, like Marlowe's drama, offers us an alternative to the usual histories of Christian–Jewish relation, with their pious thrust. While Christianity claims to replace dead Jewish materialisms with living Christian "stones," while ritual-murder libels shift from a demonized Jewish home to a sanctified Christian church, and while desecration libels raze Jewish homes and replace them with chapels, 31 Catteaton Street tells the story of an English merchant inhabiting a former Jewish built environment. Here the relationship of Jew to Christian isn't one of supersession; rather a Christian benefits from the material splendor of a home previously owned by a Jew. The physical grandeur of the thirteenth-century home is such that, some three centuries later, it merits repeated reference to its "fair" chambers on the part of Treswell. Instead of undermining Christian piety, "Jewish" materialisms assist Christian trade. To be sure, as is the case in *The Jew of Malta*, with its staging of Ferneze's appropriation of Barabas's home, this perspective is bound up with anti-Jewish activity, that is, the expulsion of London's medieval Jewish population. Appreciating goods formerly owned by Jews is a far cry from renouncing any oppressive stance toward Jews and, moreover, offering Jews the prospect of open, neighborly cohabitation. Still, in Treswell's admiration of the Catteaton property, we gain a glimpse—albeit flawed, problematic, and glancing—of the possibility for a perspective grounded not on religious judgment but on a secular, mercantile appreciation for the material aspects of lived experience.

# CHAPTER 6

# Readmission and Displacement

*Menasseh ben Israel, William Prynne, John Milton*

An Amsterdam rabbi raised by Sephardic émigrés from Portugal, Menasseh ben Israel (1604–57) was a renowned and well-connected scholar, teacher, orator, and publisher. His passions encompassed messianism, the cabal, and, in a more political vein, the problem of Jewish oppression.[1] Famously, that latter pursuit entailed Menasseh's September 1655 journey from Amsterdam to England "in behalfe of the Jewish Nation" to convince Cromwell to, in Menasseh's words, "grant us place in your Countrey, that we may have our Synagogues, and free exercise of our Religion."[2] Two months later, the Lord Protector convened English "Divines, Lawyers, and Merchants, of different persuasions, and opinions" in the council chamber of Whitehall Palace to consider "Whether it be lawful at all to receive in the Jews" and "if it be lawfull, then upon what tearms its meet to receive them."[3] Unfortunately, Menasseh spurred no formal pronouncement from Cromwell. The five Whitehall meetings that began on 4 December 1655 and disbanded on 18 December did not issue any statements on readmission.[4] Jews did immigrate to England in increasing numbers and attained by the end of the century permission to build in London what would become Bevis Marks Synagogue. But the status of that modestly expanding Jewish community was, in James Shapiro's words, "provisional and subject to challenge."[5] During the next year Cromwell granted a petition permitting London Jews to "meete at owr said private devotions in owr Particular houses without feere of Molestation," a "right" that in reality differed little from the options already available to crypto-Jews in England.[6] Some eight years later, during the Restoration, Charles II generated the first written document authorizing Jews to live in England "so long as they demeane themselves peaceably & quietly with due obedience to his Maties Lawes & without scandall to his Governement."[7] The qualified nature of both Cromwell's and Charles II's actions shows just how tenuous the lives of British Jews after Whitehall continued to be throughout the seventeenth century. Menasseh's experience is a case in point. Some two years after his arrival, the now broken and penniless rabbi left England, only to pass away shortly after in Amsterdam.[8]

How can we account for both the appearance in England of a climate amenable to readmission—so amenable as to prompt Menasseh's mission to Cromwell—and the resistance with which that prospect met? Those questions aren't easy to answer. As Achsah Guibbory puts it, "there were important differences in the attitudes and assumptions of the people who engaged in the controversy over Jewish readmission," and "the wide range of attitudes expressed cannot be easily categorized."[9] Among the factors favoring Menasseh's mission and the conference were the following: the shift from a monarchy to a commonwealth; a philosemitic interest in Hebrew, the Old Testament, and Jerusalem; a millenarian stress on conversion; a mercantilist investment in profiting from Jewish traders; a national desire to rethink "what it meant to be English during a period marked by social, religious and political instability"; and a national belief that "England was fulfilling the history of biblical Israel."[10] A host of phenomena also militated against readmission. Those factors included an interest in Jews solely as converts, fears over the economic harm wrought by Jewish businessmen, anxieties about Christians converting to Judaism, a concept of England as homogeneously Christian, and widespread belief in a slew of antisemitic stereotypes. As those two necessarily incomplete lists indicate, the question of why the English did not welcome Jews is just as complex as the reasons why the English pondered opening the nation to Jewish immigrants in the first place.

Regardless of where one stood, one thing was clear: debates over readmission pivoted on questions of space, such as where would Jews live and how would those places intersect with larger issues of location and Jewish global dispersal?[11] While my point may seem obvious, situating a foreign population in a host country is always a fraught endeavor. Consider the spatial metaphor employed by David Katz in his account of how, "once Cromwell and Charles II realized that the Jews as a nation could never be admitted through the front door, they were anxious to go around the back themselves and let them in through the entrance reserved for tradesmen."[12] Katz conceives of readmission as a project in which ideas of home and hospitality are writ large on a national scale. That prospect revises traditional English antisemitisms: the myth of Jews performing crimes behind closed doors gives way to the possibility of welcoming Jews into the "front door" of the house that is England. But that door, like that of the demonized Jewish home, proves to be closed. The secrecy long associated with Jews appears in a national, Christian, and elitist guise, as England quietly lets Jews in through an inconspicuous side "entrance." Ultimately, Jews enter England in the manner of a menial worker whose labor is hidden from respectable guests.

Katz's notion of multiple entrances into the "house" of England suggests how a geographic approach can shed light on the complexities of a fundamental crux of readmission: more Jews are living in England as never before, yet they are neither fully evident nor welcomed outright into the nation. In this chapter, I consider how that tension between Jewish presence and absence emerges in work by two personages closely identified with readmission debates—Menasseh and polemicist William Prynne—and another figure rarely tied to readmission, John Milton. Crucial to Menasseh's campaign for readmission were several texts. A prolific writer, Menasseh argued for readmission first through an English edition of his messianic treatise, *The Hope of Israel* (1650), and later through another, occasionally apologetic, work, the *Humble Addresses* (1655), which he presented to Cromwell. Prynne vociferously argued against Menasseh through his highly polemical text, the *Short Demurrer To the Jewes long discontinued barred remitter into England* (1656), penned during the Whitehall conference. Menasseh then published his riposte to Prynne and other contemporary attacks against Jews, the *Vindiciae Judaeorum*.[13] While both Menasseh and Prynne directly addressed readmission, and at times even responded directly to each other's claims, Milton took no part in the debates. I argue, however, that his closet drama *Samson Agonistes*, published as a companion piece to *Paradise Regain'd* in 1671, presents us with an indirect yet important Miltonic statement on readmission. It's no surprise that scholars have not read *Samson Agonistes* as a text about readmission. Milton's drama refers neither to contemporary Jews nor to readmission, and it was published, moreover, fifteen years after the Whitehall conference. Yet scholars have profitably read *Samson Agonistes* as a means by which Milton could voice his feelings about contemporary political issues under the cover of a biblical play. Those political issues most obviously relate to Milton's precarious positioning in the wake of the Restoration, with Samson's demolition of Dagon's temple serving as an allegory for what the poet would like to happen to the new monarchic order.[14] Yet Milton's careful and nuanced attention to space in this play, along with his characters' capacity to figure contemporary Jews, urge reading *Samson Agonistes* alongside Menasseh's and Prynne's works.

In what follows, I trace how all three writers' works iterate the spatial contradiction evinced by readmission as a phenomenon in which a heightened Jewish presence on English territory is qualified or undermined. Offering various contexts and motivations for such a contradictory pairing of Jewish presence and Jewish absence, their texts help us tease out some of the complex reasons why Menasseh failed to garner from Cromwell a secure "place in your Countrey" for the Jews. Turning first to *Hope*, I track how Menasseh generates a remarkable narrative in which God has deemed that his chosen people quite literally inhabit the entire earth, from China and the East, to southern sites like Ethiopia, points north such as Tartary, and the Americas in the west, where Jews share territory with Indians. Through *Hope* and *Vindiciae Judaeorum*, which documents the lives of Jews living in Europe, Menasseh creates an archive testifying to a world Jewish presence whose sole missing link is England. The admission of Jews into England, the rabbi contends, will form the final step in God's providential plan, before the Messiah's arrival. Yet, as we shall see, at the same time that the rabbi maps Jews throughout the globe, he qualifies that Jewish habitation by invoking the restoration of Zion. Thanks to his idea of the Jews as a chosen people tied ultimately to Jerusalem, Menasseh paradoxically locates Jews in and distances them from locations outside Israel.

Turning to Prynne, I consider how he similarly creates an archive of Jewish habitation, albeit one limited to England, by packing his *Demurrer* with citations of legal documents pertaining to Anglo-Jews in the twelfth and thirteenth centuries. Rightly described by Lucian Wolf as "a monument of research," Prynne's work testifies as never before to the fact that Jews lived in England, and even served as "the chief printed source" on the medieval Anglo-Jewry into the late nineteenth century.[15] But Prynne, like Menasseh, conjures a Jewish presence only to affirm ultimately Jewish absence. Invoking a notably hostile version of the Christian reading of Jewish dispersal as divine punishment, Prynne highlights Jews' inability to find a stable dwelling both in England and elsewhere on earth. Thus Prynne's and Menasseh's respective theories of diaspora disassociate Jews from global territory for radically different reasons: while the former denigrates Jews as God's rejects, the latter elevates them as God's chosen people.

Years after Menasseh fashioned his messianic geography and Prynne wrote his documentary history, Milton published *Samson Agonistes*, a masterpiece whose complex engagement with Jewish presence and absence demands our sustained attention. Due to its focus on the hero from Judges and his people, Milton's drama places Jews at center stage. Yet the generic form of Milton's work exiles Jews (at least, actors playing Jews) from England; *Samson Agonistes* is a closet drama never intended for performance on a physical stage. I argue that the spatial contradictions exhibited by the play's form, in tandem with its fraught representation of Jewish homelessness, offer a nuanced meditation on contemporary Jews that confirms how the great Hebraist possessed the "disturbing anti-Jewish attitude" evident in other Miltonic works.[16] Milton, like Prynne, demonized contemporary Jews—whom I argue the play's Philistines represent—by ascribing to them a certain placelessness. And yet the poet attacks those Philistine figures of Jewishness through Samson, a Jew who at times seems admirably Hebrew or proto-Christian but on other occasions seems to represent the very contemporary Jews Milton derides. As a hero, Samson possesses an agency that resonates with Menasseh and his leadership role in the readmission campaign. But while Menasseh ultimately acts on his deep investment in a Jewish presence in Israel, Samson exhibits no such interest in restoration. Rather, and disturbingly, Samson directs his heroic agency toward eradicating Jews—including himself—from space altogether.

## Jews and the (Mis)use of Space in Seventeenth-Century England

Various and contradictory ideas about the geography of Jewish identity emerged both during and after the Whitehall conference, forming an important backdrop to the readmission debates. At one extreme, highly negative stereotypes circulated about a Jewish misuse of space, and especially the abuse of houses. Those stereotypes encompassed the boy-martyr libel. Early modern writers like Shakespeare perpetuated the myth, if in muted form, through images like Shylock's sober house, while public records and chronicles ensured the popularity of ritual murder "well into the seventeenth century."[17] No charges were issued during the period, yet the private existence of London's crypto-Jews, which echoed the secret nature of the homes portrayed in ritual-murder texts, may have made them seem suspicious to gentiles. Menasseh, Prynne, and Milton were well aware of the libel, with the latter two writers directly engaging it.[18]

The ritual-murder libel clearly worked against readmission. Further support for keeping Jews out of England came from the legend of the Wandering Jew, which gained currency during the seventeenth century. A myth whose prominence resulted from an oft-translated 1602 German pamphlet, the legend recounts the story of the ill-fated actions of a Jew—often called Ahasuerus—who lived during the time of Christ.[19] According to the myth, while bearing his cross to Calvary, Jesus paused to lean against the home of Ahasuerus, who pushed him away and told Jesus to continue toward his destination. Jesus, in a move that resonates with the Christian idea of diaspora as a divine punishment, responds by dooming Ahasuerus to wander the earth without any rest, rest being understood both temporally (he never dies) and spatially (he traces and retraces the earth without ever having a lasting dwelling place).[20] As Richard Brathwaite puts it in his *Whimzies* (1631), "the wandring Iew" can "finde no place to abide in, but only to sojourne in."[21] The homeless Ahasuerus appears in various European cities, where he speaks of the Crucifixion and subsequent historical events.

A convert to Christianity, Ahasuerus nevertheless is always already Jewish due to his eternal wanderings and their disciplinary function.[22] A figure who "stood for the whole Jewish nation . . . condemned to wander until the end of time," Ahasuerus recalibrates long-standing notions of the accommodated Jew.[23] In medieval England, boy-martyr and host-desecration fantasies provided an imagined rationale for expulsion by suggesting how Jews, in their houses, privately reenacted versions of the Crucifixion. The Wandering Jew understands Jewish dispersal, however, by constructing a foundational scene of Jewish inhospitality staged at the time of, and in direct relation to, deicide: Ahasuerius wanders forever because he refused to allow Jesus to lean against his house and pushed him back on the road to Calvary. Insofar as Ahasuerus served as a metonym for all Jews, he implies that because a Jew wouldn't open his home to Christ, Christians shouldn't provide homes for Jews. Readmission is from this perspective out of the question.

By the time of the Whitehall debates, English anxieties over Jewish misuse of space had in certain respects escalated. Rumors circulated about Jews abusing not just homes, but also treasured national monuments. In 1649, former secretary of state to Charles I, Edward Nicholas, wrote to the Marquis of Ormond, "I hear . . . that the Jews proffer 600,000 l. for Paul's and Oxford Library, and may have them for 200,000 l. more."[24] In 1650, the doge received from the Royalist living in Venice a letter claiming that the "church of St. Paul, comparable with St. Peters at Rome, remains desolate and is said to have been sold to the Jews as a synagogue."[25] And Menasseh writes in *Vindiciae Judaeorum* that "it hath been rumoured abroad, that our nation had purchased S. Pauls Church for to make it their Synagogue."[26] As Katz puts it, the "accusation" about St. Paul's "was one of the most frequently heard calumnies against the Jews until well after the Restoration."[27] In addition to seeking to buy St. Paul's and the Bodleian, Jews were said to have made cash offers on other buildings such as Norwich Cathedral and Whitehall Palace. Such rumors partly testify to how nations generally distrust outsiders. Seventeenth-century fears over losing iconic built environments like St. Paul's adumbrate the 1980s rumors about the Japanese "buying up" U.S. monuments. The rumors also reflect concerns over Puritans—on the rise since the civil war—and their ascetic rejection of architectural excess.

At the same time, though, the rumors engage long-standing ideas about the geography of Jewish identity. I refer to ideas not of Jewish home life but of Jews' associations with the grandest of all built environments, Solomon's Temple. Thanks to a slew of often intersecting phenomena, including a revival of mnemonics, messianic theories of restoration to Jerusalem and the rebuilding of the temple, associations of James I and the Anglican church with Solomon, a rising Hebraism, and the popularizing efforts of Rabbi Jacob Judah Leon (Templo) of Amsterdam (1603–75), an interest in the Jewish temple was widespread.[28] Evidence of that popularity appeared in the design of English theaters, colleges, churches, and masonic lodges; in utopian writings by Francis Bacon and other authors; in geographical works like Thomas Fuller's *A Pisgah-Sight of Palestine* (1650); and in poetry including George Herbert's *The Temple* (1633). That interest in the temple necessarily entailed a heightened awareness of Jews' affiliation with grand built environments. Thus a broadside celebrating St. Paul's has a Jew who figures as the ultimate architectural connoisseur proclaim "Indéed I have travel'd Kingdomes farre, / and séen their famous Fabricks all, / Yet never a one could be compar'd / unto the Cathedrall Church of *Pauls*."[29] Rumors about Jews buying English edifices similarly imagine them as architectural connoisseurs, presumably due to their ancient relationship to the temple. They imply that, given the Jews' original possession of the finest real estate, they will jump at the chance to purchase England's great buildings. The rumors thus reveal a fear over a Jewish architectural appetitiveness that, far from creating a wondrous New Jerusalem, will through its seizure and transformation of real estate effectively erase from the island those buildings that make England "England." Jewish presence threatens a monumental English absence.

However, as Menasseh's mission affirms, alongside derogatory notions of Jews and built environments, a shift in attitude had begun to occur. "One of," in Cecil Roth's formulation, "the many harbingers and preparatives of the Readmission" were notably celebratory accounts of Jewish home life that challenged both the Wandering Jew and older stereotypes about accommodated Jews.[30] Especially pertinent to the readmission debates was a widely read account text written ca. 1616 by Venetian rabbi Leone da Modena. Leone's *Historia degli riti hebraici* was the first guide to Jewish customs and beliefs written in a European language by a Jew for gentile readers, and is a text with many important English associations. The manuscript was written originally for an Englishman and first circulated among English readers; Edmund Chilmead published his English translation of the *Riti* in 1650, at the same time that Moses Wall's translation of Menasseh's *Hope* appeared in print.[31] As Mark Cohen demonstrates, Leone wrote the *Riti* mainly to overcome negative representations of Jewish life and "advance the social integration of Jews into Christian society."[32] Foremost among such derogatory notions were those pertaining to Jewish houses. The *Riti* opens with a chapter called "Of their Houses, and Places of Dwelling."[33] The chapter first describes how builders of Jewish houses "leave one part of it unfinished, and lying rude" to memorialize the loss of Jerusalem and the temple, then turns to the content and location of mezuzot in Jewish homes, and closes by discussing the absence of "Figures, Images, nor Statues, in their houses; much lesse in their Synagogues, and Holy places."[34] The next chapter elaborates further on Jewish domesticity by describing how Jews use "Utensils, and Vessels, in their houses" in order to abide by the dietary laws of kashrut.[35]

Leone, like Menasseh, doubtless knew that libels about Jewish houses circulated in England and elsewhere; perhaps one of his English interlocutors—thinking of the libels, or wondering perhaps about the lives of London's crypto-Jewish community—asked Leone a question about Jewish home life that prompted him to write the *Riti*. Regardless of the circumstances of the composition of the *Riti*, when Chilmead's translation appeared, that text unquestionably challenged negative stereotypes through its account of Jewish domesticity. While the ritual-murder libel and the Ahasuerus myth locate inhospitality and violence in the Jewish home, Leone's "insider's look" reveals the Jewish house as a place of religious devotion. And the Jewish building practices portrayed in the *Riti* are the antithesis of big real estate purchases Jews were rumored to seek. Far from purchasing highly public and monumental English buildings, Jews construct homes that are so modest as to be unfinished. By "leav[ing] one part of" their homes "unfinished, and lying rude," Jews privately and modestly remake their domiciles in the image of a "Desolate" Jerusalem and temple. Thus, while the Jews of the *Riti* don't suffer Ahasuerus's homelessness, they experience—intentionally—in their domiciles a certain instability and material incompleteness.

Ultimately, the architectural insufficiency of the homes portrayed in the *Riti* reveals the fraught nature of the Jewish quest for accommodation in England and elsewhere. While their unfinished houses serve, along with other domestic details like the mezuzah, to undermine stereotypes about sinful, dangerous, and property-hungry Jews, those dwellings also reveal a teleology of

Jewish habitation whose culmination is the restoration of Zion. In a sense, then, while Jews seek host countries in which to live, that project is qualified by their ultimate investment in Israel.

## Menasseh ben Israel and the Mapping of Jewish Election

An especially rich example of how this ambivalence played out in England appears in the life and writings of Menasseh ben Israel. To begin with one side of the dynamic, Menasseh responded to the issue of Jews meriting habitation in England in an unprecedentedly personal and public manner. I refer to Menasseh's noteworthy choice of residence while living in England as an advocate of readmission. As Wolf points out, the most likely location for the rabbi to inhabit was the new Jewish quarter in the City, located on streets such as Bevis Marks, Leadenhall Street, Bishopsgate Street, Duke's Place, Shoemaker's Row, and Gravel Lane. Menasseh's son Samuel likely was living close to that area, with his uncle David Abarbanel Dormido, whose home was in St. Helen's, near one of two secret synagogues.[36] But instead of living with family and friends, the rabbi opted to occupy a house "at the other end of town," on the Strand (figure 23).[37] By living at such a remove from the Jewry, Menasseh in a sense did what many Anglo-Jews did before him. Before the expulsion, Jews were not segregated from but lived side by side with Christians in England. It's unlikely, though, that medieval Anglo-Jewish housing practices were on Menasseh's mind when he moved into his London residence.

Convenience may have figured into his decision, since the Strand served as a major artery connecting political Westminster to commercial London. But while its proximity to Westminster, where Cromwell and other men pondered readmission, surely made the Strand appealing, other factors also explain his choice. The oft-used roadway was lined during the period with townhouses and palaces owned by aristocrats like the Dukes of Northumberland and Earls of Salisbury. Menasseh's house also was across the street from the New Exchange, a galleried, two-story structure that was designed by Inigo Jones in 1609, built by Robert Cecil, and contained around a hundred pricey shops.[38] In short, Menasseh's lodgings enjoyed a prominence that departed markedly from the hidden nature of the Jewish enclave his son inhabited. As we saw in chapter 5, at least since the time of Henry VIII, Jews had been living in London as part of a tiny community of Marranos or crypto-Jews who officially had converted to Christianity but secretly maintained their faith.[39] In contrast, Menasseh's life in London was highly public,

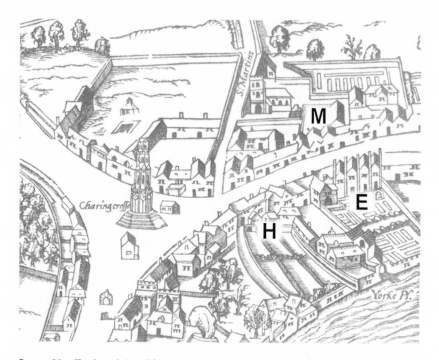

**FIGURE 23.** The Strand. Detail from Agas map. *Source:* Agas, *Plan of London*. By permission of the University of Iowa Libraries, Iowa City. E: New Exchange, H: Hungerford House, M: Menasseh's Home.

as he stresses in the final sentence of his *Humble Addresses*, where he refers to himself as "Rabbi Menesse Ben-Israel, a Divine, and Doctor Physick, in the *Strand* over against the *New-Exchange* in *London*" (103).

By specifying his housing "in the *Strand* over against the *New-Exchange* in *London*," the rabbi maps himself onto a public, Christian, and fashionable space that is of a piece with his request to Cromwell in the *Humble Addresses* that Jews have a "place in your Countrey" where they can enjoy an open existence marked by "free exercise" of their faith (77). The open habitation Menasseh displayed via his high-profile house on the Strand stood in metonymic relation to the public life that the rabbi and diplomat sought for all Jews in England. By living on such a prominent thoroughfare, the rabbi hazarded on a small scale the larger-scale project promised by readmission: ending the hidden nature of current Jewish habitation and allowing Jews to live openly as Jews among Christians.

Through his Strand residence, Menasseh seems to have enacted his desire not simply for a public Jewish presence but also for a fuller, more companionable relationship between Jews and Christians. In his writings, he alludes to such a relationship when he describes Jewish hospitality toward English Protestants and vice versa. The *Humble Addresses* describe how, once news arrived in Holland about the prospect of readmission, he "did congratulate and entertaine" in his home "their Excellencies, the Ambassadors of *England*," while the Jewish community received those same diplomats into the Amsterdam synagogue with "great pomp and applause" (77). Menasseh's account of hosting in Amsterdam and England adds another nuance to celebratory accounts of Jewish built environments such as that offered by Leone da Modena. The home Leone describes as a site of private piety emerges in Menasseh's work as a place that opens its doors to Christians in the manner of the Amsterdam synagogue. Challenging the idea of Jewish hostility promulgated by myths such as the Wandering Jew legend and the ritual murder libel, Menasseh describes Jewish hospitality directed to English Christians. Menasseh also stresses English fellowship toward Jews. In a letter written before he left Amsterdam, Menasseh tells Jews in Italy and Holstein how "this English nation . . . has become excellently affected to our nation."[40] He describes in his *Vindiciae Judaeorum* (1656) how, upon arriving in England, he was "very courteously received, and treated with much respect" by his hosts.[41] And the *Humble Addresses* opens by referring to how the "People of England" have received the Jews "into their bosomes," and how he had personal "experience of" the "loving kindnesse" of the "Learned and Pious men in this Nation" (79).[42] Menasseh's London residence proves pivotal to this rhetoric of courteous English welcoming; by placing himself "amongst strangers" in a gentile neighborhood, he registered his investment in finding hospitality among not only Jews but also gentiles in London.

But to assert, in his writings and via his abode, the mere presence of good feeling between Jews and the English is one thing; to account for that fellowship and hospitality is another. On the question of why the English should welcome Jews, Menasseh provides several answers, one of which involves singling Jews out for their particular virtues.[43] Thus, in the *Humble Addresses* Menasseh celebrates Jewish profitability and loyalty, and in his *Vindiciae Judaeorum* he describes Jews as faithful economic advisors.[44] Yet the case for a reciprocal relation of hospitality and warmth between Jews and the English is, for Menasseh, much more than a matter of good business practice. Menasseh portrays readmission as nothing less than the fulfillment of a special, divinely ordained relationship between Jews, England, and virtually all of the "places & Countreyes of the World" (*Humble Addresses*, 79). In the *Humble Addresses*, after explaining that he "first and formost" has come to England to advocate for the open practice of Judaism, Menasseh describes his second, and closely related, "Motive" (78–79). His starting point in articulating that rationale is the "opinion of many Christians and mine" that the restoration of Jews "into their Native Countrey" of Jerusalem "is very neer at hand" (79). A messianic thinker, Menasseh agrees with English millenarians that Jews would soon be restored to Israel, but refrains from addressing stickier issues related to millenarian ideas about the end of the world, a second coming of Christ to earth, and the attendant conversion of Jews.[45] Menasseh then puts a fascinating twist on the meaning of diaspora, by claiming that the restoration is predicated on the fulfillment of the prophesy in Daniel 12:7, "And when the dispersion of the Holy people shall be compleated in all places, then shall all these things be compleated," which Menasseh interprets as "signifying therewith, that before all be fulfilled, the People of God must be first dispersed into all places & Countreys of the World" (79). In other words, before the Jews can return to Jerusalem, that "People of God" must live everywhere else in the world (79), "as if," in Guibbory's words, "centrifugal movement, reaching its limit in the finite world God had created, would produce a centripetal countermovement."[46] Thus, to return to Menasseh's Strand address, his high-profile abode was sutured to not only the space of England as a home for Jews but also the entirety of the Earth, where Jews were destined by God to dwell.

Indeed, the providentially ordained centrifugal movements described by Menasseh assume the most extreme form imaginable. "All places & Countreys" inhabited by Jews, quite literally, means all locations in the world, as Menasseh's English readers would have well known, thanks to the popularity of *Hope*.[47] In that widely read text, Menasseh locates Jews in Europe, Africa, Asia, and—most surprisingly—the Americas. That final location renders Jewish dispersal especially far-flung. Creating a verbal map of the Middle East, Northern Asia, Europe, and the Americas, Menasseh describes how members of the ten tribes journey out of Tartary, over a miraculously dried up Euphrates to Greenland, Labrador, and, finally, South American "Countries farre remote" from Jerusalem.[48] *Hope* features the tale of one Antonio di Montezinos (Aaron Levi), a Portuguese Marrano who claimed to have found in Peru members of the ten lost tribes of Israel.[49] The occupation of South America by members of the lost tribes, deduces Menasseh, taken together with the habitation of nearly all of the rest of the world by other members of the tribes, means that the titular hope of Israel is near at hand. Soon the Messiah shall arrive, "the scattering of the holy people shall have an end," and "Those Tribes then shall be gathered from all quarters of the earth" to "goe into their Country," that is, Jerusalem (52, 44).

Through his messianic theory of diaspora, Menasseh radically redefines popular conceptions of the Wandering Jew. While Ahasuerus is a figure

whose itinerancy signifies his rejection by God, Menasseh's Jews are a chosen people whose global movements comprise part of a divine plan. While
Ahasuerus is irremediably homeless, the Jews of *Hope* look toward returning
to their homeland. Moreover, Menasseh's Jews enjoy a stable dwelling, at least
until God decides otherwise. The rabbi refers to "relics of the Jews of the
tribe of Naphtali" in Tartary who "are not Nomades, as the Huns who are
unconstant in their dwelling, and eate up one place after another; but they
inhabite one certaine place" (32). Menasseh's revision of popular conceptions
of Jewish itinerancy is twofold in this passage, involving both an image of
Jews who inhabit a single location and a reminder of other ethnic groups
who wander, such as the Huns.

The Jews described by Menasseh also create impressive built environments. In *Hope*, Menasseh speculates that the stone building "of a very
great pile" and "dedicated to the Maker of the World" in Tiahuanaco, Peru,
described by Garcilaso de la Vega and Jesuit missionary José de Acosta, was
"a Synagogue, built by the Israelites," and that the ancient and "vast building"
in the Peruvian city of *Guamanga*" (that is, Ayacucho in the Huamanga province) described by Spanish chronicler Pedro Cieza de León, was erected by
the Israelites as well (21–22, 23). Those edifices are architectural wonders: a
single stone from the building measured by de Leon is thirty-eight feet long,
eighteen feet high, and six feet thick; de la Vega describes how "the court,
the Wall, the Pavement, the Chamber, the Roofe of it, the entrance, the posts
of the 2 gates of the Chamber, and of the entrance building" in Tiahuanacu
"are made only of one stone" (22, 21). The magnificent form, dimensions,
and materials of the South American buildings recall Solomon's Temple. In
other words, like the Jewish home described in Leone's *Riti*, Jewish buildings
in *Hope* serve as virtual Jerusalems. But while the unfinished home of the *Riti*
recalls the dissolution of the temple, the South American edifices of *Hope*,
constructed by members of ancient tribes who were unaware of the fall of
the temple, are monuments to its ingenuity and magnificence. In keeping
with the hopeful teleology of his text, Menasseh locates in Peru buildings
that implicitly adumbrate the restoration to Jerusalem of Jews, despite their
situation in South America, "farre remote" from their homeland.

While even remote sites in the Americas witness God's scattering of the
Jews, Menasseh stresses in his *Humble Addresses*, "onely . . . this considerable
and mighty Island"—that is, England—has yet to serve such a providential
function (79). Tapping into English national feeling, Menasseh imbues England
with the special status of the final, "mighty" stop in the Jewish peoples'
journey outward into all four corners of the earth before their gathering in
Jerusalem. In *Vindiciae Judaeorum*, Menasseh refines his claims about England's

providential role. "I conceived," he writes, that when Moses claimed in Deu-
teronomy 28:64 that Yahweh would scatter the Israelites "amongst all people,
from the one end of the earth even unto the other," the prophet's reference to
"the end of the earth might be understood [as] this island."[50] Katz observes
how Menasseh plays in this passage with *qeṣeh ha-'ares* or end of the earth,
which is "the classical name for England in medieval Jewish literature."[51] But
the English themselves also had long stressed their geographic marginality,
and often in a celebratory manner.[52] Engaging with that national sentiment,
Menasseh claims that geographic isolation grants England a distinguished
and culminating place in salvation history.

Through his idea of the Jews' providential relationship with England,
Menasseh cannily reformulates contemporary English messianic theories.
Two major strands of messianism were at play in seventeenth-century
England: messianists who advocated a Jewish restoration, and millenarians
who claimed that the English themselves were the true and elect "Jews"
chosen by God to lead the world on the last days.[53] Menasseh's geography of
dispersal and restoration somewhat bridges the gap between ideas of English and
Jewish chosenness, by claiming that God has brought *both* England and the
Jews together as the world moves closer to its Messianic Age. By welcoming
Menasseh and the Jews, the English testify to the chosenness of both their
guests and their marginal island. Menasseh's understanding of readmission
sheds further light on his choice of residence in London. The imminent
arrival of Jews in the English territory providentially chosen for them merits
no low or obscure location for their spokesman's residence but rather a distinguished and high site on the order of the Strand.

Yet this is not the whole story regarding Menasseh's theory of providential diaspora. If Jews' chosenness merits an open existence on the English
world border, it necessitates something altogether different in another far-
flung locale, South America. Of South American Jews, Menasseh writes in
*Hope* that they "are not only farre off from the Holy Land, but also they
live in the extremities and ends of Countries" (41). That isolation accords
with Montezinos's report, which recounts how he never visited the actual
home of the Jews "behind the Mountaines Cordilleræ" of Peru, that is,
the Andes; rather, over the course of several days, members of the ten tribes
mysteriously meet with Montezinos at a designated location on the Ama-
zon and then depart from him with equal mystery (11). Montezinos tries
but fails to follow the Peruvian Jews, who warn him to "attempt not to
passe the River" (14). Members of the tribes living near Caracas, Venezuela,
prove similarly inaccessible to German conquistador Philip d'Utre (Phillipp
von Hutten) and subsequent explorers. Citing Franciscan chronicler Pedro

Simon, Menasseh writes that, "to this day, none go to that people neither is it known which way to go to them" (24). Menasseh's Jews are thus both everywhere—inhabiting all four corners of the world—and nowhere, "cast-out" in the secret "extremities and ends of Countries" of the Americas.

The hidden nature of South American Jews in a sense returns us to the secretive Jewish dwellings of English antisemitic lore, but with a key difference: while boy-martyr and related tales deploy isolation to demonize Jews, *Hope* uses isolation to connote Hebrew election. As an Indian puts it to Montezinos, "*the* Sons of Israel" were "brought thither by the providence of God, who for their sake wrought many Miracles" (15). Their isolation imbues the ten tribes with mystery and gives them a secure way station until their restoration. A privileged isolation and miraculous invincibility merge in the Venezuelans whom Philip d'Utré seeks to not only find but also conquer (24). Menasseh surmises "it is probable that," due to their invincibility, those hidden Venezualans "are Israelites *whom God preserves in that place against the day of redemption*" (24). That section of *Hope* ends by citing poetry by Alonso de Erzilla, which elaborates on Menasseh's understanding of the ten tribes as providentially protected from foreign discovery, conquest, and commerce, "till God shall please / To manifest his Secrets" (24).

There is a darker side to the twofold placelessness of South American Jews—dwellers of hidden sites in the far-flung "New World"—in Menasseh's writings. Placelessness in *Hope*, as it turns out, doesn't only safeguard the ten tribes from Spanish aggressors and enable them to "better observe their Law" without gentile interference; it also protects Jews from any interaction whatsoever with what Menasseh perceives to be an inferior people (20). I refer here to Menasseh's racialist account of American Indians, whom he takes pains to distinguish from Jews. Contradicting English writings on the ten tribes, which often equated American Indians with Jews, Menasseh stresses in *Hope*, as he puts it in a letter to his friend, Scottish millenarian John Dury, "our Israelites were the first discoverers of America."[54] Jews arrived first; their magnificent temples testify to that initial habitation. Indians are peoples who appear later in America as violent invaders who prompt the Jews' movement into isolated locations.

Why would Menasseh take pains to separate Jews from Indians? An answer appears near the end of *Hope*, where he says of American Indians:

> They who will have them of Peru to have come out of Norwey, or Spain, may be confuted by their very form, manners and the unlikenesse of their Languages. But that is more false, that they are Israelites, who have forgot circumcision, and their rites. For they are of a comly

body, and of a good wit, as saith Doct. Johannes Huarte, in his book which is called, *Examen ingenior.c.*14. But contrarily all men know that the Indians are deformed, dul, and altogether rude. And we have abundantly shown, with how great study, and zeal, the Israelites have kept their Language, and Religion, out of their Country.

*(54)*

Citing Spanish physician Juan Huarte de San Juan as an authority, Menasseh claims that Indians can't be Jews, because Jews "are of a comly body, and of a good wit," in contrast to Indians who, "all men know," are "deformed, dul, and altogether rude." Menasseh's stereotyping of American Indians as inherently possessing deformed bodies, slow minds, and barbarous behavior attaches to those first peoples versions of the very traits Christians had long associated with Jews. At least since Augustine of Hippo, Christians had denigrated Jews through "knowledge" of their physical deformity (e.g., the menstruating Jewish male), their mental incapacity (e.g., the hermeneutic Jew), and barbaric rituals (e.g., the blood libel). As Menasseh's claim demonstrates, gentiles don't hold a monopoly on prejudice. In his work on the Jews in seventeenth-century Amsterdam, Yosef Kaplan has traced such a perspective back to Spanish ideologies of racial purity. Catholics in Spain (and later, Portugal) combatted a host of upheavals through *conservación*, a term that referred to the conservation or protection of identity and the closely related laws of *pureza de sangre* or purity of blood. Upon leaving Portugal for Amsterdam, Jews adopted such notions "from their persecutors, for it now helped them define their own identity" during a time of marked upheaval.[55] As Menassah's reference to Jewish "comly" and Indian "deformed" bodies demonstrates, defining Jewish identity in *Hope* leads at times to a stress on physiognomy that resonates with the Spanish racialist thinking adopted by Portuguese Sephardic Jews. American Jews prove recognizable as "white and bearded" men "of tall stature, comely in presence," physical features that contrast with the Indians as men "of brown colour and without beards" (21, 25–27).[56]

Defining Jews also leads to a parsing out of built environments. For example, Menasseh opines in *Hope* that the aforementioned magnificent edifice found by Garcilaso de la Vega is "a Synagogue built by the Israelites" because of Indian backwardness: "the Authors who write about the Indies, tell us, that the Indians never use Iron, or Iron weapons" (21). Elsewhere Menasseh oddly merges bodily and architectural grandeur, describing how the Spanish conquistador Aguirre saw while canoeing down the Marañón River "tall, and white houses" that, we learn in the next section of *Hope*, are inhabited by "men of tall stature, comely in presence," who "have as great beards as the Spanish have" (25).

Menasseh's elevation of Jewish people and built environments, and his denigration of their American Indian counterparts, reveal racialist complexities and contradictions within his theory of diaspora. God's decision that Jews must live everywhere in the world means that they must share space with—and risk contagion from—dangerously heathen others. The isolation of South American Jews resolves this problem. While Menasseh is willing to consider some Indian–Israelite mixing (he does devote a brief section to shared cultural practices that the Indians may have picked up from the members of the ten tribes), he is ultimately bent on distinguishing a dark and base Indian population from a white and advanced Israelite population. The mysterious inaccessibility of the sons of Israel serves as a divine protection against their going "Indian" and mixing with racial others.

Clearly, no such fears seem to have informed Menasseh's stay in England, despite the fact that for centuries, the English were reputed to be barbarous and backward due to their isolation from civilized social centers. Suggesting instead that, for the rabbi, isolation exalted the English in somewhat the same way that it exalts the American Jews of *Hope*, Menasseh sought a public life in England marked by hospitable interaction with gentiles. Menasseh did enjoy a warm and refined reception by distinguished Christians in both London and elsewhere. Thanks in part to his involvement with apocalyptic thinkers before his arrival and the publication of *Hope*, Menasseh was "wined and dined by leading English Millenarians" such as Lady Ranelagh, Katherine Jones (1615–91).[57] In her mansion in Westminster on Pall Mall, a refined street near the Strand that was lined with expensive shops and mansions, the intellectual and activist Ranelagh held dinner parties for Menasseh attended by her younger brother, chemist and millenarian Sir Robert Boyle (1627–91).[58] Later, Menasseh stayed at the Oxford home of Edward Pococke (1604–91), a Hebraist and translator of the rabbi's treatise on free will, *De Termino Vitae*.[59] Menasseh also met, at his Strand residence and elsewhere, important personages such as Cambridge professor Ralph Cudworth (1617–88), scholar Herbert Thorndike, theologian Henry Jessey (1603–63), and Polyglot Bible editor Brian Walton (1600–61).[60] It may even be the case that Menasseh was "once civilly entertain'd" by Oliver Cromwell himself "at his Table."[61] Menasseh's residence on the Strand, and what hospitality he enjoyed while in England, countered myths of Christian–Jewish animosity with contemporary examples of Christian–Jewish neighboring.

However, as we have seen, Menasseh's time at the Strand was in the end unsuccessful. In February 1657, finding himself penniless, the diplomat sought financial support from Cromwell, whom he terms "the alone suc- courer of my life, in this land of strangers."[62] The rabbi's characterization of England as a "land of strangers" departs radically from his earlier claims about how the "English nation . . . has become excellently affected to our nation." The Lord Protector provided Menasseh with some funding but not enough, and in 1657, after the death of his son Samuel and himself having become "A broken and beggared man," Menasseh returned to Amsterdam and perished two months later.[63] Menasseh's mission to Cromwell is ulti- mately, then, a story of failed hospitality and failed territorialization at the scale both of his London home and of his national mission. I don't intend to paint an overly pessimistic picture. The failure of the mission doesn't altogether cancel out Menasseh's companionable interactions with English Protestants. And after the rabbi left the island, the Anglo-Jewish community did expand so much as to merit the erection of the Bevis Marks Synagogue, whose open presence in London represents an important milestone. For the purposes of my argument, the most important lesson to take away from Menasseh's quest for readmission is the fact that, even were the rabbi to succeed in garnering an open and secure habitation for Anglo-Jews, even though the rabbi seemed to perceive the English as a worthy people meriting a special place in God's plan and a companionable relation to God's chosen people, such tendencies only went so far. According to the teleology of his messianism, Menasseh never sought permanent residence in England either for himself or his people. Qualifying the rabbi's passionate plea for Jewish presence in England is a future when the Jews absent themselves from all locations in the world but Israel.

## Archiving God's "Off-Scowring": The Spatial Paradoxes of Prynne's *Demurrer*

It is undeniable that, regardless of the English hospitality enjoyed by Menasseh, the idea of living alongside Jews offended many English people, and perhaps no one more than Puritan lawyer William Prynne. An inveterate bachelor born to a Somerset farmer, Prynne was a prolific and polemical writer whose attack on readmission comprises just one of a slew of practices, ideas, and institutions he criticized, often to his detriment. Together, Prynne's *A Short Demurrer To the Jewes long discontinued barred remitter into England* and *The second part of a Short demurrer* make him the foremost opponent of readmis- sion.[64] In the *Demurrer*, Prynne opposes readmission by repeating all of the old English stereotypes about usury, coin-clipping, ritual murder, obduracy, and greed. But his most overarching and crucial argument directly counters Menasseh's theory of diaspora.

While Menasseh's geography of Jewish identity looks ahead to the Messiah, Prynne's geography of Jewish identity in the *Demurrer* looks back to the deicide myth, and with a vengeance. In his notably harsh evocation of the view of diaspora as punishment—what he describes as "the saddest Spectacles of divine Justice"—Prynne intensifies Jewish culpability by terming Jews "malitious" and calling their acts a "crying sinne." Most notably, he directly counters notions of Jewish election by characterizing Jews as the "very off-scowring of the world." Prynne's descriptor appropriates the image of the Jews after the fall of Jerusalem in Lamentations 3:45 as "the filthiness of the world, the offscouring of all things" and takes that idea of the Jews as global garbage to its extreme conclusion. Human embodiments of the "matter out of place" described by Mary Douglas, Prynne's Jews are the ultimate outcasts, possessed of "no place . . . in any corner of the Universe," globally unassimilable.[65]

The outcast Jews of the *Demurrer* utterly contrast with Menasseh's vision of a "holy people" under a God who, far from refusing them habitation, has disseminated them to every place in the world as a prelude to their return to its most sacred city of Jerusalem. While Menasseh's God maps Jews onto the world as his chosen people, Prynne's God voids Jews from the world as trash. Yet if we turn from the broad outline of Menasseh's messianism to its particular form in South America, we see that Menasseh's and Prynne's respective interpretations of diaspora aren't so much opposed but rather occupy flip sides of the same coin. Thanks to their extreme geographic isolation from other inhabitants, Menasseh's South American Jews share with Prynne's Jews a certain placelessness. Taken together, Prynne and Menasseh's works reveal how placelessness or isolation can be marshaled either to denigrate or to exalt. If placelessness in *Hope* safeguards Jews from barbarian contamination, in the *Demurrer* it indicates the Jews' status as filth itself.

England is no exception to Prynne's theory of diaspora. At one point in the *Demurrer*, citing Matthew 5:13 and Luke 14:34–35, Prynne writes that "The Jews, who have lost both their Saviour and their favor" are "not fit for *our Lord, nor yet for our dunghils*; but to be kept and *cast out* from amongst us."[66] Prynne's offensive characterization of Jews as unfit even for "our"—that is, English—"dunghils," clarifies the national ramifications of the Jews as global "offscowrying." The global scale of Jewish unassimilability entails that they cannot be jettisoned even into English dumps but must be cast out from the world altogether. To prove his point, Prynne turns to Anglo-Jewish habitation during the twelfth and thirteenth centuries, an enterprise whose politics, practices, and eventual failure imply that Jews should never have entered England in the first place.

Housing practices play a crucial role in Prynne's argument. Unlike boy-martyr myths, the *Demurrer* does not stress how the Jews strategically employ their domiciles as a cover for crime. Instead, and in keeping with his conception of Jews as global waste, Prynne stresses how Jews lack any control over their homes, which are governed instead by the Crown. Far from the divinely empowered people of *Hope*, Prynne's Jews are "wholly at the Kings disposal" when it comes to "their real and personal estates." "Confined to live and abide only in such places as the King and his Justices" assigned them, Jews "could not sell any of their Houses . . . without the Kings special license," and "were translated from place to place at the Kings pleasure."[67] Prynne cites multiple examples of John, Henry II, and Edward I seizing Jewish domiciles and granting them to Christians. Rendering Jewish habitation still more unstable are Christian attacks on homes in cities including London and Canterbury, where perpetrators "broke open their doores, beat them, and intended to burn their houses with fire."[68] Prynne's Jews thus don't so much settle in England, but figure as "unwelcom Guests to all Towns and places in England."[69]

The tenuous relation between Jews and English territory serves in the *Demurrer* as a symptom of a national unassimilability that both adumbrates and accounts for the Jews' forced migration from the island. Prynne emphatically stresses the finality and complete nature of the expulsion, repeatedly calling it "total," "actual," "universal," and, above all, "final."[70] The best evidence of the finality of the expulsion proves to be the fate of Jewish houses.[71] For example Prynne stresses how the *Carta de Judaismo* "wherein are near one hundred particular Patents of sales" of homes presents the reader with a "unanimous irrefragable verdict" that the Jews "were *legally and judicially Banished out* of England."[72] "Patents of sales," that is, documents confirming possession, serve as the inevitable outcome of the teleology Prynne creates through his tale of insecure Anglo-Jewish habitation; ensuring that Jews have no home to return to, the patents provide "patent" or clear proof that Jews are "never to return again" without the king's "special license."[73]

For all its offensiveness, the *Demurrer* is a significant historical achievement. Drawing on his legal training, Prynne supported his claims by publishing for the first time hundreds of documents from public records from the turn of the twelfth century to 1290. That noteworthy scholarly effort complicates the geography of Jewish identity in the *Demurrer*. For by trying through such documentary ends to keep Jews out of England, Prynne paradoxically created an *archival space* for Jews in English print culture. "A monument of research," the *Demurrer* became such a valued resource for scholars that it ironically rendered Prynne "the father of medieval Anglo-Jewish historiography, and not only by Gentile historians."[74] Wolf, writing in 1901, states that "until a generation ago," Prynne's work "was the chief printed source of our knowledge of the medieval history of the English Jews."[75] And in 1908, Solomon Levy, president of the Jewish Historical Society of England, praised the *Demurrer* as valuable "because it is based on bedrock material, obtained and rescued from oblivion" by Prynne, and furthermore claimed that the book "is still indispensable to the student of Anglo-Jewish history."[76]

Prynne's status as both a vociferous antisemite *and* a pioneer of Anglo-Jewish history makes him a fraught figure, to say the least. Ironically, Menasseh's great opponent proves to be equally relevant to the story of the Jews' English past. Perhaps with that paradox in mind, Levy, in the same address in which he praises Prynne's text, hazards that Menasseh and Prynne "must have been personally acquainted and entertained a feeling of mutual respect."[77] Levy even speculates that the rabbi issued Prynne "a friendly invitation to dinner, and beginning most affectionately, 'My dear Willie:—Oh, come round and dine with Me-nasseh. / O, do, dear Willie Prynne.'"[78] Levy reimagines Menasseh's Strand home as a place where not only Hebraists and millenarians but also an anti-readmission polemicist could break bread with the Amsterdam rabbi. Could Menasseh have hosted Prynne? As Saltman points out, "Prynne's diurnal perambulations between" his quarters in "Lincoln's Inn and Westminster" very likely entailed travel on the Strand.[79] Thus, at the very least, Menasseh might have found himself close enough to Prynne to call out from his window or doorstep a version of Levy's invitation.

But of course Levy's imagined meal between "Willie" and "Me-nasseh" tells us less about the two men's relationship than Prynne's charged prominence among Anglo-Jewish historians. After all, Prynne's theory of diaspora suggests that if Menasseh extended such an invitation, the lawyer would likely have refused it. Indeed, the rabbi's very habitation of England repelled Prynne, as a passage from the *Demurrer* demonstrates. After citing as spurious Menasseh's claim that Jews have "been invited hither" to England "by divers EMINENT PERSONS ex|celling both in Piety and Learning, as well as power," Prynne facetiously states that the rabbi is now "inqui|ring after a convenient Summer-house, intending to settle himself at least, if not his exiled Nation, here among us: whereas Pierce Gaveston, a Forraigner, and the two Spencers, great Potent Englishmen, have heretofore lost their lives and heads for returning into England, without the Parliaments and Nobles license, though by the Kings own invitation, and license, when banished thence by Parlia|ment; which this Jewish Rabbi, and his banished Coun|trimen may do well advisely to consider, for fear of af|terclaps."[80] Prynne makes the prospect of readmission tangible to readers by telling them that already one of them—Menasseh—is endeavoring "to settle himself . . . here among us." Prynne makes Menasseh's presence all the more jarring by imbuing the rabbi with an ambition for English pastoral life on the scale enjoyed by the gentry, that is, a country home dedicated to summer "Rec-reation and pastime."[81] Prynne then undermines the idea of a Jew enjoying English summer weather by warning how that same Jew may suffer from thunderous "afterclaps" of the 1290 expulsion. Far from enjoying the com-forts of the English gentry, Menasseh should take care that he doesn't meet the grisly and undignified demise suffered by other exiles, "two . . . great Potent Englishmen" who "have heretofore *lost their lives and heads for returning into England*" after their banishment.

Why was Prynne so set against welcoming Menasseh and other Jews to England? Alongside the ready explanations contained in the litany of anti-semitic slurs recorded in the *Demurrer*, I would add Prynne's own housing situation. In other writings, Prynne complains of numerous upheavals to his home life. One such disturbance occurred in 1649, when "some thirty" unruly soldiers from Cromwell's army demanded lodging from Prynne, who was at that time living at his family farm in Swainswick. Prynne describes how the soldiers, "shouting and hollowing in a rude manner climbed over my walls, forced my doors, beat my servants and workmen without any provocation, drew their swords upon me . . . using many high provoking Speeches, brake some of my windows, . . . ransacked some of my chambers under pretext to search for Arms . . . hollowed, roared, stamped, beat the Tables with their Swords and Muskets like so many Bedlams, swearing, curs-ing, and blaspheming at every word."[82] While bribery convinced the soldiers to depart, the next day they "re-entered the house" and renewed their rau-cous disruptions to the household.[83] Still more telling than this episode are the some twenty years during which he found himself in and out of English prisons for publications that offended first the Crown, and then the Com-monwealth. Those imprisonments notoriously were coupled with physical punishments that included the removal of Prynne's ears and the branding of his cheeks. Nearest to the readmission debates was an almost three-year imprisonment for plotting the restoration of the monarchy.[84]

Prynne's repeated imprisonment and torturous punishments suggest how the religious and political tensions at play in the seventeenth century—like the medieval conflicts affecting Piers Gaveston and the Despensers—rendered certain Christians no less alien or demonized than certain Jews. Far from enjoying the hospitality (however short-lived) bestowed on Menasseh, Prynne seems to have experienced a version of the very domestic upheavals he attributes to the medieval Anglo-Jewry. Indeed, his complaint in one work of how he was "tossed up and down … like a Tennis-Ball, from one Castle, and *illegal Prison* to another, to my greater trouble and expence" closely approximates his claim in the *Demurrer* that Jews "were translated from place to place at the Kings pleasure."[85] The *Demurrer* thus may represent the "wandering" polemicist's effort to foist onto a demonized population his own domestic disturbances. Such a practice was hardly original to Prynne; when John Donne wrote his sermon on wandering Jews, the poet had experienced many years of poverty, hardship, and dependence upon others for housing and sustenance.[86] And, as we shall see, *Samson Agonistes* coincided with Milton's tenuous existence after the Commonwealth's demise. During a time of socioreligious upheaval in England, the prospect of accommodating the Jew seems to have especially repelled those Christians who were finding themselves unaccommodated.

Prynne's own domestic upheavals undermine his effort to single out Jews from English Christians in terms of their unstable relationship to place. A somewhat similar message emerges at one point in *Hope*, when Menasseh compares how members of the ten tribes were "forced" by Indians "up unto the mountains, and the in-land Countries, as formerly the Brittaines were driven by the Saxons into Wales" (20). Likening the Anglo-Saxons to the Indians invading the Americas, Menasseh compares the plight of the Israelites to that of the Britons. As that passage and Prynne's biography show, the experience of exile and displacement was hardly unique to Jews but was shared by Christians such as the Britons during the Middle Ages and Englishmen during the seventeenth century.

## Jews and Milton's Spatial Prohibitions

While Prynne and Menasseh are clear candidates for exploring the spatial contradictions of readmission, Milton may seem irrelevant to that topic. This is not to deny Milton's interest in Jews. Such factors as Milton's understanding of England as a new Israel, his study of Hebrew, his use of typology, and the congruence of his theology and rabbinic interpretation all demonstrate his "rich cultural exchange" with Jews and Judaism.[87] Yet despite his Hebraism, Milton refrained from speaking out on readmission. Rendering his silence all the more puzzling is Milton's cognizance of the debates. He was privy to the business of the Protectorate, thanks to his position as Latin secretary. He also knew Wall, the English translator of *Hope*, and other millenarians invested in converting Jews.[88] It is clear that the poet not only was aware of the debates but also had heard arguments for either side from friends and colleagues.

Still another aspect of Milton's life may have made him cognizant of readmission: his own housing history. Milton often lived in relative proximity to old or new Jewish neighborhoods. During the debates, Milton lived in Petty France, Westminster, and while traveling to conduct business in Whitehall he frequently would have passed by Menasseh's home on the Strand. And, before and after the goings-on at Whitehall, Milton lived in other homes, many of which placed him in close proximity to Jews and/or Anglo-Jewish spaces. Milton often lived about half a mile away from the new Jewish neighborhood near Aldgate and also often lived immediately beside and even within the old preexpulsion Jewish quarter. Both Milton's childhood home on Bread Street and a later house on Aldersgate Street were located a block or two from the medieval Anglo-Jewry. After the fall of the Commonwealth, from 1661 to 1663, Milton rented a home located beyond the city wall, where the medieval Jewish cemetery existed.[89] The street on which he lived during that time—called Jewin Street or Jew's Garden—bore a name that memorialized its prior use as a burial ground during the twelfth and thirteenth centuries.[90] Milton's proximity to the spaces of current and historical Jewish habitation in London would have driven home to him the fact that, for better or worse, England had made a home for Jews in the past and, after openly debating the issue, was tacitly doing so in the present.

A hint at how Milton felt about the diaspora appears in the *Christian Doctrine*. On the question of evidence that "a God does exist," Milton cites how the Jews "have been reserved in their scattered state, among the rest of the nations, through the revolution of successive ages, and even to the present day" not only "on account of their sins" but also "to be a perpetual and living testimony to all people under heaven, of the existence of God, and of the truth of the Holy Scriptures."[91] While Milton, like Prynne, links dispersal with punishment, he does not denigrate Jews as global waste. Rather, Milton's language suggests an Augustinian take on dispersal and toleration. Echoing Augustine's idea of Jews as embodied instances of the Old Testament prophesies about Christ, Milton writes that Jews have been and continue to be "reserved" by God as a "living testimony" to him and to the bible. The writer therefore might have supported readmission, insofar as it both enabled Jews to advertise "the truth of the Holy Scriptures" in England and perhaps, in a more monist vein, affirmed God's dispersal throughout the created world.[92]

However, if Milton supported readmission, why is his name, as N. I. Matar puts it, "conspicuously missing from the list of Cromwell's supporters on the

project of the Jews' admission in 1655"?[93] While we can never know for certain how Milton felt about readmission, work by several scholars has shown
that despite his valuation of Jews as "living testimony" to God's existence,
Milton probably opposed Jewish settlement in England. Guibbory, studying
Milton's antimonarchical writings and apologies on behalf of the Commonwealth during the 1640s and 1650s, identifies "a disturbing anti-Semitic
attitude emerging," which "suggest[s] that it was unlikely that he would
have welcomed the Jews or expected their conversion any time soon."[94] And
Matar demonstrates how Milton's writings on Jewish restoration, with their
stress on conversion, reveal how Jews "pleading for settlement in 1655 did
not interest him."[95] Milton, in other words, seems to have had contradictory
impulses on the question of readmission; while his Augustinian position in
the *Christian Doctrine* theorizes tolerance for God's "living letters of the law,"
other texts indicate that he rejected the idea of sharing space with Jews in
England. Milton's failure to voice that negative stance may reflect his awareness of the political impropriety of publicly opposing a proposal favored by
his master, the Lord Protector.

I argue that Milton's position on Jews, readmission, and tolerance emerges
in its most charged yet elusive form in *Samson Agonistes* (1671). Those issues
are at least one remove from the overt subject of the play, an episode from
the book of Judges. Milton provides us, however, with a heuristic to his play
in other prose writings where he intertwines larger questions of coexistence
with the particular issue of Protestant–Jewish relations. I refer in particular to three of his polemical tracts penned during the 1640s: *Areopagitica*
(1644), *Of Reformation* (1641), and *The Reason of Church Government* (1642).
As Guibbory has shown, Milton's prose works of the 1640s and 1650s are
vital to any investigation of his attitude toward contemporary Jews, as well
as the writer's fraught identification of England with Israel.[96] In what follows, I focus on a particular component of those early works, Milton's use
of building metaphors. Milton's employment of architectural figures to
think through issues of tolerance, Christianity, and Judaism reflects—like
Katz's formulation of the house of England to characterize readmission—
the important role of space in conceptualizing cohabitation. Instead of the
house, however, Milton's preferred metaphor is that which was favored,
some eight hundred years earlier, in Bede's exegeses: Solomon's Temple.
Milton's early and charged evocation of the Jewish temple, as a device both
for organizing the Christian church and for distinguishing Christians from
Jews, offers a means of unpacking the antisemitic valences of the writer's
representation, many decades later in *Samson Agonistes*, of a pagan temple
and other built environments.

In a passage in *Areopagitica*, Milton relates how, when erecting the contemporary house of God,

> there must be many schisms and many dissections made in the quarry
> and in the timber. . . . And when every stone is laid artfully together,
> it cannot be united into a continuity, it can but be contiguous in this
> world; neither can every piece of the building be of one form; nay
> rather the perfection consists in this, that out of many moderate variet-
> ies and brotherly dissimilitudes that are not vastly disproportional, arises
> the goodly and the graceful symmetry that commends the whole pile
> and structure. Let us, therefore be more considerate builders, more wise
> in spiritual architecture, when great reformation is expected.[97]

In the same way that Bede reads Solomon's Temple as a figure of strong
Christian practice in England, Milton riffs on 1 Kings 5–6 in order to conceive of the role played by religion in his national community. With his
attention to the temple's physical form—the cutting and piecing together
of its marble and timber—as a way of conceiving of "spiritual architecture,"
Milton emerges here not as the monist of the divorce tracts and other writings, but as a dualist invested in separating out matter from spirit, outer from
inner.[98] As Milton later would put it in *Paradise Lost*, God prefers "before
all Temples . . . th'upright heart and pure."[99] Milton seeks to locate the living church—the collectivity of faithful souls—figured in the matter of the
temple.

But unlike Bede, who stresses the unification of a single catholic church
in England, Milton's living church in England—in keeping with the changes
wrought in the realm after the Reformation—tolerates heterogeneity and
dissent. The "graceful symmetry" of the spiritual architecture thus paradoxically involves disproportion, "varieties," and "dissimilitudes." But crucially,
those divergences are qualified. They are "not vastly" asymmetrical, but are
only "moderate" and—most tellingly—"brotherly," descriptors that reflect
Milton's embrace of religious diversity only as it appears within the siblinghood of the Protestant church.[100] Milton's English temple thus connotes,
some ten years before the debates, an idea of communal heterogeneity that
is radically different from the English house used in Katz's account of what
actually happened. While historically the English went "around the back
themselves and let" Jews into the house of England, Catholics, pagans, Muslims, and Jews play no part in the erection of Milton's national temple.

The outliers from Milton's temple technically constitute anyone who isn't
a Protestant; yet Jews occupy a unique and charged place in his formulation, thanks to its basis in their holy edifice. The Jewish temple is both

the valued springboard for Milton's conception of the reformed Christian church even as it, in classic typological fashion, also represents an outdated literal and physical mode of being. Here and elsewhere in his work Milton endorses a version of the Pauline supersession of Christianity over Judaism in which, to cite Daniel Boyarin, the "carnal, physical, material, and literal," nature of Jewish existence—the status of the Jews as a people of the flesh who read according to the flesh (i.e., literally)—is supplanted by Christian spirituality and its figurative take on the bible.[101] Jews, therefore, are a people linked to the older, literal, and physical temple, which has given way to the new spiritual temple of the Protestant church. Milton, it might then seem here, takes us away from the interest in material built environments that we've tracked in Menasseh and Prynne, and toward something approximating Paul's "living stones" (1 Pet. 2:5; 1 Cor. 3:16). Further confirmation for that possibility appears in an antiepiscopal tract, *Of Reformation*, in which Milton decries "the Idolatrous erection of Temples beautified exquisitely to out-vie the Papists" in England.[102] In the passage Milton clearly aligns Jewishness with a debased carnality—for example, the Anglican ceremonials and building practices of Archbishop William Laud (1573–1645)—that England must renounce.[103] Voicing his puritanical outrage at Laud, who, like the Pope, is "Jewish" in his "Idolatrous erection of Temples," Milton seems bent on keeping England free not only of Jews like Menasseh, but also of any persons and buildings that smack of a "Jewish" carnality.[104] It seems clear that Milton would hardly have approved of the stone churches and monasteries that defined the faith during Bede's time.

However, while Milton's engagement with supersession adds a crucial, complicating element to our investigation of his stance on readmission, it hardly means that the writer actually has jettisoned carnality altogether. To return to *Areopagitica* and its reading of Solomon's Temple, Milton's investment in Christian living stones over the physical temple has its material dimensions: the metaphor of the reformed "spiritual" church serves as a means of physically exiling non-Protestants from England. The claim that reformers alone make up the new house of God allows for the physical presence of Protestants in England, where they occupy, of course, material built environments.[105] A full comprehension of Milton's stance on readmission and diaspora involves attending carefully to both the rhetoric of Christian spirituality the writer explicitly endorses and his Christian materialisms, many of which lie just beneath the surface of Milton's discourse of supersession.

That tension between Christian spirituality and Christian materialism emerges in striking form in a passage from *The Reason of Church Government* that will prove pivotal to my reading of *Samson Agonistes*. In this passage,

Milton registers explicitly his animosity toward the Jewish temple. Again he deploys the temple as a figure of the Christian church, here in relation to the new temple prophesied by Ezekiel, where "from the 40 Chapt. onward, after the destruction of the Temple, God, by his Prophet, seeking to weane the hearts of the Jewes from their old law, to expect a new and more perfect reformation under Christ, sets out before their eyes the stately fabrick & constitution of his Church, with all the ecclesiastical functions appertaining: indeed, the description is as sorted best to the apprehension of those times, typicall and shadowie, but in such a manner as never yet came to passe, nor never must literally, unless we mean to annihilat the gospel."[106] Milton, not unlike Augustine in his reading of Ezekiel in *City of God*, exhibits a marked vehemence toward the literal fulfillment of the prophesy about rebuilding the temple. The erection of another physical temple so opposes Christian thinking that its very presence would "annihilat" the gospel, that is, obliterate Christianity altogether. Milton's conception of the utter incompatibility of the old physical and the new spiritual temples partly speaks to his rejection of the "Jewish" materialisms of Laud and other Anglicans seeking to remake a new temple in the new "Israel" of England. Here Milton insists, in Guibbory's words, "that the Christian church is no temple, and that its government and worship must have nothing in common with the Temple of Jerusalem."[107] The writer also registers his animosity toward Jews and Judaism. Milton clearly would have rejected Menasseh's messianic claim that God has sent Jews into the world as a prelude to their restoration to—and rebuilding of—Jerusalem.[108]

This passage goes beyond the excerpt from *Areopagitica* in contradicting the toleration hinted at in the *Christian Doctrine*. Far from living letters of the Hebrew Bible who helpfully embody prophesies like that of Ezekiel, the Jews of *Reason* assume an outmoded approach to prophecy and religious practice that utterly opposes Christian thinking. Milton's attribution of a massive destructive power to the physical temple resonates less with Augustinian tolerance than with antisemitic notions of Jewish danger present in ritual-murder and host-desecration libels. Indeed, Milton exhibits in this passage an intolerance akin to that of Prynne. Like the Jews of the *Demurrer*, the Jewish temple of *Reason* is an abject entity whose carnality or filth must be exiled from England.[109] Milton's prohibition against rebuilding the temple speaks to how he, at some level, wished, like Prynne, to empty the earth of both Jews and Jewish buildings. Indeed, Milton evinces a worry over Jewish materiality that harkens back to Bede and Cynewulf, and their respective invocations of images of entombment and burial to connote Jewish carnality.

Yet if Christianity transcends carnality, should the erection of a physical temple have the destructive force Milton ascribes to it? While Christians engaging in "Jewish" materialisms clearly would contradict their spiritual allegiances, what harm would an actual Jewish temple present for a Christian society, if that society has moved beyond carnal investments? Milton's worry over the erection of temples, I'm suggesting, contradicts his claims about Christian supersession. Instead of affirming the transcendent spiritualism of Christian society, the writer acknowledges a Christian vulnerability to materialism, one witnessed by Laud and others. Moreover, we should note how that worry is itself literal, materialist, and therefore what Milton would understand as "Jewish." The materialism implied by the passage from *Areopagitica*—with its implicit ban of non-Protestants from England—comes to the fore in *Reason*. Milton paradoxically is "Jewish" in his harsh ban against literally fulfilling Ezekiel's prophecy.

Milton was perhaps cognizant—however inadvertently—of those contradictions, as the challenging hermeneutics of *Samson Agonistes* suggests. The closet play is famously difficult to pin down. As Stanley Fish puts it, "Milton finds in Samson a figure of deep hermeneutical trouble, and in his play troubles are not removed but multiplied."[110] An important yet underacknowledged instance of that "deep hermeneutical trouble" entails questions of tolerance and diaspora—of coexistence and locatedness—that emerge via representations of built environments in the play. Milton's drama culminates in its titular hero's demolition of Dagon's temple. That act of violence against both a pagan building and its occupants closely relates, I contend, to the writer's fraught stance toward Jews and Jewish spaces in works like *Reason* and *Areopagitica*. Namely, by attacking the materialism of the temple and its inhabitants in a highly physical manner (its literal destruction), Samson embodies his author's paradoxical stance toward the Christian church and Jewish outsiders.

Such a claim, of course, runs against the overt meaning of the temple in the drama. Dagon's temple is a pagan site where not Jews but Philistines worship. Moreover, it figures in *Samson Agonistes* as a "place abominable" to Jews, a building whose Jewish occupation violates biblical ritual laws of pollution.[111] As Samson puts it to the officer who calls on him to perform in the temple, "Thou knowst I am an *Ebrew*, therefore tell them, / Our Law forbids at thir Religious Rites / My presence" (1319–21). Yet despite this apparent difference between Jews and Philistines, the two peoples are very much one and the same. In her analysis of a slew of Miltonic works including *Samson Agonistes*, Rachel Trubowitz has tracked Milton's orientalist tendency to conflate Jews and Asians in terms of their shared bondage to carnal and idolatrous thinking.[112] A look at a passage from the text Milton partnered with *Samson Agonistes*, *Paradise Regain'd*, is instructive here.[113] Offering the reader something of an interpretive guide to *Samson Agonistes*, *Paradise Regain'd* depicts Jesus telling Satan that the Israelites are "distinguishable scarce / From Gentiles but by Circumcision vain, / And God with Idols in their worship join'd."[114] The Jews/gentiles denigrated by Jesus in Milton's poem are also the flawed Jews of Milton's play; that is, they are Philistinian, oriental, and "Jewish" in their servitude to an idolatrous materialism. "Time and time again in *Samson Agonistes*, Milton emphasizes the likeness between the two peoples," especially through the near interchangeability of Samson's father Manoa and his wife Delilah.[115]

Dagon's temple figures in such a conflation, ironically, in terms of the Jewish dictate against entering it. That is, the rhetoric of purity and danger that informs the Jewish taboo speaks to a mindset that is literal and carnal: a fear over physically entering the space of the other. Adherence to the old law thus signifies a bondage to a materialism not unlike that practiced by the Philistines in Dagon's temple. Paradoxically, then, the Jews' avoidance of the pagan temple signals their affinity with its carnality. To put it another way, Dagon's temple figures a "Jewish" materialism present in the Jews' own literal-mindedness.[116] There is more to the story, however, since, as we've seen, Milton himself participates in a carnal discourse of purity and danger in his account of the temple in *Reason*. Milton's dictate in that text against *never* rebuilding a new Jewish temple isn't altogether different from the Hebrew prohibition against entering Dagon's temple. In the same way that the Jews appear like Philistines in barring themselves from Dagon's temple, Milton ironically is "Jewish" in prohibiting Christians from erecting the literal temple. This doesn't mean of course that Milton endorses the Jewish prohibition in *Samson Agonistes*, but rather that, when it comes to the question of Jewish carnality (and Christian spirituality), Milton is fraught. At the same time that the poet endorses transcendence of the literal, his notion of toleration is ultimately quite literal and carnal. That contradiction between Milton's theory of the spiritual Christian temple and the materialisms upon which that theory relies emerges when we set the respective spatial prohibitions of *Reason* and *Samson Agonistes* alongside each other.

And those contradictions come to a head when Samson enters and subsequently demolishes the temple. As Trubowitz, Fish, and other critics observe, Samson's decision to "obey" the Philistines' order that he participate in the festival honoring Dagon—and yet perform that task "freely"—is a pivotal moment in the play (1372–73). While the Jewish avoidance of the temple paradoxically registers the literalism that binds Jews to Philistines, Samson's consensual entry into the pagan temple, prompted by "some rousing motions" within, suggests his association with a proto-Christian—or, more precisely, proto-Protestant—spiritual freedom (1382). By deciding to enter the temple, Samson shifts from Jewish subservience to a Christian liberty unfettered by anxieties over pollution. In Fish's words, "Samson has shaken himself free of the prisons to which he earlier clung—the prisons *of the law*, of the centered self, and of an unyieldingly jealous God" (my emphasis).[117] As Trubowitz puts it, Samson "breaks away from all that naturally and historically precedes him" when he chooses not to follow the old law.[118] We might add to those observations the claim that, by entering the temple, Samson does what his seventeenth-century (re-)creator refuses to do. In *Reason*, as we have seen, Milton construes the Jewish temple as so dangerous and polluting that it cannot be rebuilt. Samson, it would seem, enacts a more authentic supersession when he freely roams into the pagan temple. A figure of Jewish materialisms generally and the Jewish temple in particular, Dagon's temple proves to be a place that Samson, in his proto-Christian transcendence of "Jewish" carnality, can enter and inhabit without suffering from the annihilation that Milton threatens in *Reason*. Samson is so proto-Christian that he doesn't have to worry about Jewish materiality tainting or corrupting him. He embodies Milton's earlier Pauline sentiment (Titus 1:15), articulated in *Areopagitica*, that "to the pure all things are pure."[119]

Yet if Samson's entry into the temple transcends the carnal, what of his subsequent actions in that built environment? Feigning exhaustion from the feats of strength he has performed there, Samson leans against the pillars supporting the temple and, empowered with a near seismic force,

> those two massy Pillars
> With horrible convulsion to and fro
> He tugg'd, he shook, till down they came and drew
> The whole roof after them, with burst of thunder
> Upon the heads of all who sat beneath.
>
> *(1648–52)*

In part, Samson's action shows how he continues to oppose materialism and carnality, thus pointing further to his new, proto-Christian subjectivity. The site of idolatrous pagan rites, the temple to Dagon epitomizes the materialism that enslaves both Philistines and Jews. By pulling the edifice down on the Philistines' heads, Samson enacts what Trubowitz has described as a "space clearing" directed not simply at pagans and pagan buildings but also their carnal Jewish doubles.[120] Samson's action thus also conforms to the animosity toward "Jewish" materialism witnessed in Milton's celebration of a purely Christian church in *Areopagitica*, his denigration of Laud's "Idolatrous erection of Temples" in *Of Reformation*, and his aggression in *Reason* toward the literal fulfillment of Ezekiel's prophecy. That Samson's action entails his own demise—thus echoing Jesus' sacrificial death—would seem only to support its Christian valences.

And yet, as critics including Jeffrey Shoulson point out, the bloodthirsty human violence associated with Samson's act opposes the ostensibly pacific nature of Christian salvation.[121] Several aspects of *Paradise Regain'd* imply such a criticism of Samson. Jesus denigrates "Conquerors, who leave behind / Nothing but ruin wheresoe'er they rove" and advocates "deeds of peace" that clearly depart markedly from the devastation wreaked by Samson (78–79, 91). While Jesus passively submits to his death, Samson actively produces death and destruction. Moreover, the relationship between Jesus and the temple in *Paradise Regain'd* belies any supersessionist aspect of Samson's actions. In that poem Jesus stands firmly atop the temple (541–61), both leaving it unharmed and visually manifesting—as Abigail does in the convent scene in *The Jew of Malta*—the "positioning of superstructure over foundation, Church over Synagogue, the architecture of typology itself."[122] Samson's demolition of a figure of the temple performs no such typological relation.[123] Rather, his destruction of Dagon's temple and its inhabitants, far from rising above the material as a problem, testifies to its existence and power. Samson's destruction of the temple is itself a brutally physical action. Unlike Samson's entry into that building (which transcends any fear of the carnal), but like the prohibition against the temple in *Reason*, Samson's action construes the temple and its inhabitants as so dangerous as to require their literal or material banishment. Samson thus attacks "Jewish" materialisms through "Jewish" means. Like the prohibition against literally entering the temple, Samson's literal demolition of that structure resonates with the carnality of that building; both the temple and its attacker share an investment in the physical and material. And that paradox makes Samson quintessentially Miltonic, at least in terms of the aggressive materialism that attends the writer's discourse of spiritual supersession in the prose tracts.

Samson brings to the forefront the aggressive and Miltonic materialism that belies the author's overt embrace of the spiritual temple elsewhere in his works. But that contradiction in Milton's thinking—that is, the "Jewishness" of Christian antisemitism—must necessarily remain opaque. Any explicit embrace of Samson would destabilize Milton's overall effort in the play to separate Christians from Jews in terms of the latter's carnality and the former's spirituality. Were Milton to celebrate categorically Samson's act, he would acknowledge his own affiliation with the very Jewish carnality he claims to transcend as a Christian. Samson's standing as a part of Milton that the author must disavow—as a figure from whom Milton must distance himself—may help account for what Michael Schoenfeldt has identified as the most significant building program of the play: the "wall" of silence separating the reader from Samson's relationship to God just before he tears down the temple.[124] While in Judges, Samson prays to God for renewed strength to wreak vengeance on the Philistines, we don't directly witness that prayer in Milton's text. The entire temple scene occurs "offstage" and is told through the secondhand report of a Hebrew messenger, who doesn't hear Samson pray but sees how "with head a while inclined / And eyes fast fixed he stood, as one who prayed, / Or some great matter in his mind revolved" (1636–38). Thanks to Milton's modification of Judges—the replacement of Samson's prayer with silence—an ambiguity emerges regarding Samson's actual thoughts; in Fish's words, "'as one who prayed' says neither that he is or is not praying."[125] Critics have shed light on the many possible meanings that might accrue to Samson's silence. Among such valences are Milton's qualms about the violent act his protagonist goes on to perform, the status of Samson's prayer as a given, and Milton's transformation of Samson from mere human into a "vessel of divine will."[126] In addition to those and other important readings, I would suggest that Samson's silence might have appealed to Milton insofar as it enabled him to distance himself from his protagonist's "Jewishness." Through the interpretive gap opened up by Samson's silence, Milton avoids any direct clash between the spiritual and material components of his thinking on Christian–Jewish relations. Samson's silence doesn't mean that Milton queries the destruction of the temple; as we have seen, the biblical hero's action conforms to the aggressive materialisms of Milton's antisemitic prose writings. Rather, Samson's silence speaks to Milton's qualms about the "Jewish" associations of his hero's (and the writer's own) carnality. The interpretive gap created by this scene covers or "walls" over the contradictory nature of a Miltonic rhetoric that deploys claims of spiritual supersession to effect brutal materialisms.[127]

Milton's fraught relation to "Jewish" materialisms may also help account for his interest in Samson as a suicidal figure, whose violent destruction of things Jewish leads to his own death. Samson's demise, that is, enables the demolition of his own lingering carnality or Jewishness. Unlike Judas in Cynewulf's *Elene*, whose carnal investment in his own life prevents him from dying for his carnal people, Samson, the self-destructing Jew, sets Jewish carnality against itself. Samson serves, in this regard, as Milton's ideal Jew: a figure who, by voluntarily evacuating himself from what we might call, following Husserl, the life-world imagined by the play, willingly accedes to Milton's wish for a purely Christian world order, where the literal temple and its Jewish faithful "never" exist.[128] Samson, in effect, does to himself precisely what Englishmen like Milton or Prynne wish contemporary Jews would do: exit from world territory.

Samson's destruction of himself along with the temple, in fact, represents only the culmination of an embrace of placelessness on his part that he demonstrates from the start of the play.[129] Troping on the Wandering Jew legend, Samson emerges in Milton's play as an itinerant Jew who cannot quell his "restless thoughts" (19). Like Ahasuerius and the contemporary Jews he metonymically signifies, Samson constantly wanders; but by restricting that movement to "wand'ring *thought*" (302, my emphasis), Samson poses none of the problems of cohabitation posed by diaspora. Instead of dispersing throughout the world like the Jews of Menasseh's *Hope*, the contemplative Samson travels only in his own head. Coupled with Samson's mental movements is his physical placelessness. Samson's thoughts wander while he is out of doors and isolated, in search of rest in an "unfrequented place" outside of the walls of the prison (17). Samson's departure from the prison doesn't mean he seeks another, more hospitable built environment in which to dwell. When his father Manoa offers to contrive a means of bringing his son home, Samson refuses "to sit idle on the household hearth" (566). Later, when Manoa's Asian double, Delilah, similarly invites Samson to solace himself at her "home in leisure and domestic ease," Samson again rejects that invitation (917). Those repeated offers of housing to the "wandering Jew" Samson resonate with the asylum-seeking Jews of Milton's world, Jews like those for whom Menasseh advocated. Unlike those Jews, or Menasseh (who, as we have seen, was quite attached to his English residence on the Strand), Samson jettisons the domestic comforts of home.[130]

Here the similarities and differences between *Samson Agonistes* and *Paradise Regain'd* again prove telling. Jesus, unlike Samson, is a homebody. While throughout most of *Paradise Regain'd* he is placeless in the desert, after vanquishing Satan, "the Son of God . . . unobserved / Home to his Mother's house private return'd" (636–39). Milton's decision to end the poem with Jesus going home—to find the rest and comfort denied him by the Wandering Jew of legend—makes clear just how much the author endorsed notions of rootedness and place. It's worth noting here that, during the 1660s, when Milton probably wrote both texts, he—like Prynne—suffered from considerable domestic upheavals. After the Restoration, in 1660, the poet spent several weeks in the Tower, and while living in his new home in Jewin Street near Aldersgate he "was in Perpetual Terror of being Assasinated."[131] Familial and economic tensions between Milton and his daughters made his home "coldly unpleasant" during the 1660s.[132] Such factors demonstrate how Milton may have yearned for a warm and secure home life, one like that which Jesus enjoys in *Paradise Regain'd*.[133] *Samson Agonistes* repeats the ending of its companion text, but with a crucial difference. After vanquishing the Philistines, Samson, like Jesus, returns to his parental domicile (i.e., Manoa's house). But while Jesus comes "Home to his mother's house" alive, Samson returns "Home to his Father's house" as a corpse (1733). Both Manoa's home and its Marian counterpart speak metonymically to Milton's understanding of the relationship of Christians and Jews to space. Christians, not Jews, merit domestic comforts. A site of idolatry (Manoa states that "there will I build him / A Monument," 1733–34) and the place where Samson's dead body lies, Manoa's home recalls the built environment that Bede compares to the stubbornly literal-minded Jew.[134] Both home and sepulcher, Manoa's domicile bridges the domestic spaces of antisemitic libels and Bede's tomb-like Jew.

Above and beyond his portrayal of Samson as a homeless one-man wrecking crew, Milton ascribes placelessness to his hero—and, indeed, all the Jews and "Jewish" Philistines of his play—through genre. A closet drama, *Samson Agonistes* abjures "the Stage (to which this work never was intended)."[135] Milton's choice of genre has yielded an array of important responses by critics. Those answers include the rejection by the author of *Eikonoklastes* of Restoration theatricalism (both on the stage and as enacted by political leaders like Charles I) and Milton's attraction to a medium that enabled voicing radical actions while resisting "conclusive judgments" about them.[136] Alongside such rationales I would include one that reflects the writer's antisemitism: the capacity of the closet drama to prevent the characters and places it depicts from entering physical space. If *Samson Agonistes* were a stage play, it would allow for "Jews" in the form of actors to inhabit a theater in London or elsewhere. Antitheatrical tracts—most famously, Prynne's *Histrio-matrix*—castigated plays for corrupting men by having them play women.[137] Milton may have found the idea of an English Christian playing a Jew even more disturbing, not only due to its blurring of identities but also because of how it situated "Jews" in England and allocated to them the space of the English stage. Thus while Milton is willing to place Samson, Manoa, and the other Jews of his play—both literal and figurative—within the mind's eye of his readers, he forever refuses their "admission" to England. The writer generically closes the doors to Jews in England in a manner not unlike the *Demurrer*, with its repeated insistence that medieval Jews received a "total, final banishment . . . out of England, never to return again."[138] Milton's decision to have the temple episode occur offstage is of a piece with this impulse, insofar as it locates the "Jewish" space of the temple—and Samson's "Jewish" destruction of himself and that built environment—at a further remove from his reader's imagination.

The generic finality of *Samson Agonistes* returns us to all of the other violent, carnal, and "Jewish" positions I have associated with Milton. Milton's generic prohibition against staging *Samson Agonistes* echoes the Jewish prohibition against entering the pagan temple first invoked by Samson. The writer's refusal to allow his characters to exist on the dramatic stage also echoes his refusal in *Reason* to allow the temple prophesied by Ezekiel to ever exist. Most importantly, perhaps, Milton's "act" of making a closet drama returns us to the destruction wreaked by his biblical hero. In the same way that *Reason* exposes a deep animosity toward a literal Jewish presence, *Samson Agonistes* performs a kind of generic violence that places Milton's literary method on a par with the destruction wreaked by the biblical hero. Like Samson's annihilation of the temple, Milton's refusal to represent Jews on a stage in England constitutes an extreme form of renunciation and aggression. Genre perhaps gives us our strongest indicator of Milton's covert affinity with Samson's violence even as it affirms his aggression toward Samson as a Jew. Milton's prohibition against staging Jews, in the end, only shores up his identity as a "Jewish"—that is, carnal and literal-minded—poet in England.

I end by returning to Manoa's home, to register one final—and crucial—twist in Milton's "staging" of Jewish placelessness in *Samson Agonistes*. As I note above, Manoa's home fosters idolatry insofar as, after receiving Samson's corpse, the father plans to "build him/ A Monument," to which "shall all the valiant youth resort," and "The Virgins also shall on feastful days / Visit" (1733–34, 1738, 1741–42). The play ends with Manoa erecting yet another "temple," where not Dagon but Samson is worshipped. Samson the living man may be absent, but the "Jewish" materialisms he opposed live on, via the monument Manoa erects in his honor. *Samson Agonistes* thus concludes by acknowledging the impossibility of ever truly creating a space devoid of "Jewish" materialisms. Manoa's actions speak to the ongoing presence in Milton's England of "Jewish" Protestants, of actual Jewish immigrants from Amsterdam and elsewhere, and even of Milton's own "Jewishness."

Taken together, Menasseh, Prynne, and Milton speak profoundly to the spatial contradictions that inform the problem of Jewish habitation in England during the seventeenth century. They reveal how Jews may be allotted and denied space by the least likely candidates: Prynne, the most vociferous opponent of readmission, ironically creates a documentary space for Jews; Menasseh, the foremost proponent of readmission, paradoxically distances Jews from the sites they inhabit. And in Milton's drama—a text renowned for its interpretive slipperiness—we arguably find the most fraught and nuanced meditation on the problem of where contemporary Jews belong. For all of its multilayered effort to empty the world of Jews, *Samson Agonistes* ultimately testifies to an ongoing Jewish presence. What we witness in all three texts, therefore, is a relationship between history and literature that seems to oppose models such as those of Fredric Jameson and Kenneth Burke.[139] Both Jameson and Burke describe how literary texts offer imaginative resolutions to historical problems. Milton, Prynne, and Menasseh, however, far from magically overcoming the dilemma of where Jews should live, offer complex intensifications of that very problem in their texts. In these writers' works we see how the Jewish entry "through the back door" of England was part of a multidimensional and irresolvable ambivalence on the part of both Jews and Christians endeavoring to understand identity along spatial lines.

# Coda

A central aim of this book has been demonstrating how antisemitic texts merit our critical attention for what they tell us about the utility of the imagined Jew in producing English capitalist space. By taking seriously their geographic dimensions, I have shown how such texts respond to historical change in a contradictory manner that at times challenges received ideas of Christian identity. Not only straightforward statements about Jew-hatred, these texts contain offensive fantasies about a supposed "Jewish" menace that stand in tension with counternarratives about an English Christian reliance on, desire for, and similitude to the "Jewish" materialisms Christianity claims to reject. Geography highlights that fraught multiplicity. Careful attention to space shores up both an English obsession over the Jew's house as a cover for malevolence and the urban-based flows and mixings that undermine that imagined domestic Jewish threat. Representations of the accommodated Jew thus reveal both an offensive politics of rejection and an ideological embrace of the Jew as a tool for accommodating the English to their messy urban materialisms.

I close by considering the implications my study has for later English images of the Jew as they appear in the work of Charles Dickens (1812–70). Writing some 150 years after Milton, Dickens returns to the question of Jewish accommodation in *Oliver Twist* (1837–39). By the time Dickens published the novel, about twenty thousand Jews were living in London and about half that number resided elsewhere in the realm.[1] Some members of the Jewish community thrived. Since the late eighteenth century or earlier, families such as the Cohens, Mocattas, and Rothschilds had achieved wealth and prominence through financial occupations such as stockbroking, trade, and banking.[2] In 1837, the prominent banker Moses Haim Montefiore (1784–1885) became sheriff of London and was knighted by Queen Victoria the following year.[3] A growing group of Jewish professions gained still more civil privileges. In 1830, Jews could become freemen and run retail businesses in the City; in 1833, Francis Henry Goldsmid (1808–78) was admitted to Lincoln's Inn as a barrister.[4]

Alongside such advances, however, were sociopolitical problems and challenges. Jews were barred officially from many professions and political positions, including membership in Parliament. The official debates over Jewish political rights that began in 1830 led to no ready resolution but instead the presentation and rejection of multiple bills in Parliament, followed by a protracted period of incremental gains such as the Reform Act of 1865 and the Universities Tests Act of 1871.[5] Arguments for and against "emancipation," which hinged primarily on ideas about religious freedom and the separation of church and state, at times drew on long-standing spatial tropes.[6] In his famous 1830 inaugural speech before Parliament, a young Thomas Macaulay (1800–59) advocated abolishing Jews' civil disabilities by evoking the privileged architecture of the Hebrew Bible. Contrasting early English barbarity with ancient Jewish society, he reminded opponents that "in the infancy of civilisation, when our island was as savage as New Guinea, . . . when scarcely a thatched hut stood on what was afterwards the site of Rome, this contemned people had their fenced cities and cedar palaces, their splendid Temple."[7] When we push back in time far enough, Macaulay asserted, we find that the only sophisticated and exalted space on earth belonged to Jews. If Macaulay supported Jewish emancipation by recalling the divine house of Solomon's Temple, Matthew Arnold's father, Thomas (1795–1842), would take the reverse spatial tack. Offering an analogy that connoted the geographic impermanence of diaspora, Arnold stated in 1834 that the "Jews are strangers in England, and have no more claim to legislate for it than a lodger has to share with the landlord in the management of his house . . . For England is the land of Englishmen, not of Jews."[8] For Arnold, only Christians—not the wandering, exiled, and always-foreign Jews—can truly occupy and possess English territory in any meaningful way.

Tangible evidence against Arnold's argument existed throughout Victorian London in the ample properties held by Jews. As Macaulay facetiously commented, "The Jew must not sit in Parliament: but he may be the proprietor of all the ten pound houses in a borough.'"[9] Both Anglo-Jewish property ownership and the presence of grand Jewish dwellings in fashionable areas such as Finsbury Square belied Arnold's characterization of Jews as mere boarders.[10] However, most Jews in Dickens's London were far from real estate magnates or the dwellers of fine homes. Instead they comprised members of poor and uneducated families that immigrated to England in the wake of the Napoleonic and Revolutionary Wars. Poverty was so widespread among those families that "at a minimum, half of the Jews in London were impoverished or barely making a living."[11] Poor Jewish immigrants lived in squalor, mainly in London's East End, and practiced peddling and other low occupations in locales such as Middle Row in Holborn and Monmouth Street in Seven Dials. As Todd Endelman points out, "Jewish poverty went hand in hand with crime, squalid surroundings, low-status trades, and coarse behavior."[12] Such factors hardly helped the emancipation effort.

Dickens registered a widespread English revulsion at the shabby mercantilism of an indigent London Jewry when he declared in *Sketches by Boz*: "Holywell-street we despise; the red-headed and red-whiskered Jews who forcibly haul you into their squalid houses, and thrust you into a suit of clothes, whether you will or not, we detest."[13] Here the accommodated Jew forces his Christian "guest" to undergo, not ritual murder, but secondhand clothes shopping. But of course Dickens's most notorious and extensive rejection of a London Jew emerges in his portrayal of Fagin, the Jewish antagonist of *Oliver Twist*. Unlike the miserable Jews about whom "Boz" complains—merchants who are annoyingly pushy but at least aren't breaking any laws—Fagin offered literary confirmation of the popular reputation of Jews as disreputable petty traders, tricksters, and criminals. Fagin offered rich support for opponents of emancipation through his behavior as a pimp, a fence, a kidnapper, and an accessory to murder. Such aspects of Dickens's character suggested that Jews, due to their corruption and corrupting influence, should not only be denied emancipation but also be eliminated violently and publically in the manner of Fagin's hanging outside Newgate.[14]

Only second to Shylock among the notorious Jews concocted by English writers, Fagin demonstrates the long literary life of both English antisemitism and English antisemitic geographies. Like Shakespeare's villain, Fagin is a figure whose characterization closely intertwines with the nature of his lodgings. Starting with the famous image of the Jew before his stove as the Artful Dodger introduces the "'spectable old genelman" to Oliver, multiple domestic set pieces connote Fagin as, first and foremost, a homebody.[15] Possessed of "great high wooden chimney-pieces and large doors, with panelled walls and cornices to the ceilings," all "ornamented in various ways," Fagin's house,

Oliver surmises, was originally "quite gay and handsome" (126).[16] But, like the Jewish temple, that was "a long time ago" (126). Now filthy, ruined and decrepit, Fagin's domicile mirrors the Jew's own "old" and "shrivelled body" (65, 131). Fagin's house would seem to undermine Macaulay's celebration of ancient Jewish built environments. Instead of connoting the venerable architectural grandeur of the Jew, the house is a ruined site worthy of demolition, a Victorian account of Jewish space as old and superseded.

But the primary characteristic of Fagin's house isn't so much its ruined state but its closure and confinement. Recalling Shylock's shut-up house and the closed dwellings of boy-martyr libels hailing back to Thomas of Monmouth, Fagin's lodging is abidingly private, secretive, and enclosed. It is what Dickens alternately calls a "den" or "lair": a secluded site off Field Lane, a narrow alley south of Saffron Hill beyond Greville Street, in one of London's most infamous slums, located only half a mile from the two homes where Dickens lived both before and when he wrote the novel (131, 311).[17] Dickens introduces the house by drawing attention to its apertures and their closure, describing how the Dodger "pushed open the door of a house near Field Lane; and drawing him [Oliver] into the passage, closed it behind them" (64). The most concerted scrutiny of the Jew's house occurs after Oliver's recapture and imprisonment at Fagin's lair in Whitechapel, in the East End, a place densely populated by Jewish immigrants. "A week or so" after Oliver's arrival, Fagin "left the room-door unlocked; and [Oliver] was at liberty to wander about the house" (126). Oliver tours the premises to find that in "all the rooms, the mouldering shutters were fast closed: the bars which held them were screwed tight into the wood" (126), an architectural detail that echoes the closed casements of Shylock's house. The one partially obstructed view that Oliver does find, from "a back-garret window with rusty bars outside, which had no shutter," opens onto a "confused and crowded mass of house-tops, blackened chimneys, and gable-ends" (126). The only opening in the house thus ironically looks onto yet another closure, writ large: a massive, monstrous urban ceiling of roofs and coverings that seal London dwellers off from the air and sky above them.

The way Oliver's circumscribed view only magnifies the closed nature of Fagin's house suggests that the Jew's dwelling is an exemplary part of a larger urban whole. In its metonymic capacity, Fagin's decrepit house speaks to issues particular to the Victorian period. Overcrowding, bad sanitary conditions, fog, smoke, and "covered ways and yards" made much of Dickens' London stultifying and confining, a place where "the air was impregnated with filthy odours" (64). But at the same time that Fagin's house speaks to its historical moment, it also returns us to the habit of thinking that first appears in Thomas of Monmouth's twelfth-century city text. Thomas's *Life of William* concerns, as we have seen, urban problems like crowding, privacy, and disorder as much as it does fantasies of Jewish ritual murder. And subsequent texts like the *Prioress's Tale*, Croxton, and *The Jew of Malta* reveal the persistent tradition of employing the Jew to imagine urban space on the part of English writers. Such texts demonstrate how, counter to Thomas Arnold's idea that Jews are alien to English space—mere "renters" to their Christian landlords—Jews (at least imagined Jews) proved fundamental to conceiving of English space and especially English cities. Dickens responds to and modifies this tradition in *Oliver Twist*.

On the question of why Dickens, after receiving complaints about Fagin, didn't eradicate Fagin's Jewish identity altogether from the text, Susan Meyer has argued that the deep interplay of Christian and Jew at the core of *Oliver Twist* prevented him from doing so.[18] But it is also the case that Fagin proves essential to the novel due to the long-standing English literary practice of imagining the city via Jewish spaces. To put it another way, given the precedent set by Thomas and later English writers, it is no surprise that in *Oliver Twist*, his second novel, Dickens shifts from the country adventures of the *Pickwick Papers* to the preoccupation with London that would inform so many of his later novels. Dickens initiates his long-standing fascination with the city via a novel featuring a Jew because his native literary canon had in some ways rendered Jewishness and the urban inseparable.

Dickens follows English antisemitic precedent through not only the seclusion of Fagin's house, but also the Jew's hosting of Christian youths. Indeed the fearful prospect of a boy entering a Jew's house multiplies in *Oliver Twist*, as not only the young Oliver but also the Dodger and other boys crowd within the domicile. However, the threat posed by Fagin's house isn't primarily a matter of physical attack. No second Calvary lurks within the Jew's house; no Christ-like boys undergo another crucifixion there. Rather, Fagin's domicile is the place where he endeavors to destroy any prospect of his young guests growing into normative and moral Victorian males. Telling "droll and curious" tales of his past robberies, playing pickpocket games, and leaving Oliver under house arrest and with little else but his "own sad thoughts," Fagin "slowly instill[s] into his soul the poison which he hoped would blacken it, and change its hue for ever" (131). Instead of ritually murdering boys, Fagin converts them into card-playing criminals, child-men who smoke, drink, and enact a quasi-pedophilic relationship with their effete Jewish host.

Fagin's house is sealed up, then, not to hide anti-Christian violence but to cultivate manifold forms of social impropriety and related "filth": the grime darkening its walls, the vermin crawling its floors, and the improper slippages and excesses of its inhabitants, boys and men who cross lines of propriety regarding gender, age, consumption, hygiene, labor, entertainment, and sexuality. Cloistering enables the creation of an alternative, decadent, and all-male Victorian "family." Almost anything goes in the house of Fagin, as long as his boys bring him spoils from the pockets they have picked. The Jew erects hard boundaries around his house to make it safe for the multiple transgressions that occur there.

Oliver Twist follows earlier English libels in juxtaposing its sealed and dangerous Jewish dwelling with beneficent Christian counterpoints, above all the Brownlow house. "White" and "neat," the domicile exemplifies the ideal Victorian house as haven (213, 81). Providing its inhabitants with shelter from the physical burdens, mental taxations, and moral cost of commerce, the Brownlow home is a site for developing the intellect and virtuous manhood. There, "in a little back room . . . with a window, looking into some pleasant little gardens," Oliver "marvel[s]" at a great number of "books as seemed to be written to make the world wiser," and is schooled by Mr. Brownlow about "honest trade[s]" like book writing or brick laying (97). Such a scene contrasts starkly with Fagin's house, the setting for multiple scenes of base consumption and greedy hoarding that affirm long-standing stereotypes about Jewish carnality. Fagin, Barabas's (albeit petty) inheritor, hoards costly watches and jewelry in "some trap in the floor" of his house (67). The maintainer of no "sober house" on the order of Shylock's home, Fagin hungrily munches on sausages in his abode. Thus while Fagin's house merely feeds the body and other low appetites, the Brownlow house feeds the mind.

To only stress that opposition, though, would neglect the complex and fraught mapping of identity onto the imagined spaces of Oliver Twist. Throughout the novel, Dickens portrays Christian dwellings that are in many respects far more lethal and dangerous than the Jew's house. While, for example, Fagin does strike Oliver once, the boy receives a more serious injury from a gun in the Christian abode of the Maylies. And while no boys die in Fagin's house, mortality abounds in both the infant pauper farm of Mrs. Mann and the workhouse.[19] In the latter place, the new gruel-based dining system there prompts an "increase in the undertaker's bill" and shrinks the bodies of the paupers so much that their clothes "fluttered loosely on their wasted, shrunken forms" (26). When Oliver moves to the undertaker's home, he sleeps among coffins and again is poorly fed with "dainty viands that the dog had neglected" (41).

Oliver's malnourishment by Christians complicates the depiction of the Brownlow house, reminding us that man doesn't live on books alone. The orphan's wish for "more" renders food a vital human right. Oliver's starvation, moreover, creates ambiguity in the famous initial image of Fagin in his house. The portrayal, in both the text and Cruikshank's illustration, of the red-haired and ugly-visaged Jew "with a toasting-fork in his hand" before a fire obviously makes Fagin demonic. However, the victuals frying on the pan over the blaze—food that Oliver soon gets to eat—also make Fagin a source of much welcomed sustenance. And the fire whose infernal resonance so many critics have stressed is also indubitably inviting and cozy, particularly given the days Oliver has just spent on the road. Ironically, Fagin's house is a site of both juvenile corruption *and* juvenile nurturance. In *Oliver Twist*, the ritual-murder house of English myth—or even the closed tombs of Bede, Cynewulf, and Milton—has become a place that fosters life.

But perhaps the most significant way that *Oliver Twist* complicates received notions of the Jewish house is through the spatial tension traced throughout this book: the juxtaposition of scenes of locking, containment, and enclosure with the portrayal of unwieldy and transgressive flows, circulations, and currents. The novel proliferates in episodes where Oliver and other boys are wrongfully imprisoned in rooms inside gentile buildings. At the baby farm, Oliver and other children are "locked up for atrociously presuming to be hungry" (21). At the undertaker's house Mrs. Sowerberry and Noah Claypool drag Oliver "into the dust-cellar, and there locked him up" (53). At the police office Oliver is "locked up" in a "stone cell" (75).[20] The preponderance of locking in the novel implies how, if Fagin is an encloser like Marlowe's Barabas, those practices of entrapment partake in a broader phenomenon practiced by many Christians in what is at times a more nefarious manner.[21] Fagin's impulse toward locking invokes not so much Jewishness as habits of secrecy and confinement that are endemic to the English world. Even Mr. Brownlow exhibits this tendency when he instructs his attendants to "Lock the door on the outside" of the room where he interrogates Monks. Earlier English works, such as Thomas of Monmouth's depiction of the choir screen at William's funeral or Marlowe's portrayal of Barabas's capture, also indicate the cloistering and trapping practices of Christians. Dickens goes beyond such portrayals in the multitude of locked spaces of *Oliver Twist*.[22] Through such images, Dickens worries over privacy, secrecy, and the institutionalized abuse of children, hallmarks of his Victorian society.

Alongside its representation of enclosure, the novel portrays flows that create mixings and contaminations that belie any effort, on the part of either Fagin or any gentiles in the novel, to erect and maintain boundaries. Fagin's association with such currents emerges when he ventures outside his home to visit Sikes, creeping through mist and on "mud" that "lay thick upon the stones . . . like some loathsome reptile, engendered in the slime and darkness through which he moved" (132). Fagin's status as an abject being made of "mud"—that is, the equine waste that blanketed London's thoroughfares—looks back to stereotypical associations of the Jew with filthy flows such as Barabas in the sluice of Malta and the Jewish privy of the *Prioress's Tale*. But in the same way that "mud" was endemic to nearly all of London's streets, Dickens packs his novel with myriad destabilizing urban circulations, such as the illicit movement of watches and other goods; the itineraries of Oliver, Fagin, Sikes, Nancy, and other characters within and without the city; the savage press of mobs on Oliver, Sikes, and (most tellingly) Fagin; and the tides that ebb in and around both the riverside building where Monks negotiates with Mr. Bumble and the site on Jacobs Island where Sikes hangs himself. The spectacle of currents and mixings renders urban circulations so prevalent as to define the city as a space of destabilizing flows, to adapt Manuel Castells's phrase.

The irrepressible flows of London help explain why Dickens's happy ending necessitates shifting all the virtuous or reformed characters to the country and suburbs. And yet, for over twenty years after the publication of *Oliver Twist*, Dickens himself opted not to retire to the country but to live and work in the heterogeneous, dirty—yet undeniably vital—capital of England. The writer's choice not to engage in an early Victorian version of "white flight" suggests the appeal of the city, while the final image of *Oliver Twist*—of Agnes Fleming's closed, empty, and alabaster tomb inside the village church—seems to deride rural space for its morbid and pristine removal from the lively if messy circulations of the urban.[23]

Dickens did, eventually, move to the country. During the final ten years of his life, his permanent residence was at Gads Hill Place, a mansion in Kent. But what concerns me here—and the scene of Jewish accommodation with which I end my study—is the London home Dickens left behind, Tavistock House (figure 24).

In 1860, a Jewish couple, Eliza Davis and her husband, solicitor James Davis, purchased and moved into the residence, located in Bloomsbury. That property transfer initially provoked offensive antisemitism on Dickens's part. Writing to a friend, "If the Jew Money Lender buys (I say 'if' because of course I shall never believe in him until he has paid the money.)," Dickens constructs James Davis as an economic Jew along the lines of Fagin and his shady business dealings.[24] Dickens's doubts about payment may even hint at an unspoken resistance to handing his home over to Jews. Dickens, however,

**FIGURE 24.** Tavistock House, London. *Source:* Forster, *Life of Charles Dickens*, 150.

went on to recant his racist slur and state of Davis "I cannot call to mind any occasion when I have had money-dealings with a Christian that have been so satisfactory, considerate, and trusting.[25] Interaction with Jews thus prompts a reform in Dickens, leading him to offer an account that radically departs from the antisemitic images of *Oliver Twist*.

Dickens's interaction with the Davises did not end with the sale of Tavistock House. In 1863, Eliza Davis would initiate a correspondence with Dickens that would last until his death in 1870. Her habitation of Dickens's erstwhile house clearly made such an exchange possible. The headings of Davis's letters all proclaim their composition in Tavistock House, and Davis explains in her first missive that she writes because she is "Emboldened by [Dickens's] Courtesy throughout my correspondence with you, on the transfer of Tavistock House to Mr. Davis."[26] No insubstantial notes filled with empty pleasantries, the letters reveal, quite remarkably, how moving into Dickens's house enabled Eliza Davis to move into Dickens's house of fiction.

In two letters, Mrs. Davis criticized Fagin's characterization as a Jew and wondered over the fact that "Charles Dickens the large hearted . . . has encouraged a vile prejudice against the despised Hebrew."[27] Mrs. Davis's correspondence actually led Dickens to remove many references to Jews in the 1867 edition of *Oliver Twist*.[28] Moreover, as Murray Baumgarten stresses, Eliza Davis's complaint over negative stereotyping in *Oliver Twist* "apparently led Dickens, who was planning out and writing *Our Mutual Friend* at the time —to invent the character of "Riah as a benevolent Jew."[29] Dickens foregrounds Riah as Fagin's spatial opposite; the first thing we learn about this good Jew is that he has a penchant for entertaining on a rooftop where, taking in the air and a view of the city, his guests enjoy precisely what Oliver lacks in Fagin's confined house.[30] Dickens's alterations were, to be sure, far from revolutionary; they hardly overturned the antisemitic stereotyping of his own fiction or subsequent English works.[31] Riah's rooftop perch above "the people who are alive, crying, and working" below him in London maps out how he is too good to be true, not so much a real-life person than, as the benevolent Jew's guest Jenny Wren puts it, "dead."[32] But such factors shouldn't prevent us from acknowledging how the purchase of Dickens's house enabled Eliza Davis to directly challenge the great writer—to speak back to his literary mythology—and alter nothing less than the shape of the English literary canon.

Beyond its impact on Dickens's writing, the correspondence in and of itself merits our attention as a text. Taken together, the eight letters exchanged between Davis, Dickens, and his daughter Mamie function as an epistolary novella of sorts that challenges antisemitic stereotyping far more than *Oliver Twist* or *Our Mutual Friend*. Eliza Davis conveys through her letters an image of the accommodated Jew that explodes the demonized houses of such literary Jews as Fagin, Barabas, and the pushy salesman on Holywell Street derided by Boz. The letters situate Tavistock house as a base for demonstrating, as Eliza Davis puts it in her first letter, that "we Wanderers from the far East desire to shew that we have found friends in the land in which we have pitched our tents."[33] Davis's notable erudition, moral compass, and warm civility emerge throughout her exchanges, in which she not only queries Dickens's image of the Jew but also asks—and receives—his support for a convalescent home for indigent Jews, and schools him in particulars of Jewish religion and culture. Tavistock House, in short, is a domestic locale that offers a suitable close to this study. No base, carnal, and dangerous site, the home is a place from which emanate ameliorating, intellectual flows, letters that offer a visionary conception of Jewish–Christian companionability and fellowship.

# ❧ NOTES

## Introduction

1. On the influence of Shylock, see Gross, *Shylock*; Felsenstein, *Anti-Semitic Stereotypes*, chap. 7; Shapiro, *Shakespeare and the Jews*, chaps. 3 and 4; Julius, *Trials of the Diaspora*, 178–92.

2. Bevington, *Shakespeare*, 229. Shylock's reference to the "wry-necked fife" could refer to the instrument or its player's twisted neck.

3. Garber, *Shakespeare After All*, 299. Garber describes how Shylock's "anti-comic repression" leads to his tragic downfall and punishment (ibid).

4. Bevington, *Shakespeare*, 229.

5. "What Belmont and gallant Venice alike hold against the Jew is not so much his usury, much less his denial of Christ, but his puritan austerity and his insistence that men are finally accountable" (Fiedler, *Stranger in Shakespeare*, 131). See also C. Richardson, *Shakespeare and Material Culture*, 50–51.

6. Calhoun, *Affecting Grace*, 187. While Shakespeare attacks puritanical denigrations of the theater by aligning a sober asceticism with the Jew, Shylock's criticisms of revelry aren't entirely unfounded in the play.

7. De Sousa, "'My Hopes Abroad,'" 50.

8. Booth, "Shylock's Sober House," 23, 26–27.

9. Ibid., 23.

10. For patristic and medieval examples, see J. Cohen, *Living Letters of the Law*. But see also Lipton, *Dark Mirror*, on patristic writers' stress on the visual capacity of "the Jew" as witness to Christ's life and crucifixion.

11. Foxe, *A sermon*, B3r. Adelman analyzes the sermon and *Merchant* in *Blood Relations*.

12. Foxe, *A sermon*, R6v–R7r.

13. Ibid.

14. Tiffany, "Names in the *Merchant of Venice*," 358.

15. On the Jew and stone, see chapter 1 and J. J. Cohen, *Stone*, 150–53.

16. Peter the Venerable, *Adversus Judeorum*, 58.

17. The first quarto of *Merchant* was printed in 1600.

18. Yaeger, "Introduction," 15. In this book I primarily invoke "space" not in reference to abstract space but rather to space as a meaningful yet unstable entity that is constructed through culture and society. Space in this book thus at times carries the sorts of valences that certain scholars attach to the term "place" (for example, Tuan, *Space and Place*; Cresswell, *In Place/Out of Place*). My terminology and methodology roughly align with that of Lefebvre, *Production of Space*, Soja, *Postmodern Geographies*, Smith, *Uneven Development*, and Yaeger, ibid., note 5.

19. *OED*, s.v. accommodate.

20. On the English medieval origins of the Wandering Jew legend and its eventual popularity, see chapter 6 and Anderson, *Legend of the Wandering Jew*. Lisa Lampert-Weissig is completing a book on the wandering Jew legend that will complicate received ideas about the literary history of the legend, by demonstrating its currency in medieval England.

21. Bale, *Feeling Persecuted*.

22. Stacey discusses "the precocious development of medieval English anti-Semitism" in "Anti-Semitism and the Medieval English State," 163. See also the works cited ibid., 162n1.

23. Some archaeological and documentary evidence—none definitive—suggests that Jews visited and inhabited both Roman Britain and Anglo-Saxon England, but not in any substantial manner. See Mundill, *King's Jews*, 1–4; Applebaum, "Were There Jews in Roman Britain?," 198–99; Roth, *History of the Jews in England*, 1–2; Baron, *Social and Religious History of the Jews*, 6:76; Golb, *Jews in Medieval Normandy*, 112–14.

24. Stacey, "Anti-Semitism and the Medieval English State," 166; J. Campbell, "Was It Infancy in England?," 14; Agus, *Urban Civilisation*, 61; and H. Richardson, *English Jewry under the Angevin Kings*, 1n4.

25. Golb, *Jews in Medieval Normandy*, 112–15.

26. On the prospect of Jewish–Christian neighboring and friendly relations, see Rutledge, "Medieval Jews of Norwich and Their Legacy," 122–24; and J. J. Cohen, "Future of the Jews of York."

27. On the York massacre, see Rees Jones and Watson, *Christians and Jews in Angevin England*.

28. On Lateran IV and the English use of the badge, see especially Despres, "Protean Jew in the Vernon Manuscript," 147–48; Bale, *Jew in the Medieval Book*, 15; and Mundill, *England's Jewish Solution*, 49–50.

29. On Meir, see Einbinder, "Meir b. Elijah of Norwich"; Krummel, *Crafting Jewishness in Medieval England*; and Pim, "Introduction."

30. Meir b. Elijah of Norwich, "A Liturgical Poem," lines 19–20, in *Into the Light*, 30–37 at 32.

31. Meir b. Elijah of Norwich, "Poem Six," lines 1–2, in *Into the Light*, 98.

32. I place "readmission" in scare quotes because Jews were never truly absent from England. For example, after the expulsion Jews continued to live in England in the *Domus Conversorum* established by Henry II and, during the sixteenth century or even earlier, crypto-Jewish communities dwelled in London and elsewhere. But only when Cromwell convened the Whitehall Conference did the question of literally accommodating Jews in English space receive new, official attention. Shapiro offers a helpful account of scholarship problematizing both the notion of expulsion and the idea of readmission in Anglo-Jewish history in *Shakespeare and the Jews*, 43–88. See also Kelly, "Jews and Saracens in Chaucer's England," 130–45.

33. Bale stresses this aspect of antisemitic culture in *Feeling Persecuted*.

34. Stacey, "Anti-Semitism and the Medieval English State," 164–65.

35. Thomas of Monmouth, *Life*, I.6, ed. and trans. Jessopp and James, 25, trans. Rubin 19.

36. Heng, "Jews, Saracens, 'Black Men,'" 253.

37. As Bale points out, "the fact that the label [antisemitism] did not exist does not mean that antisemitism was absent; it simply had not yet been categorized" ("Fictions of Judaism in England," 129). I depart from Langmuir and other scholars—and those who originally coined the term antisemitism—in viewing as antisemitic not only the "irrational" libels that first emerged in the High Middle Ages but also earlier more theological, yet still mythic and offensive, conceptions promulgated by church fathers and other writers about Judaism (Langmuir, *Toward a Definition of Antisemitism* and Chazan, *Medieval Stereotypes*).

38. Nirenberg, "'Judaism' as a Political Concept," 1.

39. Nirenberg, *Communities of Violence*, 6–7; Rubin, *Gentile Tales*, 1–5. Hannah Johnson offers an important account of the complex ethical ramifications of various scholarly takes on historical contingency and agency regarding one of the major antisemitic narratives, the ritual-murder charge, in *Blood Libel*.

40. Smith and Katz, "Grounding Metaphor," 68.

41. *Timaeus*, 70b, 69; Plato's full account of the body as polis appears in 68C–72B. On fortification in Plato and in Prudentius's *Psychomachia*, see Cornelius, "Figurative Castle," 25, 40, 58, 79, 89, 92, 111, 201.

42. Mann, "Allegorical Buildings in Medieval Literature," 197; Cornelius, "Figurative Castle," 20; and Whitehead, *Castles of the Mind*, 10–12, 40–43.

43. Mann, "Allegorical Buildings in Medieval Literature," 191. Important English works include the *Ancrene Wisse*, *Sawles Warde*, *The Castle of Perseverance*, the Digby *Mary Magdalene*, and Spenser's *Faerie Queene* (Cornelius, "Figurative Castle," 22–23, 27–29, 63–66; Whitehead, *Castles of the Mind*, 91–93, 111–16).

44. Smith and Katz, "Grounding Metaphor," 67–79.

45. Mann, "Allegorical Buildings in Medieval Literature," 199. However, Mann stresses the problematic *stasis* of buildings in her study.

46. With Smith and Katz, I don't mean to reject spatial metaphors altogether—I employ them myself—but to urge their use in a manner that attends to the full richness and complexity of space ("Grounding Metaphor," 79).

47. Lefebvre, *Production of Space*, 27.

48. Jameson, *Political Unconscious*; Eagleton, *Against the Grain*; Newman, *Medieval Crossover*. See also Besserman, *Biblical Paradigms in Medieval English Literature*. Scholars on Christian writings on Jews stressing oppositional readings include Rubin, *Gentile Tales*, 3; Lampert, *Gender and Jewish Difference*; Bale, *The Jew in the Medieval Book*; Fradenburg, "Criticism, Antisemitism, and the Prioress's Tale," especially 69–77.

49. Important work on the mapping of self and other on the map includes Leshock, "Religious Geography," 202–12; Heng, "The Invention of Race in the European Middle Ages II," 338–41; Friedman, *Monstrous Races*, 45–58; Mittman, *Maps and Monsters*, 27–60; and Gates, "Hats and Naked Jews."

50. Leshock, "Religious Geography," 211–12. On the foundational role of antisemitism in denoting Muslim identity during the Middle Ages, see Akbari, *Idols in the East*, 112–54.

51. Augustine, *City of God*, 18.46, 892.

52. Augustine, *Sermon* 199.1.2; *Works of Saint Augustine*, 80. In that sermon, which is for the epiphany, Augustine is specifically referring to the directions to Jerusalem

given by the Jews to the Magi. J. Cohen discusses how this passage exemplifies one of Augustine's six arguments about Jewish utility to Christians in *Living Letters of the Law*, 35–36.

53. Biddick demonstrates how Victorines like Hugh of St. Victor complemented their use of "local rabbis as intimate artifacts of the Old Testament" with the cartographic containment of Jews, who are increasingly identified with the enclosed peoples of Gog and Magog over the course of the twelfth century (*Typological Imaginary*, 28–29). On Gog and Magog and Jewish enclosure, see also Higgins, *Writing East*, 178–202; and Leshock, "Religious Geography," 220. On the erasure of Jews and Jewish space in medieval encyclopedias in Mandeville's *Travels*, English *Siege of Jerusalem* texts, and other works, see Akbari, *Idols in the East*, 112–54. On Jews and maps in Mandeville manuscripts, see Mittman, "A Blank Space."

54. Westrem, *Hereford Map*, 783.

55. P. Harvey, *Mappa Mundi*, 7.

56. Hillaby and Hillaby, *Palgrave Dictionary of Medieval Anglo-Jewish History*, 174. On the Lincoln Jewish community, see ibid., 203–10; J. Hill, *Medieval Lincoln*, 217–38; Stocker, *City by the Pool*, 177–79, 212–13.

57. Hillaby and Hillaby, *Palgrave Dictionary of Medieval Anglo-Jewish History*, 174.

58. Ibid., 209.

59. Ibid., 208–9.

60. Ibid., 209.

61. Ibid., 205.

62. Parkes, "Hereford Map." Factors indicating a Lincoln provenance include the cosmopolitan nature of the city, its cathedral library, and its artistic workshops, which were both Jewish and Christian before 1290 (ibid.; Morgan "Hereford Map"; works cited in Kline, *Maps of Medieval Thought*, 55n8). But see Westrem, *Hereford Map*, 306; and Birkholz, who offers in "Biography after Historicism" a critical account of scholarly investigations of the "micro-dynamics of medieval relationships with the Hereford Map" (170).

63. Kline, *Maps of Medieval Thought*, 55n8.

64. Roth, *History of the Jews in England*, 123.

65. Hourihane, *Grove Encyclopedia of Medieval Art and Architecture*, 78; Rees Jones, "Stones, Houses, Jews, Myths."

66. Rees Jones, *York*, 208–10; Schofield and Vince, *Medieval Towns*, 83–86.

67. M. Wood, *English Mediaeval House*, 1–6.

68. The term ghetto was first used in 1516 to describe a segregated Jewish community in Venice, Italy, and medieval Europeans created "compulsory, segregated and enclosed" Jewish quarters starting in the fifteenth century (Ravid, "The Significance of the Ghetto," 381).

69. Lipman, *Jews of Medieval Norwich*, 114; J. J. Cohen, "Future of the Jews of York."

70. Allen and Evans, *Roadworks*.

71. Urry, "Mobile Sociology," 197. See also Finke, Shichtman, and Kelly, "The World Is My Home When I'm Mobile."

72. D. Harvey, *Consciousness and the Urban Experience* and *Spaces of Capital*; Castells, *Informational City* and *Urban Question*.

73. Schofield and Vince, *Medieval Towns*, 152–53; Hilton, "Warriors and Peasants," 93–94; Bolton, *Medieval English Economy*, 246–86.

74. Hannah, *London Literature*, 57; Butterfield, "Introduction," 14; Wallace, *Chaucerian Polity*, 156–81; Turner, "Greater London."

75. Freedman offers an incisive, theoretically canny overview of discussions of the economic Jew in pre- and postholocaust scholarship in *Temple of Culture*, 55–69.

76. On Paul, see D. Boyarin, *Radical Jew*; Nirenberg, *Anti-Judaism: The Western Tradition*, especially 51–86.

77. Marx, "On the Jewish Question," 17.

78. Ibid., 14.

79. Nirenberg, "Shakespeare's Jewish Question," 78.

80. E.g., Stacey, "Jewish Lending and the Medieval English Economy," 90–91.

81. Israel, *European Jewry in the Age of Mercantilism* and *Diasporas within a Diaspora*.

82. Israel, *Diasporas within a Diaspora*; Ruderman, *Early Modern Jewry*, 26–36.

83. E.g. the complex view presented in Shatzmiller, *Shylock Reconsidered*.

84. On entanglement and Jewish–Christian relations in England, see Kaufman, *English Origins*, 24–25; Kim, "Entangled Jewish/Christian Relations." Mell, in her acute analysis of medieval exempla, similarly demonstrates not the differences between but the overlap of Christians and Jews on the topic of money in "Cultural Meanings of Money in Medieval Ashkenaz."

85. Stacey, "Jewish Lending and the Medieval English Economy."

86. Hillaby, "Jewish Colonization in the Twelfth Century," 18.

87. Roth, *History of the Jews in England*, chapter 3.

88. Stacey, "Parliamentary Negotiation." On the causes of the expulsion see also Barkey and Katznelson ("States, Regimes and Decisions"), who argue that, regardless of its economic strengths or lack thereof, the medieval Anglo-Jewry became expendable to the crown thanks to geopolitical occurrences that led to the rise of a civil society in England. Important scholarship on the causes of the expulsion includes Roth, *History of the Jews in England*; Mundill, *England's Jewish Solution* and *The King's Jews*; Huscroft, *Expulsion*; and Stacey, "1240–1260."

89. See, for example, Cicero, *Orator* 8.24, 323.

90. Kruger's *Spectral Jew* offers an incisive Derridean analysis of how medieval efforts to set Christians apart from Jews through conversion are haunted by a Jewish presence, insofar as conversion paradoxically entails both a conjuring away and a conjuring up of the other. See also Robbins, *Prodigal Son, Elder Brother*, 4–5; Lampert, *Gender and Jewish Difference*, 10–11; Rowe, *The Jew, the Cathedral and the Medieval City*, 17–18; Krummel, *Crafting Jewishness in Medieval England*, 2–3; Narin van Court, "Hermeneutics of Supersession."

91. An important and oft-studied example of a monumental architectural space used to denigrate Jews are the sculptures of *Synagoga* and *Ecclesia* flanking the portals of cathedrals. See Rowe, *The Jew, the Cathedral and the Medieval City*; Lipton, *Images of Intolerance*, 129–64; Bale, *Jew in the Medieval Book*, 1–5; Lampert, *Gender and Jewish Difference*, 44–45. Important analyses of the racialist dynamics of medieval architecture include Heng, "The Invention of Race, II" and Strickland, *Saracens, Demons and Jews*.

92. My project has affinities with Freedman's analysis of Jews, affect, and the marketplace. While Freedman (*Temple of Culture*, 69) stresses the affective pleasures engaged via the Jew during the nineteenth century, I take seriously the spatial element implied

by arguments about the Jew as a means of "distancing" Christians from capital and its effects.

93. A. Smith, *An Inquiry into the Nature and Causes of the Wealth of Nations*, IV.vii.c.63, 358.

## 1. Sepulchral Jews and Stony Christians

1. Bede, *Ecclesiastical History*, 5.24, ed. Colgrave and Mynors, 567; future citations by book, chapter, and page number from this edition appear in the text. On Bede's biography, see M. Brown, "Bede's Life in Context."

2. Fulk, "Cynewulf."

3. For a recent assessment of Bede, Cynewulf, and other figures' interest in conversion, see Karkov and Howe, *Conversion and Colonization*.

4. Scheil, *In the Footsteps of Israel*; Zacher, *Rewriting the Old Testament in Anglo-Saxon Verse*.

5. D. Boyarin, *Radical Jew*, 29.

6. Biblical citations in chapters 1–4 are taken from the Douay-Rheims translation, with minor modifications.

7. See J. Cohen's discussion of the hermeneutical Jew in *Living Letters of the Law*.

8. Scheil, *In the Footsteps of Israel*, 101–94; Zacher, *Rewriting the Old Testament in Anglo-Saxon Verse*; Wormald, "Bede, the *Bretwaldas* and the Origins of the *Gens Anglorum*"; S. Harris, *Race and Ethnicity in Anglo-Saxon Literature*; Howe, *Migration and Mythmaking*.

9. These works exemplify a notable interest in Jerusalem by Christians located on the western margins of Europe, witnessed also by Adomnan of Iona's *On the Holy Places* (ca. 680) and Bede's *On the Holy Places* (ca. 702–3), which relies heavily on the earlier work. On the geographic sensibility of Bede's *On the Holy Places*, see Howe, *Writing the Map of Anglo-Saxon England*, 137–41.

10. On the dating of those works, see O'Reilly, "Introduction," xvii; and Fulk, "Cynewulf."

11. Scholarship in archaeology, history, literary criticism, and other disciplines has clarified the role of a distinctive and rich material culture in Anglo-Saxon England. See, for example, Hines and Frantzen, *Cædmon's Hymn and Material Culture*; Loveluck, "Wealth, Waste and Conspicuous Consumption"; Cramp, *Wearmouth and Jarrow Monastic Sites*; Hyer and Owen-Crocker, *Material Culture of Daily Living*; Karkov and Damico, *Aedificia Nova*.

12. *OED*, s.v. "accommodate," v., 2.d. "Tractaturi igitur iuuante domino de aedificatione templi et in structura materiali spiritalem Dei mansionem" (*On the Temple* 1.2: Bede, *De tabernaculo, De Templo*, ed. Hurst, 148; *On the Temple*, ed. and trans. Connolly, 6). Subsequent page citations of Hurst's Latin edition and Connolly's translation appear in the text.

13. As an inanimate and hard object that, according to classical authorities, occupied the bottom rung of the Great Chain of Being, stone served as an apt means of critique in the bible. As Jeffrey Jerome Cohen puts it, "rock seems as inhuman a substance as can be found" ("Stories of Stone," 58). Cohen uses the ambivalent status of stone to rethink received notions of medieval English Jewish–Christian relations in "Future of the Jews of York"; he also problematizes the seemingly inert Christian narrative of the stony Jew in his ecological study of lithic liveliness, *Stone*.

14. 2 Cor. 3:14–18. The Vulgate stresses dull senses ("Sed obtusi sunt sensus eorum") while the Greek emphasizes hardened minds. The Hebrew Bible criticizes the occasional wrongdoings of Israel and the ongoing cruelty of other people (like Pharaoh) by referring to their "heart of flint" (Zech. 7:12) or "heart of stone" (Ezek. 11:19). Paul reframes that analogy in a Christian context.

15. Jeremy Cohen discusses early and medieval Christian perceptions of Jewish interpretive insufficiency in *Living Letters of the Law*.

16. J. J. Cohen, *Stone*, 150; Scheil discusses Anglo-Saxon invocations of the trope in *In the Footsteps of Israel*, 32, 41, 227.

17. Stacey, "Anti-Semitism and the Medieval English State," 166; J. Campbell, "Was It Infancy in England?," 14; Agus, *Urban Civilisation*, 61; H. Richardson, *English Jewry under the Angevin Kings*, 1n4. Campbell and Stacey postulate that fears over competition on the part of Anglo-Saxon merchants may account for any official policy excluding Jews from England. My speculation about the political import of Bede's and Cynewulf's sepulchral Jews complements arguments by Akbari, Biddick, Leshock, and others about the geographic effects of supersession.

18. On the dating of the homilies, see Martin, "Introduction," xi. On their manuscript context, see Hurst, "Introduction," in Bede, *Homiliarum*, 2:xvii–xxi.

19. Martin, "Bede and Preaching," 165.

20. "Notum iuxta historiam est narrante euangelista Matheo quia descendens de caelo angelus reuoluit lapidem ab ostio monumenti non quidem ut exeunte domino uiam faceret sed ut apertus uacuusque monumenti locus hominibus eum resurrexisse proderet" (Bede, Homily II.10, *Homiliarum*, ed. Hurst, 247; *Homilies*, trans. Martin and Hurst, 90) further citations of those editions appear in the text and include book, sermon, and page numbers.

21. "Mystice autem reuolutio lapidis sacramentorum est reuolutio diuinorum quae quondam littera legis claudebantur occulta. Lex enim in lapide scriptum est" (247–48).

22. Kruger, "Times of Conversion."

23. "Etenim et nobis singulis cum fidem dominicae passionis et resurrectionis agnouimus monumentum profecto illius quod clausum fuerat apertum est" (247).

24. "Ac uero Iudaeus ac paganus qui mortem quidem redemptoris nostri quam credunt inrident triumphum uero resurrectionis eius prorsus credere recusant quasi clausum lapide adhuc monumentum permanet nec ualent ingredi ut ablatum resurgendo corpus domini respiciant quia duritia suae infidelitatis repelluntur ne animaduertant quia non potest in terris mortuus inueniri qui destructo mortis aditu iam caelorum alta penetrauit" (247–48).

25. Bede, like other Christian writers, does portray pagans at times as hard-hearted, a phrasing that demonstrates the application of the more central trope of Jewish hard-heartedness to other non-Christians.

26. See Bede, *Two Lives of Saint Cuthbert*, ed. Colgrave, 96–97.

27. Estes, "Colonization and Conversion," 138.

28. Borgehammar, *How the Holy Cross Was Found*, chaps. 8–9.

29. The Vercelli Book is no. CXVII in the Eusebian Archives. On the date and manuscript context of *Elene*, which probably was written during the 970s, see Cynewulf, *Elene*, ed. Gradon, 1–2; and Lucas, "Vercelli Book Revisited."

30. Scheil, *In the Footsteps of Israel*, 202.

31. Scragg, *Vercelli Homilies*, 270, lines 82–85.

32. Ibid., 270, lines 91–93; cf. Scheil, *In the Footsteps of Israel*, 213–14, 227.

33. Informed by Gradon's work on the sources of *Elene* and the Latin and Greek recensions of the *Acta Cyriaci*, critics have made a persuasive case for closely comparing *Elene* to the St. Gall MS (e.g., Klein, "Reading Queenship in Cynewulf's *Elene*," 82n20). On Cynewulf's sources, see also S. Rosser, "Sources of Cynewulf's *Elene*," and Whatley, "Figure of Constantine the Great." In *Christ II*, Cynewulf links the Jew's stony heart ("heortan staenne") to an inability to see a figure for Christ's Ascension in Job 28:7 (*Christ II*, 641b, in Muir, *Exeter Anthology of Old English Poetry*, 70). Future line citations of *Christ II* come from this edition. On Bede's influence on that poem, see Kramer, *Between Heaven and Earth*, 124–28.

34. All citations of *Elene* are by line number and from the Gradon edition; translations are my own.

35. Holder, *Inventio Sanctae Crucis*, 5. Following Gradon's assessment of the possible sources of *Elene*, I cite the Latin version of the legend that appears in St. Gall 225, as transcribed by Holder (Cynewulf, *Elene*, ed. Gradon, 15–22, esp. 18–19).

36. Gardner, *Construction of Christian Poetry*, 93.

37. The *Acta Cyriaci* only relates how the Jews "did not want to speak the truth" ("nihil uerum uoluerunt dicere"; Holder, *Inventio Sanctae Crucis*, 558, line 185).

38. Whatley, "Bread and Stone," 558.

39. Scheil, *In the Footsteps of Israel*, 226. On the Jew as eternal enemy of Christians, see J. Cohen, *Christ Killers*; Lampert-Weissig, "Once and Future Jew"; Bale, *Feeling Persecuted*.

40. Scheil, *In the Footsteps of Israel*, 40–41.

41. Whatley, "Bread and Stone"; T. Hill, "Bread and Stone, Again"; Sharma, "Reburial of the Cross." Cf. the *Acta Cyriaci*: "Et quis in solitudinem constitutes panibus adpositis lapides manducet" (Holder, *Inventio Sanctae Crucis*, 7, lines 196–97).

42. Whatley, "Bread and Stone," 552.

43. Ibid.

44. Ibid., 556.

45. Ibid.

46. Important interpretations of Helena's use of physical violence include Regan, "Evangelicalism as the Informing Principle"; V. Fish, "Theme and Pattern in Cynewulf's *Elene*"; Whatley, "Bread and Stone"; and T. Hill, "Sapiential Structure and Figural Narrative" and "Bread and Stone, Again."

47. Cf. how a converted Judas describes God hurling the devil into the abyss in language that recalls his hurling into the dry well by Helena (939–45a; Whatley, "Bread and Stone," 554).

48. It is the case that in *Elene*, Judas eventually leaves the pit, helps the queen, and even becomes a Christian bishop. The pit thus serves in certain respects as not only a means of exile but also a torturous tool of conversion. However, were Judas to not convert and remain faithful to his people, his "living death" in the pit would inevitably have shifted to a permanent, literal death. The fact that *Elene* depicts a Jew escaping his sepulchral confinement hardly means that the poem does not reiterate the geopolitics—the radical brand of exile and eradication—encoded in Bede's tomb-like Jew.

49.  "Maestis autem de ablato corpore Iesu mulieribus" (248).

50.  "cum de longitudine praesentis incolatus ac de praesentia nostri conditoris salubriter afflicti repente supernorum ciuium quae sint gaudia aeterna recolimus ac recordata illorum beatitudine in qua etiam nos futuros speramus exilii quam patimur aerumnam leuius ferre incipimus" (ibid.).

51.  *Christ II*, 499b–502a; see also ibid., 537b–540a.

52.  "apparuerunt angeli qui illis patefacta resurrectione consolationis remedia ferrent. Quod nunc quoque inuisibiliter nobiscum agi minime dubitare" (248).

53.  "Maxime tamen angelici nobis spiritus adesse credendi sunt cum diuinis specialiter mancipamur obsequiis, id est cum ecclesiam ingressi uel lectionibus sacris aurem accommodamus uel psalmodiae operam damus uel orationi incumbimus uel etiam missarum sollemnia celebramus.... Nec dubitare licet ubi corporis et sanguinis dominici mysteria geruntur supernorum ciuium adesse conuentus qui monumentum quo corpus ipsum uenerabile positum fuerat et unde resurgendo abscesserat tam sedulis seruant excubiis" (249).

54.  The earliest manuscripts of the *EH* are the ca. 737 Moore Bede (Cambridge University Library, MS Kk. V. 16), the ca. 746 Leningrad codex (National Library of Russia, Q. I. 18), and the eighth-century London Cotton codex (British Library, MS Cotton Tib. C. II). Nearly 150 copies of the *EH* were made during the Middle Ages, attesting to its tremendous influence. Holder affirms the "great significance for Bede" churches had "as concrete manifestations of missionary advance" ("Allegory and History in Bede's Interpretation," 121).

55.  Citations of the *EH* are from the Colgrave and Mynors edition.

56.  Holder, "Allegory and History in Bede's Interpretation," 121.

57.  Other examples include the church that memorializes Alban's martyrdom (1.7, 34–35) and the rebuilding of churches after the Diocletian persecution (1.8, 34–35).

58.  "Si ergo ambulare uoluit in templo in quo caro et sanguis brutorum animalium offerebatur, multo magis nostram orationis domum ubi carnis ipsius ac sanguinis sacramenta celebrantur uisitare gaudebit. Si perambulare non despexit porticum in qua rex quondam mortalis ac terrenus quamuis potentissimus ac sapientissimus ad orandum stare solebat, quanto magis penetralia cordium nostrorum inuisere atque inlustrare desiderat, si tamen ea porticum esse Salomonis, hoc est si ea timorem suum quod est initium sapientiae habere perspexerit. Necque enim putandum est quia domus solummodo in qua ad orandum uel ad mysteria celebranda conuenimus templum sit domini et non ipsi qui in nomine domini conuenimus multo amplius templum eius et appellemur et simus cum manifeste dicat apostolus: *Vos estis templum Dei uiui sicut dicit Deus, inhabitabo in eis et inter illos ambulabo*" (358–59).

59.  In particular, Bede refrains from reading allegorically Christian buildings (Holder, "Allegory and History in Bede's Interpretation," 131; O'Reilly, "Introduction," li).

60.  On the dating of *On the Tabernacle* and *On Ezra and Nehemiah*, see Holder, "Introduction," in Bede, *On the Tabernacle*, xvi; and DeGregorio, "Introduction," in Bede, *On Ezra and Nehemiah*, xlii.

61.  O'Reilly, "Introduction," xviii. She refers to two sermons on the anniversary of the dedication of the church at Jarrow, and a Lenten homily on the cleansing of the temple. Bede also included allegories of the tabernacle and/or temple in his

commentary on Genesis, his commentary on the Apocalypse, and his *Thirty Questions on the Book of Kings* (Holder, "Allegory and History in Bede's Interpretation," 118).

62. On Jewish interpretations of the temple, see Whitehead, *Castles of the Mind*, 7–10.

63. DeGregorio, "Bede and the Old Testament," 136, 131.

64. *On the Tabernacle* appears in sixty-eight, *On the Temple* appears in forty-five, and *On Ezra and Nehemia* appears in thirty-two extant manuscripts from the ninth to fifteenth centuries (Laistner and King, *Hand-List of Bede Manuscripts*, 39–40, 70–77). One manuscript, Orléans, Bibliothèque municipale, 42, may be of eighth-century provenance (ibid., 40). On the prospect that Bede "may have possibly exercised an influence upon later sculpture," see Whitehead, *Castles of the Mind*, 18.

65. Beyond the rationales discussed in what follows, still more reasons include Bede's interest in charting new territory in the tradition of religious writing established by church fathers and his desire, as outlined in the apparent letter to Bishop Acca at the start of *On the Temple*, to console religious figures who had suffered affliction and exile in England by fostering meditation on heavenly existence (DeGregorio, "Bede and the Old Testament," 132; O'Reilly, "Introduction," in Bede, *On the Temple*, ed. and trans. Connolly, xxxi; I. Wood, *Most Holy Abbot Ceolfrid*, 11–12).

66. The *Codex Grandior* is no longer extant. On the evidence—most of which appears in Bede's writings—referring to its presence in Jarrow, see Meyvaert, "Bede, Cassiodorus, and the Codex Amiatinus." On the *Codex Amiatinus*, see Corsano, "First Quire of the Codex Amiatinus"; Meyvaert, "Bede, Cassiodorus, and the Codex Amiatinus"; Carruthers, *Craft of Thought*, 234–37 and 347n32; M. Brown, *The Book and the Transformation of Britain*, 46–49, and 162n94.

67. While scholars don't know precisely where the two images appeared originally, it's clear that they were "conceived to be initiatory to the text" (Carruthers, *Craft of Thought*, 234).

68. Ibid., 222.

69. Ibid., 230.

70. Meyvaert, "Bede, Cassiodorus, and the Codex Amiatinus," 883. Sanctuary images like that in the *Codex Grandior* have Jewish roots. In his *Institutiones*, Cassiodorus relates how a wise blind man from Asia, Eusebius, spurred him to insert the sanctuary image at the start of the pandect (I.5.2, ed. Mynors, 22–23). Roth describes how illuminated codices depicting biblical sanctuaries appeared in Jewish bibles during the first centuries of the Common Era, and how social contact led to the migration of the Jewish iconographic practice to Christians ("Jewish Antecedents of Christian Art"). While later scholarship stresses the complex lines of influence between Jews and Christians in Syria, Egypt, Byzantium, Italy, and further west (Meyvaert, "Bede, Cassiodorus, and the Codex Amiatinus," 848n95), Roth's essay remains "an important demonstration, not just of the earliest influences of Jewish traditions on Christian traditions, but of their continuing influence on aspects of Christian art throughout the later Middle Ages" (Carruthers, *Craft of Thought*, 347n30). Intriguingly, while Roth suggests the Jewishness of a figural method grounded in symbolic biblical buildings, Revel-Neher argues that the Amiatinus diagram offers a more literal view of the sanctuary than its Jewish precedents ("Du Codex Amiatinus et ses rapports," 16).

71. DeGregorio, "Bede and the Old Testament," 136.

72. Translation by Spiegel in "The *Tabernacula* of Gregory the Great," 2n3.

73. Spiegel, "The *Tabernacula* of Gregory the Great," 4.

74. Ibid.

75. Ibid., 5–6.

76. Ibid., 5. On Gregory's complex attitude toward Jews, and especially the relationship between his correspondence and his theological writings on Jews, see J. Cohen, *Living Letters of the Law*, 73–94. Regardless of his promotion of the pseudo-Sukkot ritual in his correspondence, Gregory "harbored no love for the Jews" (ibid., 79).

77. Spiegel, "The *Tabernacula* of Gregory the Great," 6; Hope-Taylor, *Yeavering*, 100–102.

78. "Tractaturi igitur iuuante domino de aedificatione templi et in structura materiali spiritalem Dei mansionem" (148).

79. Bede, *On the Tabernacle*, 2.1, *De taburnaculo, De temple*, ed. Hurst, 43, *On the Tabernacle*, ed. and trans. Holder, 47.

80. Meyer, *Medieval Allegory*, 21.

81. Kramer. "'Ðu Eart se Weallstan,'" 98. Bede associates the temple with the four senses of scripture (historical, allegorical, anagogical, and tropological) in *De schematibus et tropes* (Holder, "Allegory and History in Bede's Interpretation," 118). O'Brien elucidates the "plurality of interpretations" Bede offers in his architectural exegeses (*Bede's Temple*, 6).

82. "Latitudo etenim tabularum dilatatio est fidei et sacramentorum quae prius in una Israhelitica plebe latebat sed horum ministerio ad totius orbis amplitudinem peruenit" (60).

83. "sermo euangelicus iuuante domino per apostolos uniuersas in breui mundi plagas impleuit" (217).

84 "Habet ergo altare Dei in medio sui craticulam ad suscipienda holocausta paratam quia praeparant electi locum domino in intimo sui cordis affectu ubi deuotas ei cogitationes collecent" (82).

85. On Paul, see Whitehead, *Castles of the Mind*, 10.

86. A more extensive discussion of the spatial aspects of Bede's exegeses is Lavezzo, "Building Antisemitism in Bede."

87. Cf. Augustine's account of biblical Jew's failure to read figuratively the prophesy on the rebuilding of the temple in Haggai 2:9. In the same way that Bede's Jew suffers devastating spatial effects for his carnal unbelief, Augustine's Jew suffers devastating temporal effects for his literal-minded take on the space of the temple: due to their failure to realize that Haggai foretold a spiritual temple, Augustine claims, God deprived them of their ability to prophesy altogether (Augustine, *City of God*, 18.45, 888).

88. Robbins, *Prodigal Son, Elder Brother*. Kruger's book opens by discussing how "even as it is made to die, to disappear," in Christian narratives of supersession, "Judaism comes to occupy our field of vision" (*Spectral Jew*, xvi–xvii).

89. Auerbach, "Figura," 58. Auerbach's theory of *figura* insists "that each event must be treated as actual, as within "the stream of historical life," and not as a mere idea or concept (Howe, "Figural Presence of Erich Auerbach," 139; thanks belong to Andrew Scheil for drawing my attention to this piece). We should also note, with Howe, that "there was good reason . . . to insist on the here and now of events rather than the then and there of interpretive systems," since, as a Jewish émigré writing in

the late 1930s, he "had a political and moral responsibility in the late 1930s to assert the continuing presence of the historical events of the Hebrew bible and thus of the Jewish people" (ibid., 139–40).

90. Jones, "Some Introductory Remarks," 157. See also DeGregorio, "Introduction," in Bede, *On Ezra and Nehemiah*, xxi).

91. *De tabernaculo, De templo*, ed. Hurst, 5; *On the Tabernacle*, ed. and trans. Holder, 1.

92. Holder, "Allegory and History in Bede's Interpretation," 121.

93. Cf. Bede, *De tabernaculo, De templo*, ed. Hurst, 65, 82; *On the Tabernacle*, ed. and trans. Holder, 72, 92. On Bede's use of Josephus and Cassiodorus, see Holder, "New Treasures and Old," 241–42; and Meyvaert, "Bede, Cassiodorus, and the Codex Amiatinus."

94. "Tractaturi igitur iuuante domino de aedificatione templi et in structura materiali spiritalem Dei mansionem" (148). Frantzen, "All Created Things," 119.

95. Relevant here is Darby's discussion of *On the Temple* and Bede's support of images in "Bede, Iconoclasm and the Temple of Solomon."

96. Bede thus offers an early, architectural version of the virtual Jew found in post-expulsion English writings. See Tomasch, "Postcolonial Chaucer and the Virtual Jew."

97. Whitehead, *Castles of the Mind*, 8.

98. Ibid.; Holder, "Allegory and History in Bede's Interpretation," 131.

99. That proximity to the divine emerged in other aspects of biblical accounts of Jewish life. In Maccabees, angels on horses ride alongside Judas Maccabeus and other guerilla fighters as they oppose the Hellenic occupiers of the temple. Such narratives suggest how, during biblical times, no chasm or wall sundered earthly from heavenly space but rather a porous landscape or open door between the two locations allowed for easy passage on the part of divine entities into the human world. Zacher discusses the representation in the OE Exodus of a "God of presence" in *Rewriting the Old Testament in Anglo-Saxon Verse*, 61–70.

100. "specialiter domino adhaerere nouerimus quos inuincibili mentis stabilitate quasi quadratos quodammodo atque ad omnes temptationum incursus immobiles perdurare" (155–56).

101. Cf. *Christ I*, which hails Christ as the cornerstone "Binding with firm fastening the wide walls, the flint unbroken" ("gesomnige side weallas / fæste gefoge, flint unbræcne"; lines 6–7, in Muir, *Exeter Anthology of Old English Poetry*, 46).

102. Such favorable associations of stones with Christian leaders also appear in *On Genesis*, 236; and *On Ezra and Nehemiah* as well, in which Bede likens the *latomi* or stonecutters of the new temple to spiritual stonecutters, and the *cementarii* or builders of the Second Temple to preachers (Bede, *De tabernaculo, De templo*, ed. Hurst, 273–74; *On Ezra and Nehemiah*, ed. DeGregorio, 56). An especially fraught celebration of stone is in *On the Tabernacle*, where the stone of the Ten Commandments figures the preservation of the faith in Christian hearts (Bede, *De tabernaculo, De templo*, ed. Hurst, 6; *On the Tabernacle*, ed. and trans. Holder, 3).

103. "fortitudine fidei in unam eandemque regulam sibimet agglutinati" (174).

104. "Verum quia lex in lapide scripta doctrina uero euangelii per lignum est dominicae passionis confirmata unde et populus lapide circumcidebatur in praeputio nos signo crucis consecramur in fronte. Possunt non incongrue parietes templi lapidei siue pauimentum pretiosissimo marmore stratum eorum qui in lege fideliter ac

perfecte uixerunt typum gerere, tabulae uero cedrinae siue abiegnae noui testamenti iustos indicare qui uolentes post dominum uenire abnegant semet ipsos et sumpta cruce sua cotidie sequuntur illum" (174).

105. The Incarnation epitomizes the materialism at the heart of Christian practice, which encompasses the doctrine of transubstantiation and the cults of relics. Bede demonstrates the kind of concrete and material use of *figura* Auerbach describes in his discussion of Tertullian ("Figura," 28–32). In one of his church dedication homilies, Bede links the Incarnation to the temple (Homily II.24, *Homiliarum*, ed. Hurst, 375, *Homilies*, trans. Martin and Hurst, 250).

106. Though it is worth noting, with Howe, how timber buildings in the Anglo-Saxon Chronicle are linked with impermanence (*Writing the Map of Anglo-Saxon England*, 49–51).

107. Cf. Bede, *De tabernaculo, de templo*, ed. Hurst, 161; *On the Temple*, ed. and trans. Connolly, 23.

108. "Nec contrarium debet uideri quae supra diximus porticum quae erat ante templum antiquorum ipsum fidelium figuram gestare templum uero eorum qui post incarnationis dominicae tempus in mundum uenerunt" (175).

109. "Multiplex namque est in diuersis rebus earundem repetitio figurarum" (175).

110. "maiori perfectione" (175).

111. Bede, *De tabernaculo, de templo*, ed. Hurst, 175–76; *On the Temple*, ed. and trans. Connolly, 42–43.

112. Recent work on stone in Anglo-Saxon England includes Karkov and Orton, *Theorizing Anglo-Saxon Stone Sculpture*.

113. Blair, *The Church in Anglo-Saxon Society*, 137. My argument complements Mayr-Harting, who notes how "Bede's explanation in moral terms of the stones used in the building of the Temple may have another side in his interest to say in the *EH* when actual churches were built of stone" (*Venerable Bede*, 20). Inverting the approaches of critics like O'Reilly and Holder, who stress the spiritualism linking both texts, Mayr-Harting implies a materialism lurking in *De templo* that emerges more clearly in the stone churches of the *EH*.

114. Turner et al., *Wearmouth and Jarrow*, 107.

115. D. Brown, *Anglo-Saxon England*, 68. On the Upper Permian Magnesian Limestone (aka Roker Dolomite), glacier erratics, Coal Measure Sandstone, and ashlar from Roman sites used at Monkwearmouth, see Turner et al., *Wearmouth and Jarrow*, 141. Jarrow's buildings were composed entirely of cut and dressed stones taken from Roman sites, such as "the Roman wall and fort at Wallsend, across the Tyne to the north-west, and the remains of the substantial supply fort at South Shields to the east" (ibid., 146). Today, a museum called Bede's World centers around the remains of St. Peter's and other buildings of the monastic precinct. See http://www.bedesworld.co.uk.

116. Howe, *Writing the Map of Anglo-Saxon England*, 131; Turner et al., *Wearmouth and Jarrow*, 131; Cramp, "Monkwearmouth and Jarrow: The Archaeological Evidence," 10–11, 15–17; Cramp, "Monkwearmouth and Jarrow in Their Continental Context."

117. Eusebius of Caesaria, *Historia Ecclesiastica*, 10.4.39, and Lactantius, *De mortibus persecutorum*, 12, cited in Holder, "Allegory and History in Bede's Interpretation," 123–24.

118. Cramp, *Wearmouth Jarrow Monastic Sites*, 98.

119. Meyvaert, "Bede, Cassiodorus, and the Codex Amiatinus," 854n115.

120. Meyvaert, "Bede and the Church Paintings at Wearmouth-Jarrow," 65n3.

121. Holder, "Allegory and History in Bede's Interpretation," 124–25.

122. I. Wood, *Most Holy Abbot Ceolfrid*, 15–16.

123. See Carruthers, *Craft of Thought*, 272–76.

124. Bede stresses his lifelong habitation of Jarrow in an oft-cited passage from the *EH*, 5.24, 566–67.

125. O'Reilly, "Introduction," li; Holder, "Allegory and History in Bede's Interpretation," 131.

126. Kramer, *Between Heaven and Earth*, 15.

127. Ibid.

128. Ælfric, *Lives of Saints*, 123, line 822.

129. The poem occupies from line 6 of fol. 104v to the end of fol. 106r of the Vercelli Book.

130. Krapp, ed. *The Dream of the Rood*, lines 6b–17b.

131. A national rationale for the cult is suggested by Constantine's supposed birth in Britain (Estes, "Colonization and Conversion," 138).

132. On English pilgrimage to Jerusalem and the cross in *Elene*, see I. Wood, "Constantinian Crosses in Northumbria."

133. On the sensitivity of *Elene* to the geographic particulars of the Christian *imperium* and Anglo-Saxon England, see Zollinger, "Cynewulf's *Elene* and the Patterns of the Past."

134. *Elene* in a sense adumbrates the religious warfare of the Crusades, with the Jews it depicts—unlike the proximate Jewish victims of European pogroms—occupying the eastern location inhabited by the crusaders' Muslim opponents.

135. On the idea that *Elene* figures the battle of the Church Militant with Synagoga, see Regan, "Evangelicalism as the Informing Principle," 29.

136. Cf. Heckman's argument that *Elene* portrays a Christian reliance on the privileged wisdom of the Jews in "Things in Doubt."

137. In *Dark Mirror*, Lipton offers an acute analysis of the tension between how Christ "walked the earth in full sight" of Jews and Christian ideas of Jewish blindness (6).

138. While, once Judas changes positions and assists Helena, he does pray for a sign from God, it remains the case that he is the invaluable medium for this divine revelation. On the "mutual need" of Judas and Helena for each other, see Regan, "Evangelicalism as the Informing Principle," 31.

139. Klein, "Reading Queenship in Cynewulf's *Elene*," 55.

140. Cf. how architectural materialisms were central to Constantine, who sent his mother to Jerusalem and other territories precisely in order to build churches and make Christianity a visible presence in his expanding empire (ibid., 62; Drijvers, *Helena Augusta*, 66–70).

141. Klein, "Reading Queenship in Cynewulf's Elene," 54. Many important figural readings have followed Thomas Hill's seminal "Sapiential Structure and Figural Narrative," including ibid; Whatley, "Bread and Stone"; V. Fish, "Theme and Pattern in Cynewulf's *Elene*"; J. J. Campbell, "Cynewulf's Multiple Revelations"; Regan, "Evangelicalism as the Informing Principle"; Herman critiques figural readings of *Elene* in *Allegories of War*, 101–18.

142. Critics who see Christic valences in Judas include DiNapoli, "Poesis and Authority"; Calder, "Strife, Revelation, and Conversion," 203–6; and Stepsis and Rand, "Contrast and Conversion," 275–76.

143. Judas also resembles Christ insofar as his presence in the empty pit figures the desert where Christ was tempted (T. Hill, "Sapiential Structure and Figural Narrative," 172–73; Regan, "Evangelicalism as the Informing Principle," 39).

144. Hill, "Sapiential Structure and Figural Narrative," 172.

145. Krapp, ed. *The Dream of the Rood*, lines 74b–75a. Critics often adopt an "either or" approach when discussing the Jewish or Christian qualities of Judas. See Whatley ("Bread and Stone") on the former and T. Hill ("Bread and Stone, Again") on the latter. Woolf argues that the "inverted passion" in *Elene* reflects Cynewulf's intensification of an already contradictory source ("Saints' Lives," 47). Regan argues that Judas's Christ-like qualities don't so much contradict his Jewishness but look toward the "profound spiritual conversion" he "undergoes," and figure the "relationship between the teaching church and the individual soul" ("Evangelicalism as the Informing Principle," 34–35, 44–46). With Sharma, who stresses how "the metaphorical vectors of *Elene* are bidirectional" ("Reburial of the Cross," 281), I argue that Cynewulf, instead of successfully achieving *concordia discordiarum* or the reconciliation of apparently ineluctable oppositions, allows such tensions to stand in *Elene*.

146. T. Hill, "Bread and Stone, Again," 256. Critics who liken Helena to the tyrants of hagiography and view her as even less sympathetic than Judas include DiNapoli, "Poesis and Authority"; Heckman, "Things in Doubt," 470–71, and the works cited in n. 44.

147. Klein, "Reading Queenship in Cynewulf's *Elene*," 62; Regan "Evangelicalism as the Informing Principle"; and J. J. Campbell, "Cynewulf's Multiple Revelations," 267.

148. Isidore, *Etymologies*, IX. v. 4, trans. Barney et al., 206. On the medieval Christian association of the Jew with woman, see Lampert-Weissig, *Gender and Jewish Difference*.

149. Scheil, *In the Footsteps of Israel*, 226.

150. Cf. the stress at the end of *Christ II* on the unstable and shifting nature of the space of Christian earthly existence, which Cynewulf likens to a ship tossing on a heaving sea (850a–858a).

151. Scheil, *In the Footsteps of Israel*, 327. On the inescapable nature of materialism and the worldly in *Elene*, see Heckman, "Things in Doubt," 479; and Sharma, "Reburial of the Cross," 281, 297.

152. Holder, *Inventio Sanctae Crucis*, 10.

153. See also how Judas's eventual discovery of the *physical* nails prompts the creation of a *spiritual* edifice in Helena, who "was filled with grace of wisdom, and the holy, heavenly Spirit kept a dwelling in her noble heart" ("gefylled wæs / wisdomes gife, ond þa wic beheold / halig heofonlic Gast / . . . æðelne innoð"; 1142b–1145a). In many respects, *Elene* is a work that seems comfortable with such contradictions.

154. Cf. Cynewulf's unique descriptors for Helena. While the *Acta Cyriaci* stresses Helena's holiness by almost always calling her "beata Aelena," Cynewulf calls her the more secular "cwen" and "hlæfdige," and describes her as "æðele" (Klein, "Reading Queenship in Cynewulf's *Elene*," 58). While such adjectives may heighten Helena's social status, does Cynewulf avoiding calling her holy because he questions her piety?

155. DiNapoli, "Poesis and Authority," 622.

156. Ibid., 623.

157. But on Cynewulf's sympathy for Jews, see Fleming, "*Rex regum et cyninga cyning.*"

158. Cheyette, *Constructions of "the Jew" in English Literature and Society*; Freedman, *Temple of Culture.*

## 2. Medieval Urban Noir

1. Golb, *Jews in Medieval Normandy*, 112–15.

2. Elijah refers to two men wounded "outside the city" in a responsum on authenticating a husband's death (Roth and Zadoff, "Talmudic Community," 198). As Roth and Zadoff note, Elijah also exhibits an investment in urban sophistication, authority, and know-how (ibid., 199).

3. Mundill, *King's Jews*, xiv, 6–8; Hillaby, "Jewish Colonisation in the Twelfth Century."

4. Dominic of Evesham, *Miracles of the Virgin*, 258.

5. Holt, "Society and Population," 93–94; Hillaby and Hillaby, *Palgrave Dictionary of Medieval Anglo-Jewish History*, 311–12.

6. Lipman, *Jews of Medieval Norwich*, 17.

7. Ibid., 114; Lilley, *Urban Life in the Middle Ages*, 246–48.

8. Lilley, "Mapping Cosmopolis," 689, and *City and Cosmos.*

9. Lilley, "Mapping Cosmopolis," 688. On Jerusalem as the center of the world, increasingly from the thirteenth century, see Kupfer, "Mappaemundi."

10. J. Campbell, "Norwich before 1300," 39–41; J. J. Cohen, *Hybridity, Identity, and Monstrosity in Medieval Britain*, 113–38.

11. E.g., Hugh of St. Victor (ca. 1096–1141), Richard of Saint-Victor (d. 1173), Adam of Dryburgh or Adam Scotus (ca. 1140–1212), and Peter of Celle (ca. 1115–83). That outpouring stemmed partly from a renewed interest in Jerusalem during the Crusades, an ongoing monastic interest in meditation, and an emerging investment in organizing and cataloging for purposes of reform, renewal, and scholastic criticism (Whitehead, *Castles of the Mind*, 19).

12. Smalley, *Study of the Bible*. Andrew of St. Victor refers in his writings to what "the Jews say" ("Iudei dicunt") or what "my Jew told me" ("Hebreus meus dicit") about biblical passages (*Expositio in Ezechielim*, xxviii–xxxiii, in McKane, *Selected Christian Hebraists*, 42–75). Scholars diverge on whether rabbinic interpretations or more predictable Christian typologies emerged from such contact. See Nisse, "A Romance of the Jewish East," 518; Biddick, *Typological Imaginary*, 28; Abulafia, *Christians and Jews*, 94. Architects also, sometimes drawing on Bede, incorporated aspects of Solomon's Temple when erecting churches and cathedrals (Whitehead, *Castles of the Mind*, 18).

13. On the antisemitism of English Marian tales, see Ihnat, "Mary and the Jews"; Carter, "Historical Content of William of Malmesbury's Miracles"; Southern, "English Origins of the 'Miracles of the Virgin'"; Rubin, *Gentile Tales*, 7–39; and A. Boyarin, *Miracles of the Virgin in Medieval England.*

14. "As maisuns as jueus feluns" (Adgar, *Gracial*, 145 verse 103). On Adgar, see Shea, "Adgar's *Gracial* and Christian Images of Jews." The Jews' abuse of the image

(they nail the body to a cross, slap it, crown it with thorns, spit upon it, and pierce it with a lance) leads to their immediate execution. Early analogues of "Toledo" are in Gregory of Tours's *Glory of the Martyrs*, 40, and a Greek legend ascribed to Pope Athanasius of Alexandria (Ihnat, "Mary and the Jews," 192). Latin versions of "Toledo" were recounted by Anselm of Bury around 1120 and by William of Malmesbury in the 1140s; William Adgar generated an Anglo-Norman version in 1165.

15. "The Jewish Boy" appears in the *Historia Ecclesiastica* of the Syrian Evagrius Scholasticus (536–600). The legend, set in either in Greece, Bourges, or Pisa, traveled west via Gregory of Tours (538–93), was first told in England in a Latin sermon by Herbert de Losinga, the first bishop of Norwich (d. 1119), and then appeared in several Marian miracle collections by Anselm of Bury, Nigel of Canterbury (late twelfth century), William of Malmesbury (ca. 1095/96–ca. 1143), and others.

16. Herbert di Losinga, *Life, Letters, and Sermons*, 32–33.

17. Marian antisemitic tales of course register other concerns, including the possibility that ongoing Jewish unbelief might foster doubts on the part of Christians who come into contact with Jews.

18. Chazan, *European Jewry*; Moore, *Formation of a Persecuting Society*; Riley-Smith, "Christian Violence and the Crusades"; Chazan, "Anti-Jewish Violence of 1096"; Nisse, "A Romance of the Jewish East" and "'Your Name Will No Longer Be Aseneth,'" 739–40.

19. Chazan stresses how crusader ideology drew on the initial papal call for crusade and how "the majority of crusading armies show no evidence whatsoever of anti-Jewish sentiment or behavior" ("Anti-Jewish Violence of 1096," 25; *European Jewry*, 76–84).

20. Abulafia, *Christians and Jews*, 58, 119–21; J. Cohen, "Jews as Killers of Christ"; Shea, "Adgar's *Gracial* and Christian Images of Jews," 195.

21. Eidelberg, *The Jews and the Crusaders*, 121; Chazan, *European Jewry*, 170; Riley-Smith, *First Crusade*, 49–57.

22. All Jews who witness the miracle convert, except the father, who perishes in the furnace where he placed his son (Herbert di Losinga, *Life, Letters, and Sermons*, 32–33).

23. Langmuir, *Toward a Definition of Antisemitism*, 220. See also Stacey, "Anti-Semitism and the Medieval English State," 166–67.

24. All Latin citations of the *Life* are from the Jessop and James edition, by book, chapter, and page number, in consultation with Miri Rubin's transcription of the manuscript (http://yvc.history.qmul.ac.uk/passio.html). Translations are from Rubin's translation with minor changes and are cited by page number. The starting date for composition of the *Life* rests largely on how Thomas, in book 2, criticizes Stephen of Blois (ca. 1092/96–25 October 1154) so harshly as to suggest that he wrote after the king's death, in late 1154 or 1155 (II.92, Rubin 60–61); as McCulloh notes, book 2 forms an organic unit with book 1. The ending date for the composition of the *Life* reflects its dedication to William Turbe, who died in January 1174 (*Life*, I.1, Rubin 3). See Stacey, "Anti-Semitism and the Medieval English State," 167; and McCulloh, "Jewish Ritual Murder," 706–7.

25. On Cistercian knowledge and dissemination of William's cult, see Rubin, "Introduction," xxxi–xxxii.

26. Thomas's text appears at the start of the manuscript, on fols. 1–77r. Other saints' lives in the volume are the Cistercian John of Forde's life of the anchorite Wulfric of Haselbury (fols. 81r–119v) and a version of the Benedictine monk Reginald of Durham's life of Godric of Finchale (fols. 119v–168r). The manuscript also contains several letters, a copy of the Cistercian abbot Isaac of Stella's commentary on the Canon of the Mass, and a lapidary entry on the emerald. On the relationship of the *Life* to CUL Add. MS 3037, see Blurton, "Language of the Liturgy."

27. For the controversial claim that the charge first emerged in the Rhineland, when Jewish patriarchs persecuted by crusaders opted to kill themselves and their families (in *Kiddush ha-shem*, or the sanctification of God's name) rather than surrender, see Yuval, *Two Nations in Your Womb*, 135–204. McCulloh modifies Yuval, suggesting parallel lines of transmission in England and the continent ("Jewish Ritual Murder"); Langmuir offers an overview of earlier theories of origin and transmission in *Toward a Definition of Antisemitism*, 282–98.

28. Later English boy-martyr cults emerged around Harold of Gloucester (1168), Robert of Bury St. Edmunds (1181), and Hugh of Lincoln (1255). Allegations also arose in Winchester (in 1225 and 1232) and in London (1244), but led to no lasting cults. On Gloucester, see Hillaby, "Ritual-Child-Murder Accusation." On Bury, see Bale, *Jew in the Medieval Book*, 105–44; and Lampert-Weissig, " Once and Future Jew." On Hugh, see Langmuir, *Toward a Definition of Antisemitism*, 237–62; and Heng, "England's Dead Boys." On the tale of Adam of Bristol, see Cluse, "*Fabula Ineptissima*"; and Stacey, "Ritual Crucifixion and the Social Structure of Mediaeval Anglo-Jewry."

29. Booth, "Shylock's Sober House," 26.

30. Langmuir, *Toward a Definition of Antisemitism*, 477–79. As Rubin points out, versions of the libel have been invoked in polemics against Jews and Judaism in "every century since it appeared . . . right up to its grotesque appropriation by the Nazis" ("Introduction," viii).

31. *Life*, I.6, 25, Rubin 19. Cf. *Life*, I.16, 47, Rubin 33. On these and related passages, see H. Johnson, *Blood Libel*, 59–61, who discusses the medieval usage of the Latin verb "exterminare," and J. J. Cohen, *Hybridity, Identity, and Monstrosity in Medieval Britain*, 173.

32. In addition, during the preaching of the Second Crusade in 1146, and largely due to the efforts of a Cistercian monk named Ralph, violence against Jews occurred in northern France and Germany (Phillips, *Second Crusade*, 83–84). On the York pogrom and its context, see Rees Jones and Watson, *Christians and Jews in Angevin England*.

33. On the disturbing historical agency of the boy-martyr myth, see Dobson, *Jews of Medieval York*, and Heng, "Jews, Saracens, 'Black Men,' Tartars," 251–52.

34. Hillaby, "Ritual-Child-Murder Accusation," 81; Langmuir, *Toward a Definition of Antisemitism*, 209–36; J. J. Cohen, *Hybridity, Identity, and Monstrosity in Medieval Britain*, 139–74; H. Johnson, *Blood Libel*, 30–58; Despres, "Adolescence and Sanctity"; Bale, *Feeling Persecuted*, 50–58; Rose, *Murder of William of Norwich*.

35. This is not to ignore the depiction of rural spaces in the *Life*, namely Thorpe Wood, which lay northeast of the town, on the site of Mousehold Heath. William's body was hidden by Jews in the forest, discovered there through miracles, and originally buried there, according to Thomas. Later, a chapel called St. William in the Wood was erected in the wood. Popular legend linked William closely with the forest,

as images of William crucified in a wooded background on medieval rood screens attest. Half of Thorpe Wood belonged to the cathedral priory, where it was a source of tension between the monks and the bishop. See Herbert di Losinga, *Life, Letters, and Sermons*, 141; Crosby, *Bishop and Chapter in Twelfth-Century England*, 180–81.

36. Fitz Stephen, *Vita Sancti Thomae*, iii. 2–13; Lucian, *Liber Luciani*.

37. J. Campbell, "Norwich before 1300," 39–41.

38. On the Norwich economy, see Ayers, "Urban Landscape," 20; and Rutledge, "Economic Life." On the role played by the bishop and cathedral close in the town, see Tanner, "Cathedral and the City."

39. Ayers, "Urban Landscape," 10; Rutledge, "Immigration and Population Growth in Early Fourteenth-Century Norwich"; J. Campbell, "Norwich before 1300," 29.

40. Gilchrist, *Norwich Cathedral Close*, 236.

41. On monastic hospitality, see Kerr, *Monastic Hospitality*; on hospitality and Norwich cathedral, see Gilchrist, *Norwich Cathedral Close*, 44, 131–32.

42. Stacey, "Anti-Semitism and the Medieval English State," 166.

43. On the links between the *Cronicon* and the *Life*, see Partner, *Serious Entertainments*, 177–78; Allin, "Richard of Devizes," 36. In addition to the similarities discussed by Partner, details such as the Christian nurse, the stress on urban crime, and the emphasis on the Jewish house make the prospect that Richard is lampooning Thomas compelling.

44. See above, note 28. Roth points to an 1193 Pipe Roll entry regarding a fine paid by Winchester Jews as possible evidence that the boy-martyr allegation occurred there (*History of the Jews in England*, 22).

45. *Cronicon*, 64–65. Translations are from Appleby with silent modifications.

46. Ibid. On Richard's reliance on Horace's *Satires* 1.2, as well as for an argument that medieval London was not as disreputable as Richard claims it is, see Scattergood, "London and Money," 172. On the terminology employed by Richard to identify the members of the London underworld, see Johansson, "London's Medieval Sodomites," 158–62.

47. *Cronicon*, 64–65.

48. Ibid., 68–69.

49. Partner, *Serious Entertainments*, 144–45; Bale, "Richard of Devizes and Fictions of Judaism," 56; Blurton, "Richard of Devizes's *Cronicon*, Menippean Satire, and the Jews of Winchester," 267.

50. Blurton, "Richard of Devizes's *Cronicon*, Menippean Satire, and the Jews of Winchester," 272. As Bale and others have observed, the friend's words parody the boy-martyr myth insofar as his sordid language pokes fun at the fantasy of the innocent Christian boy (Bale, "Richard of Devizes and Fictions of Judaism," 63).

51. *Cronicon*, 67–68.

52. Partner, *Serious Entertainments*, 159–60. This is not to say that Richard admired Jews. The *Cronicon* opens by describing the 1189 pogrom, which Richard calls "a sacrifice of the Jews to their father the devil" (4). On the false praise of Jews in the *Cronicon* and other English texts, see Levine, "Why Praise Jews."

53. This is not to say that Christian crime is nonexistent in Thomas's ritual-murder fantasy. For example, the Jewish financier in whose home the martyrdom purportedly occurs is murdered outside of town, in Thorpe Wood, by the servants

of one his debtors, Sir Simon de Novers. Thomas interprets that crime as a form of divine retribution for William's murder. See *Life*, II.13, 97–99, Rubin 63–65.

54. Thomas associates William's family with the Norfolk village of Havering-land, located about nine miles northwest of Norwich (*Life*, I.2, 13, Rubin 12).

55. *Life*, I.4, 17, Rubin 14.

56. *Life*, I.4, 17–19, Rubin 14–15.

57. *Life*, I.5, 19, Rubin 16. The fact that women—William's cousin and, later, a maid—serve as detectives in this text is significant. As many a noir film and detective novel demonstrate, tracking and spying on a criminal is "dirty work," to be sure; investigating, listening in on, and infiltrating a criminal's space threatens to contaminate the detective and even confirm the shared identity of the suspect and pursuer. Contact with Jews was perceived as especially dangerous, given their status as untouchables (Bale, *Feeling Persecuted*, 90–117; Kruger, "Bodies of Jews"). Women can perform the dirty work of making contact with Jews in the *Life* because they are already like Jews: tainted, dangerous, and problematic (Lampert-Weissig, *Gender and Jewish Difference*).

58. *Life*, I.5, 19–20, Rubin 16. My translation.

59. *Life*, I.5, 20, Rubin 16. The boy's torment entails a gag that is elaborately strapped in place; a "strange instrument of torture" ("insolitum tormentum") involving tying a knotted rope around William's forehead, neck, and chin; shaving and pricking William's head with thorns; crucifying him; and wounding the boy's left side (*Life*, I.5, 20–21, Rubin 16).

60. *Life*, I.5, 20–21, Rubin 16–17. Rose notes how William's death mirrors the tortures used during the civil war in *Murder of William of Norwich*, 18–19.

61. *Cronicon*, 65.

62. Jeremy Cohen discusses how the ritual-murder libel gave new support for long-standing associations of Jews with deicide in *Christ Killers*, 93–117. On the name used by Thomas, "*Deus-adiuvet*," see Rose, *Murder of William of Norwich*, 75.

63. J. Campbell, "Norwich," 10.

64. Lipman, *Jews of Medieval Norwich*, 38; cf. Holt, "Society and Population," 94.

65. Lipman, *Jews of Medieval Norwich*, 3.

66. Ibid., 120.

67. Hillaby and Hillaby, *Palgrave Dictionary of Medieval Anglo-Jewish History*, 170, 283–84.

68. Langmuir, *Toward a Definition of Antisemitism*, 209.

69. J. J. Cohen, "Future of the Jews of York," 283.

70. *Life*, I.5, 21–22, Rubin 17.

71. The Jewish door contradicts both Jewish theology and lived experience. The holy capsule called a mezuzah (Hebrew for doorpost), affixed to doorways since the days of the Second Temple, marked the Jewish home as a sacred space protected by God. Worth noting here also are the mitzvoth stressing an open-door policy of hospitality. The commandments draw on rabbinic commentary on Gen. 18:1–5, where Abraham's house has four *open* gates facing in all of the cardinal directions to ensure that any weary traveller could find respite in his home. Medieval hospitality was mainly directed at fellow Jews, but in England as elsewhere, "Neighborly and even friendly relations between individual Jews and Christians always occurred, despite oppressive rules and the ideologies held by both sides" (J. Katz, *Exclusiveness*

*and Tolerance*, 24). Jeffrey Cohen considers rare and transitory moments in English texts that evoke nonhostile, neighborly cohabitation in "Future of the Jews of York."

72. Doors in hagiography surely inspired Thomas. Cf. the doors and the bodily apertures (like an eye or the Virgin's hymen) in Gregory of Tours's miracle stories, and the miracles of Saint Columban (*Glory of the Martyrs*, 21, 24; Jonas, *Life of St. Columban*, 21–22).

73. *Life*, II.9, 89, Rubin 58.

74. *Life*, II.9, 90, Rubin 58.

75. *Life*, II.9, 89–90, Rubin 59. The door also emerges as a charged threshold when the Jews bury the body in a secret place and "retired to their house as if they had done nothing; all their doors were left open" (*Life*, II.9, 91, Rubin 60).

76. Rees Jones, "Building Domesticity in the City," 76.

77. Douglas, *Purity and Danger*, 4.

78. On friendly interaction between Jews and Christians in medieval Norwich, see Rutledge, "Medieval Jews of Norwich and Their Legacy," 122–24.

79. See also book 5, when William miraculously frees a Norfolk man imprisoned in a house by a tyrannous knight whose servants "lock all the doors to the house" and "barricade them with benches and other kinds of obstacles," a detail that may have been inspired by Jonas's *Life of St. Columban* (*Life*, V.10, 198–200, Rubin 131; Jonas, *Life of St. Columban*, 21–22).

80. Isidore, *Etymologies*, XV.vii.4, trans. Barney et al., 311.

81. Cf. *Life*, I.8, 28, Rubin 22; I.16, 44, Rubin 31; II.2, 63, Rubin 43; II.4, 71, Rubin 47. It is impossible to confirm Thomas's intentions, since medieval writers often placed an "h" at the beginning of Latin words beginning with an "o."

82. *Life*, I.5, 22, Rubin 17.

83. Cf. Gregory of Tours, *Glory of the Martyrs*, 24, where the sound of a door being unlocked pertains to the miraculous cure of a blind girl.

84. *Life*, I.5, 20, Rubin 16.

85. Isidore, *Etymologies*, XI.i.49, trans. Barney et al., 234.

86. *Life*, I.5, 20, Rubin 16.

87. Bale, *Feeling Persecuted*, 54; the other moment is a reference to a *luce* in *Life*, I.1, 11.

88. Bale, *Feeling Persecuted*, 54.

89. "Teasels 'that longyn to the office of fullers' were cultivated on a large scale from at least the early 13th century in England" (Walton, "Textiles," 332). Thomas's description of the teasel as a "ligneum tormentum" or "a wooden instrument of torture" may indicate the thistle or a nap-raising man-made device of wood. The teasel reappears again later in the *Life*, when William's grandfather uses it to profit from the boy's cult (*Life*, V.5, 192–93). Rubin suggests possible Christic associations of the teasel ("Introduction," xxi).

90. Walton, "Textiles," 347; Rutledge, "Economic Life," 160.

91. Lipman, *Jews of Medieval Norwich*, 79–94.

92. J. J. Cohen, *Hybridity, Identity, and Monstrosity in Medieval Britain*, 158.

93. *Life*, I.6, 26, Rubin 20.

94. *Life*, I.18, 50–51, Rubin 35–36.

95. *Life*, I.19, 54, Rubin 38.

96. See Peter the Venerable, *Adversus Iudeorum*, lines 835–51, ed. Friedman, 65. Cf. Abulafia, *Christians and Jews*, 128–29.

97. Stacey, "From Ritual Crucifixion to Host Desecration," 24.

98. *Life*, I.9, 54, Rubin 38; J. J. Cohen, *Hybridity, Identity, and Monstrosity in Medieval Britain*, 163–64.

99. J. Campbell, "Norwich before 1300," 39.

100. Ibid., 41, 34.

101. Fernie, "The Building," 51.

102. Ibid.

103. Secular government also consolidated its power during the period. On religious and secular consolidations and the persecution of Jews and other disenfranchised persons, see Boswell, *Christianity, Social Tolerance and Homosexuality*, and Moore, *Formation of a Persecuting Society*.

104. See Duggan, "From the Conquest to the Death of John."

105. Harper-Bill, "Medieval Church and the Wider World," 285.

106. Ibid.

107. Gilchrist, *Norwich Cathedral Close*, 82.

108. Ibid.

109. Ibid., 82, 252; Heywood, "Romanesque Building," 111.

110. Abulafia, *Christians and Jews*, 52–53; Haskins, *Renaissance of the Twelfth Century*; Moore, *Formation of a Persecuting Society* and *War on Heresy*.

111. Abulafia, *Christians and Jews*, 54–55.

112. 12 March 1173 Bull of Pope Alexander III, in Douglas and Greenhaw, *English Historical Documents*, 914–15.

113. *Life*, II.1, 59–60, Rubin 41.

114. Ibid.

115. Justin Martyr, *Dialogos*, 27.4, cited and discussed in J. Cohen, *Living Letters of the Law*, 12.

116. On the Protocols of Zion, see Bronner, *A Rumor about the Jews*.

117. *Life*, II.11, 93–94, Rubin 61–62.

118. Twelfth-century Narbonne was a seigneurial capital noted for its vital literary and mercantile activity and its habitation by the most important and the oldest Jewish community in the Midi (Caille, *Medieval Narbonne*). Possibly because it was a major Roman administrative and commercial center, Narbonne appears on early twelfth-century *mappae mundi* such as those by Lambert of St. Omer (1120–25) and Guido of Pisa (1119). On Christian ideas of a Jewish "pope" or high priest at Narbonne and their transmission to Thomas, see Rubin, "Introduction," xxiii–xxiv, xliv n77.

119. *Life*, III.1, 117, Rubin 77. See also *Life*, VI.14, 249–50, Rubin 163–65, in which a woman describes her miraculous cure by William in Rome before the English pope Nicholas Breakspear (Adrian IV).

120. Astill, "General Survey," 46.

121. *Life*, I.3, 15, Rubin 13.

122. *Life*, I.1, 10, Rubin 10.

123. Ibid.

124. Jews are associated with thorns such as the teasel and the thorns used to puncture William's head (cf. *Life* 1.18, Rubin 36–37) But those Jewish associations are not at all clear at the start of the *Life* when the rose image appears. We gain a more accurate understanding of Thomas's antisemitism by insisting on the dual referents for *spina*.

125. *Life*, I.12, 36–37, Rubin 26–27.

126. E.g., Matt. 9:36; Mark 6:34; Matt. 27:17, 20, 25; McClelland, *Crowd and the Mob*, 54; Canetti, *Crowds and Power*, 155.

127. Canetti, *Crowds and Power*, 155.

128. J. J. Cohen, *Hybridity, Identity, and Monstrosity in Medieval Britain*, 163.

129. Canetti, *Crowds and Power*, 18.

130. Ibid., 16, 155.

131. Ibid., 155.

132. *Life*, I.15, 41, Rubin 30.

133. *Life*, I.15, 42, Rubin 30.

134. Gregory of Tours, *Glory of the Martyrs*, 30. The parallels between the mothers of "The Jewish Boy" and the *Life* speak to how, as Lampert-Weissig has shown, a concern over women intertwines with medieval antisemitism (*Gender and Jewish Difference*).

135. Cf. a moment later in the *Life* when a crowd unites in its worship of William upon the miraculous healing of a hysterical blind woman (*Life*, VI.8, 229–31, Rubin 151–53). On the complexities of fact and faith in the *Life*, see H. Johnson, *Blood Libel*, 30–58.

136. Isidore, *Etymologies*, VII.xiii.1, trans. Barney et al., 172.

137. The Benedictine rule enjoined all monks to be hospitable, but "within a cathedral-priory the scale of hospitality required was very considerable, and it was combined with the need for charitable and educational activities" (Gilchrist, *Norwich Cathedral Close*, 44). To meet those needs, Norwich contained a hostelry, or guest hall, that was located along the western portion of the ranges that surrounded the cloister (ibid., 131–20).

138. Gilchrist, *Norwich Cathedral Close*, 241.

139. Crowds also feature regularly in the later books of the *Life*, where they testify to the sweep of William's cult (e.g. III.27, 158, Rubin 103; VI.5, 225, Rubin 149; VI.9, 231, Rubin 153).

140. Canetti, *Crowds and Power*, 155.

141. *Life*, I.18, 51, Rubin 36.

142. Cf. the myth of Jephonius, a Jew who touches Mary's bier during her funeral (Bale, *Feeling Persecuted*, 90–117). Later in the *Life*, William complains in a vision that "some" of the pilgrims who visit his shrine "are not ashamed to touch the stone of my tomb or its cloth with muddy feet and even to stain it; and the pavement around me is dirty with the disgusting spittle of many" (*Life*, IV.7, 171, Rubin 112). Crowds also prove troublesome to the monks, prompting repeated translations of William's remains, from the chapter house to the cathedral, and then to a new location in the cathedral (north of the high altar) via a fourth translation. See Jessopp and James, "Introduction," in *Life*, xxiv; *Life*, V.1, 185–86, Rubin 122; VI.1, 220–21, Rubin 146.

143. In Norwich Cathedral, a heavily restored late medieval choir screen stands on the site of the now lost original Romanesque structure. The *pulpitum* is a medieval monument that has received increasing attention over the last decade by scholars who have shown how choir screens "fulfilled a wide variety of incorporative functions" during the medieval Christian liturgy (Jung, "Beyond the Barrier," 624; thanks belong to Marcia Kupfer for calling this essay to my attention). But in the case of Thomas, we find evidence supporting the older view that the *pulpitum* separated the

laity from the clerical performers of church rituals (Gillerman, *Clôture of Notre-Dame*; Jung, "Beyond the Barrier," 622).

144. Cf. Gregory of Tours's stress on closed doors preventing sinners from entering a holy sight (*Glory of the Martyrs*, 29).

145. Tanner, "Cathedral and the City," 261, 258.

146. Ibid., 258.

147. *Life*, I.12, 36, Rubin 27.

148. Hillaby provides an overview of the path of the attacks in "Prelude and Postscript to the York Massacre."

149. Important scholarly discussions of the pogroms include Dobson, *Jews of Medieval York*, "Medieval York Jewry Reconsidered," and "Decline and Expulsion"; Rees Jones and Watson, *Christians and Jews in Angevin England*; Roth, *History of the Jews in England*, 19–28; Mundill, *King's Jews*, 75–81; Bale, *Feeling Persecuted*, 170–74.

150. Diceto, *Historical Works* II, 75; Hillaby, "Prelude and Postscript to the York Massacre," 45.

151. Latin citations of William's *History* are from the Howlett edition, by book, chapter, and page number; translations are from Stephenson's translation with minor changes and are cited by page number. On the importance of William's account, see Watson, "Introduction," 4. Other medieval accounts of the pogroms include one of William's major sources, the *Annals* (ca. early 1170s–1201) of Roger of Howden (d. 1201). William's text massively expands on Howden; his account of the pogroms is three to four times as long. Important discussions of the relationship between the two works include Gillingham, "Two Yorkshire Historians Compared"; Vincent, "William of Newburgh, Josephus, and the New Titus," 60; and Kennedy, "'Faith in the one God,'" 143. For Roger of Howden's account of the pogroms, see *Annals*. On the sources for the pogroms beyond Howden and William, see Roger of Howden, *Gesta*, 83–84, 107–8; Roger of Howden, *Chronica*, 33–34. On the dating of William's *History*, see Partner, *Serious Entertainments*, 55, 60.

152. The priory was located twenty miles from the nearest city, York. While the priests of the priory served neighboring churches, William seems to have lived what was to all intents and purposes a life of isolation. As a young man he began to live at the priory and in all likelihood never left it. See *History*, I.15, 51, Stevenson 419; Kennedy, "'Faith in the one God,'" 139; Partner, *Serious Entertainments*, 56.

153. Partner, *Serious Entertainments*, 80–91. William, as mentioned above, was an Augustinian. On the elusive character of Augustinian piety, see ibid., 52–54. Partner stresses how William's use in the History "of the word *vulgus* seems to carry all its modern connotations" (74).

154. *History*, IV.9, 316, Stevenson 568.

155. Augustine, *City of God* 18.46, 891–92.

156. "The Jews are not to be persecuted," writes Bernard, because they "are for us the living words of Scripture, for they remind us always of what our Lord suffered" (*The Letters of St. Bernard of Clairvaux* [London, 1953], 460–62; cited in Chazan, *Church, State and Jew in the Middle Ages*, 103).

157. *History*, IV.9, 316, Stevenson 568. In equating Jews with Christ on the cross, William may be invoking the Jewishness of Christ, as he does in his commentary on the Song of Songs. See Kennedy, "'Faith in the one God,'" 150–51.

158. *History*, IV.9, 316–17, Stevenson 568.

159. *History*, IV.ix, 312–13, Stevenson 566.

160. *History*, IV.9, 317, Stevenson 568.

161. *History*, IV.9, 316–17, Stevenson 568.

162. *History*, IV.9, 313, Stevenson 566.

163. *History*, IV.1, 296, Stevenson 557.

164. *History*, IV.9, 314, Stevenson 567.

165. Another, related rationale William offered for the attacks is that they offer a harbinger of Richard I's future successes in the Third Crusade, making him a second Titus. See Vincent, "William of Newburgh, Josephus, and the New Titus," 61–62.

166. *History*, III.10–20, 240–66, Stevenson 526–42. Partner, *Serious Entertainments*, 105–6; Kletter, "Politics, Prophecy, and Jews," 103–4.

167. *History*, IV.7, 309, Stevenson 563.

168. *History*, IV.10, 320, Stevenson 570. On the transmission of Josephus in the Middle Ages and William's knowledge and use of Josephus, see Vincent, "William of Newburgh, Josephus, and the New Titus," 63–90; Kletter, "Politics, Prophecy, and Jews," 102–5; and Nisse, "'Your Name Will No Longer Be Aseneth,'" 739–40. While, as Vincent points out, William knew Josephus not through the Greek but through a Latin translation, the Latin Josephus "was fluent and comprehensive" in its translation of the Greek ("William of Newburgh, Josephus, and the New Titus," 64); Thackeray's English translation of the Greek, cited in the following discussion, therefore provides us with a solid sense of how William knew Josephus.

169. Kletter, "Politics, Prophecy, and Jews," 99; Millar, *Siege of Jerusalem*, 42–60.

170. Blurton describes how William and other chroniclers of the pogroms invoke not only the siege but also biblical depictions of Jewish exile (e.g., Exodus) in order to urge expulsion ("Egyptian Days").

171. Kennedy, "'Faith in the one God,'" 146; Vincent, "William of Newburgh, Josephus, and the New Titus," 74–75.

172. Vincent, "William of Newburgh, Josephus, and the New Titus," 62, cf. 74–75.

173. Partner, *Serious Entertainments*, 226.

174. *History*, IV.9, 317, Stevenson 568.

175. *History*, IV.7, 309, Stevenson 563. On the ironies at play in this passage, see Vincent, "William of Newburgh, Josephus, and the New Titus," 61–62.

176. Narin van Court, "*The Siege of Jerusalem* and Augustinian Historians," 239. Levine, however, claims that "the operative emotion in William of Newburgh's description of riots against the Jews in London is repugnance towards the mob, not positive feeling for Jews" ("Why Praise Jews," 291).

177. *History*, IV.9, 312, Stevenson 565. On the Jewishness of the mob in William's text, see Vincent, "William of Newburgh, Josephus, and the New Titus," esp. 75 (on blindness) and Kennedy (on blindness) in "'Faith in the one God,'" 147.

178. E.g., *History*, IV.1, 295, Stevenson 556; *History* IV.1, 298, Stevenson 558; IV.10, 320, Stevenson 570. On William's wholesale condemnation of mobs, see Rajak,"The *Against Apion*."

179. Mason, "Revisiting Josephus's Pharisees," 30–31; Kletter, "Politics, Prophecy, and Jews," 101.

180. Keene, "London from the Post-Roman Period to 1300," 195–96.

181. *History*, IV.1, 298, Stevenson 558; IV.1, 297, Stevenson 557.

182. On the crusade comparison of English kings (including Richard I) and other figures to Titus, see Vincent, "William of Newburgh, Josephus, and the New Titus," 79–90.

183. *History*, IV.1, 294–95, Stevenson 556. Here as elsewhere, William draws upon Roger of Howden's account of the riots in his *Annals of English History*, which state that the new sovereign forbade Jews from entering the "king's court" during the coronation (119).

184. History, IV.1, 295, Stevenson 556. Compare with Howden, who describes how the riots commence when Jewish leaders disregard the ordinance by approaching the king with presents, thus rousing the fury of the Christian commoners (*Annals*, 119).

185. Canetti, *Crowds and Power*, 29.

186. *History*, IV.10, 321–22, Stevenson 571.

187. *History*, IV.1, 296, Stevenson 557.

188. Canetti, *Crowds and Power*, 27. In the same way that "fire spreads," William describes the rapid spread of aggression from the initial Christian attacker at the royal palace to the enraged Christian populace, whose zeal (*zelus*) is *accensus* (kindled or enflamed). See Newburgh, IV.1, 308, Stevenson 556.

189. Canetti, *Crowds and Power*, 76; *History*, IV.1, 296, Stevenson 557.

190. Cf. William's account of the Lynn pogrom, in which he turns from describing a mob of Jews attacking a church to portraying Christian crowds attacking homes, suggesting how urban problems aren't so much tied to particular groups as they are to the dense groupings that define cities (Newburgh, IV.7, 309, Stevenson 564).

191. *History*, IV.9, 314, Stevenson 566. As Rees Jones points out, precisely what structure this *arx* was is subject to conjecture. The building may well not have been the wooden keep where Clifford's Tower now stands ("Neighbours and Victims in Twelfth-Century York," 32). Vincent links William's vocabulary here to Josephus's account of Masada in the *Jewish Wars* ("William of Newburgh, Josephus, and the New Titus," 75–76).

192. *History*, I.10, 318, Stevenson 569.

193. Josephus, *Jewish War*, 7.9.1, 416–19. Cf. Kletter, "Politics, Prophecy, and Jews," 102.

194. *History*, IV.10, 320, Stevenson 570.

195. Josephus, *Jewish War*, 7.9.1, 416–19.

196. Castells, *Rise of the Network Society*, 407–99.

### 3. The Minster and the Privy

1. Partly due to the challenge of generating hard evidence on key issues, research on medieval economies offers various and conflicting accounts of the expansion and/or rise of commerce (Britnell and Campbell, "Introduction," 3). However diverse, much of the recent work does challenge Postan's claim that from one thousand to three thousand English markets stagnated (ibid.; Postan, *Medieval Economy and Society*, 41–72).

2. Duby, *Early Growth of the European Economy*, 270.

3. Critics including Duby (*Early Growth of the European Economy*) and Hodges (*Dark Age Economics*) cite state consolidation as enabling commercial development.

On urbanization and commerce, see the works cited by Britnell in "Commercialisation and economic development in England," 9–12. On towns and the English state, see Palliser, "Towns and the English State."

4. Lopez, *Commercial Revolution of the Middle Ages*; Masschaele, *Peasants, Merchants, and Markets*; Duby, *Early Growth of the European Economy*.

5. Bolton, *Money in the Medieval English Economy*; Britnell, *Commercialization of the English Economy*, 5–52, 79–127.

6. Lefebvre, *Production of Space*, 265.

7. Masschaele, "Public Space of the Marketplace," 388–89.

8. Lilley, *Urban Life in the Middle Ages*, 146–50.

9. Saalman, *Mediaeval Cities*, 28.

10. Lefebvre, *Production of Space*, 265. The networks connecting the medieval city to the country show how urban space did not oppose but was an essential outcome of rural sites and their surplus grain production; cities were "closely integrated with all strata of the rural population" (Hilton, "Warriors and Peasants," 89). On the "urban field," see Schofield and Vince, *Medieval Towns*, 152.

11. Mundill describes "the topographical evidence which shows Jews inhabiting the main mercantile areas of towns" as "overwhelming" (*England's Jewish Solution*, 129–30).

12. Ibid., 130. Further evidence of that economic basis is the fact that, when Jews began to settle outside London during the first half of the twelfth century, they generally lived in towns and cities possessed of minting rights and proximity to fairs (Stacey, "Jewish Lending and the Medieval English Economy," 86).

13. Lipman, *Jews of Medieval Norwich*, 114–22.

14. The other key consideration motivating settlement patterns was royal protection, an issue that prompted many Jews to live near castles.

15. Stacey, "Jewish Lending and the Medieval English Economy," 79, 82. However "if these were the Conqueror's expectations, they were almost certainly not fulfilled," due to already established "currents of English commerce" (ibid., 82).

16. Ibid., 87.

17. Ibid., 88. Stephen's reign witnessed the loss of Normandy (which halted trade with Rouen), the disruption of trade routes, and other events that probably "encouraged the exchange of domestic plate" and heightened the need for loans (ibid.).

18. Ibid.

19. Ibid., 89.

20. Ibid., 90–92.

21. Thomas of Monmouth, *Life*, I.7, 26, II.13, 97, Rubin 20, 64. All Latin citations of the *Life* are from the Jessop and James edition, by book, chapter, and page number, in consultation with Miri Rubin's transcription of the manuscript (http://yvc.history.qmul.ac.uk/passio.html). Translations are from Rubin's translation with minor changes and are cited by page number. On the Latin word used by Thomas to refer to the financier, "Deus-adiuvet," see Rose, *Murder of William of Norwich*, 75.

22. Though as Rubin stresses, Deulesalt isn't singled out as guilty by Thomas, who stresses the collective nature of the crime ("Introduction," xxii).

23. Thomas of Monmouth, *Life*, II.13, 98–99, Rubin 64.

24. Le Goff, *Your Money or Your Life*, 10. On greed as a sin, see Little, *Religious Poverty and the Profit Economy*, 35–40; Little, "Pride Goes before Avarice." On discussions of greed prior to a profit economy, see Newhauser, *Early History of Greed*.

25. Thomas of Monmouth, *Life*, I.4, 16–17, Rubin 14.

26. Thomas of Monmouth, *Life*, I.4, 18–19, Rubin 15.

27. Thomas of Monmouth, *Life*, I.13, 50, III.1, 117–20, Rubin 27–28, 77–79.

28. Morris, *History of Urban Form*, 75.

29. Also noteworthy is the fact that from the thirteenth century on, cathedral households began "relaxing their dependence upon their estates and increasing their reliance upon the market," though manorial estates remained crucial to ecclesiastical economies (B. Campbell, "Measuring the Commercialisation of Seigneurial Agriculture," 186).

30. G. Rosser, "Urban Culture and the Church," 352.

31. Ibid.

32. Gilchrist, *Norwich Cathedral Close*, 236, 189.

33. Thomas of Monmouth, *Life*, V.5, 192–93, Rubin 126–27.

34. While scholars of medieval architecture, most famously Gimpel (*Cathedral Builders*), have taught us much about the material culture of church building by delineating the labor it entailed, we typically don't think about the construction of churches in light of the history of English commerce. Yet the "basic question," asked by Bennett Hill about Rievaulx Abbey remains pressing: "one wonders how the abbots paid for their renovations?" "The implication," Hill points out, "is that they borrowed." See B. Hill, Review of *Rievaulx Abbey*, 93. On the fraught role of emerging economies and social forms in the erection of gothic cathedrals, see Abou-Ei-Haj, "Artistic Integration inside the Cathedral Precinct" and "Urban Setting for Late Medieval Church Building"; Lopez, "Economie et architecture médiévale"; Kraus, *Gold Was the Mortar*; Williams, *Bread, Wine and Money*; and Eklund et al., *Marketplace of Christianity*, 197–224.

35. Stacey, "Aaron of Lincoln," 1. A man who epitomized the new economies of his era, Aaron engaged in lending, mortgages, bond trading, pawn broking, property development, commodity brokering, and crop speculation.

36. Mundill, *King's Jews*, 25.

37. Jacobs, "Aaron of Lincoln," 635.

38. Roth, *History of the Jews in England*, 109; Jacobs, "Aaron of Lincoln," 633–37; H. Richardson, *English Jewry under the Angevin Kings*, 90–91.

39. Stacey, "York, Aaron of."

40. Adler, "Aaron of York," 133–35.

41. See the recent evidence uncovering a deed detailing the receipt of funds from Jews in exchange for land which was signed on behalf John Romanus, the controller of fabric for the North Transept (where the Jewish Window exists): https://yorkminster.org/geisha/assets/files/fact-sheet-the-principal-windows.pdf.

42. On the Christian response to Jewish alterity as necessary, intimate, and/or internal, see Boyarin, "The Other Within," in *Storm from Paradise*, 77–98; and Smith, "What a Difference a Difference Makes," in *Relating Religion*, 251–302.

43. Ironically, the cathedrals bore facades, stained-glass windows, and other features depicting derogatory images of Jews, including Ecclesia and Synagoga, deicidal Jews at the Crucifixion, and myths like Theophilus (Rowe, *The Jew, the Cathedral and the Medieval City* and Strickland, *Saracens, Demons and Jews*).

44. Walsingham, *Gesta*, 193–94: "Unde Aaron Judaeus, qui nos tenuit sibi obligatos, ad Domum Sancti Albani, in superbia magna et jactantia, cum minis, veniens,

jactitabat se feretrum Beato Albano nostro fecisse, et ipsi, dehospitato, hospitium de pecunia sua praeparasse."

45. The noun *mina*, used to indicate Aaron's threatening stance, with its roots in the Latin term for battlements and parapets, links the lender with buildings not unlike the imposing mansions denigrated by William of Newburgh (Lewis and Short, *Latin Dictionary*, s.v. "mina").

46. Oman, "The Shrine of St. Alban," 241; Jacobs, "Aaron of Lincoln," 636. Both the window and the chest are no longer extant, but we do have a drawing of the inner layer of the shrine, which Matthew Paris used to illustrate his ca. 1230–40 life of St. Alban. Oman speculates that the image in Alban's *vita* may be that of the inner shrine in "Shrine of St Alban."

47. We don't know how much such ironies apply directly to Norwich Cathedral, though we might wonder if Deulesalt helped fund the erection of the church, which was completed in 1145. Thomas's ritual-murder fantasy reflects a larger cultural trend (of demonizing Jewish homes and celebrating Christian churches) that exceeds the particulars of his Norwich context.

48. Aaron's provision of shelter for an otherwise "homeless" Alban is all the more charged given the fact that Alban became England's first native saint after being martyred for housing a fugitive priest (Bede, *Ecclesiastical History*, ed. Colgrave and Mynors).

49. Chaucer, *Riverside Chaucer*, 7.572. Subsequent citations by fragment and line number of the *Canterbury Tales* and line citations of other works by Chaucer are from the Riverside edition and appear in the text.

50. Hawkins, "Chaucer's Prioress and the Sacrifice of Praise"; Fradenburg, "Criticism, Antisemitism, and the Prioress's Tale"; Kruger, "Bodies of Jews"; Lampert-Weissig, *Gender and Jewish Difference*. See also Bale, *Jew in the Medieval Book*.

51. Kruger, "Bodies of Jews," 306; see also Lampert-Weissig, *Gender and Jewish Difference*, 79.

52. Bale, *Jew in the Medieval Book*, 84.

53. E.g., ibid., 84–85; Fradenburg, "Criticism, Antisemitism, and the Prioress's Tale," 106; Kruger, "Bodies of Jews," 307; Lampert-Weissig, *Gender and Jewish Difference*, 79; Patterson, "'Living Witnesses of Our Redemption,'" 511.

54. Kolve, *Chaucer and the Imagery of Narrative*, 85–157; Kruger, "Passion and Order."

55. Stanbury considers how the anonymous city might be Prague, the site of a 1389 host-desecration allegation, in "Host Desecration."

56. Regardles of the expulsion, Chaucer may have met Jews in England as visitors to the island or as residents of the London *Domus Conversorum* (Kelly, "Jews and Saracens in Chaucer's England"; Delaney, "Chaucer's Prioress, the Jews and Muslims"); he also may have encountered Jews in his travels abroad (Besserman, "Chaucer, Spain, and the Prioress's Antisemitism," 339–50).

57. Heng, "England's Dead Boys," S59. England was not utterly absent of Jews after the expulsion. Nearly continuously until the seventeenth-century readmission debates, Jews were present in England as, among other things, physicians (for Edward II, Henry IV, and Elizabeth I), inhabitants of the *Domus Conversorum* (a residence for converts from Judaism almost continuously until its decline in the early seventeenth century), Hebrew scholars, military hostages, and royal advisors (e.g., Henry VIII's divorce case). See Wolf, "Jews in Elizabethan England" and "Jews in Tudor England."

58. For an overview of critical conceptualizations of the virtual and imaginary Jew in medieval Christian thought and especially postexpulsion English discourse, see Johnson and Blurton, "Virtual Jews and Figural Criticism." See also Krummel, *Crafting Jewishness in Medieval England*.

59. The appellation "little" set the boy martyr apart from the English saint who shared his name, Hugh of Lincoln (d. 1200).

60. Langmuir, "Knight's Tale of Young Hugh," 477–78.

61. On the antisemitic temporality employed by the Prioress, see Archer, "Structure of Anti-Semitism," 48.

62. A setting unique to boy-singer legends, "Asye" in the *Prioress's Tale* may mean Asia (the eastern half of the world as depicted in T-O maps like the Hereford map) or Asia Minor (i.e., Turkey, Iraq, Syria, and Iran). As Delaney points out, Chaucer employs the former meaning of Asia elsewhere in his work (Delaney, "Chaucer's Prioress, the Jews and Muslims," 43).

63. On the centrality of Hugh of Lincoln to the *Prioress's Tale*, see Dahood, "Historical Narratives of Jewish Child-Murder."

64. Kruger, "Times of Conversion," 24. See also Kruger, *Spectral Jew*.

65. Fradenburg, "Criticism, Antisemitism, and the Prioress's Tale," 92.

66. See the quitclaim deed, dated 19 June 1381, in which Chaucer sells his father's home: Husting Roll 110, no. 8, now in the London Metropolitan Archives, printed in Crow and Olson, *Chaucer Life-Records*, 10. On the location of Chaucer's family home, see Bestul, "Did Chaucer Live at 177 Upper Thames Street?"

67. Hillaby, "London," 91.

68. Bestul, "Did Chaucer Live at 177 Upper Thames Street?," 6–7.

69. Hillaby, "London Jewry," 5.

70. Strohm, *Theory and the Premodern Text*, 4.

71. On the ambiguous role of the street name Old Jewry in Stow's *Survey*, see J. Harris, *Untimely Matter*, 95–118.

72. J. Stow, *Survey of London*, 113; Hillaby and Hillaby, *Palgrave Dictionary of Medieval Anglo-Jewish History*, 221.

73. Strohm reconstructs the phenomenology of Chaucer's lived experience in London in *Chaucer's Tale*.

74. Dahood, "Punishment of the Jews," 478; Langmuir states that Chaucer likely knew the story from Matthew Paris ("Knight's Tale of Young Hugh," 464). The sources are Matthew Paris, *Chronica majora*, 5:516–19, 546, 552; *Burton Annals* (Luard, *Annales Monastici*, 1:340–46, 348); Waverly Annals (ibid., 2:346–48); and the ballad that appears in Michel, *Hughes de Lincoln*, 1–16.

75. Broughton, "Prioress's Prologue and Tale," 593. While Broughton calls this subgroup "lily miracles," I follow Bale in terming them miracles of the boy singer.

76. Bale, *Jew and the Medieval Book*, 59.

77. Langmuir points out that the Hugh of Lincoln myth may stress how the crime occurred in a home and was deposited elsewhere in order to link the crime more concretely to Jews ("Knight's Tale of Young Hugh," 467).

78. C. Brown, *Study of the Miracle of Our Lady*, 7.

79. E.g., the Anglo-Norman ballad describes how Hugh's mother "went weeping through the Lincoln Jewry asking at the Jews' doors: 'Where is my child?' But the door where the child had entered was firmly closed so that no Christian might

learn their secrets" (Michel, *Hugues de Lincoln*, 2, lines 26–32, translated by Brown in *A Study of the Miracle of Our Lady*, 91). The Burton Annals describe how, upon Henry III's arrival in Lincoln to investigate Hugh's death, the Jews attempted to resist Henry's officers by bolting their doors and how the officers broke the doors open, seized the Jews and brought them to court (Luard, *Annales Monastici*, 344–45, summarized by Brown in *A Study of the Miracle of Our Lady*, 93). A boy-martyr myth emphasizes how the boy's mother tries but fails to enter the "guilty and treacherous house" where the boy died, and describes how an archbishop breaks down the doors of the house to find the boy ("De cantu Alma redemptoris Mater," Trinity College, MS 0.9.38, in Broughton, "Prioress's Prologue and Tale," 638–47 at 642–43.)

80. Despres, "Protean Jew in the Vernon Manuscript," 152.

81. Broughton, "Prioress's Prologue and Tale," 625, lines 48–49.

82. Michel, *Hugues de Lincoln*, 7, line 158. Langmuir suggests that the privy in the ballad reflects the influence of the boy-martyr myths and the general association of Jews with privies ("Knight's Tale of Young Hugh," 467).

83. London, British Library, MS Harley 957, fols. 19r–27r at 20r; Cluse, "*Fabula Ineptissima*," 308. The legend describes how an angel with a fiery sword guards the latrine where the boy's corpse is hidden, and how the latrine emits an odor of sanctity and the sound of an angelic host that has gathered around Adam's body. On the myth, see Stacey, "From Ritual Crucifixion to Host Desecration."

84. Cf. Matthew Paris's Hugh of Lincoln tale, which stresses Jewish secrecy when it relates how a Jew named Copin tells Christians that few Christians become aware of the "fact" that Jews yearly sacrifice boys "for they [i.e., Jews] only carry on these proceedings privately, and in out of the way places" (*Chronica majora*, 5:519).

85. Elias, *The Civilizing Process*, 111. As Susan Morrison observes, "the idea of a modern subjectivity emerging from the dung heap of the Middle Ages seems misguided, since private acts certainly occurred in the medieval period" (*Excrement in the Late Middle Ages*, 132). See also Shaw, "Construction of the Private" and Bayless, *Sin and Filth in Medieval Culture*, 178–82.

86. Isidore, *Etymologies*, XV.iii.9, trans. Barney et al., 308–9. Ironically, in Thomas's *Life*, the idea of hiding William's body in a privy is rejected because of the likelihood that if the home—a rental—was given over to Christian occupants, they would wish to empty the home of Jewish waste and while cleaning the latrine would discover William's body. The Christian impulse to cleanse a space of Jewishness, in other words, would inevitably lead to the exposure of Jewish perfidy (*Life*, I.6, 24–25, Rubin 19.

87. *MED*, s.v. "prive." The third definition, "an intimate, a friend, confidant; an adviser, a counselor," also speaks to the term's association with secrecy.

88. "De cantu Alma redemptoris Mater," in Broughton, "Prioress's Prologue and Tale," 638–47 at 640–41; Cluse "*Fabula Ineptissima*," 308; MS Harley 957, fols. 20r–21v; Broughton, "Prioress's Prologue and Tale," 625, line 46.

89. Isidore, *Etymologies*, IX.i.105, trans. Barney et al., 237–38.

90. Schofield, *Medieval London Houses*, 86.

91. Sabine, "Latrines and Cesspools of Mediaeval London," 319; Schofield, *Medieval London Houses*, 33; Chew and Kellaway, *London Assize of Nuisance*; Riley, *Liber Albus*, 323–34.

92. Nicholas, *Later Medieval City*, 332.

93. "De cantu Alma Redemptoris Mater," Broughton, "Prioress's Prologue and Tale," 640–41; Alphonsus a Spina, "De expulsion Judeorum de regno Anglorum," in Broughton, "Prioress's Prologue and Tale," 632–37 at 634–35.

94. Broughton, "Prioress's Prologue and Tale," 612–13, 628–29.

95. Ibid., 624–25.

96. Douglas, *Purity and Danger*, 36.

97. The earliest systematic attack on Christian tenets by a Jewish writer characterizes the Incarnation as the belief that God "dwelt in the innards [of a woman], in the filth of menstrual blood and in the dark confinement of the womb" (Cuffel, *Gendering Disgust in Medieval Religious Polemic*, 77). The most concise manifestation of the association emerges in the replacement of Mary's name with *hari'a*—a word that means excrement—in twelfth- and thirteenth-century Jewish polemics (ibid., 130). On the place of Mary in both Jewish arguments against and Christian defenses of Christianity, see also Rubin, *Mother of God*, 161–68.

98. Matthew Paris, *Chronicle*, 142–43.

99. Despres, "Protean Jew in the Vernon Manuscript," 152.

100. W. Cohen, "Locating Filth," ix.

101. On how the 1290 expulsion produced Jews as filth, see S. Morrison, *Excrement in the Late Middle Ages*, 147.

102. Important work on filth and the Prioress includes S. Morrison, *Excrement in the Late Middle Ages*; Price, "Medieval Antisemitism and Excremental Libel" and "Sadism and Sentimentality."

103. Matthew Paris, *Chronica majora*, vol. 5, 518.

104. Broughton, "Prioress's Prologue and Tale," 626, line 129.

105. Lefebvre, *Production of Space*, 222–27.

106. Isidore, *Etymologies*, VIII.i.1, trans. Barney et al., 173.

107. C. Brown, *Study of the Miracle of Our Lady*, 23; Broughton, "Prioress's Prologue and Tale," 604–8, 610–12. Debt collection is a metaphor for hunger in one analogue (ibid., 638–39).

108. Luard, *Annales Monastici*, vol. 1, 345; Matthew Paris, *Chronica majora*, 5:519.

109. *MED*, s.v. "Foule."

110. The phrase "turpe lucrum" derives from Paul (1 Tim. 3:8). Yunck stresses the technical differences between usury and profiteering ("'Lucre of Vileynye'").

111. On the associations of Jews with filth, see Kruger, "Bodies of Jews"; Bayless, "Story of the Fallen Jew"; W. Johnson, "Myth of Jewish Male Menses"; Bale, *Jew in the Medieval Book*, 23–54, 82–88; Tomasch, "Judecca, Dante's Satan, and the *Dis*-placed Jew"; Price, "Medieval Antisemitism and Excremental Libel."

112. Le Goff, *Your Money or Your Life*, 10.

113. Lipton, *Images of Intolerance*, 31; Yunck, "'Lucre of Vileynye'"; Shatzmiller, *Shylock Reconsidered*, 45. Writers often defined usury as any profit above and beyond the principle, though other definitions emerged as medieval authorities debated the precise nature of the loans prohibited by medieval theology and canon law. See Luke 6:34–35; Gratian, *Decretum*, C. 14, q. 3; Shatzmiller, *Shylock Reconsidered*; Noonan, *Scholastic Analysis of Usury*, 19; Nelson, *Idea of Usury*; Helmholz, "Usury and the

Medieval English Church Courts"; Langholm, *Economics in the Medieval Schools*; K. Stow, "Papal and Royal Attitudes toward Jewish Lending"; Seabourne, *Royal Regulation of Loans and Sales in Medieval England*. For an overview of the various and conflicting church attitudes toward usury, see Lipton, *Images of Intolerance*, 31–52.

114. Roberts, *Studies in the Sermons of Stephen Langton*, 115; Le Goff, *Your Money or Your Life*, 64.

115. The most famous Christian lenders were Italian bankers who, by the later Middle Ages, engaged in moneylending on a scale that far exceeded that of their Jewish counterparts (Shatzmiller, *Shylock Reconsidered*, 88). The papacy was indirectly involved in lending money at interest through taxes and fees, whose exactions in England Matthew Paris records (*Chronica majora*, 3:184, 328–32). Richard fitz Nigel refers matter-of-factly to "a clerk who is employed in usury" in his *Dialogue of the Exchequer* (550). Bishop Walter Langton (d. 1321) and Archbishop William Melton (d. 1340) were usurers (Shatzmiller, *Shylock Reconsidered*, 85; cf. a thirteenth-century legal case where a witness let slip that the defendant "took less than the archbishop takes from his debtors," cited in Helmholz, "Usury and the Medieval English Church Courts," 377). Christian lenders were perceived at times as harsher than their Jewish counterparts (Shatzmiller, *Shylock Reconsidered*, 91, 97).

116. Strickland, *Saracens, Demons and Jews*, 142; Lipton, *Images of Intolerance*, 31–40.

117. Lipton, *Images of Intolerance*, 33–34; Shatzmiller, *Shylock Reconsidered*, 47.

118. *MED*, s.v. "Jeuerie."

119. Lipton, *Images of Intolerance*, 22.

120. Cf. Lipton on a roundel in the *Bible moralisée* depicting a "moneylender, who can be read as a Jew or as a Christian exhibiting 'Jewishness' because of his occupation" (Lipton, *Images of Intolerance*, 35).

121. Chazan, *Church, State and Jew in the Middle Ages*, 217.

122. Strickland, *Saracens, Demons and Jews*, 166; Leshock, "Religious Geography," 210–12.

123. Patterson, *Chaucer and the Subject of History*, 322.

124. Just how commercialized was Chaucer's England? The population losses that happened after the economic peak of 1300 led to a decline in aristocratic income (especially for landowners), producers "pull[ing] back from the market," and the end of many village street markets (Dyer, *An Age of Transition?*, 131, 210, 154). But "in general exchange relationships survived," merchants gained a higher share of overseas trade and witnessed generally "an important period of growth," nonaristocrats enjoyed rising income, and consumerism rose (ibid., 210, 191).

125. Schofield, *London 1100–1600*, 127. On both internal and overseas trade, see Barron, *London in the Later Middle Ages*, 45–120.

126. Schofield, *London 1100–1600*, 115. Some streets were named after trades even though often the tradespeople had moved on to other areas (ibid., 116).

127. Ibid., 159.

128. Teresa, "Chaucer's High Rise."

129. For a map of the main religious houses in London, see Schofield and Lea, *Holy Trinity Priory, Aldgate*, 146, fig. 141.

130. On the Augustinian priory, see ibid.

131. Butterfield, "Introduction," 13.

132. Ibid., 14. See also Turner, "Greater London."

133. Crow and Olson, *Chaucer Life-Records*, 147. See also Jonathan Hsy's linkage of Chaucer's Aldgate Residence to the Customs House where the poet worked as two "sites of urban 'rekenynges,' each location implicated (in its own way) in everyday business and trade" (*Trading Tongues*, 42).

134. Meyer-Lee, "Literary Value and the Customs House," 381.

135. Pearsall, *Life of Geoffrey Chaucer*, 100–101; Carlson, *Chaucer's Jobs*, 5–15.

136. Pearsall, *Life of Geoffrey Chaucer*, 211; Carlson, *Chaucer's Jobs*, 28.

137. Pearsall, *Life of Geoffrey Chaucer*, 221–23. On Maghfield, see Galloway, "The Account Book and the Treasure." Chaucer's service as an esquire of the king's chamber—a job that involved a three-month trading mission in Italy, a land renowned for its bankers—enlightened him further about lending practices as they existed elsewhere in Europe (Childs, "Anglo-Italian Contacts in the Fourteenth Century"). The 1372–73 mission took Chaucer to Genoa and Florence; he also traveled to Lombardy on another lengthy Italian visit (Pearsall, *Life of Geoffrey Chaucer*, 102, 106–7).

138. I adapt the phrase from Middleton, "'New Men' and the Good of Literature."

139. Eberle, "Commercial Language and Commercial Outlook," 171.

140. Gower, *Confessio Amantis*, 5.7727–29, page 163.

141. Ganim, "Double Entry in Chaucer's *Shipman's Tale*," 299.

142. Marlowe, *The Jew of Malta*, 1.1.19, page 5.

143. Fulton, "Mercantile Ideology in Chaucer's *Shipman's Tale*," 318.

144. Galloway, "The Account Book and the Treasure," 99.

145. Lampert-Weissig, *Gender and Jewish Difference*, 83, 58.

146. Krummel, *Crafting Jewishness in Medieval England*, 91, 101.

147. Besserman, "Chaucer, Spain, and the Prioress's Antisemitism," 351.

148. *Statutes of the Realm*, 2:59.

149. Crow and Olson, *Chaucer Life-Records*, 413–29; Pearsall, *Life of Geoffrey Chaucer*, 210.

150. Crow and Olson, *Chaucer Life-Records*, 490–93.

151. On the assize, see Shaw, "Construction of the Private." See also Bayless, *Sin and Filth in Medieval Culture*, 29–64.

152. Chew and Kellaway, *London Assize of Nuisance*, 121, 102; see also 94.

153. Ibid., 121. The complaint precisely concerns a gate, probably located on the south side of the vicarage of the church, between the north yard of the church and the Guildhard yard (Bowsher et al., *London Guildhall*, 1:180).

154. Bowsher et al., *London Guildhall*, 1:55–56. See also ibid., 164, and 2:397.

155. Schofield, *London 1100–1600*, 174; Bowsher et al., *London Guildhall*, 1:55–56.

156. The exposure of the privy registers how the spaces associated with oppressed groups such as Jews are always susceptible to violation. In examples such as Thomas of Monmouth's voyeuristic gaze into Deulesalt's home, the royal confiscation of Jewish synagogues in thirteenth-century England, and the 1290 expulsion, Jews suffer spatial disenfranchisement.

157. Wordsworth, *Prioress's Tale*, 35–44, lines 121–22.

158. Bale, *Jew in the Medieval Book*, 57.

159. Anyone familiar with boy-singer legends would be attuned to the child's contact with ordure. For example, the Vernon analogue describes how the child is "fful depe I-drouned in fulþe of fen" and how upon discovery he is "Wiþen and

ffulþe riht foule bi-whorven" (Broughton, "Prioress's Prologue and Tale," 626, lines 109 and 111).

160. In the Anglo-Norman ballad, the body is so repellant that a priest makes several failed attempts to approach the boy (Michel, *Hugues de Lincoln*, 10, lines 228–31), and only does so after his corpse is washed (ibid., 11, lines 264–67). See Heng, "England's Dead Boys," S63.

161. Bernard primarily took aim at the excesses of Cluniac monasticism, especially Abbot Suger's construction program at Saint-Denis.

162. Rudolph, *"Things of Greater Importance,"* 281. For Bernard the monks' expenditure on architecture and ornament leads, in a usurious manner, to the marvelous production of more money from churchgoers, thus rendering the church yet another commercial site in the emerging medieval city.

163. Ibid., 313–14.

164. Ibid., 278–79, 281. Bernard, the first Christian writer to use *judaizare* to signify usury, frequently invests sinful actions with Jewish resonance (Baron, *Social and Religious History of the Jews*, 4:206; Rudolph, *"Things of Greater Importance,"* 278–79; and Berger, "Attitude of St. Bernard toward the Jews," 104). See also Ælred of Rievaulx (d. 1167) who, influenced by Bernard, writes in his *Mirror of Love* that grand church architecture and ornamentation will make the monk "feel like one expelled from paradise and imprisoned in a dungeon of filth and squalor" (Draper, *Formation of English Gothic*, 45).

165. A similar response to church materialisms appears in the Vernon manuscript version of the "The Jewish Boy," when the boy's attraction to material or carnal splendor in a Christian minster marks him out as stereotypically Jewish even as it may suggest, like Bernard's *Apology*, the problematically "Jewish" materialism of church ornament (Boyd, *Middle English Miracles of the Virgin*, 39, lines 51–56).

166. Kruger, "Bodies of Jews," 306.

167. I use "refrain" in the sense established by Deleuze and Guattari in their work on sound and territory (*A Thousand Plateaus*, 310–50). Bale considers the *Alma redemptoris mater* as a refrain more extensively in *Jew in the Medieval Book*, 68.

168. Broughton, "Prioress's Prologue and Tale," 589.

169. Hawkins, "Chaucer's Prioress and the Sacrifice of Praise," 615–18; see also Chaucer, *The Prioress's Tale*, ed. Boyd, 160–61; Patterson, "'Living Witnesses of Our Redemption,'" 510.

170. Noonan, *The Scholastic Analysis of Usury*, 57, 92; Langholm, *Economics in the Medieval Schools*, 56.

171. Wenzel, *Fasciculus Morum*, 350–53.

172. Maloney, "Teaching of the Fathers on Usury," 255.

173. Conrad of Saxony (Pseudo-Bonaventure), qtd. in Derbes and Sandona, "Barren Metal and the Fruitful Womb," 281–82. The following discussion of Mary is indebted to Derbes and Sandona's contextualization of Giotto's Arena Chapel.

174. Qtd. in Derbes and Sandona, "Barren Metal and the Fruitful Womb," 282. Following Aristotle, medieval thinkers defined usury as the perverse breeding of money from money (Langholm, *Economics in the Medieval Schools*, 263–65). In a Latin translation of Aristotle that was influential in the Middle Ages, the term for interest is *tokos*, a word whose Greek origins signify offspring or breed, because interest entails a sort of (artificial) reproduction.

175. Kristeva, *Powers of Horror*, 4.

176. *MED*, s.v. "wondren." See Gayk's nuanced discussion of wonder in the *Prioress's Tale* in "'To wondre upon this thyng.'"

177. On the torturous effects of badly performed music—"*musica humana* [human music] gone awry"—see Holsinger, "Pedagogy, Violence, and the Subject of Music," 190.

178. Retroactive support for this interpretation may appear at the close of the *Tale of Sir Thopas*, where Harry Bailey cuts Chaucer off in midsentence, recalling the abbot's silencing of the boy. When Harry condemns Chaucer's tail-rhyme romance as "crappy" rhyming that is "nat worth a toord!" (7.930), the excremental qualities associated with the privy and usury by the Prioress are linked to, of all things, Chaucer's poetry. But insofar as Harry's words mirror the abbot's interruption of the boy's song, we might read them as Hamel has interpreted other aspects of the *Tale of Sir Thopas*: a parodic commentary on the Prioress's performance. As Hamel has suggested, by following the *Prioress's Tale* with the adventures of the Marian devotee Thopas, Chaucer spoofs themes related by the nun. Most pointedly, Hamel shows how the fantastic nature of the Prioress's Jews emerges in their bogeyman counterpart in the *Tale of Sir Thopas*, an absurd three-headed giant whose "parodic ridicule awakens us from [the] nightmare" offered in the nun's dark tale ("And Now for Something Completely Different," 258). Similarly, Harry's interruption of Chaucer is a send-up of the abbot's interruption of the boy. When Harry dismisses Chaucer's tale as worse than filth, the Host offers a lighthearted version of the thinking behind the abbot's squelching of the miracle.

179. The enclosure of the corpse "in a tombe of marbul stones cleere" (7.681), as Bale observes, "rescinds the 'free and open' urban spaces and denies the flux of signification between Christian and Jew" (*Jew in the Medieval Book*, 85). The Ellesmere manuscript of the Canterbury Tales replaces "tombe" with "temple," a move that may suggest the "Jewishness" of the built environment in which the boy rests as well as the possible status of the dead boy as an object of idolatry. On the Ellesmere's variants, see Chaucer, *The Prioress's Tale*, ed. Boyd, 71–73.

180. Bale, *Jew in the Medieval Book*, 85; Morrison, *Excrement in the Late Middle Ages*.

181. On the different ways in which Jews are treated in analogues, see Kelly, "Prioress's Tale in Context" and Dahood, "Punishment of the Jews."

## 4. In the Shadow of Moyse's Hall

1. See the overview of scholarly debates over the late medieval English economy in Dyer, *An Age of Transition?*, 8–17. The account of the fifteenth-century English economy that follows is indebted to Dyer's book.

2. Ibid., 176–78.

3. Ibid., 228.

4. Ibid., 175. See also Bolton, *Money in the Medieval English Economy*, 227–57.

5. Dyer, *An Age of Transition?*, 178.

6. Ibid., 177.

7. Ibid., 190.

8. Ibid., 191.

9. Ibid., 126–57.

10. Ibid., 229. Merchants faced challenges that included clashes with their Hanseatic peers and the notorious mid-fifteenth-century trading slump; moreover, they didn't employ the advanced commercial techniques of Italian traders (ibid., 191–92.). But merchants were served well by their own techniques, such as the bill of sale, and formed alliances like the Merchant Adventurers and Merchants of the Staple, which imported goods (especially wool and cloth) to the Low Countries and other sites (ibid., 130, 191).

11. Warner, *Libelle of Englysche Polycye.*

12. "The Childe of Bristowe" and "The Merchant and His Son," in Hazlitt, *Remains of the Early Popular Poetry*, 110–31, 132–52.

13. "The Child of Bristowe," in Hazlitt, *Remains of the Early Popular Poetry*, 113, line 62.

14. Mann, *Chaucer and Medieval Estates Satire*, 99–102; Ladd, *Antimercantilism in Late Medieval English Literature.*

15. Dean, *Medieval English Political Writings*, 183.

16. "London Lickpenny," in Dean, *Medieval English Political Writings*, 222–25.

17. Ibid., 225, line 110.

18. While the single sixteenth-century manuscript refers to *the Play of the Conversyon of Ser Jonathas the Jewe by the Myracle of the Blyssed Sacrament* (fol. 339r), all modern editions and most critics call the play the Croxton *Play of the Sacrament* (Sebastian, *Croxton Play of the Sacrament*, line 80, s.d., and n). Subsequent line references to the play come from this modernized edition.

19. The terminus a quo appears on fol. 356, where a note describes how the miracle occurred "in the forest of Aragon, in the famous cite. Eraclea, the yere of owr Lord God M cccc. lxj." On the terminus ad quem, and the manuscript's links with print culture, see Atkin, "Playbooks and Printed Drama." Readings that, in light of the date of the Trinity manuscript, discuss the Tudor reception of Croxton include Lerer, "'Representyd now in yower syght,'" 52–55; and M. Jones, "Theatrical History."

20. Coletti, "Paupertas est donum Dei," 368–69.

21. In the earliest allegation, Latin and French texts describe how a Parisian Jew, often called Jonathan, procured in 1290 the host from either his maidservant or a poor woman seeking a pawned piece of clothing. Rubin, who cautions against viewing this charge as an origin, describes the texts (which include a sermon, the *Grandes chroniques de France*, court rulings, and liturgical books) and provides an overview (*Gentile Tales*, 40–45). A possible source for Croxton, the early fifteenth-century play *Le mistere de la Sainte Hostie*, portrays a Jewish moneylender and merchant, Jacob Mousse, acquiring the host from a poor woman, as does a sixteenth-century analogue, the *Miracolo del Corpo di Cristo* (Petryszcze, *Le Mistere de la Saincte Hostie*; Newbigin, "Dieci sacre rappresentazioni").

22. A. Schwartz, "Economies of Salvation," 9.

23. Scherb, *Staging Faith*, 72.

24. Higginbotham, "Impersonators in the Market," 179. See also Ciobanu, "City of God?"

25. A. Schwartz, "Economies of Salvation"; Lawton, "Sacrilege and Theatricality," 299; Parker, *Aesthetics of Antichrist*, 126–35. Schwartz examines the depiction of

a money economy and the doctrine of transubstantiation in both Croxton and Paolo Uccello's 1467–68 predella for the church in Urbino.

26. Parker, *Aesthetics of Antichrist*, 238; Lawton, "Sacrilege and Theatricality," 303; Beckwith, "Ritual, Church and Theatre."

27. A. Schwartz, "Economies of Salvation," 9.

28. Lawton posits that the relation between "the sacramental and the mercantile" in the play is "cognate with that between Christian and Jew" ("Sacrilege and Theatricality," 299). Implicitly aligning the sacramental with the Christian, and money with the Jew, Lawton suggests how the four concepts make up a kind of Greimasian square reflective of "the chain of dramatic semiosis" at work in the play (ibid., 297). I explore in Croxton not so much the semiotic interplay of the Jew with other signs, but the instability of the Jew as connoted in and through space.

29. Dox's important spatial reading stresses the imagined space of the spectator's mind's eye and the play's orthodox orientation ("Theatrical Space, Mutable Space, and the Space of Imagination"); Spector sheds light on the collapse and conversion of time, space, and identity ("Time, Space and Identity").

30. Some "place and scaffold" plays could have been performed in a church (Twycross, "Theatricality of Medieval English Plays," 61). As Lawton observes, the manuscript on which Croxton appears "never uses the word scaffold at all, only the less grandiose word stage" ("Sacrilege and Theatricality," 294).

31. Gibson, *Theater of Devotion*, 40. On Croxton and East Anglian ideas of the city, see Ciobanu, "City of God?"

32. A 1522 military muster indicates an estimated size of 6,514 for Bury (Gottfried, "Bury St Edmunds and the Population," 12–13).

33. Gibson, *Theater of Devotion*, 34–41; Lampert-Weissig, "Once and Future Jew." While he doesn't focus on Croxton, Bale stresses the nature of Christian piety (and its attending antisemitism) in Bury and its environs in "'House Devil, Town Saint,'" 185–210, and *Jew in the Medieval Book*, 105–43.

34. Thus while Lawton criticizes critics whose "townscape fantasies" promote a misleadingly "triumphalist view" of the play's orthodox Christianity ("Sacrilege and Theatricality," 295), I argue that a city setting could support the play's oppositional elements.

35. Ibid.

36. Gibson, *Theater of Devotion*, 34. The scope of this essay prevents any extensive engagement with Croxton's Spanish setting, whose importance Lampert-Weissig explores in *Gender and Jewish Difference*, 109–11.

37. Dutton, "Croxton Play of the Sacrament," 57.

38. Wasson considers the logistics of a performance in Croxton in "English Church as Theatrical Space," 31–32.

39. Dutton, "Croxton Play of the Sacrament," 57.

40. Bevington, *Medieval Drama*, 756; Gibson, *Theater of Devotion*, 34–35; Wasson, personal communication, 19 November 1981, quoted in Gibson, *Theater of Devotion*, 35; Lampert-Weissig, "Once and Future Jew," 236; Beckwith, "Ritual, Church and Theatre," 70, 85n25. Some work suggests that the claim on fol. 356 that "IX may play yt at ease" confirms that the play was not originally performed at Croxton, where such advice was unnecessary. While Atkin refutes this claim by demonstrating how the note reflected sixteenth-century print conventions, a Bury provenance remains possible ("Playbooks

and Printed Drama," 202). Scholars who dispute a Bury provenance include Lawton "Sacrilege and Theatricality," and Lerer, "'Representyd now in yower syght.'"

41. Gibson, *Theater of Devotion*, 35. Gibson speculates that lay and religious members of a confraternity performed the play. On "Mustowe," see Statham, "Medieval Town of Bury St Edmunds," 101. On Corpus Christi, which occurred in May and was celebrated annually starting in 1319, see Rubin, *Corpus Christi*. On the links between the feast and Bury, see Gibson, *Theater of Devotion*, 35–40.

42. Gibson, *Theater of Devotion*, 35, 38. Dox meditates on the changes regarding perception and space that might have occurred for playgoers shifting from Angel Square into St. James Cathedral in "Theatrical Space, Mutable Space, and the Space of Imagination," 173–77.

43. Cutts, "Croxton Play"; Gibson, *Theater of Devotion*, 36.

44. Gibson, *Theater of Devotion*, 36.

45. See also Beckwith, "Ritual, Church and Theatre"; Walker, "Medieval Drama"; Scherb, "Violence and the Social Body," 69–78; Nichols, "Lollard Language"; E. Campbell, "'Be Ware of the Key.'"

46. Thanks belong to John Sebastian for alerting me to how the date of Croxton challenges the Lollard thesis.

47. Early studies that attend to the play's antisemitism include Strohm, "Croxton *Play of the Sacrament*," 43; Clark and Sponsler, "Othered Bodies," 69; and Spector, "Time, Space and Identity." Ethan Campbell provides an overview of the debate over whether Croxton depicts Jews as Jews in "'Be Ware of the Key,'" 4–5.

48. Bale, *Jew in the Medieval Book*, 106.

49. Cf. Bury poet John Lydgate's Mass manual, *Merita Missae*, which urged meditating during the Fraction on "the sorrow and the woo" that Christ endured "whan the Iewyse his vaynis brake" (cited in Lampert-Weissig, "Once and Future Jew," 244).

50. "IVDEI : RISERE : DEI : PENAM : MOR[IENTIS]" (Parker and Little, *Cloister's Cross*, 13–14, 44, 52, 169, 242). On the antisemitism of the cross and its links with Bury politics, see Hoving, "Bury St Edmunds Cross" and Scarfe, *Suffolk in the Middle Ages*, 81–98. Lampert-Weissig describes other aspects of the abbey that would have contributed to antisemitism such as a series of wall paintings commissioned by Samson, with Latin verses written by him, on antisemitic legends such as Theophilus and the Jew of Bourges. The use of an oven by the father to kill his son in the latter tale resonates strongly with the scene in Croxton when Jonathas and his cohort place the host in an oven ("Once and Future Jew," 241).

51. Bale, *Jew in the Medieval Book*, 118.

52. Carefully analyzing manuscripts containing Lydgate's poem, Bale reveals Little Robert's cult as a domestic endeavor involving women recounting the Bury child's "passion" in homes before family members and servants (*Jew in the Medieval Book*, 112–18). Evidence including a reference to *cantores* in a *feretrar*'s account role suggests that Robert's remains were housed at the chapel "at least until 1520" (Lampert-Weissig, "Once and Future Jew," 240). Bale suggests that the *cantores* may have enacted a play, especially since the abbey was the setting in 1509 for a drama about St. Edmund (Bale, *Jew in the Medieval Book*, 112).

53. See Lampert-Weissig, "Once and Future Jew"; Hsia, *Myth of Ritual Murder*, 54–56; Spector, "Time, Space, and Identity," 190; and M. Jones, "Theatrical History," 230. Bale highlights the antisemitic elements of other East Anglian dramas, such as the

Macro plays, Digby plays, and N-Town plays. Croxton is part of a larger devotional trend in the region that "bequeathed a raft of antisemitic texts and images" (*Jew in the Medieval Book*, 141).

54. Palliser et al., "Topography of Towns," 164.

55. The refashioning of Bury after 1066 (which, like Norwich, entailed brutal demolitions and evicting Anglo-Saxons) persists today (Scarfe, *Suffolk Landscape*, 159). The project likely was influenced by a Norman tradition hailing to tenth-century Rouen (Gauthier, "Planning of the Town of Bury St Edmunds"). On the difficulty of pinpointing the abbots' precise contribution, see Statham, "Medieval Town of Bury St Edmunds," 102–3. On Bury versus other abbeys in the region, see Brodt, "East Anglia," 643. On Bury's grid form, see Gauthier, "Planning of the Town of Bury St Edmunds"; Fernie, "Romanesque Church," 12–14; and J. Smith, "Note on the Origin of the Town-Plan."

56. Lilley, *City and Cosmos*, 71. Abbeygate likely comprised a second axis (Gauthier, "Planning of the Town of Bury St Edmunds," 90).

57. The transverse axis only became significant after the abbey was completed, since "the building of St James' Gate, the west front and nave of the abbey church is later than the layout of the new urban area" (Gauthier, "Planning of the Town of Bury St Edmunds," 94).

58. Bury's layout made it a "stage set for a processional landscape," one single huge shrine for the town's namesake, Saint Edmund (ibid., 81). Antrobus examines how "the shrine lay at the heart of concentric markers through the landscape on the approach to the settlement and the presence of the Saint and his powers would have been a physical reality, a corporeal presence at the heart of the area" in "Urbanisation and the Urban Landscape," 267.

59. On the multiplicity of Bury's topography, which carried with it religious, social, commercial, and political valences, see Antrobus, "Urbanisation and the Urban Landscape," 258–74.

60. Gottfried, *Bury St. Edmunds and the Urban Crisis*, 94. On the relationship between Bury and other cloth markets in the region, see ibid., 100–101.

61. Ibid., 9.

62. Statham, "Medieval Town of Bury St Edmunds," 103.

63. Ibid. Statham relies on evidence drawn from both a 1295 list of taxable properties and a 1433 rental list, discussed in detail by Redstone in "St Edmunds Bury and Town Rental."

64. Statham, "Medieval Town of Bury St Edmunds," 101.

65. Redstone, "St Edmunds Bury and Town Rental," 198.

66. Gottfried, *Bury St. Edmunds and the Urban Crisis*, 29.

67. Ibid., 26–28.

68. Positing the original Anglo-Saxon market south of the abbey as the site for the postconquest market, Gauthier speculates that the Great Market may "have developed in the rear of the houses along Skinner Street" ("Planning of the Town of Bury St Edmunds," 93). Statham posits Angel Hill as the location of the original market ("Medieval Town of Bury St Edmunds," 101). Antrobus postulates that the Great Market was part of a later expansion of the town ("Urbanisation and the Urban Landscape," 172–73). Gottfried views the Great Market as postdating the conquest and originating in the twelfth century (*Bury St. Edmunds and the Urban Crisis*, 30).

While Gottfried doesn't explain this dating, he may be referring to Jocelin of Brakelond's reference to an interest in shifting the market location to increase rents for the monks (*Chronicle*, ed. and trans. Butler, 77,78); cf. Statham, "Medieval Town of Bury St Edmunds," 101–2.

69. Brodt, "East Anglia," 643. The other market was in Salisbury.

70. Antrobus, "Urbanisation and the Urban Landscape," 265; Statham, *Book of Bury St. Edmunds*, 12. On the name, see Statham, "Medieval Town of Bury St Edmunds," 103.

71. Redstone, "St Edmunds Bury and Town Rental," 198–99; Statham, "Medieval Town of Bury St Edmunds," 103–4; Statham, *Book of Bury St. Edmunds*, 142.

72. Gottfried, *Bury St. Edmunds and the Urban Crisis*, 87.

73. Ibid. Redstone, relying on the 1295 rental list, identifies in the market "rows occupied by cheesemongers, butter merchants, poulterers, as well as stalls for butchers in shambles and hog market" ("St Edmunds Bury and Town Rental," 198–99).

74. By the eighteenth century, the sculpture was in the niche on the northwest side of the archway through the Norman Tower. It is now at Moyse's Hall museum. On this sculpture, see Zarnecki, *Romanesque Lincoln*, 68 and 69, fig. 91; Zarnecki, "Romanesque Objects at Bury St Edmunds," 407–13, fig. 3; Scarfe, *Suffolk in the Middle Ages*, 82; Statham, *Book of Bury St. Edmunds*, 32.

75. Statham, "Medieval Town of Bury St Edmunds," 101.

76. Lobel, *Borough of Bury St. Edmunds*, 16–18; Gottfried, *Bury St. Edmunds and the Urban Crisis*, 77–78. The primary figures who collected income for the abbey were the cellarer and the sacrist (ibid., 16–60). On the various forms of income garnered by the abbey, see ibid., 73–84.

77. Gottfried, *Bury St. Edmunds and the Urban Crisis*, 78.

78. Eaglen, "Mint at Bury St Edmunds."

79. See Gottfried, *Bury St. Edmunds and the Urban Crisis*, esp. 215–36; Lobel, *Borough of Bury St. Edmunds*, 118–70.

80. Gottfried, *Bury St. Edmunds and the Urban Crisis*, 89. See also ibid., 89–90, 135–43.

81. Ibid., 140.

82. Gibson, *Theater of Devotion*, 23–38.

83. Vasquez makes a similar point in *Sacred Players*, 93.

84. Strickland, *Saracens, Demons and Jews*, 142; Lipton, *Images of Intolerance*, 30–53.

85. The earliest evidence of a Jewish community in Bury is a pipe role recording an 1158 payment *pro judeis* (Hillaby and Hillaby, *Palgrave Dictionary of Medieval Anglo-Jewish History*, 68).

86. On the Jews of Bury and the successful efforts of the Benedictine monk Samson of Tottington to expel them from the city, see Jocelin of Brakelond, *Chronicle*, ed. and trans. Butler; Bale, *Jew in the Medieval Book*, 105–43; Lampert-Weissig, "Once and Future Jew"; Hillaby and Hillaby, *Palgrave Dictionary of Medieval Anglo-Jewish History*, 68–72.

87. Statham, "Medieval Town of Bury St Edmunds," 104.

88. Strickland, *Saracens, Demons and Jews*, 142. See also the description of Judas as a merchant in vernacular homiletic literature (Ross, *Middle English Sermons*, 98–99).

89. Thanks belong to Lisa Lampert-Weissig, who first drew my attention to Moyse's Hall.

90. Halliday, "Moyse's Hall, Bury St. Edmunds," 27. The description of Moyse's Hall that follows relies on ibid.; M. Wood, "Moyse's Hall"; Tymms and Thompson, *Handbook of Bury St. Edmunds*, 109–11; and Antrobus, "Urbanisation and the Urban Landscape," 224–31. Roland Harris suggests that Moyse's Hall originally consisted of two separate buildings, built at the same time ("Origins and Development of English Medieval Houses," 66). Antrobus refutes this idea in "Urbanisation and the Urban Landscape," 226–28.

91. Halliday, "Moyse's Hall, Bury St. Edmunds," 27; M. Wood, "Moyse's Hall," 165.

92. Antrobus, "Urbanisation and the Urban Landscape," 229.

93. M. Wood describes the windows in "Moyse's Hall."

94. On what remains of the original Norman architecture and the changes made to the building, see Halliday, "Moyse's Hall, Bury St. Edmunds."

95. Gottfried, *Bury St. Edmunds and the Urban Crisis*, 32.

96. Gollancz, "Ramble in East Anglia." On debates about converting the building to a fire station and the eventual use of Moyse's Hall as a museum, see Samuel, "Was Moyse's Hall, Bury St. Edmunds, a Jew's House?" and Halliday, "Moyse's Hall, Bury St. Edmunds."

97. Haes, "Moyse Hall, Bury St. Edmunds," 19–20. In January 1896 a panel of three officials of the Jewish Historical Society, following Haes, rejected the idea that the building was a synagogue, though they admitted that the building may have been originally used by Jews (Martin, et al., "A Report of the Sub-Committee on Moyse's Hall"). Newspapers dismissed "Haes' thesis, but published his paper for public discussion" (Halliday "Moyse's Hall, Bury St. Edmunds," 38).

98. Gottfried, *Bury St. Edmunds and the Urban Crisis*, 31–32, repeating Redstone, "St Edmunds Bury and Town Rental," 200. Hillaby and Hillaby (*Palgrave Dictionary of Medieval Anglo-Jewish History*, 70) note the use of Barnack stone to construct both the hall and the stone houses built by Abbot Samson.

99. Hillaby and Hillaby, *Palgrave Dictionary of Medieval Anglo-Jewish History*, 70.

100. Gottfried, *Bury St. Edmunds and the Urban Crisis*, 31; Haes, "Moyse Hall, Bury St. Edmunds."

101. Lipman, *Jews of Medieval Norwich*, 120.

102. Samuel, "Was Moyse's Hall, Bury St. Edmunds, a Jew's House?," 44.

103. Lipman, *Jews of Medieval Norwich*, 3.

104. The full passage is: "About midnight on St. Helen's Day of this year, Thomas de Thornham with many fugitives and outlaws came to the town of St. Edmund's, and forcibly seized the keys of all the gates, and no man of the town hindering them, they hastened to Moyse's Hall (*ad aulam Moysii*) to breakfast, killing Roger Peasenhall a servant of the Abbey on the way. The men of the town being re-joiced at their coming, made them a famous breakfast with many gifts" (Arnold, *Memorials*, 349). The name is mentioned again in 1474 in the will of Andrew Scarbot as the tenement called "Moyse's Hall" (Tymms and Thompson, *Handbook of Bury St. Edmunds*, 97). See Haes, "Moyse Hall, Bury St. Edmunds," 23.

105. Samuel, "Was Moyse's Hall, Bury St. Edmunds, a Jew's House?," 46–47.

106. Among other evidence cited by Samuel in support of a Jewish affiliation is the presence in the Oxford Jewry of another Moyse's Hall (ibid., 46).

107. Harper-Bill, *Register of John Morton*, 4.

108. Ibid., 215. The entry is also translated and discussed in Northeast, "Superstition and Belief"; see also Halliday, "Moyse's Hall, Bury St. Edmunds," 28.

109. Harper-Bill, *Register of John Morton*, 215.

110. Ibid. While the record is in Latin, "Moises Halle" appears in English.

111. Ibid.

112. Ibid. In medieval England, particularly during wartime, people did bury treasure hoards. "Two major coin hoards of 13th-century silver pennies" were deposited in Colchester—about forty miles from Bury—during times of intense gentile–Jewish strife in England (M. Campbell, "A British Perspective," 32). On European Jewish treasure hoards, see Descatoire, *Treasures of the Black Death*.

113. Marlowe, *The Jew of Malta*, 1.2.296, page 19; Dickens, *Oliver Twist*, 67.

114. Mesler, "Legends of Jewish Sorcery," 263. The association of Jews with magic extends back to the Greeks and Romans. Mesler's dissertation, which offers an important critique of Trachtenburg's *Jewish Magic and Superstition*, elucidates the complex and manifold uses to which the concept of Jews as sorcerers was put in England and elsewhere during the Middle Ages.

115. Girouard, *English Town*, 18. Grenville, *Medieval Housing*, 159. Statham, *Accounts of the Feoffees of the Town Lands of Bury St. Edmunds*, xxxviii.

116. Gottfried, *Bury St. Edmunds and the Urban Crisis*, 23.

117. Even here, however, Aristorius's Christian faith proves problematic; after calling Christ "our Creatour," he asks God's protection from a notably secular problem, "shame" (81).

118. Sebastian, *Croxton Play of the Sacrament*, note to lines 81–124.

119. On the "lip service" paid by Aristorius to Christianity in his monologue, see also Lampert-Weissig, *Gender and Jewish Difference*, 112.

120. The European sites cited by Aristorius are Catalonia, Geneva, Calabria, Denmark, the kingdom of Navarre, Naples, Dordrecht, Genoa, Salerno, Catalan, Prussia, Rheims, Hamburg, Holland, Milan, Galicia, Maine, France, Rome, Lombardy, Orleans, Pontevedra, and Portugal; and the eastern locales are Syria, Chaldea, Alexandria, Turkestan, Antioch, Jericho, Turkey, Saba (in Arabia), and Jerusalem (95–116). Some of the referents of the place names mentioned in the speech are unclear. Pontevedra may be indicated by "Pondere" (line 111); Turkestan or possibly Tharsia or the biblical Tarsus or Tarshish may be meant by "Taryse" (line 114).

121. On the world economic system during the fifteenth century, see Tracy, *Rise of Merchant Empires*; Hugill, *World Trade Since 1431*; A. K. Smith, *Creating a World Economy*; Wallerstein, *Modern World-System*, 1:14–65; Braudel, *Civilization and Capitalism*.

122. Neither did Spanish traders; Aristorius claims a global commercial presence enjoyed only perhaps by Italian merchants during the period.

123. Gottfried, *Bury St. Edmunds and the Urban Crisis*, 91–92. See also Carus-Wilson, *Medieval Merchant Venturers*, 91. At times during the fifteenth century, Bury men joined Londoners for continental ventures (Gottfried, *Bury St. Edmunds and the Urban Crisis*, 91). On the cloth and wool trade in England, see Power, *Wool Trade*; Lloyd, *English Wool Trade*; Bridbury, *Medieval English Clothmaking*; Hanham, *The Celys and Their World*.

124. Gottfried, *Bury St. Edmunds and the Urban Crisis*, 91–92.

125. Another point of connection would have been Aristorius's boast about buying massive quantities of real estate, since members of Bury's mercantile elite such as Jankyn Smith (d. 1481) and John Edward (d. 1441) were real estate magnates (Gottfried, *Bury St. Edmunds and the Urban Crisis*, 136–66).

126. Gottfried, *Bury St. Edmunds and the Urban Crisis*, 136–66.

127. *MED*, s.v. "rennen."

128. *MED*, s.v. "temple." The second meaning of the word, which refers to the Temple of Jerusalem, may suggest the "Jewishness" of St. Peter's as a place implicated in Aristorius's trade.

129. On the play's staging of Aristorius's relationship with his priest, which superficially supports Christian supremacy (234) but in fact affirms the merchant's control over Isidore, see Sebastian, *Croxton Play of the Sacrament*, ll. 120, 232–36.

130. Gottfried, *Bury St. Edmunds and the Urban Crisis*, 140.

131. Aristorius calls Jonathas "gentyll and trew" while welcoming him into his home (377); Jonathas instructs members of his cohort to "be Jewys jentyll" with the host once they have acquired it (385; cf. 389).

132. A tonal shift could alter the meaning of the line. A sardonic reference to the "gentle Jew" would imply that Jews aren't gracious but brutish. Delivered in the Great Market, those lines could in turn have reflected critically on Moyse's Hall, whose monumental positioning might have carried a valence akin to the York mansions described by William of Newburgh. Yet the subsequent action of the play negates such a prospect.

133. Sebastian, "Introduction," *Croxton Play of the Sacrament*, 15.

134. See 143–45, where Jonathas refers in a familiar manner to Aristorius's hall, and 157, where he greets the merchant's servant Peter Paul by name.

135. For a different view, that Jonathas exhibits a "morbid materiality," see Clark and Sponsler, "Othered Bodies," 72. "The interest in the Jews here seems more worldly than theological. Like Barabas for Marlowe, Jonathas seems to function as an exemplar of the arts of wealth and power, and of self-projection": M. Jones, "Theatrical History," 233.

136. Greenblatt, "Marlowe, Marx, and Anti-Semitism," 296.

137. Spector notes how Jonathas's lines ironically invoke a blind-folded Synagoga in "Time, Space and Identity," 193.

138. Echoing the economic thrust of *Winnere and Wastoure*, Jonathas ponders whether attaining the host is a matter of acquisition or expenditure. On *Winnere and Wastoure* and mercantilism, see D. Smith, *Arts of Possession*, 72–107. On the confusion of material goods and "the moral Good" in Croxton, see Parker, *Aesthetics of Antichrist*, 128.

139. Risbygate was the most populous Bury ward (Gottfried, *Bury St. Edmunds and the Urban Crisis*, 30–33, 41).

140. On the term "burgeis," see Riddy, "'Burgeis' Domesticity in Late-Medieval England," 18–19.

141. Riddy, "'Burgeis' Domesticity in Late-Medieval England," 21; Goldberg, "Fashioning of Bourgeois Domesticity in Later Medieval England," 134. The revolution involved technologies related to the erection of larger timber-framed homes (Rees Jones, "Building Domesticity in the City," 68).

142. Wills listing a host of goods ("chairs, benches, chests, wall hangings and screens as well as eating utensils, bed linen and the like") demonstrate how bourgeois

city dwellers "placed greater value (culturally and economically) on household goods" than their rural counterparts, thus altering consumption and leading "to new patterns in the acquisition and use of material goods, which had a wider impact on the whole economy" (Goldberg, "Fashioning of Bourgeois Domesticity in Later Medieval England," 128).

143. Ibid., 133–34.

144. Gardiner, "Buttery and Pantry and Their Antecedents," 60.

145. Tymms, *Wills and Inventories*, 23.

146. Riddy, "'Burgeis' Domesticity in Late-Medieval England," 21. Coletti explores the intersection of medieval drama and issues related to domesticity in *Mary Magdalene and the Drama of Saints*.

147. Gottfried, *Bury St. Edmunds and the Urban Crisis*, 41.

148. Ibid., 106. The primary exports in England were raw wool and finished cloth, with the latter overtaking the former in importance during the fifteenth century. Most of the laborers in Bury had textile-related occupations (ibid., table 3.5, 111). Domestic demand was even greater; by the end of the century, it was "double that of exports, about 4 million yards annually" (Dyer, *An Age of Transition?*, 150). The Bury economy—and particularly, trade within the Great Market and Risbygate Ward—echoed those national trends. Bury was primarily a site not for the production but for the sale of cloth produced in the Stour Valley, though it was not the only such market (Gottfried, *Bury St. Edmunds and the Urban Crisis*, 94–101).

149. The hanging resonates instead with such items listed in Bury wills as a hanging stained with the seven ages of man and a cloth painted with the history of Robert of Sicily (Tymms, *Wills and Inventories*, 12, 33). On the hall as a site where feudal lords displayed their aristocratic eminence, see Grenville, *Medieval Housing*, 89.

150. On the magnificence displayed via household hospitality in noble homes, see Mertes, *English Noble Household*, 114. Cf. Caxton's stress in his *Dialogues in French and English* (ca. 1422) on artisanal objects and the making of mercantile identity, as analyzed by Lisa Cooper in "Urban Utterances."

151. On the role of commerce, including industrial work, in homes, see also Grenville, *Medieval Housing*, 181; Britnell, "Markets, Shops, Inns," 117–19. On medieval notions of the incommensurability of trade and piety in a house, ideas that drew on biblical passages such as John 2:16, see Davis, *Medieval Market Morality*, 123.

152. Grenville, *Medieval Housing*, 181.

153. On these shops, see Grenville, *Medieval Housing*, 173; Davis, *Medieval Market Morality*, 6; K. Morrison, *English Shops and Shopping*, 19–22. On the use of "window shutters" in Bury, see Redstone, "St Edmunds Bury and Town Rental," 203.

154. Rees Jones, "Building Domesticity in the City," 69. Gardiner discusses the centrality of the hall to the bourgeois home and its spatial layout in "Buttery and Pantry and Their Antecedents," 38.

155. Thrupp, *Merchant Class of Medieval London*, 180. On the value of orderliness and differentiation in the bourgeois home, see Riddy, "'Burgeis' Domesticity in Late-Medieval England," 29.

156. Gardiner, "Buttery and Pantry and Their Antecedents," 38.

157. Thus while, as Riddy stresses, multiple rooms allowed for the division of activities in individual rooms in the bourgeois home, individual rooms were themselves

given to multiplicity, instability, and a blurring of boundaries ("'Burgeis' Domesticity in Late-Medieval England," 21).

158. Bale, "'House Devil, Town Saint,'" 198.

159. On the use of cushions in the urban household, see Goldberg, "The Fashioning of Bourgeois Domesticity in Later Medieval England," 132.

160. Ariès, *Centuries of Childhood*, 385. Rybczynski, *Home*, 28.

161. Riddy, "'Burgeis' Domesticity in Late-Medieval England," 34. See also Rees Jones, "Building Domesticity in the City," 76.

162. Britnell, "Town Life," 139.

163. Rees Jones, "Building Domesticity in the City," 69, esp. n. 13.

164. Cf. Upton, "Seen, Unseen, and Scene." Thanks belong to Seeta Chaganti for referring me to Upton's essay. While most homes appeared from the street to be similar, they in fact had varying dimensions. Merchant homes often occupied nearly identical narrow plots (often of no more than twenty feet facing the street), and extended upward and backward. Aristorius's home also would have resonated with more imposing stone houses in Bury, described in Gottfried, *Bury St. Edmunds and the Urban Crisis*, 13, 32 (cf. Redstone, "St Edmunds Bury and Town Rental," 204).

165. Davis, *Medieval Market Morality*; Bateson, *Borough Customs*. On the practice of trade beyond the official system of boroughs and markets and their regulatory controls, see also Dyer, "Hidden Trade of the Middle Ages."

166. Davis, *Medieval Market Morality*, 177; Bateson, *Borough Customs*, lxxiv. Britnell claims that due to the "imposition of the Ordinance of Labourers in 1349," "private negotiations" were compatible "with measures of public control," in "Markets, Shops, Inns," 120.

167. Britnell, "Markets, Shops, Inns," 115.

168. See Lampert-Weissig, *Gender and Jewish Difference*, 112–13; Spector, "Time, Space and Identity," 193; M. Jones, "Theatrical History," 239.

169. Lampert-Weissig acknowledges the complexity of Croxton's depiction of Christianity, and how "the play takes the risk of showing . . . ostensible Christians . . . whose inner corruption is equally destabilizing to the Christian community as they join forces with Jews" (*Gender and Jewish Difference*, 122). On Aristorius's Judas-like qualities, see Spector, "Time, Space and Identity," 194; and Nichols, "Lollard Language," 24–25.

170. Bynum, *Wonderful Blood*, 81.

171. Sebastian, *Croxton Play of the Sacrament*, 76, note to line 391.

172. On the liturgical dimensions of Croxton, see Maltman, "Meaning and Art."

173. Goldberg, "The Fashioning of Bourgeois Domesticity in Later Medieval England," 134.

174. Beckwith, however, describes Jonathas as a "priest" whose "grotesque" nature destabilizes clerical authority in "Ritual, Church and Theatre," 75.

175. Yaeger, "Introduction."

176. Grantley, "Producing Miracles," 84.

177. Thomas of Monmouth, *Life*, I.5, 21, Rubin 17. Presumably, the post to which Jonathas and the host are nailed is meant to be some part of his house, either a post supporting the walls or ceilings of the house or possibly a doorpost (*MED*, s.v. "post"). On the prospect that the nailing occurred in the *platea*, see Dox, "Theatrical Space, Mutable Space, and the Space of the Imagination," 175.

178. Bede, *Homilies on the Gospels* II.10, 90; Shakespeare, *The Merchant of Venice*, 2.5.34.

179. Nisse, *Defining Acts*, 113. Lampert-Weissig, like Nisse, stresses the destruction of interpretive or hermeneutic agency in this moment, i.e., how Jonathas is punished for viewing the host carnally, as a mere object (Lampert, *Gender and Jewish Difference*, 101–37).

180. On medieval processes of miniaturization, see Mitchell, *Becoming Human.*

181. Tymms, *Wills and Inventories*, 36, 41. The nailing of a tiny Christian object constituting Christ's body to a post in Croxton ironically resonates with the affixing of the small Jewish object representing God—the *mezuzah*—to the doorpost of a Jewish home. Jonathas's hand's affixing to the host even recalls the ritual touching of the mezuzah. Especially ironic is the thirteenth-century Viennese rabbi Isaac ben Moses's complaint that Jews must cover over their *mezuzot* because "the Christians, out of malice and to annoy us, stick knives into the mezuzah openings and cut up the parchment" (Trachtenburg, *Jewish Magic and Superstition*, 4). Thanks belong to Lawrence Besserman for suggesting that I consider Croxton in relation to mezuzot.

182. On the host as holy matter, see Bynum, *Wonderful Blood.*

183. Homan, "Devotional Themes," 331–32; see also Bevington, *Tudor Drama and Politics*, 38.

184. On other slippages at play in this scene, see Lampert-Weissig, *Gender and Jewish Difference*, 117–19; Clark and Sponsler, "Othered Bodies," 72.

185. On medieval industry and labor, see Lopez, *The Commercial Revolution of the Middle Ages*, 125–47; Le Goff, *Time, Work, and Culture*; and Postone, *Time, Labor, and Social Domination*, 201–12.

186. On how the dismemberment and healing of Jonathas's hand and other medieval representations of "the stricken hand" function as a supersession narrative "writ small," see Lampert-Weissig, *Gender and Jewish Difference*, 102–3, 107–8, 126–28.

187. As Homan observes, the fact that Christ appears in the form of a bleeding child echoes the focus on tortured boys in ritual-murder myths ("Devotional Themes," 338–39).

188. Homan stresses how Jonathas's praise echoes the thrust of the *Arma Christi* ("Devotional Themes," 336–37).

189. Cf. the first and subsequent continental libels, where "the space which had previously been inhabited by Jews was almost always razed and reallocated for the erection of chapels after the killing or banishment of Jews" (Rubin, *Gentile Tales*, 148, 90–91). The two "virtual" desecrations staged in continental dramas, namely the French and Italian analogues to the play, repeat the pattern (Newbigin, "Dieci sacre rappresentazioni," 97; *Le Jeu*, lines 1327–28a, in Petryszcze, *Le Mistere de la Saincte Hostie*). In contrast, Croxton has Jonathas's home remain standing, due to the intersecting conversions of its occupant with that structure.

190. Lampert-Weissig, "Once and Future Jew," 247; Lampert-Weissig, *Gender and Jewish Difference*, 115; Clark and Sponsler, "Othered Bodies," 73.

191. On how Croxton's diasporic turn resonates with the nomadism of the traveling theatrical troupe, see Nisse, *Defining Acts*, 122; M. Jones, "Theatrical History," 236.

192. Cf. Lampert-Weissig, *Gender and Jewish Difference*, 115.

193. Rubin, *Gentile Tales*, 91.

194. Cf., Nisse, who views Croxton as a "profoundly anti-urban play" that culminates in an apocalyptic vision in which "the wealthy secular city falls in anticipation of the Final Judgment" (*Defining Acts*, 122). Nisse postulates the play's staging "from outside the walls" of East Anglian cities, a vantage point from which its final image of a now "desolate" city can be envisioned (ibid.).

## 5. Failures of Fortification and the Counting Houses of *The Jew of Malta*

1. Bartels, *Spectacles of Strangeness*, 83. Bartels links the "Jew" and "Malta" in terms of their indefinite and cosmopolitan multiplicity (ibid., 100). Hopkins discusses the association of Malta with renowned Jews (such as Saul/Paul) in *Christopher Marlowe*, 89–91.

2. Marlowe, *Jew of Malta*, ed. Gill, 8. All citations of the play come from this edition.

3. Cf. Hunter, "Theology of Marlowe's *The Jew of Malta*," 214.

4. Nicholas de Nicolay, *The nauigations, peregrinations and voyages*, fol. 131r. On Nicolay as Marlowe's source, see Thomas and Tydeman, *Christopher Marlowe*, 301.

5. The following year, Foxe published first the Latin sermon and then an English translation. On Menda and Foxe, see Shapiro, *Shakespeare and the Jews*, 140–42.

6. Adelman, *Blood Relations*, 148n69. Adelman qualifies Achinstein's view of the sermon in "John Foxe and the Jews," 96.

7. Foxe, *A sermon*, P1v, C4r, L4v. On the medieval tradition behind Foxe's rhetoric, see Akbari, *Idols in the East*, 112–54.

8. Foxe, *A sermon*, L4v.

9. Ibid., D1v.

10. Ibid., C6r, E6r.

11. Shapiro, *Shakespeare and the Jews*, 46–55.

12. On the *Domus* during the sixteenth century, see Adler, "History of the 'Domus Conversorum,'" 41–48.

13. Roth, "Jews of Malta," 207.

14. However, as I discuss later in this chapter, neither England nor Malta were truly devoid of Jews during the period.

15. Hoppen, *Fortification of Malta*, 10.

16. On English understandings of Malta as a defense against the spread of Islam, see Hunter, "Theology of Marlowe's *The Jew of Malta*," 228–29, and Vaughn, "Maltese Factor," 344.

17. Hoppen, *Fortification of Malta*, 10.

18. Nicholas de Nicolay, *The nauigations, peregrinations and voyages*, 17r. OED, s.v. "inexpugnable."

19. Hughes, *Fortress*, 26. The ring of high walls and towers that encircled St. Angelo followed traditional medieval methods of fortress building. Future structures adopted the newer, bastioned system of fortification, which developed during the late Middle Ages in response to the cannon and consisted of a solid triangular platform extending from the main line of the fortifications to offer gunmen a wide range of fire. Italian engineer Pietro Prado designed St. Elmo as a four-pointed star, whose points consisted of bastions that protected the curtain wall of the fort. Other forts, including Vittoriosa, St. Michael, and Senglea, also used the bastion method.

20. Hughes, *Fortress*, 42.

21. Closely related to Ferneze's investment in Jewish exile is his status as the primary character who affirms the association of Malta with fortification and the Muslim threat that spurred martial building programs on the island. After a heated exchange with the Turkish Bashaw about Malta's prospective invasion, the governor instructs his men to "Close your Port-cullise, charge your Basiliskes" (3.6.31). Ferneze reiterates his investment in bulwarks in act 5, which opens with the governor telling the knights to "see that *Malta* be well fortifi'd" in hopes that the Turks "dye before the wals" of the city (5.1.2, 5). Some sixty lines later, for a third and final time, the governor stresses Maltese fortification when he orders the knights to "fortifie the Towne" (5.1.60).

22. See also Sullivan, "Geography and Identity in Marlowe," 238. Barabas's insistent presence in Malta complicates Greenblatt's claim that the merchant embodies a "transcendental homelessness" and is "the quintessential alien" (*Renaissance Self-Fashioning*, 196).

23. Hunter, "Theology of Marlowe's *The Jew of Malta*." On Marlowe's ironic citation of Christian theology, see also Deats, "Biblical Parody in *The Jew of Malta*."

24. Hunter, "Theology of Marlowe's *The Jew of Malta*," 216.

25. Garber, "'Infinite Riches in a Little Roome,'" 13.

26. Ibid., 9.

27. Greenblatt, *Renaissance Self-Fashioning*, 195.

28. Ibid., 198. "The great fear, in Barabas' words, is 'That I may vanish o'er the earth in air, And leave no memory that e'er I was' (1.499–500)" (ibid., 197).

29. Bartels, *Spectacles of Strangeness*, 15.

30. Ibid., 91.

31. See also Hiscock, "Enclosing 'Infinite Riches in a Little Room'" and Sullivan, "Geography and Identity in Marlowe." I do not mean to imply that materialism is separable from cosmopolitanism, colonialism and secularization.

32. Greenblatt, "Marlowe, Marx, and Anti-Semitism," 296.

33. Parker offers a recent and provocative reading of Christian materialism and *The Jew of Malta*, one that suggests that by centering his play on Barabas, a man *traded* for Jesus, Marlowe exposes how Christianity embraced commerce from its very inception (*Aesthetics of Antichrist*, 193–209).

34. Machiavelli, *The Prince*, 87. Machiavelli criticizes fortifications largely because they don't protect leaders who are despised by their subjects; he goes so far as to "blame anyone who, trusting in fortresses, thinks little of being hated by the people" (ibid.).

35. Machiavelli, *Discourses on Livy*, 186.

36. Machevil's "Prologue is aimed at deceiving the spectator" since "Machiavelli's real opinions on the desirability of some governments govern the plot" (Borot, "Machiavellian Diplomacy," 8). Machevil's reference to Phalaris in his prologue implies its falsity. While Machevil claims that Phalaris would have avoided his own demise if he had relied on "strong-built" defenses, Phalaris doesn't support but questions the utility of fortified structures. The tyrant rose to power by double-crossing the very citizenry who hired him to enrich their citadel (Polyaenus, *Stratagems of War*).

37. On *The Jew of Malta* and Malta's fortifications, see Hills, "Was Marlowe's 'Malta' Malta?"; Kocher, "Marlowe's Art of War," 213.

38. Hughes, *Fortress*, 48.

39. Ibid., 52.

40. Hoppen, *Fortification of Malta*, 30. Built on the northern side of the Grand Harbor opposite to Birgu and west of St. Elmo, Valletta's origin lay in defense; the Latin inscription on the foundation stone for the city refers to the necessity of "fortifying" it "by walls, ramparts, and towers" to withstand another Turkish siege (Hughes, *Fortress*, 61).

41. Hoppen, *Fortification of Malta*, 44.

42. Ibid., 39–40.

43. Donkin and Vorholt, *Imagining Jerusalem in the Medieval West*.

44. English texts also associated contemporary, Muslim-controlled Jerusalem with fortification; travel writer Biddulph describes how "the Citie [is] walled about with strong wals, and fortified with foure strong gates and a Castle, (built by *Sultan Soliman)*" (*Travels*, 116, 125). The widely read *Peregrinatio in terram* (1486) of Bernhard von Breydenbach included Erhard Reuwich's woodcut of Jerusalem, which featured the walled city. Biddulph took pains to disassociate the Ottoman stronghold from its Jewish predecessor. He queries whether contemporary Jerusalem even occupies the same space as the earlier city and stresses how the siege utterly "razed" the city, fulfilling Matthew 27:25 (Biddulph, *Travels*, 116, 125).

45. Fortresses loom large in the Hebrew Bible. Alongside the many invocations of the fortress as a metaphor for divine protection (e.g., "God is my strong fortress," 2 Samuel 22:33; "O Lord . . . Be my rock of protection, a fortress where I will be safe. You are my rock and my fortress," Psalm 31) is a repeated stress on Jerusalem as a "mighty fortress" (e.g., Jeremiah 21:13). After the fall of the First Temple, the prophets promoted the city's restoration, which Nehemiah took up by "build[ing] up the walls of Jerusalem" (Nehemiah 2:17). The Hebrew Bible ultimately relates an epic tale of the building, demolition, and rebuilding of Jerusalem and its defensive walls.

46. On the popularity of Josephus (who describes both Herod's building programs in Jerusalem, including the Antonia fortress, and the demolition of those defenses during the siege), see P. Burke, "Survey of the Popularity of Ancient Historians" and Feldman, *Studies in Hellenistic Judaism*, 239–40. On Peter Morwyn's translation of a medieval Hebrew text attributed to Yosippon (Joseph Ben Gorian), which was printed first in 1558 and often reprinted, see Reiner, "English Yosippon." On dramatizations of the fall of Jerusalem, see Groves, "'They repented at the preaching of Ionas,'" 146. On the popularity of traveller's accounts of the holy land during the early modern period, see Noonan, *Road to Jerusalem*.

47. Rotenberg-Schwartz, "Early Modern Jewish Prayer," 197–98.

48. Shulhan 'arukh at Orah Hayim 560:1. Karo, *Code of Hebrew Law*.

49. In recent decades much work on early modern Hebraism has been published, including Coudert and Shoulson, *Hebraica veritas?*

50. On Marlowe's possible consultation of De Bellay's *Instructions for the warres* in having Barabas lead the Turks into Malta through a sewage vault, see Kocher, "Marlowe's Art of War," 222.

51. Kermode, "'Marlowe's Second City,'" 223.

52. To the extent that Barabas helps the Turks (of course he goes on to betray them), he reflects how some Jews living in the Ottoman world worked together with

Muslims, as, for example, go-betweens, travel companions, and financial advisors (Vitkus, *Turning Turk*, 180). While it's unclear if any Jews actually assisted the Turks during the 1565 siege of Malta, a rumor that they helped finance the attack and served as spies for the Turks did circulate (Roth, "Jews of Malta," 216).

53. Dugan, "*Coriolanus* and the 'rank-scented meinie.'"

54. Ibid., 143.

55. Ibid., 140.

56. Ibid., 143.

57. On More, Crowley, and Lever, see N. Wood, *Foundations of Political Economy*.

58. Wager, *A comedy or enterlude intituled, Inough is as good as a feast*, line 1443. Subsequent line citations of the play are taken from this edition. On Wager, see Eccles, "William Wager and His Plays."

59. Wilson, *A right excellent and famous comedy, called The three ladies of London*, 2.104–5. Subsequent act and line citations of *The Three Ladies* appear in the text.

60. Games, "England's Global Transition," 24.

61. D. Harvey, "Globalization in Question," 2. Wallerstein, *Modern World-System*.

62. Vitkus, "'Common Market of All the World,'" 23. My account of England's role in the sixteenth-century world economy is indebted to Vitkus, "'Common Market of All the World'" and "New Globalism."

63. Andrews, *Trade, Plunder and Settlement*, 8.

64. Frederick, *A true and faithful narrative*; Rye, *England as Seen by Foreigners*, 7.

65. Howard, *Theater of a City*, 1. On English global commerce, see Brenner, *Merchants and Revolution*; Andrews, *Trade, Plunder and Settlement*. On London's role in English expansion, see Howard, *Theater of a City*, 1–2, and works cited on 217n5.

66. Vitkus, "'Common Market of All the World," 23–24; Skilliter, *William Harborne and the Trade with Turkey*, 34–138.

67. Agnew, *Worlds Apart*.

68. Bartolovich, "'Baseless Fabric,'" 18.

69. Schofield, "Topography and Buildings of London," 319. Friedrichs discusses how not early modernity but the Middle Ages was one of the "truly creative and transforming epochs in the history of the European city" in *Early Modern City*, 10.

70. Vitkus, "New Globalism," 34. Schofield, "Topography and Buildings of London," 300. The deterioration of the walls related both to the absence of any military threat (ibid.) and the rapid expansion of the population in the later decades of the sixteenth century (Friedrichs, *Early Modern City*, 24–25).

71. Andrews, *Ships, Money, and Politics*, 16–17, appendix A.

72. Commerce had a similar effect on Malta, whose central location in the Mediterranean, at the crossroads of multiple commercial routes, rendered the island an important trading center. When it came to business, Malta opened itself—to a far greater degree than did its English insular counterpart to the northwest—to the flow of goods, persons, and persons-as-goods. Thus in the *Navigations*, shortly after Nicholas de Nicolay celebrates the "inexpugnable" nature of Malta's forts, he describes how "shee is inhabited & peopled with a great number of Commaunders, Knights and Merchants of all nations: and aboue all there is great aboun | daunce of Curtisans, both Greeke, Italian, Spaniards, Moores, and Maltez" (*The nauigations, peregrinations and voyages*, fol. 17r). Malta's commercial impulses even allowed, as Roth shows, for the presence there of Jews, in the form of slaves and the occasional merchant ("Jews of

Malta," 213–16). Barabas shares little with those Jews, whose habitation of Malta was radically circumscribed, even in the case of merchants (ibid., 242–43).

73. Howard, *Theater of a City*, 10. Bartolovich helpfully articulates the disclocation entailed by global commerce in "'Baseless Fabric,'" 19–20.

74. Howard, "Introduction," 19. Howard offers a sustained reading of the Royal Exchange in *Theater of a City*, 29–67.

75. Howard, *Theater of a City*, 9. The term "foreigner" referred to residents of London who had migrated from elsewhere in England. About 13 percent of the "stranger" population in London consisted of merchants. Most immigrants from abroad worked in the cloth industry. Of course many immigrants to England also were escaping religious persecution. The slave trade also involved bringing foreign persons as "goods" into the metropolis (Selwood, *Diversity and Difference*, 1, 25–26, 34).

76. Kirk and Kirk, *Returns of Aliens*, 396.

77. Selwood, *Diversity and Difference*, 1, 25–26.

78. For an overview of the history of the construction of purpose-built playhouses, see Bowsher and Miller, *The Rose and the Globe*, 19–21; on the economics of the Elizabethan theater and the composition of audiences at the Rose, see Gurr, *Playgoing in Shakespeare's London*, 70–78.

79. Howard, *Theater of a City*, 5, 219n16.

80. Mullaney, *Place of the Stage*; see also Bly's revision of Mullaney's thesis in "Playing the Tourist in Early Modern London."

81. Schofield, *London 1100–1600*, 38.

82. Most ships docked east of the bridge, due to its limited clearance. Four quays lay west of London Bridge to Three Cranes Wharf, where one could find important ports such as Queenhithe, and the Steelyard, where Hanse merchants congregated until 1597, when Elizabeth expelled them from the port (Schofield, *London 1100–1600*, 132).

83. Schofield, *London 1100–1600*, 132.

84. J. Stow, *Survey of London*, 167.

85. Wolf, "Jews in Elizabethan England." On the term Marrano, a Spanish word for "swine" that functioned at the time as a pejorative descriptor for suspect converts, see Farinelli, *Marrano*. For an overview of scholarship on Jews in early modern England, see Shapiro, *Shakespeare and the Jews*, 67–76.

86. Campos, "Jews, Spaniards, and Portingales," 603.

87. Wolf, "Jews in Elizabethan England," 19; J. Harris, *Sick Economies*, 68–71. References not only to Dutch but also Portuguese aliens mentioned in lists of "returns" may refer to Jews.

88. Israel, *European Jewry in the Age of Mercantilism*; Ruderman, *Early Modern Jewry*; and Cohen et al., *Jewish Culture in Early Modern Europe*. Ruderman's groundbreaking book criticizes Israel's thesis that gentile majority societies were the impetus behind key aspects of Jewish culture.

89. Ruderman, *Early Modern Jewry*, 19.

90. By calculated I refer to gentile nations' interest in not benefiting Jews per se but advancing their own economic interests. This is not to deny that at times gentiles have welcomed Jews for more genuinely benevolent reasons. On the ambiguous, complex, and contingent nature of philosemitism as a concept, see Sutliffe and Karp, "Introduction."

91. Ruderman, *Early Modern Jewry*, 14.

92. Ibid., 25.

93. Ibid., 34.

94. Ibid. See also Israel, *Diasporas within a Diaspora*. As Israel points out, this economic function was performed not only by Jews but also by members of "the Armenian diaspora, of the Greeks outside Greece, and post-1685 Huguenots, as well as all sections of the Jewish people" (ibid., 2).

95. On these men, see Wolf, "Jews in Elizabethan England," 8–33.

96. On Marlowe and Norton Folgate, where he likely settled due to its contiguity to Halliwell or Holywell, the center of theatrical activity in London during the 1580s, see Kuriyama, *Christopher Marlowe*, 74–81; and Eccles, *Christopher Marlowe in London*, 114–27.

97. Lancashire, *London Civic Theatre*, 132–38; Manley, *Literature and Culture in Early Modern London*, 223.

98. The informant, Pedro de Santa Cruz, had lived in London for ten months. The entire deposition appears in Wolf, "Jews in Elizabethan England," 45–49; a translation of the relevant passage appears in Baron, *Social and Religious History of the Jews*, 13:129.

99. On Nunez, see Meyers, "Dr Hector Nunez" and "Debt in Elizabethan England." Nunez was the first Jew named in Pedro de Santa Cruz's testimony (Katz, *Jews in the History of England*, 64).

100. In 1582 "his household" on Mark Lane "consisted of his wife, three clerks, a butler and two negresses" (Wolf, "Jews in Elizabethan England," 9).

101. Roth, *History of the Jews in England*, 140.

102. Meyers, "Debt in Elizabethan England," 125–26.

103. Meyers, "Dr Hector Nunez," 129.

104. Inquisition informant Pedro de la Cruz relates an anecdote about how, while dining with the wife of an English merchant, Nunez received letters from Jeronimo Pardo brought by one of his ships and "rose from the table without finishing his dinner and took them to Senor Gualzingham" (Wolf, "Jews in Elizabethan England," 23–24, 46–47; cf. Roth, *History of the Jews in England*, 140).

105. Gill notes that Kirriah Jairim seems to reference the city Kiriáth-iearím (1 Chron. 2:50) and Obed the father of Jesse (1 Chron. 2:12): Marlowe, *Jew of Malta*, ed. Gill, 99.

106. Griffin, *English Renaissance Drama and the Specter of Spain*, 118.

107. Ibid.

108. See especially Lunney, *Marlowe and the Popular Tradition*, 93–124.

109. "The riches commended to the audience's attention are not entirely to be rejected: the 'heaps of gold' add some glamour to the scene, summoning dreams of 'infinite riches'" (Lunney, *Marlowe and the Popular Tradition*, 110).

110. Bullinger, *Fiftie godlie and learned sermons*, iii. ii. sig. Cc.iijv/2. See also Turberville et al., *Tragicall tales*, 117.

111. Thomson, "Marlowe's Staging of Meaning," 19; Lupton, *Citizen-Saints*, 67.

112. On the rapidity with which Marlowe shifts audience attention from the counting house to the space of the theater and then the greater world of Malta, see also Lupton, *Citizen-Saints*, 67, and Cheney, *Marlowe's Counterfeit Profession*, 145.

113. Jardine, *Reading Shakespeare Historically*, 97–98.

114. Barabas's "pursuit of wealth does not mark him out but rather establishes him—if anything, rather respectably—in the midst of all the other forces in the play" (Greenblatt, "Marlowe, Marx, and Anti-Semitism," 296).

115. Honan, *Christopher Marlowe*, 260.

116. Marlowe would have learned about the appropriations entailed by the expulsion by reading accounts in texts such as Holinshed, *Chronicles*, 285.

117. *Three Ladies* exhibits a kind of philosemitism, but one predicated on how the good Jewish lender becomes "Christian."

118. Marlowe's work influenced later notions of the destructive "Jewishness" of merchants, such as the anonymous 1593 Dutch Church Libel, which states that foreign merchants "like the Jewes . . . eate us vp as bread," "leave vs all for dead," and "Cutthroate like in selling . . . vndoe / vs all" ("A Libell, fixte upon the French Church Wall. Anno 1593," lines 8, 6, 23–24, in Freeman, "Marlowe, Kyd and the Dutch Church Libel," 50). Shakespeare would help keep alive the offensive idea of the lethal, greedy Jew in *Merchant*, where Shylock proves willing to kill Antonio for violating his bond with the banker. On Marlowe, the Dutch libel, and the association of Jews with the "threat" posed by aliens, see Shapiro, *Shakespeare and the Jews*, 184–85.

119. Horstmann, *Nova legenda Anglie*, 452–54; Görlach, *Kalendre of the Newe Legende*, 174–75; Holinshed, *Chronicles*, 56, 253; Foxe, *Actes and Monuments*, 213; Schedel, *Liber chronicarum*, fol. cci b. On Schedel's chronicle, see Hsia, *Myth of Ritual Murder*, 46–48; and Shapiro, *Shakespeare and the Jews*, 103–4. The account of Simon in Schedel's book—whose press run in Latin and German was a colossal 2,500—was so influential that it attracted English tourists to Trent (ibid., 257n55). Visual images of William of Norwich's "martyrdom" also survived the Reformation in Norfolk churches (Jessopp and James, "Introduction," lxxxvi–lxxxvii). A much-reprinted translation of a work by Socrates Scholasticus claimed that Jews practiced ritual murder even before the medieval period, in fifth-century Syria (Shapiro, *Shakespeare and the Jews*, 104).

120. On the prevalence of the ritual-murder myth even up to the twentieth century (and published refutations of the charge), see Shapiro, *Shakespeare and the Jews*, 100–111; Hsia, *Myth of Ritual Murder*, esp. table 1 (p. 3) and 111–35.

121. Before his confinement in Zacharie's home, a drunken Jack falls into the cellar door of another Jew, Zadoch. Evincing a stereotypical greed, Zadoch claims Jack as his slave and sells him to Zacharie, whose quasi-erotic groping of Jack's naked body resonates with the queer elements of several ritual-murder tales (Nashe, *The vnfortunate traueller*, M2r–M3v).

122. Booth, "Shylock's Sober House," 23.

123. *OED*, s.v. "harbour," v., 3 a.

124. On this tradition, see Whitehead, *Castles of the Mind*, 90–100.

125. Ibid., 101.

126. Abigail's commodification resonates with the history of Bankside as a locus of many "stews" or brothels (including one named the Rose), which were closed in 1546 (Bowsher and Miller, *The Rose and the Globe*, 14–16). On the libidinal aspects of Barabas's commercial embrace of Abigail, see Freedman, *Temple of Culture*, 70–71.

127. The use of the tiring house wall to portray both Barabas's house and the convent might have strengthened this correlation between the two structures. On the

ironic conflation of spaces like the tiring house wall through rapid plot shifts in the play, see Thomson, "Marlowe's Staging of Meaning," 30.

128. Greenblatt, "Marlowe, Marx, and Anti-Semitism," 296.

129. Cf. Kitch, "Shylock's Sacred Nation," 146.

130. Cook, *Letters to Cromwell*, 243.

131. Ibid.

132. Schofield, "Topography and Buildings of London," 305.

133. On the conversion of a convent to secular uses in Marlowe's boyhood home of Canterbury, see Riggs, *World of Christopher Marlowe*, 15n1. On the prospect that such buildings would revert back to their Christian uses, see Parker, "Barabas and Charles I."

134. Schofield, "Topography and Buildings of London," 313. The hospital for the mentally ill in St. Mary's Bethlehem (i.e., Bedlam) was retained by the city as was the church of St. Mary's Ovarie (i.e., Southwark Cathedral).

135. Schofield, *London 1100–1600*. On the use of monastic complexes as theaters, see Mullaney, *Place of the Stage*.

136. Schofield writes of the London craftsmen who "cannibaliz[ed]" monastic buildings, "the livery companies were as avaricious as anybody else" (*London 1100–1600*, 118). This is not to say that appropriations of monastic lands were motivated entirely by greed. See for example Bernard, *King's Reformation*, 455–56.

137. Lupton, *Citizen-Saints*, 69.

138. Cf. Freedman, *Temple of Culture*, 69–73.

139. Earlier in the play, Mathias first conjures the idea of the besieged lover when he tells Lodowick that Abigail is so "matchlesse beautifull," "As had you seene her 'twould haue mou'd your heart, / Tho countermin'd with walls of brasse, to loue, / Or at the least to pitty (1.2.25–29). Mathias's formulation reverses gender roles, with Lodowick's fortified heart submitting to the onslaught of Abigail's exceptional good looks. Mathias recalls the long dramatic tradition of staging the siege of a castle of love (Loomis, "Allegorical Siege in the Art of the Middle Ages," 255–58). His metaphor also has historical and material dimensions. When he describes Lodowick's heart as "*countermin'd* with walls of brasse" (my emphasis), Mathias uses a military term for the erection of a wall beyond or within another wall to provide additional defense against an enemy in the event of the breaching of the first wall. The concept of the countermining, like related military terms such as countermure (a defensive excavation cited in 2 *Tamburlaine* 3.2.73) and counterscarping (a wall built upon a defensive ditch, cited in 2 *Tamburlaine* 3.2.68), affirms the defensive function of fortifications even as it admits a vulnerability to rupture that requires multiple defensive structures in the fort. One wall never suffices, but rather multiple ramparts, ditches, tunnels, and bulwarks are needed when facing an enemy, a fact made especially pertinent since the advent of the cannon in England in the fourteenth century.

140. Such mergings of built environment and person suggest that Abigail is deluded when, after learning that her father engineered her suitors' deaths, returns to the "new-made convent." Speaking to Jacomo, Abigail professes a true revolution within her self; no longer "chain'd to follies of the world," she has a newfound ability to "see the difference of things" (3.3.63–65). Reflecting long-standing antisemitic notions of Jewish blindness and Christian supersession, Abigail seems to have risen to an enlightened, Christian spirituality that the convent will foster. But in the play, there really isn't a "difference of things." Merchant house merges with religious

house, and Jew merges with non-Jew in the greedy give-and-take of Marlowe's Malta. When, after Barabas poisons the convent, Abigail dies, Bernardine indicates her status as a commodified sexual object, when he laments that she died a virgin. Then, asking Jacomo to "help to bury this," the friar refrains from naming Abigail or, for that matter, referring to her as a dead nun or person.

141. See for example, Broughton, "Prioress's Prologue and Tale," 610–11, 614–15.

142. On the meaning of "gallery" (which could refer to a passage, a lobby, or a long room) see Schofield, *Medieval London Houses*, 84–86. The balcony at the back of the stage (situated directly above the discovery space) must have been use to indicate Barabas's gallery.

143. Barabas thus resembles the Sicilian tyrant cited by Machevil in the prologue, Phalaris, who ended up dying in the brass bull he created to torture his enemies.

144. This plot detail of course resonates with the fate of the father in "The Jewish Boy," who is placed in the scalding oven where he earlier had shut up his child.

145. Marshe, *Records of the Worshipful Company of Carpenters*, 146.

146. Schofield, *Medieval London Houses*, 74.

147. Counting houses were placed in a variety of locations, including the ground floor of homes, behind warehouses and at the back of shops, and on the second floor (ibid.).

148. Schofield, *London Surveys of Ralph Treswell*, 54, and *Medieval London Houses*, 170.

149. Schofield, *London Surveys of Ralph Treswell*, 94, item 29.

150. On the dimensions of the discovery space and other components of the stage of the Rose, see Gurr, *Shakespearean Stage*.

151. E.g., Topsell, *Times lamentation*, 166; the anonymous broadside *The daunce and song of death*; Udall, *The state of the Church of Englande*, 2v; Humpston, *A sermon preached at Reyfham*, 22v.

152. Schofield describes the presence of counting houses in Southampton, King's Lynn, and other towns (*Medieval London Houses*, 74).

153. Schofield, *London Surveys of Ralph Treswell*, 54.

## 6. Readmission and Displacement

1. Méchoulan and Nahon, "Introduction," 26–28; Kaplan et al., *Menasseh ben Israel*.

2. Menasseh ben Israel, *Humble Addresses*, in Wolf, *Menasseh ben Israel's Mission to Oliver Cromwell*, 73, 76. Subsequent citations of Wolf's facsimile reprint of the *Humble Addresses* appear in the text.

3. Menasseh ben Israel, *Vindiciae Judaeorum*, in Wolf, *Menasseh ben Israel's Mission to Oliver Cromwell*, 144; Jessey, *Narrative of the Late Proceeds*.

4. Factors such as the presence of Marranos make the term "readmission" a misnomer (Shapiro, *Shakespeare and the Jews*, 59). I nevertheless use the term because it registers how the Whitehall debates considered officially making a place for openly practicing Jews in England.

5. Shapiro, *Shakespeare and the Jews*, 60.

6. The 24 March petition is reprinted in Wolf, *Menasseh ben Israel's Mission to Oliver Cromwell*, lxxxv–lxxxvi.

7. Domestic State Papers, Charles II, PRO, CI, Aug. 22 Whitehall, cited in Pollins, *Economic History of the Jews*, 38–39; and Roth, *History of the Jews in England*, 167–72.

8. John Sadler, letter on behalf of Rachel Abrabanel (wife of Menasseh ben Israel) to Richard Cromwell, in Wolf, *Menasseh ben Israel's Mission to Oliver Cromwell*, lxxxviii.

9. Guibbory, *Christian Identity, Jews, and Israel*, 231.

10. Shapiro, *Shakespeare and the Jews*, 57; Guibbory, *Christian Identity, Jews, and Israel*, 220; D. Katz, *Philo-Semitism and the Readmission of the Jews to England*; Samuel, "Readmission of the Jews to England."

11. Another key issue was the contested yet shared claims of Jews and Christians on Israel (Guibbory, *Christian Identity, Jews, and Israel*, 230–39).

12. D. Katz, *Philo-Semitism and the Readmission of the Jews to England*, 244.

13. Another response to the *Demurrer* was D. L., *Israels Condition and Cause Pleaded*.

14. Work on *Samson Agonistes* as a political work that responds to the Restoration includes Mueller, "The Figure and the Ground"; Achinstein, "*Samson Agonistes* and the Drama of Dissent"; Loewenstein, *Representing Revolution in Milton and His Contemporaries*, 269–91; and Lewalski, *The Life of John Milton*, 525–36.

15. Wolf, "Introduction," in *Menasseh ben Israel's Mission to Oliver Cromwell*, xxxvii.

16. Guibbory, "England, Israel and the Jews in Milton's Prose," 19.

17. Shapiro, *Shakespeare and the Jews*, 103; the cults of William of Norwich and Hugh of Lincoln did weaken (D. Katz, *Philo-Semitism and the Readmission of the Jews to England*, 41).

18. Wolf, *Menasseh ben Israel's Mission to Oliver Cromwell*, 101, 110–24; Prynne, *A Short Demurrer*, A3v; Prynne, *The second part of a Short demurrer*, 45–46.

19. On the origins and spread of the legend, see Anderson, *Legend of the Wandering Jew*.

20. The earliest English versions are Roger of Wendover's and Matthew Paris's thirteenth-century accounts of how Pilate's porter Cartaphilus (who may be a Roman or a Jew) mocks Christ as he goes out the door of Pilate's court (Anderson, *Legend of the Wandering Jew*, 18–19). Thirteenth-century visual images of Cartaphilus, including one from Paris's *Chronica Majora*, set the scene outside on the road to Calvary (Lewis, *Art of Matthew Paris*, 300–304).

21. Brathwaite, *Whimzies*, 149. The passage makes the Jew an emblem of all travelers.

22. Cf. how Donne in a sermon implicitly cites the Wandering Jew when he describes how God's "inexorableness" determined that all Jews "must lose their rest, they must have no rest" (*Sermons*, 185–86; cf. Matar, "Date of John Donne's Sermon"; Shapiro, *Shakespeare and the Jews*, 177).

23. Shapiro, *Shakespeare and the Jews*, 178.

24. Hinds, *Calendar of State Papers*, 138.

25. Rollins, *Pack of Autolycus*, 58–59.

26. Menasseh ben Israel, *Vindiciae Judaeorum*, in Wolf, *Menasseh ben Israel's Mission to Oliver Cromwell*, 118.

27. D. Katz, *Philo-Semitism and the Readmission of the Jews to England*, 179; cf. ibid., 178–80.

28. Guibbory, *Christian Identity, Jews, and Israel*, 52–55, 74–88, 187–88.

29.  "The Jew's Commendation of St. Paul's," in Rollins, *Pack of Autolycus*, 59–61 at 59. Tellingly, the Jew does not mention Solomon's Temple, though it certainly informs the poem; perhaps the balladeer knew better than to elevate the cathedral over the privileged temple.

30.  Roth, "Leone da Modena and England," 215.

31.  Leone wrote his guidebook at the prompting of an "English nobleman," very likely Sir Henry Wotton, who intended to present it to James I (Marcus, *Jew in the Medieval World*, 406–8; Roth, "Leone da Modena and England"). Manuscripts circulated among Hebraist William Boswell, Jewish legal scholar John Seldon, and others well before its 1637 printing in Paris (Roth, "Leone da Modena and England" and "Leone da Modena and His English Correspondents").

32.  M. Cohen, "Leone da Modena's *Riti*," 288. Cohen qualifies Roth's take on the *Riti* as "one of the many harbingers and preparatives of the Readmission" that evinces a "friendly interest in the Jews" by Protestant Hebraists (Roth, "Leone da Modena and England," 215).

33.  Leone da Modena, *The history of the rites, customes, and manner of life*, 4.

34.  Ibid., 5, 7.

35.  Ibid., 8.

36.  Wolf, "Menasseh ben Israel's Study in London," 145–46.

37.  Ibid.

38.  The New Exchange was built on the former grounds of Durham Palace and was based on Thomas Gresham's Royal Exchange in the center of the city (Peck, "Building, Buying and Collecting in London," 277–79). While the Puritans had done much to diminish the grandeur of the Strand by 1655, "it was still the centre of such fashion as remained" (Wolf, "Menasseh ben Israel's Study in London," 146).

39.  On Jews in seventeenth-century London, see D. Katz, *Philo-Semitism and the Readmission of the Jews to England*, 1–10; Guibbory, *Christian Identity, Jews, and Israel*, 221–22. On how England's Marrano community became more open, see Endelman, *Jews of Britain*, 15–19.

40.  Trans. Roth in "New Light on the Resettlement," 116.

41.  Menasseh ben Israel, *Vindiciae Judaeorum*, in Wolf, *Menasseh ben Israel's Mission to Oliver Cromwell*, 144.

42.  Guibbory discusses the role of a reciprocal lovingkindness in *Hope* in *Christian Identity, Jews, and Israel*, 225–26.

43.  Menasseh also argued that God rewards those who protect and punishes those who mistreat Israel (D. Katz, *Philo-Semitism and the Readmission of the Jews to England*, 160, 167).

44.  Menasseh ben Israel, *Vindiciae Judaeorum*, in Wolf, *Menasseh ben Israel's Mission to Oliver Cromwell*, 139–43. On Jewish tolerationist Simone Luzzatto's influence on Menasseh's arguments, see Kaplan, "Political Concepts in the World of the Portuguese Jews of Amsterdam during the Seventeenth Century," 51.

45.  On Menasseh's messianism and Christian millenarianism, see Popkin, "Jewish Messianism and Christian Millenarianism"; and Fisch, " Messianic Politics of Menasseh ben Israel." Some English millenarians believed in a restoration of the Jews not to Israel but to the heavenly Jerusalem (Guibbory, *Christian Identity, Jews, and Israel*, 186–90).

46.  Guibbory, *Christian Identity, Jews, and Israel*, 225.

47. Published in Hebrew, Spanish, Latin, and English, *Hope* offered an appealing mix, "of explorer literature, Jewish history, anthropological speculation about human dispersions, and prophetic interpretation of human history" (Popkin, "Jewish Messianism and Christian Millenarianism," 75). Wall's 1650 translation enjoyed several printings and reprintings before Menasseh arrived in London.

48. Menasseh ben Israel, *Hope of Israel*, in Wolf, *Menasseh ben Israel's Mission to Oliver Cromwell*, 20. Subsequent citations of Wolf's facsimile reprint of the 1652 second corrected version of *Hope* appear in the text. As Méchoulan and Nahon point out, "this was the text available to English readers at the time of the public controversy" over readmission ("Introduction," 97).

49. Montezino's narrative also appeared in Thorowgood, *Ievves in America*.

50. Menasseh ben Israel, *Vindiciae Judaeorum*, in Wolf, *Menasseh ben Israel's Mission to Oliver Cromwell*, 143.

51. D. Katz, *Philo-Semitism and the Readmission of the Jews to England*, 147; cf. Roth on *Angleterre* in "New Light on the Resettlement," 114.

52. Lavezzo, *Angels on the Edge of the World*.

53. Popkin, "Jewish Messianism and Christian Millenarianism," 70; Guibbory, *Christian Identity, Jews, and Israel*, 21–55, 221–39.

54. "Doceo autem quomodo primi fuerint Americae inventores Israelitae nostri; aliorum nilmoratus opiniones, quas breviter tantum refutare visum fuit" ("Van der Wall, "Three Letters," 60). Thorowgood claims in *Ievves in America* that "the Westerne Indians be of Jewish race" (3), and Dury similarly promotes a Jewish Indian theory ("An Epistolicall Discourse Of Mr. IOHN DURY, TO Mr. THOROWGOOD," in Thorowgood, *Ievves in America*, after preface).

55. Kaplan, "Political Concepts in the World of the Portuguese Jews of Amsterdam during the Seventeenth Century," 53.

56. Cf. Menasseh's argument that the English should welcome the Jew due to the "purity" of their blood (*Vindiciae Judaeorum*, in Wolf, *Menasseh ben Israel's Mission to Oliver Cromwell*, 81; see Kaplan, "Political Concepts in the World of the Portuguese Jews of Amsterdam during the Seventeenth Century," 50–52).

57. Popkin, *Christian Jews and Jewish Christians*, 63. See also D. Katz, *Philo-Semitism and the Readmission of the Jews to England*; Roth, *Life of Menasseh ben Israel*, 183–90; Toon, *Puritans, the Millennium and the Future of Israel*, 117–20.

58. Roth, *Life of Menasseh ben Israel*, 252.

59. Popkin, "Christian Jews and Jewish Christians," 63.

60. D. Katz, "Menasseh Ben Israel's Christian Connection," 118–19 and (on Jessey) passim; Hesseyon, "*Gold Tried in the Fire*," 386.

61. Menasseh ben Israel, *Of the Term of Life*, iv, cited in D. Katz, "Menasseh Ben Israel's Christian Connection," 118; cf. Popkin, "Christian Jews and Jewish Christians," 63.

62. *Domestic State Papers, Commonwealth*, London PRO, cliii, entry 122, Feb. 19, 1657, cited in Wolf, *Menasseh ben Israel's Mission to Oliver Cromwell*, lxxxvi.

63. Ibid., lxix.

64. Second in importance to Prynne is William Hughes, whose *Anglo-Judaeus* (1656) Guibbory discusses in *Christian Identity, Jews, and Israel*, 234–37. On the printing history of the *Demurrer*, see Saltman, *Jewish Question in 1655*, 22–24.

65. Prynne, *A Short Demurrer*, 2; Douglas, *Purity and Danger*, 36.

66. Prynne, *A Short Demurrer*, 72.

67. Prynne, *The second part of a Short demurrer*, 130. Prynne does write that children could make "a special Fine with the Kings Iustices for" their deceased ancestors' property and gain "a special Writ of restitution awarded to give them actuall possession of them" (ibid., 28).

68. Ibid., 48, 53.

69. Ibid., 24.

70. E.g., ibid., title page, 2, 33, 59, 103, 116, 125, 128, and 136.

71. Ibid., 104.

72. Ibid., 105, 124; cf. 104.

73. Ibid., 36.

74. Ibid.; Saltman, *Jewish Question in 1655*, 19.

75. Wolf, *Menasseh ben Israel's Mission to Oliver Cromwell*, lvii.

76. Levy, "Anglo-Jewish Historiography," 6–7.

77. Ibid., 4.

78. Ibid., 7.

79. Saltman, *Jewish Question in 1655*, 20.

80. Prynne, *The second part of a Short demurrer*, 4.

81. See R. Holme's 1688 definition of "Summer Houses, Bowers" in *The Academy of Armory* (iii. xii. 453/1) as "Places to which the Gentry resort, and abide there dureing the Summer season, for their Recreation and pastime" (cited in *OED*, s.v. "summer house").

82. Prynne, *A Legall Vindication Of the Liberties of England*, 25–26.

83. Ibid., 26.

84. On 30 June 1650, he was arrested and transported to Dunster Castle, sixty miles southwest of his home. Due to correspondence with Charles I, Prynne was later "removed to a more secure prison" about twenty miles away in Taunton Castle (Kirby, *William Prynne*, 109).

85. Prynne, *A new discovery of free-state tyranny*, 29.

86. In 1601, after marrying Anne More, and incurring her uncle's wrath, Donne was unemployed and homeless. During the next ten years his family struggled and often sought charity to secure shelter. Only in 1615, upon taking Anglican orders, did Donne begin to experience the financial security entailed by preferment (Bald, *John Donne*, 128–320). Thanks belong to Michael Schoenfeldt for alerting me to Donne's housing troubles.

87. Guibbory, *Christian Identity, Jews, and Israel*, 3. See also Shoulson, *Milton and the Rabbis*; Rosenblatt, *Torah and Law in Paradise Lost*; and Brooks, *Milton and the Jews*. On the critical controversy over Milton's "Jewishness," see Biberman, *Masculinity, Anti-semitism, and Early Modern English Literature*, 121–45.

88. Guibbory, "England, Israel and the Jews in Milton's Prose," 13.

89. The cemetery was bounded by Jewin St., Barbican, Aldersgate St., and Red Cross St. (Honeybourne, "Pre-Expulsion Cemetery of the Jews").

90. Ibid.; J. Stow, *Survey of London*, 241.

91. Milton, *Complete Prose Works*, 6:132.

92. On Milton's monism in *Christian Doctrine*, see R. Schwartz, *Remembering and Repeating*; Kendrick, *Milton*; Fallon, *Milton among the Philosophers*; and Walker, "Milton's Dualistic Theory of Religious Toleration."

93. Matar, "Milton and the Idea of the Restoration," 111.

94. Guibbory, "England, Israel and the Jews in Milton's Prose," 19, 34.

95. Matar, "Milton and the Idea of the Restoration," 121. On Milton and toleration, see also Wolfe, "Limits of Miltonic Toleration."

96. Guibbory, "England, Israel and the Jews in Milton's Prose."

97. Milton, *Complete Prose Works*, 2:555.

98. On the tension between monism and dualism in Milton, see Guibbory, *Ceremony and Community from Herbert to Milton*, 211–15; Walker, "Milton's Dualistic Theory of Religious Toleration"; Rosenblatt, *Torah and Law in Paradise Lost*, 71–137.

99. Milton, *Complete Poems*, 1.18, p. 212. Milton may be drawing on George Herbert, who states in "Sion," that "All Solomons sea of brasse and world of stone / Is not so deare to thee as one good grone" (*The Temple*, 99). Thanks belong to Michael Schoenfeldt for these citations.

100. Guibbory, "England, Israel and the Jews in Milton's Prose," 18; Donnelly, *Milton's Scriptural Reasoning*, 59.

101. D. Boyarin, *Radical Jew*, 31. On English rhetorics of supersession and Milton's writings, see Guibbory, *Christian Identity, Jews, and Israel* and "England, Israel and the Jews in Milton's Prose," 24–25; Stollman, "Milton's Dichotomy of 'Judaism' and 'Hebraism.'"

102. Milton, *Complete Prose Works*, 1:590.

103. On "Jewish" ceremonials and building practices in England, see Guibbory, *Christian Identity, Jews, and Israel*, 74–82.

104. By yoking together "idolatry, the Jewish Temple, and popish worship" Milton articulates a "staple of English post-Reformation discourse" at least since Spenser's *Faerie Queene* (ibid., 83).

105. Milton acknowledges those material exigencies in *Of Reformation*, where he urges that English funding not be "profusely throwne away in trash" in the form of Laud's "Jewish" temples, but instead be spent on "*Churches* and *Schools*" (*Complete Prose Works*, 1:590). Milton thus is very much invested in built environments as shelters for members of the Protestant siblinghood. Cf. *Il Penseroso*, whose speaker, like the wandering Jew commending St. Paul's in the broadside, desires to always "love the high embowed Roof / With antique Pillars massy proof" of gothic churches (*Complete Poems*, 76).

106. Milton, *Complete Prose Works*, 1:757.

107. Guibbory, "England, Israel and the Jews in Milton's Prose," 16.

108. Milton likely would have felt the same about the expectations of Jewish restoration that emerged during the mid-1660s, around the time *Samson Agonistes* was published, and were spurred by Sabbatai Sevi's messianism. On millenarians and Sevi, see Popkin, "Jewish Messianism and Christian Millenarianism," 79–83, and Guibbory, *Christian Identity, Jews, and Israel*, 198–202.

109. Stollman, "Milton's Dichotomy of 'Judaism' and 'Hebraism,'" 111.

110. S. Fish, "Spectacle and Evidence in *Samson Agonistes*," 580.

111. Milton, *Complete Poems*, 584, line 1359. Subsequent line citations from this edition appear in the text.

112. Trubowitz, "'The people of Asia and with them the Jews.'"

113. *Paradise Regain'd* was published together with the play in a 1671 volume whose title page reads *Paradise Regain'd. A poem in IV books. To which is added Samson Agonistes*. Both the labeling of *Samson Agonistes* as a text that "is added" to *Paradise*

*Regain'd* and their pairing suggest how they inform each other and should be read together.

114. Milton, *Complete Poems*, 515, lines 424–26. Subsequent line citations of the poem from this edition appear in the text.

115. Trubowitz, "The people of Asia and with them the Jews," 173.

116. Cf. how Samson's actions recall and refigure the Wandering Jew. He leans on the temple for respite in the manner of an exhausted Christ resting against Ahasuerius's house (see the King James edition of Judges 16:26, and *Samson Agonistes* 1630–34). Moreover, Samson's act of leaning, like that of Christ, serves as a prelude to his own sacrificial death. Such parallels suggest how this scene in Milton's play would have conjured up the popular myth for readers. Additionally, Milton's stress on the material magnificence of the temple may speak to the association of Jews with grand yet outdated and repudiated edifices.

117. S. Fish, "Spectacle and Evidence in *Samson Agonistes*," 578.

118. Trubowitz, "'The people of Asia and with them the Jews,'" 177.

119. Milton, *Complete Prose Works*, 2:512.

120. Trubowitz, "'I was his nursling once,'" 167.

121. Shoulson, *Milton and the Rabbis*, 250–51.

122. Lupton, "*Jew of Malta*," 153.

123. In certain respects, Samson's action makes him less a type of Christ than another Barabas (who blows up an old monastery filled with Turkish soldiers in Marlowe's play) or Shylock (whose vengeance takes the physical form of carving out the heart of the merchant Antonio). For a different reading of Samson as enacting Milton's idea of Christian works, see Stollman, "Milton's Understanding of the 'Hebraic.'"

124. Schoenfeldt, personal conversation, April 2013.

125. S. Fish, "Spectacle and Evidence in *Samson Agonistes*," 567.

126. Mohamed, *Milton and the Post-secular Present*, 115. Mohamed provides a cogent overview of the many critical takes on Samson's silence (ibid., 113–21).

127. Samson's silence also suggests Milton's qualms about Samson as Jew turned proto-Christian. By refusing to portray Samson praying aloud to God, Milton builds a wall around his hero's supposed rejection of his bondage to Jewish literalism. Samson's silence raises the possibility that, despite Samson's seemingly proto-Christian transformation, he is still a Jew. Samson is both a figure of Christian conversion and a testimony to persistent Jewish remainders in the convert. We might speculate, then, that Samson's persistent carnality—like the unending nature of the "Christian" Ahasuerus's punishment—speaks to a concern over the inexorable nature of Jewishness, even within the convert.

128. Husserl, *Crisis of European Sciences and Transcendental Phenomenology*.

129. The play opens with Samson finding in an "unfrequented place" beyond the jail in Gaza "Ease to the body some," but "none to the mind / From restless thoughts" (17–19). "Rashly" querying "Divine Prediction" (43–44), the blind and weak prisoner worries over "times past, what once I was, and what am now" (22). Oppressed by "shame and sorrow," possessed of a "Soul, that suffers not" his "thoughts to rest" (457–59), Samson exemplifies those who find God's edicts "contradicting / Then give the reins to wand'ring thought" (301–2).

130. Another meaning of Samson's placelessness is how this once powerful warrior cannot accept a life of inaction, a sentiment Milton may have shared after the

Restoration. Samson's repudiation of Manoa's invitation to come home may echo how a blind Milton, living in a world where the dream of a commonwealth had vanished, may have similarly scorned his own home-bound existence as a man "Inglorious, unemploy'd, with age out-worn" (580). Milton thus may have identified with his hero in terms of both Samson's sufferings and his attack in the temple, an attack that registers the writer's animosity toward the restored monarchy and contemporary Jews.

131. St. John, "Preface," xxxix.

132. Forsyth, *John Milton*, 154.

133. Milton's domestic investments appear in "When assault was intended to ye City." Written three months into the civil war, when Londoners feared a Royalist seizure of the city, the sonnet addresses whatever soldier—"Captain or Colonel, or Knight in Arms,"—might come upon the "defenseless doors" of Milton's home in Aldersgate (Milton, "Sonnet VIII," in *Complete Poems*, 140, lines 1–2.). Milton implores the reader to mimic Alexander the Great and the Spartan Lysander in refraining from architectural demolition out of respect for great poetry. Milton's title replaces a heading written by an amanuensis on the manuscript in which the sonnet appears: "On his door when the City expected an Assault." Situated just beyond the city walls, Milton's home could have been the first to fall during an invasion. Milton uses the verses to protect the otherwise "defenseless doors" of his home in somewhat the same way that "sad *Electra's* Poet had the pow'r / To save th' *Athenian Walls* from ruin bare" (Milton, "Sonnet VIII," in *Complete Poems*, 140, lines 13–14). The attachment of the poem to the portal fortifies in the manner of iron bars over windows. That deep Miltonic investment in home departs from Samson's rejection of his home and suggests how the biblical hero's position presents no easy reflection of the poet's point of view. The Christian poet who cherished his own home seems to have wished no such domesticity for Jews.

134. On Manoa's idolatry, see Knoppers, *Historicizing Milton*, 61, and Shore, *Milton and the Art of Rhetoric*, 101.

135. Milton, *Complete Poems*, 550.

136. Sauer, "Politics of Performance in the Inner Theater," 203. On Milton and Restoration theater, see Zwicker, "Milton, Dryden and the Politics of Literary Controversy."

137. Sauer, "Politics of Performance in the Inner Theater," 203–4. As Lampert-Weissig points out in her reading of the Croxton *Play of the Sacrament*, having an English Christian play a Jew proves powerfully destabilizing in its merging of identities.

138. Prynne, *A Short Demurrer*, title page.

139. Jameson, *Political Unconscious*; K. Burke, *Philosophy of Literary Form*.

## Coda

1. Endelman, *Jews of Britain*, 79.

2. Ibid., 93. Montefiore was related by marriage to the Mocattas.

3. On Montefiore, see Green, *Moses Montefiore*.

4. Endelman, *Jews of Britain*, 101, 94.

5. On emancipation in England, its piecemeal nature, distinct character, and the ambivalence of Christians and Jews to the process, see Endelman, *Jews of Britain*, 101–10, and Alderman, "English Jews or Jews of the English Persuasion?"

6. On the term "emancipation," see Alderman, "English Jews or Jews of the English Persuasion?," 128.

7. Macaulay, *Miscellaneous Writings and Speeches*, 550.

8. Quoted in Cheyette, *Constructions of "the Jew" in English Literature and Society*, 16.

9. Macaulay, *Miscellaneous Writings and Speeches*, 546.

10. On affluent Jewish settlement in nineteenth-century London, see Endelman, *Jews of Britain*, 94–95.

11. Endelman, *Jews of Britain*, 81.

12. Ibid., 82.

13. Dickens, *Sketches by Boz*, 74.

14. As opposed to the private and accidental death of Sikes.

15. Dickens, *Oliver Twist*, ed. Kaplan, 63. Subsequent page references to the Kaplan edition appear in the text.

16. Oliver describes here Fagin's second house in Whitechapel.

17. From 1834 to 1837 Dickens lived at Furnivall's Inn in Holborn, and from 1837 to 1839 he lived at 48 Doughty Street in Holborn (Slater, *Charles Dickens*, 46, 97).

18. S. Meyer, "Antisemitism and Social Critique," 240.

19. Cf. her answers to Mr. Bumble's inquiry about Mann's inmates: "they're as well as can be, the dears! Of course, except the two that died last week. And little Dick" (120).

20. Mr. Brownlow would seem to counter this trend by extricating Oliver from his cell. Later he engages in a "just" act of imprisonment when he has himself locked in the room where he interviews the nefarious Monks (325). Though does Brownlow's private tête-à-tête to discuss dirty business with Monks at some level taint Oliver's liberator and benefactor?

21. When Sikes "double-locked the door" to his rented room, "lifting a heavy table against it," he outdoes even Fagin's multiple acts of locking (315). The most dangerous site in the novel by far is Sikes's weapon-laden apartment in Bethnal Green. While Nancy is neither a boy nor crucified, Dickens's depiction of her "nearly blinded with the blood that rained down from a deep gash in her forehead," kneeling and holding Rose Maylie's white handkerchief "high towards Heaven in prayer," is the closest approximation to ritual murder in the novel (316–17). Fagin is implicated in this death, but the greater criminal is Sikes.

22. Dickens possibly encodes locking in Oliver's family line, in the pivotal moment when Monks obtains a bag containing a wedding ring and "a little gold locket: in which were two locks of hair" (253). Those objects confirm Oliver's real genealogy and enable his adoption by Brownlow. The echo of the word "lock" in Agnes Fleming's locket and lock of hair speaks to how those objects enable Oliver's disentanglement from the criminal pseudo-family headed by Fagin, "locking" him out from that murky world and "sealing up" his relation to a more proper human network. At the same time, though, does the "lock" in locket and lock of hair encode the presence of Fagin—or Shylock—in Oliver's Christian genealogy?

23. During the last ten years of his life, Dickens's primary residence was outside the city, at Gad's Hill Place in Kent; five months before his 8 June death, during his public lectures in London, he lived in a rental at 5 Hyde Park Place.

24. Dickens to Thomas Mitton, 19 August 1860, in Dickens, *Letters*, 289.
25. Dickens to W. H. Wills, 4 September 1860, ibid., 303.
26. Davis to Charles Dickens, 22 June 1863, in Baumgarten, "Other Woman," 64.
27. Ibid.
28. S. Meyer, "Antisemitism and Social Critique," 240.
29. Baumgarten, "The Other Woman," 57.
30. Dickens, *Our Mutual Friend*, 287–93.
31. Baumgarten, "The Other Woman," 60–62.
32. Dickens, *Our Mutual Friend*, 292–93.
33. Baumgarten, "The Other Woman," 64.

## ❧ BIBLIOGRAPHY

### Primary Sources

Adgar, William. *Le Gracial*. Edited by Pierre Kunstmann. Publications Mediévales de l'Université d'Ottawa 8. Ottawa: Editions de l'Université d'Ottawa, 1982.

——. *Lives of Saints*. Vol. 2. Edited by Walter Skeat. EETS o.s. 94, 114. London: Oxford University Press, 1966.

Arnold, Thomas, ed. *Memorials of Bury St. Edmunds*. Vol. 2. Cambridge: Cambridge University Press, 1892.

Augustine. *The City of God Against the Pagans*. Edited and translated by R. W. Dyson. Cambridge: Cambridge University Press, 1998.

——. *The Works of Saint Augustine: A Translation for the 21st Century*. Pt. III, vol. 6: *Sermons*. Translated by Edmund Hill and edited by John E. Rotelle. New Rochelle, NY: New City Press, 1993.

Bede. *De tabernaculo, De templo, In Ezram et Neemiam*. Edited by D. Hurst. Corpus Christianorum, Series Latina 119A. Turnhout: Brepols, 1969.

——. *Bede's Ecclesiastical History of the English People*. Edited by Bertram Colgrave and R. A. B. Mynors. Oxford: Clarendon Press, 1969.

——. *Homiliarum evangelii libri II*. Edited by D. Hurst. Corpus Christianorum, Series Latina 122. Turnhout: Brepols, 1955.

——. *Homilies on the Gospels: Book Two: Lent to the Dedication of the Church*. Translated by Lawrence T. Martin and David Hurst. Kalamazoo: Cistercian Publications, 1991.

——. *On Ezra and Nehemiah*. Edited and translated by Scott DeGregorio. Liverpool: Liverpool University Press, 2006.

——. *Bede: On Genesis*. Translated by C. Kendall. Liverpool: Liverpool University Press, 2008.

——. *On the Tabernacle*. Edited and translated by Arthur Holder. Liverpool: Liverpool University Press, 1994.

——. *On the Temple*. Edited and translated by Seán Connolly. Liverpool: Liverpool University Press, 1995.

——. *Two Lives of Saint Cuthbert: A Life by an Anonymous Monk of Lindisfarne and Bede's Prose Life*. Edited by Bertram Colgrave. Cambridge: Cambridge University Press, 1940.

Biddulph, William. *The Travels of Certain Englishmen into Africa, Asia, Troy, Bythinia, Thracia, and to the Blacke Sea*. London, 1609.

Boyd, Beverly, ed. *The Middle English Miracles of the Virgin*. San Marino: The Huntington Library, 1964.

Brathwaite, Richard. *Whimzies, or, A nevv cast of characters*. London, 1631.

Bullinger, Heinrich. *Fiftie godlie and learned sermons.* Vol. 3. Translated by H. I. London, 1577.

Cassiodorus. *Institutiones.* Edited by R. A. B. Mynors. Oxford: Clarendon Press, 1961.

Chaucer, Geoffrey. *The Prioress's Tale.* Edited by Beverly Boyd. Norman: University of Oklahoma Press, 1987.

———. *The Riverside Chaucer.* Edited by Larry D. Benson. London: Houghton, 1987.

Chew, Helena M., and William Kellaway, eds. *London Assize of Nuisance, 1301–1431.* London: London Record Society, 1973.

Cicero, *Orator.* Translated by H. M. Hubbell. Loeb Classical Library. Cambridge, MA: Harvard University Press.

Cluse, Christoph. "*Fabula Ineptissima*: Die Ritualmordlegende um Adam von Bristol nach der Handschrift, London, British Library, Harley 957." *Aschkenas: Zeitschrift für Geschichte und Kultur der Juden* 5, no. 2 (1995): 293–330.

Cook, G. H., ed. *Letters to Cromwell on the Suppression of the Monasteries.* London: Baker, 1965.

Crow, Martin M., and Clair C. Olson, eds. *Chaucer Life-Records.* Austin: University of Texas Press, 1966.

Cynewulf. *Elene.* Edited by P. O. E. Gradon. London: University of Exeter Press, 1977.

*The daunce and song of death.* London, 1569.

Dean, James, ed. *Medieval English Political Writings.* Kalamazoo: Medieval Institute Publications, 1996.

Diceto, Ralph de. *The Historical Works of Master Ralph de Diceto, Dean of London.* Edited by W. Stubbs. Vol. 2. RS 68. London, 1876.

Dickens, Charles. *The Letters of Charles Dickens.* Vol. 9. Edited by Graham Storey. Oxford: Clarendon Press, 1997.

———. *Oliver Twist: Norton Critical Edition.* Edited by Fred Kaplan. New York: Norton, 1993.

———. *Our Mutual Friend.* New York: Modern Library, 1960.

———. *Sketches by Boz, illustrative of every-day life and every-day people.* London: Oxford University Press, 1957.

D. L. *Israels Condition and Cause Pleaded.* London, 1656.

Dominic of Evesham. *Miracles of the Virgin.* "El libro '*De Miraculis Sanctae Mariae*" de Domingo de Evesham (m. c. 1140)." Edited by José Canal. *Studium Legionense* 39 (1998): 247–83.

Donne, John. *Sermons.* Edited by George R. Potter and Evelyn M. Simpson. Vol. 5. Berkeley: University of California Press, 1962.

Douglas, David C., and George W. Greenhaw, eds. *English Historical Documents, 1042–1189.* New York: Routledge, 1981.

fitz Stephen, William. *Vita Sancti Thomae.* In *Materials for the History of Thomas Becket, Archibishop of Canterbury,* edited by James Cragie Robertson, 3:2–13. RS 67. London: Longman, 1885.

Forster, John. *The Life of Charles Dickens.* Leipzig: B. Tauchnitz, 1872–74.

Foxe, John. *Actes and Monuments.* London, 1570.

———. *A sermon preached at the christening of a certaine Iew at London, Conteining an exposition of the xi. chapter of S. Paul to the Romanes.* Translated by James Bell. London, 1578.

Frederick of Wirtemberg. *A true and faithful narrative of the bathing excursion.* Tübingen, 1602.

Görlach, Manfred, ed. *The Kalendre of the Newe Legende of Englande.* Heidelberg: Winter, 1994.

Gower, John. *Confessio Amantis.* Edited by G. C. Macaulay. EETS e.s. 81. London: Paul, 1901.

Gregory of Tours. *Glory of the Martyrs.* Translated by Raymond Van Dam. Liverpool: Liverpool University Press, 1988.

Hazlitt, W. Carew, ed. *Remains of the Early Popular Poetry of England.* Vol. 1. London, 1864.

Herbert di Losinga. *The Life, Letters, and Sermons of Bishop Herbert de Losinga.* Edited and translated by E. M. Goulburn and Henry Symonds. Oxford, 1878.

Herbert, George. *The Temple: Sacred Poems and Private Ejaculations.* Cambridge, 1633.

Hinds, Allen B., ed. *Calendar of State Papers Relating to English Affairs in the Archives of Venice,* Vol. 28, 1647–1652. London: His Majesty's Stationer's Office, 1927.

Holder, Alfred, ed. *Inventio Sanctae Crucis.* Leipzig, 1889.

Holinshed, Raphael. *The Third volume of Chronicles, beginning at duke William the Norman ....* London, 1587.

Horstmann, Carl, ed. *Nova legenda Anglie.* Vol. 2. Oxford: Oxford University Press, 1901.

Humpston, Robert. *A sermon preached at Reyfham in the countie of Norfolk the 22 of September, an. Do. 1588.* London, 1589.

Isidore of Seville. *The Etymologies of Isidore of Seville.* Translated by Stephen Barney et al. Cambridge: Cambridge University Press, 2006.

Jonas, *Life of St. Columban.* Charleston: BiblioLife, 2009.

Josephus, Flavius. *The Jewish War.* Translated by H. St. J. Thackeray. 2 vols. London: Heinemann, 1927–28.

Karo, Joseph ben Ephraim. *Code of Hebrew Law: Shulhan 'aruk.* Translated by Chaim N. Denburg. Montreal: Jurisprudence Press, 1954.

Kirk, R. E., and Ernest F. Kirk, eds. *Returns of Aliens Dwelling in the City and Suburbs of London from the Reign of Henry VIII to that of James I.* Vol. 3. Aberdeen: Huguenot Society, 1907.

Krapp, George Philip, ed. *The Dream of the Rood. The Vercelli Book.* New York: Columbia University Press, 1932. 61–65.

Leone da Modena. *The history of the rites, customes, and manner of life, of the present Jews, throughout the world.* Translated by Edumund Chilmead. London, 1650.

Luard, Henry Richards, ed. *Annales Monastici.* RS 36. Vol. 1. London, 1864.

Lucian. *Liber Luciani De Laude Cestrie.* Edited by M. V. Taylor. London: Record Society, 1912.

Macaulay, Thomas Babington. *The Miscellaneous Writings and Speeches of Lord Macaulay.* London, 1871.

Machiavelli, Niccolò. *Discourses on Livy.* Translated by Harvey Mansfield and Nathan Tarcov. Chicago: University of Chicago Press, 1996.

——. *The Prince.* Translated by Harvey Manfield. Chicago: University of Chicago Press, 1998.

Marcus, Jacob R. *The Jew in the Medieval World.* 1938; repr. Cleveland: Meridian, 1960.

Marlowe, Christopher. *The Jew of Malta.* Edited by Roma Gill. Oxford: Oxford University Press, 1995.

Marshe, Bower, ed. *Records of the Worshipful Company of Carpenters.* Vol. 3: *Court Book: 1533–73.* Oxford: Oxford University Press, 1915.

Marx, Karl. "On the Jewish Question." In *Early Writings*, translated and edited by T. B. Bottomore, 1–40. London: Watts, 1963.

Matthew Paris. *Chronica majora.* Edited by Henry Richards Luard. RS 57. 7 vols. London, 1972–73.

——. *The Chronicle of Matthew Paris: Monastic Life in the Thirteenth Century.* Translated and edited by Richard Vaughan. Stroud: A. Sutton, 1984.

Meir b. Elijah of Norwich. *Into the Light: The Medieval Hebrew Poetry of Meir of Norwich.* Edited by Keiron Pim. Translated by Ellman Crasnow and Bente Elsworth. Norwich: East, 2013.

Michel, Francisque. *Hugues de Lincoln.* Paris, 1834.

Milton, John. *Complete Poems and Major Prose.* Edited by Merritt Y. Hughes. New York: Odyssey Press, 1957.

——. *Complete Prose Works of John Milton.* Edited by Don M. Wolfe et al. 8 volumes in 10. New Haven: Yale University Press, 1953–82.

Muir, Bernard, ed. *The Exeter Anthology of Old English Poetry.* Vol. 1. Exeter: University of Exeter Press, 1994.

Nashe, Thomas. *The vnfortunate traueller. Or, The life of Iacke Wilton.* London, 1594.

Newbigin, Nerida. "Dieci sacre rappresentazioni del Quattro e Cinquecento." *Letteratura italiana antica* 10 (2009): 21–397.

Nicholas de Nicolay. *The nauigations, peregrinations and voyages, made into Turkie by Nicholas Nicholay Daulphinois, Lord of Arfeuile.* Translated by T. Washington. London, 1585.

Nigel, Richard fitz. *Dialogue of the Exchequer. English Historical Documents.* Vol. 2, *1042–1189.* Edited by David C. Douglas and George W. Greenaway. London: Eyre, 1968. 490–569.

Peter the Venerable. *Petri Venerabilis, Adversus Iudeorum inveteratam duritiem.* Edited by Y. Friedman. Corpus Christianorum Continuatio Mediaevalis 58. Vol. 3. Turnhout: Brepols, 1985.

Petryszcze, Camille Salatko, ed. *Le Mistere de la Saincte Hostie introduction, édition du texte et notes.* http://www.sites. univrennes2.fr/celam/cetm/Edition%20 Hostie/ostie. html. 29 July 2014.

Plato. *Timaeus and Critias.* Translated by Robin Waterfield. Edited by Andrew Gregory. Oxford: Oxford University Press, 2008.

Polyaenus. *Stratagems of War.* Translated by R. Shepherd. Chicago: Ares, 1974.

Prynne, William. *A Legall Vindication Of the Liberties of England, against Illegal Taxes and pretended Acts of Parliament.* London, 1649.

——. *A new discovery of free-state tyranny.* London, 1655.

——. *The second part of a Short demurrer to the Ievves long discontinued remitter into England.* London, 1656.

——. *A Short Demurrer to the Jewes Long discontinued Remitter into England.* London, 1656.

Richard of Devizes. *Cronicon Richardi Divisensis de tempore Regis Richardi Primi.* Edited and translated by John T. Appleby. London: Nelson, 1963.

Riley, Henry Thomas, ed. *Liber Albus.* London, 1859.

Roger of Howden. *The Annals of Roger de Hoveden: Comprising the History of England and of other Countries of Europe from A.D. 732 to A.D. 1201.* Translated and edited by H. T. Riley. Vol. 2. London, 1853.

——. *Chronica Magistri Roger de Houedene.* Edited by W. Stubbs. 4 vols. London, 1868–71.

——. *Gesta Regis Henrici Secundi et Gesta Regis Ricardi: The Chronicle of the Reigns of Henry II and Richard I, AD 1169–1192.* Edited by W. Stubbs. RS 49. Vol. 2. London, 1867.

Ross, W. O., ed. *Middle English Sermons.* EETS o.s. 209. Oxford: Oxford University Press, 1940.

Schedel, Hartmann. *Liber chronicarum.* Nuremberg, 1493.

Schofield, John, ed. *The London Surveys of Ralph Treswell.* London: London Topographical Society, 1987.

Scragg, D. G., ed. *The Vercelli Homilies and Related Texts.* EETS o.s. 300. Oxford: Oxford University Press, 1992.

Sebastian, John, ed. *The Croxton Play of the Sacrament.* Kalamazoo: Medieval Institute Publications, 2012.

Shakespeare, William. *The Merchant of Venice.* Edited by M. M. Mahood. Cambridge: Cambridge University Press, 2003.

Smith, Adam. *An Inquiry into the Nature and Causes of the Wealth of Nations.* Edited by Kathryn Sutherland. Oxford: Oxford University Press, 1993.

*Statutes of the Realm.* Vol. 2. London: Dawsons, 1810.

Stow, John. *The Survey of London, containing the originall, antiquitie, encrease, moderne estate, and description of that Citie.* London, 1598.

Thomas of Monmouth. *The Life and Miracles of St. William of Norwich.* Edited and translated by Augustus Jessopp and Montague Rhodes James. Cambridge, 1896.

——. *The Life and Passion of William of Norwich.* Edited and translated by Miri Rubin. London: Penguin, 2014.

——. "[Vita et Miraculi Sancti Willelmi Martyris Norwicensis]." Transcription of Cambridge University Library Ms. Add. 3037, fols. 1–77r. Transcribed by Miri Rubin. http://yvc.history.qmul.ac.uk/WN-joined-17-08-09.pdf.

Thorowgood, Thomas. *Iewes in America or, Probabilities that the Americans are of that race.* London, 1650.

Topsell, Edward. *Times lamentation: or An exposition on the prophet Ioel, in sundry sermons or meditations.* London, 1599.

Turberville, George, et al. *Tragicall tales translated by Turberuile in time of his troubles out of sundrie Italians, with the argument and lenuoye to eche tale.* London, 1587.

Tymms, Samuel, ed. *Wills and Inventories from the Registers of the Commissary of Bury St. Edmunds and the Archdeacon of Sudbury.* London, 1850.

Udall, John. *The state of the Church of Englande laide open in a conference betweene Diotrephes a bishop, Tertullus a papist, Demetrius an vsurer, Pandocheus an in-keeper, and Paule a preacher of the word of God.* London, 1588.

Wager, William. *A comedy or enterlude intituled, Inough is as good as a feast.* London, 1570.

Walsingham, Thomas. *Gesta abbatum monasterii sancti Albani.* Edited by H. T. Riley. Vol. 1. London, 1867.

Warner, George Frederic, ed. *The Libelle of Englysche Polycye: a poem on the use of sea-power, 1436.* Oxford: Clarendon Press, 1926.

Wenzel, Siegfried, ed. and trans. *Fasciculus Morum: A Fourteenth-Century Preacher's Handbook.* University Park: Pennsylvania State University Press, 1989.

William of Newburgh. *Historia rerum Anglicarum.* In *Chronicles of the Reigns of Stephen, Henry II, and Richard I.* Edited by Richard Howlett. Vols. 1–2. RS 82. London, 1884–89.

——. *History of English Affairs.* In *The Church Historians of England.* Translated by Joseph Stevenson. Vol. 4.2. London, 1856. 397–672.

Wilson, Robert. *A right excellent and famous comedy, called The three ladies of London.* London, 1592.

Wolf, Lucien, ed. *Menasseh ben Israel's Mission to Oliver Cromwell.* London: Mac-Millan, 1901.

## Secondary Sources

Abou-Ei-Haj, Barbara. "Artistic Integration inside the Cathedral Precinct: Social Concensus Outside?" In *Artistic Integration in Gothic Buildings,* edited by Virginia Chieffo Raguin et al., 214–35. Toronto: University of Toronto Press, 1995.

——. "The Urban Setting for Late Medieval Church Building: Reims and Its Cathedral." *Art History* 11 (1988): 17–41.

Abulafia, Anna Sapir. *Christians and Jews in the Twelfth-Century Renaissance.* London: Routledge, 1995.

——, ed. *Religious Violence between Christians and Jews: Medieval Roots, Modern Perspectives.* Houndmills: Palgrave, 2002.

Achinstein, Sharon. "John Foxe and the Jews." *Renaissance Quarterly* 54 (2001): 86–120.

——. "*Samson Agonistes* and the Drama of Dissent." In *The Miltonic Samson,* edited by Albert C. Labriola and Michael Lieb. Special issue of *Milton Studies* 33 (1996): 133–58.

Adelman, Janet. *Blood Relations: Christian and Jew in the Merchant of Venice.* Chicago: University of Chicago Press, 2008.

Adler, Michael. "Aaron of York." *TJHSE* 13 (1932–35): 113–55.

——. "History of the 'Domus Conversorum' from 1290 to 1891." *TJHSE* 4 (1899–1901): 16–75.

Agnew, Jean-Cristophe. *Worlds Apart: The Market and the Theater in Anglo-American Thought, 1550–1750.* Cambridge: Cambridge University Press, 1985.

Agus, I. A. *Urban Civilisation in Pre-Crusade Europe.* Vol 1. New York: Yeshiva University Press, 1965.

Akbari, Suzanne Conklin. *Idols in the East: European Representations of Islam and the Orient, 1100–1450.* Ithaca, NY: Cornell University Press, 2009.

Alderman, David. "English Jews or Jews of the English Persuasion? Reflections on the Emancipation of Anglo-Jewry." In *Paths of Emancipation: Jews, States and Citizenship,* edited by Pierre Birnbaum and Ira Katznelson, 128–56. Princeton, NJ: Princeton University Press, 1995.

Allen, Valerie, and Ruth Evans, eds. *Roadworks: Medieval Britain, Medieval Roads.* Manchester: Manchester University Press, 2016.

Allin, Patricia. "Richard of Devizes and the Alleged Martyrdom of a Boy at Winchester." *TJHSE* 27 (1978–80): 32–39.

Anderson, Ben, and Colin McFarlane. "Assemblage and Geography." *Area* 43, no. 2 (2011): 124–27.

Anderson, George K. *The Legend of the Wandering Jew.* Hanover: Brown University Press, 1991.

Andrews, Kenneth. *Ships, Money, and Politics: Seafaring and Naval Enterprise in the Reign of Charles I.* Cambridge: Cambridge University Press, 1991.

———. *Trade, Plunder and Settlement: Maritime Enterprise and the Genesis of the British Empire, 1480–1630.* Cambridge: Cambridge University Press, 1984.

Antrobus, Abbey L. "Urbanisation and the Urban Landscape: Building Medieval Bury St Edmunds." PhD dissertation, Durham University, 2009. http://etheses.dur.ac.uk/1948/.

Applebaum, Shimon. "Were There Jews in Roman Britain?" *TJHSE* 17 (1951–52): 189–205.

Archer, John. "The Structure of Anti-Semitism in the *Prioress's Tale*." *Chaucer Review* 19, no. 1 (1984): 46–54.

Ariès, Philippe. *Centuries of Childhood: A Social History of Family Life.* Translated by Robert Baldick. London: Jonathan Cape, 1996.

Astill, Grenville. "General Survey, 600–1300." In Palliser, *Cambridge Urban History*, 27–51.

Atherton, Ian, Eric Fernie, Christopher Harper-Bill, and Hassell Smith, eds. *Norwich Cathedral: Church, City and Diocese, 1096–1996.* London: Hambledon, 1996.

Atkin, Tamara. "Playbooks and Printed Drama: A Reassessment of the Date and Layout of the Manuscript of the Croxton *Play of the Sacrament*." *Review of English Studies*, n.s. 60, no. 244 (2009): 194–205.

Auerbach, Erich. "Figura." In *Scenes from the Drama of European Literature*, 11–78. Minneapolis: University of Minnesota Press, 1984.

Ayers, Brian. "The Urban Landscape." In Rawcliffe and Wilson, *Medieval Norwich*, 1–28.

Bald, R. C. *John Donne: A Life.* Oxford: Oxford University Press, 1970.

Bale, Anthony. *Feeling Persecuted: Christians, Jews and Images of Violence in the Middle Ages.* London: Reaktion, 2010.

———. "Fictions of Judaism in England before 1290." In Skinner, *Jews in Medieval Britain*, 129–44.

———. "'House Devil, Town Saint': Anti-Semitism and Hagiography in Medieval Suffolk." In Delaney, *Chaucer and the Jews*, 185–210.

———. *The Jew in the Medieval Book: English Antisemitisms, 1350–1500.* Cambridge: Cambridge University Press, 2007.

———. "Richard of Devizes and Fictions of Judaism." *Jewish Culture and History* 3, no. 2 (2000): 55–72.

Barkey, Karen, and Ira Katznelson. "States, Regimes, and Decisions: Why Jews Were Expelled from Medieval England and France." *Theory and Society* 40 (2011): 475–503.

Baron, Salo Wittmayer. *A Social and Religious History of the Jews.* 2nd ed. 18 vols. New York: Columbia University Press, 1952–93.

Barron, Caroline. *London in the Later Middle Ages: Government and People, 1100–1500.* Oxford: Oxford University Press, 2005.

Bartels, Emily. *Spectacles of Strangeness: Imperialism, Alienation, and Marlowe.* Philadelphia: University of Pennsylvania Press, 1993.

Bartolovich, Crystal. "'Baseless Fabric': London as a 'World City.'" In *"The Tempest" and its Travels,* edited by Peter Hulme and William H. Sherman, 13–26. Philadelphia: University of Pennsylvania Press, 2000.

Bateson, Mary. *Borough Customs.* Vol. 2. London: Quaritch, 1906.

Baumgarten, Murray. "'The Other Woman': Eliza Davis and Charles Dickens." *Dickens Quarterly* 32, no. 1 (2015): 44–70.

Bayless, Martha. *Sin and Filth in Medieval Culture: The Devil in the Latrine.* New York: Routledge, 2012.

———. "The Story of the Fallen Jew and the Iconography of Jewish Unbelief." *Viator* 34 (2003): 142–56.

Beckwith, Sarah. "Ritual, Church and Theatre: Medieval Dramas of the Sacramental Body." In *Culture and History 1350–1660: Essays on English Communities, Identities and Writings,* edited by David Aers, 65–89. New York: Harvester, 1992.

Berger, David. "The Attitude of St. Bernard toward the Jews." *Proceedings of the American Academy for Jewish Research* 40 (1972): 89–108.

Bernard, G. W. *The King's Reformation: Henry VIII and the Remaking of the English Church.* New Haven: Yale University Press, 2005.

Besserman, Lawrence. *Biblical Paradigms in Medieval English Literature: From Caedmon to Malory.* New York: Routledge, 2012.

———. "Chaucer, Spain, and the Prioress's Antisemitism." *Viator* 35 (2004): 329–53.

Bestul, Thomas H. "Did Chaucer Live at 177 Upper Thames Street? The Chaucer-Life-Records and the Site of Chaucer's London Home." *Chaucer Review* 43, no. 1 (2008): 1–15.

Bevington, David. *Medieval Drama.* Boston: Houghton Mifflin, 1975.

———. *Shakespeare: The Seven Ages of Human Experience.* Malden: Blackwell, 2002.

———. *Tudor Drama and Politics: A Critical Approach to Topical Meaning.* Cambridge, MA: Harvard University Press, 1968.

Biberman, Matthew. *Masculinity, Anti-semitism, and Early Modern English Literature: From the Satanic to the Effeminate Jew.* Aldershot: Ashgate, 2004.

Biddick, Kathleen. *The Typological Imaginary: Circumcision, Technology, History.* Philadelphia: University of Pennsylvania Press, 2003.

Birkholz, Daniel. "Biography after Historicism: The Harley Lyrics, the Hereford Map, and the Life of Roger De Breynton." In *The Post-Historical Middle Ages,* edited by Elizabeth Scala and Sylvia Federico, 161–90. New York: Palgrave Macmillan, 2009.

Blair, John. *The Church in Anglo-Saxon Society.* Oxford: Oxford University Press, 2005.

Blurton, Heather. "Egyptian Days: From Passion to Exodus in the Representation of Twelfth-Century Jewish-Christian Relations." In Rees Jones and Watson, *Christians and Jews in Angevin England,* 222–37.

———. "The Language of the Liturgy in the *Life and Miracles of William of Norwich.*" *Speculum* 90, no. 4 (2015): 1053–75.

——. "Richard of Devizes's *Cronicon*, Menippean Satire, and the Jews of Winchester." *Exemplaria* 22, no. 4 (2010): 265–84.

Bly, Mary. "Playing the Tourist in Early Modern London: Selling the Liberties Onstage." *PMLA* 122, no. 1 (2007): 61–71.

Bolton, J. L. *The Medieval English Economy, 1150–1500*. London: Dent, 1980.

——. *Money in the Medieval English Economy: 973–1489*. Manchester: Manchester University Press, 2012.

Booth, Roy. "Shylock's Sober House." *Review of English Studies*, n.s. 50, no. 197 (1999): 22–31.

Borgehammar, Stephan. *How the Holy Cross Was Found: From Event to Medieval Legend*. Bibliotheca Theologiae Practicae 47. Stockholm: Almquist, 1991.

Borot, Luc. "Machiavellian Diplomacy and Dramatic Developments in Marlowe's *Jew of Malta*." *Cahiers Elisabethains* 33 (1988): 1–11.

Boswell, John. *Christianity, Social Tolerance and Homosexuality: Gay People in Western Europe from the Beginning of the Christian Era to the Fourteenth Century*. Chicago: University of Chicago Press, 1981.

Bowsher, David, Tony Dyson, Nick Holder, and Isca Howell. *The London Guildhall: An Archeological History of a Neighbourhood from Early Medieval to Modern Times*. 2 vols. London: Museum of London Archaeology Service, 2007.

Bowsher, Julian, and Pat Miller. *The Rose and the Globe, Playhouses of Shakespeare's Bankside, Southwark: Excavations 1988–91*. London: Museum of London Archaeology, 2009.

Boyarin, Adrienne Williams. *Miracles of the Virgin in Medieval England: Law and Jewishness in Marian Legends*. Cambridge: D. S. Brewer, 2004.

Boyarin, Daniel. *A Radical Jew: Paul and the Politics of Identity*. Berkeley: University of California Press, 1994.

Boyarin, Jonathan. *Storm from Paradise: The Politics of Jewish Memory*. Minneapolis: University of Minnesota Press, 1992.

Braudel, Fernand. *Civilization and Capitalism, 15th–18th Century*. New York: Harper and Row, 1982–84.

Brenner, Robert. *Merchants and Revolution: Commercial Change, Political Conflict and London's Overseas Traders, 1550–1653*. Princeton, NJ: Princeton University Press, 1993.

Bridbury, R. *Medieval English Clothmaking: An Economic Survey*. London: Heinemann, 1982.

Britnell, Richard H. *The Commercialization of the English Economy*. Cambridge: Cambridge University Press, 1993.

——. "Commercialisation and Economic Development in England, 1000–1300." In Britnell and Campbell, *Commercialising Economy*, 7–26.

——. "Markets, Shops, Inns, Taverns and Private Houses in Medieval English Trade." In *Buyers and Sellers: Retail Circuits and Practices in Medieval and Early Modern Europe*, edited by Bruno Blondé et al., 109–23. Turnhout: Brepols, 2006.

——. "Town Life." In *A Social History of England, 1200–1500*, edited by Rosemary Horrox and W. M. Ormrod, 134–78. Cambridge: Cambridge University Press, 2006.

Britnell, Richard H., and Bruce Campbell, eds. *A Commercialising Economy: England 1086–c. 1300*. Manchester: Manchester University Press, 1995.

——. "Introduction." In Britnell and Campbell, *Commercialising Economy*, 1–6.

Brodt, Bärbel. "East Anglia." In Palliser, *Cambridge Urban History*, 639–56.

Bronner, Stephen Eric. *A Rumor about the Jews: Reflections on Antisemitism and the Protocols of the Learned Elders of Zion.* New York: St. Martin's, 2000.

Broughton, Laurel. "The Prioress's Prologue and Tale." In *Sources and Analogues of the Canterbury Tales*, edited by Robert M. Correale and Mary Hamel, 2:583–648. Cambridge: Brewer, 2005.

Brown, Carleton. *A Study of the Miracle of Our Lady Told by Chaucer's Prioress.* London: Chaucer Society, 1910.

Brown, David P. *Anglo-Saxon England.* Totowa, NJ: Rowman and Littlefield, 1978.

Brown, Michelle. "Bede's Life in Context." In DeGregorio, *Cambridge Companion to Bede*, 3–24.

——. *The Book and the Transformation of Britain, c. 550–1050.* London: The British Library, 2011.

Burke, Kenneth. *The Philosophy of Literary Form: Studies in Symbolic Action.* Baton Rouge: Louisiana State University Press, 1941.

Burke, Peter. "A Survey of the Popularity of Ancient Historians, 1450–1700." *History and Theory* 5 (1966): 135–52.

Butterfield, Ardis, ed. *Chaucer and the City.* Cambridge: Brewer, 2002.

——. "Introduction: Chaucer and the Detritus of the City." In Butterfield, *Chaucer and the City*, 3–24.

Bynum, Carolyn Walker. *Wonderful Blood: Theology and Practice in Late Medieval Northern Germany and Beyond.* Philadelphia: University of Pennsylvania Press, 2007.

Caille, Jacqueline. *Medieval Narbonne: A City at the Heart of the Troubadour World.* Aldershot: Ashgate, 2005.

Calder, Daniel G. "Strife, Revelation, and Conversion: The Thematic Structure of *Elene*." *English Studies* 53 (1972): 201–10.

Calhoun, Kenneth S. *Affecting Grace: Theatre, Subject, and the Shakespearean Paradox in German Literature from Lessing to Kleist.* Toronto: University of Toronto Press, 2013.

Campbell, Bruce. "Measuring the Commercialisation of Seigneurial Agriculture c. 1300." In Britnell and Campbell, *Commercialising Economy*, 132–93.

Campbell, Ethan. "'Be Ware of the Key': Anticlerical Critique in the Play of the Sacrament." *Fifteenth-Century Studies* 36 (2011): 1–22.

Campbell, Jackson J. "Cynewulf's Multiple Revelations." *Medievalia et Humanistica* 3 (1972): 262–67.

Campbell, James. "Norwich." In *The Atlas of Historic Towns, Volume Two*, edited by Mary D. Lobel, 1–15. London: Scholar Press, 1975.

——. "Norwich before 1300." In Rawcliffe and Wilson, *Medieval Norwich*, 29–48.

——. "Was It Infancy in England? Some Questions of Comparison." In *England and Her Neighbours, 1066–1453: Essays in Honour of Pierre Chaplais*, edited by Michael Jones and Malcolm Vale, 1–17. London: Hambledon, 1989.

Campbell, Marian. "A British Perspective: The Black Death, Treasure Hoards and Anglo-Jewish Material Culture." In Descatoire, *Treasures of the Black Death*, 28–33.

Campos, Edmund Valentine. "Jews, Spaniards, and Portingales: Ambiguous Identities of Portuguese *Marranos* in Elizabethan England." *ELH* 69, no. 3 (2002): 599–616.

Canetti, Elias. *Crowds and Power*. New York: Viking, 1963.

Carlson, David R. *Chaucer's Jobs*. New York: Palgrave, 2004.

Carruthers, Mary. *The Craft of Thought: Meditation, Rhetoric, and the Making of Images, 400–1200*. Cambridge: Cambridge University Press, 1998.

Carter, Peter. "The Historical Content of William of Malmesbury's Miracles of the Virgin Mary." In *The Writing of History in the Middle Ages: Essays Presented to Richard William Southern*, edited by Davis and Wallace Hadrill, 127–65. Oxford: Oxford University Press, 1981.

Carus-Wilson, E. M. *Medieval Merchant Venturers: Collected Studies*. 1954; repr. London: Routledge, 2004.

Castells, Manuel. *The Informational City: Information Technology, Economic Restructuring, and the Urban-Regional Process*. Oxford: Blackwell, 1989.

———. *The Rise of the Network Society*. Oxford: Blackwell, 2000.

———. *The Urban Question: A Marxist Approach*. Cambridge, MA: MIT Press, 1977.

Chazan, Robert. "The Anti-Jewish Violence of 1096: Perpetrators and Dynamics." In Abulafia, *Religious Violence between Christians and Jews*, 21–43.

———, ed. *Church, State and Jew in the Middle Ages: A Sourcebook*. New York: Behrman House, 1979.

———. *European Jewry and the First Crusade*. Berkeley: University of California Press, 1987.

———. *Medieval Stereotypes and Modern Antisemitism*. Berkeley: University of California Press, 1997.

Cheney, Patrick, ed. *The Cambridge Companion to Christopher Marlowe*. Cambridge: Cambridge University Press, 2004.

———. *Marlowe's Counterfeit Profession: Ovid, Spenser, Counter-Nationhood*. Toronto: University of Toronto Press, 1997.

Cheyette, Bryan. *Constructions of "the Jew" in English Literature and Society: Racial Representations, 1875–1945*. Cambridge: Cambridge University Press, 1993.

Childs, Wendy. "Anglo-Italian Contacts in the Fourteenth Century." In *Chaucer and the Italian Trecento*, edited by Piero Boitani, 65–88. Cambridge: Cambridge University Press, 1983.

Ciobanu, Estella A. "City of God?: City Merchants, Bloody Trade and the Eucharist in the Croxton *Play of the Sacrament*." In *Images of the City*, edited by Agnieszka Rasmus and Magdalena Cieślak, 50–70. Newcastle upon Tyne: Cambridge Scholars, 2009.

Clark, Cumberland. *Charles Dickens and His Jewish Characters*. London: Chiswick Press, 1918.

Clark, Robert L. A., and Claire Sponsler. "Othered Bodies: Racial Cross-Dressing in the *Mistere de la Sainte Hostie* and the Croxton *Play of the Sacrament*." *JMEMS* 29, no. 1 (1999): 61–87.

Cohen, Jeffrey Jerome. "The Future of the Jews of York." In Rees Jones and Watson, *Christians and Jews in Angevin England*, 278–93.

———. *Hybridity, Identity, and Monstrosity in Medieval Britain: On Difficult Middles*. New York: Palgrave Macmillan, 2006.

———. *Stone: An Ecology of the Inhuman*. Minneapolis: University of Minnesota Press, 2015.

——. "Stories of Stone." *postmedieval: a journal of medieval cultural studies* 1 (2010): 56–63.

Cohen, Jeremy. *Christ Killers: The Jews and the Passion from the Bible to the Big Screen.* Oxford: Oxford University Press, 2007.

——. "The Jews as Killers of Christ in the Latin Tradition, from Augustine to the Friars." *Traditio* 39 (1983): 1–27.

——. *Living Letters of the Law: Ideas of the Jew in Medieval Christianity.* Berkeley: University of California Press, 1999.

Cohen, Mark R. "Leone da Modena's *Riti*: A Seventeenth-Century Plea for Social Toleration of Jews." *Jewish Social Studies* 34, no. 4 (1972): 287–321.

Cohen, Richard I., Natalie B. Dohrmann, and Adam Shear, eds. *Jewish Culture in Early Modern Europe: Essays in Honor of David B. Ruderman.* Pittsburgh: University of Pittsburgh Press, 2014.

Cohen, William A. "Locating Filth." In *Filth: Dirt, Disgust, and Modern Life*, edited by Cohen and Ryan Johnson, vii–xxxvii. Minneapolis: University of Minnesota Press, 2005.

Coletti, Theresa. *Mary Magdalene and the Drama of Saints: Theater, Gender, and Religion in Late Medieval England.* Philadelphia: University of Pennsylvania Press, 2004.

——. "*Paupertas est donum Dei*: Hagiography, Lay Religion, and the Economics of Salvation in the Digby Mary Magdalene." *Speculum* 76, no. 2 (2001): 337–78.

Cooper, Lisa H. "Urban Utterances: Merchants, Artisans, and the Alphabet in Caxton's *Dialogues in French and English*." *New Medieval Literatures* 7 (2005): 127–61.

Cornelius, Roberta. "The Figurative Castle: A Study in the Mediaeval Allegory of the Edifice with Especial Reference to Religious Writings." PhD dissertation, Bryn Mawr, 1930.

Corsano, Karen. "The First Quire of the Codex Amiatinus and the *Institutiones* of Cassiodorus." *Scriptorium* 41 (1987): 3–34.

Coudert, Allison P., and Jeffrey S. Shoulson, eds. *Hebraica veritas? Christian Hebraists and the Study of Judaism in Early Modern Europe.* Philadelphia: University of Pennsylvania Press, 2004.

Cramp, Rosemary. "Monkwearmouth and Jarrow in Their Continental Context." In *Churches Built in Ancient Times*, edited by Kenneth Painter, 279–94. London: Society of Antiquaries of London, 1994.

——. "Monkwearmouth and Jarrow: The Archaeological Evidence." In *Famulus Christi: Essays in Commemoration of the Thirteenth Centenary of the Birth of the Venerable Bede*, edited by Gerald Bonner, 5–18. London: SPCK, 1976.

——. *Wearmouth and Jarrow Monastic Sites.* Vol. 1. Swindon: English Heritage, 2005.

Cresswell, Tim. *In Place/Out of Place: Geography, Ideology and Transgression.* Minneapolis: University of Minnesota Press, 1996.

Crosby, Everett U. *Bishop and Chapter in Twelfth-Century England: A Study of the "mensa episcopalis."* Cambridge: Cambridge University Press, 1994.

Cuffel, Alexandra. *Gendering Disgust in Medieval Religious Polemic.* Notre Dame: University of Notre Dame Press, 2007.

Cutts, Cecelia. "The Croxton Play: An Anti-Lollard Piece." *Modern Language Quarterly* 5 (1944): 45–60.

Dahood, Roger. "Historical Narratives of Jewish Child-Murder, Chaucer's *Prioress's Tale*, and the Date of Chaucer's Unknown Source." *SAC* 31 (2009): 125–40.

——. "The Punishment of the Jews, Hugh of Lincoln, and the Question of Satire in Chaucer's Prioress's Tale." *Viator* 36 (2005): 465–91.

Darby, Peter. "Bede, Iconoclasm and the Temple of Solomon." *Early Medieval Europe* 21, no. 4 (2013): 390–421.

Davis, James. *Medieval Market Morality: Life, Law and Ethics in the English Marketplace, 1200–1500.* Cambridge: Cambridge University Press, 2011.

Deats, Sara Munson. "Biblical Parody in *The Jew of Malta*: A Re-examination." *Christianity and Literature* 37 (1988): 27–48.

DeGregorio, Scott. "Bede and the Old Testament." In DeGregorio, *Cambridge Companion to Bede*, 127–41.

——, ed. *The Cambridge Companion to Bede.* Cambridge: Cambridge University Press, 2010.

Delaney, Sheila, ed. *Chaucer and the Jews: Sources, Contexts, Meanings.* New York: Routledge, 2002.

——. "Chaucer's Prioress, the Jews and Muslims." In Delaney, *Chaucer and the Jews*, 43–58.

Deleuze, Gilles, and Felix Guattari. *A Thousand Plateaus: Capitalism and Schizophrenia.* Translated by Brian Massumi. London: Athlone, 1988.

Derbes, Anne, and Mark Sandona. "Barren Metal and the Fruitful Womb: The Program of Giotto's Arena Chapel in Padua." *Art Bulletin* 80, no. 2 (1998): 274–91.

Descatoire, Christine, ed. *Treasures of the Black Death.* London: Holberton, 2009.

Despres, Denis L. "Adolescence and Sanctity: *The Life and Passion of Saint William of Norwich." Journal of Religion* 90 (2010): 33–62.

——. "The Protean Jew in the Vernon Manuscript." In Delaney, *Chaucer and the Jews*, 133–64.

DiNapoli, Robert. "Poesis and Authority: Traces of an Anglo-Saxon *Agon* in Cynewulf's *Elene." Neophilologus* 82 (1998): 619–30.

Dobson, R. Barry. "The Decline and Expulsion of the Medieval Jews of York." *TJHSE* 26 (1979 for 1974–78): 34–52.

——. *The Jewish Communities of Medieval England: The Collected Essays of R. B. Dobson.* Edited by Helen Birkett. York: Bothwick, 2010.

——. *The Jews of Medieval York and the Massacre of March 1190.* Borthwork Papers 45. York: St. Anthony's Press, 1974.

——. "The Medieval York Jewry Reconsidered." In Skinner, *Jews in Medieval Britain*, 145–56.

Donkin, Lucy and Hanna Vorholt, eds. *Imagining Jerusalem in the Medieval West.* Oxford: Oxford University Press, 2012.

Donnelly, Phillip J. *Milton's Scriptural Reasoning: Narrative and Protestant Toleration.* Cambridge: Cambridge University Press, 2009.

Douglas, Mary. *Purity and Danger: An Analysis of Concepts of Pollution and Taboo.* 1966; repr. London: Ark, 1984.

Dox, Donnalee. "Theatrical Space, Mutable Space, and the Space of Imagination: Three Readings of the Croxton *Play of the Sacrament*." In *Medieval Practices of Space*, edited by Barbara A. Hanawalt and Michal Kobialka, 167–98. Minneapolis: University of Minnesota Press, 2000.

Draper, Peter. *The Formation of English Gothic: Architecture and Identity.* New Haven: Yale University Press, 2006.

Drijvers, Jan Willem. *Helena Augusta: The Mother of Constantine the Great and the Legend of Her Finding of the True Cross.* Leiden: Brill, 1992.

Duby, Georges. *The Early Growth of the European Economy: Warriors and Peasants from the Seventh to the Twelfth Century.* Translated by Howard B. Clarke. Ithaca, NY: Cornell University Press, 1974.

Dugan, Holly. "*Coriolanus* and the 'rank-scented meinie': Smelling Rank in Early Modern London." In *Masculinity and the Metropolis of Vice, 1550–1650,* edited by Amanda Bailey and Roze Hentschell, 139–59. New York: Palgrave Macmillan, 2010.

Duggan, Charles. "From the Conquest to the Death of John." In *The English Church and the Papacy in the Middle Ages,* edited by C.H. Lawrence, 63–116. 1965; repr. New York: Sutton Publishing, 1999.

Dutton, Elisabeth. "The Croxton Play of the Sacrament." In *The Oxford Handbook of Tudor Drama,* edited by Thomas Betteridge and Greg Walker, 55–71. Oxford: Oxford University Press, 2012.

Dyer, Christopher. *An Age of Transition? Economy and Society in England in the Later Middle Ages.* Oxford: Oxford University Press, 2005.

———. "The Hidden Trade of the Middle Ages: Evidence from the West Midlands of England." *Historical Geography* 18, no. 2 (1992): 141–57.

Eaglen, R. J. "The Mint at Bury St Edmunds." In Gransden, *Bury St. Edmunds,* 111–21.

Eagleton, Terry. *Against the Grain: Essays 1975–1985.* London: Verso, 1986.

Eberle, Patricia J. "Commercial Language and Commercial Outlook in the *General Prologue.*" *Chaucer Review* 18, no. 2 (1983): 161–74.

Eccles, Mark. *Christopher Marlowe in London.* Harvard Studies in English 10. New York: Octagon Books, 1967.

———. "William Wager and His Plays." *English Language Notes* 18 (1981): 258–62.

Eidelberg, Shlomo, trans. *The Jews and the Crusaders.* Madison: University of Wisconsin Press, 1977.

Einbinder, Susan L. "Meir b. Elijah of Norwich: Persecution and Poetry among Medieval English Jews." *Journal of Medieval History* 26, no. 2 (2000): 145–62.

Eklund, Robert B., Jr., Robert F. Hébert, and Robert D. Tollison. *The Marketplace of Christianity.* Cambridge, MA: MIT Press, 2006.

Elias, Norbert. *The Civilizing Process: Sociogenetic and Psychogenetic Investigations.* Oxford: Blackwell, 1994.

Endelman, Todd M. *The Jews of Britain, 1656–2000.* Berkeley: University of California Press, 2002.

Estes, Heide. "Colonization and Conversion in Cynewulf's *Elene.*" In Karkov and Howe, *Conversion and Colonization in Anglo-Saxon England,* 133–52.

Fallon, Stephen M. *Milton among the Philosophers: Poetry and Materialism in Seventeenth-Century England.* Ithaca, NY: Cornell University Press, 1991.

Farinelli, Arturo. *Marrano: storia de un vituperio.* Geneva: Olschki, 1925.

Feldman, Louis H. *Studies in Hellenistic Judaism.* Leiden: Brill, 1996.

Felsenstein, Frank. *Anti-Semitic Stereotypes: A Paradigm of Otherness in English Popular Culture, 1600–1830.* Baltimore: Johns Hopkins University Press, 1995.

Fernie, Eric. "The Building: An Introduction." In Atherton et al., *Norwich Cathedral*, 47–58.

———. "The Romanesque Church of Bury St. Edmunds Abbey." In Gransden, *Bury St. Edmunds*, 1–15.

Fiedler, Leslie A. *The Stranger in Shakespeare*. New York: Stein and Day, 1972.

Finke, Laurie A., Martin B. Shichtman, and Kathleen Coyne Kelly. "'The World Is My Home When I'm Mobile': Medieval Mobilities." *Postmedieval* 4, no. 2 (2013): 125–35.

Fisch, Harold. "The Messianic Politics of Menasseh ben Israel." In Kaplan, Méchoulan, and Popkin, *Menasseh ben Israel*, 228–39.

Fish, Stanley. "Spectacle and Evidence in *Samson Agonistes*." *Critical Inquiry* 15, no. 3 (1989): 556–86.

Fish, Varda. "Theme and Pattern in Cynewulf's *Elene*." *NM* 76, no. 1 (1975): 1–25.

Fleming, Damian. *"Rex regum et cyninga cyning:* 'Speaking Hebrew' in Cynewulf's *Elene*." In *Old English Literature and the Old Testament*, edited by Michael Fox and Mannish Sharma, 229–52. Toronto: University of Toronto Press, 2012.

Forsyth, Neil. *John Milton: A Biography*. Oxford: Lion, 2008.

Fradenburg, L. O. Aranye. "Criticism, Antisemitism, and the Prioress's Tale." *Exemplaria* 1, no. 1 (1989): 69–115.

Frantzen, Allen J. "All Created Things: Material Contexts for Bede's Story of Cædmon." In *Cædmon's Hymm and Material Culture in the World of Bede*, edited by Frantzen and John Hines, 111–49. Morgantown: West Virginia University Press, 2007.

Freedman, Jonathan. *The Temple of Culture: Assimilation and Anti-Semitism in Literary Anglo-America*. Oxford: Oxford University Press, 2000.

Freeman, Arthur. "Marlowe, Kyd and the Dutch Church Libel." *English Literary Renaissance* 3 (1973): 44–52.

Friedman, John Block. *The Monstrous Races in Medieval Art and Thought*. Cambridge, MA: Harvard University Press, 1981.

Friedrichs, Christopher R. *The Early Modern City, 1450–1750*. London: Longman, 1995.

Fulk, Robert. "Cynewulf: Canon, Dialect, and Date." In *Cynewulf: Basic Readings*, edited by Robert E. Bjork, 23–55. New York: Garland, 1996.

Fulton, Helen. "Mercantile Ideology in Chaucer's *Shipman's Tale*." *Chaucer Review* 36, no. 4 (2002): 311–28.

Galloway, Andrew. "The Account Book and the Treasure: Gilbert Maghfield's Textual Economy and the Poetics of Mercantile Accounting in Ricardian Literature." *SAC* 33 (2011): 65–124.

Games, Alison. "England's Global Transition and the Cosmopolitans Who Made It Possible." *Shakespeare Studies* 35 (2007): 24–31.

Ganim, John M. "Double Entry in Chaucer's *Shipman's Tale*: Chaucer and Bookkeeping before Pacioli." *Chaucer Review* 30, no. 3 (1996): 294–305.

Garber, Marjorie. "'Infinite Riches in a Little Roome': Closure and Enclosure in Marlowe." In *Two Renaissance Mythmakers: Christopher Marlowe and Ben Jonson*, edited by Alvin Kernan, 3–21. English Institute, n.s. 1. Baltimore: Johns Hopkins University Press, 1977.

——. *Shakespeare After All.* New York: Random House, 2004.

Gardiner, Mark. "Buttery and Pantry and Their Antecedents: Idea and Architecture in the English Medieval House." In Kowaleski and Goldberg, *Medieval Domesticity*, 37–66.

Gardner, John. *The Construction of Christian Poetry in Old English.* Carbondale: Southern Illinois University Press, 1975.

Gauthier, Bernard. "The Planning of the Town of Bury St Edmunds: A Probable Norman Origin." In Gransden, *Bury St. Edmunds*, 81–97.

Gayk, Shannon. "'To wondre upon this thyng': Chaucer's *Prioress's Tale*." *Exemplaria* 22, no. 2 (2010): 138–56.

Gibson, Gail McMurray. *The Theater of Devotion: East Anglian Drama and Society in the Late Middle Ages.* Chicago: University of Chicago Press, 1989.

Gilchrist, Roberta. *Norwich Cathedral Close: The Evolution of the English Cathedral Landscape.* Woodbridge: Boydell, 2005.

Gillerman, Dorothy. *The Clôture of Notre-Dame of Paris and Its Role in the Fourteenth-Century Choir.* New York: Garland, 1977.

Gillingham, John. "Two Yorkshire Historians Compared: Roger of Howden and William of Newburgh." *Haskins Society Journal* 12 (2003): 15–37.

Gimpel, Jean. *The Cathedral Builders.* New York: Grove, 1961.

Girouard, Mark. *The English Town: A History of Urban Life.* New Haven: Yale University Press, 1990.

Golb, Norman. *The Jews in Medieval Normandy: A Social and Intellectual History.* Cambridge: Cambridge University Press, 1998.

Goldberg, P. J. P. "The Fashioning of Bourgeois Domesticity in Later Medieval England: A Material Culture Perspective." In Kowaleski and Goldberg, *Medieval Domesticity*, 124–44.

Gollancz, Hermann. "A Ramble in East Anglia." *TJHSE* 2 (1894–95): 106–40.

Gottfried, Robert S. "Bury St Edmunds and the Population of Late Medieval English Towns, 1270–1530." *Journal of British Studies* 20, no. 1 (1980): 1–31.

——. *Bury St. Edmunds and the Urban Crisis, 1290–1539.* Princeton, NJ: Princeton University Press, 1982.

Gransden, Antonia, ed. *Bury St. Edmunds: Medieval Art, Architecture, Archaeology and Economy.* London: British Archaeological Association, 1998.

Grantley, Darryll. "Producing Miracles." In *Aspects of Early English Drama*, edited by Paula Neuss, 78–91. Cambridge: D. S. Brewer, 1983.

Green, Abigail. *Moses Montefiore: Jewish Liberator, Imperial Hero.* Cambridge, MA: Harvard University Press, 2010.

Greenblatt, Stephen J. "Marlowe, Marx, and Anti-Semitism." *Critical Inquiry* 5, no. 2 (1978): 291–307.

——. *Renaissance Self-Fashioning: From More to Shakespeare.* Chicago: University of Chicago Press, 1980.

Grenville, Jane. *Medieval Housing.* London: Leicester University Press, 1997.

Griffin, Eric. *English Renaissance Drama and the Specter of Spain: Ethnopoetics and Empire.* Philadelphia: University of Pennsylvania Press, 2009.

Gross, John. *Shylock: A Legend and Its Legacy.* New York: Simon and Schuster, 1992.

Groves, Beatrice. "'They repented at the preaching of Ionas: and beholde, a greater then Ionas is here': *A Looking Glass for London and England*, Hosea and the

Destruction of Jerusalem." In *Early Modern Drama and the Bible: Contexts and Readings, 1570–1625*, edited by Adrian Street, 139–55. New York: Palgrave, 2012.

Guibbory, Achsah. *Ceremony and Community from Herbert to Milton: Literature, Religion and Cultural Conflict in Seventeenth-Century England*. Cambridge: Cambridge University Press, 1998.

——. *Christian Identity, Jews, and Israel in Seventeenth-Century England*. Oxford: Oxford University Press, 2010.

——. "England, Israel and the Jews in Milton's Prose, 1649–1660." In *Milton and the Jews*, edited by Douglas A. Brooks, 13–34. Cambridge: Cambridge University Press, 2008.

Gurr, Andrew. *Playgoing in Shakespeare's London*. Cambridge: Cambridge University Press, 2004.

——. *The Shakespearean Stage, 1574–1562*. Cambridge: Cambridge University Press, 2009.

Haes, Frank. "Moyse Hall, Bury St. Edmunds: Whence Its Name—What It Was—What It Was Not." *TJHSE* 3 (1896–98): 18–24.

Halliday, Robert. "Moyse's Hall, Bury St. Edmunds." *Suffolk Review*, n.s. 25 (1995): 27–44.

Hamel, Mary. "And Now for Something Completely Different: The Relationship between the *Prioress's Tale* and the *Rime of Sir Thopas*." *Chaucer Review* 14, no. 3 (1980): 251–59.

Hanham, Alison. *The Celys and Their World: An English Merchant Family of the Fifteenth Century*. Cambridge: Cambridge University Press, 1985.

Hannah, Ralph. *London Literature, 1300–1380*. Cambridge: Cambridge University Press, 2005.

Harper-Bill, Christopher. "The Medieval Church and the Wider World." In Atherton et al., *Norwich Cathedral*, 281–313.

——, ed. *The Register of John Morton, Archbishop of Canterbury, 1486–1500*. Vol. 3: *Norwich Sede Vacante, 1499*. Woodbridge: Boydell, 2000.

Harris, Jonathan Gil. *Sick Economies: Drama, Mercantilism and Disease in Shakespeare's England*. Philadephia: University of Pennsylvania Press, 2004.

——. *Untimely Matter in the Time of Shakespeare*. Philadelphia: University of Pennsylvania Press, 2009.

Harris, Roland. "The Origins and Development of English Medieval Houses Operating Commercially on Two Levels." PhD dissertation, University of Oxford, 1994.

Harris, Stephen. *Race and Ethnicity in Anglo-Saxon Literature*. New York: Routledge, 2003.

Harvey, David. *Consciousness and the Urban Experience: Studies in the History and Theory of Capitalist Urbanization*. Baltimore: Johns Hopkins University Press, 1985.

——. "Globalization in Question." *Rethinking Marxism* 8, no. 4 (1995): 1–17.

——. *Spaces of Capital: Towards a Critical Geography*. Edinburgh: Edinburgh University Press, 2001.

Harvey, Paul D. A., ed. *The Hereford World Map: Medieval World Maps and Their Context*. London: British Library, 2006.

——. *Mappa Mundi: The Hereford World Map.* Toronto: University of Toronto Press, 1996.

Haskins, Charles Homer. *The Renaissance of the Twelfth Century.* Cambridge, MA: Harvard University Press, 1955.

Hawkins, Sherman. "Chaucer's Prioress and the Sacrifice of Praise." *JEGP* 63, no. 4 (1964): 599–624.

Heckman, Christina M. "Things in Doubt: *Inventio,* Dialectic, and Jewish Secrets in Cynewulf's *Elene," JEGP* 108, no. 4 (2009): 449–80.

Helmholz, R. H. "Usury and the Medieval English Church Courts." *Speculum* 61, no. 2 (1986): 364–80.

Heng, Geraldine. "England's Dead Boys: Telling Tales of Christian-Jewish Relations Before and After the First European Expulsion of the Jews." *MLN* 127, no. 5 Supplement (2012): S54–S85.

——. "The Invention of Race in the European Middle Ages II: Locations of Medieval Race." *Literature Compass* 8, no. 5 (2011): 275–93.

——. "Jews, Saracens, 'Black Men,' Tartars: England in a World of Racial Difference." In *A Companion to Medieval English Literature and Culture, c.1350 — c.1500,* edited by Peter Brown, 247–69. Malden: Blackwell, 2007.

Herman, John P. *Allegories of War: Language and Violence in Old English Poetry.* Ann Arbor: University of Michigan Press, 1989.

Hesseyon, Ariel. *"Gold Tried in the Fire": The Prophet Theaurau, John Tany and the English Revolution.* Aldershot: Ashgate, 2007.

Heywood, Stephen. "The Romanesque Building." In Atherton et al., *Norwich Cathedral,* 73–115.

Higginbotham, Derrick. "Impersonators in the Market: Merchants and the Premodern Nation in the Croxton *Play of the Sacrament." Exemplaria* 19, no. 1 (2007): 163–82.

Higgins, Iain Macleod. *Writing East: The "Travels" of Sir John Mandeville.* Philadelphia: University of Pennsylvania Press, 1997.

Hill, Bennett. Review of *Rievaulx Abbey: Community, Architecture, Memory* by Peter Fergusson and Stuart Harrison. *Catholic Historical Review* 87, no. 1 (2001): 92–94.

Hill, J. W. F. *Medieval Lincoln.* Cambridge: Cambridge University Press, 1948.

Hill, Thomas D. "Bread and Stone, Again: *Elene* 611–18." *NM* 81, no. 3 (1980): 611–18.

——. "Sapiential Structure and Figural Narrative in the Old English *Elene." Traditio* 27 (1971): 159–77.

Hillaby, Joe. "Jewish Colonisation in the Twelfth Century." In Skinner, *Jews in Medieval Britain,* 15–40.

——. "London: The 13th-Century Jewry Revisited." *JHS* 32 (1990–92): 89–158.

——. "The London Jewry: William I to John." *JHS* 33 (1992–94): 1–44.

——. "Prelude and Postscript to the York Massacre: Attacks in East Anglia and Lincolnshire, 1190." In Rees Jones and Watson, *Christians and Jews in Angevin England,* 43–56.

——. "The Ritual-Child-Murder Accusation: Its Dissemination and Harold of Gloucester." *JHS* 34 (1994–96): 69–109.

Hillaby, Joe, and Caroline Hillaby. *The Palgrave Dictionary of Medieval Anglo-Jewish History.* Houndmills: Palgrave Macmillan, 2013.

Hills, David Farley. "Was Marlowe's 'Malta' Malta?" *Journal of the Faculty of Arts* 3, no. 1 (1965): 22–28.

Hilton, Rodney. "Warriors and Peasants" [review of Georges Duby, *Early Growth of the European Economy*]. *New Left Review* 83 (1974): 83–94.

Hiscock, Andrew. "Enclosing 'Infinite Riches in a Little Room': The Question of Cultural Marginality in Marlowe's *The Jew of Malta*." *Forum for Modern Language Studies* 35 (1999): 1–22.

Hodges, Richard. *Dark Age Economics: The Origins of Towns and Trade, A.D. 600–1000.* London: Duckworth, 1982.

Holder, Arthur. "Allegory and History in Bede's Interpretation of Sacred Architecture." *American Benedictine Review* 40, no. 2 (1989): 115–31.

———. "New Treasures and Old in Bede's 'De Tabernaculo' and 'De Templo.'" *Revue Benedictine* 99 (1989): 237–49.

Holsinger, Bruce. "Pedagogy, Violence, and the Subject of Music: Chaucer's *Prioress's Tale* and the Ideologies of 'Song.'" *New Medieval Literatures* 1 (1997): 157–92.

Holt, Richard. "Society and Population 600–1300." In Palliser, *Cambridge Urban History*, 79–104.

Homan, Richard. "Devotional Themes in the Violence and Humor of the 'Play of the Sacrament.'" *Comparative Literature* 20, no. 4 (1986–87): 327–40.

Honan, Park. *Christopher Marlowe: Poet and Spy.* Oxford: Oxford University Press, 2005.

Honeybourne, Marjorie B. "The Pre-Expulsion Cemetery of the Jews in London." *TJHSE* 20 (1959–61): 145–59.

Hope-Taylor, Brian. *Yeavering: An Anglo-British Centre of Early Northumbria.* Department of the Environment Archaeological Reports 7. London: Her Majesty's Stationary Office, 1977.

Hopkins, Lisa. *Christopher Marlowe: A Literary Life.* New York: Palgrave, 2000.

Hoppen, Allison. *The Fortification of Malta by the Order of St. John, 1530–1798.* Edinburgh: Scottish Academic Press, 1979.

Hourihane, Colum, ed. *The Grove Encyclopedia of Medieval Art and Architecture.* Vol. 2. New York: Oxford University Press, 2012.

Hoving, Thomas P. F. "The Bury St Edmunds Cross." *Metropolitan Museum of Art Bulletin* 22 (1964): 317–40.

Howard, Jean. "Introduction. Forum: English Cosmopolitanism and the Early Modern Moment." *Shakespeare Studies* 35 (2007): 19–23.

———. *The Theater of a City: The Places of London Comedy, 1598–1642.* Philadelphia: University of Pennsylvania Press, 2009.

Howe, Nicholas. "The Figural Presence of Erich Auerbach." *Yale Review* 85 (1997): 136–43.

———. *Migration and Mythmaking in Anglo-Saxon England.* New Haven: Yale University Press, 1989.

———. *Writing the Map of Anglo-Saxon England: Essays in Cultural Geography.* New Haven: Yale University Press, 2008.

Hsia, R. Po-Chia. *The Myth of Ritual Murder: Jews and Magic in Reformation Germany.* New Haven: Yale University Press, 1988.

Hsy, Jonathan. *Trading Tongues: Merchants, Multilingualism, and Medieval Literature.* Columbus, OH: Ohio State University Press, 2013.

Hughes, Quentin. *Fortress: Architecture and Military History in Malta*. London: Lund Humphries, 1969.

Hugill, Peter J. *World Trade Since 1431: Geography, Technology, and Capitalism*. Baltimore: Johns Hopkins University Press, 1993.

Hunter, G. K. "The Theology of Marlowe's *The Jew of Malta.*" *Journal of the Warburg and Courtauld Institutes* 27 (1964): 211–40.

Huscroft, Richard. *Expulsion: England's Jewish Solution*. Stroud: Tempus, 2006.

Husserl, Edmund. *The Crisis of European Sciences and Transcendental Phenomenology: An Introduction to Phenomenological Philosophy*. Translated by David Carr. 1954; repr. Evanston: Northwestern University Press, 1977.

Hyer, Maren Clegg, and Gale R. Owen-Crocker. *The Material Culture of Daily Living in the Anglo-Saxon World*. Exeter: University of Exeter Press, 2011.

Ihnat, Kati. "Mary and the Jews in Anglo-Norman Monastic Culture." PhD dissertation, Queen Mary, University of London, 2011.

Israel, Jonathan Irvine. *Diasporas within a Diaspora: Jews, Crypto-Jews and the World Maritime Empires (1540–1740)*. Leiden: Brill 2002.

——. *European Jewry in the Age of Mercantilism, 1550–1750*. London: Littman, Library of Jewish Civilization, 1998.

Jacobs, Joseph. "Aaron of Lincoln." *The Jewish Quarterly Review* 10 (1898): 629–48.

Jameson, Fredric. *The Political Unconscious: Narrative as a Socially Symbolic Act*. Ithaca, NY: Cornell University Press, 1981.

Jardine, Lisa. *Reading Shakespeare Historically*. London: Routledge, 1996.

Jessey, Henry. *A Narrative of the Late Proceeds at White-Hall Concerning the Jews*. London: Chapman, 1656.

Jessopp, Augustus and Montague Rhodes James. "Introduction." In Thomas of Monmouth, *The Life and Miracles of St. William of Norwich*, ed. Jessopp and James, ix–lxxxviii.

Johansson, Warren. "London's Medieval Sodomites." In *History of Homosexuality in Europe and America*, edited by Wayne R. Dynes, 159–64. New York: Routledge, 1992.

Johnson, Hannah. *Blood Libel: The Ritual Murder Accusation at the Limit of Jewish History*. Ann Arbor: University of Michigan Press, 2012.

Johnson, Hannah, and Heather Blurton. "Virtual Jews and Figural Criticism: Recent Scholarship on the Idea of the Jew in Western Culture." *PQ* 92, no. 1 (2013): 115–30.

Johnson, Willis. "The Myth of Jewish Male Menses." *Journal of Medieval History* 24, no. 3 (1998): 273–95.

Jones, Charles W. "Some Introductory Remarks on Bede's Commentary on Genesis." *Sacris Erudiri* 19 (1969): 115–98.

Jones, Michael. "Theatrical History in the Croxton *Play of the Sacrament.*" *ELH* 66, no. 2 (1999): 223–60.

Julius, Anthony. *Trials of the Diaspora: A History of Anti-Semitism in England*. Oxford: Oxford University Press, 2010.

Jung, Jacqueline. "Beyond the Barrier: The Unifying Role of the Choir Screen in Gothic Churches." *Art Bulletin* 82, no. 4 (2000): 622–57.

Kaplan, Yosef. "Political Concepts in the World of the Portuguese Jews of Amsterdam during the Seventeenth Century: The Problem of Exclusion and the

Boundaries of Self-Identity." In Kaplan, Méchoulan, and Popkin, *Menasseh ben Israel*, 45–62.

Kaplan, Yosef, Henry Méchoulan, and Richard H. Popkin, eds. *Menasseh ben Israel and His World*. Leiden: Brill, 1989.

Karkov, Catherine E., and Helen Damico. *Aedificia Nova: Studies in Honor of Rosemary Cramp*. Kalamazoo: Medieval Institute Publications, 2008.

Karkov, Catherine E., and Nicholas Howe, eds. *Conversion and Colonization in Anglo-Saxon England*. Tempe: Arizona Center for Medieval and Renaissance Studies, 2006.

Karkov, Catherine E., and Fred Orton, eds. *Theorizing Anglo-Saxon Stone Sculpture*. Morgantown: West Virginia University Press, 2003.

Katz, David S. "Menasseh Ben Israel's Christian Connection: Henry Jessey and the Jews." In Kaplan, Méchoulan, and Popkin, *Menasseh Ben Israel and His World*, 117–38.

——. *Philo-Semitism and the Readmission of the Jews to England, 1603–1655*. Oxford: Clarendon Press, 1982.

——. *Jews in the History of England, 1485–1850*. Oxford: Oxford University Press, 1994.

Katz, Jacob. *Exclusiveness and Tolerance: Studies in Jewish-Gentile Relations in Medieval and Modern Times*. New York: Schocken, 1961.

Kaufman, Heidi. *English Origins, Jewish Discourse, and the Nineteenth-Century British Novel: Reflections on a Nested Nation*. University Park: Pennsylvania State University Press, 2009.

Keene, Derek "London from the Post-Roman Period to 1300." In Palliser, *Cambridge Urban History*, 187–216.

Kelly, Henry A. "Jews and Saracens in Chaucer's England: A Review of the Evidence." *SAC* 27 (2005): 129–69.

——. "The Prioress's Tale in Context: Good and Bad Reports of Non-Christians in Fourteenth-Century England." In *Studies in Medieval and Renaissance History*, edited by Philip M. Soergel, 71–129. New York: AMS Press, 2006.

Kendrick, Christopher. *Milton: A Study in Ideology and Form*. New York: Methuen, 1986.

Kennedy, Michael J. "'Faith in the one God flowed over you from the Jews, the sons of the patriarchs and the prophets': William of Newburgh's Writings on Anti-Jewish Violence." *Anglo-Norman Studies* 25 (2003): 139–52.

Kermode, Lloyd Edward. "'Marlowe's Second City': The Jew as Critic at the Rose in 1592." *SEL* 35, no. 2 (1995): 215–29.

Kerr, Julie. *Monastic Hospitality: The Benedictines in England, c. 1070–c. 1250*. Woodbridge: Boydell, 2007.

Kim, Dorothy. "Entangled Jewish/Christian Relations in the Middle Ages." *Frankel Institute Annual*, 2014, 34–36. http://quod.lib.umich.edu/f/fia?page=home.

Kirby, Ethyn Williams. *William Prynne: A Study in Puritanism*. Cambridge, MA: Harvard University Press, 1931.

Kitch, Aaron. "Shylock's Sacred Nation." *Shakespeare Quarterly* 59, no. 2 (2008): 131–55.

Kletter, K. M. "Politics, Prophecy, and Jews." In Utterback and Price, *Jews in Medieval Christendom*, 91–116.

Klein, Stacy. "Reading Queenship in Cynewulf's *Elene.*" *JMEMS* 33, no. 1 (2003): 47–89.

Kline, Naomi Reed. *Maps of Medieval Thought: The Hereford Paradigm.* Woodbridge: Boydell, 2001.

Knoppers, Laura Lunger. *Historicizing Milton: Spectacle Power, and Poetry in Restoration England.* Athens: University of Georgia Press, 1994.

Kocher, Paul H. "Marlowe's Art of War." *Studies in Philology* 39, no. 2 (1942): 207–25.

Kolve, V. A. *Chaucer and the Imagery of Narrative: The First Five Canterbury Tales.* Stanford: Stanford University Press, 1984.

Kowaleski, Maryanne, and P. J. P. Goldberg, eds. *Medieval Domesticity: Home, Housing and Household in Medieval England.* Cambridge: Cambridge University Press, 2008.

Kramer, Johanna. *Between Heaven and Earth: Liminality and the Ascension of Christ in Anglo-Saxon Literature.* Manchester: Manchester University Press, 2014.

——. "'Đu Eart se Weallstan': Architectural Metaphor and Christological Imagery in the Old English *Christ I* and the *Book of Kells.*" In *Source of Wisdom: Old English and Early Medieval Latin Studies in Honour of Thomas D. Hill,* edited by Charles D. Wright et al., 90–112. Toronto: University of Toronto Press, 2006.

Kraus, Henry. *Gold Was the Mortar: The Economics of Cathedral Building.* New York: Barnes and Noble, 1979.

Kristeva, Julia. *Powers of Horror: An Essay on Abjection.* New York: Columbia University Press, 1982.

Kruger, Steven F. "The Bodies of Jews in the Late Middle Ages." In *The Idea of Medieval Literature: New Essays on Chaucer and Medieval Culture in Honor of Donald Howard,* edited by James M. Dean and Christian K. Zacher, 301–22. Cranbury: Associated University Presses, 1992.

——. "Passion and Order in Chaucer's *Legend of Good Women.*" *Chaucer Review* 23, no. 3 (1989): 219–35.

——. *The Spectral Jew: Conversion and Embodiment in Medieval Europe.* Minneapolis: University of Minnesota Press, 2006.

——. "The Times of Conversion." *PQ* 92, no. 1 (2013): 19–39.

Krummel, Miriamne Ara. *Crafting Jewishness in Medieval England: Legally Absent, Virtually Present.* New York: Palgrave, 2011.

Kupfer, Marcia. "Mappaemundi: Image, Artefact, Social Practice." In *The Hereford World Map: Medieval World Maps and Their Context,* edited by P. D. A. Harvey, 253–68. London: British Library, 2006.

Kuriyama, Constance Brown. *Christopher Marlowe: A Renaissance Life.* Ithaca, NY: Cornell University Press, 2002.

Ladd, Roger A. *Antimercantilism in Late Medieval English Literature.* New York: Palgrave Macmillan, 2010.

Laistner, M. L. W., and H. H. King. *A Hand-List of Bede Manuscripts.* Ithaca, NY: Cornell University Press, 1943.

Lampert-Weissig, Lisa. *Gender and Jewish Difference from Paul to Shakespeare.* Philadelphia: University of Pennsylvania Press, 2004.

——. "The Once and Future Jew: The Croxton 'Play of the Sacrament,' Little Robert of Bury, and Historical Memory." *Jewish History* 15, no. 3 (2001): 235–55.

Lancashire, Anne. *London Civic Theatre: City Drama and Pageantry from Roman Times to 1558*. Cambridge: Cambridge University Press, 2002.

Langholm, Odd. *Economics in the Medieval Schools: Wealth, Exchange, Value, Money, and Usury according to the Paris Theological Tradition, 1200–1350*. Leiden: Brill, 1992.

Langmuir, Gavin I. "The Knight's Tale of Young Hugh of Lincoln." *Speculum* 47, no. 3 (1972): 459–82.

———. *Toward a Definition of Antisemitism*. Berkeley: University of California Press, 1990.

Lavezzo, Kathy. *Angels on the Edge of the World: Geography, Literature, and English Community, 1000–1534*. Ithaca, NY: Cornell University Press, 2016.

———. "Building Antisemitism in Bede." In *Imagining the Jew in Anglo-Saxon Literature and Culture*, edited by Samantha Zacher, 79–107. Toronto: University of Toronto Press, 2016.

Lawton, David. "Sacrilege and Theatricality: The Croxton *Play of the Sacrament*." *JMEMS* 33, no. 2 (2003): 281–309.

Lefebvre, Henri. *The Production of Space*. Oxford: Blackwell, 1991.

Le Goff, Jacques. *Your Money or Your Life: Economy and Religion in the Middle Ages*. New York: Zone, 1990.

———. *Time, Work, and Culture in the Middle Ages*. Chicago: University of Chicago Press, 1980.

Lerer, Seth. "'Representyd now in yower syght': The Culture of Spectatorship in Late-Fifteenth-Century England." In *Bodies and Disciplines: Intersections of Literature and History in Fifteenth-Century England*, edited by Barbara Hanawalt and David Wallace, 29–62. Minneapolis: University of Minnesota Press, 1996.

Leshock, David B. "Religious Geography: Designating Jews and Muslims as Foreigners in Medieval England." In *Meeting the Foreign in the Middle Ages*, edited by Albrecht Classen, 202–25. New York: Routledge, 2002.

Levine, Robert. "Why Praise Jews: Satire and History in the Middle Ages." *Journal of Medieval History* 12, no. 4 (1986): 291–96.

Levy, Solomon. "Anglo-Jewish Historiography." *TJHSE* 6 (1908): 1–20.

Lewalski, Barbara Kiefer. *The Life of John Milton: A Critical Biography*. Oxford: Oxford University Press, 2000.

Lewis, Charlton T., and Charles Short. *A Latin Dictionary founded on Andrew's Edition of Freund's Latin Dictionary*. Oxford: Clarendon Press, 1955; first ed. 1879.

Lewis, Suzanne. *The Art of Matthew Paris in the "Chronica Majora."* Berkeley: University of California Press, 1987.

Lilley, Keith. *City and Cosmos: The Medieval World in Urban Form*. London: Reaktion, 2009.

———. "Mapping Cosmopolis: Moral Topographies of the Medieval City." *Environment and Planning D: Society and Space* 22 (2004): 681–98.

———. *Urban Life in the Middle Ages, 1000–1450*. New York: Palgrave Macmillan, 2002.

Lipman, Vivian. *The Jews of Medieval Norwich*. London: Jewish Historical Society of England, 1967.

Lipton, Sara. *Dark Mirror: The Medieval Origins of Anti-Jewish Iconography*. New York: Metropolitan, 2014.

———. *Images of Intolerance: The Representation of Jews and Judaism in the Bible moralisée*. Berkeley: University of California Press, 1999.

Little, Lester K. "Pride Goes before Avarice: Social Change and the Vices in Latin Christendom." *American Historical Review* 76 (1971): 16–49.

———. *Religious Poverty and the Profit Economy in Medieval Europe*. Ithaca, NY: Cornell University Press, 1983.

Lloyd, T. H. *The English Wool Trade in the Middle Ages*. Cambridge: Cambridge University Press, 1977.

Lobel, Mary D. *The Borough of Bury St. Edmunds*. Oxford: Clarendon Press, 1935.

———, ed. *The British Historic Towns Atlas*. Vol. 3, *The City of London from Prehistoric Times to c. 1520*. Oxford: Oxford University Press, 1989.

Loewenstein, David. *Representing Revolution in Milton and His Contemporaries: Religion, Politics, and Polemics in Radical Puritanism*. Cambridge: Cambridge University Press, 2002.

Loomis, R. S. "The Allegorical Siege in the Art of the Middle Ages." *American Journal of Archeology*, 2nd series, 23 (1919): 255–69.

Lopez, Robert. *The Commercial Revolution of the Middle Ages, 950–1350*. Cambridge: Cambridge University Press, 1998.

———. "Economie et architecture médiévale: Cela aurait-il tué ceci?" *Annales, Econ-omies-Sociétiés-Civilizations* 8 (1952): 433–38.

Loveluck, Christopher. "Wealth, Waste and Conspicuous Consumption." In *Image and Power in the Archaeology of Early Medieval Britain: Essays in Honour of Rose-mary Cramp*, edited by Helena Hamerow and Arthur MacGregor, 79–130. Oxford: Oxbow Books, 2002.

Lucas, Peter J. "The Vercelli Book Revisited." In *The Genesis of Books: Studies in the Scribal Culture of Medieval England in Honour of A. N. Doane*, edited by Matthew T. Hussey and John D. Niles, 161–74. Turnhout: Brepols, 2011.

Lunney, Ruth. *Marlowe and the Popular Tradition: Innovation in the English Drama before 1595*. Manchester: Manchester University Press, 2002.

Lupton, Julia Reinhard. *Citizen-Saints: Shakespeare and Political Theology*. Chicago: University of Chicago Press, 2005.

———. "The Jew of Malta." In Cheney, *Cambridge Companion to Christopher Marlowe*, 144–57.

Maddicott, J. R., and D. M. Palliser, eds. *The Medieval State: Essays Presented to James Campbell*. London: Hambledon, 2000.

Maloney, Robert P. "The Teaching of the Fathers on Usury: An Historical Study on the Development of Christian Thinking." *Virgiliae Christianiae* 27 (1973): 241–65.

Maltman, Sister Nicholas. "Meaning and Art in the Croxton *Play of the Sacrament*." *ELH* 41, no. 2 (1974): 149–64.

Manley, Lawrence. *Literature and Culture in Early Modern London*. Cambridge: Cambridge University Press, 1995.

Mann, Jill. "Allegorical Buildings in Medieval Literature." *Medium Aevum* 63 (1994): 191–209.

———. *Chaucer and Medieval Estates Satire: The Literature of Social Classes and the* General Prologue *to the* Canterbury Tales. Cambridge: Cambridge University Press, 1973.

Martin, C. Trice, B. Lionel Abrahams, and Asher I. Myers. "A Report of the Sub-Committee on Moyse's Hall." *TJHSE* 3 (1896–98): 33–35.

Martin, Lawrence T. "Bede and Preaching." In DeGregorio, *Cambridge Companion to Bede*, 156–69.

———. "Introduction." In *Bede the Venerable: Homilies on the Gospels*, 1: xi–xxiii. Kalamazoo: Cistercian Publications, 1991.

Mason, Steve. "Revisiting Josephus's Pharisees." In *Where We Stand: Issues and Debates in Ancient Jerusalem*, edited by Jacob Neusner and Alan Jeffery Avery-Peck, 23–57. Leiden: Brill, 1999.

Masschaele, James. *Peasants, Merchants, and Markets: Inland Trade in Medieval England, 1150–1350*. New York: St. Martin's Press, 1997.

———. "The Public Space of the Marketplace in Medieval England." *Speculum* 77, no. 2 (2002): 383–421.

Matar, N. I. "The Date of John Donne's Sermon 'Preached at the Churching of the Countesse of Bridgewater.'" *Notes and Queries* 39, no. 4 (1992): 447–48.

———. "Milton and the Idea of the Restoration of the Jews." *SEL* 27, no. 1 (1987): 109–24.

Mayr-Harting, H. *The Venerable Bede, the Rule of St. Benedict, and Social Class*. Jarrow: Parish of Jarrow, 1976.

McClelland, J. S. *The Crowd and the Mob from Plato to Canetti*. London: Unwin Hyman, 1989.

McCulloh, John M. "Jewish Ritual Murder: William of Norwich, Thomas of Monmouth, and the Early Dissemination of the Myth." *Speculum* 72, no. 3 (1997): 698–740.

McKane, William. *Selected Christian Hebraists*. Cambridge: Cambridge University Press, 1989.

Méchoulan, Henry, and Gérard Nahon. "Introduction." In *The Hope of Israel: The English Translation by Moses Wall*, edited by Méchoulan and Nahon, 1–95. Oxford: Oxford University Press, 1987.

Mertes, Kate. *The English Noble Household, 1250–1600: Good Governance and Politic Rule*. London: Blackwell, 1988.

Mesler, Katelyn N. "Legends of Jewish Sorcery: Reputations and Representations in Late Antiquity and Medieval Europe." PhD dissertation, Northwestern University, 2012. ProQuest Dissertations Publishing 3508520.

Meyer, Ann R. *Medieval Allegory and the Building of the New Jerusalem*. Woodbridge: Brewer, 2003.

Meyer, Susan. "Antisemitism and Social Critique in Dickens's *Oliver Twist*." *Victorian Literature and Culture* 33 (2005): 239–52.

Meyer-Lee, Robert J. "Literary Value and the Customs House: The Axiological Logic of the *House of Fame*." *Chaucer Review* 48, no. 4 (2014): 374–94.

Meyers, Charles. "Debt in Elizabethan England: The Adventures of Dr Hector Nunez, Physician and Merchant." *JHS* 34 (1994–96): 125–40.

———. "Dr Hector Nunez: Elizabethan Merchant." *TJHSE* 28 (1981–82): 129–31.

Meyvaert, Paul. "Bede and the Church Paintings at Wearmouth-Jarrow." *Anglo-Saxon England* 8 (1979): 63–77.

———. "Bede, Cassiodorus, and the Codex Amiatinus." *Speculum* 71, no. 4 (1996): 827–83.

*Middle English Dictionary*. University of Michigan Digital Library Production Service. Print, 18 December 2001. Web, 1 December 2015. http://quod.lib.umich.edu/m/med/.

Middleton, Anne. "'New Men' and the Good of Literature in the *Canterbury Tales*." In *Literature and Society*, edited by Edward W. Said, 15–56. Baltimore: John Hopkins University Press, 1980.

Millar, Bonnie. *The Siege of Jerusalem in its Physical, Literary and Historical Contexts.* Dublin: Four Courts, 2000.

Mitchell, J. Allan. *Becoming Human: The Matter of the Human Child.* Minneapolis: Minnesota University Press, 2014.

Mittman, Asa. "A Blank Space: Mandeville, Maps and Possibility." *Peregrinations: A Journal of Medieval Art and Architecture* 5, no. 2 (2015): 1–22.

——. "Gates, Hats, and Naked Jews: Sorting out the Nubian Guards on the Ebstorf Map." *FKW: Zeitschrif für Geschlechterforschung und visuelle Kultur* 54 (2013): 89–101.

——. *Maps and Monsters in Medieval England.* New York: Routledge, 2006.

Mohamed, Feisal. *Milton and the Post-secular Present: Ethics, Politics, Terrorism.* Stanford: Stanford University Press, 2011.

Moore, R. I. *The Formation of a Persecuting Society: Power and Deviance in Western Europe, 950–1250.* Oxford: Blackwell, 1987.

——. *The War on Heresy.* Cambridge, MA: Harvard University Press, 2012.

Morgan, Nigel. "The Hereford Map: Art-Historical Aspects." In Harvey, *Hereford World Map*, 119–35.

Morris, E. J. *History of Urban Form: Before the Industrial Revolution.* New York: Wiley, 1979.

Morrison, Kathryn A. *English Shops and Shopping: An Architectural History.* New Haven: Yale University Press, 2005.

Morrison, Susan Signe. *Excrement in the Late Middle Ages: Sacred Filth and Chaucer's Fecopoetics.* New York: Palgrave, 2008.

Mueller, Janel. "The Figure and the Ground: Samson as a Hero of London Nonconformity, 1662–1667." In *Milton and the Terms of Liberty*, edited by Graham Parry and Joad Raymond, 137–62. Cambridge: Cambridge University Press, 2002.

Mullaney, Steven. *The Place of the Stage: License, Play and Power in Renaissance England.* Chicago: University of Chicago Press, 1988.

Mundill, Robin R. *England's Jewish Solution: Experiment and Expulsion, 1262–1290.* Cambridge: Cambridge University Press, 1998.

——. *The King's Jews: Money, Massacre and Exodus in Medieval England.* New York: Continuum, 2010.

Narin van Court, Elisa. "The Hermeneutics of Supersession: The Revision of the Jews from the B to the C Text of *Piers Plowman*." *Yearbook of Langland Studies* 10 (1996): 43–87.

——. "*The Siege of Jerusalem* and Augustinian Historians: Writing about Jews in Fourteenth-Century England." *Chaucer Review* 29, no. 3 (1995): 227–48.

Nelson, Benjamin. *The Idea of Usury: From Tribal Brotherhood to Universal Otherhood.* Chicago: University of Chicago Press, 1969.

Newhauser, Richard. *The Early History of Greed: The Sin of Avarice in Early Medieval Thought and Literature.* Cambridge: Cambridge University Press, 2000.

Newman, Barbara. *Medieval Crossover: Reading the Secular against the Sacred.* Notre Dame: University of Notre Dame Press, 2013.

Nicholas, David. *The Later Medieval City, 1300–1500*. London: Longman, 1997.

Nichols, Ann Eljenholm. "Lollard Language in the Croxton *Play of the Sacrament*." *Notes and Queries* 36, no. 1 (1989): 23–25.

Nirenberg, David. *Anti-Judaism: The Western Tradition*. New York: Norton, 2013.

——. *Communities of Violence: Persecution of Minorities in the Middle Ages*. Princeton, NJ: Princeton University Press, 1996.

——. "'Judaism' as a Political Concept: Toward a Critique of Political Theology." *Representations* 128, no. 1 (2014): 1–29.

——. "Shakespeare's Jewish Question." *Renaissance Drama*, n.s. 38 (2010): 77–113.

Nisse, Ruth. *Defining Acts: Drama and the Politics of Interpretation in Late Medieval England*. Notre Dame: University of Notre Dame Press, 2005.

——. "'Your Name Will No Longer Be Aseneth': Apocrypha, Anti-Martyrdom, and Jewish Conversion in Thirteenth-Century England." *Speculum* 81, no. 3 (2006): 734–53.

——. "A Romance of the Jewish East: The Ten Lost Tribes and the Testaments of the Twelve Patriarchs in Medieval Europe." *Medieval Encounters* 13 (2007): 499–523.

Noonan, F. Thomas. *The Road to Jerusalem: Pilgrimage and Travel in the Age of Discovery*. Philadelphia: University of Pennsylvania Press, 2007.

Noonan, John T. *The Scholastic Analysis of Usury*. Cambridge, MA: Harvard University Press, 1957.

Northeast, Peter. "Superstition and Belief: A Suffolk Case of the Fifteenth Century." *Suffolk Review*, n.s. 20 (1993): 44–46.

O'Brien, Conor. *Bede's Temple: An Image and its Interpretation*. Oxford: Oxford University Press, 2015.

Oman, C. C. "The Shrine of St Alban: Two Illustrations." *Burlington Magazine for Connoisseurs* 62, no. 362 (1933): 237–41.

O'Reilly, Jennifer. "Introduction." In Bede, *On the Temple*, xvii–lv.

Orlin, Lena Cowen, ed. *Material London, ca. 1600*. Philadelphia: University of Pennsylvania Press, 2000.

Palliser, D. M., ed. *The Cambridge Urban History of Britain*. Vol. 1, *600–1540*. Cambridge: Cambridge University Press, 2008.

——. "Towns and the English State, 1066–1500." In Maddicott and Palliser, *Medieval State*, 127–46.

Palliser, D. M., T. R. Slater, and E. Patricia Dennison. "The Topography of Towns, 600–1300." In Palliser, *Cambridge Urban History*, 153–86.

Parker, Elizabeth C., and Charles T. Little. *Cloister's Cross: Its Art and Meaning*. New York: Metropolitan Museum of Art, 1994.

Parker, John. *The Aesthetics of Antichrist from Christian Drama to Christopher Marlowe*. Ithaca, NY: Cornell University Press, 2007.

——. "Barabas and Charles I." In *Placing the Plays of Christopher Marlowe: Fresh Cultural Contexts*, edited by Sara Munson Deats and Robert A. Logan, 167–84. Aldershot: Ashgate, 2008.

Parkes, Malcolm B. "The Hereford Map: The Handwriting and Copying of the Text." In Harvey, *Hereford World Map*, 107–17.

Partner, Nancy F. *Serious Entertainments: The Writing of History in Twelfth-Century England*. Chicago: University of Chicago Press, 1977.

Patterson, Lee. *Chaucer and the Subject of History*. Madison: University of Wisconsin Press, 1991.

———. "'The Living Witnesses of Our Redemption': Martyrdom and Imitation in Chaucer's *Prioress's Tale*." *JMEMS* 31, no. 3 (2001): 507–60.

Pearsall, Derek. *The Life of Geoffrey Chaucer: A Critical Biography*. Oxford: Blackwell, 1992.

Peck, Linda Levy. "Building, Buying and Collecting in London, 1600–1625." In Orlin, *Material London*, 268–90.

Phillips, Jonathan. *The Second Crusade: Extending the Frontiers of Christendom*. New Haven: Yale University Press, 2010.

Pim, Keiron. "Introduction." In Meir, *Into the Light*, 8–16.

Pollins, Harold. *Economic History of the Jews in England*. Rutherford: Fairleigh-Dickenson University Press, 1982.

Popkin, Richard. "Christian Jews and Jewish Christians in the 17th Century." In *Jewish Christians and Christian Jews: From the Renaissance to the Enlightenment*, edited by R. Popkin and Gordon M. Weiner, 57–72. Dordrecht: Kluwer, 1994.

———. "Jewish Messianism and Christian Millenarianism." In *Culture and Politics from Puritanism to the Enlightenment*, edited by P. Zagorin, 67–90. Berkeley: University of California Press, 1980.

Postan, Michael. *The Medieval Economy and Society: An Economic History of Britain, 1100–1500*. Berkeley: University of California Press, 1972.

Postone, Moishe. *Time, Labor, and Social Domination: A Reinterpretation of Marx's Critical Theory*. Cambridge: Cambridge University Press, 1993.

Power, Eileen. *The Wool Trade in English Medieval History*. Oxford: Oxford University Press, 1941.

Price, Merrall Llewelyn. "Medieval Antisemitism and Excremental Libel." In Utterback and Price, *Jews in Medieval Christendom*, 177–222.

———. "Sadism and Sentimentality: Absorbing Antisemitism in Chaucer's Prioress." *Chaucer Review* 43, no. 2 (2008): 197–214.

Rajak, Tessa. "The *Against Apion* and the Continuities in Josephus's Political Thought." In *Understanding Josephus: Seven Perspectives*, edited by Steve Mason, 222–46. Sheffield: Sheffield Academic Press, 1998.

Ravid, Benjamin C. I. "From Geographical Realia to Historiographical Symbol: The Odyssey of the Word *Ghetto*." In *Essential Papers on Jewish Culture in Renaissance and Baroque Italy*, edited by David B. Ruderman, 373–85. New York: New York University Press, 1992.

Rawcliffe, Carole, and Richard Wilson, eds. *Medieval Norwich*. London: Hambledon, 2006.

Redstone, Vincent. "St Edmunds Bury and Town Rental for 1295." *Proceedings of the Suffolk Institute of Archaeology* 13 (1907–09): 191–222.

Rees Jones, Sarah. "Building Domesticity in the City: English Urban Housing Before the Black Death." In Kowaleski and Goldberg, *Medieval Domesticity*, 66–91.

———. "Neighbours and Victims in Twelfth-Century York: A Royal Citadel, the Citizens and the Jews of York." In Rees Jones and Watson, *Christians and Jews in Angevin England*, 15–42.

———. "Stones, Houses, Jews, Myths." *York 1190 in 2010* (blog). http://york1190.blogspot.com/2010/08/stones-houses-jews-myths.html.

———. *York: The Making of a City 1068–135*. Oxford: Oxford University Press, 2013.

Rees Jones, Sarah, and Sethina Watson, eds. *Christians and Jews in Angevin England: The York Massacre of 1190, Narratives and Contexts.* Woodbridge: Boydell, 2013.

Regan, Catharine A. "Evangelicalism as the Informing Principle of Cynewulf's 'Elene.'" *Traditio* 29 (1973): 27–52.

Reiner, Jacob. "The English Yosippon." *The Jewish Quarterly Review* 58, no. 2 (1967): 126–42.

Revel-Neher, Elisabeth. "Du Codex Amiatinus et ses rapports avec les plans du Tabernacle dans l'art juif et dans l'art byzantine." *Journal of Jewish Art* 9 (1982): 6–17.

Richardson, Catherine. *Shakespeare and Material Culture.* Oxford: Oxford University Press, 2011.

Richardson, H. G. *English Jewry under the Angevin Kings.* London: Methuen, 1960.

Riddy, Felicity. "'Burgeis' Domesticity in Late-Medieval England." In Kowaleski and Goldberg, *Medieval Domesticity,* 14–36.

Riggs, David. *The World of Christopher Marlowe.* London: Faber, 2004.

Riley-Smith, J. "Christian Violence and the Crusades." In Abulafia, *Religious Violence between Christians and Jews,* 3–20.

——. *The First Crusade and the Idea of Crusading.* London: Athlone, 1986.

Robbins, Jill. *Prodigal Son, Elder Brother: Interpretation and Alterity in Augustine, Petrarch, Kafka, Levinas.* Chicago: University of Chicago Press, 1991.

Roberts, Phyllis Barzillay. *Studies in the Sermons of Stephen Langton.* Toronto: Pontifical Institute of Medieval Studies, 1968.

Rollins, Hyder Edward. *Pack of Autolycus.* Cambridge, MA: Harvard University Press, 1927.

Rose, Emily M. *The Murder of William of Norwich: The Origins of the Blood Libel in Medieval Europe.* Oxford: Oxford University Press, 2015.

Rosenblatt, Jason. *Torah and Law in Paradise Lost.* Princeton, NJ: Princeton University Press, 1994.

Rosser, Gervase. "Urban Culture and the Church 1300–1540." In Palliser, *Cambridge Urban History,* 335–70.

Rosser, Susan. "The Sources of Cynewulf's *Elene* (Cameron A.2.6)." *Fontes Anglo-Saxonici: World Wide Web Register.* Oxford: Fontes Anglo-Saxonici Project, English Faculty, Oxford University, 1990. http://fontes.english.ox.ac.uk/.

Rotenberg-Schwartz, Michael. "Early Modern Jewish Prayer in and for Israel." In *Through the Eyes of the Beholder: The Holy Land, 1517–1713,* edited by Judy A. Hayden and Nabil I. Matar, 185–206. Leiden and Boston: Brill, 2013.

Roth, Cecil. *A History of the Jews in England.* Oxford: Clarendon Press, 1964.

——. "Jewish Antecedents of Christian Art." *Journal of the Warburg and Courtauld Institutes* 16, nos. 1–2 (1953): 24–44.

——. "The Jews of Malta." *TJHSE* 12 (1928–31): 187–251.

——. "Leone da Modena and England." *TJHSE* 11 (1924–27): 206–27.

——. "Leone da Modena and His English Correspondents." *TJHSE* 17 (1951–52): 39–43.

——. *A Life of Menasseh ben Israel: Rabbi, Printer and Diplomat.* 1934; repr. Philadelphia: Jewish Publication Society of America, 1945.

——. "New Light on the Resettlement." *TJHSE.* 11 (1928): 112–42.

Roth, Pinchas, and Ethan Zadoff. "The Talmudic Community of Thirteenth-Century England." In Rees Jones and Watson, *Christians and Jews in Angevin England,* 184–203.

Rowe, Nina. *The Jew, the Cathedral and the Medieval City: Synagoga and Ecclesia in the Thirteenth Century.* Cambridge: Cambridge University Press, 2011.

Rubin, Miri. *Corpus Christi: The Eucharist in Late Medieval Culture.* Cambridge: Cambridge University Press, 1991.

———. *Gentile Tales: The Narrative Assault on Late Medieval Jews.* Philadelphia: University of Pennsylvania Press, 2004.

———. "Introduction." In Thomas of Monmouth, *The Life and Passion of William of Norwich*, edited and translated by Rubin, vii–l. London: Penguin, 2014.

———. *Mother of God: A History of the Virgin Mary.* New Haven: Yale University Press, 2009.

Ruderman, David B. *Early Modern Jewry: A New Cultural History.* Princeton, NJ: Princeton University Press, 2010.

Rudolph, Conrad. *The "Things of Greater Importance": Bernard of Clairvaux's Apologia and the Medieval Attitude toward Art.* Philadelphia: University of Pennsylvania Press, 1990.

Rutledge, Elizabeth. "Economic Life." In Rawcliffe and Wilson, *Medieval Norwich*, 157–88.

———. "Immigration and Population Growth in Early Fourteenth-Century Norwich: Evidence from the Tithing Roll." *Urban History Yearbook* 15 (1988): 15–30.

———. "The Medieval Jews of Norwich and Their Legacy." In *Art, Faith and Place in East Anglia*, edited by T. A. Heslop et al., 117–29. Woodbridge: Boydell, 2012.

Rybczynski, Wytold. *Home: A Short History of an Idea.* New York: Penguin, 1987.

Rye, William Brenchley, ed. *England as Seen by Foreigners.* London, 1865.

Saalman, Howard. *Mediaeval Cities.* New York: Braziller, 1968.

Sabine, Ernest L. "Latrines and Cesspools of Mediaeval London." *Speculum* 9, no. 3 (1934): 303–21.

Saltman, Avrom. *The Jewish Question in 1655: Studies in Prynne's Demurrer.* Jerusalem: Bar-Ilan University Press, 1995.

Samuel, Edgar R. "The Readmission of the Jews to England in 1656, in the Context of English Economic Policy." *JHS* 31 (1988–90): 153–69.

———. "Was Moyse's Hall, Bury St. Edmunds, a Jew's House?" *TJHSE* 25 (1973–75): 43–47.

Sauer, Elizabeth. "The Politics of Performance in the Inner Theater: *Samson Agonistes* as Closet Drama." In *Milton and Heresy*, edited by Stephen Dobranski and John P. Rumrich, 199–215. Cambridge: Cambridge University Press, 1998.

Scarfe, Norman. *Suffolk in the Middle Ages.* Woodbridge: Boydell, 1986.

———. *The Suffolk Landscape.* London: Hodder and Stoughton, 1972.

Scattergood, John. "London and Money: Chaucer's *Complaint to his Purse*." In Butterfield, *Chaucer and the City*, 162–74.

Scheil, Andrew P. *In the Footsteps of Israel: Understanding Jews in Anglo-Saxon England.* Ann Arbor: University of Michigan Press, 2004.

Scherb, Victor. *Staging Faith: East Anglian Drama in the Later Middle Ages.* Madison: Farleigh Dickensen University Press, 2001.

———. "Violence and the Social Body in the Croxton *Play of the Sacrament*." In *Violence in Drama*, edited by James Redmond, 69–78. Cambridge: Cambridge University Press, 1991.

Schofield, John. *London 1100–1600: The Archaeology of a Capital City*. Sheffield: Equinox, 2011.

——. *Medieval London Houses*. New Haven: Yale University Press, 1994.

——. "The Topography and Buildings of London, ca. 1600." In Orlin, *Material London*, 296–321.

Schofield, John, and Richard Lea. *Holy Trinity Priory, Aldgate, City of London: An Archaeological Reconstruction and History*. London: Museum of London Archaeology Service, 2005.

Schofield, John, and Alan Vince. *Medieval Towns: The Archaeology of British Towns in Their European Setting*. 2nd ed. London: Continuum, 2003.

Schwartz, Alexandra Reid. "Economies of Salvation: Commerce and the Eucharist in *The Profanation of the Host* and the Croxton *Play of the Sacrament*." *Comitatus* 25, no. 1 (1994): 1–20.

Schwartz, Regina. *Remembering and Repeating: Biblical Creation in "Paradise Lost."* Cambridge: Cambridge University Press, 1988.

Seabourne, Gwen. *Royal Regulation of Loans and Sales in Medieval England: "Monkish Superstition and Civil Tyranny."* Woodbridge: Boydell, 2003.

Selwood, Jacob. *Diversity and Difference in Early Modern London*. Burlington: Ashgate, 2010.

Shapiro, James. *Shakespeare and the Jews*. New York: Columbia University Press, 1996.

Sharma, Manish. "The Reburial of the Cross in the Old English *Elene*." In *New Readings in the Vercelli Book*, edited by Samantha Zacher and Andy Orchard, 280–97. Toronto: University of Toronto Press, 2009.

Shatzmiller, Joseph. *Shylock Reconsidered: Jews, Moneylending and Medieval Society*. Berkeley: University of California Press, 1990.

Shaw, Diane. "The Construction of the Private in Medieval London." *JMEMS* 26, no. 3 (1996): 447–66.

Shea, Jennifer. "Adgar's *Gracial* and Christian Images of Jews in Twelfth-Century Vernacular Literature." *Journal of Medieval History* 33, no. 2 (2007): 181–96.

Shore, Daniel. *Milton and the Art of Rhetoric*. Cambridge: Cambridge University Press, 2012.

Shoulson, Jeffrey S. *Milton and the Rabbis: Hebraism, Hellenism, and Christianity*. New York: Columbia University Press, 2001.

Singh, Jyotsna G., ed. *A Companion to the Global Renaissance: English Literature and Culture in the Era of Expansion*. Chichester: Blackwell, 2009.

Skilliter, S. A. *William Harborne and the Trade with Turkey, 1578–1582: A Documentary Study of the First Anglo-Ottoman Relations*. Oxford: Oxford University Press, 1977.

Skinner, Patricia, ed. *The Jews in Medieval Britain: Historical, Literary and Archaeological Perspectives*. Woodbridge: Boydell, 2003.

Slater, Michael. *Charles Dickens: A Life Defined by Writing*. New Haven: Yale University Press, 2009.

Smalley, Beryl. *The Study of the Bible in the Middle Ages*. Oxford: Oxford University Press, 1952.

Smith, Alan K. *Creating a World Economy: Merchant Capital, Colonialism, and World Trade, 1400–1825*. Boulder: Westview, 1991.

Smith, D. Vance. *Arts of Possession: The Middle English Household Imaginary*. Minneapolis: University of Minnesota Press, 2003.

Smith, Jonathan Z. *Relating Religion: Essays in the Study of Religion*. Chicago: Chicago University Press, 2004.

Smith, J. T. "A Note on the Origin of the Town-Plan of Bury St. Edmunds." *Archaeological Journal* 118 (1951): 162–64.

Smith, Neil. *Uneven Development: Nature, Capital, and the Production of Space*. Oxford: Basil Blackwell, 1991.

Smith, Neil, and Cindi Katz. "Grounding Metaphor: Towards a Spatialized Politics." In *Place and the Politics of Identity*, edited by Michael Keith and Steve Pile, 67–83. New York: Routledge, 1993.

Soja, Edward. *Postmodern Geographies: The Reassertion of Space in Critical Social Theory*. London: Verso, 1989.

Sousa, Geraldo U. de. "'My Hopes Abroad': The Global/Local Nexus in *The Merchant of Venice*." In *Shakespeare and Immigration*, edited by Ruben Espinosa, 37–58. Surrey: Ashgate, 2014.

Southern, R. W. "The English Origins of the 'Miracles of the Virgin.'" *Medieval and Renaissance Studies* 4 (1958): 176–216.

Spector, Stephen. "Time, Space and Identity in the *Play of the Sacrament*." In *The Stage as Mirror: Civic Theatre in Late Medieval Europe*, edited by Alan E. Knight, 189–200. Rochester: D. S. Brewer, 1997.

Spiegel, Flora. "The *Tabernacula* of Gregory the Great and the Conversion of Anglo-Saxon England." *Anglo-Saxon England* 36 (2007): 1–13.

Stacey, Robert C. "1240–1260: A Watershed in Anglo-Jewish Relations?" *Bulletin of the Institute for Historical Research* 61 (1988): 135–50.

——. "Aaron of Lincoln." In *Dictionary of National Biography: Missing Persons*, edited by C. S. Nicholls, 1. Oxford: Oxford University Press, 1993.

——. "Anti-Semitism and the Medieval English State." In Maddicott and Palliser, *Medieval State*, 163–77.

——. "From Ritual Crucifixion to Host Desecration: Jews and the Body of Christ." *Jewish History* 12, no. 1 (1998): 11–28.

——. "Jewish Lending and the Medieval English Economy." In Britnell and Campbell, *Commercialising Economy*, 78–101.

——. "Parliamentary Negotiation and the Expulsion of Jews from England." In *Thirteenth-Century England VI: Proceedings of the Durham Conference*, edited by Michael Prestwich, R. H. Britnell, and Robin Frame, 77–101. Woodbridge: Boydell, 1997.

——. "Royal Taxation and the Social Structure of Mediaeval Anglo-Jewry: The Tallage of 1239–1242." *Hebrew Union College Annual* 56 (1985): 175–249.

——. "York, Aaron of (d. 1268)." In *Oxford Dictionary of National Biography*. Oxford University Press, 2004. Online edition, January 2008. http://www.oxforddnb.com.proxy.lib.uiowa.edu/view/article/38612.

Stanbury, Sarah. "Host Desecration, Chaucer's 'Prioress's Tale,' and Prague 1389." In *Mindful Spirit in Late Medieval Literature: Essays in Honor of Elizabeth D. Kirk*, edited by Bonnie Wheeler, 211–24. New York: Palgrave Macmillan, 2006.

Statham, Margaret. *Accounts of the Feoffees of the Town Lands of Bury St Edmunds, 1569–1622*. Woodbridge: Boydell, 2003.

———. *The Book of Bury St. Edmunds*. Buckingham: Barracuda, 1988.

———. "The Medieval Town of Bury St Edmunds." In Gransden, *Bury St. Edmunds*, 98–110.

Stepsis, Robert, and Richard Rand. "Contrast and Conversion in Cynewulf's *Elene*." *NM* 70, no. 2 (1969): 273–82.

St. John, J. A. "Preface." In *The Prose Works of John Milton*, edited by St. John, 1:i–xl. London, 1848.

Stocker, D., ed. *The City by the Pool: Assessing the Archaeology of the City of Lincoln*. Oxford: Oxbow, 2003.

Stollman, Samuel S. "Milton's Dichotomy of 'Judaism' and 'Hebraism.'" *PMLA* 89, no. 1 (1974): 105–12.

———. "Milton's Understanding of the 'Hebraic' in *Samson Agonistes*." *Studies in Philology* 69, no. 3 (1972): 334–47.

Stow, Kenneth. "Papal and Royal Attitudes toward Jewish Lending in the Thirteenth Century." *AJS Review* 6 (1981): 161–84.

Strickland, Debra Higgs. *Saracens, Demons and Jews: Making Monsters in Medieval Art*. Princeton, NJ: Princeton University Press, 2003.

Strohm, Paul. *Chaucer's Tale: 1386 and the Road to Canterbury*. New York: Penguin, 2015.

———. "The Croxton *Play of the Sacrament*: Commemoration and Repetition in Late Medieval Culture." In *Performances of the Sacred in Late Medieval and Early Modern England*, edited by Susanne Rupp and Tobias Döring, 33–44. Amsterdam: Rodopi, 2005.

———. *Theory and the Premodern Text*. Minneapolis: University of Minnesota Press, 2000.

Sullivan, Garrett. "Geography and Identity in Marlowe." In Cheney, *Cambridge Companion to Christopher Marlowe*, 231–44.

Sutliffe, Adam, and Jonathan Karp. "Introduction: A Brief History of Philosemitism." In *Philosemitism in History*, edited by Sutliffe and Karp, 1–26. Cambridge: Cambridge University Press, 2011.

Tanner, Norman. "The Cathedral and the City." In Atherton et al., *Norwich Cathedral*, 255–80.

Teresa, Sister Margaret. "Chaucer's High Rise: Aldgate and *The House of Fame*." *American Benedictine Review* 33, no. 2 (1982): 162–71.

Thomas, Vivien, and William Tydeman, eds., *Christopher Marlowe: The Plays and Their Sources*. London: Routledge, 1994.

Thomson, Leslie. "Marlowe's Staging of Meaning." *Medieval and Renaissance Drama in England* 18 (2005): 19–36.

Thrupp, Sylvia. *The Merchant Class of Medieval London, 1300–1500*. Chicago: University of Chicago Press, 1989.

Tiffany, Grace. "Names in the *Merchant of Venice*." In *The Merchant of Venice: New Critical Essays*, edited by John W. Mahon and Ellen Macleod Mahon, 353–68. New York: Routledge, 2002.

Tomasch, Sylvia. "Judecca, Dante's Satan, and the *Dis*-placed Jew." In Tomasch and Gilles, *Text and Territory*, 247–67.

———. "Postcolonial Chaucer and the Virtual Jew." In *The Postcolonial Middle Ages*, edited by Jeffrey Cohen, 243–60. New York: St Martin's Press, 2000.

Tomasch, Sylvia, and Sealy Gilles, eds. *Text and Territory: Geographical Imagination in the European Middle Ages.* Philadelphia: University of Pennsylvania Press, 1998.

Toon, Peter. *Puritans, the Millennium and the Future of Israel: Puritan Eschatology, 1600–1660.* Cambridge: Cambridge University Press, 1970.

Trachtenburg, Joshua. *Jewish Magic and Superstition: A Study in Folk Religion.* 1939; repr. Philadelphia: University of Pennsylvania Press, 2004.

Tracy, James D., ed. *The Rise of Merchant Empires: Long Distance Trade in the Early Modern World, 1350–1750.* Cambridge: Cambridge University Press, 1990.

Trubowitz, Rachel. "'I was his nursling once': Nation, Lactation and the Hebraic in *Samson Agonistes.*" In *Milton and Gender,* edited by Catherine Gimelli Martin, 167–83. Cambridge: Cambridge University Press, 2004.

——. "'The people of Asia and with them the Jews': Israel, Asia, and England in Milton's Writings." In *Milton and the Jews,* edited by Douglas A. Brooks, 151–77. Cambridge: Cambridge University Press, 2008.

Tuan, Yi Fu. *Space and Place: The Perspective of Experience.* Minneapolis: University of Minnesota Press, 1977.

Turner, Marion. "Greater London." In Butterfield, *Chaucer and the City,* 25–40.

Turner, Sam, Sarah Semple, and Alex Turner. *Wearmouth and Jarrow: Northumbrian Monasteries in an Historic Landscape.* Hertfordshire: University of Hertfordshire Press, 2013.

Twycross, Meg. "The Theatricality of Medieval English Plays." In *The Cambridge Companion to Medieval English Theater,* edited by Richard Beadle and Alan J. Fletcher, 26–74. Cambridge: Cambridge University Press, 2008.

Tymms, Samuel, and J. R. Thompson. *A Handbook of Bury St. Edmunds, in the County of Suffolk: "Sacrarium regis, cunabula regis."* 6th ed. Bury St. Edmunds, 1891.

Upton, Dell. "Seen, Unseen, and Scene." In *Understanding Ordinary Landscapes,* edited by Paul Groth and Todd W. Bressi, 174–79. New Haven: Yale University Press, 1997.

Urry, John. "Mobile Sociology." *British Journal of Sociology* 51, no. 1 (2000): 185–203.

Utterback, Kristine T., and Merrall L. Price, eds. *Jews in Medieval Christendom: Slay Them Not.* Leiden: Brill, 2013.

Van der Wall, E. G. E. "Three Letters by Menasseh ben Israel to John Durie: English Philo-Judaism and the Spes Israelis." *Nederlands Archief voor Kerkgeschidenis* 65 (1985): 46–63.

Vasquez, Heather Hill. *Sacred Players: The Politics of Response in the Middle English Religious Drama.* Washington, DC: Catholic University Press, 2007.

Vaughn, Virginia Mason. "The Maltese Factor: The Poetics of Place in *The Jew of Malta* and *The Knight of Malta.*" In Singh, *Companion to the Global Renaissance,* 340–54.

Vincent, Nicholas. "William of Newburgh, Josephus, and the New Titus." In Rees Jones and Watson, *Christians and Jews in Angevin England,* 57–90.

Vitkus, Daniel. "'The Common Market of All the World': English Theater, the Global System, and the Ottoman Empire in the Early Modern Period." In *Global Traffic: Discourses and Practices of Trade in English Literature and Culture from 1550 to 1700,* edited by Barbara Sebek and Stephen Deng, 19–37. New York: Palgrave Macmillan, 2008.

——. "The New Globalism: Transcultural Commerce, Global Systems Theory, and Spenser's Mammon." In Singh, *Companion to the Global Renaissance*, 31–49.

——. *Turning Turk: English Theater and the Multicultural Mediterranean, 1570–1630*. New York: Palgrave Macmillan, 2003.

Walker, Greg. "Medieval Drama: The Corpus Christi in York and Croxton." In *Readings in Medieval Texts: Interpreting Old and Middle English Literature*, edited by David F. Johnson and Elaine Treharne, 370–85. Oxford: Oxford University Press, 2005.

Walker, William. "Milton's Dualistic Theory of Religious Toleration in 'A Treatise of Civil Power,' 'Of Christian Doctrine,' and 'Paradise Lost.'" *Modern Philology* 99, no. 2 (2001): 201–30.

Wallace, David. *Chaucerian Polity: Absolutist Lineages and Associational Forms in England and Italy*. Stanford: Stanford University Press, 1997.

Wallerstein, Immanuel. *The Modern World-System*. Vol. 1, *Capitalist Agriculture and the Origins of the European World-Economy in the Sixteenth Century*. Berkeley: University of California Press, 2011.

Walton, Penelope. "Textiles." In *English Medieval Industries: Craftsmen, Techniques, Products*, edited by John Blair and Nigel Ramsay, 319–54. London: Hambledon Press, 1991.

Wasson, John N. "The English Church as Theatrical Space." In *A New History of Early English Drama*, edited by John D. Cox and David Scott Kastan, 25–38. New York: Columbia University Press, 1997.

Watson, Sethina. "Introduction." In Rees Jones and Watson, *Christians and Jews in Angevin England*, 1–14.

Westrem, Scott D. *The Hereford Map: A Transcription and Translation of the Legends with Commentary*. Turnhout: Brepols, 2000.

Whatley, E. Gordon. "Bread and Stone: Cynewulf's *Elene* 611–618." *NM* 76, no. 4 (1975): 550–60.

——. "The Figure of Constantine the Great in Cynewulf's 'Elene.'" *Traditio* 37 (1981): 161–202.

Whitehead, Christiania. *Castles of the Mind: A Study of Medieval Architectural Allegory*. Cardiff: University of Wales Press, 2003.

Williams, Jane Welch. *Bread, Wine and Money: The Windows of the Trades of Chartres Cathedral*. Chicago: University of Chicago Press, 1993.

Wolf, Lucien. "Jews in Elizabethan England." *TJHSE* 11 (1924–27): 1–91.

——. "Jews in Tudor England." In *Essays in Jewish History*, edited by Cecil Roth, 71–90. London: Jewish Historical Society of England, 1934.

——. "Menasseh ben Israel's Study in London." *TJHSE* 3 (1896–98): 144–50.

Wolfe, Don M. "Limits of Miltonic Toleration." *JEGP* 60, no. 4 (1961): 834–46.

Wood, Ian. "Constantinian Crosses in Northumbria." In *The Place of the Cross in Anglo-Saxon England*, edited by Catherine E. Karkov et al., 3–13. Woodbridge: Boydell, 2006.

——. *The Most Holy Abbot Ceolfrid*. Jarrow: St Paul's Parish Church Council, 1985.

Wood, Margaret. *The English Mediaeval House*. London: Phoenix House, 1965.

——. "Moyse's Hall: A Description of the Building." *Archaeological Journal* 118 (1951): 165.

Wood, Neal. *Foundations of Political Economy: Some Early Tudor Views on State and Society.* Berkeley: University of California Press, 1994.

Woolf, Rosemary. "Saints' Lives." In *Continuations and Beginnings: Studies in Old English Literature,* edited by Eric G. Stanley, 37–66. London: Nelson, 1966.

Wordsworth, William. *The Prioress's Tale: Translations of Chaucer and Virgil.* Edited by Bruce E. Graver. Ithaca, NY: Cornell University Press, 1998.

Wormald, Patrick. "Bede, the *Bretwaldas* and the Origins of the *Gens Anglorum.*" In *Ideal and Reality in Frankish and Anglo-Saxon Society: Studies Presented to J.M. Hadrill,* edited by P. Wormald, 99–129. Oxford: Blackwell, 1983.

Yaeger, Patricia. "Introduction: Narrating Space." In *The Geography of Identity,* edited by Yaeger, 1–38. Ann Arbor: University of Michigan Press, 1996.

Yunck, John A. "'Lucre of Vileynye': Chaucer's Prioress and the Canonists." *Notes and Queries* 7, no. 5 (1960): 165–67.

Yuval, Israel J. *Two Nations in Your Womb: Perceptions of Jews and Christians in Late Antiquity and the Middle Ages.* Translated by Barbara Harshav and Jonathan Chipman. Berkeley: University of California Press, 2006.

Zacher, Samantha. *Rewriting the Old Testament in Anglo-Saxon Verse: Becoming the Chosen People.* London: Bloomsbury, 2013.

Zarnecki, George. *Romanesque Lincoln: The Sculpture of the Cathedral.* Lincoln: Honeywood, 1988.

———. "Romanesque Objects at Bury St Edmunds." *Apollo* 85 (1967): 407–13.

Zollinger, Cynthia Wittman. "Cynewulf's *Elene* and the Patterns of the Past." *JEGP* 103, no. 2 (2004): 180–96.

Zwicker, Steven N. "Milton, Dryden and the Politics of Literary Controversy." In *Culture and Society in the Stuart Restoration,* edited by Gerald MacLean, 137–57. Cambridge: Cambridge University Press, 1995.

# ✒ INDEX

Page numbers followed by letter *f* refer to figures.

CPSIA information can be obtained
at www.ICGtesting.com
Printed in the USA
LVOW08*1908290817
546832LV00005B/109/P